Frontiers in Time Research – Einführung in die interdisziplinäre Zeitforschung

Elisabeth Schilling · Maggie O'Neill
(Hrsg.)

Frontiers in Time Research – Einführung in die interdisziplinäre Zeitforschung

Springer VS

Hrsg.
Elisabeth Schilling
HSPV NRW
Bielefeld, Deutschland

Maggie O'Neill
University College Cork
Cork, Ireland

ISBN 978-3-658-31251-0   ISBN 978-3-658-31252-7 (eBook)
https://doi.org/10.1007/978-3-658-31252-7

Die Deutsche Nationalbibliothek verzeichnet diese Publikation in der Deutschen Nationalbibliografie; detaillierte bibliografische Daten sind im Internet über http://dnb.d-nb.de abrufbar.

© Springer Fachmedien Wiesbaden GmbH, ein Teil von Springer Nature 2020
Das Werk einschließlich aller seiner Teile ist urheberrechtlich geschützt. Jede Verwertung, die nicht ausdrücklich vom Urheberrechtsgesetz zugelassen ist, bedarf der vorherigen Zustimmung des Verlags. Das gilt insbesondere für Vervielfältigungen, Bearbeitungen, Übersetzungen, Mikroverfilmungen und die Einspeicherung und Verarbeitung in elektronischen Systemen.
Die Wiedergabe von allgemein beschreibenden Bezeichnungen, Marken, Unternehmensnamen etc. in diesem Werk bedeutet nicht, dass diese frei durch jedermann benutzt werden dürfen. Die Berechtigung zur Benutzung unterliegt, auch ohne gesonderten Hinweis hierzu, den Regeln des Markenrechts. Die Rechte des jeweiligen Zeicheninhabers sind zu beachten.
Der Verlag, die Autoren und die Herausgeber gehen davon aus, dass die Angaben und Informationen in diesem Werk zum Zeitpunkt der Veröffentlichung vollständig und korrekt sind. Weder der Verlag, noch die Autoren oder die Herausgeber übernehmen, ausdrücklich oder implizit, Gewähr für den Inhalt des Werkes, etwaige Fehler oder Äußerungen. Der Verlag bleibt im Hinblick auf geografische Zuordnungen und Gebietsbezeichnungen in veröffentlichten Karten und Institutionsadressen neutral.

Planung/Lektorat: Cori Antonia Mackrodt
Springer VS ist ein Imprint der eingetragenen Gesellschaft Springer Fachmedien Wiesbaden GmbH und ist ein Teil von Springer Nature.
Die Anschrift der Gesellschaft ist: Abraham-Lincoln-Str. 46, 65189 Wiesbaden, Germany

Inhaltsverzeichnis

Time in Constructed Social Reality........................... 1
Elisabeth Schilling and Maggie O'Neill

Time, History and Biography. Zeit, Geschichte und Biografie

Umgang mit Identitätskonstruktion und Zeitwahrnehmung in der
Oral History... 11
Felicitas Söhner

„Heute kann ich nicht mehr behaupten, meine Eltern seien links
gewesen" – George Herbert Meads Zeit-Begriff und die biografietheoretische Analyse... 29
Lena Kahle

Life-Stories in Times of Uncertain Futures: How Future Narratives
are Constructed in Young Peoples' Biographies................. 55
Ingmar Mundt

Linking Time and Space in Narrative: Nostalgia as a Chronotope.... 83
Anya Ahmed

Constructing Biography—Constructing Identity: Changeable
Concept of the Future in Migrants 101
Anna Sircova, Carolyn Patterson and Elisabeth Schilling

Chrononormativität im Lebenslauf – Die sozialen Praktiken der
Herstellung und De/Stabilisierung temporaler Normalität in der
Lebensphase Alter.. 133
Anna Wanka

Biografizität als „mentale Grammatik" der Lebenszeit 161
Peter Alheit

Time and Education. Zeit und Bildung

Time, Power and Education. Zeit, Macht und Bildung............... 187
Matthew Krehl Edward Thomas and Ben Whitburn

Erweiterte institutionalisierte Freizeit an Tagesschulen und
ambivalente Bedeutsamkeit aus der Perspektive von Schülerinnen
und Schülern, sozialpädagogischen Fachkräften, Lehrkräften und
Eltern 211
Emanuela Chiapparini, Andrea Scholian, Christa Kappler und Patricia
Schuler Braunschweig

„Das muss am Gymnasium schneller gehen": Eine praxeologisch-
wissenssoziologische Rekonstruktion von „Zeit" im Kontext von
Differenzierungspraktiken im Gymnasialunterricht................. 235
Marcus Syring, Lena Brinkmann, Sabine Weiß und Ewald Kiel

Individueller Lernanspruch als temporaler Einflussfaktor –
Konzeptionell-methodische Reflexionen zur Erfassung wissenschaft-
licher Weiterbildungslernzeit mittels Leitfadeninterviews............ 263
Ramona Kahl

Construction of Schooling Time as Part of Mothers' Identities 287
Lyudmila Nurse

Time, Future and Innovation. Zeit, Zukunft und Innovationen

Wie denkt die Verwaltung über die Zukunft? Dokumentenanalyse
von Strategiepapieren zur Digitalisierung der öffentlichen
Verwaltung... 311
Malte Schophaus

Time and Futures. Zeit und Zukünfte in der Vorausschau – Konzepte
in den Zukunftswissenschaften 335
Kerstin Cuhls

Zeit-Rebounds im Arbeitsleben – Transformative Forschung zu zeitpolitischen Innovationen 355
Gerrit von Jorck und Sonja Geiger

Methodology for the Study of Time. Methodologien der Zeitforschung

Zeitforschung als vergleichende Prozessanalyse. Die Verbindung von Qualitative Comparative Analysis und Einzelfallstudien für die Untersuchung zeitlicher Dynamiken............................. 381
Simon Gordt und Thomas Laux

Verfahren zur Analyse von Alltagshandlungen 405
Doris Cornils

Kommunikative Zeit beobachten. Methodisch-methodologische Implikationen des kommunikativen Konstruktivismus 433
Ekkehard Coenen

Rough Relationing Making Time for Analysis in Ethnography 453
Clément Dréano und Markus Rudolfi

The Narrative and the Flash Fiction: Ethical and Political Temporalities in the Life Course of an Adolescent Involved with Crime in Brazil 481
Jacqueline de Oliveira Moreira, Andréa Máris Campos Guerra, Rodrigo Goes e Lima und Ana Elisa de Oliveira Drawin

Temporality in Qualitative Longitudinal Studies on Health Experience: A Review and Analysis 495
Archana Ramanujam, Christian Bröer, Stefano Giani und Gerben Moerman

Autorenverzeichnis

Professor Anya Ahmed is professor of Social Science in Manchester Metropolitan University. She studied her BA at the University of Leeds and did her PhD at the University of Central Lancashire. Her current work focuses on ageing/dementia, migration and inequality.
E-Mail: Anya.Ahmed@mmu.ac.uk

Prof. em. Dr. Dr. Peter Alheit, ehemaliger Lehrstuhl für Allgemeine Pädagogik am Pädagogischen Seminar der Georg-August-Universität Göttingen (jetzt: Institut für Erziehungswissenschaft).
E-Mail: palheit@gwdg.de

Prof. Dr. Patricia Schuler Braunschweig, Dozentin in der Abteilung Sekundarstufe I an der Pädagogischen Hochschule Zürich.
Adresse: Pädagogische Hochschule Zürich, Abteilung «Sekundarstufe I», Lagerstrasse 2, 8090 Zürich
E-Mail: Patricia.Schuler@phzh.ch

Lena Brinkmann, M.A. Wissenschaftliche Mitarbeiterin in der Abteilung Schulpädagogik an der Eberhard Karls Universität Tübingen.
Adresse: Universität Tübingen, Institut für Erziehungswissenschaft, Abteilung Schulpädagogik, Münzgasse 22-30, 72070 Tübingen
E-Mail: lena.brinkmann@uni-tuebingen.de

Christian Bröer is associate professor at the department of sociology of the university of Amsterdam. He is interested in issues of subjectivity, health and power in policy and has a related interested in online qualitative analysis. Bröer is

working on a longitudinal study on everyday practices in households with young children as mediators between socio-economic differences and health outcomes.
c.broer@uva.nl

Prof. Dr. Emanuela Chiapparini, Dozentin am Departement für Soziale Arbeit der Berner Fachhochschule.
Adresse: Berner Fachhochschule, Fachbereich Soziale Arbeit. Hallerstrasse 10, 3012 Bern
Kontakt: Emanuela.Chiapparini@bfh.ch

Dr. Ekkehard Coenen ist wissenschaftlicher Mitarbeiter am Lehrstuhl für Mediensoziologie an der Bauhaus-Universität Weimar. Seine Forschungsschwerpunkte liegen in den Methoden der qualitativen Sozialforschung, in der Thanato-, Wissens-, Kultur- und Emotionssoziologie sowie in der Soziologie der Gewalt.
Kontakt: ekkehard.coenen@uni-weimar.de

Dr. Kerstin Cuhls, studierte Japanologie, Sinologie und BWL, ist wissenschaftliche Projektleiterin im Foresight am Fraunhofer-Institut für System- und Innovationsforschung in Karlsruhe. Sie beschäftigt sich mit Vorausschau-Methoden und zukünftigen Entwicklungen in Wissenschaft, Wirtschaft und Gesellschaft.
Adresse: Breslauer Str. 48, 76139 Karlsruhe
E-Mail: kerstin.cuhls@isi.fraunhofer.de

Dr. Sonja Geiger, promoviert in Kognitionspsychologie, arbeitet heute als Umweltpsychologin am Fachgebiet Arbeitslehre/Ökonomie und Nachhaltiger Konsum der TU. Sie untersucht in transdisziplinären Forschungssettings soziale, normative und affektive Einflussfaktoren auf nachhaltiges Konsumverhalten und Umweltengagement von Menschen. Ihr Hauptinteresse gilt der integrierten Betrachtung struktureller Bedingungen und persönlicher Eigenschaften, die gemeinsam nachhaltiges Verhalten begünstigen oder auch erschweren.
Kontakt: sonja.m.geiger@tu-berlin.de

Dr. Stefano Giani is Subject librarian for Communication science, Romance languages and Sociology at the University of Amsterdam. He holds a MA in Art History from the Politecnico di Milano (Italy).
s.giani@uva.nl

Dr. Simon Gordt ist nach Stationen an der Universität Bern und der Otto-Friedrich-Universität Bamberg wissenschaftlicher Mitarbeiter am Institut für Sozialwissenschaften an der Stiftung Universität Hildesheim. Er hat in der

Abteilung Bildungssoziologie an der Universität Bern promoviert. Seine Arbeitsschwerpunkte liegen in der soziologischen und historisch-vergleichenden Bildungsforschung, in der Religions- und politischen Soziologie sowie der Sozialstrukturanalyse.
simon.gordt@uni-hildesheim.de

Gerrit von Jorck, Dipl.-Volksw., B.A., studierte Volkswirtschaftslehre, Soziologie und Philosophie. Er arbeitet als ökologischer Ökonom am Fachgebiet Arbeitslehre/Ökonomie und Nachhaltiger Konsum der TU Berlin und koordiniert die Arbeitsgemeinschaft sozial-ökologische Arbeits- und Zeitforschung der Vereinigung für ökologische Wirtschaftsforschung. Informationen zu seinem aktuellen Forschungsprojekt „Zeitwohlstand, Zeit-Rebound und Nachhaltiger Konsum" finden sich auf www.zeit-rebound.de.
Kontakt: gerrit.vonjorck@tu-berlin.de

Dr. Lena Kahle ist Post-Doktorandin an der Stiftung Universität Hildesheim. Sie hat in Frankfurt am Main in Soziologie promoviert und an der Freien Universität Berlin das Diplom in Politikwissenschaft abgeschlossen. Ihre Arbeitsschwerpunkte sind Interpretative Sozialforschung, Migrationssoziologie, Agency- und Handlungstheorie, Bildung, Erinnerungs- und Geschichtskultur.
Kontakt: kahlele@uni-hildesheim.de

Dr. phil. Ramona Kahl ist Projektkoordinatorin der Studie «Qualifizierung für eine inklusive, allgemeine Erwachsenenbildung am Beispiel von Blindheit und Sehbeeinträchtigung – iQ_EB» (2018–2020) gefördert vom Bundesministerium für Bildung und Forschung. Ihre Arbeitsschwerpunkte sind: Wissenschaftliche Weiterbildung, Teilnehmer- und Personalforschung, hermeneutische Medienanalyse und Medienrezeptionsforschung.
Kontakt: kahl@uni-marburg.de

Dr. Christa Kappler, Dozentin im Prorektorat Forschung und Entwicklung an der Pädagogischen Hochschule Zürich.
Adresse: Pädagogische Hochschule Zürich, Zentrum «Professionalisierung und Kompetenzentwicklung», Lagerstrasse 2, 8090 Zürich
E-Mail: Christa.Kappler@phzh.ch

Prof. Dr. Ewald Kiel Ordinarius für Schulpädagogik an der Ludwig-Maximilians-Universität München.
Adresse: LMU München, Lehrstuhl für Schulpädagogik, Leopoldstraße 13, 80802 München
E-Mail: kiel@lmu.de

Jun.-Prof. Dr. Thomas Laux ist Juniorprofessor für Europäische Kultur und Bürgergesellschaft am Institut für Europäische Studien und Geschichtswissenschaften (IESG) der TU Chemnitz. Zuvor Studium der Soziologie, der Politischen Wissenschaft und der Philosophie in Heidelberg, Mannheim und Aberdeen. Forschungsinteressen: Politische Soziologie, Globalisierungsprozesse, Soziale Bewegungen und Zivilgesellschaft, Menschenrechte, fallorientierte Methoden (QCA, Process Tracing).
Kontakt: Institut für Europäische Studien und Geschichtswissenschaften (IESG); TU Chemnitz, Thüringer Weg 9, 09126 Chemnitz
E-Mail: thomas.laux@phil.tu-chemnitz.de

Dr. Gerben Moerman is programme director of the BSc Sociology and senior lecturer in methodology at the University of Amsterdam. He holds a PhD in social research methodology from Vrije Universiteit Amsterdam. His expertise lies in the field of qualitative research. Specifically, he works on qualitative interviewing and different forms of qualitative analysis.
g.moerman@uva.nl

Ingmar Mundt is a Research Assistant at the Chair of Sociology of Technology and Sustainable Development at the University of Passau. He studied Economics (B.A.), Future Studies (M.A.) and Sociology (M.Sc.) in Berlin and Edinburgh. His research and work focuses on the social construction and meaning of the future as well as the influence of digital technologies, algorithms and artificial intelligence on the perception of the future from a cultural, technical and knowledge sociological perspective. He is also co-coordinator of the working group on social-ecological work and time research at the VÖW.
Contact: ingmar.mundt@uni-passau.de, Universität Passau, Innstraße 41, 94032 Passau, Germany

Maggie O'Neill is Professor and Head of the Department of Sociology & Criminology at University College Cork, Ireland. A board member and former Chair of the ESA Research Network 3, *Biographical Perspectives on European Identities*. Her recent book co-authored wth Brian Roberts is *Walking Methods:Research on the Move (Routledge)*.
Maggie.oneill@York.ac.uk

Lyudmila Nurse, PhD, Research Director of Oxford XXI think tank, UK. Previously a Research Fellow in the Department of Education, University of Oxford in 2017–2020; and visiting academic at the Centre for Global Politics, Economy and Society, Oxford Brookes University. She is Coordinator of the ESA's Research Network "Biographical Perspectives on European Societies".

She is a member of the Cultural, Scientific and Medical Advisory Board of Music Mind Spirit Trust, UK. Her research and publications include qualitative biographical methods in studies of education and families; social and educational inequalities; identities, belonging and cultural memory.
lyudmilanurse@oxford-xxi.org

Carolyn Holmes Patterson is currently a student studying at Connecticut College in the United States. She is expecting to graduate with a BA in the spring of 2021, as a Human Development and Psychology double major. Carolyn Patterson is affiliated with the Time Perspective Network and became a member through her course with DIS in the fall of 2019 semester in Copenhagen, Denmark.
E-Mail: cpatter5@conncoll.edu

Archana Ramanujam, MSc is to matriculate in the fall of 2020 as a candidate in the Sociology PhD program at Brown University in the United States. She is currently a data analyst at the Dutch government, and holds a Research MSc in the Social Sciences from the University of Amsterdam.
archana_ramanujam@brown.edu

Markus Rudolfi, M.A., ist wissenschaftlicher Mitarbeiter und Doktorand am Institut für Soziologie am Schwerpunkt für interpretative Sozialforschung an der Goethe-Universität Frankfurt am Main. Seine Arbeitsschwerpunkte sind Science & Technology Studies, Ethnographie, Umweltsoziologie und Politische Ökologie.
E-Mail: rudolfi@soz.uni-frankfurt.de

Prof. Dr. Elisabeth Schilling is professor of Social Science in the University for Police and Public Administration NRW. Her current work focuses on intersections of time, diversity, migration and education.
Address: University of Police and Public Administration NRW, Am Stadtholz 24, 33609 Bielefeld
E-Mail: elisabeth.schilling@hspv.nrw.de

MA Andrea Scholian ist Wissenschaftliche Mitarbeiterin am Departement für Soziale Arbeit der ZHAW.
Adresse: Zürcher Hochschule für angewandte Wissenschaften Soziale Arbeit, Institut für Kindheit, Jugend und Familie. Postfach 707, 8037 Zürich
E-Mail: Andrea.Scholian@zhaw.ch

Prof. Dr. Malte Schophaus ist Professor für Psychologie an der Hochschule für Polizei und öffentliche Verwaltung NRW (HSPV) in Bielefeld. Aktuelle

Arbeits- und Forschungsschwerpunkte sind: Nachhaltige Personalentwicklung und Partizipation, Reflexionskompetenz und Peer-Coaching sowie wissenschaftliche Politikberatung. Er ist Mitherausgeber der Fachzeitschrift „Umweltpsychologie".
E-Mail: malte.schophaus@hspv.nrw.de

Anna Sircova, Ph.D. in Psychology, a researcher and Head of the Board at Time Perspective Network, Denmark; an external lecturer at DIS Copenhagen, Denmark. Her current work focuses on futurization of thinking and behavior, concept of psychological time across cultures.
E-Mail: anna.sircova@gmail.com

Dr. Felicitas Söhner, Research Fellow, Department of the History, Philosophy and Ethics of Medicine, Centre for Health and Society, University of Düsseldorf. Her current work focuses on Oral History, Contemporary Social History, European Memory Culture and its Biographical Dimensions.
Email: Felicitas.Soehner@hhu.de

PD Dr. habil. Marcus Syring Vertretungsprofessor für Erziehungswissenschaft mit dem Schwerpunkt Schulpädagogik an der Eberhard Karls Universität Tübingen.
Adresse: Universität Tübingen, Institut für Erziehungswissenschaft, Abteilung Schulpädagogik, Münzgasse 22-30, 72070 Tübingen
E-Mail: marcus.syring@uni-tuebingen.de

Dr. Matthew Krehl Edward Thomas, PhD (SFHEA) is a Senior Lecturer in Pedagogy and Curriculum and the Course Director of the Masters of Teaching at Deakin University. Dr. Thomas' research explores time, power, human rights and technology. Matthew's interest in temporality is the intersection between education and surveillance capitalism. He tweets @whoseprivacy
Address: Faculty of Arts, School of Education, Deakin University, 221 Burwood Highway, Melbourne, Victoria 3125, Australia
E-Mail: matthew.thomas@deakin.edu.au

Dr.in Anna Wanka Anna Wanka obtained her PhD in sociology and is currently working as a postdoctoral researcher in the research training group ‚Doing Transitions' at Goethe University, Frankfurt am Main. Her areas of expertise comprise the social practices of doing age, life course transitions/retirement and the re/production of social inequalities across the life course.
E-Mail: wanka@em.uni-frankfurt.de

PD Dr. Sabine Weiß Akademische Rätin am Lehrstuhl für Schulpädagogik an der Ludwig-Maximilians-Universität München.
Adresse: LMU München, Lehrstuhl für Schulpädagogik, Leopoldstraße 13, 80802 München
E-Mail: sabine.weiss@edu.lmu.de

Dr. Ben Whitburn, PhD is Senior Lecturer of Inclusive Education at Deakin University and the Course Director of the Master of Specialist Inclusive Education. Dr Whitburn's research interests are aligned with critical disability studies and inclusive education. Ben's interest in temporality is to consider how teachers understand time in the context of inclusive teaching. He tweets @BenWhitburn
Address: Faculty of Arts, School of Education, Deakin University, 221 Burwood Highway, Melbourne, Victoria 3125, Australia
E-Mail: b.whitburn@deakin.edu.au

Time in Constructed Social Reality

Elisabeth Schilling and Maggie O'Neill

Time and, more precisely, time concepts are a cross-cutting issue which have been studied by different disciplines from different perspectives (see e.g. Damasio 2001 for neuroscientific research on time-induced emotions; Wittmann 2016 for psychological brain research on perception of time; Zimbardo und Boyd 2008 for socio-psychological research on time constructs and their influence on current action; Taylor 2002 on subjective time and present concepts in virtual computer games). In sociology time is often seen as a pivotal element of the social order (Elias 1984; Sorokin und Merton 1937; Bourdieu 2000; Rosa 2015, 2019; Vostal 2020). Because of this interdisciplinarity and omnipresence, dealing with the subject of time opens up diverse perspectives for looking at the construction of social reality. For example, 'Timescapes' was a five year programme of qualitative longitudinal (QL) research across five universities that examined personal lives and family relationships of 400 people across the life course on themes such as growing up, parenthood, the lives of older people to examine 'change in the making' and how it is 'lived and experienced.' By studying lives through time. 'QL research forms an important bridge between two parallel fields of enquiry – theoretical studies of time and empirically driven life course and longitudinal studies' (Neale 2012, S. 3; cf. Adam 1998).We

---

E. Schilling (✉)
University of Police and Public Administration NRW, Bielefeld, Germany
E-Mail: elisabeth.schilling@hspv.nrw.de

M. O'Neill
University College Cork, Cork, Ireland
E-Mail: Maggie.oneill@ucc.ie

conceptualize time as a meaningful and structuring category, which offers 'one, if not *the,* systematic link between actor and system perspectives' (Rosa 2015, S. 4).

However, the perspectives on the sociological view of the time are very heterogeneous. For example, time is of central importance for researching the biography. While reconstructing past biographical events and processes, we always refer to our current understanding of time and our future biographical projections (Rosenthal und Bogner 2017; O'Neill et al. 2014). Our understandings are not simply formed in a linear past-present-future, but rather time conceptions can be present-past; future-present; past-future (O'Neill and Roberts 2019). How we understand and experience time through forms of memory is a key aspect of the study of life story accounts and can be readily explored using creative methods, such as O'Neill and Roberts 'walking interview as a biographical method' (WIBM). In O'Neill and Roberts (2019, S. 245) autobiographical walks, they draw on two core themes from Benjamin's work: the concept of experience as lived moments (Erlebnis) and historical experience (Erfahrung) and the relationship of these, our histories, biographies and lived moments, to memory and involuntary memory to explore the links between memory, place and time. In the walking interview as biographical method and the sharing of experience on the move there is the everpresent potential for attunement to the landscape, other people, objects and landmarks that might spark involuntary memory. A relatively neglected dimension of the study of time in Sociology is the relationship between time and space the time/space intersections (Neale 2012; Seal and O'Neill 2019). Conducting a biographical interview whilst walking or moving enables us to record and attend to the 'enfolding and unfolding relations between body, space, place, the senses and social relations' and the lived experience of lives through time (O'Neill and Roberts 2019, S. 76).

Hence, the rapid development of the biographical paradigm in current sociology (or, in a broader perspective, the growing importance of memory studies, focused on the past) seems to reflect the growing social importance of time (re)construction and its necessity in the rapidly and unpredictably developing society. The destabilizing change in temporal structures creates the need for a balance and stabilization (Rosa 2019), among other things through the recourse to the (own) past and the restructuring of the experiences gained. The connection between the past and the present is continuously renewed and restored. In the past, people have achieved a certain degree of stability and can compensate for the loss of the familiar in an uncertain and unfamiliar present or threatening future (Lübbe 1989). The structuring or the restructuring of the past thus has an ordering and stabilizing role for the entire social structure as well as for the actors, who live within it and construct their life plans according to it (Schilling 2019).

Therefore social time does not flow linearly. The past is not always unalterable: dependent from the present and future needs it can be reflected and reconceptualized, past can turn to be more progressive and trendsetting than the future, returning might become a future goal. Therefore there are manifold interdependencies between different time modi; it is not always easy to differentiate between them. Nevertheless we structured this book in accordance with the common understanding about the flow of time. The interlinks between the chapters illustrate the holistic nature of time and the interdependencies between different focal points.

The first section of this book *Time, History and Biography. Zeit, Geschichte und Biografie* deals with the structuring of the past, which is often the subjective past, the individual biography. As we see in the chapters that make up this section biographies or life-stories have always a purpose, located in the present and future; they give stability, create identity, and offer solace. Felicitas Söhner focuses the clash of perspectives between professionals (historians) and the witnesses. The discourse on (biographical or historical) events and their interpretation affects strongly the identity issues of the involved persons. Simultaneously it allows to unveil the socio-cultural change in collective historical interpretations. The relationship between future, present and past in one's own biography as it conceptualized by George Herbert Mead is discussed in the paper by Lena Kahle. Ingmar Mundt's biographical narrative research with postgraduate students identifies two distinct ways in which the future is constructed, either through a linear perception or more episodically; both groups 'face an uncertain future after graduation' but also narrate various coping strategies in dealing with this uncertainty. Ahmed's chapter draws on interviews with women migrants to Spain in retirement, and explores nostalgia as 'chronotopic', that is to say, 'how the past is often recollected to make sense of the present and a focus on the past – and time as passing – is also a means of structuring and analysing narratives'. Sircova, Patterson and Schilling's interdisciplinary research explores subjective time concepts in relation to integration, belonging and successful acculturation strategies, through analysis of the 'cultural capital, which influences the individual's opportunities, biographies, and the feelings of belonging' and more creatively through the concept of biographical collage and 'the individual's representation of the future as an object'. The social norms in the construction of one's own life course are discussed by Anna Wanka. She argues that 'chronormativity' is stabilized and destabilized in social practices and hence form a link between the subjective and the social. Finally, Peter Alheit formulates in his paper a new concept for the biographical research "Biografizität", which helps to understand, how individuals' understand and implement social influencing.

The temporal structuring of the present, which is both, oriented towards the future and based on the past experience, is considered in the second section of this book: ***Time and Education. Zeit und Bildung.*** The diverse efforts to stabilize social time can be seen in the growing body of literature on the structuring of the present, e.g. on the time management of the private and professional life, on the temporal organization of certain activities, the search for the quality time or the attempt to slow down. In this section we focus on the time of education as it offers a perfect link between past, present and future. On the one hand, education includes the past knowledge or experience, which should be passed on to the next generation, for example in Thomas and Whitburn's chapter, the analysis of time, power and education informs wider applications of educational research.

Chiapparini, Scholian, Kappler and Schuler question the educational value of the leisure time within the institutional context of the day schools. Can more time at school bring 'more' of learning or improve its quality? Do the students perceive leisure activities at school as their leisure time as they cannot influence or shape it self-dependently? Chiapparini et al. focus these questions as the majority of the students in Switzerland spend increasingly more time at day schools and loose many options for self-determined day-time activities. They state that the students need to learn the management of this new form of leisure time. The authors conclude that the quality and the extent of the educational contents depend more from the perspectives and professional self-concepts of the pedagogues than from the school form. However time can be seen as an instrument of power in the context of the school, this fact is regarded critically by Syring et al. Emphasizing the temporal differences between the students (e.g. their processes' time) can be used by teachers as a part of the 'divide and rule' strategy. This differentiation creates new forms of inequality among the students, which is usually used by teachers in order to create and to restore the order, to synchronize the teaching between different students and classes or to coordinate the teaching. The orientation towards time teaches the students the code of conduct and homogenizes their behavior. Students might pass on this normative orientation towards time long time after they finish the school. As Kahl shows in her study, time related expectations play an important role in the educational motivation of mature students during their job continuing education and might influence its success.

Education hence always bears the future in mind: it is always the question, which contents exactly should be included into the course of instruction; which of them will be more useful, appropriate and expedient in the supposed future? Furthermore, educational processes take place in the present and they create and design the present time in form of constructing the temporal requirements, expectations, processes and structures. These temporal constructions are highly relevant for the actors' identities, their (life) satisfaction, their inclusion into the educational system and the educational success. For example Nurse explores time from the perspective of mothers, their everyday life routines (such as their walks together to primary school) associated with their identities and 'distinctive parenting styles' of their children. The dynamic of the organizational constraints and the individual logics or the contrast between the organizational (structural) and the individual (actor's) time forms the focus in this section. In these chapters we see explicitly the macro–micro link between the social structure and the individual actor.

The structuring of the future is regarded in the third section of the book: *Time, Future and Innovation. Zeit, Zukunft und Innovationen.* Innovations, planning possibilities and approaches to predicting the future are in the limelight in these chapters. The possibilities of shaping time and the future are an issue, since it can have a decisive influence on the chances and development perspectives of the single actors, organizations and complex social structures. Malte Schophaus shows in his chapter the planning practices of the German public administration on the example of digital transformation of human resources management, which is simultaneously regarded to be a potential threat for the existing processes, but also a chance for an improvement in different areas of public administration. Future plans usually project past and present constructions into the unknown future, making it less unknown, less threatening, overall more understandable and manageable. Drawing up the future plans creates the illusion of a predictable, structurable and feasible time that corresponds to the needs of the subjects, especially in the periods of uncertainty. Future plans give orientation and security. Kerstin Cuhls shows in her chapter how the structured long-term planning can work and practically help to deal with unknown future, especially in the organisational settings. Gerrit von Jork and Sonja Geiger discuss the transformative research and its potential impact on innovative and sustainable time politics. Especially their notion of time prosperity seems to be fruitful for the further discussion.

The last section of this book: *Methodology for the Study of Time. Methodologien der Zeitforschung,* deals with methodological opportunities and challenges, which are offered by a dedicated methodological analysis of time. The diversity of time-related topics and research questions seems to offer great potential for describing the nature and functioning of the social context. In particular, this potential seems to lie in the expansion of concepts for functional differentiation and social inequality to include the actor-related perspective. At the same time, the diversity of perspectives and interrelations also poses a problem for a systematic view of social time as a differentiation category. A conception of the sociology of time that would consider different research fields in a coherent manner has so far been lacking. In this chapter we attempt to give an overview about the new methodological possibilities of time research.

Gordt and Laux describe comparative process analysis as a methodology to analyze temporal dynamics. This is a qualitative analysis, which regards time as an important factor for social processes and gives researchers an important tool to unveil causalities within single cases. Also Doris Cornils reports about an innovative methodology, named VAA which she developed in order to analyze the everyday lifestyle of families with working parents and their children. It facilitates a temporal perspective on the basis of self-reporting documentation. Cornils shows a research practice, how to structure ethnographical data in a time-sensitive way. Coenen reflects the time of communication using the communicative constructivist approach. The ways to improve the quality of the data are therefore analyzed, as well as some alternatives for collecting data. Coenen proposes to include more audiovisual recordings, ethnographical observations or artefact analyses into the research setting. Moreira, Guerra, Lima and take a creative approach to understanding temporalities in the life narratives of adolescents involved in crime in Brazil by using their 'narrative memoirs' or 'flash fiction' as arguably, a more psychosocial method to understand the complexities of young lives. Dréano and Rudolfi's chapter contributes to Science and Technology Studies (STS) through a methodological technique called 'rough relationing' that is used to analyse temporalities in ethnographic research and specifically 'how time and temporalities 'mess with' our ethnographic practices'. In Ramanujam, Broer and Giani review they focus on exploring temporality within qualitative longtitudinal studies on 'experiences of sickness, health and wellbeing'. Drawing upon literature from four databases and an initial sample of 152 studies they discuss four modes of temporality across these studies: 'interrupted time, phasic time, continuous time and cyclical time'.

In summary, this book provides an overview of current advances in time related research in relation to: time, history and biography; time and education; time, future and innovation; and methodologies for the study of time. Time concepts discussed here, create the sense of social structures; they give orientation to the individual and organizational actors and structure social life. Time further creates links between social structures and individuals, between collective and individual past and possible futures. The research on time hence makes an important contribution to our understanding of social reality and our ability to form, construct or create it. Research on time is, as the chapters in this collection make clear, a vital aspect when studying societies and lives in flux; and in our current age, the age of pandemics, time related research is of the utmost importance.

References

Adam, B. (1998). Timescapes of Modernity. The environment and invisible hazards. London and New York: Routledge.
Bourdieu, P. (2000). *Die zwei Gesichter der Arbeit. Interdependenzen von Zeit- und Wirtschaftsstrukturen am Beispiel einer Ethnologie der algerischen Übergangsgesellschaft.* Konstanz: UVK.
Damasio, A. (2001). Fundamental feelings. *Nature, 413*, S. 781.
Elias, N. (1984). *Über die Zeit. Arbeiten zur Wissenssoziologie II.* Frankfurt am Main: Suhrkamp.
Neale, B. (2012) Qualitative Longitudinal research: an introduction to the Timescapes methods Guides series. https://www.timescapes.leeds.ac.uk/assets/files/methods-guides/timescapes-methods-guides-introduction.pdf (accessed 4th May 2020).
O'Neill, M. & Roberts, B. (2019) *Walking Methods:Research on the Move.* London: Routledge.
O'Neill, M. Roberts & B. Sparkes, A.C. (2014) *Advances in Biographical Methods* [Eds]. London:Routledge.
Rosa, H. (2015). *Social Acceleration: A New Theory of Modernity.* New York: Columbia University.
Rosa, H. (2019). *Resonance: A Sociology of Our Relationship to the World.* Cambridge: Polity Press.
Rosenthal, G. & Bogner, A. (2017). Biographies – discourses – figurations: Methodological considerations from the perspective of social constructivism and figurational sociology. In G. Rosenthal, & A. Bogner, *Biographies in the Global South. Life stories embedded in figurations and discourses* (S. 15–49). Frankfurt am Main: Campus.
Schilling, E. (2019). Making sense of large numbers: Biographical projects of young migrants. *Ethnicities, 19*(3), S. 575-591.
Seal, L. & O'Neill.M. (2019). *Imaginative Criminology: Of spaces past, present and future.* Bristol:Policy.
Sorokin, P. A. & Merton, R. K. (1937). Social Time. A Methodological and Functional Analysis. *American Journal of Sociology, 42*(5), S. 615–629.
Taylor, T. (2002). Living Digitally: Embodiment in Virtual Worlds. In R. Schroeder, *The Social Life of Avatars: Presence and Interaction in Shared Virtual Environments* (S. 40-62). London: Springer.
Vostal, F. (2020). *Inquiring into Academic Timescapes.* Bingley: Emerald.
Wittmann, M. (2016). *Gefühlte Zeit: kleine Psychologie des Zeitempfindens.* München: Beck.
Zimbardo, P. G. & Boyd, J. N. (2008). *The time paradox.* New York: Free Press/Simon & Schuster.

# Time, History and Biography. Zeit, Geschichte und Biografie

Umgang mit Identitätskonstruktion und Zeitwahrnehmung in der Oral History

Felicitas Söhner

Abstract

The experience in oral history shows in some cases that personal experiences and historical events are weighted differently and thus quite individual perspectives of history emerge. This contribution reflects on the conflict of interpretations between historians and eye witnesses, which can be amplified by divergent interpretive patterns between contemporary history and historical politics. The method used her is an analysis of the current discourse by means of targeted literature research. In addition to biographical self-construction, the focus is on the level of time perception. Biographical representations are discussed in their interdependence with the respective historical-social context.It can be asserted that while contemporary evidence documents to some extent historical events and processes, it rather indicates how they were perceived and classified. The article describes to what extent autobiographical narratives reflect the current zeitgeist.

Zusammenfassung

Die Erfahrung in der Oral History zeigt in manchen Fällen, dass persönliche Erfahrungen und historische Ereignisse unterschiedlich gewichtet werden und damit durchaus individuelle Perspektiven von Geschichte entstehen. Dieser Beitrag reflektiert den Deutungskonflikt zwischen Historikern und Gesprächspartnern,

F. Söhner (✉)
University of Düsseldorf, Düsseldorf, Deutschland
E-Mail: Felicitas.Soehner@hhu.de

© Springer Fachmedien Wiesbaden GmbH, ein Teil von Springer Nature 2020
E. Schilling und M. O'Neill (Hrsg.), *Frontiers in Time Research – Einführung in die interdisziplinäre Zeitforschung*,
https://doi.org/10.1007/978-3-658-31252-7_2

der durch abweichende Deutungsmuster zwischen Zeitgeschichte und Geschichtspolitik verstärkt werden kann. Methodisch stützt sich die Autorin auf eine Analyse des aktuellen Diskurses mittels gezielter Literaturrecherche. Im Fokus steht, neben der biographischen Selbstkonstruktion im Zusammenhang, die Ebene der Zeitwahrnehmung. Diskutiert werden biographische Darstellungen in ihrer Interdependenz mit dem jeweiligen historisch-sozialen Kontext.

Es zeigte sich, dass biographische Erinnerungen zwar bis zu einem gewissen Grad historische Ereignisse und Prozesse beschreiben, doch vielmehr darüber aussagen, wie diese wahrgenommen und eingeordnet wurden. Der Beitrag stellt dar, inwiefern autobiografische Narrative mehr den aktuellen Zeitgeist abbilden.

Schlüsselwörter

Geschichtsbild · Historische Methode · mündliche Geschichte · Sinnstiftung · Zeitkonstruktion

Zum Einstieg

Das Konzept der Oral History berührt Historiker, Praktiker wie Rezipienten, die sich auch außerhalb der traditionellen Geschichtswissenschaft bewegen können. Dieser Ansatz lässt es zu, sich der Geschichte ‚von unten' bzw. ‚von innen heraus' zuzuwenden. Die Literatur verweist auf die Rolle von biographischer Erinnerungen als „kommunikative Strukturierungen, […] die soziale und individuelle Zeit nutzen und erzeugen". (Fischer 2018, S. 461).

In manchen Fällen erwecken Interviewaussagen den Eindruck, persönliche Erfahrungen und historische Ereignisse unterschiedlich zu gewichten und so letztlich eine personalisierte Perspektive auf zurückliegende Zeit zu konstruieren. So im kontrastierenden Vergleich narrativer Praxen zeigt sich, dass manche Quellen ein ausgeprägtes ‚History-Fashioning' vermuten lassen (Berkhofer 2008). Dieser Effekt kann entstehen, wenn sich massenmedial repräsentiertes Bildinventar über eigene, lebensgeschichtliche Erinnerung legt – ein Phänomen, das sich etwa bei persönlichen Erinnerungen aus der NS-Zeit immer wieder zeigt, dass Aussagen letztendlich mehr über die Persönlichkeit des Befragten verraten als über die tatsächlichen historischen Fakten (Welzer 2008; Plato 2008).

Ein Aspekt in der mündlichen Geschichtsschreibung, der kritisch reflektiert werden sollte, liegt in einem Deutungskonflikt zwischen Zeitzeugen und

Historikern. An Projekten beteiligte Gesprächspartner können als Akteure von Institutionen strategische Positionen im Erinnerungsdiskurs besetzen, was einen distanzierten, retrospektiven Blick auf historische Ereignisse und Prozesse beinahe an ihre Grenzen bringen kann. Die daraus resultierende Spannung, insbesondere durch abweichende Deutungsmuster zwischen Zeitgeschichte und Geschichtspolitik, muss in der Auswertung problematisiert und berücksichtigt werden. Dessen Umsetzung fordert ein reflektiertes Forschungshandeln und wird im vorliegenden Beitrag diskutiert. Im Fokus steht neben der biographischen Selbstkonstruktion im Zusammenhang der Ebene der Zeitwahrnehmung. Betrachtet wird, wie die Darstellung von Individualbiographien als Teil eines kollektiven Gedächtnisses wirken, indem sie das Erleben politischer, kultureller und sozialer Zeiterscheinungen widerspiegeln. Der Beitrag diskutiert biographische Darstellungen in ihrer Interdependenz mit dem jeweiligen historisch-sozialen Kontext. Die Autorin konzentriert sich auf einen exemplarischen Ausschnitt aus einem Bereich der historischen Forschung.

Oral History und Zeitzeugen

Zeitzeugen generieren mit ihren Erinnerungen Geschichte und machen diese für ihre Rezipienten zugänglich. Über die Erinnerungen eröffnen biographische Dokumente die Möglichkeit, historische Perspektiven des Alltags oder auch Wahrnehmungen von Minderheiten zu erfahren. Diese alternative Perspektive erkannte Lutz Niethammer als eine Notwendigkeit und forderte eine ‚Geschichte von unten': *„Eine demokratische Zukunft bedarf einer Vergangenheit, in der nicht nur die Oberen hörbar sind"*. (Niethammer 1980).

In diesem Sinne verfolgt die Oral History das Ziel, neben bislang tradierten Narrativen (kollektives Gedächtnis) stehende Aspekte subjektiver Erfahrungsgeschichte zu untersuchen. Sie ist zu verstehen als retrospektive, heuristische Methode, durch die in einem kollaborativen Austausch (biographisches Interview) mündliche Dokumente (Erinnerungen von Menschen) generiert und analysiert werden (Söhner 2020b). Je nach Erkenntnisinteresse wird in der mündlichen Geschichtsschreibung auf unterschiedliche Interviewformen zurückgegriffen – wie das biographische, thematische oder Experteninterview (Wierling 2003, S. 109 f.). Das strukturierte Interview orientiert sich an einem Leitfaden, der Impulsfragen enthalten kann zu persönlichem Hintergrund, Lebensgeschichte und Netzwerken, persönlichen Idealen und Zielen sowie Verortung der eigenen Rolle und angehöriger Institutionen (Miethe und Laak 2018, S. 593). Gleichzeitig enthält diese Form des Interviews eine abschließende Gesprächsphase, in der Deutungsmuster, Begründungen und Bewertungen angesprochen werden können. Gleichzeitig sollen das Interviewsetting und mögliche Antworten möglichst wenig beeinflusst werden (Krischel et al. 2018). Um eine zu tiefe Vorstrukturierung des Interviews zu vermeiden, sollen die Fragen offen formuliert werden, sodass die Befragten die Möglichkeit haben, den Gesprächsverlauf auf die zu ihnen relevant erscheinende Inhalte zu lenken (Gläser und Laudel 2010).

Im Zentrum sollte die Narration von Erinnerungen stehen: Wenn Menschen über sich selbst erzählen, sprechen sie darüber, wie es zu den Erlebnissen und Ereignissen kam, warum sie sich so entwickelt und in einer bestimmten Weise gehandelt und entschieden haben und warum ihnen Vorhaben geglückt oder misslungen sind. Die Entwicklung der eigenen Biographie wird nicht nur berichtet, sondern auch erklärt und begründet. Damit setzt das Individuum sich und den eigenen Werdegang in ein Verhältnis zur Welt und die Geschichte. Die Ereignisse werden in einer sinnstiftenden Ordnung dargestellt, auch wenn diese Ordnung nicht der historischen Realität entsprechen muss (Corsten 1994). Die mit der Aufzeichnung von biographischen Erinnerungen generierten Quellen können sich dann in einer inhaltsanalytischen Auswertung auf historische und gegenwärtige Wahrnehmungs- und Verhaltensmuster analysieren lassen (Söhner 2020a).

Erinnerung als Sinnbildung

Der Erkenntniswert von mündlichen Quellen aus Zeitzeugengesprächen ist und war mehrfach Gegenstand geschichtswissenschaftlicher Debatten (Jureit 1998, 1999; Daniel 2001). Im Sinne von Wierling erscheinen mündliche Quellen in der Analyse gegenüber schriftlichen Quellen als gleichwertig, da sie *„nicht weniger, sondern anders"* als niedergeschriebene Dokumente Vergangenheit vermitteln (Wierling 2003, S. 82).

Ein epistemologisches Problem der mündlichen Geschichtsschreibung ist, dass die aufgezeichneten Erinnerungen nicht als Dokumente der Vergangenheit verstanden werden dürfen, sondern vielmehr als Ausdruck der Gegenwart.

Biographische Erinnerungen entsprechen eher lebensgeschichtlichen Konstruktionen, die sich in kollektiven und individuellen Umarbeitungsprozessen permanent wandeln und durch äußere Einflüsse vielfach geprägt werden (Halbwachs 1967). Die Oral History geht davon aus, dass jede Erinnerung vom sozialen Umfeld geprägt wird. Der Soziologe Maurice Halbwachs betonte darüber hinaus den Einfluss des gesellschaftlichen Bezugsrahmens auf individuelle Erinnerungen: *„Die Gesellschaft stellt sich die Vergangenheit je nach den Umständen und je nach der Zeit in verschiedener Weise vor: sie modifiziert ihre Konventionen.*

Da sich jedes ihrer Glieder diesen Konventionen beugt, so lenkt es auch seine Erinnerungen in die gleiche Richtung, in die sich das kollektive Gedächtnis entwickelt". (Halbwachs 1985, S. 368).

Neben gesellschaftlichen Einflüssen können Erinnerungen, insbesondere die traumatischen Ursprungs, durch Entlastungsstrategien modifiziert sein (Keilbach 2010, S. 194). In diesem Zusammenhang können *„die individuellen Vergangenheiten bis zu einem gewissen Grad erst erschaffen [werden] – durch Auslassungen ebenso wie durch Uminterpretationen"*. (Daniel 2001, S. 307).

Für die historische Analyse stellt sich damit die Frage nach der Objektivität und Authentizität der mündlichen Quelle (Mayring 2015). Es ist davon auszugehen, dass lebensgeschichtliche Interviews, ebenso wie andere Repräsentationen historischer Ereignisse und Entwicklungen, keine getreuen Abbilder vergangener Geschehnisse liefern, sondern vielmehr an Wahrnehmung, Verstehen und Deutung gebundene Auffassungen des Geschehens (Straub 2001, S. 45). Daher ist es geboten, sie kritisch einzuordnen und in der Analyse nicht unmittelbar von erzählten Erinnerungen auf eine soziale Wirklichkeit zu schließen (Jureit 1999, S. 10).

Erinnerung als Generator von Identität

Erinnerungen, insbesondere Selbstthematisierungen, hängen eng mit Identität zusammen. Für Maurice Halbwachs gelten Erinnerungen durchweg als gegenwartsbezogen und Resultat der Auseinandersetzung mit der sozialen Umwelt. Halbwachs betonte: *„Wir bewahren aus jeder unserer Lebensepochen einige Erinnerungen, die wir immer wieder reproduzieren, und durch diese hindurch hält sich wie in einer kontinuierlichen Verkettung das Gefühl unserer Identität."* (Halbwachs 1985, S. 132) Da jede – persönliche wie institutionelle – Biographie auf Erinnerungen basiert, lässt sich die Funktion ihrer Narration darin verstehen, die einzelnen Elemente und damit die eigene Vergangenheit in einem kohärenten Zusammenhang darzustellen.

Episodische Erinnerungen gleichen einer mentalen Zeitreise des Selbst (Tulving 1999, S. 278) und können durch ihren Selbstbezug die Voraussetzung für die Herstellung biographischer Kontinuität und damit Identität schaffen. Gleichzeitig konzentriert sich personale wie kollektive Identität nicht allein auf ein Gefühl von Kontinuität, sondern auch auf Entwicklungen und damit auf Veränderungen, Abgrenzungen und Brüche.

Der Terminus der ‚Identität' ist ein interdisziplinär diskutiertes Konzept. Die Debatte zu Begriff und dessen Verständnis basiert auf unterschiedlichen

Annahmen zum Wesen und zur Generierung von Identität. Während die Sozialpsychologie darunter das innere Selbstbild bzw. das repräsentionale Selbstkonzept eines Individuums versteht (Mummendey 2006), begreift die Soziologie ‚Identität' in sozialen Rollenkontexten als ein durch Situation und Interaktion geprägtes Handlungskonzept, quasi als „*Patchwork der Identitäten*". (Straus und Höfer 1998; Keupp et al. 1999; Höfer 2000).

In der soziologischen Identitätsforschung gilt die soziale Gruppe als von zentraler Bedeutung, ohne die Sinnwelten weder entstehen noch weitergegeben werden können (Erll 2017, S. 13): Die Erikson interessiert sich für ‚Ich-Identität' und ‚persönliche Identität' (Erikson 1970), Goffman beschäftigt sich mit ‚persönlicher' und ‚sozialer Identität' (Goffman 1967), bei Reck geht es um ‚Selbst-Identität' (Reck 1981), bei McCall und Simmons um ‚Rollen-Identität' (McCall und Simmons 1974). Wahrnehmungen und individuelle Erinnerungen werden sozial geprägt verstanden und jede Form der Sinnstiftung als unmöglich ohne den Bezug zu einem kollektiven Gedächtnis. Über die Kombination mehrerer sozialer und damit Identitäten konstituierender Zugehörigkeiten (Profession, Milieu, Ethnie, Geschlecht) verfügt jedes Individuum über unterschiedliche gruppenspezifische Erfahrungen und Denksysteme. So bestimmen unter anderem auch die Kombination unterschiedlicher Gruppierungen und damit zusammenhängende Erinnerungsmuster die Gedächtnisse einzelner Personen (Erll 2017, S. 13). Vertreter der Soziologie verstehen ‚Identität' als „*Krisenbegriff der Moderne*" (Heinze 2009, S. 173, Berger et al. 1975, S. 85), deren Konstruktion Arbeitscharakter habe. In diesem Zusammenhang verweist Zygmunt Bauman auf einen Wandel von Inklusionsinstanzen in der postmodernen Gesellschaft und reflektiert einen tiefgreifenden kulturellen Epochenumbruch hin zu einem spezifisch postmodernen Typus der Welt- und Selbstdeutung. Nach Baumans zeitdiagnostischen Deutungen werde soziale Identität in der Postmoderne nicht mehr über die Mitgliedschaften in Organisationen und Institutionen hergestellt, sondern über die Teilhabe an bestimmten milieugenerierenden Lebensstilen (Bauman 1999; Söhner 2013). Damit gälten sozio-ökonomische, kulturelle und personale Dimensionen auf das Engste miteinander verschränkt (Eickelpasch und Rademacher 2013, S. 40 ff.). Bauman beschreibt einen Wandel weg von einer stabilen Ich-Identität, hin zu wechselnden Selbst-Entwürfen und dem Spiel mit Identitäten.

Der Sozialpsychologe Heiner Keupp verweist auf eine universelle Notwendigkeit zur individuellen Identitätskonstruktion basierend auf einem menschlichen Grundbedürfnis nach Anerkennung und Zugehörigkeit (Keupp 1999, S. 28). Identität steht hier als ein Rahmenkonzept, in das Erfahrungen integriert und innerhalb dessen Deutungsmuster generiert werden können (Keupp 1999, S. 60).

Nach Sicht des Kulturwissenschaftlers und Erinnerungsforschers Jan Assmann entsteht Identität aus einer Wechselwirkung mit Alterität und setzt andere Identitäten voraus (Assmann 1992, S. 135). Assmann (1992, S. 132) definiert den Terminus der ‚kollektiven Identität' als ein „*Bild, das eine Gruppe von sich aufbaut und mit dem sich deren Mitglieder identifizieren.*" Über das Betonen von Differenzen nach außen und deren Vernachlässigen nach innen erhält die eigene Identität im narrativen Erinnern Gestalt. Die Literaturwissenschaft spricht von Identität ebenfalls im Zusammenhang mit der Frage nach Referentialität und Subjektivität des Erzählens (Zima 2000, S. 70–86).

Die Geschichtswissenschaft beschäftigt sich mit Identität im Verständnis einer Identitätsbildung durch Narrative in der Geschichte (Angehrn 1985), in Zusammenhang mit der Frage nach der eigentlichen Bestimmung des Menschen (Lembeck 2000) und der Rolle der Menschen als Macher ihrer eigenen Geschichte (Marx und Engels 1972). In diesem Sinne definiert Harald Welzer Identität als „*das Gefühl, über ein identisches und kohärentes Selbst zu verfügen, (das) im Wesentlichen auf expliziten, episodischen Erinnerungen an Elemente der eigenen Lebensgeschichte*" (Welzer 2002, S. 30) gründet. Der Historiker Lutz Niethammer (2000, S. 33) bemerkt vor diesem Hintergrund einen inflationären, diffusen Einsatz des Begriffes und kritisiert diesen aufgrund einer unüberschaubaren Bedeutungsfülle als „*Plastikwort*". Niethammer unterzieht den Begriff der ‚Identität' einer Fundamentalkritik: so gebe es keine „*Identität an sich*", vielmehr existiere diese nur als Konstruktion (Niethammer 2000, S. 44).

Identität und Identitätskonstruktion

Ausgehend vom Konstruktionscharakter einer jeden Biographie werden erhobene Erinnerungen in ihrer Doppelbedeutung als Quelle zur Rekonstruktion vergangener Wirklichkeit und subjektiver Erfahrungs- und Verarbeitungsprozesse zu historischen Ereignissen verstanden (Wierling 1995, S. 51; Wierling 2003, S. 81; Söhner et al. 2016, 2017). Das ‚*Skript*' eines autobiographischen Narratives ließe sich in diesem Sinne einordnen als ein gesellschaftliches, kulturell geprägtes Muster der Identitätskonstruktion. In der biographischen Erzählung werden zentrale Erlebnisse und als bedeutsam erinnerte Beziehungskonstellationen geschildert, die als identitätskonstituierend verstanden werden. Diese werden eingebettet in den sozialen Bezugsrahmen, das Lebensmilieu und den sozialgeschichtlichen Hintergrund, insofern diese als eher relevant verstanden werden. Ecarius geht davon aus, dass das erzählende Subjekt in der biographischen Rekonstruktion „*sein Leben in Form von Erfahrungszusammenhängen und*

Ereignisverkettungen darstellt, die auf biographische Lernprozesse" hinweisen (Ecarius 2006, S. 98). Diese als Lerngeschichten präsentierten Lebensgeschichten lassen sich in einem identitätskonstituierenden Zusammenhang verstehen. Erinnerte Ereignisse stellen mehr als nur Sinn- bzw. Bedeutungseinheiten eines biographischen Lernprozesses dar, sondern auch die Kategorisierung relevanter Erfahrungen vor weiteren als irrelevant erlebten Ereignissen. Damit lassen sich die in biographischen Gesprächen festgehaltenen Erinnerungen also weniger als Abbild erlebter Geschehnisse, sondern vielmehr als Indikator für die jeweilige Persönlichkeit, deren Identitätsgefühl und Verhalten, verstehen.

In Anlehnung an Hoff (1990, S. 13 ff.) kreiert ein Individuum seine Identität nach zeitlichen, inhaltlichen und sozialen Dimensionen: *Zum Ersten* werden auf einer *Zeit*linie biographische Erlebnisse und Episoden zu einer kontinuierlichen Abfolge geordnet. *Zum Zweiten* werden auf der *inhaltlichen* Ebene lebensweltliche Divergenzen und Konflikte sachlogisch in einen konsistenten Identitätsentwurf integriert. Hier stellt sich die Frage: Was sind die Merkmale, Eigenschaften oder Gefühle, über die sich Individuen charakterisieren oder über die sie charakterisiert werden? *Zum Dritten* ringt ein Individuum um die Validierung und Anerkennung der Identitätskonfiguration im *sozialen* Raum, wozu es die Unterstützung signifikanter Bezugsakteure mobilisieren und diese über performative Akte sicherstellen muss.

Das lebensgeschichtliche Narrativ ermöglicht die Kontinuierung von Identität trotz sich wandelnder Selbstbilder in einer kontextgebundenen, konsistenten Lebensgeschichte, insbesondere durch explanative Übergänge zwischen disparaten Selbstentwürfen sowie Erklärungsmustern für allmähliche oder plötzliche Veränderungen und instabile Phasen (Linville und Carlston 1994, S. 170; Straub 2000, S. 284). Aus diesen Integrationsleistungen resultieren, trotz einer Konsolidierung im höheren Lebensalter, stets nur episodenweise stabile Identitätskonstruktionen, was einen alltäglichen wie lebenslangen Prozess der Identitätsarbeit bedeutet (Leipold und Greve 2008; Roberts und Caspi 2003, 205 ff.). So lässt sich Identitätsarbeit als eine Bewältigungsstrategie verstehen und daraus resultierende Identitätskonstruktionen als kommunikative Aushandlungsprozesse (Heinze 2009, S. 174) und Ergebnis von Verarbeitungsprozessen historischer, situativer Anforderungen (Rothermund und Brandtstädter 1997, 120; Born 2002, S. 31; Leipold und Greve 2008, S. 407).

Diesem äußerst komplexen Thema begegnet der Beitrag damit, dass im Folgenden ein Teilaspekt herausgegriffen und Identität als ein individuell konstruiertes Phänomen im Zusammenhang der zeitlichen Dimension betrachtet wird.

Identität und Zeitwahrnehmung

Identitätskonstruktionen lassen sich zunächst als konfliktbehaftetes Unterfangen verstehen: Fremd- und Selbstbild stimmen nicht zwangsläufig überein und müssen, damit soziale Interaktion gelingen kann, in ein für beide Seiten passendes Verhältnis gebracht werden (Lührmann 2006, S. 192). Ein Individuum lässt sich sowohl als Objekt als auch Subjekt der Identitätskonstruktion verstehen. Es kann sich als Subjekt der Identitätskonstruktion anders beschreiben als es als Objekt der Identitätskonstruktion tatsächlich ist. Hier fallen Persönlichkeit und Identität auseinander (Reck 1981; Lührmann 2006, S. 152).

Gleichzeitig benötigt das Individuum die Anerkennung, der von ihm gewünschten Identität, von seinen Interaktionspartnern. Diese können die Anderen dem Individuum nicht um jeden Preis vorenthalten, denn auch sie benötigen wiederum die Anerkennung für die Identität, die sie in der Interaktion einnehmen möchten (Keupp 1999 214; Krappmann 2000, S. 78). Damit liegt die Einigung auf eine Identitätsbalance im Interesse der meisten Beteiligten.

Das narrative Erinnern hat neben einer identitätskonstruierenden auch eine zeitordnende Funktion inne und strebt danach *„auch heterogene Erfahrungen in einen sinnvollen Zusammenhang zu stellen."* (Bär 2014, S. 34).

Die Zeit gilt als weltordnende und -deutende Kategorie und ständiger Gegenstand geisteswissenschaftlicher Nachdenkens. Die Zeitwahrnehmung gilt als eine der fundamentalen kulturellen Kategorien, die die Konstruktion von Identität beeinflussen (Corradini 2009). Analysen verweisen im historischen wie internationalen Vergleich auf eine zutiefst kulturell geprägte Wahrnehmung von und auch im Umgang mit Zeit (Götze 2004; Levine 1999). Zeit erscheint insbesondere als ein sozio-kulturelles Konstrukt, das sich im Austausch mit naturwissenschaftlichen, ökonomischen wie philosophischen Wahrnehmungs- und Deutungsmustern von Welt und Existenz wandelt.

Zeit wird jedoch nicht objektiv erlebt. Das Phänomen ‚subjektive Zeitwahrnehmung' lässt sich umschreiben mit der Erinnerung einer schwierigen Prüfungssituation (länger) und ein fröhliches Treffen mit Freunden (kürzer). Auch ist den meisten das Phänomen bekannt, dass die Wochen vor Weihnachten für ein Kind wie eine Ewigkeit scheinen, während sie für einen Erwachsenen wie im Flug vergehen. Vor diesem Hintergrund lässt sich subjektive Zeit verstehen als die zeitliche Wahrnehmung eines Individuums in einer Situation mit Bezug auf die Dauer und die Aufeinanderfolge von Ereignissen (Richelle 1996). Gleichzeitig ist der Begriff der ‚Zeitwahrnehmung' missverständlich, da er den Eindruck verstärkt, dass Zeitempfinden ein umgrenztes, homogenes Konstrukt sei.

Mehrere Untersuchungen verstehen unter diesem Oberbegriff ein Konglomerat zeitbezogener Wahrnehmungen (Fraisse 1984; Wassenhove 2009), deren Beziehungen zueinander kontrovers diskutiert werden (Eagleman 2008; Grondin 2001; Pöppel 2009; Weiß 2012).

Der Neurowissenschaftler David Eagleman versteht subjektiv empfundene Zeit als heterogenes Phänomen. Er geht davon aus, dass unterschiedlichen zeitlichen Wahrnehmungseindrücken unabhängige neuronale Mechanismen zugrunde liegen, die in der Regel, jedoch nicht zwingend, miteinander harmonieren: „*In the domain of time perception, it is probable that duration, simultaneity, temporary order, flicker rate, and other judgments are underpinned by different mechanisms that normally concur but are not required to.*" (Eagleman 2008, S. 134).

Die Wahrnehmung der zeitlichen Dimension ist äußerst vielschichtig und bedeutet vor allem, wie Zeit an sich von Individuen und Institutionen erlebt, geplant oder erinnert wird (Giddens 2008). Die subjektive Wahrnehmung der Zeitaspekte spielt in der historischen Analyse eine wichtige Rolle, da die Akteure neben der Beschreibung von Ereignissen und Abläufen auch Wertvorstellungen, zugewiesene Bedeutungsgehalte, eingrenzende Bedingungen und situative Begleitumstände übermitteln und damit dem Narrativ ein spezifisches, weitgehend individuelles Gepräge verleihen können (Perich 1992, S. 245). Zudem spielen in der Zeiterfahrung auch Weltwissen sowie autobiographisches Gedächtnis eine wesentliche Rolle.

Gleichzeitig lässt sich die Wahrnehmung des subjektiven Jetzt, das unmittelbar für jeden Menschen erfahrbar ist (Fraisse 1963, 1984; Wittmann 2011), verstehen als breite Schwelle zwischen Zukunft und Vergangenheit – quasi Zeitintervalle, die selbst nicht unmittelbar erfahrbar sind, sondern vielmehr antizipiert oder erinnert werden. Der Psychologe Stroud entwickelte die Hypothese eines minimalen psychologischen Moments (Allport 1968; Stroud 1956, 1967), nach der Zeit im Unterschied zur individuellen Wahrnehmung und ihrer physikalischen Definition nicht kontinuierlich, sondern diskret verläuft. Dies bedeutet, dass sie sich in aufeinanderfolgende Einheiten psychologischer Momente verschiedener Längen einteilen lässt. Darüber hinaus stellte die Forschung in der Wahrnehmung der Aufeinanderfolge von Reizen häufige Fehler und Wahrnehmungstäuschungen fest (Scharlau 2007; Weiß und Scharlau 2011). Der Aspekt des Fehlers im zeitlichen Urteil ist in der subjektiven Wahrnehmung ein Aspekt, der bei der Interpretation biographischer Narration berücksichtigt werden muss (Söhner 2017).

In der biographischen Erzählung ordnen die Gesprächspartner identitätsrelevante Erlebnisse und Episoden auf einer mentalen *Zeit*linie in eine Kette von Abläufen ein. Die Zeitdimensionen können im Erzählfluss ineinander verwoben und damit die konkrete Gestaltung der Gegenwart, Vergangenheitsbewusstsein wie Zukunftskonzeption gleichzeitig dargestellt werden (Czock und Rathmann-Lutz 2016, S. 9).

Über die Rekonstruktion der Vergangenheit spiegelt das Narrativ der Erinnerungen in Anlehnung an Lührmann eine in verschiedenen Zeitdimensionen wirkende Identitätsarbeit: in einer retrospektiven Identitätskonstruktion, einer aktuellen Identitätsfiguration und einer Antizipation künftiger Identitätsinhalte (Lührmann 2006, S. 223). Damit beziehen sich Aussagen zur Zeitwahrnehmung sowohl auf die Vergangenheit als auch Gegenwart und Zukunft. Die Fragen ‚Woher komme ich?', ‚Wer bin ich?' und ‚Wohin gehe ich?' lassen sich hier als auf das Engste miteinander zusammenhängend einordnen (Lührmann 2006). In dieser Logik existiert auch keine Erinnerung, die nicht auch auf das Gegenwartsbild und die Zukunftsorientierung ausgerichtet wäre (Markus und Nurius 1986, S. 954).

Die Kulturwissenschaftlerin Astrid Erll versteht in diesem Zusammenhang das individuelle wie kollektive Gedächtnis als eine Art Schaltstelle, in der Erfahrungen prospektiv und retrospektiv organisiert werden und nach unterschiedlichen Mustern entschieden wird, welche Erinnerungen grundsätzlich in das Bewusstsein dringen und wie diese Informationen weiter verarbeitet werden. So würden erst in der deutenden Rückschau auf die Vergangenheit die Voraussetzungen dafür geschaffen, dass Erfahrungen überhaupt gemacht würden (Erll 2017, S. 124). Dessen ungeachtet kann auch die Art und Weise, wie sich ein Erzählender der Oral History-Forschung präsentieren möchte, zu inhaltlichen Verzerrungen führen. Als Aufgabe der historischen Analyse kann gesehen werden, den Zeitgeist und Zeitverständnis der mündlichen Dokumente aufzuspüren und diese in die Interpretation einzubeziehen.

Als ein nicht unerheblicher Aspekt in der historiographischen Einordnung der Erinnerungen gilt die Einflussnahme bisher publizierter Geschichtsschreibung auf deren Wahrnehmungen. So können Erinnerungen einem oft unbemerkten Wandel unterliegen. Als eindrückliches Beispiel lässt sich hier die Analyse des Historikers Helmut Schnatz (2000) anführen, der sich mit den Reminiszenzen an die Bombardierung von Dresden im Februar 1945 beschäftigte. Schnatz sammelte zum Teil höchst emotionale Zeitzeugenberichte, die von regelrechten Menschenjagden durch Tiefflieger schilderten. Gleichzeitig fand Schnatz in der Untersuchung deutscher wie alliierter Akten keine Belege für die vorliegenden Aussagen. Diese Diskrepanzen interpretiert Schnatz als typisierte, zu stereotypen Formen geronnene Versatzstücke der kollektiven Erinnerung. Sich auf Sozialpsychologie und Hirnforschung berufend sei das Erinnerungsvermögen *„alles andere als zuverlässig [und unterliege] Anlagerungsprozessen, bei denen Vorstellungen, gehörte Erzählungen, Bilder, Film- und Fernsehszenen der* *eigenen Erinnerung zugefügt und als selbsterlebt fest geglaubt"* (Schnatz 2010, S. 3) würden. Dies gelte auch für das kollektive Gedächtnis. Diese Positionen bestätigen Vertreter der Kommunikationssoziologie und Rezeptionsforschung, und verweisen darauf, dass Medien in verschiedenen Lebensphasen eine bedeutsame Rolle für die Identitätskonstruktion einnehmen (Charlton und Neumann 1986, 1990; Saxer 2012, S. 412). Auch Welzer (2008, S. 43) machte an einigen Beispielen deutlich, wie sich Erinnerungen bereits in kurzer Zeit veränderten und verwies insbesondere auf Phänomene wie die sog. Quellenamnesie und Konfabulation. Daneben kann sich der inhaltliche Zusammenhang durch neu Gelerntes verändern, auch können Aspekte vergessen werden, die einmal memoriert wurden (Kühnel 2009, S. 39).

Darüber hinaus ist die Darstellung der Zeitwahrnehmung mit einer nicht zu vernachlässigenden Komponente verbunden: dem jeweiligen Zeitgeist. Dieser gilt in der Gegenwart oft schwerer erfassbar als im Nachhinein (Herzog 2011, S. 95). So können in der Vergangenheit besetzte Themen und erwünschte Strukturen in der Gegenwart als nicht zeitgemäß angesehen werden und werden in ihrem Einfluss rückblickend anders wahrgenommen. Zudem prägen aktuelle gesellschaftspolitische Fragen und internationale Perspektiven den Zeitgeist zum Untersuchungszeitpunkt (Kleinschmidt 2002).

Grundsätzlich lässt sich festhalten, dass Zeitwahrnehmungen sich prinzipiell in allen mündlichen, schriftlichen wie gegenständlichen Quellen niederschlagen; damit ist von Zeit und deren Wahrnehmung als einen subjektiven Faktor, der allen Quellen inne wohnt, auszugehen.

Diskussion

Die im biographischen Bericht narrative Inszenierung von Erinnerung steht in einem Spannungsverhältnis zwischen der subjektiven Zeiterfahrung der Protagonisten und den Dimensionen der historisch-chronologischen Zeit. Im Erzählmuster können Ereignisse in einer veränderten Progression und Kausalität auftreten. Auch kann sich durch geänderte Akzentuierung im Narrativ eine mögliche Diskrepanz zwischen dem linearen Kontinuum der chronologischen Zeit und dem subjektiven Zeitempfinden der Individuen verstärken.

Die individuelle oder kollektive Inszenierung von Zeit in biographischen Erzählungen induziert ein orientierendes Zeitsystem. Durch die Memorierung von Ereignissen, Anekdoten und Erinnerungsmomenten werden eigene individuelle und institutionelle Identitäten ausgebildet. Die Identitätskonstruktionen bilden weniger eine statische Realität ab, sondern konstruieren sich innerhalb einer Partikulargeschichte immer wieder neu über unterschiedliche Phasen und lassen sich in das Gesamtbild einer umfassenden Gesellschaftsgeschichte einbetten (Czock und Rathmann-Lutz 2016, S. 211). Da biographische Interviews vielmehr „*die Erfahrungsdimension von Geschichte oder den historischen Sinnbildungsprozess*" (Keilbach 2010, S. 195) dokumentieren, ist es geboten, die mündlichen Quellen mit weiteren Archivalien kontrastierend zu vergleichen und die Zusammenhänge von Erinnerungsprozessen und Sinnkonstruktion mit ihren permanenten Umdeutungen, Überlagerungen und Konstruktionsleitungen zu reflektieren (Jureit 1998, S. 29). Damit verschiebt sich der Fokus der historischen Analyse von der Rekonstruktion der Vergangenheit hin zu einer Reflexion des Stellenwerts des Vergangenen in der Gegenwart der Interviewpartner (Leitner 1990, S. 362).

Die in autobiographischen Dokumenten generierten Identitätskonstruktionen lassen sich einordnen als der Versuch, das Individuum in einer Vielzahl von gesellschafts- und kulturgeschichtlichen Faktoren zu positionieren und sich einer gewünschten Identität historisch zu versichern (Beck 1986). Die dargestellte historische Lebenswelt lässt sich demnach als ‚Sinnreservoir' oder „*soziohistorisches Apriori*" (Luckmann 1980) zur Identitätsbildung bezeichnen. Um in der historischen Analyse autobiographischer Erinnerungen den Aspekten narrativer Temporalität gerecht zu werden, sollte die Existenz subjektiver Zeiterfahrung und verschiedener Zeitdimensionen angenommen und gedanklich einbezogen werden.

Über die Darstellung von Zeitstrukturen und jeweiliger Zeitvorstellungen lassen sich wertvolle Einsichten in die soziokulturellen Hintergründe und individuellen Interpretationsmuster gewinnen (Schilling 2005; O'Neill 2014). Damit steht in der historischen Analyse die Struktur der Biographie weniger im Sinne eines Ablaufs realer Ereignisse im Zentrum, sondern vielmehr ein Konglomerat sinnstiftender Momente und Muster über die erinnerte Realität präsentiert wird. Über die dargestellten Diskurse und Praktiken können unterschiedliche Zeitwahrnehmungen und -vorstellungen sichtbar gemacht werden, „*indem sie die Konstitutionsbedingungen von Zeit freilegen.*" (Czock und Rathmann-Lutz 2016, S. 21).

Vor diesem Hintergrund lassen sich die biographische Erinnerungen als Quellen verstehen, die im Rahmen eines historischen Narratives einer Konstruktion von Vergangenheit dienen, um die individuelle Gegenwart zu konsolidieren. Über die Verbindung rekonstruierter Geschichtsdarstellung mit gegenwartsbezogener Kommentierung und Interpretation vermitteln sie Informationen über die individuelle und kollektive Interpretation, Integration und Bewältigung historischer Erfahrungen und den aktuellen gesellschaftlichen

Diskursraum, in dem sich das Individuum bewegt (Sabrow et al. 2003). Damit berührt die autobiographische Darstellung in historischer Sicht nicht nur die gewünschte Identität eines Individuums sondern auch die sozialer Gruppen. Identitätskonstruktionen sind in autobiographischen Erzählungen von den ihnen zugrunde liegenden sozialen Realitäten als historische und soziokulturelle Kontexte klar zu differenzieren. Eine klare Einordnung kann oftmals schwer fallen, da davon auszugehen ist, dass es sowohl zu einem historischen Ereignis prinzipiell verschiedene Perspektiven als auch zu einem Selbst verschiedene Identitätskonstruktionen geben kann (Heinze 2009, S. 166). Eine autobiographische Lebenskonstruktion ist in der Regel selbstrepräsentierend (Individuum, Gruppe, Institution) motiviert. Prinzipiell können jeder historischen Rekonstruktion Modifikationen und Umdeutungen innewohnen, bei Erinnerungen die mit einer belasteten Vergangenheit zusammenhängen können zusätzlich sozialpsychologische Momente wirksam werden, die eine individuelle bzw. kollektive Verantwortung abwehren oder gar leugnen können (Halbwachs 1967, 1985; Jureit 1998, 1999).

Erinnerungen lassen sich historisch verankert und mit von außen wirkenden erinnerungskulturellen Kontexten verknüpft verstehen. Dabei sind die Identitätskonstruktionen als individuelle wie kollektive Erinnerungsmuster einem soziokulturellen Wandel unterworfen. Da autobiographisches Erzählen und Identitätskonstruktion sowie publikumsorientierte Identitätspräsentation eng miteinander zusammenhängen, erhält die Frage nach der historischen Implikation autobiographischer Quellen besonderes Gewicht, da die Erinnerung oftmals für sich in Anspruch nimmt, ‚authentisch', durch die scheinbare Unmittelbarkeit ‚legitimiert' und daher als ‚wahr' begründend auf der eigenen unmittelbaren Beobachtung zu gelten. In diesem Sinne ist dem Kulturanthropologen Wolfgang Reinhard (2006, S. 600) Recht zu geben, dass Erinnerungen als Vergangenheitsbearbeitungen niemals „*identitätsneutral*" seien und daher wie jede andere historische Quelle auch einer kritischen Überprüfung bedürfen.

Fazit

Dies zusammenfassend lässt sich Identität als für das Zustandekommen und Funktionieren sozialer Interaktion von essentieller Bedeutung verstehen (Lührmann 2007, S. 142). Es kann festgehalten werden, dass historische Erfahrungen, autobiographische Selbstreflexionen und die damit zusammenhängenden Identitätskonstruktionen in einer engen, sich gegenseitig beeinflussenden Beziehung stehen. Eine Lebensgeschichte kann schon allein aufgrund der unmittelbaren Befangenheit und aufgrund der von ihr geleisteten Wirklichkeitskonstruktion kaum dem Postulat der historischen Objektivität entsprechen (Heinze 2009, S. 280). Gleichzeitig lässt sich aus der autobiographischen Lebenskonstruktion und der in ihr inszenierten Identitätskonstruktion eine Reihe von Deutungsmustern erschließen. Die historische Analyse ist mit der Frage der Glaubwürdigkeit von biographischen Dokumenten konfrontiert, der sie mit der Einbeziehung weiterer Quellen begegnet, um die Validität und Reliabilität der Aussagen zu sichern. So kann narratives Erinnern in mehrerlei Hinsicht begriffen werden: Zum einen als durch den soziokulturellen Kontext beeinflusste Muster; zum anderen als Praxis der individuellen und kollektiven Gedächtnisbildung; zum dritten als Identitätskonstruktion in enger Verbindung stehend mit gegenwärtigen Interessen und Sinnbedürfnissen. Angesichts der vorhandenen unterschiedlichen Perspektiven und Einflüsse erscheint es kaum möglich, eine einheitliche Version der Geschichte zu erarbeiten, die Grundlage einer allgemeinen Erinnerungskultur sein kann. Dennoch sollte der Begriff der historischen Wirklichkeitskonstruktion nicht darüber hinwegtäuschen, dass Identitätskonstruktionen auf realen Grundlagen basieren.

Abschließend lässt sich urteilen, dass die Aussagen in biographischen Erzählungen zu einem gewissen Grad zum einen darüber aussagen, welche Ereignisse und Prozesse in der Vergangenheit geschehen sind, doch vielmehr sagen sie aus, wie diese wahrgenommen und beurteilt wurden und vor allem wie diese aktuell erinnert werden. Damit bilden autobiografische Narrative mehr den aktuellen Zeitgeist ab, und verweisen darauf, welche wirtschaftlichen, gesellschafts- und institutionspolitischen Aspekte derzeit im Fokus stehen bzw. als relevant gelten.

Literatur

Allport, D. (1968). Phenomenal simultaneity and the perceptual moment hypothesis. *Br J Psychol*, 59, 395 – 406.
Angehrn, E. (1985). *Geschichte und Identität*. Berlin, de Gruyter.
Assmann, J. (1992). *Das kulturelle Gedächtnis*. München, Beck.
Bär, J. (2014). *Zwischen „Festung Breslau" und „verlorener Heimat"*. Dissertation, Universität Frankfurt a.O.
Bauman, Z. (1999). *Unbehagen in der Postmoderne*. Hamburger Edition.
Beck, U. (1986). *Risikogesellschaft*. Frankfurt, Suhrkamp.
Berger, P., Berger, B., Kellner, H. (1975). *Das Unbehagen in der Moderne*. Frankfurt, Campus.
Berkhofer, R. (2008). *Fashioning History*. Basingstoke, Palgrave Macmillan.
Born, A. (2002). *Regulation persönlicher Identität im Rahmen gesellschaftlicher Transformationsbewältigung*. Münster, Waxman.

Charlton, M., Neumann, K. (1986). *Medienkonsum und Lebensbewältigung in der Familie.*, Weinheim, Beltz.

Charlton, M., Neumann, K. (1990) *Medienrezeption und Identitätsbildung.* Tübingen, Narr.

Corradini, R. (2009). *Zeit und Identität* Abgerufen am 15. Mai 2019, von https://www.oeaw.ac.at/gema/Wittgenstein/witt_pdf/3_2_zeitid.pdf Zugegriffen: 04. April 2019

Corsten, M. (1994) Beschriebenes und wirkliches Leben. *BIOS,* 7(29), 185 – 205.

Czock, M., Rathmann-Lutz, A. (Hrsg.) (2016). *ZeitenWelten.* Köln, Böhlau.

Daniel, U. (2001). *Kompendium Kulturgeschichte.* Frankfurt, Suhrkamp.

Eagleman, D. (2008). Human time perception and its illusions. *Curr Opin Neurobiol,* 18, 131– 132.

Ecarius, J. (2006). Biographieforschung und Lernen. In: H-H. Krüger, & W. Marotzki (Hrsg.) *Handbuch erziehungswissenschaftliche Bildungsforschung* (S. 91 – 108). Wiesbaden, Springer VS.

Eickelpasch, R., Rademacher, C. (2013). *Identität.* Bielefeld, transcript.

Erikson, E. (1970). *Jugend und Krise.* Stuttgart, Klett.

Erll, A. (2017). *Kollektives Gedächtnis und Erinnerungskulturen.* Berlin, Springer.

Fischer, W. (2018). Zeit und Biographie. In: H. Lutz et al. (Hrsg.) *Handbuch der Biographieforschung* (S. 461 – 472). Wiesbaden, Springer VS.

Fraisse, P. (1963). *The psychology of time.* Oxford, Harper & Row.

Fraisse, P. (1984). Perception and estimation of time. *Annu Rev Psychol.* 35, 1 – 26.

Giddens, A. (2008). *This Time It's Personal.* The Guardian (UK).

Gläser, J., Laudel, G. (2010). *Experteninterviews und qualitative Inhaltsanalyse als Instrumente rekonstruierender Untersuchungen.* Wiesbaden, Springer VS.

Goffman, E. (1967). *Stigma.* Frankfurt, Suhrkamp.

Götze, L. (2004). *Zeitkulturen.* Frankfurt, Lang.

Grondin, S. (2001). From physical time to the first and second moments of psychological time. *Psychol Bull,* 127, 22 – 44.

Halbwachs, M. (1967). *Das kollektive Gedächtnis.* Stuttgart, Enke.

Halbwachs, M. (1985). *Das Gedächtnis und seine sozialen Bedingungen.* Frankfurt, Suhrkamp.

Heinze, C. (2009). *Identität und Geschichte in autobiographischen Lebenskonstruktionen.* Wiesbaden, Springer.

Herzog, M. (2011). *Historisches Organisationslernen als Wegbereiter zukünftiger Lernprozesse.* Wiesbaden, Springer.

Höfer, R. (2000). *Jugend, Gesundheit und Identität.* Wiesbaden, Springer.

Hoff, E-H. (1990). Identität und Arbeit. *Psychosozial,* 13(43 III), 7 – 25.

Jureit, U. (1998). *Konstruktion und Sinn.* Oldenburg, BIS.

Jureit, U. (1999). *Erinnerungsmuster. Ergebnisse.* Hamburg.

Keilbach, J. (2010). *Geschichtsbilder und Zeitzeugen.* Münster, LIT.

Keupp, H. et al. (Hrsg.) (1999). *Identitätskonstruktionen.* Reinbek, Rowohlt.

Kleinschmidt, H. (2002). *Menschen in Bewegung.* Göttingen, V&R.

Krischel, M., Söhner, F., Fangerau, H. (2018). Zeitgeschichte der Humangenetik in Deutschland. *MedGen.* 30(3), 351 – 358.

Kühnel, S., Markowitsch, H. (2009). *Falsche Erinnerungen.* Heidelberg, Spektrum.

Leipold, B., Greve, W. (2008). Sozialisation, Selbstbild und Identität. In: K. Hurrelmann et al. (Hrsg.) *Handbuch Sozialisationsforschung* (S. 659 – 672). Weinheim, Beltz.

Lembeck, K-H. (2000). *Geschichtsphilosophie.* München, Alber.

Levine, R. (1999). *Eine Landkarte der Zeit*. Berlin, Piper.
Linville, PW., Carlston, D. (1994). Social Cognition of the Self. In: P. Devine, D. Hamilton & T. Ostrom (Hrsg.) *Social cognition* (S. 143 – 193). Sandiego Academic Press.
Luckmann, T. (1980). Persönliche Identität als evolutionäres und historisches Problem. In: T. Luckmann. *Lebenswelt und Gesellschaft* (S. 123 – 141). Paderborn, Schönigh.
Lührmann, T. (2006). *Führung, Interaktion und Identität*. Berlin, DUV.
Markus, H., Nurius, P. (1986). Possible Selves. *Am Psychol.* 41, 954 – 969.
Marx, K., Engels, F. (1972). *Werke*. Bd. 8. Berlin, Dietz.
Mayring, P. (2015). *Qualitative Inhaltsanalyse: Grundlagen und Techniken*. Weinheim, Beltz.
McCall, G., Simmons, J. (1974). *Identität und Interaktion*. Düsseldorf, Schwann.
Miethe, I., Laak, Jv. (2018). Oral-History, Ego-Dokumente und Biographieforschung. In: H. Lutz, M. Schiebel & E. Tuider (Hrsg.) *Handbuch Biographieforschung* (S. 587 – 599). Berlin, Springer.
Mummendey, HD. (2006). *Psychologie des „Selbst"*. Göttingen, Hogrefe.
Niethammer, L., Plato, Av. (Hrsg.) (1985). *„Wir kriegen jetzt andere Zeiten." Lebensgeschichte und Sozialkultur im Ruhrgebiet*. Berlin, Dietz.
Niethammer, L. (2007). *Fragen an das deutsche Gedächtnis*. Essen, Klartext.
Niethammer, L. (2000). *Kollektive Identität*. Reinbek, Rowohlt.
O'Neill, M. (2014). The slow university: Work, time and well-being. *FQS*. 15(3), 14.
Perich, R. (1992). *Unternehmensdynamik. Zur Entwicklungsfähigkeit von Organisationen aus zeitlich-dynamischer Sicht*. Bern, St. Galler Beiträge.
Plato, Av. (1991). Oral History als Erfahrungswissenschaft. *BIOS*. 4, 97 – 119.
Pollak, M. (1988). *Die Grenzen des Sagbaren*. Frankfurt, Campus.
Pöppel, E. (2009). Pre-semantically defined windows for cognitive processing. *Phil Trans*. 364, 1887 – 1896.
Reck, S. (1981). *Identität, Rationalität und Verantwortung*. Frankfurt, Suhrkamp.
Roberts, B. (2011). Interpreting photographic portraits: Autobiography, time perspectives, and two school photographs. *FQS*. 12(2), 25.
Roberts, B., Caspi, A. (2003). The Cumulative Continuity Model of Personality Development. In: UM. Staudinger, U. Lindenberger (Hrsg.) *Understanding Human Development* (S. 183 – 214). Berlin, Springer.
Rosenthal, G., Bogner, A. (2017). Biographies – discourses – figurations. In: G. Rosenthal & A. Bogner (Hrsg.) *Biographies in the Global South* (S. 15 – 49). Frankfurt, Campus.
Rothermund, K., Brandstätter, J. (1997). Entwicklung und Bewältigung. In: C. Teschrömer, C. Salewski & G. Schwarz (Hrsg.) *Psychologie der Bewältigung* (S. 42 – 57). Weinheim, PVU.
Rudnick, C. (2014). *Die andere Hälfte der Erinnerung*. Bielefeld, transkript.
Sabrow, M., Jessen, R., Große Kracht, K. (Hrsg.) (2003). *Zeitgeschichte als Streitgeschichte*. München, Beck.
Saxer, U. (2012). *Mediengesellschaft*. Berlin, Springer VS.
Scharlau, I. (2007). Perceptual latency priming. A measure of attentional facilitation. *Psychol Res*. 71, 678 – 686.
Schilling, E. (2005). *Die Zukunft der Zeit*. Aachen, Shaker.
Schnatz, H. (2010). *Nachträge zum Komplex Tiefflieger über Dresden*. Abgerufen am 15. Mai 2019, von https://www.dresden.de/media/pdf/stadtarchiv/Schnatz_100403.pdf
Söhner, F. (2020a). *Die Psychiatrie-Enquete – mit Zeitzeugen verstehen. Eine Oral History der Psychiatrie-Reform in der BRD*. Köln, Psychiatrie-Verlag.

Söhner, F. (2020b). Geschichte erinnern: Grundzüge, Entwicklung und Anwendungsfelder der Oral History in der angewandten Geschichtswissenschaft. In: M. Großmann, T. Hellmuth & T. Walach (Hrsg.) *Handbuch „Public History"*. Berlin, Springer Reference. (in Druck)

Söhner, F. (2017). Methodische Problemfelder und ethische Implikationen in der zeitzeugenbasierten Historiographie – ein Erfahrungsbericht. *BIOS* 1+2(2017), 273 – 289.

Söhner, F. (2013). *Vom Konfliktherd zur Modellregion. Selbst- und Fremdbilder entlang der Hohen Straße in Schlesien*. Dresden, Neisse.

Söhner, F. et al. (2016). Nach der „Aktion T4": „Regionalisierte Euthanasie" in der Heil- und Pflegeanstalt Günzburg. *Nervenarzt.* 88(9), 1065 – 1073.

Söhner, F., Fangerau, H., Becker, T. (2017). Der Weg zur Psychiatrie-Enquete. Rekonstruktion der politischen Vorbereitung der ersten Enquetekommission des Deutschen Bundestags. *Nervenarzt.* 89(5), 570–578.

Straub, J. (2000). Identität als psychologisches Deutungskonzept. In: W. Grewe (Hrsg.) *Psychologie des Selbst* (S. 279 – 301). Weinheim, PVU.

Straus, F., Höfer, R. (1998). Entwicklungslinien alltäglicher Identitätsarbeit. In: H. Keupp, R. Höfer (Hrsg.) *Identitätsarbeit heute* (S. 270 – 307). Frankfurt, Suhrkamp.

Stroud, JM. (1956). The fine structure of psychological time. In: H. Quastler (Hrsg.) *Information theory in psychology* (S. 174 – 207). New York Free Press.

Stroud, JM. (1967). The fine structure of psychological time. *Ann N Y Acad Sci.* 138, 623 – 631.

Wassenhove, Vv. (2009). Minding time in an amodal representational space. *Phil Trans.* 364, 1815 – 1830.

Weiß, K. (2012). *Auf der Suche nach der gewonnenen Zeit*. Dissertation, Universität Paderborn.

Weiß, K., Scharlau, I. (2011). Simultaneity and temporal order perception: Different sides of the same coin? Evidence from a visual prior entry study. *Q J Exp Psychol.* 64, 394 – 418.

Welzer, H. (2000). Das Interview als Artefakt. *BIOS*. 1, 51–63.

Welzer, H. (2008). *Das kommunikative Gedächtnis*. München, Beck.

Wierling, D. (2003). Oral History. In: M. Maurer (Hrsg.) *Aufriß der Historischen Wissenschaften*. Bd. 7. Stuttgart, Reclam.

Wittmann, M. (2011). Moments in time. *Front Neurosci.* 55, 1 – 9.

Zima, P. (2000). *Theorie des Subjekts*. Stuttgart, UTB.

„Heute kann ich nicht mehr behaupten, meine Eltern seien links gewesen" – George Herbert Meads Zeit-Begriff und die biografietheoretische Analyse

Lena Kahle

Abstract

George Herbert Mead's concept of time is based on past experiences and events, the present situation and future expectations in social interaction. This relationship between past, present and future is discussed by using biographical-narrative interviews and is thus seen as a promising reference point for biographical research. For biographical theory, time is a structuring element in the sense of experienced and narrated life stories as well as a text structuring element of narration. Four interviews will be analyzed with regard to the relationship between past, present and future.

Zusammenfassung

George Herbert Meads Zeitbegriff ist ein in der Interaktion zum Tragen kommendes Verhältnis aus vergangenen Erlebnissen und Ereignissen, der gegenwärtigen Situation und Zukunftsvorstellungen und -erwartungen. Dieses Verhältnis wird anhand biografisch-narrativer Interviews diskutiert und damit als vielversprechender Anknüpfungspunkt für die Biografieforschung angenommen. Denn für die Biografie ist Zeit ein strukturierendes Element im Sinne erlebter und erzählter Geschichte wie auch als *Text*strukturierendes Element der Erzählung. Vier Interviews werden hierfür beispielhaft analysiert im Hinblick auf das Verhältnis aus Vergangenheit, Gegenwart und Zukunft.

L. Kahle (✉)
Stiftung Universität Hildesheim, Hildesheim, Deutschland
E-Mail: kahlele@uni-hildesheim.de

© Springer Fachmedien Wiesbaden GmbH, ein Teil von Springer Nature 2020
E. Schilling und M. O'Neill (Hrsg.), *Frontiers in Time Research – Einführung in die interdisziplinäre Zeitforschung*,
https://doi.org/10.1007/978-3-658-31252-7_3

Einleitung

Zeit ist ein strukturierender Aspekt von Biografien und damit auch für deren Analyse relevant. Denn über die Analyse von Zeitlichkeit – Zeit als Textstrukturelement, Zeit als Faktor generationaler Zugehörigkeit, Zeit als wesentlicher Marker erlebter und erzählter Geschichte (Rosenthal 1995) – gelingt ein Zugang zu handlungstheoretischen Fragen in biografischen Interviews. In diesem Aufsatz soll die Bedeutung von Zeit anhand des Zeitverständnisses von George Herbert Mead grundlagentheoretisch diskutiert werden. Für die Diskussion des Ansatzes werden biografisch-narrative Interviews herangezogen und das Verhältnis aus vergangenen Ereignissen, erlebter Gegenwart und Zukunftsvorstellungen in den Blick genommen. Dabei steht die Frage im Vordergrund, welche Möglichkeiten sich über den Meadschen Ansatz für die Analyse biografischer Interviews bieten, indem Zeit als strukturierendes Merkmal von Handlungsfähigkeit begriffen wird.

Für diesen Aufsatz wurden biografisch-narrative Interviews mit Akteur*innen der Coexistence Education in Israel aus einer Studie zu Agency und Belonging in polarisierten Gesellschaften herangezogen (Kahle 2017). Der Zugang zur eigenen Biografie in den Interviews ist in fast allen Fällen ein Konversions- oder Wandlungsmoment hin zu politischem Handeln und Engagement vor dem Hintergrund der eigenen Bildungsarbeit. Die Prozessstruktur der erzählten Biografie ist also stark auf die eigene Handlungsfähigkeit bezogen. Aus den Interviews lassen sich gemeinsame Typen im Umgang und in der Verhandlung von Zeit in der biografischen Erzählung rekonstruieren.

Im Folgenden wird zuerst ein Überblick über die Biografieforschung und deren Zeitbezüge gegeben (2), woraufhin Mead als Vertreter des Symbolischen Interaktionismus und als Autor der „Philosophy of the Present" (Mead 1932) vorgestellt wird (3), um anschließend anhand von vier Interviews zwei Typen von Zeiterleben und Zeiterzählen zu diskutieren (4).

Biografie und Zeit

Die biografietheoretische Perspektive fragt nach der Art und Weise der Konstruktion von Biografien in der modernen Gesellschaft. Das Ziel ist, den Zusammenhang einer biografischen Erzählung zu rekonstruieren, da sie mehr ist als nur die Summe aller persönlichen Erlebnisse in chronologischer Reihenfolge oder ein zielgerichteter Lebenslauf (Schütze 2006, S. 10). Anders als der Lebenslauf, der auf „historische Modi der Vergesellschaftung verweist, mit denen Gesellschaften […] ihre Mitglieder funktional" (Dausien 2010, S. 363) einbinden, ist die Lebensgeschichte eine subjektive Sichtweise der Selbstdarstellung. Dieser Gegensatz aus Lebensgeschichte (als subjektive Erzählung) und Lebenslauf (als Ausdruck institutionalisierter Formen der biografischen Vergesellschaftung) wird immer wieder als erkenntnistheoretisches Problem diskutiert. Doch versucht das Biografiekonzept diesen Dualismus gerade zu überwinden, denn der Lebenslauf ist für die Betrachtung der biografischen Erzählung insofern von Interesse, als die institutionalisierte Form sich in der Biografie widerspiegeln kann (ebd.). Die individuelle Biografie wird gerade dadurch zum soziologischen Material, dass „die unterschiedlichen möglichen Beziehungen zwischen individueller Lebensgestaltung und sozialer Organisation" (Apitzsch 2006, S. 500) untersucht werden können. Der Aspekt der Zeit spielt zudem für die Frage nach dem Lebens*verlauf* und der Prozesshaftigkeit von Biografien eine Rolle.

Fischer (2018) untersucht die temporale Dimension biografischer Strukturierung. Biografie erfasse Zeit in doppelter Weise: Biografische Strukturierung birgt die Möglichkeit zeitlicher Modalisierungen, was bedeutet, dass über die autobiografische Erzählung eigener Handlungspraktiken und Lebensabschnitte beispielsweise Sinnhaftigkeit und Chronologie erlangt werden kann. Weiterhin produzieren biografische Erzählungen „gesellschaftliche, soziale und individuelle Zeit und tragen so zur Komplexitätssteigerung der Gesellschaft bei" (S. 463). Die soziale und erlebte Zeit wird zwar im Text nicht weiter ausgeführt, sind an dieser Stelle allerdings von Bedeutung für den Zusammenhang von Biografie und Zeit. Soziale Zeit lässt sich nicht einfach als das Gegenteil von physikalischer Zeit fassen, da auch die physikalische Zeit – das Bedürfnis nach der Vermessung, Einteilung und Rhythmisierung des Lebens – sozialen Ursprungs ist (Durkheim 1981, nach Brose et al. 1993, S. 18). Die soziale Zeit ist somit eine von dem jeweiligen sozialen Umfeld oder der Gesellschaft vorgegebene Zeit, wohingegen die erlebte Zeit individuelle Ereignisse im Sozialen widerspiegelt. Dabei ist zentral, dass hier angenommen wird, die Darstellung der Biografie berge „Unvereinbares und Vereinbares", das „zu einem temporalen Patchwork" zusammengebaut werde (Fischer 2018, S. 468). Eine Biografie, die in ihrer Darstellung inkonsistent ist, muss also nicht geleugnet werden oder ist per se unverständlich, sondern die einzelnen Lebensabschnitte werden stattdessen „verzeitlicht" (ebd.). Das Einfügen von Ereignissen, Handlungen und Lebensabschnitten und biografischen Veränderungen tragen zur Komplexität einer Biografie bei, die auch über ihre zeitliche Ausgestaltung rekonstruiert werden kann.

Die Biografie ist nun die Erzählung eines Lebens, die sich auf die Vergangenheit, die Gegenwart und die Zukunft individuell wie gesellschaftlich – bezieht. Ohne dass dieser Prozess immer reflektiert wird und bewusst verläuft, besteht eine Verbindung aus persönlich Erlebtem und kollektiven Ereignissen (Dausien

2000, S. 100). Rosenthal hat sich explizit mit dem Verhältnis aus erlebter und erzählter Lebensgeschichte auseinandergesetzt:

„Die dialektische Beziehung zwischen Erleben, Erinnern und Erzählen bedeutet also unter anderem: Die in der Vergangenheit liegenden Erlebnisse können sich dem Biographen in der Gegenwart des Erinnerns und Erzählens nicht darbieten, wie sie erlebt wurden, sondern nur im Wie ihrer Darbietung, d. h. nur im Wechselverhältnis zwischen dem sich in der Gegenwart der Erzählung Darbietenden und Gemeinten" (Rosenthal 2008, S. 168).[1]

Rosenthal unterscheidet grundlagentheoretisch zwischen erzählter und erlebter Zeit: Ihr zufolge sind Erzählungen über vergangene Erlebnisse an die Gegenwart des Erzählens gebunden, wobei die Gegenwart den Rückblick auf Vergangenes beeinflusst.

Prozessstrukturen des Lebenslaufs

Schütze, der die Biografieforschung in Deutschland maßgeblich beeinflusste, arbeitet heraus wie sich die individuelle Vergangenheit in der erzählten Gegenwart, in einem biografisch-narrativen Interview darstellt. Narrationen selbst erlebter Erfahrungen kommen dabei der Vergangenheit am nächsten „und die Orientierungsstrukturen des faktischen Handelns und Erleidens auch unter der Perspektive der Erfahrungsrekapitulation in beträchtlichem Maße rekonstruieren" (Schütze 1987, S. 14). In spontanen, nicht-eingeübten Narrationen, in sogenannten Stegreiferzählungen reproduziere sich im Gegensatz zu den Textsorten der Beschreibung, Bewertung oder Argumentation am ehesten das damalige Erleben.[2] Gerade in der Textsorte der Erzählung zeigen zeitliche Marker (wie zum Beispiel „jetzt", „dann" oder „heute"), wie stark Zeitlichkeit hier eingebettet ist.

Er unterscheidet vier Prozessstrukturen des Lebenslaufes, die sich aus biografischen Interviews rekonstruieren lassen. Darunter fallen institutionelle Ablaufmuster und Erwartungen, Handlungsschemata von biografischer Relevanz,

---

[1]Der komplexe gestalttheoretische Zugang Rosenthals kann hier nur angedeutet werden.
[2]Carlson et al. (2017) greifen die Debatte um die Bedeutung der Textsorten auf und zeigen, welche Bedeutung gerade auch Argumentationen bzw. Beschreibungen und Bewertungen für die Analyse narrativer Interviews haben.

negative und positive Verlaufskurven sowie letztlich Wandlungsprozesse der biografischen Gesamtformung (Schütze 1983). Prozessstrukturen zeigen die theoretische Verarbeitung von Ereignisverkettungen eines biografischen Verlaufs, und lassen sich auf unterschiedliche Weise in allen biografischen Verläufen wiederfinden (ebd., S. 284). Für das Verstehen individueller Handlungsverläufe ist sowohl die Genese als auch die Perspektive der Handelnden selbst von Bedeutung. Rosenthal stellt einen wichtigen Zugang der biografietheoretischen Analyse heraus, indem sie festhält,

„dass bei sozialwissenschaftlichen und historischen Fragestellungen, die sich auf soziale Phänomene beziehen, die an die Erfahrung von Menschen gebunden sind und für diese eine biografische Bedeutung haben, die Bedeutung dieser Phänomene im Gesamtzusammenhang ihrer Lebensgeschichte interpretiert wird." (Rosenthal 2008, S. 164)

Nur durch die Betrachtung der gesamten biografischen Erzählung können die Prozessstrukturen des Lebens rekonstruiert werden, die den Rückblick, die gegenwärtige Perspektive sowie die Zukunftsplanung bestimmen (Rosenthal 1995, S. 13).

Die Biografieforschung schließt daran an, indem sie an den Prozess- und Sinnstrukturen von Akteur*innen interessiert ist. Die biografischen Sinnstrukturen setzen sich aus individuellen Entscheidungs- und Handlungsmöglichkeiten sowie gesellschaftlichen kollektiven Sinnstrukturen und Wissensbeständen zusammen (Kleemann et al. 2009, S. 16). Sie sind durch soziale und erlebte Zeit sowie Orte strukturiert, meist jedoch nicht unmittelbar zugänglich und somit auch nicht durch Interviewte explizierbar. Dagegen können die impliziten Regeln, nach denen gehandelt, erzählt und argumentiert wird, aus dem Sinn eines konkreten Verhaltens und Kommunikation rekonstruiert werden. Demnach zielt ein struktur- und textsortenanalytisches Vorgehen bei der Interpretation von Biografien auf die gesellschaftlichen Zusammenhänge, die auf das Individuum Einfluss haben. Und um diese Zusammenhänge methodisch gesichert rekonstruieren zu können, stellen bei der Biografieanalyse unterschiedliche Textsorten ein wichtiges Element dar (Rosenthal 1995, S. 218).

Zusammenfassend bedeutet das, dass die Biografieforschung die erlebte und erzählte Lebensgeschichte des Individuums in der Gesellschaft untersucht. Der Aspekt der Zeit ist dabei als subjektives wie gesellschaftliches Zeiterleben, aber auch als ein Verhältnis aus der Vergangenheit und der Gegenwart des Erzählens, zu berücksichtigen. Zudem spielen handlungstheoretische Aspekte eine Rolle, denn es geht um die Handlungsfähigkeit der Biografieträger*innen in der Gesellschaft, die in der Lebenserzählung zum Ausdruck kommt.

George Herbert Mead – Intersubjektivität und Handeln

Der symbolische Interaktionismus und seine Vertreter*innen gehen davon aus, dass soziale Wirklichkeit durch Kommunikation und Interpretation hergestellt wird. Die soziale Wirklichkeit entsteht in der Interaktion, wobei das Individuum die Handlungen seines Gegenübers in der Interaktion deuten, entsprechend handeln und soziale Sinnstrukturen konstituieren und reproduzieren kann (Bonß et al. 2013, S. 8). Mead, der als ein Vertreter des symbolischen Interaktionismus gilt, bestimmt das soziale Handeln zum Objekt seiner Arbeiten (Joas 1989). Er verortet die Entstehung des Selbst im Interaktionsprozess, indem die Interaktionsteilnehmenden jeweils die Rolle des Anderen übernehmen und dessen Verhalten antizipieren (Mead 1968). Die Interaktion beruht auf Symbolen, die im Sozialisationsprozess erworben werden und als Zeichen und Gesten – oder auch Sprache – zum Ausdruck kommen. Die Kommunikation in einer gemeinsamen Sprache ist dabei die Voraussetzung für Gesellschaft (ebd., S. 39).[3] Mead analysiert diese symbolvermittelte Interaktion, die das Selbstbewusstsein im Interaktionsprozess überhaupt ermöglicht, in dem ein Bewusstsein für das eigene Handeln bzw. ein Selbstbewusstsein in der Rollenübernahme entwickelt wird. So schreibt Mead:

„Wo man [...] auf das reagiert, was man an einen anderen adressiert, und wo diese Reaktion Teil des eigenen Verhaltens wird, wo man nicht nur sich selber hört, sondern sich selbst antwortet, zu sich selbst genauso wie zu einer anderen Person spricht, haben wir ein Verhalten, in dem der einzelne sich selbst zum Objekt wird." (Mead 1968, S. 181)

Das Selbst, das für sich Objekt werden kann, „ist im Grunde eine gesellschaftliche Struktur und erwächst aus der gesellschaftlichen Erfahrung" (ebd., S. 182). Mit der Entwicklung des Selbst kommen aber auch eigene Erfahrungen zum Ausdruck, die innerhalb des gesellschaftlich ausgehandelten Rahmens positioniert werden.

---

[3]Signifikante Symbole lösen die gleiche Reaktion bei allen aus, haben aber bereits „einen langen Weg" hinter sich (Mead 1968, S. 107), von einer ersten Situation, einem ersten Ausruf bis zu einem allgemein anerkannten signifikanten Symbol. Sprache entsteht demnach in einem gesellschaftlichen Kontext (ebd. 109), die sich in der Rollenübernahme und in der jeweiligen Interpretation zeigt. Mead spricht dem Menschen dabei eine reflektierende Intelligenz zu, die ihn befähigt, als Teil eines gesellschaftlichen Prozesses zu denken und zu handeln (ebd., S. 184).

Zentral für die Theorie Meads ist der Interaktionsprozess, in dem das Selbst sich seiner bewusst wird. Hier treten parallel das reflektierende *Me* und das impulsive *I* auf.[4] *Me* ist das gesellschaftliche, das sich selbst als Objekt in der Interaktion erfährt (ebd., S. 216), wohingegen *I* dasjenige des Selbst ist, das körperliche und sinnliche Bedürfnisse zum Ausdruck bringt (Mead 1934, S. 261). Unerwartetes, Fehlerhaftes und Emotionales kommen in Meads Ansatz durch die im Interaktionsprozess konkurrierenden *Ichs* zum Ausdruck. Das reflexive Bewusstsein des Menschen entwickelt sich genau aus dieser „Differenz zwischen dem spontanen, unreflektierten Handeln des impulsiven Ich und der Perspektive, die sich aus der Sicht der anderen auf das Individuum, dem reflektierenden Ich" ergibt (Abels 2007, S. 366). Diese unterschiedlichen Perspektiven von *Me* und *I* setzen Reflexivität konstant frei und werden zu einem einheitlichen, aber einzigartigen Selbst synthetisiert, das sich von anderen durch die individuelle Position von *I* und *Me* unterscheidet (ebd., S. 367).

In der Handlungstheorie Meads steht die Handlung selbst im Vordergrund und nicht die Motive des handelnden Subjekts. Zu den wesentlichen Merkmalen von Handlung bei Mead gehören, so Bergmann, Zeitlichkeit und Sozialität (1981, S. 363).

Zeitlichkeit und Sozialität

Der Aspekt der Zeit ist bei Mead eine Kategorie, die nicht ohne ihren Bezug auf die Geschichte und das Handeln des Menschen auskommt und steht damit im Gegensatz zu einem metaphysischen oder abstrakten Zeitverständnis. Die Welt ist eine Welt aus Ereignissen, die in der Gegenwart die Realität anzeigen (Mead 1932, S. 1). Ereignisse, so interpretiert es Bergmann (1981), sind dabei Handlungen, die zeitkonstituierend sind, da sich mit jedem neuen Ereignis die Gegenwart herstellt (S. 353).

Meads Auseinandersetzung mit Zeitlichkeit findet hauptsächlich in seiner Textsammlung *The Philosophy of the Present*[5] von 1932 statt. Zentral ist dabei das Verhältnis aus Gegenwart – Vergangenheit – Zukunft:

---

[4]Mead selbst spricht nur von *I* und *Me*. Der Zusatz „reflektierend" und „impulsiv" ist von Abels vorgeschlagen worden und wird hier aufgenommen (Abels 2007).

[5]Alle Veröffentlichung erschienen posthum und bestehen zum größten Teil aus Texten und Vorlesungen.

„The past projected into the future, hypothetically, is justified by the result, but the future into which it is projected is an extension of the future that is actually there in the act. The future is the control of the process, and the past that which is there as an irrevocable condition of the ongoing process." (Mead 1932, S. 347 f.) Die Zukunft ist die Projektionsfläche und motiviert als (normativer) Erwartungs- und Möglichkeitsraum den Akt des sozialen Handelns, der gleichzeitig strukturiert ist durch vergangene Erfahrungen und Informationen, die sich in der Gegenwart realisieren. Der Verhältnisraum der Gegenwart bestimmt den Moment der reflexiven Bewusstseinswerdung im Interaktionsprozess (ebd.), wodurch die Komplexität sozialer Handlungen deutlich wird. Das Individuum schafft eine eigene zeitliche Ordnung innerhalb gesellschaftlicher Voraussetzungen. „Im operativen Modus der Gegenwart, des Ereignisses, Erlebens, der aktuellen Handlung, der Kommunikation werden Vergangenheit und Zukunft in Rechnung gestellt, verifiziert, modifiziert und somit hergestellt." (Fischer 2018, S. 463) Temporäre Orientierungen im Interaktionsprozess sind so durch situationelle Dringlichkeiten und Erfordernisse bestimmt. Akteur*innen beziehen sich in intersubjektiven Situationen auf den unmittelbaren Moment der Interaktion, anstatt sich auf langzeitlich ausgearbeitete Lebensziele zu fokussieren. Der Symbolische Interaktionismus interessiert sich, wie in diesem Zusammenhang noch einmal deutlich wird, besonders „für die tatsächlichen Handlungsperformanzen und die sich dort entwickelnden ad-hoc-Situationsdefinitionen" (Matthes und Schütze 1981, S. 16).

Wie bereits ausgeführt, ist der Interaktionsprozess und die währenddessen stattfindende Rollenübernahme ein Ausdruck für die Fähigkeit des Menschen, „mehrere Dinge gleichzeitig zu sein" (Mead 1969, S. 280), was für Mead Sozialität ausmacht. Sozialität ist dabei die Organisation der eigenen wie der anderen Perspektiven und gleichzeitig die Entstehung neuer Handlungsoptionen und Entscheidungen (Bergmann 1981, S. 356). Soziales Handeln entsteht durch „delayed and mutually conflicting responses" (Mead 1932, S. 71), die ein Bewusstsein des Selbst ermöglichen. Hier sind Zeit und Selbstbewusstsein in der sozialen Interaktion unverkennbar miteinander verschränkt. Sozialität ist dabei die Situiertheit der Akteur*innen in unterschiedlichen „temporal evolving relational contexts" (Emirbayer und Mische 1998, S. 969), die zur Entwicklung reflektierten Bewusstseins beitragen. Der zeitliche Aspekt von Sozialität bedeutet zum einen, verschiedene Rollen im Interaktionsprozess zu übernehmen, was von gegenwärtiger Dauer ist, und zum anderen, dass das Individuum sich kurzzeitig in verschiedenen, aufeinanderfolgenden Systemen befinden kann, worauf ein Wandlungsprozess des Individuums erfolgt (Bergmann 1981, S. 356). Die Annahme, dass alles Seiende im Prozess des Entstehens real und damit die

Gegenwart zum Ort der Realität wird, bedeutet, dass soziale Interaktion im Augenblick stattfindet und das Entstehen des Selbstbewusstseins Probleme in der gegenwärtigen Unmittelbarkeit löst. Das Moment der Interpretation im unmittelbar stattfindenden Interaktionsprozess jedoch ist nicht unabhängig von sozialen Erwartungen, weshalb ein Bezug auf Vergangenheit und Zukunft sinnvoll ist. Hier werden Erinnerung, Erwartungen und Antizipation in „a coherent sense of duration" (Flaherty und Fine 2001, S. 151) verbunden.[6]

Im Folgenden werden nun Ausschnitte biografisch-narrativer Interviews herangezogen, um zu diskutieren, wie sich der Ansatz Meads in der Biografieanalyse anwenden lässt. Ein Schwerpunkt wird dabei auf dem Aspekt des biografischen Wandels liegen sowie auf dem Aspekt des Zusammenhangs aus vergangenen Erlebnissen und deren gegenwärtiger Bewertung im narrativen Prozess. Dabei werden Begriffe wie Handlungsfähigkeit, Sozialität und Zeit für die Analyse herangezogen.

Interviewanalyse

Vier biografische Eingangserzählungen stellen nun exemplarisch zwei Typen unterschiedlicher Verhandlung von Zeitlichkeit in den Interviews dar, die analysiert werden.

Für die Darstellung von Zeitlichkeit, d.h. der Verhandlung von Vergangenheit, Gegenwart und Zukunft wurde die Stegreiferzählung der Interviews gewählt, da die spontane, unvorbereitete Erzählung vergangener Erfahrungen reproduziert (Schütze 1987, S. 14) und über das narrative Kommunikationsschema der Sachverhaltsdarstellung, hier ganz konkret die sogenannten „Zugzwänge des Erzählens", auf den Erzählstimulus der Interviewerin hin eintreten (Kallmeyer und Schütze 1977, S.162).

Eine Textsortenanalyse nach Erzählungen, Beschreibungen und Argumentationen oder Bewertungen wird in den folgenden Interviewsegmenten explizit nicht vorgenommen, da es um das Zeitverhältnis und dessen Bedeutung geht.

---

[6]Joas bezieht sich ausführlicher auf die philosophisch-naturwissenschaftliche Diskussion um den Zeitbegriff, den auch Mead reflektiert. Gerade die Frage, was denn die Gegenwart darstelle, spielt hierbei eine zentrale Rolle (Joas 1989, S. 170). Mead spricht von einer Dauer – *duration*. Die Gegenwart ist als Zeitfenster ein permanenter Zustand, denn „durations are a continual sliding of presents into each other" (Mead 1932, S. 28).

Vertraute Vergangenheit – zeitliche Chronologie und synchrone Biografien

Zwei Fälle lassen sich beispielhaft für die zeitlich synchrone Erzählung heranziehen. Synchronität wird in beiden Fällen über einen ungebrochenen Bezug auf die Familiengeschichte als tradierte Vergangenheit hergestellt. Nach einer biografischen Rahmung der Eingangserzählung durch die Geschichte der Eltern folgt in beiden Fällen eine chronologische Darstellung des Lebenslaufs: Kindheit, Schule, Armeedienst, Studium und Berufswahl. Erst spät erfolgt der recht abrupte und narrativ nicht vorbereitete Wandlungsprozess mit einer beruflichen und zum Teil politischen Neuorientierung.

Im Folgenden werden Ausschnitte aus den Eingangserzählungen von Rivka und Yotam einen Typ der Verhandlung von Zeitlichkeit in der narrativen Annäherung an die Lebensgeschichte darstellen.

Rivka beginnt ihre Stegreiferzählung mit ihren Eltern, die im Zuge des Boykotts jüdischer Geschäfte im April 1933 aus Deutschland über die Niederlande und Frankreich nach Palästina emigrierten. Ihre Eltern wohnten fortan in einer Stadt im Norden des heutigen Israels, wo auch Rivka Ende der vierziger Jahre geboren wurde. Sie selbst taucht erst ca. 15 Jahre später in ihrer eigenen Lebensgeschichte auf. Es folgt eine sehr knappe Darstellung ihres schulischen und beruflichen Werdegangs, wonach sie von zwei wichtigen Ereignissen erzählt, die zusammengenommen ihre heutige Tätigkeit in der historisch-politischen Bildung begründen: der Umzug in eine neu gegründete Ortschaft und die damit verbundene Begegnung mit palästinensisch-israelischen Kolleg*innen und das Kennenlernen der Bildungsarbeit eines US-amerikanischen Holocaust History Museums.

„*I was born in 1948 (.) much later* [...] *already to a very sick eh father eh (.) the whole situation and then: all the rumors that came about the Holocaust and siblings and my mother's siblings who eh didn't make it ah: (2) that's what I was told later (.) weren't good and when he he died my father died I was a few month old (.) I eh: (.) I did eh:(.) I don't remember him=I didn't know him*" (Z. 22–28)

Dieses Segment, das sich an die Darstellung der Emigration der Eltern anschließt, verdeutlicht die familienbiografische Rahmung ihrer Eingangserzählung, die bereits 15 Jahre vor ihrer Geburt beginnt. Sie selbst wurde „viel später" geboren, hat die Ereignisse, die ihre Familie sicherlich prägten, nur aus Erzählungen erfahren. Auch der Grund, weshalb der Vater kurz nach ihrer Geburt stirbt, wird ihr „viel später erzählt". Sie selbst kann sich nicht an ihn erinnern. Rivka vermittelt damit indirekt ein Vertrauen, dass sie gegenüber der Geschichte ihrer Familie hat.

Die eigene Biografie wird damit in eine tradierte Familiengeschichte integriert, womit angenommen werden kann, dass die Vergangenheit der Familie für sie weiterhin bedeutsam ist. Auf die Familiengeschichte folgt eine zeitlich stark kondensierte Darstellung ihres Lebenslaufs:

„I grew up in a very luxurious home and neighborhood and eh: went to a private school: and eh ehm: (.) went to the youth movement (.) eh: went '67 I graduated high school=went to the army (.) became an officer= first in [City] […] I went there because my boyfriend then my husband (.) now my husband (.) eh: started to learn in [City] so I moved we got married (1) eh: (1) lived […] in different (.) neighborhoods (1) and: ehm: (1) eh in *my early thirties* with three children already we: eh wanted to: *to do something else* and leave the city" (Z. 28–36)

Die schnell aufeinanderfolgenden Abschnitte ihres Lebens – Schule, Jugendorganisation, Schulabschluss, Armeedienst, Studienbeginn und Familienleben – sind im Gegensatz zur Familiengeschichte gerafft. Diese Lebensabschnitte gehören zur Lebensgeschichte, sind allerdings für Rivka an dieser Stelle nicht von besonderer Bedeutung und werden ihrer zeitlichen Chronologie folgend in zeitlich schnellerer Abfolge als Stationen des Lebenslaufs verhandelt. Vielmehr geht es hier offenbar darum, ihren professionellen Werdegang in den Vordergrund zu stellen. Die erzählte Zeit steht in diesem Segment in einem relational starken Gegensatz zur erlebten Zeit, denn hier werden etwa 25 Jahre in 5 Textzeilen verhandelt, wohingegen ab der folgenden Passage eine Veränderung eintritt und hier einige Jahre sehr detailliert dargelegt werden. Schütze spricht von einer „Raffung in der Erzähldarstellung" (Schütze 1984, S. 101), die besonders zwischen unterschiedlichen Prozessstrukturen – hier einmal der biografischen Eingangserzählung über die Familie und einem ersten autobiografischen Handlungsschemata, die Gründung einer neuen Lebensgemeinschaft – zum Tragen kommt. Nun in ihren „frühen 30ern" wollten sie und ihr Mann etwas Neues beginnen und sie verlassen die Stadt, in der sie groß geworden ist, in der ihre Familie in den dreißiger Jahren ankam, und gründen eine neue Siedlung[7].

---

[7]Der Begriff Siedlung ist politisch belegt, besonders wenn von Siedlungen in den besetzten Gebieten, wie dem Westjordanland oder den Golan Höhen gesprochen wird. In Rivkas Fall handelt es sich um eine neu gegründete Ortschaft innerhalb der Grenzen Israels. Inwiefern auch diese Ortschaften politische Zwecke umsetzen und staatlich subventioniert wurden, soll an dieser Stelle nicht weiter ausgeführt werden.

Diesen Aufbruch beendet sie in der Gegenwart und damit auch im Präsens „I have today four children and three eh grandchildren in my personal life I feel very (.) lucky (.) I have a nice home" (Z. 79–80). Es folgt nun eine längere Erzählung darüber, wie ihre berufliche Tätigkeit einem Wandel unterlag, in dem sie mit ihrer Familie einige Zeit in den USA verbrachte und neue Ansätze politischer Bildung kennenlernte. Interessant ist nun, dass die Zeitperspektiven nun nicht mehr eindeutig und chronologisch sind. Ein Wandlungsprozess bedeutet eine systematische Veränderung der Erlebnis- und Handlungsmöglichkeiten (Schütze 1984, S. 92) und auch, dass sich die Zeitdimensionen ändern, besonders dann, wenn die Konsequenzen des Wandels weiterhin in der Gegenwart wirksam sind.

„later: eh: nineteen ninety three nineteen ninety four eh: as a family we went to another sabbatical (.) /we were/ ((leise)) three times in the States=my husband is a researcher eh: so: we eh: (.) he was-he got a position in [City] in the States and it was the first year for the Holocaust Memorial [Museum] that it was opened and: for me: I was very curious to know: *what the Americans have to do with my Holocaust*=because: dealing with Holocaust=I am going back to Holocaust Education ah: while: eh: growing up in Israel in the fifties and sixties I: eh: *let's say I: see myself as a typical (.) a typical ehm eh: (1) product of the Israeli school system (.) and eh Holocaust was eh: (.) taught in a traditional way: as it's been taught today in most of the schools in Israel as a Jewish disaster (.) ahm: that happened to us: (.) the Jews (.) we are the victims (1) the whole world is against us* and we: -the only lesson I could eh: learn was that we have to be strong and we have to ehm go on fighting against the whole world and it won't happen to us (.) again […] and: the: crowd that were going with me in the museum (.) I didn't know where: to look first at the crowd coming with me or: at the exhibition (1) because the crowd were-they were definitely no Jews (.) they were Amish (.) they were Christians with eh: big eh: cross=they were Asians=there were-you know you could tell there were no Jews (.) and they are still interested and they are still: with a lot of respect to the issue and eh: (.) you know it was (1) a first experience (1) I couldn't leave the place on this day=I really couldn't" (Z. 106–136)

In diesem Segment reflektiert Rivka zum ersten Mal in ihrer Erzählung Aspekte der Lebensgeschichte. Folgte sie vorher einem chronologischen Ablauf, bewertet sie Erlebtes nun aus der Gegenwart: Sie war neugierig, was die Besucher*innen des Museums an „ihrem Holocaust" interessant fanden. Erklärend schließt sie hier mit der Darstellung der israelischen Holocaust-Bildung in Schulen und der Gesellschaft an, in der der Holocaust als ein exklusives Erleben von Jüdinnen und Juden dargestellt wird und omnipräsente Gedenkkultur ist (u.a. Segev 1995).[8] An dieser Stelle jedoch wird ihre heutige Sichtweise deutlich: sie betont und spricht leicht ironisierend und damit distanziert über „meinen Holocaust" und der israelischen Bildungs- und Vergangenheitspolitik. Die zeitlich synchrone Erzählung als Erlebnisse der Vergangenheit wird an dieser Stelle gebrochen durch ihre erzählte Lebensgeschichte, in der die subjektive Sichtweise der Selbstdarstellung zum Tragen kommt.

Rivkas Handeln und ihre Entscheidungen sind gerahmt von einer tradierten, kollektiven Vergangenheit, Prozesse des Wandels führen nicht zu einem Bruch oder einer Revidierung des Erlebten, sondern bestärken die eigene Handlungsmaxime und fügen sich nahtlos in das synchrone Zeitverhältnis ein. Die Vergangenheit ist dabei eine Grundlage, auf der neues verhandelt und integriert wird, die Gegenwart ist hier schlussfolgernd das Resultat aus vergangenen Erlebnissen, die eine Version zukünftigen Handelns beinhaltet.

Yotam ist ein weiteres Beispiel dieses Typs der Lebensgeschichte, in der vergangenen Erlebnissen oder Erzählungen vertraut wird. Ähnlich wie Rivka erzählt Yotam die Geschichte seiner Eltern und wie diese in den dreißiger Jahren von Österreich nach Palästina emigrieren als Einschub zu Beginn. Weiterhin ist es ihm wichtig, sein Aufwachsen im Kibbuz darzustellen und damit auch die Werte und Erziehung, mit der er großgeworden ist, darzustellen.

„Okay eh-I was born in a Kibbuz (1) it's called Kibbuz X in eh-1954 (1) eh I was the second child my eldest sister is five years older than me: (3) ehm (1) *my my two parents [...] were born in Austria (1) and eh came: eh in 1938 as a:-in the youth Aliyah (2) with the families /of course staying behind/* ((schnell)) (1) I grew up in: when it was still the quite typical Kibbuz education eh (1) living-not sleeping at home for example but in a children's house" (2/13–20)

Yotam beginnt also mit einer kurzen Erzählung über seinen Geburtsort, ein Kibbuz in Israel. Es folgt eine Erzählung über die Eltern, die als Jugendliche 1938 mit einer zionistischen Jugendorganisation aus Österreich nach Palästina

---

[8]Das Thema der Gedenkkultur über den Holocaust bzw. die Shoah in Israel wurde vielfältig untersucht. Tom Segev (1995) hat mit seinem Buch „Die siebte Million" historisch die Entwicklung der Holocaust-Erinnerung in Israel nachvollzogen, die nach wie vor einen sehr guten Überblick bietet.

gekommen sind. Er geht davon aus, dass mir der Begriff Jugendaliyah[9] bekannt ist und ebenso sein Anhang an die Erzählung, dass die Familien der beiden „*of course*" zurückgeblieben seien. Viele Verwandten haben den Holocaust nicht überlebt.

Das Kibbuz ist zentral für die chronologische Darstellung seiner Kindheit und Jugend: er wächst im „Kinderhaus" auf, was der Ideologie gemeinschaftlicher Erziehung in Kibbuzim entsprach. Er beginnt schon früh, sich in der Kibbuz-Bewegung zu engagieren, leitet Jugendgruppen und verbringt nach der Schule ein gemeinschaftliches Jahr mit anderen der Jugendbewegung seines Kibbuz[10] in einer Kommune. Danach leistet er seinen Armeedienst und beginnt dort bereits Bildungsarbeit zu leisten und ist nicht als Soldat eingesetzt. Die Eingangserzählung bis zur Conclusio verläuft dabei synchron und ohne Brüche und nur mit wenigen erklärenden Einschüben[11], ähnlich wie bei Rivka als institutionelles Ablaufmuster (vgl. Schütze 1983, S. 281). Mit dem Ende der Eingangserzählung, das durch die Koda „Ich denke, das ist der grundlegende Rahmen" markiert ist, beginnt nun der Wandlungsprozess, der erklärt, warum er nun in der historisch-politischen Bildungsarbeit arbeitet. Nun kommen gegenwärtiges Erleben und auch Vorstellung zukünftiger Zusammenarbeit in der Erzählung vergangener Ereignisse zum Ausdruck.

„*I think that's the basic framework* (.) I mean (.) along the line: (.) I had two more sons born and eh: I did my MA and my PhD: eh: but this is the:-I would I would add=*maybe that this has something to do with the fact that I'm here* is also eh: when the 2000 riots=you know about them the October 2000 riots broke out between-here in Israel not during the Intifada we're not talking about the Intifada […] (1) at that time we were on a eh: visit to [Country] where (.) my: brother-in-law lives=my eh wives' brother (.) and we heard about it from there but when I came here: (2) *I felt: well I was of course like everybody very=very surprised and disturbed* by the fact that the riots took place here in Israel" (Z. 74–84).

---

[9]Jugendaliyah bedeutet die Einwanderung nach Palästina von jüdischen Jugendlichen, die durch zionistische Organisationen in Europa betreut wurden.

[10]Kibbuzim (Plural) sind die Manifestation der Idee des gemeinschaftlichen Zusammenlebens vor dem Hintergrund zionistisch-sozialistischer Ideale (Lindenau 2007, S. 269 ff.). Die unterschiedlichen politischen Strömungen, die hinter der Gründung der Wohnsiedlungen standen, hatten organisierte Jugendgruppen.

[11]In vielen der von mir geführten Interviews in Israel finden sich erklärende Einschübe, die dem interkulturellen Kontext der Interviewsituation geschuldet sind.

Nach der Koda fügt Yotam noch drei Ereignisse an, die er vorher nicht erwähnte – zwei weitere Söhne, den MA und seine Doktorarbeit. Wie dies auch schon bei Rivka deutlich wurde, ist das familiäre, das „Privatleben", an dieser Stelle seiner autobiografischen Erzählung nicht relevant und wird nebenbei erwähnt. Mit der Eingangserzählung, die sich stark auf seinen Lebenslauf und Werdegang konzentrierte, macht er hingegen den für ihn auch weiterhin bedeutsamen klar abgesteckten Referenzrahmen – das Aufwachsen und Leben im Kibbuz deutlich. Nach der Koda allerdings beginnt eine Prozessstruktur des Wandels, die er ausdrücklich mit der Gegenwart in Verbindung bringt. Alle weiteren Ereignisse, die zwischen den beiden Prozessstrukturen noch wichtig sein könnten, werden hier zeitlich gerafft. Der Beginn dieser Darstellung des Wandlungsprozesses bedeutet nicht nur das Reflektieren über die Bedeutung für die eigene Lebensgeschichte und eigene Entscheidungen, sondern ebenso das Darstellen von Emotionen – „very surprised and disturbed" und das Verlassen geregelter institutioneller Ablaufmuster.

Zusammenfassend kann für den Fall Yotam festgehalten werden, dass Vergangenheit und Gegenwart in der Eingangserzählung in einen Prozess eingeordnet und als synchrones Aufeinanderfolgen von Ereignissen verhandelt werden.

Weitere Fälle, die im Rahmen der Studie zu biographischen Erzählungen in der israelischen politischen Bildung analysiert wurden (vgl. Kahle 2017), und in denen das Vertrauen in die eigene Lebens- und auch ebenso Familiengeschichte zum Ausdruck kommt, deuten klar auf die Relevanz des Elternhauses und die primäre Erziehung hin. Die Eltern fungieren hier als Vorbild und Grundlage für eigene Entscheidungen. Dabei ist das Zeitverhältnis synchron, weil die gesamte lebensgeschichtliche Vergangenheit ungebrochen in die erzählte Lebensgeschichte eingebunden wird und als Teil gegenwärtigen Handelns verhandelt wird.

Vertrauen in die selbst erlebte Lebensgeschichte – diachrones Zeitverhältnis

In einem zweiten Typ der Autobiografien hingegen werden zeitliche Brüche und Reflexionen über vergangene Erlebnisse schon in die frühe Erzählung eingeführt. Das Erzählen verläuft in Bezug auf das Verhältnis aus Vergangenheit-Gegenwart-Zukunft weitaus diachroner. Eine These ist, dass die Veränderung vergangener Annahmen so stark ist, dass der Geschichte der Eltern beispielsweise kein Vertrauen mehr entgegengebracht werden kann, im Gegensatz dazu ist nur noch das selbst Erlebte Teil der Erzählung.

Adayas Lebensgeschichte ist sehr stark gerahmt durch den „Verlust ihres Narrativs" und ihre Neu-Orientierung innerhalb der israelischen Gesellschaft. Sie erlebt die Zweite Intifada, die im Jahr 2000 begann, während sie einen Studiengang in Peace Studies nachholte und dafür viel in Bildungszusammenhängen arbeitete, in denen jüdische sowie palästinensische Israelis zusammenarbeiteten. Mit dieser Erfahrung und den Gesprächen, die sie aus dieser Zeit mitnimmt, entwickelt sich eine neue Sichtweise auf zuvor Gelerntes und Erzähltes. Auch die Geschichte der Eltern und wie sie diese einschätzte, änderte sich grundsätzlich.

„I was born in in a kibbutz in a very small kibbutz next to the boarder with Jordan ehm: (1) *as a child I was raised in the shadow of endless wars @(.)@* (1) ehm as little children we slept in the bomb shelter (.) not-not in normal houses because ehm: between the age of: I think (.) two (.) years old to: five or six years old there was always bombings between Israel and Jordan (.) I don't know how you call this war in eh: English (.) sixty: sixty-nine the two years between sixty-seven and sixty-nine or something like that=it was eh: bombing all the time (.) okay: I can't remember the name I will remember later (.) so eh: I was raised-this this were the first noises that I can remember and the fears that I had and eh: that there was some kind of a hole between the kindergarten to the bomb shelter (.) not in the kibbutz we don't sleep with parents but we slept in the kindergarten but we used to sleep in the bomb shelter (1) *so this is=this were the first noises that I can remember [...] my father was a soldier in the Army of Israel quite a high rank as the years went by end eh: I (.) but they both raised us (.) we are four (.) kids in the family and we were all raised eh: (.) on values of pluralism (.) humanism and so on (.) although I can't say: (.) today that my parents are-used to be left wing or something like that (.) they considered themselves like they are (.) but it's different in the way they act=I mean my father was a (.) soldier and it was a very important part of his life and of his eh: agenda and of his narrative and this was something very=very important for him (.) eh so it's complex*" (Z. 9–31)

Ihre Detaillierung der Erzählung wird unterbrochen, indem sie nach einer Validierung der Ereignisse sucht, indem sie Jahreszahlen und Namen des Krieges versucht zu erinnern. Der Detaillierungs- und Gestaltschließungszwang ihrer Eingangserzählung ist deutlich. Sie erinnert sich an die Geräusche der Bomben und an ihre Ängste und nur noch unklar an das Setting. Der Kindergarten und der Bunker, in dem sie schlief, und ein Loch, das beide Orte verband, sind ungenau. Die Darstellungsarbeit ihrer Narration ist deutlich auf das Erleben als Kind fokussiert.

Bedeutend ist zudem, dass diese ihr nicht von anderen erzählt wurde, sondern sie diese selbst erlebt hat. Anders als beispielsweise in den beiden biografischen Lebensgeschichte von Adaya und Yotam, in denen mit der Geschichte der Eltern begonnen wird, um das Verständnis für einen familiären, biografischen Gesamtzusammenhang zu ermöglichen, folgt Adaya ihrer eigenen Erinnerung. Dies ist auch eine Möglichkeit auszudrücken, dass sie nur sich selbst vertraut bzw. nicht den Geschichten und Erlebnissen ihrer Eltern, solange diese nicht von ihr selbst überprüft werden können.

Es folgt ein kurzer Bezug auf ihre Eltern und nun zudem ein erster zeitlicher Vorgriff: Sie verbleibt nicht in der Erzählung wie sie aufgezogen wurde, sondern stellt stattdessen die Grundlagen, auf denen ihre Erziehung fußte und die politischen Einstellungen ihrer Eltern infrage: *"we were all raised eh: (.) on values of pluralism (.) humanism and so on (.) although I can't say: (.) today that my parents are-used to be left wing or something like that"*. Nach damaliger Vorstellung und auch danach, was sie lange glaubte, wurden sie und ihre Geschwister nach Werten wie Pluralismus, Humanismus „und so weiter" erzogen. In dieser Passage des Interviews jedoch wird die Distanz zur Vergangenheit sehr deutlich. „Und so weiter" entwertet den Werte-Komplex, auf dessen Fundament die Erziehung ruhte. Weiterhin wird der Einstellung der Eltern kein Vertrauen mehr entgegengebracht. Das weiß sie heute: ihre Eltern waren nicht links „or something like that". Sehr deutlich durch den zeitlichen Marker „today" kommt zum Ausdruck, dass wesentliche Aspekte ihrer Familiengeschichte heute anders bewertet werden. Eine synchrone lebensgeschichtliche Erzählung ihrer Kindheit ist somit nicht mehr ohne erklärende und bewertende Einschübe und damit zeitliche Vorgriffe möglich, die Zeit fließt nicht mehr chronologisch, sondern wird stetig unterbrochen, was sich wiederum auch in den Textsorten niederschlägt.

Die folgende zentrale Stelle in ihrer Eingangserzählung belegt nun ihren Vertrauensverlust, den sie während der Zweiten Intifada erlebte und drückt damit deutlich einen Wandlungsprozess aus.

„I was eh: in a facilitation course with Arab- (.) with Palestinians who live next to me (.) so I've got two different roads of getting information (.) from the people I was with in the course in the seminar and from the eh: media in Israel (.) this is the time when I lost all the: trust (.) and all the belief and all the don't know (2) all the ability to identify with the media in Israel I just=I just lost my faith in=in=in this (.) country in this state in this: (.) because what I saw with my eyes from where I lived and what I heard from my friends from the course […] was so different like reality was so different from the media and what the government said (.) *I knew people that were killed (.) I knew how they were killed I-I knew what was happening* and I-I just lost everything it-I-I lost my narrative (.) I lost my identity (.) for a while //mhm// eh: (2) and when you are standing in this situation it's like it's like a very big hole […] (1) and you jump in (.) I mean giving up your narrative (.) giving up I mean your: in a way identity (.) ehm th-the ability to identify with your country (.) with your people with (.) the place where you were born is very difficult (.) your story the story of your parents the story of=all your people" (Z. 59–74).

Adaya stellt einen persönlichen Prozess dar, der sich nach Schütze als Wandlungsprozess der biografischen Gesamtformung im Verlauf der Erzählung charakterisieren lässt. Maßgeblich kommt der Wandel dadurch zustande, dass sie nun zwei Informationsquellen ausgesetzt ist: den Erzählungen der Kursteilnehmer*innen einerseits und den israelischen Medien andererseits. Diese beiden Quellen unterscheiden sich nicht nur im Inhalt, sondern auch in der Nähe zu ihr. Die einen sind *mit* ihr zusammen – *the people I was with* – und die Medien sind für sie ein unpersönliches Narrativ des Staates. Die Aufstände im Jahr 2000 sind als Beginn ihres biografischen Wendepunkts eingeführt, mit dem der Vertrauensverlust in den Staat einhergeht, da die offizielle Realitätsdarstellung durch die Medien mit der selbst erlebten Realität nicht mehr deckungsgleich ist. Im weiteren Verlauf stellt sie den Höhepunkt der Wende dar und benennt ihren Wandlungsprozess und die Konsequenzen. Sie verliert Vertrauen, Glauben und die Fähigkeit, sich mit dem Staat zu identifizieren. Auch hier steht wieder das eigene individuelle Wissen einer kollektiven Entität, dem nationalen israelischen Narrativ, symbolisiert durch die Medien, gegenüber – *I knew people that were killed (.) I knew how they were killed I-I knew what was happening*. Ihr Wandel beruht auf Erlebnissen, die sie selbst mitbekommt und die in ihrem unmittelbaren Umfeld geschehen. All ihre neuen Erkenntnisse führen direkt auf die Conclusio hin: *I-I just lost everything it-I-I lost my narrative (.) I lost my identity (.) for a while*. Wohingegen Adaya zu Beginn der Sequenz noch den Verlust von Vertrauen und Glauben hervorhebt und sie sich nicht mehr mit den Medien identifizieren kann, kumulieren ihre Erlebnisse, die sie aufzählt, in den Verlust ihrer Identität bzw. von allem (*everything*). Dieses „alles" ist ein Ausdruck dessen, wie sehr sie dieser Prozess beschäftigt und mitgenommen hat. Bis zu diesem Zeitpunkt empfand sie die Inkongruenz ihrer Erziehung höchstwahrscheinlich nicht. Erst ab diesem Moment des Verlusts kann sie die ersten Jahre ihrer Lebensgeschichte nicht mehr ohne die Reflexion über die Widersprüchlichkeit der Wertevermittlung erzählen. Doch Adaya schränkt den Höhepunkt ihres Wandlungsprozesses im gleichen Satz ein: Sie verliert ihre Identität nur für eine Weile, denn sie ist bereits über diesen Prozess hinweg. Ihre Erfahrungen werden von ihr bereits als Vergangenes berichtet.

Bei Adaya zeigt sich zusammenfassend, dass der Wandlungsprozess, der sie überraschte und von ihr eine Neu-Orientierung politischer Normen und Einstellungen verlangte, zu einer zeitlichen Diachronie in Bezug auf die eigene Familiengeschichte führte. Das Vergangene wird nicht ungebrochen unter die Lebensgeschichte subsumiert, wie dies bei Rivka und Yotam der Fall ist, sondern

„im Modus der Gegenwart" (Fischer 2018, S. 463) wird die Vergangenheit reflektiert, modifiziert und letztlich hergestellt.

Ähnlich nun zeigt sich die Diachronie der Zeit auch in einem weiteren Fall, der hier nur kurz vorgestellt wird. Roni durchläuft ebenso einen Wandlungsprozess, woraufhin ihr die Erzählung über ihre Kindheit, die Familie und die Erziehung nicht mehr ohne eingeschobene Bewertungen und Reflexionen gelingt.

„I was born in [City] (.) we moved to a few places (2) in Israel outside Israel (.) most of the years I grew up in a suburb called [Town] (.) a suburb of [City] (.) it was then quite small and sleepy //mhm// ehm: v-(4) very: >I'm searching for the word in English< but very (3) not diversed the other way round (.) very unified (.) very //homogenous?// homogen-oh thank you @(2)@ very homogeneous eh: people (.) middle class mostly Ashkenazi Jews very similar (.) living in apartment buildings with the kindergarten underneath >and whatever<" (Z. 17–24)

Ronis Eingangserzählung beginnt mit einer geografischen Verortung ihres bisherigen Lebens. Sie ist mit ihren Eltern häufig umgezogen und hat die meiste Zeit ihre Kindheit und Jugend in einem Vorort einer Großstadt verbracht. Wichtig ist offenbar weniger die familiäre Einordnung, ob sie Geschwister hat, was ihre Eltern machen oder wie ihre Eltern nach Israel kamen, sondern die eigene lokale Herkunft und damit, wo der Beginn der eigenen Biografie verortet ist. Der Vorort, in dem sie die meiste Zeit ihrer Kindheit und Jugend verbrachte, ist die Positionierung innerhalb eines Milieus. Sie positioniert sich hier nicht im Konflikt zu dieser Herkunft, sondern eröffnet an dieser Stelle erstmalig den normativen Horizont, der im weiteren Verlauf ausgeführt bzw. unbewusst eine bedeutende Rolle spielt in Bezug auf ihren biografischen Verlauf. Obwohl das Segment durch das Wort *then* scheinbar als Erzählung eingeleitet ist, ist dies bereits der Beginn der Beschreibung des sozialen Milieus, indem sie aufwuchs und dessen Beschreibung aus der heutigen Perspektive vorgenommen wird. Der Vorort hatte eine sozial (*middle class*) und ethnisch homogene (*mostly Ashkenazi*[12]) Anwohner*innenschaft, deren Lebensstil sich scheinbar nicht voneinander unterschied.

---

[12]Der Ausdruck „Aschkenasisch" lässt sich nur noch schwer richtig fassen. In diesem Fall ist es wichtig zu wissen, dass er in Israel vielmehr ein gesellschaftliches Verhältnis ausdrückt und es mehr um die Sichtbarkeit in der Gesellschaft geht. Aschkenasim kommen z.T. ursprünglich aus Ost- und Westeuropa. Roni möchte hier deutlich machen, dass in ihrem Viertel viele als weiß bezeichnete Menschen lebten, womit auch in Israel häufig eine gesellschaftliche Stellung, ein bestimmtes Milieu einhergeht.

Diese Beschreibung des Vororts erscheint vorweggestellt als Kontrastfolie zu dem, wie sie heute lebt oder möglicherweise leben will. Sie stellt diese Beschreibung vor den Beginn der Erzählung des eigenen Lebens. Diese Milieubeschreibung wirkt wie ein Fundament der eigenen Zugehörigkeitskonstruktion, noch bevor das biografische Ich in der Erzählung auftaucht, dennoch ist die Abgrenzung deutlich. Roni verhandelt hier nun parallel einerseits ihren familiären Bezug, das Milieu, aus dem sie kommt als Aspekt ihrer Biografie und ihrer Vergangenheit und andererseits zeitgleich ihren Wissenszuwachs *über* dieses Milieu und damit gleichzeitig ihre Abgrenzung davon.

„I think most of my life (.) I don't know exactly why=probably my mother had an interest in social issues and social justice (.) and in a very (2) general preliminary kind of way: and I liked Shirley Temple movies when she helped the poor people @stuff (.) like that@ when I was young=I don't know why but I think it's in relation to eh: (2) my mom is a very ideological person: >I think< she came from a kibbuz and (1) her father was a Jecke from Germany (.) with all that it means (.) he was like you need to do things the way they should be done and eh: (.) no discrimination no special treatments stuff like that=so that's very: eh: (2) very much him (.) didn't get my mom a musical instrument because she was the first in her groups: so she cannot do it before other people so nobody will say she'll=stuff like that but my house wasn't a political one >it was maybe I think< values had a place there (1) were important but it wasn't a political house" (Z. 24–35)

Roni stellt hier ein prinzipien- und wertorientiertes Fundamt der eigenen Biografie voraus. Sie füllt das soziale Umfeld, das zuvor eher eine Milieubeschreibung war mit Inhalt durch die Beschreibung der Ansichten, der Werte und des politischen Verständnisses ihrer Eltern und sich selbst. Sie nennt ihre Mutter als ein Beispiel für den Einfluss ihres Elternhauses auf ihre politische Einstellung. Ihre Mutter hatte ein Interesse für soziale Verhältnisse und soziale Gerechtigkeit auf eine sehr allgemeine Art und Weise. Sie selbst bewertet ihre Einstellung anhand der Filme, die sie zu der Zeit mochte – Filme mit Shirley Temple *when she helped the poor people*. Diese Selbstdarstellung ist aus der Gegenwart konstruiert und keine in der Kindheit bewusste Entscheidung für diesen Film (so scheint es). Auch heute vermutet sie nur, dass es etwas mit den Werten, die ihre Mutter und die Familie ihrer Mutter transportierten zu tun hat, denn wieder fügt sie sehr schnell *I don't know* an, mit dem sie den Erklärungszapfen vom Beginn des Segments wiederaufnimmt und auf ähnliche Weise wieder mit ihrer Mutter unterbricht, die sie immer wieder in Beziehung zu sich setzt. Ihre Mutter war eine sehr ideologische Person, die nicht nur die Werte aus dem Kibbuz in die Familie brachte, sondern auch diejenigen Werte ihres Vaters, der aus Deutschland nach Israel einwanderte. Diese Werte werden nur beispielhaft angerissen anhand der Zuschreibung „Jecke", wie man in Israel Jüdinnen und Juden nennt, die aus Deutschland eingewandert sind. Ihre Mutter wird als Ereignisträgerin eingeführt, die biografischen Sinn stiftet über ihre Herkunft und ihre Einstellung. Hier werden der nationalen Herkunft bestimmte Charaktereigenschaften zugewiesen, ein Repertoire, dass sich automatisch abrufen lässt – *with all that it means* – und das Roni für die Interviewerin mit zwei Beispielen in einer Verdichtung einschiebt. Trotzdem sind diese bestimmend, Gleichheit, keine Bevorteilung und Prinzipienorientierung werden von ihrem Großvater über die Mutter in die Familie weitergegeben und zusätzlich spielen nun auch das Interesse für soziale Ungerechtigkeit und „Nächstenliebe" eine Rolle, dargestellt anhand der Figur Shirley Temple.

Ronis Intention in diesem Segment scheint es zu sein, die politische Einstellung und die Werte ihrer Familie zu konstruieren, sie stellt diese aus ihrer heutigen Perspektive dar. Dies geschieht u.a. dadurch, dass sie einen Gegensatz zwischen Werten auf der einen und dem Politischem auf der anderen Seite schafft. Dafür steht auch die Koda dieses Segments: *my house wasn't a political one >it was maybe I think< val:ues had a place there.* Die im Kibbuz aufgewachsene Mutter, die sich für soziale Themen interessiert, ist Ronis heutiger Bewertung nach, nicht politisch.

Ronis Eingangserzählung ist ebenfalls von Reflektionen über ihre Kindheit, ihre Eltern und das Milieu, aus dem sie kommt geprägt. Das heißt der Modus der Gegenwart ist auch hier strukturgebend. Dennoch ist der Bruch, anders als bei Adaya, weniger deutlich, sondern Ronis Verhältnis bleibt ambivalent und sie betont das Fundament ihrer Erziehung und die Werte, die ihr vermittelt wurden.

Diskussion und Fazit

Der Fokus des Aufsatzes lag vordergründig auf dem Verhältnis aus Gegenwart, das heißt dem gegenwärtigen Erzählen und den vergangenen Erlebnissen, aus denen ein jeweils anderes zeitliches Verhältnis und eine andere Erzählweise hervorgegangen ist. Für Rivka und Yotam ist die Vergangenheit Teil einer konstant verlaufenden Lebensgeschichte, vergangene Erfahrungen werden, wie bereits die Geschichte der Eltern, in gegenwärtige Entscheidungen eingesponnen in der Eingangserzählung. Der später im Leben stattfindende Wandel – der Beginn des bildungspolitischen Engagements – führt zwar zu neuen Handlungsmustern und Aktivitätspotentialen, bedeutet aber nicht einen Bruch oder eine Neu-Orientierung vergangener Einstellungen oder familiärer Erziehungs- und Wertefundamente.

Adaya und Roni hingegen beginnen bereits zu Beginn der Lebensgeschichte mit Reflektionen über vergangene Erlebnisse und die Herkunftsfamilie. Das was früher zählte, kann so in der Gegenwart nicht mehr aufrechterhalten, unkommentiert oder einfach unmodifiziert erzählt werden. Es besteht eine Distanz zwischen Vergangenheit und Gegenwart, wodurch das fehlende Vertrauen in alles, was nicht selbst erlebt wurde, erklärt werden kann.

Der Zukunftsaspekt stand weniger im Vordergrund, da davon ausgegangen werden kann, dass die Zukunft als Erwartungsraum, der gegenwärtiges Handeln mitstrukturiert, im Sample der Studie durch den Bezug auf die Co-Existence Education, die Bildungsarbeit mit palästinensischen und jüdischen Israelis bestimmt ist. Dieser Bezug auf Bildung und Gesellschaft ist fallspezifisch, denn gerade innerhalb von Bildungseinrichtungen und nichtstaatlichen Organisationen in Israel ist der Bezug auf „Interaktion, Freundschaft und politische Kooperation" (Berlowitz 2012, S. 15) sehr deutlich.

Die hier herangezogenen vier Fälle entwickeln alle einen Wandlungsprozess der biografischen Gesamtformung, in deren Verlauf auch Handlungsschemata zum Ausdruck kommen (Schütze 1983). Der Wandel bedeutet in allen Fällen eine Neu-Verhandlung in Bezug auf berufliche Orientierungen aber auch politische Einstellungen, und im Fall Israels, eine neue Positionierung innerhalb gesellschaftlicher Konfliktfelder.[13] Die Lebensgeschichte jedoch wird auf unterschiedliche Weise in Bezug auf das Erleben *vor* und *nach* dem Wandel erzählt. Das ist insofern methodologisch interessant, weil so – zumindest in den Fällen mit einem dominant erzählten Wandlungsprozess – die Zeitperspektive sich in Bezug auf vergangenes Erleben ändert.[14] Die „Gleichheit einer Person" kann daher nur aus der Gegenwart rekonstruiert werden und aus dieser gegenwärtigen Situation verhalten sich die vergangenen Erlebnisse zum gegenwärtigen Handeln sinnhaft (Joas nach Brose et al. 1993, S. 164). Dennoch interessant ist gerade der Aspekt, wie sich unterschiedliche Deutungen der Vergangenheit narrativ darstellen: wird die eigene Lebensgeschichte synchron, mit wenigen Brüchen erzählt und damit das eigene Handeln in der Gegenwart als ein Produkt einer gleichen

---

[13]In der Arbeit „Agency und Belonging in polarisierten Gesellschaften" konnte dargestellt werden, inwiefern man im Falle Israels von einer gespaltenen oder polarisierten Gesellschaft aufgrund gesellschaftlicher Konfliktfelder sprechen kann (Kahle 2017, S. 64 ff.)

[14]Brose et al. (1993) verweisen demgegenüber in ihrer Studie zum Erleben von Zeitarbeit und die Gestaltung von Arbeitszeit und Lebenszeit auf eine „reduzierte" Zeitperspektive, wenn beispielsweise Hoffnungslosigkeit in Bezug auf Zukunftserwartungen rekonstruiert wird. Als Beispiel wird Arbeitslosigkeit angeführt (S. 160f.)

Person mit einer konstant verlaufenen Lebensgeschichte verhandelt oder aber diachron, auf eine notwendig zu revidierende, weil auf falschen Einstellungen beruhende Vergangenheit.

Handlungsfähigkeit entsteht durch Reflexion in einer von sozialen, politischen, kulturellen und ökonomischen Strukturen beeinflussten *Situation* in der Gegenwart. Zeit für diese Reflexion und Interpretation entsteht dabei in der von Mead erarbeiteten Interaktionssequenz, wobei die Antwort „mehr oder weniger ungewiss" ist (Mead 1934, S. 176). In dieser Ungewissheit liegt für qualitative Forschung eine Möglichkeit, Handlungen jenseits gesellschaftlicher Norm und Erwartbarkeit zu rekonstruieren, da sie Reflexivität, Kreativität und Neuheit beinhaltet (Hitlin und Elder 2007, S. 178).

Wie die Analyse zeigt, bietet die Zeit-Theorie Meads somit vielversprechende Anknüpfungspunkte für die Biografieanalyse. Dies betrifft insbesondere die Möglichkeit, der individuellen Zeitperspektive mehr Raum in der Rekonstruktion narrativer Interviews zu geben und dabei den Aspekt der Handlungsfähigkeit zu berücksichtigen. Denn Handeln ist ein gegenwärtiger Akt, der sich aus vergangenen Erfahrungen speist, zukunftsgerichtet ist und ein bestimmtes Ziel verfolgt.

Literatur

Abels, H. (2007). *Interaktion, Identität, Präsentation. Kleine Einführung in interpretative Theorien der Soziologie*. Wiesbaden: Springer VS.

Apitzsch, U. (2006). Biografieforschung und interkulturelle Pädagogik. In H.-H. Krüger, W. Marotzki (Hrsg.), *Handbuch erziehungswissenschaftliche Biografieforschung* (S. 500–514), Wiesbaden: Springer VS.

Bergmann, W. (1981). Zeit, Handlung und Sozialität bei G. H. Mead, *Zeitschrift für Soziologie* 10 (4): 351–363.

Berlowitz, S. (2012). *Die Erfahrung der Anderen. Konfliktstoff im palästinensisch-israelischen Dialog*, Konstanz: Konstanz University Press.

Bonß, W., Dimbath, O., & Maurer A. et al. (2013). *Handlungstheorie. Eine Einführung*, Bielefeld: Transcript.

Brose, H.G., Wohlrab-Sahr, M., & Corsten, M. (1993). *Soziale Zeit und Biografie. Über die Gestaltung von Alltagszeit und Lebenszeit*. Wiesbaden: VS Verlag für Sozialwissenschaften.

Carlson, S., Kahle, L., & Klinge, D. (2017): Wenn Narrationen nicht zustande kommen… Wie hochreflexive Berufsfelder dazu beitragen, dass argumentativ-evaluative Darstellungsweisen im narrativen Interview dominant werden. *Zeitschrift für Qualitative Forschung*, 18 (2): 239–262.

Dausien, B. (2000). „Biografie" als rekonstruktiver Zugang zu „Geschlecht" – Perspektiven der Biografieforschung. In D. Lemmermöhle, D. Fischer & A. Schlüter (Hrsg.). *Les-*

arten des Geschlechts. Zur De-Konstruktionsdebatte in der erziehungswissenschaftlichen Geschlechterforschung (S. 96–115), Opladen: Leske+Budrich.

Dausien, B. (2010). Biografieforschung: Theoretische Praxis und methodologische Konzepte für eine rekonstruktive Geschlechterforschung. In R. Becker, B. Kortendiek (Hrsg.). *Handbuch Frauen- und Geschlechterforschung. Theorie, Methoden, Empirie* (S. 363–375), Wiesbaden: Springer VS.

Durkheim, E. (1981). Die elementaren Formen des religiösen Lebens. Frankfurt a.M.: Suhrkamp.

Emirbayer, M., & Mische, A. (1998). What is Agency?. *American Journal of Sociology* 103 (4): 962–1023.

Fischer, W. (2018). Zeit und Biografie. In H. Lutz, M. Schiebel & E. Tuider (Hrsg.). *Handbuch Biografieforschung* (S. 461–472), Wiesbaden: Springer VS.

Flaherty, M. G., & Fine, G. A. (2001). Present, Past, and Future: cojugating George Herbert Mead's perspective on time. *Time and Society. An International Interdisciplinary Journal* 10 (2/3): 147–162.

Hitlin, S., & Elder, G. H. Jr. (2007). Time, Self and the Curiously Abstract Concept of Agency. Sociological Theory. *A Journal of the American Sociological Association* 25(2): 170-191.

Joas, H. (1989). *Praktische Intersubjektivität. Die Entwicklung des Werks von G. H. Mead*, Frankfurt a. M.: Suhrkamp.

Kahle, Lena (2017). *Agency und Zugehörigkeit in polarisierten Gesellschaften. Eine biografieanalytische Studie in Israel*, Opladen/Toronto: Barbara Budrich.

Kallmeyer, W. & Schütze, F. (1977). Zur Konstitution von Kommunikationsschemata der Sachverhaltsdarstellung. In D. Wegener (Hrsg.), *Gesprächsanalysen. Vorträge gehalten anläßlich des 5. Kolloquiums des Instituts für Kommunikationsforschung und Phonetik, Bonn, 14.–16. Oktober 1976* (S. 159–274), Hamburg: Helmut Buske.

Kleemann, F., Krähnke, U., & Matuschek, I. (2009). *Interpretative Sozialforschung. Eine Einführung*, Wiesbaden: Beltz Juventa.

Lindenau, M. (2007). *Requiem für einen Traum? Transformation und Zukunft der Kibbutzim in der israelischen Gesellschaft*, Berlin: LIT Verlag.

Matthes, J., & Schütze, F. (1981). Zur Einführung: Alltagswissen, Interaktion, und gesellschaftliche Wirklichkeit. In Arbeitsgruppe Bielefelder Soziologen (Hrsg.). *Alltagswissen, Interaktion und gesellschaftliche Wirklichkeit 1+2* (S. 11–53), Opladen: Springer VS.

Mead, G. H. (1932). *The Philosophy of the Present*, London/Chicago: University of Chicago Press.

Mead, G. H. (1934). *Mind Self and Society from the Standpoint of a Social Behaviorist*, Chicago: Lasalle.

Mead, G. H. (1968). *Geist, Identität und Gesellschaft. Aus der Sicht des Sozialbehaviorismus*, Frankfurt a. M.: Suhrkamp.

Mead, G. H. (1969). *Philosophie der Sozialität*. Frankfurt a.M.: Suhrkamp.

Rosenthal, G. (1995). *Erlebte und erzählte Lebensgeschichte. Gestalt und Struktur biografischer Selbstbeschreibung*, Frankfurt a. M./New York: Campus Verlag.

Rosenthal, G. (2008). *Interpretative Sozialforschung: Eine Einführung*, Weinheim/München: Beltz/Juventa.

Schütze, F. (1983). Biografieforschung und narratives Interview. *Neue Praxis*, 13 (3): 283–293.

Schütze, F. (1984). Kognitive Figuren des autobiografischen Stegreiferzählens. In M. Kohli & R. Günther (Hrsg.), *Biografie und soziale Wirklichkeit. Neue Beiträge und Forschungsperspektiven* (S. 78–117). Stuttgart: J.B. Metzler.

Schütze, F. (1987). *Das narrative Interview in Interaktionsfeldstudien: erzähltheoretische Grundlagen. Teil I*. Hagen: Fernuniversität Gesamthochschule Hagen.

Schütze, F. (2006). *Biography analysis on the empirical base of autobiografical narratives: how to analyze autobiografical narrative interviews*. http://www.uni-magdeburg.de/zsm/projekt/biografical/1/B2.1.pdf. Zugegriffen: 05. Juli 2019.

Segev, T. (1995). *Die siebte Million. Der Holocaust und Israels Politik der Erinnerung*. Reinbek b. Hamburg: Rowohlt.

Life-Stories in Times of Uncertain Futures: How Future Narratives are Constructed in Young Peoples' Biographies

Ingmar Mundt

Abstract

Since the 1980s, the amount of sociological publications with a negative connotation of the future in times of late-modernity have increased. Even though this phenomenon is frequently explained by the economic developments of post-Fordism in the Western World, not much research exists about how this might affect the perception of people concerning their narratives of the future. For this research, 22 postgraduate students between the age of 21 and 29 were asked, in biographical-narrative interviews, about their idea, plans and attitude about the future. In trying to grasp the future as a research field for social sciences, some theoretical thoughts and developments of the concept of future are presented here, which can offer an explanation of how the future is constructed in the respondents' biographies and lives in times of late-modernity. Analysis of the interviews identifies two groups: The first group with a linear perception of the future try to minimize uncertainty through planning and relying on stable institutional structures. The second group of episodic perception focus on the current status-quo of the present and try to avoid decision-making concerning the future. Both face an unsecure future after graduation (academic precarisation, short-term contracts etc.), but developed different coping strategies to deal with the uncertainty of the future.

I. Mundt (✉)
Universität Passau, Passau, Germany
E-Mail: ingmar.mundt@uni-passau.de

© Springer Fachmedien Wiesbaden GmbH, ein Teil von Springer Nature 2020
E. Schilling und M. O'Neill (Hrsg.), *Frontiers in Time*
Research – Einführung in die interdisziplinäre Zeitforschung,
https://doi.org/10.1007/978-3-658-31252-7_4

> **Zusammenfassung**
>
> Seit den 1980er Jahren hat die Zahl soziologischer Publikationen mit einer negativen Konnotation der Zukunft in Zeiten der Spätmoderne zugenommen. Obwohl dieses Phänomen häufig durch die wirtschaftlichen Entwicklungen des Postfordismus in der westlichen Welt erklärt wird, gibt es kaum Untersuchungen darüber, wie dies die Wahrnehmung der Menschen hinsichtlich ihrer Erzählungen der Zukunft beeinflussen könnte. Für dieses Forschungsprojekt wurden 22 junge Erwachsene im Alter zwischen 21 und 29 Jahren in biografisch-narrativen Interviews nach ihrer Idee, ihren Plänen und ihrer Einstellung zur Zukunft befragt. Beim Versuch, die Zukunft als Forschungsfeld der Sozialwissenschaften zu erfassen, werden einige theoretische Gedanken und Entwicklungen des Konzepts der Zukunft vorgestellt, die erklären können, wie die Zukunft in den Biografien der Befragten und in spätmodernen Zeiten konstruiert wird. Mehrere Kategorien mit unterschiedlichen Ausdrücken ermöglichen die Identifizierung zweier Gruppen: Die erste Gruppe mit linearer Wahrnehmung der Zukunft versucht, die Unsicherheit durch Planung und Nutzung stabiler institutioneller Strukturen zu minimieren. Die zweite Gruppe der episodischen Wahrnehmung konzentriert sich auf den aktuellen Status quo der Gegenwart und versucht, Entscheidungen über die Zukunft zu vermeiden. Beide stehen nach ihrem Abschluss in einer unsicheren Zukunft (akademische Prekarisierung, kurzfristige Verträge usw.), entwickelten jedoch unterschiedliche Bewältigungsstrategien, um mit der Unsicherheit der Zukunft fertig zu werden.

Introduction

"No wonder young people love stories about dystopias—they feel like they're in one."

This headline of a magazine article published by Laurie Penny (2014) describes a phenomena of a young generation which does not have the vision of a positive future anymore. Other recent popular articles show a growing attention for this topic (e.g. Child 2016; Adams 2015). But is this merely a new round of a steadily lamenting about 'the youth' or is there evidence for a deeper crisis going-on in young people's life?

Since the 1980s, the change in the perception of the future in early-industrialised countries has been subject to much analysis on the field of sociology. The future, once the horizon for expectations and the idea of a better time, has become something negative and a threat for individual life-plans in late-modernity. This development is often linked to rapid changes in the economic, political and societal environment. It is seen as a consequence of an accelerating world that shapes people's perception of time dramatically. If these assumptions are right, it must have influences on people's lives, identity processes and their biographies. One leading assumption for this contribution is that Western societies are 'future-orientated societies' in that sense that they need a positive narrative of the future for their self-conception. Following this, a break of this narrative must have consequences on people's perception of the future as an orientation to their lives.

The aim of this contribution is to present a theoretical and methodological profound way to understand young peoples' perception of the future and how they construct future within their life stories and individual future projections in times of late-modernity. First findings indicate that a break in the perception of the future is actually taking place among young people. This article likes to contribute a starting point for further sociological research of the role of the future within peoples' life and how it influence time perception and life decisions.

Firstly, a theoretical and contextual approach is presented to make sense of how to grasp the future as a research field for sociological research. Secondly, findings of an actual research project containing biographical-narratives interviews of 22 postgraduate students between 21 and 29 were interviewed for this study using narrative-biographical interviews to look closely into the construction process of future narratives within subjects' life-history.

Grasping the Future as a Research Field

In sociology, ideas and concepts for a social theory about how subjects construct and acquire their future self are not completely new. The idea of using narratives as a method to explore images of the future has become a broad field of academic research. Since the 'narrative turn' in social science in the late 1970s (Czarniawska 2004), several sociological studies dealt with the question of how people think about the future. The idea of using (meta) narratives is a quite common approach to research future expectations in general (e.g. Cook 2018). Carmo et al. (2014) showed that the access to and mobilisation of resources (like education) is crucial to value the future as positive or negative. In his studies,

Eckersley (1997; 1999) analysed the complexity of young people's hopes and fears for the future, showing that they have worse future expectations than the generation of their parents. Hicks (1996) states that '*[it] seems, that younger people are unable to imagine the future as something better than the present*'. Ono (2003) agrees with this view and adds that younger generations '*[...] see the past and present, about which they have some knowledge, extrapolate them into the future, and form an image of the future. But it's a darker future*'. Nordensvard (2014) mentions that educated young people do not link their very dystopian future expectations for society to their individual positive framed future vision.

A lot of research exists about how young people see the future in forms of narratives across many scientific disciplines. Most studies paint a big macro-sociological vision of the future, often describing the content of such narratives and the context in which they are constructed. But they only answer the questions of *what* people think about the future in form of present images and do not explain *how* this affects the individual perception of the future. A second group mostly concentrates on social-psychological perspectives, explaining how different expected futures affect the motivation and mood of people or how they make decisions based on uncertain outlooks. Even though both groups more or less analyse these images within the living context of their target groups, questions of *how* these future expectations influence people's identities or life-courses are left out. Micro-sociological approaches, which deal with the question of *how* subjects include future expectations or images into their own identity or life-history, could barely be found in these works. Additionally, they neglect questions about the effects of changing time perceptions in young people's life in late-modernity. The question whether the feeling of time and the idea of the future might change when living in constant times of high uncertainty, is often not even noticed in previous research. Therefore, this chapter will try to shed some light on these aspects.

Temporality, the Future and Social Theory

(1) The Phenomenological Approach

Time and temporality are seen as naturalistic and deterministic by many social scientists, even until today (Flaherty and Fine 2001). In that view, the past influences the present and the present determines the future. George H. Mead (1932) was the first who broke with this and offered a more complex view on temporality by describing time as a social phenomenon. Time has not only an objective chronological existence. It is also a subjective social category, which is reflected, appropriated and understood by subjects (Carmo et al. 2014). Following this view, time can only be analysed by distinguishing between past, present and future. But past and future cannot exist physically. Our past biography and future narratives are perceived and permanently reinterpreted in the 'now', so both temporal forms can only be constructed in the present. But for Mead (1932) the future has a special place: while the present represents what is currently happening, it is the future, with all its imaginations, beliefs or goals and the actions we undertake to achieve them, where everything could happen. Studying the future means not to examine a future present, but to understand and analyse present futures.

Luckmann (1979) asked which role temporality plays in the consciousness of people's life-world (*Lebenswelt*). In addition to Mead, he presents the idea that our perception of time is constructed, reproduced and transformed by people's everyday interactions and knowledge produced by our cultural self-image, which is shared by all members of society. The life-world is not an ontologically detached world which exists, but it is the place where individuals and society share experiences and traditions. He indicates that just like a society shares a collective memory of the way the past is seen, there is a common view on the future shared by members of society (Flaherty and Fine 2001).

For Schütz (1967), past and future are as real as the present. Both affect the present and thus the perception of the subject. The appropriation of the future in modern societies depends on decisions and therefore enters the sphere of people's availability. It becomes something to experience.

(2) The Social-Constructivist Approach

A macro-sociological view on time and temporality is given by Luhmann (1976). He describes time as '[…] *the social interpretation of reality with respect to the differences between past and future*' (p. 131). Temporality gives time an open dimension and shows the individual that the present represents one possibility among others, which would have been possible as well. The open future presents different possible futures from which one has to anticipate a narrative that is most likely to come. Bourdieu (1998, 2000) goes further and defines the future as a category of social and symbolic projections by the individual according to subjective expectations and the objective possibilities one has. These are indicated by class and social position. The feeling of not having a future, especially from lower social classes, is according to Bourdieu, the impossibility of mobilising the resources to construct a future in the present (Bourdieu 1998).

The anthropologist Helmuth Plessner (1981) argues that people need to transfer the open temporal horizon of the future into a societally closed one because they are hardly able to deal with uncertainty. He refers to the concept of social institutions by Berger and Luckmann (1966), which describes those as control systems that form, stabilise or guide social behaviour or actions of individuals, groups or societies. They are created by habitual actions, which are reciprocally adopted by (almost) all members of the society. This articles follows the assumption that the (societal) future can be defined as a social institution, which provides individuals with a societally accepted view on the future and which is communicated within the process of socialisation. The societal 'grand narrative' of the future offers individual guidance in an open and complex world. In modern societies, this narrative is the promise of a better future in which 'children will have a better life than their parents'. One can postulate that this *intergenerational promise* of the future as a qualitatively and quantitatively better condition than the past or present, is a key institution within these societies.

(3) The Epistemological Approach

Giddens (1991) describes time as a subjective category in which individuals reflectively colonise their future, constructing it by considering the potential costs and gains resulting from choices and decisions. He attributes reflectivity as a key instrument for individuals to think about the future. Narratives of the future undergo a permanent process of reflection in the present. The question arising from this is: What can individuals know about the future? While the past and the present are categories of reality, the future is subject to the category of possibility or hypotheticals. Beck et al. (1994) offer a concept of *knowing* and *not-knowing* into the discussion. Individuals cannot finally know what the future will bring, so they have to construct expectations and commit actions based on their knowledge. This characteristic of the future holds the possibility of not having or knowing all information necessary. Therefore, the future is always a risk for individuals. People try to compensate for this risk by holding to institutions that offer stability or security. This could be social or real institutions, like societal traditions or the welfare state. For Giddens (1990) and Beck (1992), risk is a main driver of modern societies as risk leads to the creation of change and a future differing from the present. It is a basic element for modern societies with an open future orientation.

(4) The Present as a Temporal Fixed-Point

For Mead, the present is the paramount form of temporality (Flaherty and Fine 2001). It is the place and time where the individual and the society negotiate, interpret and experience past and future (Luhmann 1976). A subject constructs temporality by reflecting past experiences and constructing future expectations in the present, while at the same time, past and future influence the present as well. Koselleck (2004) suggests two categories to analyse the present:

- The '*space of experience*', defined as "*[...] present past which the individual can remember. It has also an element of alien experience contained and preserved in experience conveyed by generations or institutions.*"
- The '*horizon of expectations*' defined as "*[...] present future, which is person-specific and interpersonal, expectation also takes place in the today; it directs itself to the not-yet, to the non-experienced, to that which is to be revealed*" (p. 365).

The space of experience and the horizon of expectations were almost congruent in pre-modern times. Modernity is defined as a time where both categories are drifting apart from each other. The present still is the fixed point in people's life, influenced by experiences of the past and expectations about the future. All together, it creates the present as the place of personal identity, where the individual perceives the life-world and oneself as stable. Following Rosa (2013) these '*stable structures*' cannot claim validity nowadays. This work assumes that in times of late-modernity, past, present and future are objects of permanent reinterpretation in increasingly shorter intervals, with the consequence that the present has become a space of instability. The greater the feeling of a future that is completely different to the present, the more likely is a feeling of a '*contradiction of the present*' (Lübbe 1983). This means that the present has become a shorter period of time in one's life because of permanently re-interpreted past and futures. The present can no longer offer stability, guidance or hold for the subject (Bauman 2000). As Kohli (2003) adds, the old structures of modernity are still taken, believed and communicated as stable situations by the society.

An uncertain future for Luhmann (1976) is the result of too many possibilities a subject has to (or can) choose from. They are a result of an acceleration of functional differentiations within late-modern societies. People have to make decisions; but no decision ever made hold the guarantee to last long-term under an unstable present. Decisions have to be permanently revaluated because the uncertainty and complexity is too high, so that the horizon of expectations is reduced. Late-modern society has created a situation in which the current structures and dynamics undermine the possibility to establish a perception of the present which is experienced as stable (Böschen and Weis 2007). Having no grip on the present—one must assume—will diminish the possibility of subjects to project themselves into the future. Bourdieu (1998) mentions that unstable temporal structures like the present make the future uncertain and impossible to foresee, which prevents all rational anticipation. The feeling of insecurity about one's life course never goes away. He writes that this feeling *"pervades both the conscious and the unconscious mind and stamps it with the sense that work is a 'fragile, threatened privilege' and no one 'irreplaceable"*. These *'conditions of doubt'* penetrate all aspects of the social life of young people so that the self-identity becomes fragile and a subject of constant reinterpretation. As will be shown in the following sections, the younger generation live in different life situations and economic structures, which are seen as negative and which, one must assume, have a significant impact on how the youth reconceptualise their identities. For Beck et al. (1994), this change of identities, where individuals are constantly forced to reconstruct their biographies under permanently changing circumstances, is the new normal for young adults. As identities always contain temporal structures of past, present and future, a change in identities must also have an effect on the perception of temporality and therefore an effect on the perception of the future.

The Cultural Concept of the Future

Future as a Project of Modernity

Historians and sociologists present in detail how the perception of time and individual life-time changed in Europe at the transition point from the Renaissance to Modernity (e.g. Koselleck 2004; Lombardo 2006; Weber 2001). In pre-modern times, people lived in a feudal caste and in a God-given experience-system with fixed social positions, which made social advancement almost impossible. As social and technological change was slow, people had experiences on the basis of their ancestors' experiences in the past, living in a cyclic time perceptions. It created a feeling that things *'have always been like that'*, so that the space of experiences and the horizon of expectations were almost congruent (Koselleck 2004).

With the beginning of modernity life conditions changed through the breakup of former master-servant relations. The most disruptive change was the perception of time and the awareness of an open non-deterministic future (Koselleck 2004). An accelerating and disruptive development of new technologies changed the everyday life routines of the people. Social advancement, individualisation and prosperity became a possibility for a broader part of society and a new dimension in one's life. Subjects created new structures of meaning for their own life and constructed an individual life-story—a biography. The general time perception of society changed to an on-going process of societal progress, in which the individuals obtain an own past, present and future. The future became a horizon of a better state of prosperity, a life which is quantitatively and qualitatively better than the present. Life reality between the generations started to differ from each other in a much faster pace, so that the *space of experiences* and the *horizon of expectations* drifted apart. Societal and individual change is now aligned to the future; the future itself comes closer to the present.

The Industrial Modernity

The initial period after World War II is characterised as a time of high stability, driven by an unusual high increase in economic production, high economic growth and a rising employment in the Western world, called the *"Golden Age of Capitalism"* (Maddison 2001) Even though social injustice existed, the establishment of a welfare state redistributed wealth so that almost the whole population could participate in the rising prosperity. Full employment, higher incomes and education, and a new form of mass consumption lead to a higher level of prosperity than ever before. Buchholz and Blossfeld (2009) characterise the Fordistic economy as a *system of inclusion, even so it was restricted to some societal groups (e.g. women)*. It ensured most people social improvement and established a new social milieu, the so-called middle-class. This time—the Fordistic era of industrial capitalism—was a time of stability for economic structures and personal identities, which made the future rational and in some way foreseeable. It was easier to calculate and to make plans for life: foreseeable income rises, next career steps and secured jobs made decisions of buying property or starting a family easier to manage. This rational future created structures of certainty, reduced the individual risk of an open future and in addition with a strong welfare-state and a mass-consumption based social advancement, the future was more foreseeable than ever before in the history of modernity. Kohli (2003) calls this *institutionalised biographies*.

The Future in Late-Modernity

From the 1980s onwards, more and more sociological analyses of Western societies have recognised a second fundamental change in the way that future is perceived, as something negative. This trend can be explained by two disruptive changes in late-modern societies.

(1) The Loss of Future Certainty

Beck et al. (1994) and other scholars identify the rapid break-up of former basic certainties as one characteristic feature in late-modernity, e.g. the welfare-state. Contemporary societies made experiences, which enabled them to adapt to complex environments and developments to make life-courses more predictable. Nowadays, people still act within this basic foundations of modernity that they are used to, but which do not necessarily offer an orientation in a faster changing world any longer. Bauman (1992, 2000) calls this development *liquid modernity*, where all the old foundations are blurring and nothing can provide a permanent hold, offer stability or provide guidance for the future. Although the knowledge of the world is constantly increasing in all disciplines of science, it also makes the world far more complex for subjects to grasp. For Habermas (1986), the future has become a *confusingly complex* world that alters the sense of orientation in our lives and in which "*[e]xemplary pasts, which could serve as an unobjectionable orientation for the present are faded.[...] The horizon of the future has contracted and has changed the zeitgeist and politics radically. Future is negative nowadays*" (Habermas 1986).

Rosa (2013) describes late-modernity as an on-going and in its intensity, unique process of social acceleration of almost all fields of society. Our individual history and the collective enter into a process in which they are drifting apart from each other much faster than ever before. It creates the feeling of an 'accelerating world' and an increase in the 'pace of life'. Rosa (2013) argues that "*[...] beyond a still higher, though hardly unambiguously determinable threshold value, change is no longer perceived as a transformation of fixed structures, but instead as a fundamental and potentially chaotic indeterminacy*" (Rosa 2013). He emphasizes that social change has increased its speed from an *inter*generational to an *intra*generational change. Rosa uses the term of '*slippery slopes*' to refer to a process that makes it almost impossible for subjects to keep pace, because of a much higher complexity and inconsistency of the world. For him, this must have a significant impact on the way subjects perceive their life-course and their future identity. The world does not become more complex solely because of economical dynamics, but also due to an increase of personal opportunities to design one's life. It is becoming harder to overview all the information that would be necessary for decision-making. In consequence, the future in form of an individual life-plan comes under constant pressure to avoid failure and mistakes (Rosa 2012). All of this leads to what Lübbe (1983) mentions as *Zukunftsgewissheitsschwund* (*loss of future certainty*): never before have the upcoming structures of the world been so uncertain, the dynamics of our development of civilization so changeable and the amount of events and processes per time-unit so high, that it is almost impossible to foresee in what kind of world the next generations will live in.

(2) Loss of the Grand-Narrative

The second change raises the developments of the first to another level by emphasising the general picture of the future in times of late-modernity. Lyotard (1984) writes that our time is determined by an evaporation of the 'grand narrative'—the overarching story line by means of which we are placed in history as human beings having a definite past and a predictable future. Following his argument, it is one leading hypothesis of this study that the 'grand narrative' of a better future for current and following generations is going to end without a new one in sight. Western societies have to re-negotiate and re-establish a new kind of future narrative to create stability in their relations between the individual and the society. Horn (2014) presents an interesting overview of how dystopian narratives of the future entered literature, movies and other kind of media. She diagnoses a '*lust for apocalyptical scenarios and fictions*' and the future as something terrible, as the '*end of the world as we know it*'. Positive fictions of the world are mostly limited to technological progress. Findings on other research fields show that the future has become an important element of political debate, where its rhetoric is '*preempting the future*': negative political future narratives are used to present a specific and ideologically framed picture of the future and therefore to enforce political actions in favour of a specific ideology. It is used to create a sovereignty in interpreting developments and their consequences for the future and to set lock-in effects on how society should see the future (Dunmire 2005). It shows that, as Lyotard describes, there is not one big societal meta-narrative of the future any longer. The functional differentiation of societies creates different views on the future.

Economic and Biographical Changes in Late-Modernity

Since the 1980s, almost all Western countries have undergone political and economic changes, which altered society significantly. At the same time, the economic development and growth has slowed down, unemployment has risen and working conditions have become worse, especially for younger people who are more vulnerable to economic recessions (Buchholz et al. 2009). With the neo-liberal turn, the welfare system was cut down and individual responsibility has become a new political maxim (Kotz 2002) and the dominant mode of thought (Beck and Beck-Gernsheim 2002). Buchholz and Blossfeld (2009) for example show that job-markets have become exclusive. Even well qualified young people often have to deal with precarious job conditions and short-term contracts. A university degree is no longer a guarantee for upward social mobility (Bukodi et al. 2014). The new economic environment lead to an asymmetric relationship between employers and employees. The former stable employment biographies, which once characterised adulthood, are now becoming elusive, since downward career mobility has become a real threat even for highly qualified young adults (Furlong and Cartmel 2007; Bukodi et al. 2014; Nachtwey 2016). This permanent feeling of insecurity can lead to the point that young people "*[...] struggle to establish adult identities and maintain coherent biographies*" (Buchholz et al. 2009).

Late-modernity is characterised by a two-faced development: On the one hand, subjects are free to choose the life-form which fits them best and have multiple options to design their life, while on the other hand, former certainties and guiding structures are breaking apart (Mayer 2001). Subjects are much more detached from traditional and class-orientated constraints nowadays and are relatively free to make their own decisions about their biography. On the contrary, it makes subjects responsible to deal with this freedom and therefore to bear the potential risk of their decisions and life-plans. Multi-optional possibilities to design one's own life-course create the possibilities of failure, too. Subjects cannot be sure whether a decision is the right one. Making no decision et all is not possible. While having multiple options is an element of late-modern life-realities for young people (Rosa 2013), Giddens (2001) describes this as subjects having '*no choice, but to choose*'.

Methodology: Biographical-Narrative Interviews

Theoretical Concept: Biographies and Future Narratives

The goal of this contribution is to explore a relatively new field of research, to identify approaches and categories that can help to explain how future is constructed in times of late-modernity. The concept of future is complex; and thus quite intangible if trying to find empirically determined parameters. Future is not a homogeneous construct but a product of subjects seeking for meaning in life.

Followings Giddens (1986) concept of the double-hermeneutical approach, subjects' actions have a certain intended meanings to them, and they act in a world they already have interpreted as meaningful. A researcher, therefore, has to consider and to understand people's individual construction of the future, but also has to understand the societal context in which expectations are created. This research is based on the assumption that society offers the individual a habitual view on the future in the form of a social institution. Even though those structures tend to be objective, they are so only to the subjects mind. It is the inner representation of one's individual view on the future, out of a collective accepted and appropriated future perception—called *intersubjectivity* (Zaner 1961; Reiter 2003). People are born into a world which is already pre-structured by social institutions. This research is on the exploration and reconstruction of meaningful life-histories of subjects, the relation of past, present and future. To create a temporal structure of one's life can be seen as a defining element of a biography. Even so the future is not necessarily a part of the everyday reality—a narrative of the future provides orientation knowledge for the individual and is required for life-decisions.

Future narrative ways of conveying experiences and expectations portray a future by using methods to project them. These narratives generate a hypothetical, probabilistic or wishful future, based on a subject's experiences of the past and from a present perspective (Adam 2004; Weigert 2012). They imply a sense of personal or societal change by reflecting past and present (du Plooy 2014), and making the future real in the sense of experiences and expectations (Weigert 2012). Narratives contain current societal developments and popular visions. They create reality by a subjective or collective thinking about possibilities, expectations or plausibility of a specific time. They are often images and interpretations of a social reality.

Biographical-Narrative Interviews

Considering that two other publication in this book are presenting the method of biographical-narrative interviews in more depth, this contribution therefore only refers to some basic concepts of this method and some extension to adopt the method to the current research. For general background of this method see Rosenthal (1993); Weidenhaus (2015); Corbally and O'Neill (2014)

The advantage of a biographical and narrative interview approach is that connections between what subjects think and the life-situation they are currently in can be examined in more depth. Themes, experiences and perceptions can thus be connected in this specific interview method (Labov and Waletzky 1967; Nilsen 1999). Schütze (1983) highlighted that this method combines reflections on the participant's own life (biography) with the creation of a bigger picture (narrative). Instead of only looking on specific events, the focus was on experiences and their sequential meaning in the respondent's life (Czarniawska 2004; Watson 2009). Individually perceived changes of time and the self can only be understand by dynamic patterns and experiences, while connecting all forms of temporality and the personal biography to a present narrative of one's life (De Fina and Georgakopoulou 2008; Squire et al. 2008).

Research Design

For this research, a cohort of 22 young postgraduate students between the age of 21 and 30 were interviewed. They all experienced the process of socialisation in an early-industrialised country (mainly in Germany, Austria and UK). Although there are some cultural or national differences, a cross-cultural comparison is not taken into account. Instead, the focus lies on the impact of socio-economic changes which are experienced in the three countries more or less the same. Postgraduate students were chosen as they have to occupy themselves with their own future due to the near end of their student time. The students were chosen randomly until a certain level of saturation for the sample was reached. Cross-sectional characteristics were taken into account to get a broader spectrum of different cases. A thematic analyses is used to evaluate the interviews (Guest 2012) and a Grounded Theory approach helped to build classes and types of different modes of future thinking and perception (Strauss and Corbin 1998).

The presented findings are hypotheses of how people intend to implement and reflect the future within their own life-stories. They are not final certainties, but a discussion starting point of a micro-sociological approach to explore future narratives and appropriation strategies within biographies.

Findings and Discussion

Hopefully, the findings by this sample of young students will present some indications that the future has become something highly ambiguous. It is no longer only a horizon of dreams but also a threat to personal expectations. Furthermore, one can argue that the awareness and thoughts about the future are embedded in everyday living and connected to thoughts about life in general.

Types of Future Construction

The analysis and evaluation of the gathered data allows the creation of categories. These are relevant to explain how people construct their future narratives by reflecting their own biographies. Each of these categories can be divided into two expressions. This does not mean that there exist only two possibilities. Of course, there are more variations between these expressions, but due to the limited scope of this research project, it proved useful to work this way. Furthermore, while working on this research, it showed that almost all of the respondents can be generally classified to one expression of each category. Here, categories are presented which came up during all the interviews, so that it is possible to direct every respondent of the sample to an expression of each category and to make significant statements, despite the empirical base. During the analysis process several more possible categories occurred, but they are not included into this discussion as they are irrelevant to the core of the research question, even though they would be interesting for a further, deeper examination as well.

In this section, the selected categories and expressions are presented, followed by a broader sociological context discussion for each of them. In most of the cases it will referred to type A as *linear* and type B as *episodic*, because they are the most significant and dominant characteristics due to their influence on the other categories.

Perception of Time: Linear vs. Episodic

All subjects construct time and temporality by a logical connection of past, present and future within their biography. But there exist some variations about how they construct their sense of temporality considering causalities and conditions within their lives. The leading question for this category is to what extent are the past and present perceived as the cause of the future? This question is often raised and mentioned within the interviews by reflecting about past and present decisions which will have an effect on the respondents' future.

Modernity is usually associated with the perception of time as a linear progress: The past determines the present and here we commit actions orientated towards the future. Life is like an arrow through the different forms of time leading into the future. Participants of this group, for instance, see a close connection between their completed Bachelor degree, their current postgraduate studies and their job wishes for the time after their graduation. Therefore, past and present are a relevant cause for the future.

Andrew (28 years, Political Studies) shows a linear kind of time structuring through his life very clearly by recurring on crucial factors of his past, which helps him to make sense of his present and desired future.

> "I have always been good at school, I liked the discussions in my political classes. My teacher was a very great inspiration to me. So I decided to study Political Studies, because it was something I knew I could be good at. And here I am, finishing my M.A. and then looking for a political job in the UK.
> [...] I still love politics. It has always been my dream to work for a big institution, like in the government or the European Union. And I know that all the steps I made will lead me to this.[...] Looking back, there is a logical path in my life".

As he has said, his life follows a logical way from the past into the future. Nine students can be categorized as having this kind of time perception. They all mention a life history with a progressive narrative that functions as motivation, which means that they are in a development to achieve a future they imagine for themselves. Every step they make is the preliminary step to the next one, and they all lead to a desired goal. They also tend to separate all forms of time from each other linguistically. Respondents with a linear perception of time appropriate future by '*defuturizing the future*' (Luhmann 1976) by making plans and prognoses about it in order to lower uncertainty. The future keeps its modern idea of progress, in other words: the future can be distinguished from past and present as something better.

Contrary to the linear perception of time, a second way to construct the future in one's life can be best described as *episodic*. This way to construct the future was first identified by Cavalli (1985) as a very small-scale phenomenon. He even linked this to the development of late-modern circumstances. In an episodic construction of time, past, present and future are clearly separated from each other. Even more, compared to the linear model, one can argue that the future does not play an important role in the respondent's life.

In the interview cohort, Marta (24 years, Cultural Studies) is a very good example for an episodic construction of time.

"I think there is a future I can imagine, what in fact, is currently my master studies. This is my actual episode. The next one will be the time after the university, going to work and so. I feel more comfortable thinking about the proximate future, concentrate on the episode I am in. The next one will come fast enough. And I can't imagine how my life looks like in twenty years or having a family [...] It is like in a computer game, jumping from level to level. And I guess each one will get more difficult".

For her, the present gives security and orientation. Every participant of this group is certain that the current episode will end. What comes next is not only unknown but also connoted very negatively and perceived as a possible threat to the life of the respondents. Thomas (27 years, Law Studies):

Q: "Do you have any plans for the time you leave university?"

A: "No, I don't. This is something I have to deal with after the graduation. I don't like to think about it yet…no, I really don't like to.

Q: "Why not?".

A: "Because it will come soon enough and right now I don't know what I like to do after graduation. I think my life is better now than it will be in the future".

Although the future does not play an important role, it is still something for the respondents they have to deal with. The insecurity about the future is absorbed by a diminished pertinence for them. Having the focus on present projects offers the possibility of keeping an inner distance from the future. It is a coping strategy of exclusion to handle future uncertainty.

Duration of Present: Short vs. Extended

Another important category that occurred very clearly in all interviews is the perceived duration of the present by the respondents. It describes which parts of their current life-situation are counted as the present and which help to explain the chronological extent of the present.

Many social scientists describe the *contradiction of the present* as a main characteristic of late-modernity (Harvey 1989; Rosa 2013). In fact, for twelve of the interviewees this is an appropriate way to describe their present. They tell a life-story of an accelerated world which forces them to adapt to a permanently changing environment. Therefore, a group of twelve respondents report a very short period of what they describe as present in their life, meaning that the future plays a more important role in their life than the present. For instance, in Amanda's life (26, Anthropology & Law, Politics Studies), the future plays a more important role than the present.

"It feels like I am living always two years in the future, making plans for the future. Like I am doing now. I am already applying for internships for autumn 2017, to have something to do after graduation. I am also preparing for my application for a diplomatic career in Berlin for Spring 2018."

This approach appropriates the future by making concrete plans for it and therefore pulling it closer to the present. It helps them to react to a world that is changing continuously, as Frank (28, Geography & Development) describes:

"I am a long-term thinker, I guess. But I like to concentrate on the closer future. It's what I can manage, plan and oversee. Everything else is too blurry to see and will change the next moment."

On the contrary, ten respondents report what can be best described as the extension of the present. For them, the present is not a short stage of time they have to cross. It is a place in which they try to stay as long as possible because it gives them some kind of structure, orientation and security. Like the other group they perceive the world as fast, but for them it is too fast to make stable plans or decisions.

"I enjoy being a student. I think it is what describes me best. It gives me something to do and some security. I don't think much about what comes next in life. I try to focus on the now". Han-Lee (24 years, Environmental Engineering).

"The time after I will have finished my master is a total black hole for me, there is just uncertainty and anything could happen. Right now, only my master studies gives me some kind of structure and security in life. There are no other signs or guidance which could offer a picture of what comes next. How my future will look like. That really scares me."

Sebastian (30, Social Work).

They all describe their time being students as the present, in which they feel themselves as the same person through time, even though it describes a period of several years. Personal developments are not perceived as an on-going process, like for linear respondents. Comparisons between the 'older' self and the 'actual' self are made only between different episodes in their life. Compared to the first group, respondents with an extended present try to push the future out of their life and thereby even more into the future. It is notable, that these participants avoided talking about the future too frequently during the interviews. Instead, they always came back to their present life very quickly as we will see in more detail.

Strategic Planning: Detailed vs. Avoidance

To achieve any kind of plans in the future, individuals have to commit actions in the present. Therefore, several other studies which have studied the future concentrate on plans of young people (Reiter 2003; Cook 2015). As seen before, plan-making was also an important area to talk about in this sample. Inspired by Mead (1932), one can describe the present as the *'locus of reality'*, *where* social actions pursue and generate future. The future is the time when objectives are reached or rejected by the individual. The longer it takes until objectives are realised, the longer the present lasts.

Those participants who fall into the linear type have very detailed plans about the future. The closer the future is to the present, the more detailed are their plans. Their progressive attitude appropriates the future by detailed strategic planning for their next step to a bigger goal. Ulrich (24, Philosophy & German Literature) said:

"I have a very concrete plan for the next three years, which I hope will bring me to my first goal in life [job at the university]. Then I have an idea for the next lets say five years. In the end, I hope, it will get me to what I am really looking for, even so I know, it will take a long time to achieve."

This is verified by other interviews of the sample. They have a clear linear idea for their personal future and biography. High intrinsic motivation, personal engagement and a notable resoluteness to get the right internships or scholarships characterise this group.

On the other side, students with an episodic perception of their biography do all report that they avoid any decision-making. This is often due to too many options they have to decide about.

"I am so terrified about decisions, because every decision I make can have a huge impact on my life. And I so often look back and regret decisions I have made once. Look, I don't know whether my undergrad was the right choice, don't know where it will take me. But I know I am on my way and I can't go back so easily."

Selma (23, Chinese studies).

Compared to the other group, this one concentrates more on re-thinking former decisions, regarding whether they were good choices or not. Finding themselves in some kind of permanent doubt, they project same doubt on up-coming decisions about the future. In some cases it also lead to permanent questioning and comparison of the individual capabilities, leading sometimes into fatalism. Laura (25, Mathematics):

"People should be like everyone else plus some extras, that makes one unique compared to others. We are all exchangeable. […] I have to reinvent myself on and on".

There is an even more interesting dimension in this group: The educational and occupational goals of respondents with a linear mode of biography are societally accepted and prestigious. Attitudes like high motivation, commitment to work and career targets are often mentioned by the respondents and are seen as universal values, meaning that they are true et all time for the society they life in. They provide a background of personal affirmation to be 'on the right way' in life. This type needs functioning and stable institutional framework conditions, which guarantee social appreciation, like the award of social upward mobility through education or a high motivation for performance. Following Beck and Beck-Gernsheim (2002), this 'taken-for-granted' strategy holds a strong risk of failing in late-modernity. In this case, the agent individual is responsible for his or her own actions and failure. Most of them, for instance, neither have developed an alternative plan, nor have reflected much on whether their future occupation goal is available for them. Similar results were found by Weidenhaus (2015).

For those respondents who construct their biography episodically it is more complex. Their acknowledgement depends on the current status or project in life. Partly, they do not need to rely on these institutions, they act contrarily to them or feel that they affect their lives extrinsically. But it all leads to intense reflections about their future. For example, some episodic thinkers emphasise that the society defines which behaviour is accepted. Mina (24, Sociology), for instance, makes her decision whether she likes to start a second study or a professional training depending on what the society thinks is acceptable for a woman at her age.

"I made a Bachelor in Sociology and therefore I am studying a sociology master now. I think was the best decision for future job opportunities. But to be honest, I would like to do something else, maybe another bachelor after the master. Or a professional training as a camera operator. But it is also a question of age, especially for women. I don't think that it looks good to start something new with 30. I have the feeling that my environment expect to be finish with education and start to do something real".

Thoughts like this often make them feel dislocated from the future. Some of the students report that they have *"lost their sense for the future"*, leaving them unable to form coherent plans. They are not inevitably pessimistic or fatalistic about the future, but often describe a feeling of not having the future in their own hands.

Future Development: Contingency vs. Continuity

The last category addresses how people perceive future development, dealing with the issue of how strongly the respondents believe that they have the future in their own hands. Autonomy and individuality are important values and personal rights in modern societies. The interview sample shows that the participants think about the future in the form of continuity or contingency developments for the future. But both groups see their life as a storeroom that holds so many options and possibilities, giving them all chances to lead a life they want to.

For the first group, the future is very complex and almost unable to foresee and therefore full of contingency. This has strong effects on their life-choices and decision-making. They neither tend to establish a long-term plan for the future, nor have detailed plans for the future. This leads to the feeling of having only a weak impact on one's own life. Dominick (29, Educational Sciences) for example did not believe he should have too many plans for the future:

"I don't need a grand master-plan set down for my life, because I see that there is more in life I can't influence than I actually can."

He also mentions extrinsic forces which undermine long-term thinking. For him it is the best to concentrate on his actual projects. For this group, the future is a very complex system of endless opportunities, which are, on the one hand, seen as positive but at the same time they feel that it is impossible to realise them. Therefore, they try to avoid decisions, because every decision for an opportunity will forfeit several others that could not be realised. Mina thinks:

"Compared to the generation of my parents I live in a world of endless opportunities and we all pretend to use all of them and that we can became anything we want to. But that was never true, this is all just talk. It's so frustrating, for many people."

She also claims that the high complexity of society, as seen in the last category, has eroded any certainty about the future. For students of that sample and type it is difficult to establish a consistent future narrative to build up a stable ground to project themselves into the future. On the other hand, an institutionalised biography is for this group no longer the only legitimate way to structure one's own biography.

A few positions of this group combine the 'craziness' of an accelerating world with their denial to make big plans about the future. Laura:

"Isn't making plans in a world without any plans an irrational act? Aren't short-term plans the logical answer to uncertainty? I think people with long-term plans will easier fail in their life."

Linear respondents perceive a strong implication of a societal future that does not change much et all, so that most things will remain the same. For them the future is characterised by continuity. Frank (27, Geography) shows an easy-going attitude towards the future.

"I am very relaxed and optimistic when am thinking about the future. I don't expect much to change, though there has always been change in the world. It's complex. The basics of what the society constitutes won't change so fast, I think there is more continuousness than change in the future."

This group is very self-confident of their individual abilities to achieve future goals. Their view of the future as an on-going process of present circumstances may underestimate the effects of social change. But considering the findings of the previous sections it is a logical feeling. Linear students of this sample have to rely on basic social institutions to establish their stable view of the future. They are bound to a self-imposed fixed path and there is no way to leave it. Believing in too much change could undermine their plans for the future. Even so, some of them recognise the erosion of former basic certainties of modernity. Amanda:

"I believe society will stay almost the same. On the other hand, the fight for shares on the societal wealth will increase. People don't have the feeling any longer, that the welfare state works for them."

Understanding Young People's View of the Future in Times of Late-Modernity

The majority of the respondents can be associated with what was described as an episodic perception of the future., This analysis can neither rule out nor confirm if this could become the new normal for young people. However, one can find some first evidence in current developments, which are briefly discussed in this section.

Firstly, Late-modernity has been characterised by social scientists (e.g. Castells 2000; Harvey 1989) as a time where the linear model of time has lost its original meaning. Harvey (1989) describes in his analysis of *'time–space-compression'* that time horizons have become ever shorter intervals leading to a '*shrinking of the present*'. Urry (2000) describes in his concept of '*instantaneous time*' that time has become fragmented and time horizons shortened. Findings of the current data set used in this work show that instead of expressing a short duration of the present, a majority of the respondents perceive the present as an even longer time in their life. The prospect of young students on short contract terms and precarious payment situations after graduation has a significant influence on the participants, which almost all of them emphasised several times during the interviews. For those who construct their biography episodically, this leads to a temporal extension of their present, making the current stage of life even longer, pushing an unsecure future into an even more distant time. It could be argued, that the mode of production and work in a post-Fordistic economy makes such an experience of time to become a possibility (Castells 2000; Rosa 2013). Requirements, like being mobile for jobs, are increasing for young students and shape their perception of time. If it is correct that changes in the constitution of collective and individual time patterns are bound to a change in the social structures of society and economy, then one could assume that the post-Fordistic capitalism alters these time patterns in the long run significantly (Rosa 2013).

Secondly, individuals might be obliged to develop constant and stable future narratives against the background of ever faster changing institutionalised environments and diminishing economic conditions, what Rosa (2013) calls the '*slippery slopes*' phenomenon. The validity of social structures and institutions decrease. Facing this development, it could lead to an increase of a critical questioning of the self and an on-going reorientation and reinterpretation of personal future expectations. What someone can do and knows is eventually more important than who someone actually is, as mentioned by many respondents of the episodic group.

Thirdly, this also has effects on their future-identity. While some sociologists suggest that during the Fordistic-era, the linear perception of time and individual life-plans which were aligned for a better future supported high economic growth and vice versa (Weidenhaus 2015), in times of late-modernity and low growth rates, this effect is maybe altering: long-term life-plans can be seen as development-inhibiting breaks which could delay the adjustments of subjects to an ever-changing environment. That is how the episodic type construct their future: if it is too uncertain how the future looks for them after the current episode, it is reasonable to avoid making long-term plans and keep the personal identity open to these rapid changes, to make adaptation to them less difficult. Mead (1964) describes identity as a mediation process between internalised and institutionalised expectations of the environment and individual motives. Episodic biographers tend to have what Rosa (2013) calls *situational identities*: subjects adapt differently to different situations, which makes it easy to change them if necessary. The respondents perceive signals from the economic and societal system, which awards flexibility and readiness to change. Subjects have to adapt to these changes or run the risk of permanent frustration, because former stability-orientated identities seem to lack the ability to deal with late-modern and post-fordistic circumstances. Episodic identities are less stable but easy to adapt. This leads to a lack of articulation of about their self-identity in this world. Maybe this is the main reason why young people often feel sometimes alienated from the future in times of late-modernity.

Conclusion

In conclusion, the study demonstrates that as the future itself, people's narratives about the future have become complex in times of late-modernity. With the analysis of the current data set of young postgraduate students, this chapter has shown that time patterns in people's lives are changing. One can recognise this by how people deal with the unsecure future, which is often characterised as post-Fordistic. The two identified types (linear and episodic) of how these groups perceive and construct their narrative of the future shows that both groups developed different coping strategies to deal with an unstable and open future. While the two groups recognise that time horizons get shorter, they react with different premises: the linear group follows a "taken-for-granted" strategy, which promise a high gain but depends on stable structures around them. They blind out that in times of late-modernity these structures erode. For the episodic group, plans about the future has become something to avoid. They think about the future, but are overwhelmed of all the opportunities an open future offers. Knowing that they have to make decisions, they feel unable to take required decision about the future in order to keep themselves flexible. By looking at the challenges of late-modernity and post-Fordism capitalism, one strategy is better than the other. In the end, both strategies have their own reasonable arguments to deal with uncertain futures and are therefore maybe just individual ways, to make it through life. But the findings for the episodic group tend to match with current developments described as post-Fordistic and late-modernity earlier in this contribution. Only more research can show whether this development is a general societal issue or not.

However, there are limitations of this research as well. Firstly, the scope of the actual panel is too low to allow generalizable statements at this point of current research. Secondly, even though university graduates have to face an increased challenging and competitive job market nowadays, they still have better job opportunities than young people with lower qualifications. Exclusion from societal processes and participation is nothing they have to fear in general. Therefore, the findings from this research outline only the future perception of a selected group within a specific societal context. Thirdly, this research has focused on the individual perception of time. To get a full sociological insight of how people construct the future in their lives and biographies, one has also to look at individual perceptions of space. Although this has come up in some interviews, it could not be included into this work.

The findings open the door to interdisciplinary future research possibilities. Besides an expanding research with a broader and more representative panel, the current approach of this research requires a closer analysis which considers attributes like class, race, gender or cross-cultural differences. The question of how these processes affect identities should be examined in-depth. As indicated before, there have to exist more variations between the two identified types of future perception. From the current perspective, it seems to be clear that both forms are not able to explain future perceptions for all life situations. As other studies indicated before, current societal and economical trends, which occurred in the last decades, alter the perception of time and future radically. One influential trend to mention would be the future perception of long-term unemployed persons, which should be significantly different from the sample of this research or from other parts of the society in general. Finally, social theory is still fragmented when it comes to explaining the role of the future in late-modern societies. Theorising the concept of future for social sciences would be a necessary step for further research in this field.

References

Adam, B. (2004) *Time*. Cambridge: Polity Press.
Adams, T. (2015) "'My father had one job in his life, I've had six in mine, my kids will have six at the same time'", *The Guardian*, 29 November.
Bauman, Z. (1992) *Initimations of Postmodernity*. London: Routledge.
Bauman, Z. (2000) *Liquid Modernity*. Cambridge: Polity Press.
Beck, U. (1992) *Risk Society: Towards a New Modernity*. Lodnon: SAGE Publictions Inc.
Beck, U. and Beck Gernsheim, E. (2002) *Individualization. Institutionalized Individualism and its Social and Political Consequences*. London: SAGE Publications Inc.
Beck, U., Giddens, A. and Lash, S. (1994) *Reflexive Modernization: Politics, Tradition and Aesthetics in the Modern Social Order*. Stanford: Stanford University Press.

Berger, P. L. and Luckmann, T. (1966) *The Social Construction of Reality: A Treatise in the Sociology of Knowledge*. London: Pinguin Books.

Böschen, S. and Weis, K. (2007) *Die Gegenwart der Zukunft: Perspektiven zeitkritischer Wissenspolitik*. Wiesbaden: VS Verlag für Sozialwissenschaften.

Bourdieu, P. (1998) *Acts of Resistence: Against the Tyranny of the Market*. New York: The New Press.

Bourdieu, P. (2000) *Pascalian Meditations*. Cambridge: Polity Press.

Buchholz, S. et al. (2009) 'Life Courses in the Globalization Process : The Development of Social Inequalities in Modern Societies', *European Sociological Review*, 25(1), pp. 53–71. doi: 10.1093/esr/jcn033.

Buchholz, S. and Blossfeld, H.-P. (2009) 'Beschäftigungsflexibilisierung in Deutschland – Wen betrifft sie und wie hat sie sich auf die Veränderung sozialer Inklusion/Exklusion in Deutschland ausgewirkt?', in Stichweh, R. and Windolf, P. (eds) *Inklusion und Exklusion: Analysen zur Sozialstruktur und sozialen Ungleichheit*. Wiesbaden: VS Verlag für Sozialwissenschaften, pp. 123–138.

Bukodi, E. et al. (2014) 'The mobility problem in Britain: new findings from the analysis of birth cohort data.', *The British journal of sociology*. doi: https://doi.org/10.1111/1468-4446.12096.

Carmo, R. M., Cantante, F. and de Almeida Alves, N. (2014) 'Time projections: Youth and precarious employment', *Time & Society*, 23(3), pp. 337–357. doi: 10.1177/0961463X14549505.

Castells, M. (2000) *The Rise of the Network Society*. Malden, Mass.: Blackwell Ltd.

Cavalli, A. (1985) *Time and Youth*. Bologna: Il Mulino.

Child, B. (2016) *Not the future after all: the slow demise of young adault dystopian sci-fi films*, The Guardian. Available at: https://www.theguardian.com/film/2016/mar/25/allegiant-young-adult-dystopian-films-box-office-flops (Accessed: 27 July 2016).

Cook, J. (2015) 'Young people's strategies for coping with parallel imaginings of the future', *Time & Society*, pp. 1–18. doi: https://doi.org/10.1177/0961463X15609829.

Cook, J. (2018) *Imagined Futures: Hope, Risk and Uncertainty*. Critical S. Palgrave Macmillan.

Corbally, M. and O'Neill, C. S. (2014) 'An introduction to the biographical narrative interpretive method', *Nurse Researcher*, 21(5), pp. 34–39. doi: 10.7748/nr.21.5.34.e1237.

Czarniawska, B. (2004) *Narratives in Social Science Research*. London: SAGE Publictions Ltd.

De Fina, A. and Georgakopoulou, A. (2008) 'Analysing narratives as practices', *Qualitative Research*, pp. 379–387. doi: https://doi.org/10.1177/1468794106093634.

Dunmire, P. L. (2005) 'Preempting the future: rhetoric and ideology of the future in political discourse', *Discourse & Society*, pp. 481–513. doi: https://doi.org/10.1177/0957926505053052.

du Plooy, H. (2014) 'Between Past and Future: Temporal Thresholds in Narrative Texts', *Journal of Literary Studies*, 30(3), pp. 1–24. doi: 10.1080/02564718.2014.949405.

Eckersley, R. (1997) 'Portraits of youth: Understanding young people's relationship with the future', *Futures*, 29(3), pp. 243–249.

Eckersley, R. (1999) 'Dreams and expecations: Young people ' s expected and preferred futures and their significance for education', *Futures*, 31(1), pp. 73–90.

Flaherty, M. and Fine, G. A. (2001) 'Present, Past and Future: Conjugating George Herbert Mead's perspective on time', *Time & Society*, 10(2/3), pp. 147–161.

Furlong, A. and Cartmel, F. (2007) *Young People and Social Change*. 2nd Editio, *Sociology and Social Change*. 2nd Editio. Edited by A. Warde and N. Crossley. Berkshire: Open Universtiy Press.

Giddens, A. (1986) *The constitution of society : outline of the theory of structuration*. Cambridge: Polity Press.

Giddens, A. (1990) *The Consequences of Modernity*. Cambridge: Polity Press.

Giddens, A. (1991) *Modernity and self-identity : self and society in the late modern age*. Cambridge: Polity Press.

Guest, G. (2012) *Applied thematic analysis*. Thousand Oaks, California: SAGE Publictions Ltd.

Habermas, J. (1986) 'The new obscurity: the crisis of the welfare state and the exhaustion of utopian energies: translated by phillip Jacobs', *Philosophy & Social Criticism*, 11(2), pp. 1–18. doi: 10.1177/019145378601100201.

Harvey, D. (1989) *The Condition of Postmodernity: An Enquiry into the Origins of Cultural Change*. Oxford: Basil Blackwell Ltd.

Hicks, D. (1996) 'Retrieving the dream: How students envision their preferable futures', *Futures*, 28(8), pp. 741–749.

Horn, E. (2014) *Zukunft als Katastrophe*. Frankfurt am Main: S. Fischer Verlag.

Kohli, M. (2003) 'Der institutionalisierte Lebenslauf: ein Blick zurück und nach vorn', in Allmendinger, J. (ed.) *Entstaatlichung und soziale Sicherheit: Verhandlungen des 31. Kongresses der Deutschen Gesellschaft für Soziologie in Leipzig 2002*. Opladen: Leske + Budrich.

Koselleck, R. (2004) *Futures Past: On the semantics of historical time*. New York: Columbia University Press. doi: 10.1007/s13398-014-0173-7.2.

Kotz, D. M. (2002) 'Globalization and Neoliberalism', *Rethinking Marxism*, 12(2), pp. 64–79.

Labov, W. and Waletzky, J. (1967) 'Narrative Analysis', *Journal of Narrative and Life History*, 7, pp. 1–38.

Lombardo, T. (2006) *The Evolution of Future Consciousness*. Bloomington: AuthorHouse.

Lübbe, H. (1983): Zeit-Verhältnisse: Zur Kulturphilosophie des Fortschritts, Graz: Verlag Styria.

Luckmann, T. (1979) 'Phänomenologie und Soziologie', in Knobloch, H., Raab, J., and Schettler, B. (eds) *Wissen und Gesellschaft. Ausgewählte Aufsätze 1981–2002*. Konstanz: UVK Verlag.

Luhmann, N. (1976) 'The Future Cannot Begin: Temporal Structures in Modern Society', *Social Research*, 43(1), pp. 130–152.

Lyotard, J.-F. (1984) *The Postmodern Condition: A Report on Knowledge Condition*. Theory and. Manchester: Manchester University Press.

Maddison, A. (2001): The World Economy: A Millennial Perspective, Paris: OECD Publishing.

Mayer, K. U. (2001) 'The paradox of global social change and national path dependencies: life course patterns in advanced societies', in Woodward, A. and Kohli, M. (eds) *Inclusions and Exclusions in European Societies*. London: Routledge, pp. 89–110.

Mead, G. H. (1932) *The Philosophy of the Present*. Frankfurt am Main: Suhrkamp.

Mead, G. H. (1964) *Mind, Self, and Society*. Edited by C. W. Morris. Chicago: University of Chicago Press.

Nachtwey, O. (2016) *Die Abstiegsgesellschaft. Über das Aufbegehren in der regressiven Moderne*. Frankfurt am Main: Suhrkamp Wissenschaft.

Nilsen, A. (1999) 'Where is the future? Time and space as categories in analyses of young people's images of the future', *Innovation: The European Journal of Social Science Research*, 12(2), pp. 175–194. doi: 10.1080/13511610.1999.9968596.

Nordensvard, J. (2014) 'Dystopia and disutopia: Hope and hopelessness in German pupils' future narratives', *Journal of Educational Change*, 15, pp. 443–465. doi: 10.1007/s10833-014-9237-x.

Ono, R. (2003) 'Learning from young people ' s image of the future: a case study in Taiwan and the US', *Futures*, 35, pp. 737–758. doi: 10.1016/S0016-3287(03)00025-9.

Penny, L. (2014) *No wonder teens love stories about dystopias – they feel like they're in one*, New Statesman. Available at: https://www.newstatesman.com/2014/03/no-wonder-teens-love-stories-about-dystopian-futures-they-feel-they-re-heading-one (Accessed: 26 December 2016).

Plessner, H. (1981) 'Die Stufen des Organischen und der Mensch', in Dux, G., Marquard, O., and Ströker, E. (eds) *Gesammelte Schriften, Band 4*. Frankfurt am Main: Suhrkamp.

Reiter, H. (2003) 'Past, present, future: Biographical time structuring of disadantaged young people', *Young – Nordic Journal of Youth Research*, 11(3).

Rosa, H. (2013) *Social Acceleration: a new theory of modernity*. New York: Columbia University Press.

Rosenthal, G. (1993) *Erlebte und erzählte Lebensgeschichte. Gestalt und Strutkur biographischer Selbstbeschreibung*. Frankfurt am Main: Campus Verlag.

Schütz, A. (1967) *The Phenomenology of the Social World*. Evanston: Northwestern University Press.

Schütze, F. (1983) 'Biographieforschung und narratives Interview', *Neue Praxis*, 13(3), pp. 283–293.

Squire, C., Andrews, M. and Tamboukou, M. (2008) *Doing Narrative Research*. London: SAGE Publications Ltd. doi: 10.4135/9780857024992.

Strauss, A. L. and Corbin, J. (1998) *Basics of Qualitative Research: Techniques and Procedures for Developing Grounded Theory*. Los Angeles: SAGE Publictions Inc.

Urry, J. (2000) *Sociology beyond Society. Mobilities for the Twenty-First Century*. London: Psychology Press.

Watson, C. (2009) 'Futures narratives, possible worlds, big stories: Causal layered analysis and the problems of youth', *Sociological Research Online*, 14(5). doi: https://doi.org/10.5153/sro.1969.

Weber, M. (2001) *The Protestant Ethic and the Spirit of Capitalism*. New York: Routledge.

Weidenhaus, G. (2015) *Soziale Raumzeit*. Frankfurt am Main: Suhrkamp Wissenschaft.

Weigert, A. J. (2012) 'Realizing narratives make future time real', *Time & Society*, 23(3), pp. 317–336. doi: 10.1177/0961463X11417320.

Zaner, R. M. (1961) 'Theory of Intersubjectitvity: Alfred Schutz', *Social Research*, 28(1), pp. 71–93.

Linking Time and Space in Narrative: Nostalgia as a Chronotope

Anya Ahmed

Abstract

It has long been established that nostalgia is an important feature of community and migration discourse and scholarship. Nostalgia is also important in relation to how it links time and space in narrative. Drawing upon and developing the idea of the chronotope as a compositional facet of literature linking time and space together as advanced by (Bakhtin, M. M. (1981) The Dialogic Imagination: Four Essays. Holquist, R. (ed.) (2006) Sixteenth Paperback Printing. Austin: University of Texas Press.), this chapter posits that the chronotope is also significant in and for narrative since it amplifies and conjoins time and space in myriad ways. The chapter demonstrates how nostalgia can be viewed as chronotopic as it links a lost place and also a lost time through narrative. Drawing on a study of women's migration to Spain in retirement and their search for community and belonging to theoretically situate my use of nostalgia as a chronotopic narrative device, I unravel how the past is often recollected to make sense of the present and a focus on the past – and time as passing – is also a means of structuring and analysing narratives.

A. Ahmed (✉)
Manchester Metropolitan University, Manchester, UK
E-Mail: Anya.Ahmed@mmu.ac.uk

Zusammenfassung

Es ist bekannt, dass Nostalgie ein wichtiger Bezugspunkt des soziologischen Migrationsdiskurses ist. Nostalgie ist auch wichtig in Bezug auf die Verbindung von Zeit und Raum in einer Erzählung. In diesem Kapitel wird die Idee des Chronotops als kompositorische Facette der von Bakhtin (1981) vorgebrachten Verbindung von Zeit und Raum in der Literatur aufgegriffen und weiterentwickelt. Das Kapitel zeigt, wie Nostalgie chronotopisch konzeptualisiert werden kann, da sie einen verlorenen Ort und auch eine verlorene Zeit durch Erzählung verbindet. Gestützt auf eine Studie über Migration von Frauen nach Spanien im Ruhestand und ihre Suche nach Gemeinschaft und Zugehörigkeit, um theoretisch Nostalgie als chronotopisches Erzählmittel zu verorten, analysiere ich, wie oft Vergangenheit in Erinnerung gerufen wird, um einen Sinn für die Gegenwart zu gewinnen. Eine Fokussierung auf die Vergangenheit – und die Konzeptualisierung der Zeit als vergänglich – wird dabei als ein Mittel zur Strukturierung und Analyse von Erzählungen angesehen.

Keywords

Time · Space · Narrative · Nostalgia · Chronotype · Retirement Migration

Introduction

Nostalgia is an important characteristic of community and migration discourse and it is also significant in how it links time and space in narrative (Ahmed 2015). In his exegesis of the Greek, Baroque and Gothic classical novel Bakhtin (1981) appropriates the idea of the chronotope from Einstein's theory of relativity and reformulates it as a distinct compositional facet of literature which links time and space together. The chronotope is also salient in and for narrative since, although in migration, time–space compression means that all places are ever more accessible, in narrative, through the chronotope, time and space are amplified and linked together in different ways (Ahmed 2015; Skultans 1998). In this chapter I explore how nostalgia can be viewed as chronotopic since it links a lost place and also a lost time through narrative. The past is frequently recollected to make sense of the present and a focus on the past – and time as passing – is also a means of structuring and analysing narratives (Ahmed 2015). To theoretically situate my use of nostalgia as a chronotopic device linking time and space in narrative I draw upon a study (Ahmed 2010) which focused on British women's migration to Spain in retirement and their search for community and belonging (see also Ahmed 2011, 2012, 2013, 2015, Ahmed and Hall 2016).

The chapter is structured in the following way: first I define nostalgia and discuss its relevance to community discourse; second I explain my use of narrative analysis with a focus on the importance of time; third, I explain how nostalgia can be understood to chronotopically link time and space in narratives of migration and community; fourth, I introduce the women who participated in the study; and finally I revisit how nostalgia is an important feature of community and migration and its role in linking time and space.

Nostalgia, Community and Migration

Retirement migration – or lifestyle migration (Benson and O'Reilly 2009)- to Spanish coastal resorts began in the late 1970s and peaked during the early 2000s. Precipitated by previous experiences of mass tourism, it was facilitated by EU enlargement following the Maastricht Treaty in 1992 (which permitted EU nationals to buy properties and live in EU countries (Warnes et al. 2004; Janoshka 2011; Huete and Mantecon 2012).

Retirees migrate to Spain to experience an imagined Mediterranean lifestyle (Huete 2009 cited in Huete and Mantecon 2012), and the Costa Blanca is one of the places in Spain which is heavily populated by large numbers of retired northern Europeans. Between 2000–2010 there were more houses sold to foreign nationals than to Spanish people (Huete and Mantecon 2012). Retirement migration increased due to a number of inter-related factors: increased longevity among EU citizens; increased affluence among those in early old age; and changes in people's aspirations. Other factors influencing British retirees' decisions to migrate include Spain's climate, the relatively lower cost of living, the 'social scene', the presence of other British people and the fact that English is spoken widely. In addition, mass tourism has created infrastructures which facilitate affordable and frequent travel from the UK to several parts of Spain (King, et al. 1998; Williams and Hall 2002; Casado Diaz et al. 2004; O'Reilly 2000; 2007; Warnes et al. 2004).

Decisions to migrate are underpinned by a desire to improve one's life in some way (Ahmed 2015) and retirement migrants move to experience a new lifestyle, or a better quality of later life. Mourning the loss of community is a theme in research on older people (Blakie 1999; Blokland 2003; Savage et al. 2005) and for older people, often regaining community and a sense of belonging is part of improving the quality of one's life (Ahmed 2015) as community is a key issue influencing quality of life among older people (Conway 2003). The nostalgic and romantic discourse around community evokes the past and represents it as a better time and place than the present (Ahmed 2015). Migration also involves spanning boundaries and this relates to space and time, as moving across space can also represent moving back in time (Ahmed 2015).

Nostalgia is a comparatively recent concern linked to Western conceptions of linear rather than cyclical time, and post-Enlightenment societies: 'Nostalgia, like progress is dependent on the modern conception of unrepeatable and irreversible time' (Boym 2001, p. 13). Originating from the Swiss doctor, Johannes Hofer's medical dissertation in 1688, nostalgia was originally a term used to describe the pain felt by someone who was homesick: *hiemweh*. According to Hofer, nostalgia was thought to create "erroneous representations" which meant that those suffering from it lost touch with the present and instead yearned for their native land, indicating time and space dimensions 'temporal progression [and]…spatial expansion (Boym 2001, p. 10). In the English language it later became known as nostalgia, from the Greek – 'pseudo Greek, or nostalgically Greek (Boym 2003, p. 3) – *'nostos'* and *'algia'* which can be understood as nostos, a return home (Boym 2001, Dickenson and Erben 2006); and algia, longing (Boym 2001), or pain and sorrow (Dickenson and Erben 2006).

Prevailing discourses of community in academic and policy circles in the UK are underpinned by its perceived disappearance or loss: sometimes community is deemed to be irretrievable, at others it is constructed as something which can be resurrected (Crow 2001; Delanty 2003; Ahmed 2015), but in both cases as something which is idealised both in terms of the past and the idea of community itself. In addition, successive UK Governments have used community as a panacea to social problems (Young and Lemos, 1987; Hoggett et al. 1997). Although an oversimplification, community can be broadly understood to represent different forms of belonging to place, networks and identity (Ahmed 2015). My focus here is on how community is nostalgically (re)constructed to an 'England' of the past and Spain in the present. This captures time and space and then and now dimensions in relation to belonging to place, networks and in this particular case ethnic identity. Significantly too, boundaries are a feature of community: for place there are geographical determinants; for networks boundaries apply regarding who is 'in' and who is 'out'; and for identity representations of community there are real and imagined factors which denote belonging and non-belonging (Ahmed 2015).

Nostalgia is also characterised by simultaneously lamenting and surrendering to loss (of a place and time) and in this way has gratifying and distressing implications (Boym 2001; Ahmed 2015). Although it is provoked by social change, nostalgia can also be used to guard against such vicissitudes. Significantly, migration represents a form of social change which also involves shifts in time and space (King 2012; Ahmed 2015) and nostalgia has a powerful role in linking time and space in narrative accounts of community and belonging in migration (Ahmed 2015).

Narrative 'Is'

By the late 1990 s, narrative approaches were well established in the social sciences.

Originally used in literary analysis, the study of narratives now crosses a range of disciplines including sociology, sociolinguistics, psychology, anthropology and psychiatry (Riessman 2008), and also includes many different theoretical and analytical approaches (Stanley and Temple 2008; Ahmed 2015). The 'narrative turn' in the social sciences has been construed as a reaction by some against the limits of positivist epistemologies and writers from a wide range of disciplines offer multiple and diverse labels (see for example, Plummer 2002; Riessman 1993; Bruner 1986, 1990; Gee 1985); Goffman 1975; Gubrium and Holstein 1998). There is little agreement about what narrative 'is' (Ahmed 2013, 2015; Ahmed and Rogers 2016; Riessman 1993, 2000) and there are differences in definition, both in terms of how narrative is labelled and in what it constitutes; however, there is a common theme: the consequential linking of events and ideas, therefore it is generally accepted that narratives have a storied form (Riessman 2008; Ahmed 2013, 2015). It should be noted however, that narrative analysis is only one of myriad ways of understanding people's lived experiences and it is important to note that people focus on the highs and lows of their lives when they narrate (Anthias 2002; Ahmed 2015). Further, narratives are not a special representation of reality (Atkinson 1997, 2009), instead they are subjective and an interpretation of experiences which in turn also require interpretation (Ahmed 2013; 2015).

Analysis of narrative data can be thematic, focusing on the content of a story (or what is it about) and also structural or performative (Riessman 2008; Temple 1996, 2008) although it is difficult to separate the content from the structure. Structural analysis centres on 'the telling' or how narrative is structured to fulfil the purpose of the narrator; or why the narrator is telling the story, how the narrator persuades and convinces the audience that they see events in a particular way. Here the emphasis is on the narrative itself, rather than what is narrated. There are several differing approaches to this, although these share a concern with how an account is put together or constructed. Although narratives depend on certain structures to hold them together, as with definitions of narrative, there is significant debate and little agreement about the properties that it has or how structure should be analysed (Ahmed 2013, 2015).

There are wide differences in what is analysed in terms of structure; for example, Gee (1986) draws on oral rather than text-based tradition and analyses pitch, pause and other features that punctuate speech. For Tonkin (1992), narratives have: clarity and pace; plot; stages; symbolism; subplots; metaphor and sequence, while McAdams (1993) also uses 'imagoes' to denote a central character and argues that narratives, or stories, have tone, image, theme (recurrent pattern of human intention) and ideological setting (systematic body of values and beliefs). For Denzin (1989), narratives have a plot and a story line that exists independently of the life of the storyteller or narration and a reason or set of justifications for its telling. Gubrium and Holstein (1998) maintain that narratives or stories need to have plots, characters, themes and flow, while Riessman's definition of what comprises narrative encompasses sequence and consequence.

Other approaches to structural analysis notably include Labov and Waletsky (1967) who use a 'paradigmatic structural approach' where narratives have formal properties involving the following six elements: first there is the 'abstract' which is a summary of the substance of the narrative; this is followed by 'orientation' which reveals the time, place and characters; the 'complicating action' or sequence of events; the 'evaluation' or the significance and meaning of the actors and the action; the 'resolution' or what happened of the narrative and finally the 'coda', or a return to the present. Labov and Waletsky (1967) make the distinction between narrative clauses which would be past tense, temporally ordered and would have an impact on the inferred order of events if rearranged, and free clauses which can be rearranged in a narrative sequence without altering the semantic interpretation. Analysing the performative or dialogic Riessman (2008), drawing on Bakhtin (1984), argues that other elements of narrative add a further dimension – looking at 'who' the narrative is for and how it is a joint production between the narrator and the audience[1]. This aspect of narrative analysis examines interaction between speaker and listener, the context in which the story is told and the performance of 'identity' through narrating.

Looking at thematic and structural analysis together enables an identification and analysis of common themes across (and within) cases and also, exploration

---

[1]This is sometimes included with the general term 'structure' of a narrative rather than separate from structure.

of variation in meaning (Ahmed 2013; 2015; Ahmed and Rogers 2016; Riessman 2008). With regard to the structure of a narrative, the analytical focus centres on the telling, rather than what is told. Elsewhere I have analysed narrative structure in relation to plot (Ahmed 2013, 2015; Ahmed and Rogers 2016); time (Ahmed 2015); identity and positionality (Ahmed 2015; Ahmed and Rogers 2016) and linguistic devices deployed (Ahmed 2015; Ahmed and Rogers 2016). Here I analytically bracket (Gubrium and Holstein 1998) to focus specifically on time as a dimension of narrative in relation to nostalgia as chronotopically linking time together.

Narrative and Time

The plot of a narrative brings together distinct incidents into an intelligible entity (Ahmed 2013, 2015; Ahmed and Rogers 2016). Plot can also be comprehended as constituting and organising the events in people's lives. Such events are given meaning through the 'temporal dialectic' (Ricoeur 1984, 1985, 1988) or the relating of time tenses in narrative (Ahmed 2015). Time is an important feature of migration (Ahmed 2015; Halfacree and Boyle 1993 drawing on Shotter 1984) and migration decisions are based on people's past, present and futures, as part of their biography. Analysing time in narrative provides the opportunity to make sense of people's migration experiences since the past, present and future emerge in relation to people's unique biographies (Riessman 2008; Ahmed 2015).

Time as something which passes and endures typifies narratives and, in this way, recounting lived experiences can be seen as storied and organised by and in time (McAdams 1993; Roberts 2002; Ahmed 2015). Narrative production involves organisation and sequencing and in this way plot links with time as the discrete facets of the narrative are consequential according to past, present and future (Ahmed 2015). Time and space have epistemological resonance since the context in which a narrative is produced (where and when) shapes them. Additionally, how we talk about the past reflects our concerns in the present (Day Sclater 1998) and our intentions in the future (Ahmed 2015). My focus here is on how talk of the past influences the present (then and now) and how women use nostalgia to recall and reconstruct community and belonging (here and there). 'Nostalgia – like memory – depends on mnemonic devices' (Bakhtin 1981: 346) and narrating can be understood as such a device to trigger nostalgic recollections of the past.

The Study Context

The fieldwork for the study took place between 2001–3004 (narrative interviews and ethnography), across three purpose built 'urbanisations' for residential tourists – the Spanish Government categorise European migrants as such – close to the town of Torrevieja in the Costa Blanca. The urbanisations were almost exclusively occupied by northern European migrants, and predominantly British people, with a very small number of Spanish people having purchased second homes there.

Introducing the Research Participants

Throughout this chapter I use pseudonyms for the research participants and provide some background information in the table below:

Research participant	Lives in Spain full time (FT) or part time (PT)	Intends to remain in Spain?	Marital status	Age[a]
Celia	FT	Yes	Married	58
Cynthia	FT	Yes	Married	54
Vera	FT	No – wants to return to the UK	In a couple with Deidre	59
Deidre	FT	No – wants to return to the UK	In a couple With Vera	62
Phyllis	FT	Yes	Married	77
Mabel	FT	Yes	Widowed	83
Agnes	FT	No – wants to return to the UK	Married	69
Agatha	FT	Yes	Married	60
Olive	FT	Yes	Divorced	57
Myra	FT	Yes	Divorced	60
Margot	FT	Yes	Divorced	60
Lillian	FT	Yes	Married	61
Joy	FT	Yes	Married	54
Jenny	FT	No – wants to return to the UK	Married	56

Research participant	Lives in Spain full time (FT) or part time (PT)	Intends to remain in Spain?	Marital status	Age[a]
Viv	PT	Intends to retain home in Spain	Married	54
Bernice	PT	Intends to retain home in Spain	Married	62
Enid	PT	No – wants to buy a second home elsewhere	Married	57

[a]This denotes the women's ages on the date of interview

The women featured here can be classified as falling into four related but different residential categories: those living in Spain permanently, that is without a home in the UK, who wished to remain there (Celia, Cynthia, Mable, Agatha, Joy, Myra, Margot, Olive, Lillian and Phyllis); those living in Spain permanently who wished to return to the UK (Jenny, Agnes, Vera and Deirdre); those who lived in Spain for part of the year and were happy with this arrangement (Bernice and Viv) and finally, those who live in Spain for part of the year but did not wish to retain their home there (Enid). Seven of the women were from the North of England, nine from the South and another was from Northern Ireland.

Although all the women were retired, their ages ranged from between 53 and 83 with the average being just under 62 years. Some women moved to Spain alone with Mabel, Olive, Myra and Margot falling into this category; whilst the majority – Celia, Cynthia, Joy, Agnes, Agatha, Jenny, Lillian and Phyllis – moved with their husbands. Two of the women, Vera and Deidre (the women who I knew prior to the research and who allowed me access to most of the women I interviewed), were a couple. All of the women (apart from Deidre who had parented step-children) had adult children and grandchildren residing in the UK. With regard to education, three women had gone on to higher education (Mabel, Enid and Vera), while a further two had been in further education (Deidre and Olive); the remainder, (apart from Viv) finished secondary school. Mabel, Enid, Vera, Olive, Agnes and Deidre were employed in roles traditionally considered to be 'professional', whilst Celia, Phyllis, Lillian, Margot, Myra had worked in the retail industry. Jenny and Agatha both previously worked in service industries. Neither Joy nor Viv had ever been in paid employment but had worked as homemakers. I consider the significance of these categories when I discuss how I analyse the women's narratives below

Chronotopes and Narrative

Bakhtin (1981) identifies the significance of the chronotope – understood as 'literally, "time space"' (1981:84) – as linking time and space together in literature, although time is 'the dominant principle' (1981:86) the chronotope 'expresses the inseparability of space and time' (1981: 84) and 'the intrinsic connectedness of temporal and spatial relationship that are artistically expressed in literature (1981:84).

'Spatial and temporal indicators are fused into one carefully thought-out, concrete whole. Time, as it were, thickens, takes on flesh, becomes artistically visible; likewise, space becomes charged and responsive to the movements of time, plot and history' (1981:84).

Bakhtin (1981) introduces adventure and idyllic chronotopes which link time and space together in literature in different ways. Adventure time is identified by Bakhtin as characterising classic Greek novels and occurs outside of biographical time. In other words, there is a beginning and end to the plot of such novels but the events which take place are unconnected and could actually be rearranged without altering the end point of the plot. Such events are conceptualised as 'random temporal contingencies' – a suddenly, just at that moment feature when unusual events happen (Bakhtin 1981; Skultans 1997; Ahmed 2015) and adventure time is triggered at points of biographical disruption. However, for Bakhtin, the beginning and end of a plot, although have random events occurring between them, are not merely the result of chance. The idyllic chronotope, also links time and space but it is connected to the physical landscape – life is grafted to a place or space – and time slows down when rooted to the physical environment. In this way, an idyll can therefore be understood as being suspended in time as there is a blurring of temporal boundaries (Ahmed 2015; Skultans 1998).

The women who participated in the study often presented a chronological story of their life; often they would go back in time and provide an account of time passing up to the present as the following excerpt from Enid and Cynthia's narratives illustrate:

> Ok, I'll go back and I'll tell you about how we came to be here
> (Enid)

> Well I'll go back to the beginning to when we first thought about moving here
> (Cynthia)

The decision to migrate represents a form of biographical disruption and occurs takes place in everyday adventure time (Bakhtin 1981) since it symbolises a succession of incidents triggering the migration process from the UK to Spain. As such it takes place in everyday adventure time distinguished by random contingency or abrupt associated incidents as Cynthia and Jenny's narratives illustrate:

> Well we've always loved Spain and thought each time we came on holiday we really could live there. And then, my husband was diagnosed with emphysema and then he was offered early retirement from work...my grandchildren had got to the age where they didn't need me to look after them anymore and the company I was working for at the time offered people voluntary redundancy and I thought 'why not?'...where we lived [in the north-east of England] was going down so we thought we'd move to Spain
> Cynthia

For Cynthia, the decision to move to Spain was precipitated by a number of factors: previous holiday experiences in Spain and the feeling they would be happy living there on a more permanent basis; her husband's illness; the opportunity for him to retire early; she was no longer needed to care for her grandchildren; the opportunity for her to take redundancy from work; and she was also unhappy with the way she perceived the area in which they lived was changing. The combination of these discrete but contingent incidents coalesced to precipitate the decision to move to Spain.

The random events for Jenny included the deterioration of her health; the belief that Spain's climate might improve it; her husband's wish to move to Spain; and the fact that her daughter and her family had also decided to move there:

> My arthritis was getting worse and I thought the warm weather might help me. My husband has always been itching to move to Spain and then my daughter announced that she and her husband were moving here...so it seemed like the obvious thing to do
> Jenny

The Mediterranean Idyll (Ahmed 2015) was influential in persuading the women in the study to move to Spain and idyllic chronotopes in narrative emphasise the value of nature and the physical landscape while also 'fastening' or slowing down time and linking it to space. The excerpt from Myra's narrative highlights the suspended in time/slowing down characteristics of the idyll. She talked about not needing to rush any more where the climate in Spanish space encourages relaxation and slowing down time:

> It's just so hot it just forces you to relax and take things slowly…there's no need to rush about any more
> Myra

Skultans (1998) identifies three thematic dimensions along which narratives develop a moral critique:
'The beauty and moral order of the past … The goodness, beauty and strength of childhood and youth … The innate goodness of earth, trees and animals' (Skultans (1998, pp. 86–7).

Initially at least, – and irrespective of whether they intended to remain in Spain – the women focused on the health benefits of the Spanish climate, the opportunities to relax and their relief at having left a more frenetic environment and pace of life behind in the UK as Myra and Celia's narratives illustrate:

> Being so close to the Mediterranean is wonderful…and the plants we can grow in our garden are out of this world…we've got the time now to relax and enjoy this sort of thing now
> Celia

The third moral dimension 'the innate goodness of earth, trees' as identified by Skultans (1998) is evident in Celia's narrative. Celia praised the Mediterranean climate and scenery, highlighting the beauty of the flora and fauna and the benefits of having the time to relax and enjoy the scenery.

Nostalgia as a Chronotope in Women's Narratives

Cynthia talked nostalgically about recreating a bygone era – symbolising the good old days – a golden age, that would actually have been outside of her experience. However, as Boym (2001) highlights, 'As a public epidemic, nostalgia was based on a sense of loss not limited to personal history' (2001:6):

> We have speakers who come, and we have these old-fashioned music hall evenings where everyone dresses up, like the good old days
> Cynthia

In addition to the perceived benefits of Spain's climate and physical environment which encouraged rest and relaxation, there also appeared to be other positive impacts associated with living in the Mediterranean Idyll – suspended in time. Women nostalgically recollect how 'England' used to be in terms of 'community spirit', people's willingness to engage with each other and offer help – in other words a positive impact on people's behaviour, which tended to be associated with the past as Mabel, Margot and Vera's narratives illustrate:

> It's like how England used to be…community disappeared but now it's come back in Spain
> Mabel

> People are so lovely here, everyone has time to say hello and have a chat…not like in England where everyone is rushing around, too busy for anything. It reminds me of what it was like when I was a girl
> Margot.

> Living in Spain we have to stick together in case we need any help…so it's like the old days in England really, we've recreated the old community way for want of a better word.
> Vera

This also resonates with the first of Skultans' (1998) moral critiques where the beauty and moral order of the past are emphasised. Margot's narrative has elements of the second moral critique where the goodness, beauty and strength of childhood are highlighted. A sense of community in the UK during childhood was compared to Spain in the present in terms of being a reaction against some kind of hardship where people needed to come together. For these women, living on the margins among compatriots in an isolated diasporic community (Ahmed 2015) regaining community represented a recreation of the past in another place. In the UK community had 'gone' and related to a bygone era, in Spain it had returned in the present. Idealising and nostalgically reconstructing community brings the past into the present across space.

So far, I have presented the women's narratives which focused on the place and network representations of community. I now turn to look at how shared identity, in this particular case ethnic identity is a representation of community and is nostalgically (re)constructed. Some of the women featured explained that their motivation to move to Spain in part was based on feeling non-belonging in the UK due to the presence of 'others' as Phyllis and Cynthia highlight:

> Well you know where we lived three were a lot of foreign people and we didn't feel that we belonged any more
> Phyllis
> Where we lived there were a lot of Pakistanis and …well we started to feel like it wasn't our country any more…there were hardly any English people around
> Cynthia

When in Spain however, being surrounded by their compatriots afforded a sense of belonging and community predicated on shared ethnic (or national) identity as Myra and Margot's narratives illustrate:

> I chose this area because there are a lot of English people round her
> Myra
> It's lovely here, practically everyone who lives here is English
> Margot

It is useful at this juncture to introduce both Britishness and Englishness as potential ethnic or national positionalities. Englishness is contested as an ethnic or national identity and there has been significant debate about where Englishness stops and Britishness beings (Byrne 2007; Wright 1985). Englishness can be understood as a romantic construction and as the product of a nostalgic imagination, while Britishness represents the opposite of the idyll: urban, lower-class and multi-racial.

'Englishness is somehow truly what England should be – refined, rural, white and middle class…whilst Britishness is a category which can absorb all that disturbs this nation' (Byrne 2007, p. 518).

This suggests that Britishness is inclusive, and Englishness is exclusive. Wright (1985) refers to three kinds of 'Englishness' within the context of a broader national identity. First, there is 'deep England' which denotes a nostalgic idealised attachment to a rural idyll. Second, there is 'empty Englishness' which is 'a sense of Englishness that is closed, fixed and white. Finally, there is 'evading Englishness', which can be understood as a negative regard for what is considered to be English. The women's narratives above also resonate with Delanty's (1996) 'new nationalism' which captures the crisis of national identity in the UK. New nationalism embodies a heightened hostility to immigrants rather than towards other nations, and an enhanced sense of nationality has been defined as opposing immigrants. (Rex 1996; Delanty 1996). For the women featured, a nostalgic idealised narrative reconstruction of community along the lines of place, networks and ethnic identity chronotopically links time and space. In this sense, the women left Britain to move to Spain to return to England (Ahmed 2015).

Conclusion

Nostalgia can be interpreted as chronotopic as it conjoins time and space in narrative, especially in relation to community and its different forms in migration (Ahmed 2015). Women's narratives of community and belonging in migration were characterised by time/space – here and there/then and now – in several important ways. First, the Mediterranean idyll was represented as positively influencing how people felt; relaxed, not rushed as time slows down in the idyll. Second, being in Spain in the idyll suspended in time influenced how people behaved towards one another. People were 'nicer' to each other and there was a much stronger community spirit imbuing social networks. Third, being among compatriots – drawing on notions of an England in the past and living on the margins of Spanish society provided the women with a sense of community which they felt was no longer possible in the UK. The presence of 'others' in the UK was felt to preclude this – the paradox of course is that these women were themselves immigrants, foreigners in Spain – although they did not necessarily recognise this.

As I have suggested nostalgia is an elusive concept and is often represented as an emotion or feeling (Boym 2001) which can be examined at will (Dickenson and Erben 2006) and this is reflected and constructed through narrative. Nostalgia can be understood within the context of, and as an outcome of rapid social change. However, nostalgic recollections are not necessarily individual memories from personal biographies; rather they are attempts to recreate a lost past – and this is done through narrative. Belonging and community are constructed through a sense of nostalgic intimacy with the world. If intimacy is compromised then nostalgia constructs and reflects belonging; in other words, nostalgia bridges this gap. Nostalgia encompasses space, time and time and space are linked through nostalgia as are the past and the present. Nostalgia is utilitarian, symbolic and part of the social imaginary.

The concept of nostalgia therefore is important in understanding belonging and community, in the context of retirement migration – the past representing a golden age; and, as I have already suggested, it can be understood as both an idealisation of the past and as bringing the past into the present (Dickenson and Erben 2006). Community and belonging can be a place, a time or both and nostalgia chronotopically links these. Nostos, the return home can be understood as a return to another time and can also be achieved in a different place or a different time. In this way return denotes going back in time as well as travelling across space. Algia is the longing the pain, for another past (time) as well as a lost place. This was particularly important for women featured since they were on the margins and felt dislocation in both the UK and Spain. Nostalgia provides familiarity and safety in an unfamiliar social world which is changing rapidly. It represents an antidote to modernity and social change. We cannot stop social change, but we can preserve or halt our position and relationship to the social world through nostalgia.

References

Ahmed, A. (2010) *Home and away: British women's narratives of community in Spain.* PhD Thesis, The University of Central Lancashire.
Ahmed, A. (2011) 'Belonging out of context: the intersection of place, networks and ethnic identity among retired British migrants living in the Costa Blanca', *Journal of Identity and Migration Studies*, vol. 5, no. 2, pp. 2-19.
Ahmed, A. (2012) *Networks among retired British women in the Costa Blanca: Insiders, Outsiders, 'Club Capital' and 'Limited Liability, Urbanities, vol. 2, no. 2, pp. 95 -112.*
Ahmed, A. (2013) 'Structural narrative analysis: understanding experiences of lifestyle migration through two plot typologies', *Qualitative Inquiry*, vol. 19, no. 3, pp. 232-243.
Ahmed, A. (2015) British Women's Narratives of Nostalgia, Community and Belonging. Bristol, Policy Press.
Ahmed, A. and Rogers, M. (2016) Polly's Story: using structural narrative analysis to examine a trans migration journey *Qualitative Social Work Special Issue: Narrative and Social Work*, vol. 16, no. 2, pp. 224-230
Anthias, F. (2002) 'Where do I belong?: Narrating Identity and Translocational Positionality', *Ethnicities*, vol. 2, no. 4, pp. 491-515.
Atkinson, P. (1997) 'Narrative Turn or Blind Alley?' *Qualitative Health Research*, vol. 7, no. 3, pp. 325-344.
Atkinson, P. (2009) 'Illness Narratives Revisited: The Failure of Narrative Reductionism', *Sociological Research Online*, vol. 14, no. 5. Available from www.socresonline.org.uk
Bakhtin, M. M. (1981) *The Dialogic Imagination: Four Essays.* Holquist, R. (ed.) (2006) Sixteenth Paperback Printing. Austin: University of Texas Press.
Benson, M. and O'Reilly, K. (eds.) (2009) *Lifestyle Migration: Expectations, Aspirations and Experiences.* Farnham: Ashgate.
Blaikie, N. (1999) *Approaches to Social Enquiry.* Cambridge: Blackwell.
Blokland, T. (2003) *Urban bonds: social relationships in an inner city neighbourhood.* Cambridge: Polity Press.
Boym, S. (2001) *The Future of Nostalgia.* New York: Basic Books.
Bruner, J.S. (1990) *Acts of Meaning.* Cambridge, MA: Harvard University Press.
Casado- Díaz, M. A., Kaiser, C. and Warnes, A.M. (2004) 'Northern European retired residents in nine southern European areas: characteristics, motivations and adjustment', *Ageing and Society*, vol. 24, pp. 353-381.

Casado-Díaz, M.A. (2006) 'Retiring to Spain: An Analysis of Differences among North European Nationals', *Journal of Ethnic and Migration Studies*, vol. 32, no. 8, pp. 1321-1339.

Conway, S. (2003) 'Ageing and Imagined Community: Some Cultural Constructions and Reconstructions', *Sociological Research Online*, vol. 8, no. 2. Available from www.socresonline.org.uk

Crow, G. (2002a) 'Community Studies: Fifty Years of Theorization', *Sociological Research Online*, vol. 7, no. 3. Available from www.socresonline.org.uk

Crow, G., Allan, G. and Summers, M. (2002) 'Neither Busybodies nor Nobodies: Managing Proximity and Distance in Neighbourly Relations', *Sociology*, vol. 36, no. 1, pp. 127-145.

Day Sclater, S. (1998) 'Nina's Story: An exploration into the construction and transformation of subjectives in narrative accounting', *Auto/Biography*, Vol. 6, Nos. 1 and 2, pp. 67–77.

Delanty, G. (2003) *Community*. London: Routledge.

Denzin, N.K. (1989) *Interpretive biography, Sage University Paper Reason Qualitative Research Methods*. Newbury Park, Sage.

Gee, J.P. (1986) *Units in the production of narrative discourse*. Discourse Processes, 9, 391-422

Goffman, E (1975) *Frame Analysis: An essay on the organisation of Experience*. Harmondsworth: Penguin.

Gubrium, J.F. and Holstein, J.A. (1998) 'Narrative practice and the coherence of personal stories', *The Sociological Quarterly*, vol. 39, pp. 163-187.

Gubrium, J.F. and Holstein, J.A. (2008) *Analyzing Narrative Reality*. Thousand Oaks: Sage.

Halfacree, K. and Boyle, P. (1993) 'The challenge facing migration research: the case for a biographical approach', *Progress in Human Geography* 17, pp. 333-348.

Hoggett, P. (1997) 'Contested Communities,' in Hoggett, P. (ed.) (1997) *Contested Communities. Experiences, struggles and policies*. Bristol: Policy Press.

Huete, R. and Mantecon, A. (2012) 'Residential Tourism or Lifestyle Migration: Social Problems Linked to the Non-Definition of the Situation', in Moufakkir, O. and Burns, P. (eds.) *Controversies in Tourism*. Wallingford: CABI.

Janoschka, M. (2011) 'Between mobility and mobilization – lifestyle migration and the practice of European identity in political struggles', *The Sociological Review*, vol. 58, pp. 270-290.

King, Russell (2012) *Geography and migration studies: retrospect and prospect*. Population, Space and Place, 18 (2). pp. 134-153.

McAdams, D. P. (1993) *The Stories We Live By: Personal Myths and the Making of the Self*. New York: Guilford Press.

O'Reilly, K. (2000) *The British on the Costa del Sol: Transnational Identities and Local Communities*. Routledge, London and New York.

O'Reilly, K. (2007a) 'Emerging Tourism Futures: Residential Tourism and its Implications', in Geoffroy, C. and Sibley, R. (2007) *Going Abroad: Travel, Tourism and Migration. Cross-Cultural Perspectives on Mobility*. Newcastle: Cambridge Scholars Publishing.

Plummer, K. (2001) *Documents of Life 2: An Invitation to Critical Humanism*. Sage, London.

Ricouer, P. (1984) *Time and Narrative Vol. 1.* Chicago: Chicago University Press.
Ricouer, P. (1985) *Time and Narrative Vol. 2.* Chicago: Chicago University Press.
Ricouer, P. (1988) *Time and Narrative Vol. 3.* Chicago: Chicago University Press.
Riessman, C.K. (1993) *Narrative Analysis (Qualitative Research Methods).* Thousand Oaks, CA: Sage.
Riessman, C.K. (2008) *Narrative Methods for the Human Sciences.* London: Sage.
Roberts, B. (2002) *Biographical Research.* Buckingham: Open University Press.
Salazar, N. B. (2014) Migrating Imaginaries of a Better Life ... Until Paradise Finds You, pp 119-138 in Benson, M. and Osbaldiston, N. (eds) (2014) *Understanding Lifestyle Migration: Theoretical Approaches to Migration and the Quest for a Better Way of Life,* Basingstoke: Palgrave Macmillan
Savage, M. and Bennett, T. (2005) 'Editors' introduction: Cultural capital and social inequality', The British Journal of Sociology, vol. 56, no. 1, pp. 1-12.
Skrbiš, Z. (2008) 'Transnational Families: Theorising Migration, Emotion and Belonging', *Journal of Intercultural Studies,* vol. 29, no. 3, pp. 231-246.
Skultans, V. (1998) *The Testimony of Lives: Narratives and Memory in Post-Soviet Latvia.* London: Routledge.
Stanley, L. and Temple, B. (2008) *Narrative methodologies: subjects, silences, re-readings and analyses.* Qualitative Research 2008; 8; 275 DOI: 10.1177/1468794106093622.
Tonkin, E. (1993) *Narrating Our Pasts: The social construction of oral history.* Cambridge University Press
Torkington, K. (2012) 'Place and Lifestyle Migration: The Discursive Construction of 'Glocal' Place-Identity', *Mobilities,* vol. 7, no. 1, pp. 71-92.
Warnes, A.M., Friedrich, K., Kellaher, L. and Torres, S. (2004) 'The diversity and welfare of older migrants in Europe', *Ageing and Society,* vol. 24, no. 3, pp. 307-326.

Constructing Biography—Constructing Identity: Changeable Concept of the Future in Migrants

Anna Sircova, Carolyn Patterson and Elisabeth Schilling

Abstract

Research on OECD countries shows that migrants in most regions have on average worse outcomes than the native-born population in areas such as education attainment and labour market participation (OECD, 2017). Migration, acculturation strategies, and various factors influencing the acculturation outcomes have been extensively studied in psychology as well as in sociology and further social sciences. However, most psychological studies have been carried out using the cross-cultural psychology methodology and therefore applied a static definition of culture, when culture becomes a label and not the process. The aim of the present interdisciplinary study was to explore subjective time concepts as a part of the migrants' cultural capital, which influences the individual's opportunities, biographies, and the feelings of belonging through in-depth interviews. The participants were migrants (both from EU and non-EU countries) residing in Denmark for various periods (newly arrived, 2 to 5 years, 5 to 10 years, and over 10 years).

A. Sircova (✉)
Time Perspective Network, Copenhagen, Denmark
E-Mail: anna.sircova@gmail.com

C. Patterson
Time Perspective Network, Copenhagen, Denmark
E-Mail: cpatter5@conncoll.edu

E. Schilling
University of Police and Public Administration NRW, Bielefeld, Germany
E-Mail: elisabeth.schilling@hspv.nrw.de

© Springer Fachmedien Wiesbaden GmbH, ein Teil von Springer Nature 2020
E. Schilling und M. O'Neill (Hrsg.), *Frontiers in Time
Research – Einführung in die interdisziplinäre Zeitforschung*,
https://doi.org/10.1007/978-3-658-31252-7_6

Further, participants were asked to discuss identity conflicts that arose during their time in Denmark, which could impede their integration. The theoretical concept of time-collage (Schilling, 2005, 2008) was applied, describing the diversity of time approaches and possibilities for individuals in learning a transcultural time approach. Temporal horizons (Ledgerwood, Trope, Liberman 2015) was an important concept in determining how the participants imagine their future and its role in integration. We observed various emotional responses to everyday challenges depending on if the desired image of the future could be accomplished or not. The study also explored acculturation strategies through the individual's representation of the future as an object. The meaning of the subjective time concept for a successful integration of migrants is further discussed.

Zusammenfassung

Studien zu OECD-Ländern zeigen, dass Migranten in den meisten Regionen bei Bildung und Erwerbsbeteiligung im Durchschnitt schlechter abschneiden als die im Inland geborene Bevölkerung (OECD, 2017). Migration, Akkulturationsstrategien und diverse Faktoren, die die Akkulturationsergebnisse beeinflussen, wurden ausführlich in verschiedenen Sozialwissenschaften untersucht. Die meisten psychologischen Studien wurden jedoch unter Verwendung der cross-cultural Methodologie durchgeführt und verwendeten daher eine statische Definition von Kultur, wenn Kultur zu einem Etikett und nicht zum Prozess wird. Ziel der vorliegenden interdisziplinären Studie war es, subjektive Zeitkonzepte als Teil des Kulturkapitals der Migranten zu untersuchen, die durch eingehende Interviews die Chancen, Biografien und Zugehörigkeitsgefühle des Einzelnen beeinflussen. Die Teilnehmer*innen waren Migrant*innen (sowohl aus EU- als auch aus Nicht-EU-Ländern), die für verschiedene Zeiträume (neu angekommen, 2 bis 5 Jahre, 5 bis 10 Jahre und über 10 Jahre) in Dänemark lebten. Darüber hinaus wurden die Teilnehmer*innen gebeten, Identitätskonflikte zu erörtern, die während ihrer Zeit in Dänemark aufgetreten waren und deren Integration behindern könnten. Das theoretische Konzept der Zeitkollage (Schilling, 2005, 2008) wurde angewendet und beschreibt die Vielfalt der Zeitansätze und Möglichkeiten für den Einzelnen, einen transkulturellen Zeitansatz zu erlernen. Zeitliche Horizonte (Ledgerwood, Trope, Liberman 2015) waren ein wichtiges Konzept, um zu bestimmen, wie sich die Teilnehmer ihre Zukunft und ihre Rolle bei der Integration vorstellen. Wir beobachteten verschiedene emotionale Reaktionen auf alltägliche Herausforderungen, je nachdem, ob das gewünschte Bild der Zukunft erreicht werden konnte oder nicht. Die Studie untersuchte auch

Akkulturationsstrategien durch die Darstellung der Zukunft als Objekt durch den Einzelnen. Die Bedeutung des subjektiven Zeitkonzepts für eine erfolgreiche Integration von Migranten wird weiter diskutiert.

Keywords

Identity · Future · Time concept · Migration · Integration · Cross-cultural research · Temporal horizons

Schlüsselwörter

Identität · Zukunft · Zeitvorstellungen · Migration · Integration · cross-cultural research · Zeithorizonte

Introduction

When arriving at a new place—people have a particular image of the future or how their life is going to unfold in that new place. The current study explores what happens to that image of the future when various factors come into play, such as: cultural distance (how far or close is their home country from Denmark according to the Inglehart's World Values Survey map; (Ingelhart et al. 2014)), the challenges they face due to the administration rules, and their length of stay in the new country.

The overall idea of our study was to explore, if the subjective time concepts can be conceptualized as a part of the migrants' cultural capital, which influences the individual's changes, biographies and feelings of belonging. Additionally, we also aimed to explore the concept of time as a factor influencing successful integration for different groups of migrants.

Our main research questions were: How the image of the future new life in Denmark changes over time? What plays a role in this change? What are the challenges and stressor factors people face within their first year in Denmark, during the adaptation period between 1–2 years, 3–10 years and over 10 years.

The study investigates a possibility to access high-quality data about migration and adjustment to the host society. We propose to conceptualize time as an informative frame for social movements and changes. When asking through narrative interviews about time issues, we gained access to: complex sense structures of the individual life world and the interpersonal, social, transferable structures of time use. In our study we asked our participants about the image of their future as an object. The results visualize the hidden structures of their mindset concerning the prospects they believe they have in a new country. The images provide a deeper understanding of participants' self-position, which is hard to unveil through verbal interaction alone.

Background

Background: Acculturation: Transition, Identity, Adaptation

The importance of time concepts for the understanding of migration and acculturation processes have been rarely discussed in the social sciences. First we can refer to Elias and Scotson (1994) and Schütz (1944) as classic sociological texts. They describe subjective time concepts as one of the important expressions of the social life, which are implicit and often unconscious for the insiders and strange, alienating for the newcomers (cf. Schütze 1992). The ability to adjust to the new social life is hence interconnected with the ability to understand and to take on new time concepts. In this chapter we would like to discuss the processes, which make this change and adjustment possible.

Märtsin and Mahmoud (2012) view migration as rupture: "Migration is a rupturing experience that introduces a break into a person's normal and taken-for-granted flow of being and produces a diversity of ever-changing outcomes ranging from pain and trauma to feelings of exhilaration, excitement, relief and self-discovery" (p. 733). With other words we can describe migration as time anchored: interrupting a continuum of the 'usual or normal' time rhythms and causing the emergence of empty spaces and the need to process them and to fill with new meanings and actions. Migrants fill the empty spaces with various positive and negative feelings, cognitions and actions, thus creating the collage of the worldview. This collage contains some aspects from their past (learned in their home country), some new elements, adapted from the host country and many creative elements interconnecting the both in a subjective and individual way (Schilling 2005). Encountering the new environment can bring a lot of excitement as we see especially in the beginning, upon arrival—new beginning, new opportunities, moving in, settling in, feeling of joy and being excited as a kid and welcoming this newness. Many describe it as a 'honeymoon' stage with settling in. However, it can also bring a sense of loss, especially if the migration was forced due to natural disaster or war.

According to OECD (2017) "migration has become a major issue on the international agenda, and better measures of migrants' well-being are needed to support governments' efforts to integrate migrants, address their needs and leverage their capacities." The report shows that migrants' life satisfaction is lower compared to that of the native-born in most European countries. The largest differences were observed in Estonia, Austria, Poland, Iceland, Lithuania, Denmark and Slovenia. The report further specifies that many migrants are overqualified for their jobs, due to the barriers they face in recognizing their qualifications. That might cause not only a loss of life satisfaction, but also create deep identity crises related to one's future personal projections. The identity of an individual is also seen to carry over to their societal role, which can increase life satisfaction and purpose. The roles individuals play in society become part of one's self identity and each time an individual enters or exits a role, self-identity is threatened.

We see identity as the integration of self over time. During the process of identity development a person might deal with various conflicting images of the self, social roles and relationships with others, to keep a coherent picture of oneself, integrating images of the past and present experiences and future hopes and expectation (van Schalkwyk 2010; Habermas and Bluck 2000; Hermans 2001; McAdams 2001).

Leaving a country and settling in a new place brings with it a particular ending, sometimes social roles that were at play in the home-country would never be activated again in a new place. So the person has to deal with a role ending and a 'hangover' identity (Ebaugh 1988). To become well integrated and a whole person, a cultural traveler must incorporate the personal past history (biography) into the current identity, creating a new identity that incorporates their past social status and the future projected biography with a possible, desired and pursued social status. The process of role exiting involves the tension between an individual's past, present and future. If a specific role has ended, it can be experienced like a small death, which the person needs to make sense of. In order to continue further, they must create a new meaning from their experience. This might be connected to the individual understanding of meaning of life: it is one of the most subjective notions and at the same time important for self-affirmation of an individual: forming her or his conviction in the correctness of his actions and self-confidence. According to Frankl, people can find the meaning of life in different ways. It might be an action with which they create something; or an important experience, for example if they meet somebody or witness something or finally it can be a special attitude or a standing that they take towards things that they cannot avoid, like for example suffering from nostalgia. Frankl describes suffering as "the last of the human freedoms—to choose one's attitude in any given set of circumstances" (Frankl 1985). The coping with the termination of some attractive life phases and the current suffering might be mastered in a positive way, if a person discovers a meaning in their own biographical trajectory, constructing a coherent story from the past to the future. It might promote the individual's understanding and meaning of life, specifically through self-confidence and integration.

In addition, the experience of migration can also promote further understanding, helping individuals find a meaning in life. As Märtsin and Mahmoud (2012, p. 732) put it, "migration is a threat, yet also a promise; it is a painful, yet possibly exhilarating experience that makes us lose our center of security and familiarity, yet also opens up opportunities for transformation and reinvention."

The different ways of acculturation can be studied within a framework developed by Berry (Berry 2006). He proposed a two-dimensional structure of acculturation attitudes, which was based on two issues: the degree to which individuals wish to maintain (or change) their heritage cultural and identity, and the degree to which individuals wish to have active contact and participation with others in the larger society (Berry and Sabatier 2011).

Among the factors influencing acculturation process we can name the following: the length of stay, personality, gender, age, marital status, social support (i.e. family, friends and important others), host country language proficiency, country of origin (cultural distance to the host country), finding work, policies in the host country, social and socio-economic status, perceived discrimination (stereotypes threat), visibility of difference, and the reason for migration (Sircova 2017; Heine 2012; Smith and Khawaja 2011).

For the purposes of our study we took the framework of the ABC model of cultural shock (Bochner 2003). This model distinguishes between the Affective, Behavioural and Cognitive components of cross-cultural interaction. In other words this model describes how individuals feel, behave, perceive and think. It regards the response to an unfamiliar cultural setting as an active process of coping with a new situation (Ward et al. 2001).

Background: Time Concepts: Mental Horizons, Possible Selves

One's ability to make future plans depends on the concept of what is possible and feasible for them under the current circumstances, in the present situation. A person might create a variety of different drafts of their own futures based on their own experience, family history, available role models, sociocultural context, and mass media (Markus and Nurius 1986). This concept of possible selves creates a link between cognition and motivation. In our study we hoped to explore the differences between our participants' ability to imagine a desired future, to build a trajectory and their capability to attain it.

A further concept, which might be fruitful in this regard, is of mental horizons and psychological distance (Trope and Liberman 2010). Psychological distance refers to the removal of the event from a direct experience. For migrants coming from a very different cultural background, imagining their host country as their new life might be psychologically distant, so they are not able to imagine a concrete trajectory towards it (Schilling 2018). The main problem that people face, when they try to imagine a psychologically remote event is that they lack the specific, detailed knowledge about it, so the ways to this goal remain vague, insecure, the goal remains unavailable and the people tend to lose their motivation. They prefer to stay within their short-termed plans or low level of construal (Ledgerwood et al. 2015). As Sircova et al. stated, the tendency to short-termed planning grows during the times of social instability and crises, which can be also applied to the transition time of migration (Sircova et al. 2015). Short-term planning can serve as a coping mechanism with the uncertainty that arises due to feeling of future being insecure and unpredictable, as various structures, social relations, and norms in the new country are not yet comprehensible, and perspective of the permanent residency status is not clear. This strategy might have long-term consequences for the further generations: children in the families with the unsecured future learn not to plan too far ahead (ebd.), which might impede their progress at school and in the labor market.

It is also important to regard the relationship between the psychological distance and the level of construal (Ledgerwood et al. 2015): high-level construals, i.e. sophisticated plans, detailed, concrete and more distant visions of the future help to broaden individual mental horizons and enhance the self-regulation. A person's behavior can facilitate how well they are able to align their ability to achieve such goals of future plans and present day life. Vice versa making only short-termed plans narrows the mental horizons and traps an individual in here-and-now routines.

Methodology

The purpose of this study was to examine individual's time perspectives when introduced to a new home country, Denmark. This study investigated how changes in identity influenced their integration to the foreign culture, while exploring the meaning behind time perspectives in terms of belonging. In relation to time perspective, future achievement and happiness in reference to Denmark was also discussed through: cultural distance, administration rules, and length of stay in the new country.

To guide this study, 25 biographies were analyzed to determine feelings towards belonging during their stay in Denmark. Within these biographies, 16 countries were represented, and grouped into three categories: U.S. participants, Non E.U participants, and E.U. participants. The data was collected through narrative interviews, which allowed access to complex individual structures and verbalized delicate issues for the participants. Lastly, the data was computed through MAXQDA Coding, Retranscriptions, and Google Analytics.

Hypotheses

In order to structure the data analysis we formulated four hypotheses based on our literature review.

H1.: Migrants coming from turbulent societies with high level of uncertainty and risk will adjust better to life in the host country.
H2.: Migrants coming from a similar cultural context would adjust better to life in the host society.
H3.: People with lower levels of construal have a harder time adjusting to the host society.
H4.: The future concepts of migrants are formed through a high degree of uncertainty about their environment.

Sample

The overall sample consisted of 25 migrants in Denmark, both women and men, aged between 18 and 50, living in Denmark between 6 months to 35 years. The respondents had different qualifications, professions, and career interests. For the purposes of this study we evaluated and contrasted six cases, including: Erik, Cristofer, Eva, Karen, Dorte, and Daniel. These participants were chosen due to their various living situations in Denmark, personal experiences, among other factors such as occupation and gender. We contrasted participants with similar length of stay in Denmark who either opted to further stay in Denmark or decided to leave the country.

Erik, a 26-year-old male from Baalbek, Lebanon. He moved from Lebanon to France when he was 15, graduated from the Pierre et Marie Curie University in Paris and then moved to Denmark two years ago as a result of poor economic conditions in France. He speaks French, Arabic, and English. After a period of unsuccessful job search he decided to leave Denmark.

Eva, a 25-year-old, female from the USA, who lived one year in Denmark to the time of the interview and who opted to marry and stay.

Cristofer, a 38 years old male, described his migration through multiple countries. This included: Greece, UK, Saudi Arabia, Canada, and Denmark. He spent a total 5 years living in Denmark. He found a job, according to his qualifications. He is married and has two children. Cristofer was interviewed twice in his second and third years in Denmark.

Karen, a 40-year-old female, who migrated from Canada to Germany. Karen then moved to Denmark and stayed for 4.5 years, she was working according to her educational qualifications. Later on her family relocated again due to the new job appointment of her husband.

Daniel, a 38-year-old male participant, who migrated from Germany and has currently lived in Denmark for 10.5 years.

Dorte, a 31-year-old female described her past migrations from Algeria, Hungary, Spain, and ending in Denmark. She strongly identifies her heritage and family within Iraqi roots, although she has currently been in Denmark for 19 years.

Results

The findings indicated that multiple participants expressed feelings of alienation, frustration, and discomfort when transitioning to the host country. Increased levels of acculturative stressors were produced through work difficulties, social isolation, and language barriers. Further we describe the results according to our hypotheses.

Adjustment and Uncertainty

We predicted that migrants would exhibit traces of uncertainty in relation to their home country's beliefs, which would influence their decisions and adaptation to the new host country.

Erik, who came from a society with high uncertainty levels didn't adjust to life in Denmark and opted out, to leave the country. On the other hand, Eva, who was coming from a society with lower levels of uncertainty managed to successfully adapt and stayed. Erik hopes for the government to provide necessary changes, as he blames the Danish society for his failure:

> "If there is any change that can be done, it has to come from the government. (…) You can shit on immigrants for taking from the welfare state, but you won't even let them apply their education here. Can someone explain that logic to me? The 'hardships' associated with moving to Denmark all come from Danish mentality of superiority over others. The Danish communities and the Danish government can only solve the problem if they change their attitude, because no policy will be helpful if they don't reevaluate the basic psychology behind it."

Erik shows a widespread strategy for coping with failure and uncertainty, giving up his control and responsibility. He perceives himself as helpless in a disadvantageous situation and he blames the Danish society and government for his adaptation problems. His experiences with high uncertainty and ambiguity, which could help him to adjust in the new society, cannot be recalled. This can be due to the host society not valuing ambiguity coping skills.

Eva, who is American, and feels more American, although she "likes to pretend she is Danish" after less than one year in the country. It might be connected with her European appearance, which makes it easier for her to be accepted by the Danish majority, while Erik is strongly confronted with the problem of looking different and being perceived as a stranger. He claims of being permanently misunderstood and wrongly categorized, which forces him to seek for other contact and social groups in other minority groups. In result, this possibility hindered his ability to find a connection to Danish society.

> "I do not feel Danish et all. In fact, being in Denmark has made me connect more to the Lebanese culture. I had never really seen Lebanon as having a distinct culture, but since I felt so unwelcome here, I could only connect with minorities. It's funny because I'm not even Muslim but I always get shit for being Muslim and get associated with that stereotype, just because of my skin color. I would say I can't really compare feeling more Lebanese or French because in France you can be both French and Lebanese. Here in Copenhagen, either you are Danish or you're not. You can't be both."

In Berry's model logic we see the process of separation, i.e. rejecting the host culture and getting closely identified with the home culture, which happens for Erik as a response to the host country's attitudes (Berry 2006). Erik further refers about the otherness in the Danish society, which he perceives to be very closed and monocultural.

Eva, who is better adapted, stresses the importance of a Danish gatekeeper, a guide, who would lead a stranger through all pitfalls of the adaptation process.

> "I'm currently in the process of extending my visa, and that has been a hassle and a half, because without help, without somebody there to hold your hand as you do it, it's you, it's so hard to understand."

This connection to a gatekeeper seems to be important also for the other respondents in all stages of migrational adaptation. It can be assumed that the information and support a new migrant receives from such a pathfinder might be important in various senses: it minimizes the insecurity and delivers a clear future vision with increased and concrete details (cf. 4.3).

Karen—also coming from a society with a lower level of uncertainty, managed to successfully adapt. However, at the end of her journey she chose to leave the country. Cristofer, who has lived in various countries, can be viewed as a very adaptive personality and manages various levels of uncertainty well. He has a high level of self-confidence which helps him to withstand the frequent relocations, organized by himself, that would usually disorient a person. For both Karen and Cristofer, their migration to Denmark was not the first migration experience, which might have helped them to adjust.

Karen reports that she lives in Denmark in a kind of bubble, for a limited time, not trying to adjust, not investing in her future there and not imagining it in the host country. She follows her husband from country to country due to his job requirements, floating in between the locations.

> "Interviewer: Did you encounter any unforeseen problems related to your immigration status in Denmark?
> Karen: No, quite the opposite. I actually don't quite know how I'm living here legally. But, no, it was very easy.
> Interviewer: Okay.
> Karen: Like, very easy. Much easier than Germany."

Karen finds herself in a very privileged position, where the job of her husband acts as a gatekeeper, taking over all the everyday life issues (like the paperwork associated with the relocation, housing, etc.), so the problems are not that urgent. It can be stated that not (or not only) her experience with insecurity helps her in her adjustment process, but also the support of the company, which minimizes the insecurity. In the following passage we see that the adjustment problems are rather minimal and do not impair essential issues:

> "Interviewer: Okay. And then when, when you first arrived in Denmark, what shocked you the most? Denmark, or I guess Germany, too, as well.
> Karen: Oh Germany as well? Little things. For example, like if you've been, if you've had your groceries bagged for you your entire life and suddenly, I was standing there in the grocery store and the stuff was piling up and I didn't understand why."

Cristofer stresses that he was already prepared for the immigration to Denmark through his previous experiences. However he reports about a personal crisis after two years: he lost the security of the job, safe social network, friends, professional skills and abilities. Some unresolved issues from his childhood came to the surface and caused feelings of frustration and stress. However even during the crisis Cristofer keeps a positive attitude towards his life and feels welcomed in Denmark.

> "… Another thing that I did miss moving to Denmark was having my bearings around work and somehow having a lot of job security there, a very high status in my work, that I enjoyed, that somehow when I came to Denmark, this was taken away. That's what I missed, but on the other hand, it was a spiritual opportunity for growth that now, if I could turn back time, I would do it again somehow, taking away your safety net. And you get caught in your bubble and coming to Denmark let me break that bubble."

After three years he managed to find an alternative structure and a new meaning in his life. Cristofer identifies his children as his gatekeepers to this success.

> "Also I think, having kids in Copenhagen though, is having the responsibility of needing to bring up a family, changes somehow your relationship to the country, because somehow it is not about you, but it is about another generation or so that you're bringing up. So that in itself is a shift, you can say that the underlying reason is psychological, you can say "look family, of why I'm in a particular country, and I've come here by choice, and it wasn't… I didn't come here as a refugee, or as a refugee to look for work. So I think adapting to Denmark somehow hasn't been that difficult because I've come here for a bigger thing than myself, which is my children."

Dorte, who had the highest amount of insecurities and uncertainty in her life, in addition to her appearance as Iraqi, managed to adapt very well to life in Denmark. Her interview shows how her positive personality provides an increased set of resources during her migration, focusing less on the possible uncertainties.

> "For me, I come from a place that has two cultures, from that place grows a new culture. for me-- that's --I've taken things from my own culture, from the Danish

culture which I find really really beautiful and amazing, and I build up what is my culture. For some people I seem more Danish; for other people I will seem more Iraqi because of the way I look and that I cannot control. What they think of me how they define me. I've honestly stopped trying to define myself into what nationality I am because when it comes down to it, it doesn't matter, honestly it really doesn't. I know myself, I know who I am, I know my values, I know my culture and for me my culture is a mix of both Danish and Iraqi; I've taken the best from both worlds, I really have and I like it the way it is, I wouldn't change it."

Dorte manages to balance the ambiguity for herself and tries to fade out detrimental categorizations from her environment. Her ability to deal with the uncertainty seems not to be required in the host society and does not help her in the adaptation process.

Further, like Eva and Karen, Daniel shows that coming from a country with low levels of uncertainty was able to successfully adapt.

"I feel as integrated as it can get. Not being married to a Dane or otherwise linked to the Danish family, I feel accepted. So, I feel respected, I don't feel judged because of my nationality, the country where I come from. Of course there's typical job and there's stereotypes and some of it may be offensive to someone but as I said, I'm not a super emotional person so I'm not very often offended. And sometimes it crosses a line, but then I can just ignore it because it's not sort of directed personally against me, it's just in general, or I say simply say it's just not okay to say that."

Although Daniel does not report any personal problems, he notices barriers other migrants might face. These migrants might be more emotional than him, having a difficult time obtaining professional standing or looking differently from the majority:

"Interviewer: I guess, in terms of immigration status was it fairly easy for you to move here?
Daniel: No, that wasn't a problem et all. Since then it has changed a little bit, of course, obviously. As long as you have your work contract. As long as you're a caucasian, European there are no issues."

In our participants the level of uncertainty attributed to their country of origin did not play a significant role for adaptation to the host country. Generally, the participants who personally did not have stability in their lives were not ready to tolerate it. It was important for them to attain it. Often it was the reason for the migration decision, to reach more stability in the host country. A very important factor, which could help to stabilize the life setting was a significant other, a gatekeeper, who provided some knowledge about the life in the host society, explained conventions and helped to construct a detailed future prospect. Our cases did not fully support our first hypothesis, as we see that it is more the factor of understanding in the host society that plays a role, than the levels of uncertainty in the country of origin.

Adjustment, Otherness and the Similarity of the Cultural Contexts

When looking at the group of new migrants, Erik came from a very different cultural context, while the context of Eva was rather a similar one. At the same time, we have also observed the impact of visibility here: not only the cultural context, but also the visible otherness. It has been seen that belonging to a visible minority makes it harder to both be accepted and to find an anchor:

> "I do not feel like a man here. I feel inferior to Danes, even to those loud high schooler shits on the bus even though I have an education from one of the most competitive schools in Europe. I work at Netto's where I feel I have a lower status than my co-workers just because of my skin color. I am polite, quiet and respectful. I could not have tried harder to be part of the culture. I am doing everything I can to learn the language because I think it is a big social barrier, but I don't think people make an effort to try with me. I am going home to Paris because there people treat you as a human no matter your skin color or social status."

It remains a question if the problems of Erik arose only due to his visible otherness or were based on the differences of cultural context between his home and his host countries. It might also be a self-enhancing dynamic, which forces Erik to oppose himself to the rest of the Danish society.

On the contrary Eva reports only funny details of everyday life, such as *"nobody speaks in public transportation"* or less variety of goods in the grocery store and absence of microwaves. She does not report about big problems with these issues and can get accustomed to them quite quickly. Eva shares this perspective with other respondents from similar cultural contexts (here Karen, Cristofer and Daniel).

Furthermore, Karen notices small everyday issues, which seem both interesting and significant in the greater context. She compares three cultures at once (Canadian, German and Danish) and makes it rather unemotionally: she seems to be impressed but not suppressed by the differences, sometimes she even likes them.

> "But in Denmark you have much less of a personal identity here, and individual identity. You have more of that in Germany. And so, and you have less hierarchy

here in Denmark. And so that also impressed me, actually, that it had suddenly changed. I had been working in the university in Denmark. In Germany you have to say, like, these very formal way of speaking in German to talk to people. And like you can't use your first name, you have to be Mrs. and Mr. and so on. And here suddenly that was all dissolved."

For Cristofer the system of Danish education and health care were initially a challenge, especially in the beginning of his stay, especially concerning his children. Generally he regarded it concerning his youngest son, who was labeled as autistic by a government protocol. Cristofer reported about a massive opposition towards the official school system and about his attempts to exit it:

"So we needed to fight the system a lot. So, these were part of the problems, which caused a lot of stress with the kids, and how do the kids fit in within this because our, now we took the youngest out of the Danish system and put him into a British system. The oldest is continuing into the Danish system. And the Danish system is a lot about following the rules. Maybe I can even say, you know, blindly at times."

In this case the rules played against Cristofer, he opposed himself and fought the system. In his third year of stay in Denmark however, after the school problems of his son were successfully solved, Cristofer was lucky to find himself in a privileged group, taking advantage of the governmental regulations. Hence he supported these rules and blamed those, who criticized them for being not responsible enough:

"I kind of think Denmark is a well-functioning society. Government represents somehow you can say in my head, this big father, this symbol up there that… and somehow this government has responsibility to do something towards me, but I don't see it that way. You get free Danish classes when you come to Denmark, that's good enough, so then you need to make your own way, I'm not expecting the Danish government to give me a job, I am expecting from the Danish government to have good schooling for my children, and a good healthcare system, and that's what I'm expecting from the government, but I would be expecting that from any government I think. Education and health care should be free to every citizen just because of equality, (…) I think these two basic things that the Danish government is doing is more than enough, everything else should be your responsibility. When I hear people complaining that the government is not big enough, it annoys me sometimes. (…) I think we're not entitled to anything, and it's our responsibility to go out and get it."

For Dorte the migrational and ethnic context is more important than the cultural context per se. Her visible otherness causes quite a few problems for her in her daily life in Denmark. Similarly to Erik she states:

> "I never thought my name or looks could be a problem, but um.... it is here in Denmark. It's very -- people don't talk about it. But it is there and we know it."

After many years in the country Dorte had adopted the practice of silence, as she hesitates to label it as racism. However, this unsaid accusation marks her wish and effort to adjust to the society and also the opposition of the society, which keeps her out.

The system and the inflexible rules are a great challenge for Dorte as well, although she successfully lives in Denmark since 19 years, which is the major part of her life.

> "I felt welcome -- felt safe, there was a good introduction into society, but then there was also a lot of -- but then started a lot of rules and regulations what one should do when they're here in the country. Which were really difficult ... (...) There were a lot of clashes between the systems, but otherwise it; a great country."

Dorte makes an effort not to judge or speak about racist claims. In addition to this challenge, she misses the communal empathy and understanding from her social surroundings, as she does not have close friendships or a tight network in the host country. The statement about cultural differences between what she expects and what she gets in her social life remains unsaid in this interview, however they are pointed out and seem to build a barrier between Dorte and her full adjustment in Denmark.

Some differences between basically similar societies also can make the adaptation challenging. Sometimes it causes antagonism of values between migrants and the host society. The barrier however remains rather low, if the societies are similar. As Daniel puts it:

> "In the sense that if you were invited to a birthday party, whatever, someone's home, and there is a bigger group of people that they have invited, it is more or less strictly uncommon to just bring friends. You should really ask about it. And be okay with-- or expect that they're basically going to say no. It's you we have invited, not anyone else."

In this quotation we see that the problem is annoying but rather unimportant: Daniel reports that he is used to being invited to birthday parties, hence to have friends, who value him personally and want to communicate with him.

To sum up we can state that migrants from similar cultural contexts find it generally easier to adjust to a host society. However even migrants from very similar cultures notice differences and are sometimes offended by them. Further,

Constructing Biography—Constructing Identity ... 117

there are some aspects, which influence the perception of migrants from more distant countries and lead to false, stereotypical assumptions. Ethnicity seems to be very important as migrants, who look differently, are othered and treated in a different way, which makes it especially hard for them to adapt.

Future Plans and their Impact on the Adjustment

The importance of the concrete and detailed future plans becomes especially visible in the case of Erik, who finds it difficult to imagine a detailed trajectory towards his goal as he lacks detailed knowledge about it. Although Erik is a very well-educated, bright young man, he comes to Copenhagen in order to find *"a job"* without any concrete plan. He hopes that he will be lucky and does not perceive his behavior as hazardous:

> "When I graduated, I decided to move to Denmark because the economy in Paris is shit even with a degree from such a good school [Pierre and Marie Curie University]. I knew the economy was a lot better in Copenhagen and I would have better luck finding a job. I still haven't found anything good though, which is why I am still working at Netto's. That's why I am moving back to Paris."

According to our hypothesis we see in this case that the goal of Erik remains vague and hence unavailable. He cannot describe what kind of work he is aiming for exactly, what are the appropriate steps towards it. We observe him to stay within his short-termed plans (working at Netto) and to lose his motivation (returning to France).

Just the opposite is the case of Eva: due to her relationship to a Danish man Eva managed to receive a very detailed description of her way into the Danish society. A marriage and the establishment of the family as a goal were defined through a social and gender role, which she adopted for herself and which were similar in her home and host societies. Also her goal to finish her studies was rather clearly defined through the curriculum of her university. All these factors enabled Eva to make long-termed, realistic plans and keep her motivation in pursuing them.

It is important to note that the detailed plans seem to be especially important and critical at the beginning of adjustment. They may turn on the adaptation process in a positive and negative way and then develop a self-fulfilling dynamics. Cristofer, who was interviewed twice, reported about his attempts and a hard way to find a clearly defined goal. The passage below shows his disorientation during the first interview:

> "[Migrants miss] sense of safety around them. And the newspaper when you can buy your newspaper from, your local newspaper, or knowing how to get around and not getting lost, what is safe, what isn't safe. This aspect of not knowing, I think. And I think I've experienced it coming to Copenhagen so somehow I can say I was used to it but coming to Copenhagen and not knowing what the expectations are or what are you going to do. It was different. In London, I had the safety that I knew what I was going to do was I was going to be a student. But on the other hand, yeah, coming to Denmark I didn't have a concrete control in terms of what work I would do. Yeah, I was a psychologist in the UK but I knew I was coming to a country that doesn't speak English as it's primary language so that added a lot of stress somehow to the change. But on the other hand, you have more life experience so you're more secure with the end all. But it was a difficult... somehow I could say coming to Denmark was mixed emotions and the sense of the unknown."

The problems after two years of migrations seem to be merged: it is the language, the unclear professional expectation, the overall feeling of insecurity. Cristofer knows that he can rely on his experience, but seems not to be quite sure, how he can use this resource. Only one year later Cristofer clearly finds his goal. His narrative is a very different one in this second interview, there is a clear structure and a message. He wants to understand better the Danish system and to be able to work in a more efficient way.

> "What I miss in Denmark is my ability to maneuver my profession. It's been difficult for me still to maneuver as well as I was able to do so in the UK. But I think this is a matter of time. I think 5 years down the line from now, things will have changed substantially in terms of my ability, my knowledge of the Danish system, and yeah, that would be the thing that could have been easier. But this is not something that is the fault of Denmark, it's the process of change into a new culture."

In this passage we see a definite timeline, a concrete goal and some clear steps, which should be done towards this goal. In this interview Cristofer also expresses a clear vision not only of his professional life, but also for his family and his personal development. Also remarkable that in the second interview he seems not to recall all the problems about which he reported only one year ago. His perspective changes and the whole narrative shifts. Cristofer can hardly remember that he was disorientated and aimless only a short time before. We see this situative dependency of the narrated past in every other interview in our sample. It seems to be especially difficult to recall the phases without future plans; they are only visible in the moment. The respondents, who stayed longer time in Denmark, did not report such passages, although they must have gone through them as well.

To sum up, we can conclude that the development of concrete and detailed future plans is very important for the integration and the motivation to stay in the host country. A high level of construals allows them to understand the system of their surroundings and to build their plans according to their reality. Respondents however can hardly remember the time they had a low level of construals, they do not realize their deficit, but they just develop and expand their mental horizons during the time.

The Interplay Between Uncertainty and Concept of the Future, Expansion of the Mental Horizon

Conception of the future is very much formed by the interaction of the two factors—the uncertainty of the future situation and one's tolerance for this uncertainty. Previous research shows that uncertainty and dealing with it taps into important dimension of subjective well-being by causing a particular level of distress, it connects to notions of stability or 'being in transit', sense of control or powerlessness, being the author of own biography or it constantly depending on the policies of the host country (El-Shaarawi 2015; Lawrie et al. 2019; Daftary 2020). For the newly arrived into the country it is very important that the paperwork related to the status would be resolved, so that there is certainty, if they can stay, or if they should go? There is a lot of frustration associated with waiting and not knowing the outcome of that process. Therefore there is no concrete image of the future, no defined time horizon, no future plan.

As Eva puts it:

"A future to believe in would be a future that's, like, very clear, not, I mean, you know where you're going, you know your status in the country, you know…you know 'I can stay here forever' or 'I can't,this is when I have to go back,' and then something concrete that you can actually work with… a future to believe in is something that you… you know will happen, you're not just waiting on an answer".

For Erik the conception of the future is very much linked to the country's policies; as a person belonging to a visible minority, this is crucial for him. He expresses a lot of frustration with the "Danish ways", concentrated on the negative present he finds himself in, doesn't see his future unfolding further in Denmark, plans to return to France as described earlier (see Sect. 4.2. in this chapter).

Both Eva and Erik are expressing concerns for their future in relation to the country's policies, as this becomes the 'figure'—will they be able to actually stay in the country and have a fulfilling life?

Cristofer expresses a much more proactive approach to his future—*"Change happens only through action"*; his personal future is very much interlinked with the family, which becomes an anchor and creates an image of a much more concrete future. He is bringing up his kids in Denmark, but it is still important for him to pass on the heritage culture:

> "I think I am bringing up my children with my wife, we have helped them being Greek is important, but it's not something I'm putting down their throats. That's part of me and they will develop a new identity."

Having family allows him and in a certain way also pushes him to plan for a longer time. It opens a new, much longer, intergenerational time horizon for him, e.g. with the topics of developing the new identity of his kids. It also allows Cristofer a much more positive evaluation of the Danish society:

> "I don't stay in my own cocoon, I experience life, so I think these changes have been quite positive. (…) There will always be something better, or better career, and somehow I think it is also up to me and up to the family to say, 'well, this is good enough'. So no, I wouldn't have an expectation of people or a society somehow doing things differently for me. I think Denmark is an open society, it's been good to me, of course there are difficulties, but these difficulties are part of change and part of living."

In this quote Cristofer claims a credit for his good adaptation. In his view it is not only his Caucasian appearance, Danish spouse or established professional environment, which have helped him to adapt, but also his own flexibility, activity and attempts. In his second year Cristofer was rather stressed and confused, still comparing many things to his previous more comfortable and secured stay in London, which was lost due to the relocation to Denmark. In his third year he has settled for the idea that the moving was done due to something bigger than himself, it was for their kids and their future.

> "…the shift occurs somehow, you always feel foreign, because you're not from there, but somehow you feel that you have a sense of ownership where you are at."

In his case we can see how the meaning is created.

For Karen the future is linked with personal development and the ability to view it in a positive way. It is more about finding her own true values and not really related to the country she lives in currently.

> "A future to believe in. For me, it means that I can see myself developing in my future in positive ways, meaningful ways. Intellectually, but also personally with

friends and family and with myself. And I believe that I stay more and more, more and more understand what are my true things in life that make me happy".

For both Cristofer and Karen, many practical issues were resolved, such as sorted out living permits, housing, and having a fulfilling work life, thus creating a more stable ground on which the future can possibly unfold. And similarly, their futures are linked with development, either own or their children's.

Dorte's future horizon is very much embedded in the collective past of the community she identifies herself with, she expresses hope that various political conflicts will be resolved and that:

> "A perfect scenario is to have stability…. the ultimate future is that people live in peace and respect each other and there isn't all this prejudice and stupidity and ignorance and people can live with each other with respect-- and the majority already do-- and the problem is that there are people in the outer lines that don't have an interest in it".

Dorte's future then also encompasses the transgenerational link:

> "when it comes to the future I'm mostly worried about our language. We don't speak it well because of our vocabulary just has not developed. When my children will be born and raised here I will teach them my language but their Danish will be stronger than their mother tongue, and there's not something I can do about that. I accept it."

Similarly to Erik, she belongs to a visible minority and also to a religious minority and therefore might have experienced more challenges compared to Eva, Karen or Daniel. She defines concrete certain steps for the rather distant future, here: bilingual upbringing of her still unborn, presumed children. Based on her experience in Denmark Dorte also defines her goals: what is important for her and what is dispensable, what she is going to pursue and what she is ready to accept.

Daniel just generally expresses a very positive outlook for the future:

> "I'm, in general, more optimistic than pessimistic. And, I'm not saying it's going to be easier. I think it's going to be brighter as a nation. It would be sad, if not".

We see that our respondents do experience various degrees of uncertainty and deal with it in different ways. In some cases uncertainty is so great that a person terminates their stay in the country, as the future becomes impossible. We can of course, argue, that it is not only the uncertainty, but also personal expectations that play a role here.

Future Object

During the interviews participants were asked a question "If your future would be an object—what would it be?". With this question we tap into their inner metaphor of their future situation. We believe that metaphors are not only a linguistic ornamentation, but an expression of the structure of thought, they also structure and influence action and communication processes (Lakoff and Johnson 1980; Ottati et al. 1999).

Metaphors can unfold a personal narrative and contain many beliefs that are otherwise untouched by the regular questions in the interview. The following future objects illustrate the social and cultural origins of the metaphor, they reflect the current situation of an individual (the context) and they will change over time, therefore it is like a photograph, capturing a moment in time.

Erik describes his object as:

> "It would probably be Marcel Duchamp's LHOOQ (Mona Lisa with a Mustache). Like the painting, you take something as prestigious as my education and make it laughable from being a minority in Denmark. The fact that I work at Netto's is a joke. I also always laugh when I hear Danes talking about how great Bansky is. Don't you get it's all a social critique of your culture? I could also see my future as Banksy's 'Follow your Dreams-Cancelled.'"

In these two images we see a lot of disappointment with the environment, reactions of others to him, himself as having been made ridiculous. The obstacles are too big for him and not possible to overcome, therefore it communicates a very negative mood and hopelessness. This can be interpreted as a reaction to the current pressing situation. Erik had many expectations with this move to Denmark that were not fulfilled and he does not see any possibility to make those dreams come true, they 'have been cancelled'. The first image is embedded in his cultural context, Erik indicates that he is coming from France, also showing off his education as well—the image is very specific and one has to be well educated to relate to it. The other image stems from the popular underground culture—indicating also his interest in street art and graffiti, which are also a particular way of communicating contents that otherwise could not be heard. With these images Erik communicates both his high level of education, but also his feelings of marginalization and frustration.

Karen describes her future as a compass:

> "Because I definitely have strong associations with travel and adventure, and also I don't know where I will end up. I know what the plan is for the next year or so, but I have no idea what five, where in five years I will be. Or in 10 years or, you know. All of these things are completely up in the air and I'm actually quite happy about that. But yeah, maybe a compass that sort of just, yeah, open to possibilities".

This is a much more positive metaphor, open to possibilities, adventures ahead, and a guiding compass to follow, however, there is no authorship of own life narrative. Due to her situation Karen cannot decide how her future will unfold, but she is open to various experiences that it might bring. It gives a feeling of safety despite everything being 'up in the air'.

In Cristofer's case we see the change of the metaphor across time. In his first interview, two years of living in Denmark, he has described his future as an olive branch and in his second interview, three years in Denmark, he described it as a barbecue.

Time 1:

> "I'll go back to my Greek roots. You asked me where I'm from. Maybe an olive branch. (…) it represents peace and I think that that's the first step around changing the world is, I think that's a very big step and peace around communities amongst themselves. The tension in the US, you have the, a lot of tension amongst your communities, but on a wider scale. So somehow trying to bridge these divides. And so it would be an olive branch."

Time 2:

> "My family makes fun of me, because we have a joke in the family, so every week I say 'It's barbecue Sunday', so I barbecue, but sometimes I barbecue on Tuesday, and say 'Oh, it's barbecue Tuesday'. It's a joke, my wife sends me pictures of barbecues as a present, and…[unclear]. And the psychology behind it, my parents

had a barbecue restaurant, when I was growing up, so maybe this is a way of me keeping a link with my past, so yeah, a barbecue."

We see the development of his personal situation in these two metaphors. There were various challenges and confusion for him during his second year of living in Denmark and the representation of an olive branch helps him to distance himself from it, he goes all the way back to his ancient Greek roots to find support there. It is a celebration of traditions and a symbol for peace, growth and being alive, but simultaneously it is very distant. It creates a feeling of safety, it is from the distant cultural heritage past and it survived till the present day, therefore gives a feeling of stability that Cristofer is currently seeking for. During his third year of living in Denmark many of the challenges and confusions were resolved for him and his future became more playful and personal—the barbecue reflects more the personal narrative, a family joke, and there is still a vague link to the familial past, but it is much closer than the abstract olive tree branch. Cristofer sees his future as joyful time with this family, enjoying good food and bearing in mind the family tradition.

For Dorte the future is represented by a palm tree:

> "I would like it to be a palm tree. I've always been fascinated with palm trees. For me they represent my country, and also palm trees they are something sacred. They are so beautiful, no matter where you have them and they're very very strong. They can get really small or really tall. They bear fruit, so they give food -- life. Whether it's dates or coconuts, they hydrate or nourish, they also give shade in the hot weather."

Here, similar to Cristofer, we see the traces of the home country, socio-cultural context, but also a safe way to think about the future, more abstract and less personal. The image is communicating strength, growth, giving life and shelter, which can be interpreted in a way that these are qualities she is seeking for at the moment, a stability stemming from the cultural traditional past.

For Daniel the future is something "that gets better with age":

> "I would tend to say that my future-- not me, but my future-- it will probably be something that gets older and, I don't know… Like a wine or whiskey that get better with age. Something that learns and gets better. Like, a machine doesn't sound so bright… No, I'd go with the wine or whiskey."

This image communicates growth, getting better, hope, but also a natural process of transformation over time. The image is not too specific in terms of his culture of origin, it is embedded in a wider western cultural context. Daniel communicates stability of his situation—as both the wine and whiskey have to be left for some time in the same conditions to mature and reach a certain taste. It also absorbs the flavor of the barrel in which the drink is placed. If we extend the metaphor, Daniel feels stable and calm in his environment and is gradually absorbing the context around him to get to a particular state.

In these images we can observe various cultural and historical contexts, reflections of the personal situation and might have a glimpse of how the lives of our respondents will unfold in the future, at least from the standpoint of the expressed metaphor in this particular point of time. It is interesting to see that when the challenges are very big and the respondents do not see any way of overcoming them, the images become very 'loud' and provocative, like Banksy's 'Follow your Dreams-Cancelled.' For other people, traveling back into the distant cultural past, finding their roots there that can support them in the current situation becomes a way of getting the support they need and once tensions are released the image becomes closer to the person, comes from more recent past, originates from the personal narrative and might even become a personal joke.

Discussion

One of the first striking observations of this study was how the patterns around migration are changing. For many of our respondents it was not the first migration in their lives, and the reasons were different from previous decades when the most common motive was to escape the current unbearable situation (due to societal drastic changes or escaping the war zone; or hard political and economic conditions) and to find a new place to build a better life. This is still seen, but is less prevalent. There is now more information available for people to travel and find points of reference, thus creating a possibility to join someone and not to be alone. Such not-a-first-time-movers can foresee some of the difficulties they might encounter in this new relocation and already have some ideas of how to overcome those.

The search for stability, however, hasn't changed in this new type of migration. Stability allows for the future horizon to expand. Uncertainty and instabilities are managed through the previous experiences and personal resources, but also through the help of 'gatekeepers', and we observed that if the gatekeeper is present, or was eventually found, then the adaptation process is much more smooth and is et all possible.

Our single case with two interviews, Cristofer, allowed us to see an important phenomenon: it is difficult to recall the phases without the future plans; they are visible only in the moment. Many pass through such phases, but once they are resolved, they do not stay in the narrative, as per the classical Zeigarnik effect (Zeigarnik 1927). This process of personal change is not always visible for the person themselves. It is rather difficult to notice own inner changes, however, the external ones are much easier to see.

Successful integration depends on many factors, which have been extensively discussed in various literature reviews. However, the notion of time and the subjective time concept is not widely studied. When moving to a country, a person not only leaves behind a physical place but also social roles they used to have. In very general terms, they become an 'ex', an expatriate. All that was normal and common before can transform into something not normal in the new place. Simultaneously we also observe certain alienation tendencies towards the home societies. Especially among the emigrants from the USA we often observed the strict opposition to the social system or the political development. The longer these emigrants stayed outside of their home country the more harsh criticism they expressed. This might be explained through the adaptation to the host society but also through the availability and selection of the respondents: those individuals who oppose themselves to their home society might tend to stay longer in the host country. This question cannot be answered conclusively in this paper, so future research is needed.

Erik's case resembles the study done in China on rural–urban migration, when high aspirations about the future conditions create frustration with the current situation as the desired future is unattainable (Knight and Gunatilaka 2010). Upon arrival, the first question is "can I be here?" and if it is resolved and basic needs are settled, then the future starts to expand—we observe more narration about development, be it personal or transgenerational. And in some cases the future concept is very much linked with the collective past and a particular cultural identity.

Immigration raises a lot of basic existential questions, such as: "Can I live in this environment?", "Can I stay here as I am, or do I have to change?", "Those changes proposed by the environment, are they possible for me to do and do I agree to modify myself in such a way?", "Can I belong to this environment?" or "This environment creates an 'other' out of me?". It is a constant interaction between the dialogue of the individual and their environment. All individuals have some past that they bring with them; therefore the process of integration also includes the process of managing those past identities. Additionally, sometimes when leaving a country, negative feelings can be associated with a loss. It is an important question, if a person allows herself to grieve for that loss and if he or she really leaves one place and arrives at a new place.

We can then say that successful integration includes the following processes. The process of disengagement and disidentification can be very painful, and in some cases, doesn't ever fully get resolved. Following disengagement, the process of incorporating past history of oneself into the current identity can be linked to disidentification. This involves looking into one's own past and possibly creating a new meaning under the present conditions and potentially building a projection of a future image. However, the research shows that under stress and uncertainty (Muzdybaev 2000; Misko and Tarabrina 2004) the totality of the personal time perspective breaks down, there is no more coherent connection between ones own past, present, and future. Very often it manifests itself as a foreshortened future as it is impossible to plan long-term. It may be experienced as anticipation that normal life events won't occur (e.g., access to education, ability to have a significant and committed relationship, good opportunities for work, etc.) and if the situation doesn't change for a long time, then it can lead to losing a sense of hope. Emotional and cognitive deformations can take place in the concept of the future. The past may become the most dominant temporal zone as it gives support and foundation for the own identity. Such a disintegrated time perspective has profound impact on one's well-being, physical and psychological health (Sircova and Mitina 2008; Boniwell et al. 2010; Åström et al. 2014, 2018, Marczak et al. 2020). This can lead to higher levels of anxiety, depression, suicidality, aggression, substance abuse, personal neglect, gambling, and other negative issues (Stolarski et al. 2015). The more one's identity is threatened under these new circumstances, the greater the temporal disintegration will be, especially if traumatic events also occurred.

Therefore, the consistency of the personal narrative is crucial for one's well-being during the process of acculturation. The more consistent individuals are in their evaluation of the personal past, present, and future, the more balanced past, present, and future will become (Kazakina 1999). Then there is a possibility for a coherent life story in which different parts come together in a meaningful way, and therefore, create the possibility for the future to unfold. If a person sees an opportunity to resolve the tension between their past, present, and future in hopes of integrating their past hangover identity into their current identity, then the processes of adjustment and adaptation to the new cultural setting commence. It, of course, involves the process of creating a new meaning.

Future time concept becomes possible when an individual is able to cope with uncertainty, as the future encompasses hope, happiness, and personal well-being. This requires some stability, control, and possibility of extension. In our study we observed if the pressure of the current situation is unbearable, the past often cannot be viewed as a resource but is filled with regrets (or becomes sort of an alibi as in Erik's case). If in the current situation a person is successful, they may feel more like the author of their own life and then their past becomes a resource, a place where they learned lessons and obtained skills, which can be used now and in the future.

Our study shows the process of how people resolve those existential questions. Our initial questions were: Do they find new meanings and new support? What becomes their anchor? What are the tensions between their own aspirations and current conditions? What choices do people make under these circumstances? In our study we see that children can serve as an anchor, a spouse, family traditions or a stable job situation.

A certain amount of change is needed in order to create stability. Similarly to the Red Queen's statement to Alice: "Now, here, you see, it takes all the running you can do, to keep in the same place. If you want to get somewhere else, you must run at least twice as fast as that!" Does a person have enough resources to make that change and if such a change is et all possible? There was a lot of frustration voiced with being visibly different from Danish majority—this change seems not to be possible. The physical look in this environment quite automatically creates 'the other'. How is a person expected to manage this? As shown, Dorte is more embedded in the Danish context, but also encounters a feeling of otherness. She deals with it differently than Erik, but they are both disappointed and express frustration. Lastly, Erik voices hostility, as he assumes that Danes and their government are fully responsible for his misfortunes. The result is that he decides to give up his migration project and to finally leave Denmark.

Our study illustrates various aspects of the process of psychological adjustment during acculturation. We have observed their time-collage, how various aspects of their past interact with the present situation and create the possible futures. The process of adjusting one's self concept often includes the following:

1. incorporating the hangover identity, various ex-statuses, and personal expectations that originate from there (e.g. Cristofer's ex-Londoner status and ex-Greek roots; Erik's sophisticated educational background that can't find application in the new place);
2. learning to deal with social reactions to their ex-status, including stereotypes associated with the labeling process (Erik being labeled as Muslim, and unexpectedly becoming a Lebanese due to the pressure from others; Dorte staying a stranger even after growing up in the country and having no other homeland);

3. often becoming a member of a minority group due to the otherness (as in case of visible minority), but also in case of invisible minority, just the fact that one's native tongue is not Danish, already puts a person in a minority group;
4. shifting networks of friends as seen in the cases of Cristofer and Daniel;
5. relating to members who are still part of the former group (e.g. Dorte and her identification as Christian Iraqi);
6. learning a new language (including the language of time and social conventions);
7. learning new interpersonal and social behaviors (Eva, Karen, Cristofer, Daniel)
8. becoming accustomed to new norms and values.

It is a very complex process and therefore there is no single solution to it. Each person has their own unique journey filled with their unique challenges and their personal choices. Therefore it is always an interaction of three components: one's cultural background (collective past), one's personality (with various weights in the personal past, present and future) and the context of the present situation.

Limitations and Future Research

Although this research signifies a pattern among migrant's emotions during their assimilation to a new host country, we encountered multiple limitations during the study. To begin, we focused on six participants from our population set. Evaluating six individuals does not gauge a large variety of answers or analysis. For future studies, a larger sample of participants would benefit the results and discussion for a study such as this. Another limitation of our participant pool was the lack of age differences. Many of our participants were middle-aged adults, which left our interviewees unable to gauge the age differences people might experience when assimilating to a new culture.

The study review presented above outlines a common trend seen in migrants today. Feelings of isolation, confusion, and frustration cause obstacles for migrants during their acculturation process. In result, their transition into the new culture can be extremely difficult and psychologically tasking, leaving some of them feeling hopeless. Our project evaluates the acculturation strategies and difficulties people face today, discussing how as a society, the human race can do better. Future policy oriented research should focus on such factors to create a more bearable migration from home country to host country, creating a safe place for everyone. Furthermore, future research could aim to apply longitudinal design, as in our case we had a possibility to interview one person twice and important insights were revealed in this process.

We hope that this particular study can provide insight and discussion points for migrants moving to a new country, or better yet, provide resources for host country individuals to be an ally for those migrating. Creating a smooth transition is key when migrating to a new destination, and many organizations are making this their purpose (cf. McAuliffe and Ruhs 2017).

References

Åström, E., Wiberg, B., Sircova, A., Wiberg, M. & Carelli, M. G. (2014). Insights into features of anxiety through multiple aspects of psychological time. *Journal of Integrative Psychology and Therapeutics, 2.*

Åström, E., Seif, A., Wiberg, B. & Carelli, M. G. (2018). Getting "stuck" in the future or the past: relationships between dimensions of time perspective, executive functions, and repetitive negative thinking in anxiety. *Psychopathology, 51*(6), p. 362-370.

Berry, J. (2006). Acculturative stress. In P. Wong & L. Wong, *Handbook of multicultural perspectives on stress and coping. International and Cultural Psychology* (p. 287–298). Boston: Springer.

Berry, J. & Sabatier, C. (2011). Variations in the assessment of acculturation attitudes: Their relationships with psychological wellbeing. *International Journal of Intercultural Relations, 35*, p. 658-669.

Bochner, S. (2003). Culture Shock Due to Contact with Unfamiliar Cultures. *Online Readings in Psychology and Culture, 8*(1), Artikel 7.

Boniwell, I., Osin, E., Linley, A. & Ivanchenko, G. V. (2010). A question of balance: Time perspective and well-being in British and Russian samples. *The Journal of Positive Psychology, 5*(1), p. 24-40.

Daftary, A. M. (2020). Living with Uncertainty: Perceptions of Well-being Among Latinx Young Adults in Immigrant Family Systems. *Family Relations, 69*(1), p. 51-62.

Ebaugh, H. (1988). *Becoming an Ex: The process of role exit.* Chicago: University of Chicago Press.

Elias, N. & Scotson, J. L. (1994). *The Established and the Outsiders.* London: Sage.

El-Shaarawi, N. (2015). Living an uncertain future: Temporality, uncertainty, and well-being among Iraqi refugees in Egypt. *Social Analysis, 59*(1), p. 38-56.

Frankl, V. E. (1985). *Mas's search for meaning.* New York: Simon and Schuster.

Habermas, T. & Bluck, S. (2000). Getting a life: the emergence of the life story in adolescence. *Psychological Bulletin, 126*(5), p. 748-769.

Heine, S. (2012). Living in multicultural worlds. In S. Heine, *Cultural Psychology* (S. 383-422). New York: W.W. Norton and Company.

Hermans, H. (2001). The dialogical self: Toward a theory of personal and cultural positioning. *Culture & Psychology, 7*, p. 243-281.

Ingelhart, R., Haerpfer, C., Moreno, A., Welzel, C., & Kizilova, K. E. (2014). *World Values Survey: Round Six-Country-Pooled Datafile 2010-2014.* Madrid: JD Systems Institute.

Kazakina, E. (1999). *Time perspective of older adults: Relationships to attachment style, psychological well-being and psychological distress.* Doctoral dissertation: ProQuest Information & Learning.

Knight, J. & Gunatilaka, R. (2010). Great expectations? The subjective well-being of rural-urban migrants in China. *World development, 38*(1), p. 113-124.

Lakoff, G. & Johnson, M. (1980). *Metaphors we live by.* Chicago: University of Chicago Press.

Lawrie, S. I., Eom, K., Moza, D., Gavreliuc, A. & Kim, H. S. (2019). Cultural Variability in the Association Between Age and Well-Being: The Role of Uncertainty Avoidance. *Psychological Science*, S. DOI: https://doi.org/10.1177/0956797619887348.

Ledgerwood, A., Trope, Y. & Liberman, N. (2015). Construal level theory and regulatory scope. In R. Scott, S. Kosslyn, & M. Buchman, *Emerging Trends in the Social and Behavioral Sciences.* New York: John Wiley and Sons.

Marczak, M., Sorokowski, P. & Sobol-Kwapińska, M. (2020, March 30). Balanced Time Perspective as a Facilitator of Immigrants' Psychological Adaptation: A Study among Ukrainian Immigrants in Poland. https://doi.org/10.31234/osf.io/ybprf

Markus, H. & Nurius, P. (1986). Possible Selves. *American Psychologist, 41*(9), p. 954-969.

Märtsin, M. & Mahmoud, H. W. (2012). Never "at-home"?: Migrants between societies. In J. Valsiner, *Oxford library of psychology. The Oxford handbook of culture and psychology* (p. 730–745). New York, NY, US: Oxford University Press.

McAdams, D.P. (2001). The psychology of life stories. *Review of General Psychology, 5*(2), p. 100-122. DOI: https://doi.org/10.1037/1089-2680.5.2.10010.1037/1089-2680.5.2.100

McAuliffe, M., & Ruhs, M. (2017). World migration report 2018. Geneva: International Organization for Migration.

Misko, E. A. & Tarabrina, N. V. (2004). Peculiarities of life perspective in veterans of Afghanistan war and liquidators of accident at Chernobyl atomic power station. *PSIKHOLOGICHESKII ZHURNAL, 25*(3), p. 44-52.

Muzdybaev, K. (2000). Perezhivanie vremeni v period krizisov [The experience of time in period of crises]. *Psihologicheskij zhurnal, 4*, p. 5-21.

Ottati, V., Rhoads, S. & Graesser, A. (1999). The Effect of Metaphor on Processing Style in an Persuasion Task: A Motivational Resonance Model. *Journal of Personality and Social Psychology, 77*(4), p. 688-697.

OECD. (2017). Chapter 3: Migrants' well-being: Moving to a better life? In OECD, *How's Life? 2017-Measuring Well-being.* Paris: OECD Publishing.

Schilling, E. (2005). *Die Zukunft der Zeit: Vergleich von Zeitvorstellungen in Russland und Deutschland im Zeichen der Globalisierung.* Aachen: Shaker.

Schilling, E. (2008). Future Concepts in Russia and Germany. Different approaches to planning in the global society. *21st Century Society, 3*(2), p. 131–142.

Schilling, E. (2018). Between Statistical Odds and Future Dreams: Biographical Drafts of Young Migrants' Futures. *Migration Studies*, DOI: https://doi.org/10.1093/migration/mny028.

Schütz, A. (1944). The stranger: an essay in social psychology. *American Journal of Sociology, 49*(6), p. 499-507.

Schütze, F. (1992). Pressure and Guilt: War Experiences of Soldier and their Biographical Implications. Part 1 and 2. *International Sociology, 7*(2), p. 187–208 and 7(3), p. 347–367.

Sircova, A. (2017). Acculturation. *Public lecture.* Copenhagen.

Sircova, A., van de Vijver, F., Osin, E., Milfont, T. L., Fieulaine, N., Kislali-Erginbilgic, A. et al. (2015). Time Perspective Profiles of Cultures. In M. Stolarski, N. Fieulaine, & W. van Beek, *Time Perspective Theory; Review, Research and Application* (p. 169-187). Cham, Heidelberg, New York, Dordrecht, London: Springer.

Smith, R. & Khawaja, N. (2011). A review of acculturation experiences of international students. *International Journal of Intercultural Relations, 35*(1), p. 699-713.

Stolarski, M., Fieulaine, N. & van Beek, W. (2015). *Time perspective theory; Review, research, and application.* . Cham: Springer International.

Trope, Y. & Liberman, N. (2010). Construal level theory of psychological distance. *Psychological Review, 117*, p. 440-463.

van Schalkwyk, G. J. (2010). Collage life story elicitation technique: a representational technique for scaffolding aoutobiographical memories. *The Qualitative Report, 15*(3), p. 675-695.

Ward, C., Bochner, S. & Furnham, A. (2001). *The psychology of culture shock.* Hove, UK: Routledge.

Zeigarnik, B. (1927). Das Behalten erledigter und unerledigter Handlungen. *Psychologische Forschungen, 9*, p. 1-85.

Chrononormativität im Lebenslauf – Die sozialen Praktiken der Herstellung und De/Stabilisierung temporaler Normalität in der Lebensphase Alter

Anna Wanka

Abstract

In contemporary societies, chronological age is widely used as a temporal basis for organising social processes. The standardised sequence of life stages that constitute our life courses, and their close ties to chronological age, are constituted and stabilised by social institutions, like work, family, or retirement, and their respective policies and organisations. Elizabeth Freeman (2010). Time Binds: Queer Temporalities, Queer Histories(Perverse Modernities). Durham [NC]: Duke University Press.) describes this normative temporal regime that orchestrates the life course as chrononormativity. This paper follows the question how chronormativity is constituted and (de-) stabilized in social practices, and why no fundamental resistance against chronormative temporal regimes (yet) exists.

From a practice-theoretical perspective, chronormativity can be understood as a processual practical accomplishment that is continuously reproduced through the iterative performance of its constitutive practices, and these practices take place at multiple sites and involve a variety of elements. Based on a longitudinal qualitative study following 30 adults through the transition from work to retirement, the paper discusses three dimensions of this practical accomplishment: first, the historical emergence of life stages and their relations; second, the wide array of elements that contribute to the

---

A. Wanka (✉)
Goethe Universität Frankfurt am Main, Frankfurt am Main, Deutschland
E-Mail: wanka@em.uni-frankfurt.de

© Springer Fachmedien Wiesbaden GmbH, ein Teil von Springer Nature 2020
E. Schilling und M. O'Neill (Hrsg.), *Frontiers in Time*
Research – Einführung in die interdisziplinäre Zeitforschung,
https://doi.org/10.1007/978-3-658-31252-7_7

constitution and (de-)stabilisation of chronormativity; and third, the diversity of sites its constitutive practices take place at. Consequently, to destabilise chonormativity and hence contribute to a "queering" of age, this complexity of actors, elements, and sites – from the workplace to the body – must be taken into account.

Zusammenfassung

Das kalendarische Alter stellt eine zentrale Basis für die Organisation gesellschaftlicher Prozesse dar. Konstituiert und abgesichert wird der altersgradierte Lebenslauf durch implizite und explizite Normen und Wissensordnungen, die sich in sozialen Institutionen wie Arbeit, Familie oder Rente, sowie den zugehörigen Organisationen und gesetzlichen Bestimmungen, materialisieren. Elizabeth Freeman (2010). Time Binds: Queer Temporalities, Queer Histories(Perverse Modernities). Durham [NC]: Duke University Press.) beschreibt dieses normative Zeitregime, das den Lebenslauf orchestriert, als Chrononormativität. Der vorliegende Beitrag geht dabei der Frage nach, wie Chrononormativität in sozialen Praktiken hergestellt und (de-)stabilisiert wird, und wieso (noch) keine grundsätzliche Revolte gegen das chrononormative Zeitregime stattfindet.

Praxistheoretisch kann Chrononormativität als ein prozesshaftes Vollzugsgeschehen verstanden werden, das, an mehreren Schauplätzen und unter Beteiligung verschiedener Elemente, durch kontinuierliche Wiederholung immer wieder aufs Neue hergestellt und gestaltet wird. Basierend auf einer qualitativen Längsschnittstudie, die 30 Erwachsene im Übergang von der Erwerbs- in die Nacherwerbsphase begleitet, diskutiert der Beitrag drei Dimensionen dieses Vollzugsgeschehens: erstens, die historische Emergenz von Lebensphasen und ihrer Zusammenhänge; zweitens, die Fülle von Elementen, die an der Herstellung und (De-)Stabilisierung von Chrononormativität beteiligt sind; und drittens, die verschiedenen Schauplätze, an denen sich die konstituierenden Praktiken vollziehen. Um Chrononormativität zu destabilisieren, so die Schlussfolgerung, muss diese Komplexität an verschiedensten Akteur*innen, Elementen und Schauplätzen, an denen sie vollzogen wird – vom Arbeitsplatz bis in den Körper – berücksichtigt werden.

Schlüsselwörter

Alter · Chrononormativität · Norma-/temporalität · Praxistheorien · Übergang in die Nacherwerbsphase · Queering Time

Einleitung

In heutigen westlichen Gesellschaftlichen stellt das kalendarische Alter eine zentrale Basis für die Organisation und Regulierung gesellschaftlicher Prozesse dar. Martin Kohli (1985; 2007) nennt die standardisierte und primär an das chronologische Alter gebundene Abfolge von Lebensphasen – und damit den Lebenslauf – sogar das primäre Sozialisationsprogramm unserer Zeit. Konstruiert und abgesichert wird diese Sequenzierung, so die aktuelle Lebenslaufforschung, von impliziten und expliziten Normen und Wissensordnungen, die sich in sozialen Institutionen wie Arbeit, Familie, oder Rente, sowie den zugehörigen Organisationen und gesetzlichen Bestimmungen, materialisieren. Elizabeth Freeman (2010) beschreibt dieses normative Zeitregime, das den Lebenslauf orchestriert, als Chrononormativität.

Chrononormativität bezeichnet insbesondere (aber nicht ausschließlich) Vorstellungen über die „richtige" Zeit für spezifische Lebensphasen und –übergänge, etwa um zu beginnen, in die Schule zu gehen, eine Familie zu gründen, oder in Rente zu gehen. Diese Vorstellungen manifestieren und stabilisieren sich über rechtliche Regelungen und exekutive Organisation, etwa die an das Lebensalter gekoppelte Schulpflicht und das entsprechende Schulsystem, das Recht, zu heiraten, oder das Renteneintrittsalter. Die eigene Positionsbestimmung in diesem Lebenslauf ermöglicht es, (Lebens-)Ereignissen biographische Bedeutungen zuzuschreiben, Orientierung zu finden, und Identitäten zu konstruieren. Trotz zunehmender De-Standardisierung verlieren solche Verständnisse eines „richtigen Zeitpunkts" im Lebenslauf kaum an individueller und gesellschaftlicher Bedeutsamkeit (vgl. Kohli 2007; Biesta et al. 2010).

Doch wie entsteht und wie besteht Chrononormativität – wie wird sie hergestellt und stabilisiert? Wieso findet keine grundsätzliche Revolte gegen das chrononormative Zeitregime statt? Diesen Fragen geht der vorliegende Beitrag aus einer praxistheoretischen Perspektive nach. Praxistheoretisch können „Zeit" und ihre multidimensionalen Erscheinungsformen als zentraler konstitutiver Bestandteil sozialer Praktiken verstanden werden (Blue 2017). Diese Praktiken verbinden und stabilisieren sich durch ihre Wiederholung und Wiederholbarkeit, beziehungsweise – um mit Derrida (1982) zu sprechen – ihre Iterabilität[1].

---

[1]Iterabilität bezeichnet nach Derrida Wiederholung mit Andersartigkeit – so wird in jeder neuen Performanz einer sozialen Praxis eine bereits bestehende Praxis "zitiert", welche wiederum nur durch die andauernde erneute Performanz bestehen bleibt. Somit wird das Konzept der Wiederholung (etwas bereits Dagewesenen) mit dem Konzept des Neuen und Andersartigen (in der aktuellen Performanz) verbunden.

Der vorliegende Beitrag erkundet die Herstellung und (De-)Stabilisierung des chrononormativen Lebenslaufs am Beispiel des Übergangs von der Erwerbs- in die Nacherwerbsphase. Neben existierender Literatur werden dabei Ausschnitte aus dem Habilitationsprojekt „The Social Practices of Transiting into Retirement and the Distribution of Transitional Risks" (2017–2021) diskutiert. Das Projekt ist Teil des DFG-finanzierten, interdisziplinären Graduiertenkollegs „Doing Transitions", das an der Goethe Universität Frankfurt am Main und der Universität Tübingen angesiedelt ist. Es verbindet in einem Mixed-Methods Design quantitative Zeitverwendungsdaten mit einer qualitativen Längsschnittstudie, die 30 ältere Erwachsene bei ihrem Übergang in die Rente begleitet[2].

Der Beitrag ist in drei Teile gegliedert: Zuerst wird dargelegt, wie die temporale Organisation des Lebenslaufs aus einem praxistheoretischen Verständnis erfasst werden kann, und dabei das Konzept der Chrononormativität praxistheoretisch ausbuchstabiert. Im Anschluss wird dieser Zugang am Beispiel des Übergangs in die Nacherwerbsphase mittels empirischer Daten illustriert. Im dritten und letzten Teil werden die Ergebnisse diskutiert.

Soziale Praktiken und die Temporale Organisation des Lebenslaufs

Das diesem Beitrag zugrunde liegende Verständnis von Zeit und Zeitlichkeit basiert auf einer praxistheoretischen Ontologie. Zeit wird dabei weder als ein externes (Natur-)Phänomen, das menschliches Verhalten reguliert, noch als eine subjektive Wahrnehmung, die aus bestimmten Lebensumständen und Arten der Lebensführung resultiert, konzipiert. Stattdessen wird Zeit als konstitutiver Bestandteil sozialer Praktiken verstanden – „time is practice" (Blue 2017: S. 23).

Doch was sind diese sozialen Praktiken? Der Sozialphilosoph Ted Schatzki (1996) identifiziert soziale Praktiken als jene Einheit des Sozialen, anhand derer wir am meisten über die soziale Welt erfahren können. Soziale Praktiken werden dabei

---

[2]Zu drei Erhebungszeitpunkten (2017/18, 2018/19, und 2019/20) wurden bzw. werden mit 30 Erwachsenen zwischen 56 und 71 Jahren jeweils episodische Interviews durchgeführt und diese gebeten, für jeweils eine Woche ein Foto- und Aktivitätentagebuch zu führen. Interviews werden vollständig transkribiert und mittels Analysesoftware MAXQDA 12 codiert. Der vorliegende Beitrag bezieht sich auf Material der ersten zwei Erhebungswellen von September 2017 bis April 2018 (Welle 1) sowie Dezember 2018 bis Mai 2019 (Welle 2).

definiert als „von einem praktischen ‚Verstehen' zusammengehaltene Verhaltensroutinen" (Reckwitz 2003, S. 289), die sowohl Sprechakte („sayings") als auch Vollzugsakte ohne Sprache („doings") umfassen. Sie folgen einer impliziten Logik, die statt auf theoretischen und expliziten Wissensbeständen auf praktischem Können beruht, das häufig routiniert, habitualisiert und inkorporiert ist. Entsprechend werden als „Trägerinstanzen" von Praktiken verschiedene menschliche und nichtmenschliche Elemente definiert, z. B. „mit inkorporierte(m) Wissen ausgestattet(e) Körper" oder „Artefakte, in denen sich […] Praktiken über Zeit und Raum hinweg verankern lassen" (ebd., S. 291), aber auch diskursive Bedeutungselemente (vgl. Shove et al. 2012). Soziale Praktiken haben also immer mehrere unterschiedliche Partizipand*innen. Sie sind somit multi-agentiale Vollzugsgeschehen.

Wenn Zeit nun als Praxis zu verstehen ist, dann bestehen alle temporalen Phänomene und Erscheinungsformen von Zeitlichkeit (z. B. Dauer, Geschwindigkeit) aus sozialen Praktiken. Der Lebenslauf als Abfolge von Lebensphasen ist damit ebenso als Konstellation sozialer Praktiken zu verstehen wie eine Stunde, ein Tag, oder ein Jahr. Ganz grundsätzlich beruhen Praxistheorien auf einer „flachen Ontologie", was impliziert, dass aus ihrer Perspektive nichts außerhalb von Praktiken existiert (Schatzki 2016). Das heißt, alle Begriffe, die wir aus den Sozialwissenschaften kennen – soziale Kategorien wie Alter und Geschlecht, soziale Gefüge wie Institutionen oder „unsichtbare" Phänomene wie Diskurse, Macht, oder eben Zeit – bestehen aus Praktiken. Oder wie Nicolini (2016: S. 100) es formuliert: „when it comes to the social, it is practices all the way down". Das bedeutet auch, dass soziale Phänomene zwar als semantische Einheiten existieren können, analytisch jedoch jeweils in soziale Praktiken – die ihrerseits immer inhärent temporal sind – auflösbar sind.

Alles besteht in dieser Ontologie also aus Praktiken, auch größere soziale Phänomene. Ermöglicht wird diese Denkfigur dadurch, dass Praktiken immer in ein Netz anderer Praktiken eingebettet sind – Schatzki nennt dieses den „nexus of doings and sayings" (1996). Mehrere miteinander verbundene Praktiken formen „Bündel" (lose und einfache Verbindungen, z. B. Kaffee trinken und rauchen) oder „Komplexe" (festere, komplexere Verbindungen, z. B. Autofahren), können sich in sozialen Feldern (z. B. Finanzmärkten) oder Lebensstilen (z. B. Jugendkulturen) organisieren, oder zu Institutionen (z. B. Arbeit) verdichten (vgl. Schatzki 2017; Shove et al. 2012; Reckwitz 2003). Soziale Phänomene als eine Verbindung verschiedener sozialer Praktiken finden damit an verschiedenen „Schauplätzen" (sites) statt, sie sind somit nicht nur multi-agential, sondern auch „multi-sited".

Praxistheoretiker*innen haben bisher verschiedene soziale Phänomene in unterschiedlichen „Größenordnungen" auf ihre temporale Performanz hin untersucht – vom Wäschewaschen bis hin zur wissenschaftlichen Arbeitsorganisation oder den Temporalitäten innerhalb des Finanzsektors (vgl. Laube 2016; Spurling 2015; Southerton 2006). In Analogie dazu können auch Lebensphasen, wie Kindheit und Alter, und ihre sequentielle Abfolge im Lebenslauf, als komplexe Praxiskonstellationen gefasst werden, die ihrerseits wiederum in Feldern, Lebensstilen, Institutionen, Komplexen und Bündeln organisiert sind. Die Lebensphase „Alter" wird aus einer solchen Perspektive also von einer Vielzahl sozialer Praktiken hergestellt, die typischerweise als „alt" erkannt werden – dazu gehören etwa altersstereotype Praktiken wie Bingo spielen, Nordic Walking oder Kreuzfahrten machen, aber auch eine bestimmte Art, sich zu kleiden („Rentnerbeige") oder die Geschwindigkeit, in der Praktiken durchgeführt werden (vgl. Schröter 2012). Wie Alter „getan" wird unterscheidet sich dabei nicht nur inter-generational – also in Abgrenzung von anderen Lebensphasen – sondern auch intra-generational zwischen sozialen Schichten, Lebensstilen und Milieus (vgl. Amrhein 2008).

Bezugnehmend auf Eviatar Zerubavels (1987) Konzept temporaler „Codes" bezeichnet Clary Krekula (2010) solche Praktiken, die eine bestimmte Alters- oder Lebensphase erkennbar machen und sie somit mit-konstituieren, als „age-coded". Alterskodierung bezeichnet "practices of distinction that are based on and preserve representations of actions, phenomena, and characteristics as associated with and applicable to demarcated ages" (S. 7). Der Lebenslauf kann somit aus praxistheoretischer Perspektive als großflächige Konstellation alterskodierter Praktiken verstanden werden.

Verstehen wir den Lebenslauf als eine solche Praxiskonstellation, so stellt sich die Frage, was diese Praktiken in der „richtigen" zeitlichen Abfolge zusammenhält. Warum gehen wir nicht direkt aus der Kindheit in die Lebensphase Alter über? Wie werden Lebensphasen in ihrer Ausgestaltung und Reihenfolge, also in ihrer Koppelung an ein bestimmtes chronologisches Alter, hergestellt? Wie stabilisieren sie sich? Und (wie) werden sie infrage gestellt?

In diesem Beitrag soll sich diesen Fragen mithilfe des von Elizabeth Freeman (2010) formulierten Konzepts der Chrononormativität angenähert werden. Chrononormativität wurde ursprünglich in der queer theory formuliert und bezeichnet "interlocking temporal schemes necessary for genealogies of descent and for the mundane workings of everyday life" (Freeman 2010, S. xxii), die insbesondere (aber nicht ausschließlich) Vorstellungen über die „richtige" Zeit für spezifische Lebensphasen und –übergänge beinhalten (Riach et al. 2014). Chrononormativität bezeichnet also ein zeitliches Organisationsprinzip, das soziale Praktiken in einer spezifischen temporalen Ordnung hält und somit den Lebenslauf als soziale Institution herstellt und absichert.

Praxistheoretisch betrachtet besteht Chrononormativität aber auch selber aus sozialen Praktiken – die Ordnung, die sie herstellt, muss also immer wieder praktisch vollzogen werden. Diese Praktiken involvieren verschiedene Elemente und finden an verschiedenen Schauplätzen statt, sind also multi-agential und multi-sited: in jenen politischen und verwaltenden Institutionen, die gesetzliche Regelungen formulieren und beschließen, in Wirtschaftsbereichen und Firmen, Familien und sozialen Netzwerken, in Konsumangeboten, Literatur, Medien, und so weiter. Chrononormativität wird somit auch im ganz alltäglichen Leben hergestellt und vollzogen. Dem nachgehend haben Clary Krekula und Kolleg*innen (2017) das Konzept der Chrononormativität von der Ebene des Lebenslaufs auf die Alltagsebene „übersetzt". Mit dem Begriff „Norma-/Temporalität" bezeichnen sie die Herstellung und Stabilisierung von temporaler Normalität im Alltag. Es besteht demnach nicht nur eine „richtige Zeit", um in Rente zu gehen, sondern auch eine „richtige Zeit", um morgens aufzustehen, um Mittag zu essen, oder um aus der Arbeit zu gehen.

Die Praktiken, die diese temporale Normalität im Alltag aufrechterhalten, sind dabei ebenfalls alters- bzw. lebensphasen-kodiert: Morgens lange zu schlafen wird eher als eine Jugendpraxis verstanden, ein frühes Zubettgehen der Kindheit oder dem höheren Alter zugeordnet; eine hohe Geschwindigkeit bei der Durchführung von Alltagspraktiken ist ebenfalls eher mit Jugend, Langsamkeit dagegen eher mit höherem Alter assoziiert, etc. Somit vollziehen sich Alltagspraktiken keinesfalls unabhängig von jenen Praktiken, die temporale Normalität im Lebenslauf konstituieren. Lebenslaufinstitutionen wie die Schule, die Arbeit oder die Familie bestimmen in großem Maße mit, wie ein „normaler" Alltag in einer spezifischen Lebensphase ausgestaltet ist.

Lebenslaufinstitutionen fungieren damit als „Zeitgeber" für die Alltagsgestaltung. Mit diesem Begriff bezeichnen Parkes und Thrift (1979) jene Einheiten, die anderen Praktiken bestimmte Formen temporaler Organisation (z. B. Zeitpunkt, Geschwindigkeit, Dauer) vorgeben können. Zeitgeber für das Nachtleben können etwa die Öffnungszeiten von Lokalen sein, Zeitgeber für Essenspraktiken die Arbeits- und Pausenzeiten in einem Unternehmen, etc. Entsprechend gehen Übergänge im Lebenslauf mit einer Restrukturierung des Alltags einher – Norma-/Temporalität verändert sich. Wenn Erwachsene etwa in Rente gehen, so verlieren sie bestimmte Zeitgeber hinsichtlich dessen, wann sie aufstehen und das Haus verlassen müssen, wann und wo sie einkaufen (z. B. am Weg von der Arbeit), oder wann sie Mittagessen können. Aber auch umgekehrt können Alltagsroutinen zu „Zeitgebern" für den Lebenslauf werden – Veränderungen in Lebensstilen und Ausgestaltungen von Partnerschaften führen etwa dazu, dass Menschen später oder gar nicht zusammenziehen, heiraten, oder Kinder bekommen.

Elizabeth Freeman streicht dabei die herrschaftsstabilisierende Wirkweise von Chrononormativität hervor, die sie, in Anleihe an Michel Foucaults Konzept von Biopolitik, auch als „Chronobiopolitik" bezeichnet: Chrononormativität bezeichnet eine Orchestrierung von Zeit, die menschliche Körper zur maximalen Produktivität hin normiert. Diese Kontrolle ist, mit Foucault gesprochen, weniger Disziplinierung als Gouvernementalität: Menschen internalisieren Chrononormen und unterwerfen sich ihnen nicht nur, sondern setzen sie auch gegenüber anderen durch. Mit Judith Butler ist eine solche Unterwerfung immer auch emanzipatorisch – sie ermöglicht Handlungsfähigkeit erst, konstituiert Subjekte, soziale Gruppen, und geteilte Identitäten. Dadurch ermöglicht die Unterwerfung unter Chrononormativität, sich selbst als „jung" oder „alt" zu beschreiben, und sich der Gruppe der „Kinder" oder „Erwachsenen" zugehörig zu fühlen.

Trotzdem sollten weder Chrononormativität noch Norma-/Temporalität als deterministische Zeitregimes verstanden werden, von denen keinerlei Abweichung möglich ist. Abweichungen auf beiden Ebenen umfassen etwa „zu früh" oder „zu spät", „zu langsam" oder „zu schnell" zu sein: Eine Person kann ebenso „zu früh" in Rente gehen, wie sie morgens „zu spät" aufstehen kann. Abweichungen von temporalen Normalitäten können verschiedene Hintergründe haben: Im Konzept des „Queering Time" (vgl. Halberstam 2005) wird der Verstoß gegen Chrononormativität als politischer Akt der Kritik am heteronormativen Lebenslauf verstanden. In vielen Fällen entstehen temporale Abweichungen jedoch nicht aus individuellen und intentionalen Widerständen, sondern resultieren aus Asynchronizitäten zwischen sozialen Praktiken. Leonard et al. (2018) verdeutlichen dies in ihrer Forschung zu älteren Lehrlingen, die Arbeitsabläufe und Arbeitsrhythmen in jenen Unternehmen irritierten, in denen sie tätig waren. Sie taten das jedoch nicht absichtsvoll, um Altersstereotype infrage zu stellen, sondern rein durch ihre Teilnahme an Arbeitspraktiken, die für gewöhnlich von jüngeren Menschen ausgeführt wurden.

Tatsächlich sind geringfügige Abweichungen von Chrononormativität und Norma-/Temporalität weit verbreitet und führen nicht notwendigerweise zu wie immer gearteten negativen Konsequenzen (vgl. Wanka 2019). Viel eher ist die Aufrechterhaltung von temporalen Normalitäten sogar auf ihre zeitweise Störung angewiesen. Henri Lefebvre ([1984] 2004) hat dies in seinem Konzept von „Polyrhythmik" verdeutlicht, die allen sozialen Phänomenen zugrunde liegt und die immer aus dem wellenartigen Zusammenspiel von Eurhythmik und Arrhythmik besteht. Eurhythmik bezeichnet dabei die synchronen, „gesunden" oder „normalen" Rhythmen eines Phänomens, während Arrhythmik die desynchronisierenden, pathologischen und andersartigen Rhythmen beschreibt. Abweichung ist damit normaler und sogar notwendiger Bestandteil aller zeitlichen Phänomene (Blue 2017).

Was bedeutet dies nun für den Übergang von der Erwerbsphase in die Nacherwerbsphase? Zum einen können wir davon ausgehen, dass sich dieser ebenso durch verschiedene soziale Praktiken, mithilfe verschiedenster Partizpand*innen

– also multi-agential – und an verschiedenen Schauplätzen – also multi-sited – vollzieht. Chrononormativität, so die Arbeitshypothese dieses Beitrags, ist dabei einer der Stoffe, die diese Praktiken zusammenhalten und ihre „richtige" Reihenfolge gewährleisten. Doch wie, wann und wo wird Chrononormativität am Übergang in die Nacherwerbsphase konkret hergestellt? Welche sozialen Praktiken stabilisieren sie, welche laufen ihnen zuwider? Wie wird der richtige Zeitpunkt, um in Rente zu gehen, bestimmt, und wie verändert sich die Alltagsgestaltung, wenn der „Zeitgeber" Erwerbsarbeit wegfällt?

Die performative Herstellung von Chrononormativität am Übergang in die Nacherwerbsphase Die Emergenz des „Ruhestands" und seine Institutionalisierung

Verstehen wir den Lebenslauf als eine Konstellation alterskodierter sozialer Praktiken und fragen nach seiner Herstellung und (De-)Stabilisierung, so können wir dies erstens aus einer historischen Perspektive, die die Emergenz verschiedener Lebensphasen – wie Kindheit oder eben Ruhestand – und ihrer zeitlichen Verortung im Lebenslauf nachzeichnet, tun. Wie Martin Kohli (1985) argumentiert, wird die Chronologisierung des Lebenslaufs durch die ab dem 19. Jahrhundert entstehenden altersgeschichteten Systeme öffentlicher Rechte und Pflichten vorangetrieben – im Zivilrecht etwa durch den Code Napoleon mit seinem ausdifferenzierten System von chronologischen Altersstufen, das bald in andere Rechtsgebiete übernommen wurde. Nicht nur Bürgerrechte wie das aktive und passive Wahlrecht, sondern auch Pflichten (z. B. die allgemeine Schulpflicht), Kosten (etwa für die Fahrt in öffentlichen Verkehrsmitteln) und Schutzregelungen im Arbeitsmarkt (z. B. Verbot von Kinderarbeit) werden seither an das chronologische Alter geknüpft. Kohli nennt jedoch insbesondere das Bildungs- und das Rentensystem als „die organisatorischen Träger der Ausdifferenzierung der wichtigsten Lebensphasen; auf ihrer Grundlage konstituiert sich die Dreiteilung des Lebenslaufs" (S. 504).

Die Lebensphase „Alter", wie wir sie heute verstehen, ist dabei im institutionalisierten Lebenslauf relativ neu[3] – ihre Geburtsstunde kann mit der Einführung des staatlichen Rentensystems gleichgesetzt werden. Das deutsche

---

[3]Als Vorläufer des Ruhestandes nennt Kohli hier die bäuerliche Hofübergabe, die jedoch weniger an ein bestimmtes chronologisches Alter als an die Arbeitsfähigkeit geknüpft war, meist kein abruptes Ende der Arbeitstätigkeit bedeutete und außerdem nicht sonderlich weit verbreitet war (vgl. Held, 1993).

öffentliche Altersrentensystem wurde als erstes System der Altersabsicherung 1889 als Arbeiterrentenversicherung eingeführt und 1911 auf Angestellte sowie 1972 auf Selbstständige ausgeweitet. Heute sind grundsätzlich alle Arbeitnehmer*innen, sowie bestimmte Arten von Selbstständigen, in Deutschland pflichtversichert. Entsprechend ist die Altersphase in ihrer historischen Entwicklung zu einer erwerbslosen Phase geworden – waren 1895, kurz nach Einführung der Arbeiterrentenversicherung, noch 79 % der 60 bis 70-jährigen Männern erwerbstätig, so waren es 2018 noch 65,5 % der 60 bis 64-jährigen und 21,1 % der 65 bis 69-jährigen Männer[4] (Kohli 1985; Statistisches Bundesamt 2018).

Der Eintritt in die Nacherwerbsphase ist im deutschen Rentenversicherungssystem insbesondere an zwei temporale Einheiten geknüpft, mittels derer Chrononormativität institutionalisiert wird: an das chronologische Alter (mindestens 63 Jahre) und an die Dauer der vorherigen Erwerbstätigkeit bzw. Einzahlungsperiode (mindestens 3 Jahre). Die Altersgrenze für den Eintritt in die Regelaltersrente wird dabei zwischen 2012 und 2029 schrittweise von 65 Jahren auf 67 Jahre angehoben (Seibold 2017). Das faktische durchschnittliche Rentenzugangsalter lag dagegen 2017 bei 61,7 Jahren (Männer) bzw. 61,9 Jahren[5] (Frauen; vgl. Deutsche Rentenversicherung 2018), und das faktische durchschnittliche Erwerbsaustrittsalter noch deutlich niedriger. 2014 wechselten etwa nur ein Drittel der neuen Altersrentner*innen aus einer versicherungspflichtigen Beschäftigung in die Rente, die Mehrheit wechselte aus einer Arbeitslosigkeit oder einem passiven Versicherungsverhältnis (z. B. Hausfrauen mit früher erworbenen Rentenansprüchen; vgl. Bundeszentrale für politische Bildung 2016).

Der „richtige" Zeitpunkt für den Übergang in die Nacherwerbsphase

Die Entstehung des öffentlichen Rentenversicherungssystems stellt somit eine historisch gewachsene Institutionalisierung von Chrononormativität dar. Doch beein-

---

[4]Hier werden zur besseren Vergleichbarkeit nur die Erwerbsquoten von Männern verglichen, da Daten zur Frauenerwerbsbeteiligung 1895 noch nicht erhoben wurden. Die Frauenerwerbsbeteiligung lag 2018 bei 55,6 % der 60 bis 64Jährigen und 13,2 % der 65 bis 69Jährigen (Statistisches Bundesamt 2018).
[5]Das durchschnittliche Rentenzugangsalter aufgrund von Erwerbsminderung lag dabei bei 52,4 Jahren (Männer) bzw. 51,4 Jahren (Frauen), das durchschnittliche Rentenzugangsalter bei Altersrenten bei 64 (Männer) bzw. 64,1 Jahren (Frauen).

flusst sie auch die gegenwärtige Vorstellung eines „richtigen" Zeitpunkts, um in Rente zu gehen? Auf Basis des repräsentativen European Social Survey zeigte Jansen (2018) auf, dass das gesetzliche Renteneintrittsalter zwar das persönlich angestrebte Renteneintrittsalter beeinflusst, dieses aber nicht vollständig erklären kann.

Qualitative Interviewausschnitte aus dem Projekt „Doing Retiring" können dabei weitere Hinweise darauf geben, wie ältere Menschen ein für sie „richtiges" Renteneintrittsalter ermitteln und damit Chrononormativität stabilisieren oder infrage stellen. Dazu wurden die Forschungsteilnehmenden gefragt, wann sie zum ersten Mal darüber nachgedacht hatten, in Rente zu gehen. Das „Nachdenken" steht in diesem Fall für die Initiierung einer Vielzahl unterschiedlicher Übergangspraktiken, wie finanzielle Kalkulationen, Gespräche mit der Familie, oder Wissenstransfer in der Firma, auf die im Folgenden näher eingegangen werden soll.

Die meisten Forschungsteilnehmenden hatten dabei eine klare Vorstellung eines „richtigen" Zeitpunkts, um in Rente zu gehen. Häufig war dieser an ein bestimmtes kalendarisches Alter gekoppelt. Harald (*1955), ein ehemaliger Maschinenbauer, erzählte etwa, dass er schon immer mit 55 Jahren in Rente gehen wollte, während Herbert (*1954), ein ehemaliger Projektmanager, das Erreichen des 60. Lebensjahrs als Trigger, um über die Rente nachzudenken, beschrieb. Wieder andere Teilnehmende berichteten, dass sie bereits ihr ganzes Leben darüber nachgedacht hatten, in Rente zu gehen, doch erst konkrete Schritte unternahmen, als sie sich an das gesetzliche Renteneintrittsalter annäherten.

Allerdings wichen die meisten Forschungsteilnehmenden de facto vom gesetzlichen Renteneintrittsalter ab – von 29 Personen waren nur zwei bei Erreichen der Regelaltersgrenze aus einer versicherungspflichtigen Erwerbstätigkeit in den Ruhestand gegangen, zwölf waren auf verschiedenen Wegen (z. B. Erwerbsminderung, Arbeitslosigkeit) in eine Form der Frührente gegangen, sieben hatten eine Altersteilzeitregelung in Anspruch genommen, und zwei hatten über das gesetzliche Renteneintrittsalter hinaus gearbeitet[6]. Woraus ergeben sich diese Asynchronizitäten, diese Abweichungen von Chrononormativität?

Ein Faktor liegt in der Kreuzung mehrerer Lebensläufe mit jener der in den Ruhestand übertretenden Person – etwa jener Lebensläufe von Partner*innen oder Kindern. Diese Verbundenheit der Lebensläufe mehrerer Personen bezeichnen Glen Elder und Kolleg*innen (2003) als "linked lives". Tom (*1958), ein ehemaliger Entwicklungsingenieur, beschreibt etwa die Gedanken, die ihm in Bezug

---

[6] Die übrigen Forschungsteilnehmenden waren in der zweiten Erhebungswelle noch erwerbstätig.

auf den Ruhestand als Erstes durch den Kopf gingen, wie folgt: "[…] wann sind die Kinder aus dem Haus, wann kannst machen, was du willst, wie alt ist deine Frau […]?" Dabei kann die Lebenslaufposition von Kindern als auch von Partner*innen sowohl ausschlaggebend dafür sein, „zu früh" in Rente zu gehen, wie über das gesetzliche Renteneintrittsalter hinaus zu arbeiten. Wenn Kinder sich etwa noch in Ausbildung befanden, so war das für viele Studienteilnehmende ein Grund, länger zu arbeiten, um sie weiterhin finanziell zu unterstützen. Planten die Kinder dagegen, selber bald Kinder zu bekommen, so begründete das für manche einen frühzeitigen Erwerbsaustritt, um sich um die Enkelkinder kümmern zu können. Für Anna (*1949), eine ehemalige Lehrerin, waren ihre Kinder ausschlaggebend dafür, zwei Jahre über das gesetzlichen Rentenalter hinaus zu arbeiten:

"[…] ich wollte meinen Kindern zeigen, jetzt wo mein Mann nicht mehr da ist, dass ich eben arbeite. Dass das Leben eben aus (lachend) Arbeit besteht und nicht aus im Sessel sitzen […] dass er [Anm.: der Sohn] sah, die Mutter, die hat noch eine Aufgabe. Die geht noch in die Schule." (Anna, *1949)

Während manche ihren Renteneintritt mit jenem ihres Partners oder ihrer Partnerin synchronisieren wollten, erfuhren andere ungewollten Druck aus ihrer Partnerschaft, entweder frühzeitig in Rente zu gehen oder aber noch (gegen den eigenen Willen) länger zu arbeiten, damit nicht beide Partner*innen gleichzeitig plötzlich „zu Hause" wären. Jane, eine ehemalige Bankangestellte, sorgte sich entsprechend über einen möglichen gleichzeitigen Renteneintritt mit ihrem Mann: *"Was kommt wenn wir beide relativ unvorbereitet von jetzt auf gleich zuhause sind?"* (Jane, *1957).

Dass mit dem Ende der Erwerbsarbeit antizipiert wurde, vermehrt Zeit zu Hause zu verbringen, löste bei vielen Forschungsteilnehmenden Angst davor aus, dass einem „die Decke auf den Kopf" fallen könnte. Dabei führte gerade auch der Umstand, mehr Zeit zu Hause zu verbringen, etwa aufgrund von Stundenreduktionen oder Home-Office-Stunden, zu einer affektiven Entfremdung von der Arbeit. Marie-Kristine, eine ehemalige Sozialarbeiterin, reduzierte mit Mitte 50 ihre Arbeitsstunden um einen Tag und fühlte, wie sie dadurch eine distanziertere Perspektive zu ihrer Arbeit entwickelte. Jane (*1957) musste ein halbes Jahr vor ihrem Berufsende ihr Büro ausräumen, um Platz für ihren Nachfolger zu machen, und arbeitete seither vermehrt von zu Hause aus. Dies, so beschrieb sie, erleichterte ihr den Abschied, und sie fühlte sich bereits ab diesem Zeitpunkt nicht mehr als ihrer Firma zugehörig.

Janes Erzählung weist bereits darauf hin, dass auch Unternehmenspraktiken Chrononormativität stabilisieren oder unterlaufen können. Häufig war Letzteres der Fall: Viele Forschungsteilnehmende erzählten etwa von routinierten (und häufig algorythmisierten) Prozessen in ihrer Firma, durch die Angestellten bestimmter Geburtskohorten automatisch Frühverrentungsmöglichkeiten angeboten wurden. Tina, eine ehemalige Marketingassistentin, erinnert sich wie folgt daran:

> „Ja, also dieses Angebot kam wirklich aus heiterem Himmel und damals gabs ja noch das alte Rentengesetz. Also ich hätte bis 65 und sieben Monate arbeiten müssen. Und als die dann gesagt haben, ich kann mit 60 da raus, hab ich gedacht, Mensch, das sind ja SECHS, also fast sechs geschenkte Jahre." (Tina, *1955).

Tinas Aussage verdeutlicht dabei bereits einen weiteren Faktor, der für die Bewertung des „richtigen" Zeitpunkts, in Rente zu gehen, eine bedeutsame Rolle spielt: die Einschätzung der noch verbleibenden Lebenszeit. Ein weit verbreitetes Narrativ unter den Forschungsteilnehmenden war folgende Erzählung: Ursprünglich hatten sie nicht an einen (frühzeitigen) Rentenantritt gedacht, doch dann war überraschend eine etwa gleich alte Person aus ihrem Bekanntenkreis verstorben. Dieser Todesfall initiierte Gedanken darüber, wie lange man selber wohl noch zu leben hätte; ob man die eigenen Lebenspläne auf eine spätere Rentenphase aufschieben sollte (in der sie sich aufgrund von Krankheit oder Tod eventuell gar nicht mehr realisieren lassen würden); und ob man stattdessen nicht lieber „zu früh" in Rente gehen sollte, anstatt das Risiko einzugehen, „rechtzeitig" in Rente zu gehen, dann aber „viel zu früh" zu sterben. Dana (*1954), eine ehemalige Sozialarbeiterin, beschreibt diese Gedanken so:

> "[...] auch noch 'n anderer Kollege, wo das ähnlich passiert ist, der zwei, drei Jahre in Rente war und kriegte 'ne Langzeiterkrankung. 'N Jahr später (.) weg. Und das war auch so mit ein Anlass für mich, drüber nachzudenken ‚Okay, kannst dich ja ganz wohlfühlen in deinem Beruf, aber was passiert, wenn dich 'ne Krankheit überfällt und du kannst dein Rentendasein gar nicht so GENIEßEN, wie ich es mir vorstelle?'" (Dana, *1954).

Der "richtige" Zeitpunkt, in Rente zu gehen, wird also einerseits vor dem Hintergrund der eigenen Positionierung im Lebenslauf und der noch verbleibenden Lebenszeit ermittelt, resultiert aber andererseits auch aus der Kreuzung mehrerer (ungleichzeitiger) Lebensläufe und der Einschätzung des „richtigen" Zeitpunkts vonseiten der Partner*innen, Kinder, oder Vorgesetzten. Und auch nicht-menschliche Akteur*innen wie Dinge und Räume, der Arbeitsplatz und das Zuhause, spielen im Vollzugsgeschehen zur Ermittlung eines „richtigen" Renteneintrittszeitpunkts eine bedeutsame Rolle.

Die „richtige" Zeitverwendung in der Nacherwerbsphase

Unabhängig davon, ob eine Person „zu früh" oder „zu spät" in Rente geht, erleben fast alle Neurentner*innen dieselbe Herausforderung, wenn sie aufhören, zu arbeiten: Ohne den „Zeitgeber" Erwerbsarbeit muss die Alltagsgestaltung grundsätzlich neu verhandelt und eine neue temporale Normalität im Alltäglichen hergestellt werden.

Zeitverwendungsdaten geben einen detaillierten und repräsentativen Einblick, wie sich die Alltagszeitgestaltung im Alter verändert. Nach der letzten deutschen Zeitverwendungsstudie 2012/13 wendeten Personen über 65 Jahre im Altersgruppenvergleich die meiste Zeit für Fernsehen und Lesen auf (Statistisches Bundesamt 2016). Daneben nehmen aber auch scheinbar banale Alltagstätigkeiten der Regeneration (z. B. Schlafen, persönliche Hygiene) und der Hausarbeit im Alter mehr Zeit in Anspruch (Köller 2007). Diese Tätigkeiten definiert Küster (1998) als persönliche Zeit und grenzt sie damit von familialer Zeit (Tätigkeiten, die für Familienmitglieder erbracht werden) und öffentlicher Zeit (Tätigkeiten, die für andere außerhalb der Familie erbracht werden), ab. Öffentliche Zeit, die Aktivitäten wie Erwerbsarbeit, Bildungsbeteiligung oder ehrenamtliches Engagement umfasst, nimmt im Alter am stärksten ab.

Qualitative Forschungen zur Zeitgestaltung im Alter machen demgegenüber die Ambivalenzen subjektiver Zeitperspektiven im bzw. am Übergang in den Ruhestand sichtbar (vgl. Wolf 1988; Burzan 2002; Köller 2007). So wird einerseits die Konstruktion von Routinen von vielen Rentner*innen als essenziell für ein funktionierendes Alltagsleben angesehen: Wochen und Monate werden durch feste Termine rhythmisiert und aufgabengebundene Zeiten im Alltag institutionalisiert; andererseits werden eine erweiterte Zeitsouveränität und die Möglichkeit, in Muße zu leben, als größte Gewinne des Ruhestands angesehen (Wolf 1988, 205 f.). Diese Ambivalenzen treten auch deutlich im Projekt „Doing Retiring" zutage, und zwar insbesondere entlang zweier Dimensionen: temporaler Selbstbestimmtheit versus temporaler Fremdbestimmtheit, sowie temporaler Expansion versus temporaler Strukturierung.

Temporale Selbstbestimmtheit versus temporale Fremdbestimmtheit

Zuerst erfuhren viele der Forschungsteilnehmenden mit dem Wegfall des „Zeitgebers" Erwerbsarbeit eine Zunahme ihrer temporalen Selbstbestimmung: Arzt-termine müssen nicht mehr in den übervollen Arbeitstag integriert werden, und man kann auch schon einmal mittags und ohne Termin zum Friseur gehen. Ulrich (*1955), ein ehemals selbstständiger Softwareentwickler, war froh, endlich dem Druck seines Arbeitslebens entkommen zu sein:

> "Der wesentliche Unterschied für mich ist, dass man keinerlei Termindruck mehr hat, ja. Und das ist das was ich mich erhofft habe. Ich möchte auch meine Zeit in der Zukunft nicht mehr so gestalten durch Aktivitäten, dass da ein Termindruck entsteht. […] da denke ich, das brauche ich jetzt in den letzten Lebensjahren so nicht mehr. Und deswegen möchte ich mich auch (.) nirgends (..) ja, mich irgendwo engagieren, wo wieder Termindruck entsteht, ne. (Ulrich, *1955).

Wie Ulrich achteten entsprechend viele Forschungsteilnehmende sorgfältig darauf, ihre Zeit im Ruhestand nicht erneut zu stark in fixierten, langfristigen Verpflichtungen zu binden, sondern Herr über ihre Zeitgestaltung zu bleiben. Richard (*1954), ein ehemaliger Schwerbehindertenvertreter, betonte: *"Wichtig dabei is, äh dass ich die Zeit entscheiden möchte, wann ich das tue. Ich möcht nich im/in' n Konzept gepresst werden"*.

Jedoch erfuhren nicht alle Forschungsteilnehmenden einen derartigen Zuwachs an temporaler Selbstbestimmtheit. Ganz im Gegenteil machten einige die Erfahrung, dass ihre Zeit im Ruhestand zum öffentlich verfügbaren Gut wurde -*„da stellen jetzt die anderen fest, huch wir haben ja einen der hat viel Zeit!"* (Tina, *1955). Insbesondere Frauen berichteten von ihrem Renteneintritt, dass sich ihre Partner*innen vollständig aus der Hausarbeit zurückzogen; dass ihre Kinder es für selbstverständlich hielten, sie nun jederzeit als Babysitter*innen einzusetzen; und dass ihre (Schwieger-)Eltern sich plötzlich mehr Unterstützung und Besuche von ihnen erwarteten. Zeit für sich selber, für Freizeitaktivitäten oder Regeneration, erfuhr wenig Verständnis. Dana beschreibt die Reaktionen ihres sozialen Umfelds auf ihre Zeitverwendung im Ruhestand folgendermaßen: *"[…] die sagen "Was? Hast schon wieder keine Zeit? Gehste zum Chor? Muss das denn sein?"* (Dana, *1954). Hermine (*1955), eine ehemalige kaufmännische Angestellte, erklärt ihren Widerstand gegenüber derartigen temporalen Übergriffen mit ähnlichen Worten:

> "Ich bin ja jetzt diejenige die Zeit hat, ne. Und ich kriege dann immer so Aufgaben zugeteilt, ne. Ach das kannst du doch mal machen. Kannst dich dann einfach drum kümmern. (…) Die lachen sich immer tot, wenn ich sage, dafür habe ich keine Zeit. (.) Aber ich weiß jetzt, warum Rentner keine Zeit mehr haben.[…] Klar, wenn ich morgens um sieben aufstehen würde (.) hätte ich natürlich zwangsläufig mehr Zeit, ja. Will ich aber nicht." (Hermine, *1955).

Temporale Expansion versus temporale Strukturiertheit

Neben der Frage nach temporaler Selbst- bzw. Fremdbestimmtheit berichteten die Forschungsteilnehmenden von einer Veränderung im gefühlten Tempo ihres Alltagslebens. Einige, wenn auch nicht alle, erfuhren diese Veränderung als Entschleunigung – wie Anna (*1949) es ausdrückt: *"[...] das alles hat sich jetzt so ein bisschen entzerrt."* Tess, (*1956), eine ehemalige Sachbearbeiterin, erklärt:

> "[…] was sich ganz konkret geändert hat, ist dieses, es geht alles viel langsamer. Ja? Weil früher hat man das ja alles nebenbei, ja? Vollzeit und Kind und/und/ und/und trotzdem einkaufen und Haushalt und (holt kurz Luft) Kochen und Freizeitaktivitäten und ich weiß nicht was, das/das/ ich weiß nicht mehr wie das früher in den Alltag gepasst hat, also es geht heute alles langsamer […] weil man sich eben selbst diesen Stress nich mehr macht. Weil das is, ich sag ma, Entschuldigung, aber scheiß egal, ob dieser Korb heut oder morgen weggebügelt wird." (Tess, *1956).

Die Forschungsteilnehmenden konnten eine Reihe an Praktiken benennen, die ihr Tempo geändert hatten, seit sie nicht mehr arbeiteten: Aktivitäten mit Freund*innen und Familienmitgliedern, Reisen, sportliche Betätigung, Kursbesuche, Gartenarbeit oder andere Hobbies. Allerdings wurden drei alltägliche Praxiskomplexe als besonders Zeit-expansiv beschrieben: Frühstücken, Lesen, sowie Haushaltstätigkeiten. Hermine (*1955) beschreibt die Veränderungen in diesen Praktiken, sowie ihre Zusammenhänge, wie folgt:

> "Ich habe mich auch insofern umgestellt, ich bin/gehöre jetzt ja nicht zu den Frühaufstehern und ähm, ich genieße es wirklich sehr, aufzuwachen, nicht nach dem Wecker unbedingt.[…] Und dann stehe ich auf, mache mir einen Kaffee und gehe mit dem Kaffee und der Zeitung wieder ins Bett. (lacht) Und dann lese ich erstmal meine Tageszeitung von vorne bis hinten. Und da geht ja schon viel Zeit bei drauf, ne.[…] Und dann bin ich ganz erschrocken, ah, mein Gott, es ist schon zehn Uhr. So verschiebt sich das, ja." (Hermine, *1955).

Während die temporale Expansion bestimmter Praktiken einerseits als angenehm erlebt wurde, so löste sie andererseits auch Angst, die Kontrolle über die eigene Zeitgestaltung zu verlieren, aus. Dementsprechend wurde die Erarbeitung einer neuen Zeitstruktur von vielen Forschungsteilnehmenden als zentrale Aufgabe gesehen, die am Übergang in die Nacherwerbsphase zu bewältigen sei. „*Weil die Struktur ist ja im Prinzip das Gerüst, was jetzt hält, was um einen herum ist. Und die will neu aufgebaut werden.*" (Jane, *1957). Mithilfe bestimmter

Strukturierungspraktiken[7] sollten bestimmte andere Praktiken davon abgehalten werden, sich unkontrolliert auszudehnen.

> "[...]eine Struktur zu schaffen. Also ich hab eine Arbeitsstruktur in meinem Arbeitsleben und die so gut es geht auch irgendwie weiter zu behalten. Vielleicht' n Level niedriger, aber das wär mir ganz wichtig, ähm also irgendeine, ja, Struktur, Aufgabe. Und da kommen eben diese Beispiele. Neue Sprache lernen, Musikinstrument, studieren, Ehrenamt..." (Harald, *1955).

Das obige Zitat verdeutlicht dabei auch die temporale Ambivalenz zwischen Zeitstrukturierung und Zeitfreiheit, die Rentner*innen bei der Neustrukturierung ihrer Alltagstätigkeiten erlebten. Diese Ambivalenz ist geprägt von einem geteilten Verständnis von „sinnvoll verwendeter" oder aber „verschwendeter" Zeit. Zeit sollte strukturiert werden, damit bestimmte Praktiken sich nicht ungebührlich ausdehnten und somit keine Zeit verschwendet würde.

Während viele Forschungsteilnehmende verschwendete Zeit als das Gegenteil von sinnvoll verwendeter Zeit definierten, verdeutlicht ein genauerer Blick, dass vor allem Praktiken des „Nichtstun" und der „Muße" als verschwendet angesehen wurden. Danach gefragt, wie eine typische Woche in ihrem Leben aussieht, war es den Forschungsteilnehmenden wichtig, zu betonen: *„ne, ist nicht so, dass ich jetzt auf der faulen Haut liege"* (Ulrich, *1955). Bemüht, sich selbst davon abzugrenzen, erzählten sie Geschichten von anderen, die ihr späteres Leben „verschwendet" hätten. Marina (*1953), eine ehemalige selbstständige Steuerberaterin, berichtet über ihre Mutter:

> "Also ich würde schon ein [...] aktives Leben beanspruchen.[...] Also ich hab' das äh bei meiner Mutter gesehen. Meine Mutter, die hat mit sechsundfünfzig ihren Mann verloren. (.) Dann hat sie auch ihre Mutter gepflegt und die war auch im Alter/gut die Siebzig, wie sie jetzt in meiner Position war. Wo praktisch alles (.) versorgt war und alles irgendwie geregelt war und wo sie dann selbst entscheiden konnte, wie sie ihr Leben ähm gestalten wollte. Und die hat nichts draus gemacht,

---

[7]Auch die Interviews selber wurden von manchen Forschungsteilnehmenden als solche Strukturierungspraktiken eingesetzt. Beispielsweise wurden die Zeiträume zwischen den Erhebungswellen (etwa 12 Monate) herangezogen, um zu berechnen, wann man welche seiner Zukunftspläne umgesetzt haben müsste, um beim kommenden Interview darüber berichten zu können.

ne. (..) Sie ist nirgendwo hingegangen. Sie hat sich keine Bekanntschaften, keine Freunde gesucht und keine Hobbys gehabt. Also das find' ich dann 'n bisschen traurig, ne. Wenn man dann einfach so die Zeit verstreichen lässt. Das würd' ich/ würd' ich nicht machen." (Marina, *1953).

Die Affekte, die die Forschungsteilnehmenden gegenüber solchen Praktiken des "Nichtstuns" ausdrückten, reichten von Ablehnung über Verleugnung bis hin zu Ekel, wie das Zitat von Charlotte verdeutlicht:

> " Die meisten [anderen Rentner*innen] fressen sich fett und sind irgendwo depressiv und hängen rum vor der Glotze, konsumieren und machen lauter blödes Zeug […] Ach, Arzt rennen, das ist auch ein (.) Thema, das braucht alles furchtbar viel Zeit. (.) Ich nicht." (Charlotte, *1957).

Andere beschrieben einen „schuldbewussten Genuss"', den sie empfanden, wenn sie Zeit in dieser Definition „verschwendeten". Ute, eine ehemalige Journalistin, beschreibt den verschwenderischen Umgang mit Zeit als einen Luxus, den sie erst lernen müsse, sich zu gönnen:

> "Hätte eigentlich gerne noch mehr Zeit so, mich/einfach zum Lesen, so wie Sonntag auf dem Balkon zu lesen, in die Sonne. Das sind so diese kleinen Luxusdinge. Die eigentlich mein Leben sein sollten.(.) Und wo ich noch so ein bisschen lernen muss, mir die zu gönnen." (Ute, *1957).

Zum einen drückten die Forschungsteilnehmenden das Gefühl aus, keine Muße zu „verdienen", nachdem sie nun in ihrer Selbsteinschätzung ja auch nicht mehr produktiv arbeiteten. Zum anderen bewerteten sie ihre alltägliche Zeitverwendung vor dem Hintergrund der ihnen (vermeintlich) noch verbleibenden Lebenszeit. Das Gefühl, dass diese Lebenszeit sich dem Ende zuneigte, erzeugte Druck, die noch verbleibende Zeit möglichst sinnvoll zu verwenden. Mia (*1952), eine ehemalige Sozialarbeiterin, erzählte von einer Erkrankung ihrer Schwester, die sie zu folgenden Überlegungen angeregt hatte:

> "[…] das hat's auch wieder so bewusst gemacht, wie kostbar auch diese Zeit jetzt noch is. Und dass man ja generell, aber ab 'nem bestimmten Alter umso mehr, nit so alles in die Zukunft verschieben kann. Also och dann mehr im Jetzt zu leben." (Mia, *1952).

Das Bewusstsein über die wahrgenommene Nähe zum Tod führte dazu, dass manche Forschungsteilnehmende ihre Alltagsaktivitäten und die Personen, mit denen sie diese Aktivitäten ausübten, stärker ausselektierten. Es rief bei einigen aber auch ein gewisses Gefühl der Zukunftslosigkeit hervor. Petra beschreibt diese augenzwinkernd als „*Endzeitstimmung. Und die Leute, die feiern mehr oder die feiern anders.[...] Also das hat/nimmt ganz andere Ausmaße an, hätt ich vorher gar nich so gedacht.*"

Diskussion
Der vorliegende Beitrag hat die temporale Organisation des Lebenslaufs aus praxistheoretischer Perspektive erkundet. Die jene temporale Organisation stabilisierende Chrononormativität kann aus einer solchen Perspektive als ein prozesshaftes Vollzugsgeschehen verstanden werden, das, an mehreren Schauplätzen und unter Beteiligung verschiedener Elemente, durch kontinuierliche Wiederholung der sie konstituierenden sozialen Praktiken immer wieder aufs Neue hergestellt und gestaltet wird. Chrononormativität bezeichnet somit die praktische Herstellung und Stabilisierung des Normallebenslaufs. Am Beispiel des Übergangs von der Erwerbs- in die Nacherwerbsphase folgte der Beitrag einigen jener Praktiken, die Chrononormativität in Bezug auf die Lebensphase „Alter" herstellen und ihren Platz im Lebenslauf (de-)stabilisieren.

Eine praxistheoretische Perspektive ermöglicht es, die Komplexität von Chrononormativität als Vollzugsgeschehen in verschiedenen Dimensionen zu fassen – hier soll zusammenfassend auf drei davon eingegangen werden: erstens, auf die historische Emergenz von Lebensphasen und ihrer Zusammenhänge; zweitens, auf die Fülle von Elementen, die an der Herstellung und (De-)Stabilisierung von Chrononormativität beteiligt sind; und drittens, auf einige der verschiedenen Schauplätze, an denen sich ihre Praktiken vollziehen.

Dabei zeigt sich erstens, aus historischer Perspektive, dass der Ruhestand an sich eine eher rezente soziale Konstruktion ehemaliger Industriegesellschaften ist (Kohli 1985). Der Eintritt in diese Lebensphase ist dabei in Deutschland an zwei temporale Einheiten geknüpft: das chronologische Alter und die Dauer der vorherigen Erwerbstätigkeit bzw. Einzahlungsperiode (Seiber 2017). Die Entstehung des öffentlichen Rentenversicherungssystems stellt also eine historisch gewachsene Institutionalisierung von Chrononormativität dar, die auch gegenwärtige Vorstellungen eines „richtigen" Zeitpunkts, in Rente zu gehen, maßgeblich mit beeinflusst (Jansen 2018). Das Projekt „Doing Retiring" zeigt jedoch auf, dass auch andere Zeitlichkeiten abseits des chronologischen Alters und der bisherigen Erwerbsdauer bei dieser Bewertung eine Rolle spielen und zu Abweichungen vom gesetzlichen Renteneintrittsalter führen können.

Diese sind, zweitens, teilweise auf Verstrickung mehrerer Lebensläufe zurückzuführen. Rick Settersten und Asia Thogmartin argumentieren entsprechend, dass es einen „individuellen Lebenslauf" überhaupt nicht gäbe (2018, 361). Die

Lebenslaufposition von Partner*innen (in- oder außerhalb der Erwerbsphase) oder Kindern (in- oder außerhalb der Ausbildungsphase) ist ebenso ausschlaggebend für die Ermittlung eines „richtigen" Renteneintrittsalters wie die respektive Einschätzung von Vorgesetzten, die meist auf tradierten Unternehmenspraktiken beruht. So ist es in manchen Unternehmen automatisierter Usus, bestimmten Geburtskohorten Frühverrentungsmöglichkeiten anzubieten und ihnen damit zu verdeutlichen, dass es für sie „Zeit" wird, aus der Arbeit auszuscheiden. Allerdings werden auch mögliche Abweichungen bei anderen Übergängen antizipiert: Das Risiko, „zu früh" zu sterben, setzt das angestrebte Renteneintrittsalter in Relation zu der (vermeintlich) noch verbleibenden Lebenszeit.

Der „richtige" Zeitpunkt für den Übergang von der Erwerbs- in die Nacherwerbsphase wird also nicht allein von dem in Rente gehenden Individuum bestimmt, sondern in einem Netzwerk unterschiedlicher Akteur*innen, Elemente und Diskurse verhandelt. Dabei spielen neben Personen auch Dinge und Räume eine Rolle – das Ausräumen des Arbeitsplatzes kann so ein affektiv aufgeladenes Praxisbündel sein, das den Abschied von der Arbeit erleichtert. Diese kollektiven Verhandlungen führen in vielen Fällen zu Abweichungen von Chrononormativität, die in manchen Fällen trotzdem als „richtig" bewertet werden, z. B. im Fall, „zu früh" in Rente zu gehen, um dem Risiko, „zu früh" zu sterben und somit den Ruhestand nicht ausreichend auskosten zu können, präventiv entgegenzuwirken.

Drittens, wird Chrononormativität nicht nur in den oben genannten sozialen Institutionen des Lebenslaufs, wie der Familie oder der Arbeit (Kohli 1985), hergestellt und (de-)stabilisiert, sondern auch im Alltag (vgl. Norma-/Temporalität: Krekula et al. 2017). Unabhängig davon, ob eine Person „zu früh" oder „zu spät" in Rente geht, steht sie irgendwann vor der Herausforderung, ihren Alltag ohne den Zeitgeber Erwerbsarbeit zu gestalten. Die Herstellung temporaler Normalität im Alltag wurde im Beitrag entlang von zwei Dimensionen verhandelt: temporaler Selbstbestimmtheit versus temporaler Fremdbestimmtheit, sowie temporaler Expansion versus temporaler Strukturierung. Zuerst erfuhren viele der Forschungsteilnehmenden eine Zunahme ihrer temporalen Selbstbestimmtheit in der Nacherwerbsphase. Diese Selbstbestimmtheit wurde allerdings nicht nur von anderen Personen herausgefordert, sondern auch von scheinbar unkontrollierter Expansion bestimmter Praktiken, die nun in der Nacherwerbsphase plötzlich mehr Zeit in Anspruch nahmen als zuvor. Die Angst, Kontrolle über die eigene Zeitverwendung zu verlieren, verdeutlicht sich besonders an der Bewertung bestimmter Praktiken als „sinnvoll verwendete" bzw. „verschwendete" Zeit. Venn und Arber (2011) beschreiben dies auf ähnliche Weise für Tagesschlaf im Ruhestand:

"Retirement from paid work was not seen as an excuse for being inactive, and sleeping during the day was regarded as: (a) an indication of idleness, (b) a waste of valuable and limited time, and (c) counter to the inherently. strong moral work ethic of their upbringing." (S. 207).

Doch wie hängen diese komplexen Vollzugsgeschehen nun miteinander zusammen? Die oben diskutierte Bewertung bestimmter Praktiken als „Zeitverschwendung" ist eine jener Mechanismen, die Chrononormativität über mehrere Schauplätze hinweg stabilisieren. Sie verbindet die Ebene des Lebenslaufs mit der Ebene des Alltags: Durch ein erhöhtes Bewusstsein über die eigene Position auf der „Linie" des Lebenslaufs, wird die Frage, wie die verbleibende (und abnehmende) Lebenszeit verbracht wird, zur zentralen Distinktionskategorie. Statt scheinbar "inaktive" Praktiken mit positiver Bedeutung aufzuladen, wie wir es aus bestimmten Jugendkulturen kennen (z. B. „Chillen" als gemeinsame Freizeitaktivität), wird das „Nichtstun" im Alter abgewertet. Durch das Konzept der Zeitverschwendung wird Chrononormativität damit im Alltag reproduziert.

Neu-Rentner*innen strukturieren ihren Alltag mit entsprechender Disziplin: Sie stehen früh auf, machen sich Termine, und suchen nach produktiven Praktiken (z. B. ehrenamtliches Engagement) – verkürzt könnte man sagen, sie bauen einen Arbeitsalltag nach. David Ekerdt bezeichnet den daraus resultierenden ständigen Druck, aktiv zu sein (oder jedenfalls zu scheinen), als "Geschäftigkeitsethik" des Alters (1986). Dies greift allerdings zu kurz: Manche Praktiken, die statt Produktivität oder Aktivität Muße darstellen, wie etwa genüssliches Frühstücken, scheinen notwendige Elemente in der Zeitstrukturierung der Nacherwerbsphase zu sein. Diese ist damit inhärent ambivalent – Strukturiertheit und Offenheit sind in ihrem Wechselspiel für sie kennzeichnend. Und diese Ambivalenz ist nach Lefebvre konstitutiv für die Polyrhythmik von Praxis und die Herstellung und Stabilisierung temporaler Normalität ([1984] 2004). Die Struktur, die um Praktiken (bzw. Zeit) gebaut wird, muss also bis zu einem gewissen Grad flexibel bleiben, damit bestimmte Praktiken sich bis zu einem gewissen Grad ausdehnen können – insbesondere solche Praktiken, die das „gute Leben" ohne Zeitdruck verdeutlichen. Dabei existiert ein schmaler Grat zwischen Inaktivität und Faulheit auf der einen und verbissener Geschäftigkeit auf der anderen Seite. Für die Lebensphase Alter hat Stephen Katz (2000) drei Bereiche von Praktiken definiert, die besonders anfällig dafür sind, als „Zeitverschwendung" bewertet zu werden: passive Aktivitäten, wie Schlafen oder Fernsehen, unmoralische Aktivitäten, wie Geschlechtsverkehr oder Alkoholkonsum, und konzeptuelle Aktivitäten, wie Nachdenken (S. 134 f.).

Fraglos werden diese Aktivitäten von Menschen aller Altersgruppen ausgeführt. Im Alter werden sie jedoch besonders stark abgewertet. Dementsprechend fungiert Zeitverschwendung im Alter als Distinktionsmerkmal, durch das bestimmte Personengruppen abgewertet werden und dem mit Ablehnung, teils Abscheu begegnet wird – oder sie werden als „schuldbewusster Genuss" (*guilty pleasure*) beschrieben. Das gleichzeitige Auftreten von Genuss und Schuld kann als eine Form affektiver Ambivalenz verstanden werden, die auf Widersprüchen zwischen „Sich-Gehen-Lassen" und Selbstdisziplinierungsmaßnahmen beruht (Miao 2011). Dies weist darauf hin, dass Affekte, wie etwa Ekel, Schuld, oder eben Genuss, ebenso Elemente jener sozialer Praktiken sind, die dazu beitragen, die Chrononormativität des Lebenslaufs zu stabilisieren oder infrage zu stellen. Die Herstellung und (De-)Stabilisierung von temporaler Normalität umfasst also auch affektive Elemente. Schon Bourdieu (1979) erkannte die zentrale Rolle von Affekten, wie Ekel, als internalisiertes Mittel zur Legitimation der Reproduktion sozialer Ungleichheiten. Neu ist, dass sie sich lebensphasenspezifisch ausgestaltet. Stine Adrian nennt dieses Zusammenkommen mehrerer Elemente, um Affekte in Praktiken zu erzeugen, „emotionale Choreographie" (2015). Durch eine solche sich prozesshaft über den Lebenslauf vollziehende emotionale Choreographie wird temporale Normalität im Alltag und im Lebenslauf abgesichert.

Die Ambivalenz zwischen Produktivität und Selbstoptimierung auf der einen und Muße und Entschleunigung auf der anderen Seite, muss vor dem Hintergrund einer größeren diskursiven Arena verstanden werden. In den Medien, in Policy-Dokumenten und auch der Alter(n)sforschung selber stehen defizitäre Vorstellung über das Alter als eine Lebensphase des sozialen Rückzugs und der Passivität neueren Altersbildern, die den Anschein ewiger Jugend, Aktivität und Produktivität erwecken, gegenüber (vgl. Katz 1996; Powell 2001). Seit den 1980ern hat sich ein Aktivitäts- und Aktivierungsparadigma in Bezug auf das Alter manifestiert und ausgebreitet, das in den 1990ern von einem gesteigerten Anspruch, nicht nur aktiv, sondern auch produktiv zu bleiben, angereichert wurde (van Dyk und Lessenich 2009; Marshall 2018). Stephen Katz (2000) formuliert dazu: "The aged subject becomes encased in a social matrix where moral, disciplinary conventions around activity, health, and independence appear to represent an idealized old age" (S. 140).

Dieses Aktivitätsparadigma wurde zuerst auch in der Alter(n)sforschung selber positiv aufgenommen, da es eine willkommene Abkehr vom ehemals defizitorientierten, naturalisierten Altersbild darstellte und aufzeigte, dass die Lebensphase Alter nicht notwendigerweise mit einem „Ruhestand" gleichzusetzen sei. In ihm wurde eine Destabilisierung des chrononormativen Lebenslaufregimes gesehen, quasi eine Revolte gegen die soziale Institution des Ruhestands. Paul und Mathilda

Riley (1994) beschrieben darauf aufbauend ihre Utopie einer „altersintegrierten Gesellschaft", in denen Phasen der Ausbildung, der Arbeit und der Muße sich im Lebensverlauf unabhängig vom kalendarischen Alter abwechseln könnten. Diese Utopie kann als frühe Form eines „Queering" von Zeit (vgl. Halberstam 2005) gelesen werden. Allerdings sind auch die im „aktiven Alter(n)" transportierten Bilder und Vorstellungen in hohem Maße hetero- und chronormativ: fokussiert werden zumeist Praktiken gesunder, weißer, heterosexueller Paare aus der oberen Mittelschicht (vgl. Marshall 2018). Das Alter wird somit nicht mehr als passive, zurückgezogene Lebensphase dargestellt, sondern vollständig negiert und unsichtbar gemacht – „erfolgreich" zu altern bedeutet heute, überhaupt nicht zu altern.

Damit destabilisieren Praktiken des aktiven und insbesondere des produktiven Alters den chrononormativen Lebenslauf tatsächlich in gewisser Hinsicht, denn sie stellen einen an das kalendarische Alter gekoppelten Renteneintritt an sich infrage. Und diese Diskurse manifestieren sich nicht nur in der Veränderung von Alltagsroutinen als der Disziplinierung alltäglicher Zeitverwendung, sondern auch in der Veränderung institutionalisierter Markierungen im Lebenslauf: So haben Länder wie die USA oder Großbritannien gesetzliche Renteneintrittsalter bereits abgeschafft, und Deutschland geht mit dem 2016 beschlossenen Flexirentengesetz ebenfalls einen Schritt in Richtung eines individualisierten Renteneintrittsalters. Andererseits stabilisiert das produktive Alter(n) den chrononormativen Lebenslauf aber auch in vielerlei Hinsicht: Gerade die Großelternrolle, die von einer Mehrheit (82 %) der Europäer*innen als zentrale soziale Rolle im Alter gesehen wird, trägt erheblich dazu bei, die Erwerbstätigkeit junger und mittelalter Erwachsener zu ermöglichen (Vidovicová 2018).

Sandberg und Marshall (2017) plädieren demgegenüber für ein interdisziplinäres Unterfangen, das sie „queering aging futures" nennen. Klaus Schröter (2018) spricht von einem „doing age in other ways" sowohl auf der Ebene von routinierten Alltagspraktiken, als auch auf der Ebene institutionalisierter Lebenslaufregimes. Solche Bestrebungen sind zu begrüßen, und doch höchst voraussetzungsreich – denn sie müssen die verschiedensten Akteur*innen, Elemente und Schauplätze, an denen Chrononormativität vollzogen wird – vom Arbeitsplatz bis in den Körper – berücksichtigen.

Literatur

Adrian, S.W. (2015). Psychological IVF: conceptualizing emotional choreography in a fertility clinic. Distinktion: *Journal of Social Theory* 16(3), 302–317. DOI: https://doi.org/10.1080/1600910X.2015.1091780.

Amrhein, L. (2008). *Drehbücher des Alter(n)s*. Wiesbaden: VS Verlag für Sozialwissenschaften.
Blue, S. (2017). Institutional rhythms: Combining practice theory and rhythmanalysis to conceptualise processes of institutionalisation. *Time & Society*: 0961463X1770216. DOI: https://doi.org/10.1177/0961463X17702165.
Benson, D. (2008). Consuming and Producing Culture. *Philosophy now*: https://philosophynow.org/issues/65/Consuming_And_Producing_Culture [DOA: 12/04/2019],
Biesta, G., Field, J. & Tedder, M. (2010). A time for learning: representations of time and the temporal dimensions of learning through the lifecourse. *Zeitschrift für Pädagogik* 56 (3), 317-327.
Bourdieu, P. (1979). *La Distinction: Critique Sociale Du Jugement. Le Sens commun*. Paris: Éditions de Minuit.
Bundeszentrale für politische Bildung (2016). Erwerbsaustritt und Renteneintritt. URL: https://www.bpb.de/politik/innenpolitik/rentenpolitik/223233/erwerbsaustritt-und-renteneintritt [DOA 24.04.2019, 17:00]
Butler, J. (2004). *Undoing Gender*. New York ; London: Routledge.
Burzan, N. (2002). *Zeitgestaltung im Alltag älterer Menschen. Eine Untersuchung im Zusammenhang mit Biographie und sozialer Ungleichheit*. Opladen: Leske + Budrich.
Derrida, J. (1982). *Margins of Philosophy*. Chicago: University of Chicago Press.
Deutsche Rentenversicherung (2018). Rentenversicherung in Zeitreihen, Oktober 2018. URL: https://www.deutsche-rentenversicherung.de/Allgemein/de/Inhalt/6_Wir_ueber_uns/03_fakten_und_zahlen/03_statistiken/02_statistikpublikationen/03_rv_in_zeitreihen.pdf?__blob=publicationFile&v=22 [DOA 24.04.2019, 17:00]
Ekerdt, D.J. (1986). The Busy Ethic: Moral Continuity Between Work and Retirement. *The Gerontologist* 26(3), 239–244. DOI: 10.1093/geront/26.3.239.
Elder, G.H., Johnson, M.K. & Crosnoe, R. (2003). The Emergence and Development of Life Course Theory. In J.T. Mortimer & M.J. Shanahan (Hrsg.), Handbook of the Life Course (S. 3–19). Boston, MA: Springer US.
Foucault, M. (2010). *The Birth of Biopolitics: Lectures at the Collège de France, 1978–79*. Paperback edition. In M. Senellart (Hrsg.), Michel Foucault's lectures at the Collège de France. New York, NY: Palgrave Macmillan.
Freeman, E. (2010). *Time Binds: Queer Temporalities, Queer Histories(Perverse Modernities)*. Durham [NC]: Duke University Press.
Halberstam, J. (2005). *In a Queer Time and Place: Transgender Bodies, Subcultural Lives.*, New York: New York University Press.
Jansen, A, (2018), Work-retirement cultures: A further piece of the puzzle to explain differences in the labour market participation of older people in Europe? *Ageing and Society* 38 (8), 1527–1555. https://doi:https://doi.org/10.1017/S0144686X17000125
Katz, S. (1996). *Disciplining Old Age: The Formation of Gerontological Knowledge*. Charlottesville: University Press of Virginia.
Katz, S. (2000). Busy Bodies: Activity, aging, and the management of everyday life. *Journal of Aging Studies* 14(2), 135–152. DOI: 10.1016/S0890-4065(00)80008-0.
Köller, R. (2007). *Ruhestand – mehr Zeit für Lebensqualität? Die Bedeutung von Erwerbstätigkeit und Zeiterfahrungen im Lebenslauf für die individuelle Gestaltung des Ruhestandes*. Bremen (Dissertation an der Universität Bremen).

Kohli, M. (1985). Die Institutionalisierung des Lebenslaufs. Historische Befunde und theoretische Argumente. *Kölner Zeitschrift für Soziologie und Sozialpsychologie* 37, 1–29.

Kohli, M. (2007). The Institutionalization of the Life Course: Looking Back to Look Ahead. *Research in Human Development* 4(3-4), 253–271. DOI: 10.1080/15427600701663122.

Krekula, C. (2010). Age coding – on age-based practices of distinction. *International Journal of Ageing and Later Life* 4(2), 7–31. DOI: 10.3384/ijal.1652-8670.09427.

Krekula, C., Arvidson, M., Heikkinen, S., et al. (2017). On gray dancing: Constructions of age-normality through choreography and temporal codes. *Journal of Aging Studies* 42, 38–45. DOI: 10.1016/j.jaging.2017.07.001.

Küster, C. (1998). Zeitverwendung und Wohnen im Alter. In: Deutsches Zentrum für Altersfragen (Hrsg). Wohnbedürfnisse, Zeitverwendung und soziale Netzwerke älterer Menschen. Expertenband 1 zum zweiten Altenbericht der Deutschen Bundesregierung (S. 51–175). Frankfurt a.M..

Laube, S. (2016). *Nervöse Märkte. Materielle und leibliche Praktiken im virtuellen Finanzhandel*. Berlin: De Gruyter.

Laz, C. (1998). Act Your Age. *Sociological Forum* 13(1), 85–113.

Lefebvre, H. (2004). *Rhythmanalysis: Space, Time, and Everyday Life*. London ; New York: Continuum.

Leonard, P., Fuller, A. & Unwin, L. (2018). A new start? Negotiations of age and chrononormativity by older apprentices in England. *Ageing and Society* 38(8), 1667–1692. DOI: 10.1017/S0144686X17000204.

Marshall, B.L. (2018). Happily ever after? 'Successful ageing' and the heterosexual imaginary. *European Journal of Cultural Studies* 21(3), 363–381. DOI: 10.1177/1367549417708434.

Miao, L. (2011). Guilty Pleasure or Pleasurable Guilt? Affective Experience of Impulse Buying in Hedonic-Driven Consumption. *Journal of Hospitality & Tourism Research* 35(1), 79–101. DOI: 10.1177/1096348010384876.

Nicolini, D. (2017). Is small the only beautiful? Making sense of 'large phenomena' from a practise-based perspective. In: A. Hui, T. Schatzki & E. Shove (Hrsg.) The Nexus of Practices. Connections, constellations, practitioners (S. 98–113). London ; New York: Routledge.

Parkes, D. & Thrift, N. (1979). Time spacemakers and entrainment. *Transactions of the Institute of British Geographers* 4, 353–372.

Powell, J.L. (2001). Theorising Social Gerontology: The Case Of Social Philosophies Of Age. *The Internet Journal of Internal Medicine* 2(1). DOI: https://doi.org/10.5580/15d1.

Reckwitz, A. (2002). Toward a Theory of Social Practices: A Development in Culturalist Theorizing. *European Journal of Social Theory* 5(2), 243–263. DOI: 10.1177/13684310222225432.

Reckwitz, A. (2017). Practices and their affects. In: A. Hui, T. Schatzki & E. Shove (Hrsg.) The Nexus of Practices. Connections, constellations, practitioners (S. 114–125). London ; New York: Routledge.

Riach, K., Rumens, N. & Tyler, M. (2014). Un/doing Chrononormativity: Negotiating Ageing, Gender and Sexuality in Organizational Life. *Organization Studies* 35(11), 1677–1698. DOI: 10.1177/0170840614550731.

Sandberg, L. & Marshall, B.L. (2017). Queering Aging Futures. *Societies* 7(3), 21. DOI: 10.3390/soc7030021.

Schatzki, T.R. (1996). *Social Practices: A Wittgensteinian Approach to Human Activity and the Social*. New York: Cambridge University Press.

Schatzki, T.R. (2010). *The Timespace of Human Activity: On Performance, Society, and History as Indeterminate Teleological Events*. Toposophia. Lanham, Md: Lexington Books.

Schatzki, T.R. (2016). Practice theory as flat ontology. In: G. SpaargarenD. Weenink & M. Lamers (Hrsg.), Practice theory and research: exploring the dynamics of social life (S. 28–42). Abingdon: Routledge.

Schilling, O.K. (2016). Distance-to-Death Research in Geropsychology. In: N.A. Pachana (Hrsg.), Encyclopedia of Geropsychology (S.1–13). Singapore: Springer Singapore,.

Schroeter, K.R. (2012). Altersbilder als Körperbilder: Doing Age by Bodyfication. In: F. Berner, J. Rossow,& K.P. Schwitzer (Hrsg.), Individuelle und kulturelle Altersbilder (S.153–229). Wiesbaden: VS Verlag für Sozialwissenschaften.

Schroeter, K.R. (2018). Doing Age in Other Ways – Formen "anderen Alterns". Weitere Facetten der Verwirklichung des Alterns. In: H.P. Zimmermann (Hrsg.), Kulturen der Sorge: Wie unsere Gesellschaft ein Leben mit Demenz ermöglichen kann (S. 99–126). Frankfurt a.M.: Campus,.

Seibold, A. (2017). Statutory Ages as Reference Points for Retirement: Evidence from Germany. London School of Economics. URL: https://www.iipf.org/papers/Seibold-Statutory_Ages_as_Reference_Points_for_Retirement-440.pdf [DOA 24.04.2019, 17:00]

Shove, E., Pantzar, M. & Watson, M. (2012). *The Dynamics of Social Practice: Everyday Life and How It Changes*. Los Angeles: SAGE Publications.

Southerton, D. (2003). `Squeezing Time': Allocating Practices, Coordinating Networks and Scheduling Society. *Time & Society* 12(1), 5–25. DOI: 10.1177/0961463X03012001001.

Southerton, D. (2006). Analysing the Temporal Organization of Daily Life:: Social Constraints, Practices and their Allocation. *Sociology* 40(3), 435–454. DOI: 10.1177/0038038506063668.

Spurling, N. (2015). Differential experiences of time in academic work: How qualities of time are made in practice. *Time & Society* 24(3), 367–389. DOI: 10.1177/0961463X15575842.

Statistisches Bundesamt (2018). Erwerbstätige und Erwerbstätigenquote nach Geschlecht und Alter 2008 und 2018. Ergebnis des Mikrozensus. . URL: https://www.destatis.de/DE/Themen/Arbeit/Arbeitsmarkt/Erwerbstaetigkeit/Tabellen/erwerbstaetige-erwerbstaetigenquote.html [DOA: 28.08.2019; 12:00]

Statistisches Bundesamt (2016). *Wie die Zeit vergeht. Analysen zur Zeitverwendung in Deutschland*. Beiträge zur Ergebniskonferenz der Zeitverwendungserhebung 2012/2013 am 5./6. Oktober 2016 in Wiesbaden.

van Dyk, S. & Lessenich, S. (2009). Ambivalenzen der (De-)Aktivierung: Altwerden im flexiblen Kapitalismus. *WSI-Mitteilungen* 62 (10), 540-546.

Venn, S. & Arber, S. (2011). Day-time sleep and active ageing in later life. *Ageing and Society* 31(02), 197–216. DOI: 10.1017/S0144686X10000954.

Vidovićová, L. (2018). The Expected, Evaluated, Perceived, Valued and Prevalent Social Roles of Older People: Are They by Consent? In: A. Zaidi, S. Harper, K. Howse, et al.

(Hrsg.), Building Evidence for Active Ageing Policies (S. 39–54). Singapore: Springer Singapore.

Wanka, A. (2019). Change Ahead—Emerging Life-Course Transitions as Practical Accomplishments of Growing Old(er). *Frontiers in Sociology* 3. DOI: 10.3389/fsoc.2018.00045.

West, C. & Zimmerman, D.H. (1987). Doing Gender. *Gender & Society* 1(2), 125–151. DOI: 10.1177/0891243287001002002.

Wolf, J. (1988). Langeweile und immer Termine. Zeitperspektiven beim Übergang in den Ruhestand. In: G. Göckenjan & H.J. Kondratowitz (Hrsg.), Alter und Alltag (S. 200–218). Frankfurt a.M.: Suhrkamp,.

Zerubavel, E. (1987). The Language of Time: Toward A Semiotics of Temporality. *The Sociological Quarterly* 28(3), 343–356. DOI: 10.1111/j.1533-8525.1987.tb00299.x.

Biografizität als „mentale Grammatik" der Lebenszeit

Peter Alheit

Abstract

The following considerations raise the cautious claim to get to the bottom of the difficult sociological problem, how biographical experience arises and how it happens that social individuals develop their very own "experience code", which in a temporal perspective is "constituted" by social influences and at the same time remains a highly personal construction of each individual, i.e. how structure and emergence, social constitution and individual construction form a specific blend in a lived life. The stimulating influence of modern neurobiology will be discussed first. Subsequently, time will be given to innovations and restrictions of a system theoretically reformulated biography theory. Its self-referentiality blocks can be illustrated particularly clearly by the problem of the social construction of "gender", in which we also come up against the limits of the interactionist concept of construction. This theoretical discourse gives rise to a concept of its own, which at least implicitly follows on from the previously only vaguely developed concept of "biographicity".

Zusammenfassung

Die folgenden Überlegungen erheben den vorsichtigen Anspruch, dem schwierigen soziologischen Problem auf die Spur zu kommen, wie biografische Erfahrung entsteht und wie es dazu kommt, dass soziale Individuen

P. Alheit (✉)
Georg-August-Universität Göttingen, Göttingen, Deutschland
E-Mail: palheit@gwdg.de

einen je eigenen „Erfahrungscode" entwickeln, der in temporaler Perspektive als durch soziale Einflüsse „konstituiert" gedacht werden muss und doch zugleich eine höchst persönliche Konstruktion jedes einzelnen Individuums bleibt, wie also Struktur und Emergenz, soziale Konstitution und individuelle Konstruktion in einem gelebten Leben eine spezifische Melange ausbilden. Dabei soll zunächst der anregende Einfluss der modernen Neurobiologie diskutiert werden. Im Anschluss daran soll auf Innovationen und Bornierungen einer systemtheoretisch reformulierten Biografietheorie eingegangen werden. Deren Selbstreferenzialitätsblockaden lassen sich besonders anschaulich am Problem der sozialen Konstruktion von „Geschlecht" verdeutlichen, bei der wir allerdings auch an die Grenzen des interaktionistischen Konstruktionsbegriffs stoßen. Aus diesem theoretischen Diskurs entsteht ein eigenes Konzept, das zumindest implizit an den bisher nur vorläufig entfalteten Begriff der *Biografizität* anschließt.

Keywords

Biography · Constructivism · Neurobiology · Systems theory · Gender · Generative transformation grammar · Semantics · Biographicity

Schlüsselwörter

Biografie · Konstruktivismus · Neurobiologie · Systemtheorie · Gender · Generative Transformationsgrammatik · Semantik · Biografizität

Das Konzept der „Biografizität" schließt im soziologischen Diskurs an konstruktivistische Überlegungen an. Einen ersten Hinweis finden wir in einem Überblicksartikel von Martin Kohli, in dem er *Biografizität* als „Code von personaler Entwicklung und Emergenz" definiert (Kohli 1988, S. 37). Diese sehr vorläufige Charakterisierung muss präzisiert und auf den konstruktivistischen Diskurs bezogen werden.

In der Biografieforschung selbst sind konstruktivistische Ansätze seit den 1980er Jahren *en vogue*. In einem interessanten Aufsatz hat Uwe Schimank (1988) im Anschluss an Luhmanns Autopoiesis-Konzept die provokante These vertreten, dass „das Verhältnis zwischen den gesellschaftlichen Kommunikationen, denen eine Person ausgesetzt ist, und ihrem biografischen Bewusstsein … strikt *konstruktivistisch*" verstanden werden müsse (Schimank 1988, S. 58). „Die Konstruktion der je eigenen Biografie durch eine Person vollzieht sich", so Schimank, „im radikalen Sinn des Wortes autonom. Alle Einflüsse aus der gesellschaftlichen Umwelt, ob gezielt oder absichtslos, werden gemäß den internen Strukturen des personalen Systems verarbeitet, gleichsam von *withinputs* abgefangen und eskortiert und können allein so überhaupt biografische Bedeutung erlangen." (ibid.)

Dieser Gedanke kann plausibel auf eine Reihe empirisch beobachtbarer Phänomene zurückgreifen – so beispielsweise auf die triviale Tatsache, dass bestimmte soziale Einflüsse in einer Biografie geradezu gegenteilige Wirkungen zeitigen können wie dieselben Inputs in einer anderen Biografie. Deshalb ist es sinnvoll, „Sozialität" konsequent aus der biografischen Perspektive wahrzunehmen – nicht um den „objektiven" Charakter struktureller Außeneinflüsse zu dementieren, sondern um die Semantik zu verstehen, mit der „psychische Systeme" Soziales zu codieren pflegen. Dass also „gesellschaftliche Kommunikationen", wie Schimank sich ausdrückt, eher als selbstreferenzielle *intakes* begriffen werden müssen und gerade nicht als *inputs*, die erwartbare *outputs* hervorbringen, erscheint überzeugend. Wie nun freilich der einzigartige „Code" der biografischen Erfahrungsverarbeitung seinerseits zustande kommt, wie er in temporaler Perspektive durchaus als durch soziale Einflüsse „konstituiert" gedacht werden muss, wie also Struktur und Emergenz, soziale Konstitution und individuelle Konstruktion in einem gelebten Leben eine spezifische Melange ausbilden, darüber lässt uns Schimanks intelligente Abhandlung noch im Unklaren.

Die folgenden Überlegungen erheben den vorsichtigen Anspruch, diesem schwierigen soziologischen Problem auf die Spur zu kommen. Dabei soll zunächst der anregende Einfluss der modernen Neurobiologie diskutiert werden. Im Anschluss daran soll auf Innovationen und Bornierungen einer systemtheoretisch reformulierten Biografietheorie eingegangen werden. Deren Selbstreferenzialitätsblockaden lassen sich besonders anschaulich am Problem der sozialen Konstruktion von „Geschlecht" verdeutlichen, bei der wir allerdings auch an die Grenzen des interaktionistischen Konstruktionsbegriffs stoßen. Aus diesem theoretischen Diskurs entsteht ein eigenes Konzept, das zumindest implizit an den bisher nur vorsichtig entfalteten Begriff der *Biografizität* anschließt.

Anregungen und offene Fragen des neurobiologischen Konstruktivismus

[1]Die Kritik an der autobiografischen Rekonstruktion sozialer Wirklichkeit, die gerade in der Soziologie artikuliert worden ist, der Vorwurf, es handele sich dabei um schlichte „Illusion" (Bourdieu 1990), wiederholt eine klassische Debatte

---

[1]Die folgenden beiden Abschnitte dieses Aufsatzes sind im Wesentlichen Auszüge aus dem gemeinsam mit Bettina Dausien publizierten Essay „*Die biographische Konstruktion der Wirklichkeit. Überlegungen zur Biographizität des Sozialen*" (2000), allerdings von mir allein verantwortet.

der modernen Erkenntnistheorie: der Wahrnehmung von Wirklichkeit aus der Sicht biografischer Erzähler hafte etwas Subjektives und Partikulares an; und es erscheine durchaus fragwürdig, ob sich daraus allgemeine Erkenntnisse über soziale Wirklichkeit gewinnen lassen.

Diese zumindest implizit am erkenntnistheoretischen Standpunkt des kritischen Rationalismus orientierte Position, die auch das Alltagshandeln in modernen Gesellschaften beeinflusst hat, erscheint aus dem Blickwinkel jüngerer Forschungen der Neurobiologie zumindest ergänzungsbedürftig.[2] Bei allem Misstrauen gegenüber der Genauigkeit subjektiver Wahrnehmung – gerade wenn beträchtliche Zeitabschnitte zwischen Ereignis und Rekapitulation liegen – bleibt doch die Tatsache, dass das Gedächtnis (allgemeiner: das Gehirn als synthetisches „Wahrnehmungsorgan") einen unmittelbaren Zugang zur Wirklichkeit habe, völlig unproblematisiert.

Genau diese Skepsis ist indessen notwendig, wenn man mit der jüngeren Neurobiologie Wahrnehmungsvorgänge sozusagen aus der Perspektive des Gehirns betrachtet. Dann nämlich erscheinen die Informationen der verschiedenen Sinnesorgane nicht als unmittelbare Eindrücke von Auge und Ohr, Geruchs- oder Tastsinn, sondern als prinzipiell unspezifische neuronale Informationen, die erst vom Gehirn selbst in eindeutige „Sinneseindrücke" verwandelt werden. „Für das Gehirn existieren [...] nur die neuronalen Botschaften, die von den Sinnesorganen kommen, nicht aber die Sinnesorgane selbst, genausowenig wie für den Betrachter eines Fernsehbildes die Aufnahmekamera existiert." (Roth 1987a, S. 234)

Die Möglichkeit des Gehirns, gewissermaßen „richtige" Bedeutungszuschreibungen vorzunehmen, resultiert allein aus einer relativ frühen räumlichen Differenzierung neuronal übermittelter Erregungszustände. Z.B. werden alle neuronalen Impulse, die am Hinterhauptcortex verarbeitet werden, als *Seh*eindrücke gedeutet. Sie würden auch dann als Informationen des Gesichtssinns, etwa als rote Farbe, „wahrgenommen", wenn der neuronale Reiz dieser Gehirnpartie nicht durch das Auge übermittelt worden wäre, sondern von der Manipulation des Hinterhauptcortex durch eine künstlich eingeführte Elektrode stammte. „All dies führt zu der merkwürdigen Feststellung, daß das Gehirn, anstatt weltoffen zu sein, ein kognitiv in sich geschlossenes System ist, das nach eigenentwickelten

---

[2]Ich beziehe mich hier vor allem auf die Arbeiten von Humberto R. Maturana und seinen Mitarbeitern (stellvertretend Maturana 1970, 1978, 1987a, 1987b; Maturana et al. 1975, 1987; Varela 1979, 1981, 1987; Varela et al. 1974, 1991) und auf die kongenialen und z.T. modifizierenden Fortsetzungsstudien der Forschungsgruppe um Gerhard Roth (z.B. Roth 1985, 1987a, 1987b; Roth und Schwegler (eds.) 1981; An der Heiden et al. 1986).

Kriterien neuronale Signale deutet und bewertet, von deren wahrer Herkunft und Bedeutung es nichts absolut Verläßliches weiß." (Roth 1987a, S. 235)

Freilich, indem das Gehirn im radikalen Sinn selbstreferenziell verfährt und Wirklichkeit eben nicht abbildet, sondern konstruiert, schafft es sich auch Kriterien zur Überprüfung seiner Konstruktionsergebnisse. Denn um überleben zu können, benötigt das Gehirn nicht nur *eine* kognitive Welt, sondern gleichsam drei „Welten": eine Welt um uns herum, die man *Dingwelt* nennen könnte, eine Art *Körperwelt*, die sich auf sensorische und motorische Erfahrungen mit unserem Körper bezieht, und die nichtkörperliche Welt unserer Gedanken und Gefühle (vgl. ibid., S. 236 ff). Diese Welten stehen in Beziehung zueinander, bilden füreinander Innen- und Außendimensionen und korrigieren sich gewissermaßen wechselseitig, obgleich jede im strengen Sinn nur ein kognitives Konstrukt ist, also mit dem realen materiellen „Außen" *unmittelbar* keine Verbindung hat.

Gerhard Roth hat unser Gehirn mit einer Person verglichen, die durch ein fremdes Land reist, dessen Sprache sie nicht versteht, und die deshalb auf einen Dolmetscher angewiesen ist (vgl. ibid., S. 242 ff). Zur Einschätzung der Zuverlässigkeit des Übersetzers hat die Person mehrere Strategien zur Verfügung: Sie kann z.B. in vorausgegangenen Situationen mit dem Dolmetscher ausgezeichnete Erfahrungen gemacht haben, die ihr die Verlässlichkeit des kulturellen Vermittlers verbürgen. Auch die Organisation unseres Gehirns verweist auf ein lange zurückliegendes und offensichtlich äußerst erfolgreiches phylogenetisches Erbe. Die „Dolmetscherleistungen" verdienen also Vertrauensvorschuss. Die Person könnte zur Kontrolle auch *mehrere* Dolmetscher verpflichten. Auch mit dieser Strategie ist unser Gehirn vertraut, wenn zur Ratifizierung ein und desselben Zustandes mehrere Sinnesareale aktiviert werden. Jener Reisende hat schließlich die Möglichkeit, jede vom Übersetzer hinzugefügte Information mit bereits vorhandenen Informationen zu vergleichen und auf ihre Konsistenz hin zu prüfen. Diese Funktion übernimmt beim Gehirn das Gedächtnis.

Dies bedeutet aber: Strikte Selbstreferenzialität führt keineswegs zu einer prinzipiellen Abschottung des Gehirns von Außeneinflüssen. Solche *„Perturbationen"*, wie Maturana und Varela sie nennen, müssen ständig verarbeitet werden und verändern das verarbeitende Gesamtsystem durchaus. Aber sie beeinflussen es nicht nach den Gesetzen des „Eindringlings", sondern ausschließlich nach den bis dahin entwickelten internen Regeln des Systems (Maturana & Varela 1987, S. 108 f). Diese Disposition scheint in immer komplexer werdenden Umwelten wesentlich erfolgreichere Überlebenschancen zu garantieren als die prinzipielle Weltoffenheit des Wahrnehmungsapparates (vgl. ausführlicher Roth 1985, 1987a; Maturana et al. 1987).

Herausfordernd an diesem neurobiologischen Konzept der Kognition ist die Vorstellung, dass jede Verarbeitung von Wirklichkeit, selbstverständlich auch die Rekapitulation biografischer Erfahrung, als selbstreferenzielle Leistung des kognitiven Systems betrachtet werden müsste. Sympathischerweise zeigt sich allerdings, dass bei den Vertretern dieser reizvollen These durchaus noch Dissens darüber besteht, wie eng jener Prozess phylogenetisch und ontogenetisch mit dem Prinzip der *Autopoiese* verknüpft und erklärt werden kann. Während Humberto Maturana, der eigentliche Entdecker der konzeptionellen Idee, Leben und Kognition in eins setzt und für beide das Prinzip der zirkulären Selbstherstellung und Selbsterhaltung (Autopoiese) reklamiert (vgl. das Maturana-Zitat in Roth 1987b, S. 262), betont z.b. die Forschungsgruppe um Gerhard Roth den nur *relativ* autopoietischen Charakter aller Organismen, die immer auch von ihren Umwelten definiert werden (An der Heiden et al. 1986), und besteht zudem auf einer durch die Evolution bedingten *strukturellen Differenzierung* zwischen den Selbsterhaltungsprinzipien des Gesamtorganismus und den zwar selbstreferenziellen, aber keineswegs autopoietischen Funktionsweisen höherer Nervensysteme (Roth 1987b, S. 266 ff).

Pointierter noch: Kognition ist, neurobiologisch betrachtet, umso leistungsfähiger für die Autopoiese des Organismus, je eindeutiger sie von den Zwängen zirkulärer Selbstherstellung und Selbsterhaltung ihrer Komponenten frei bleibt. Diese Eigenschaft macht nämlich Lernprozesse möglich, die jedes kognitive System „selbst-explikativ" entwickeln muss. „Der Umstand, daß das kognitive System nicht autopoietisch ist, konstituiert also zum einen [...] die Möglichkeit der selbstreferentiellen Entfaltung, aber zugleich die Notwendigkeit, individuell stets wieder ‚von vorn' anzufangen." (ibid., S. 281) Dieses „Immer-wieder-von-vorn-Anfangen" ist im Grunde identisch mit der Einzigartigkeit des jeweiligen biografischen Prozesses. Auf diese konzeptionell wesentlichen Affinitäten der kritischen Einsichten der jüngeren neurobiologischen Diskussion mit soziologischer und pädagogischer Biografieforschung soll später explizit eingegangen werden.

Biografietheoretisch relevant ist ohne Frage die Entdeckung, dass kognitive Wirklichkeitsverarbeitung, also die synthetischen Codierungsleistungen unseres Gehirns, *selbstreferenziell* strukturiert sind, sich eben nicht durch den Charakter von äußeren Einflüssen, sondern allein durch eine zuvor bereits existente innere „Logik" bestimmen lassen. Dieser Vorgang scheint jedoch – folgt man Gerhard Roth und seiner Arbeitsgruppe – gerade nicht „autopoietisch" zu sein, sondern von der relativen Autopoiese einer umgebenden Systemstruktur (Organismus) abzuhängen, deren Überleben wiederum von den selbstreferenziellen Leistungen des Gehirns profitiert. Wir hätten es gewissermaßen mit der relativen (inneren) Autonomie einer prinzipiellen Abhängigkeitsstruktur zu tun – ein soziologisch zweifellos hochinteressantes Modell.

Konzeptionelle Aporien biografietheoretischer Erklärungen der Systemtheorie

Eine gewisse soziologische Radikalisierung erfährt die Konstruktivismusdebatte zweifellos in der jüngeren Systemtheorie. Dabei soll hier weniger interessieren, dass Luhmann mit seiner „Theorie selbstreferentieller Systeme" (Luhmann and Niklas 1984, S. 24) das von ihm zuvor konzeptionell entfaltete Verhältnis von System und Umwelt drastisch modifiziert. Die Binnendifferenzierung des Systems wird nun nicht mehr als Ergebnis umweltbedingten Komplexitätsdrucks, sondern ausschließlich als Effekt selbstreferenzieller Operationen gedeutet (ibid., S. 25). Der Anschluss an Maturanas Autopoiesis-Konzept relativiert die Dynamik von Kontingenz und Selektivität zugunsten einer „mitlaufenden Selbstreferenz", wie Luhmann sich ausdrückt[3]. Für unsere Zwecke sind vielmehr nur diejenigen Aspekte der Theorieentwicklung von Interesse, die sich unmittelbar auf biografietheoretische Fragen beziehen lassen.

Dazu erscheint es sinnvoll, sich knapp die entscheidende Pointe der Luhmannschen Modernitätsdiagnose noch einmal zu vergegenwärtigen. Die primäre vertikale Differenzierung vormoderner Gesellschaften, die sozialen Akteuren, von Ausnahmefällen abgesehen, ihren eindeutigen Platz in einem Teilsystem der Gesellschaft zuwies (vgl. Luhmann 1980, S. 30), ist einer funktionalen Differenzierung gewichen, in der soziale Teilsysteme wie Wirtschaft, Familie, Politik, Recht, Religion oder Erziehung nebeneinander treten und die Individuen nötigen, sich *gleichzeitig* in mehrere Teilsysteme einzugliedern (ausführlicher Nassehi 1994a, b). Damit wird das Selbstverständnis sozialer Akteure nicht mehr durch ihre eindeutige Platzierung in einem hierarchisch strukturierten sozialen Feld bestimmt, sondern in gewisser Weise durch individuelle Selbstbeschreibung. „Die Identität der Person gründet also gerade nicht auf dem Prinzip sozialer Differenzierung; sie steht vielmehr quer zu ihr." (Nassehi und Weber 1990, S. 164)

Diese „Multiinklusivität" *(Nassehi/Weber)*, die es unmöglich macht, aus der einfachen Zugehörigkeit zu einem Teilsystem der modernen Gesellschaft Identität zu gewinnen, zwingt das Individuum zu permanenter Selbstbeobachtung und Selbstbeschreibung, d.h. zur selbstreferenziellen Verarbeitung sozialer Erfahrung

---

[3]Ibid., S. 605. Es erscheint übrigens für den vorliegenden Theorieaufriss ebenfalls sekundär, ob sich Luhmann damit, wie Wagner und Zipprian (1992) in einer interessanten Analyse nachweisen, ungewollt der klassischen Bewusstseinsphilosophie annähert.

(Luhmann 1985). Und was in klassischen Sozialisationstheorien als „Balance" zwischen sozialer und personaler Identität beschrieben wird (stellvertretend Krappmann 1982), zeigt sich aus systemtheoretischer Perspektive als schlichter Reflex auf die Tatsache, dass moderne soziale Akteure gezwungen sind, „sich in mehrere Selbsts, mehrere Identitäten, mehrere Persönlichkeiten zu zerlegen, um der Mehrheit sozialer Umwelten und der Unterschiedlichkeiten der Anforderungen gerecht werden zu können" (Luhmann 1989, S. 223). In Wahrheit ist die Aufspaltung in soziale und personale Identitätsanteile ein Ergebnis „selbstreferenzieller Selbstbeobachtung des psychischen Systems" (Nassehi und Weber 1990, S. 165).

Allerdings bleibt die Frage bestehen, wie das „Soziale" überhaupt zum Gegenstand der Selbstbeschreibung werden kann. Die der neurobiologischen Kognitionsidee nachgebildete Vorstellung, dass das „reflexive Selbstbewußtsein" *(Schimank)* sozialer Akteure nicht als „selbstreferentielle *Umwelt* beobachtung, das Konstruieren einer Innenwelt aus Materialien der Außenwelt, sondern (als) selbstreferentielle *Selbst* beobachtung, also das Konstruieren einer besonderen Innenwelt aus Materialien der Innenwelt" (Schimank 1988, S. 61) betrachtet werden müsse, löst nicht die Herkunftsproblematik jenes „Materials der Innenwelt".

Tatsächlich greifen Luhmann und seine Nachfolger auf eine Hierarchisierung der Bewusstseinsphänomene zurück[4]: „Das Primärphänomen ist die riesige Zahl der extern oder intern veranlaßten Erlebnisse und Handlungen, die, obwohl in einer Bewußtseinskontinuität enthalten und insofern aufeinander beziehbar, doch keinen Sinnzusammenhang bilden, weil es unmöglich ist, jedes mit jedem abzustimmen." (Luhmann und Schorr 1982, S. 237) Eine Art „basales Selbstbewußtsein" *(Schimank)* muss durch Reflexivität gleichsam „gebändigt" werden. Dass dieser Prozess nicht widerspruchslos verläuft, sondern durch „Umweltbedingungen" drastisch beeinflusst wird, kann problemlos an Schimanks Hilfskonstrukt des „biografischen Inkrementalismus" (Schimank 1988, S. 67 f) gezeigt werden. Denn die „evolutionäre Dynamik biografischer Transitorität auf der Ebene des basalen Selbstbewußtseins" (ibid., S. 67), Schimanks erstaunlich unspezifische Reformulierung für den Einfluss sozialen Wandels in modernisierten modernen

---

[4]Dabei ist der Hinweis, dass solche Abstufung natürlich zum Inventar der klassischen Bewusstseinsphilosophie gehört, relativ belanglos; auch Schimanks Verweis auf Tugendhat (1988, S. 69, Anm.11) oder Nassehi et al. (1990, S. 156 ff) belegen den Anschluss an bewusstseinphilosophisches Erbe und verstärken die Skepsis gegenüber einer Apriorizität der Autopoiese psychischer Systeme (vgl. dazu auch die vorsichtige Kritik an Luhmann bei Nassehi & Weber 1990, S. 166).

Gesellschaften, beschreibt die biografische Disposition des „Sich-Durchwurstelns" *(Schimank)* angesichts riskanter gewordener Außenbedingungen. Hier bricht das „Soziale" gleichsam hinterrücks in die selbstreferenzielle Selbstbeschreibung des psychischen Systems ein, ohne *konzeptionell* integriert zu werden.

Ein entscheidender Grund für diesen blinden Fleck systemtheoretischer Biografiekonzeptionen ist die kritiklose Hypostasierung der Autopoiese des Bewusstseins bei Luhmann. Bewusstseinsprozesse werden in der Systemtheorie nämlich – angefangen von den basalen Operationen bis hin zu den höherstufigen Selbstbeschreibungen und Selbstbeobachtungen – als zirkulär produziert und aus sich selbst konstruiert begriffen. In gewisser Weise reproduziert Luhmann hier auf soziologischer Ebene eine Schwäche, die Maturanas emphatische Autopoiesis-Idee bereits neurobiologisch begrenzt hatte: die Blockade, zu verstehen, dass das Gehirn für die Autopoiese des Gesamtorganismus gerade dann funktionaler ist, wenn es seinerseits von Autopoiesis „freigestellt", also zur Selbstherstellung und Selbstreproduktion seiner Komponenten *nicht* gezwungen wird (vgl. dazu noch einmal Roth 1987b). Dieser Einwand dementiert durchaus nicht den selbst referenziellen Charakter der Operationen des Gehirns, aber er erlaubt den Gedanken an eine systematische *Öffnung* für ein wie immer zu konzipierendes „Außen" – gleichsam eine Semantik, die *Perturbation* von außen und „inneres" *Coping* so ausbalanciert, dass die Außeneinflüsse zwar selbstreferenziell verarbeitet werden können, ihre Eigenart aber auch nach der Verarbeitung semantisch noch decodierbar bleibt.[5]

Eine konzeptionelle Parallele ließe sich zwischen Biografie und sozialer Umwelt konstruieren. Biografien besitzen die Struktur einer *nach außen offenen Selbstreferenzialität* (vgl. Alheit 2009). Diese Öffnung „zur Gesellschaft hin" setzt eine gemeinsame Semantik voraus[6], die „Soziales" biografisch codierbar und „Biografisches" sozial transponierbar macht. Wie deutlich „Soziales" in das personale System einbricht und die Unterstellung einer interaktiven Semantik zwischen Individuum und Gesellschaft notwendig macht, soll am Beispiel der Gender-Kategorie gezeigt werden.

---

[5]Auf das Phänomen „semantischer Codierung" wird später ausführlicher eingegangen.
[6]Habermas hat in einer prinzipiellen Kritik der Systemtheorie dieses Problem diskurstheoretisch aktualisiert: „Semantisch geschlossene Systeme können nicht veranlaßt werden, aus eigener Kraft die gemeinsame Sprache zu erfinden, die für die Wahrnehmung und Artikulation gesamtgesellschaftlicher Relevanzen und Maßstäbe nötig ist." (Habermas 1992, S. 427)

„Doing Gender" als Prüfstein eines soziologischen Konstruktivismus[7]

An dieser Stelle nun wird die feministische Diskussion unmittelbar für eine empirische Kritik systemtheoretischer Biografiekonzeption relevant. Gildemeister und Wetterer (1992) z.b. schlagen eine Forschungsperspektive vor, die an einer „De-Konstruktion" essentieller Genderkonzepte interessiert ist, dieses Vorgehen jedoch zunächst als wissenschaftliche *Re-Konstruktion* begreift.[8] Sie fordern, die „Geschlechterklassifikation als generatives Muster der Herstellung sozialer Ordnung" (ibid., S. 229) zu analysieren. Damit rückt der Modus des *Konstruierens* selbst in den Mittelpunkt. Er wird jedoch weder als kognitiver Akt eines individuellen Bewusstseins, noch als „Effekt" eines Diskurses ohne Subjekte betrachtet, sondern als *soziale Praxis,* mit der die Individuen in ihrem Alltagshandeln die Kategorie Geschlecht (in der Form der Zweigeschlechtlichkeit) fortgesetzt produzieren und reproduzieren (vgl. auch Wetterer 1995a). Die Analyse des sozialen Geschlechts wird mit dem Konzept des *doing gender* (West und Zimmerman 1987) gewissermaßen empirisch „situiert".

In diesem Ansatz, der explizit an die handlungstheoretische Tradition des Symbolischen Interaktionismus und der Ethnomethodologie anschließt, werden *Interaktionsprozesse* und nicht Individuen (geschlossene „personale Systeme") zur „Basiseinheit" der (empirischen) Analyse gemacht. Studien z.B. zum „Krisenexperiment" Transsexualität (Garfinkel 1967; Kessler und McKenna 1978; Hirschauer 1993b; Lindemann 1993b) decken die subtilen Regeln auf, mit denen die Individuen ihre Zugehörigkeit zu einem der beiden Geschlechter in den verschiedensten Handlungsfeldern und Alltagssituationen „darstellen" und damit *en passant* ratifizieren, aber auch in gewissen Spielräumen variieren. Diese Alltagspraktiken und Regeln sind dem Bewusstsein der Akteure nur begrenzt zugänglich. Sie wirken eher als Routinen, die erst da zur Disposition stehen, wo „Störungen" auftreten, wo unerwartete oder unbekannte Interaktionsverläufe die

---

[7]Der gendertheoretische Abschnitt dieses Aufsatzes ist ein Auszug aus dem gemeinsam mit Bettina Dausien publizierten Essay *„Die biographische Konstruktion der Wirklichkeit. Überlegungen zur Biographizität des Sozialen"* (2000) und wurde von Bettina Dausien verantwortet. Ich danke ihr für die Möglichkeit, die Passage in diesen Essay aufzunehmen.

[8]Vgl. hierzu Hirschauers Position (1993a), der ähnlich wie Gildemeister und Wetterer die Frage der De-Konstruktion in erster Linie als empirisch fundierte Rekonstruktion betrachtet und mit seiner eigenen Studie zur Transsexualität (1993b) hierfür einen Beitrag leistet.

Teilnehmer dazu zwingen, ihre Handlungen zu reflektieren, z.b. dann, wenn ein Mensch mit einer „männlichen" Körpergeschichte und einer „weiblichen" Identität die flexible Handhabung der Regeln lernt, die „er" benötigt, um in sozialen Situationen als „Frau" erfolgreich mit anderen interagieren zu können. Dieses „Wissen" um die Regeln des *doing gender* ist gerade deshalb so nachhaltig, weil es im Normalfall weitgehend präkognitiv bleibt, als Erfahrungswissen aus unzähligen Interaktionssituationen gewissermaßen im Hintergrund einer je neuen Handlungssituation wirksam wird und dem handelnden Subjekt deshalb als „fraglos gegeben", als „natürlich" erscheint (vgl. Schütz und Luckmann 1979).

Wie Erving Goffman in seiner immer noch aktuellen Studie von 1977 zeigt, betreffen die Regeln des *doing gender* gerade auch jene vermeintlich einfachen Merkmale, die „rein biologisch" zu sein scheinen wie etwa die Körpergröße. Die dem Alltagsbewusstsein „natürlich" erscheinende Relation „größerer Mann – kleinere Frau" ist erst das im Prozess der Paarbildung interaktiv hergestellte Ergebnis eines subtilen sozialen Regelsystems, das „hinter dem Rücken" der Beteiligten wirkt (Goffman 1994, S. 141 ff) und dazu führt, dass selektiv soziale Situationen aufgesucht bzw. inszeniert werden, „in denen sich Frauen und Männer ihre angeblich unterschiedliche ‚Natur' gegenseitig wirkungsvoll vorexerzieren können" (ibid., S. 143).[9] Das Beispiel zeigt, dass soziale Konstruktionsprozesse einerseits in hohem Maß auf die flexible Selbstorganisation der Individuen angewiesen sind, die sich in wechselnden Alltagssituation mit den verschiedensten funktionalen und personalen Bezügen und Handlungsspielräumen immer wieder neu als Frau bzw. als Mann rekonstruieren müssen. Andererseits ist zugleich deutlich geworden, dass dieser Prozess gewissermaßen in der Interaktion „zwischen" den Akteuren lokalisiert ist.

Bis zu diesem Punkt können die Befunde zur Geschlechtskonstruktion als anschauliche und überzeugende Bestätigung für das angedeutete Modell einer nach außen offenen Selbstreferenzialität gelesen werden. Nun führt uns das Beispiel aber einen Schritt weiter. Wenn wir die These der interaktiven Konstruktion von Geschlecht akzeptieren, dann stellt sich die Frage nach den *Regeln* dieser

---

[9]Hinsichtlich der Körpergröße, die selbst kein umweltunabhängiger Faktor ist, gibt es lediglich Differenzen *der Durchschnittswerte* zwischen den beiden Geschlechtsgruppen, die deutlich geringer sind als die Varianzen *innerhalb* der Gruppen. Paarbildungen, in denen die Frau größer ist als der Mann, wären also praktisch durchaus in großer Zahl möglich. Dass sie die „Ausnahme" bleiben, wird durch soziale Normen und subtile Handlungsstrategien garantiert.

Konstruktion. Offensichtlich handelt es sich dabei nicht um starre Muster, die den Individuen „übergestülpt" werden. Andererseits sind sie auch nicht beliebig von Situation zu Situation veränderbar. Goffman weist darauf hin, dass die Akteure in ihrem interaktiven Handeln in übergeordnete *soziale Rahmen* eingebunden sind, die je nach Situation bestimmte Sets von Regeln vorgeben. So gelten beispielsweise in einer als erotisches „Spiel" definierten Situation teilweise andere Regeln als in einer Bewerbungssituation auf dem Arbeitsmarkt.[10]

Doch auch hinter diesen situationsübergreifenden Rahmungen scheint sich eine weitere generative Struktur zu verbergen. Goffman gibt überzeugende Beispiele dafür, wie die Gesellschaftsmitglieder in den verschiedensten Typen von Alltagssituationen immer wieder neu dasselbe hierarchische Geschlechterverhältnis hervorbringen: in Beruf, Familie oder Ehe, bei Sport und Freizeit, beim Benutzen öffentlicher Räume, beim Aufsuchen von Bars oder Toiletten, beim Flirten, beim Betreten von Klassenräumen, in Situationen von Hilfsbedürftigkeit und Hilfeleistung usw. (vgl. Goffman 1977, 1994). Die soziale Konstruktion muss offensichtlich als reflexiver Prozess zwischen dem interaktiven Handeln der Individuen in kontingenten Situationen und der äußerst stabilen „Institution" Geschlecht interpretiert werden. Goffman (1994) verwendet hierfür den Begriff der „institutionellen Reflexivität" (ibid., S. 107) und beschreibt die entsprechende soziale Praxis als *Genderismus* (ibid., S. 113).[11]

An diesem Punkt wird aber deutlich, dass die Stärke des interaktionistischen Zugriffs, jene subtilen mikrosozialen Herstellungspraktiken in Alltagssituationen aufzudecken, zugleich seine Grenzen bestimmt. Wenn der Zeithorizont der Situation überschritten wird, bleibt nur noch die Annahme eines abstrakt wirksamen „Genderismus". Der historische Ursprung des Klassifikationssystems selbst erscheint dann kaum noch relevant. Nun ist der *binäre Geschlechtercode* in modernen Gesellschaften zweifellos zu einer Institution *sui generis* geworden (vgl. Gildemeister und Wetterer 1992, S. 237 ff). Feministische Forschungen liefern eine Fülle von Belegen dafür, dass die patriarchale Struktur des Geschlechterverhältnisses über verschiedenste „soziale Rahmen"

---

[10]Diese Beobachtung entspricht Luhmanns ‚funktionaler Differenzierung' (s. o.).

[11]„Schon vom Anbeginn einer Interaktion gibt es also eine Tendenz dazu, Dinge in geschlechtsbezogenen Begriffen zu formulieren; auf diese Weise stellt die Geschlechtsklasse ein Gesamtprofil oder einen Behälter zur Verfügung, auf das die unterschiedenen Merkmale zurückgeführt oder in den sie hineingeleert werden können." (Goffman 1994, S. 138) Geschlecht wird damit zum Prototyp sozialer Klassifikation überhaupt (vgl. ibid., S. 108).

hinweg konstant bleibt. Sie zeigen aber auch, dass diese Rahmen spezifischen historischen, ökonomischen und kulturellen Veränderungsprozessen unterliegen. Dem interaktionistischen Konzept des *doing gender* fehlt gewissermaßen diese historische „Tiefendimension". Die nämlich verlangt die Einbeziehung gesellschaftsgeschichtlicher Analysen[12], aber sie braucht – konzeptionell – noch eine andere Ebene: die Perspektive *lebenszeitlicher* Prozessstrukturen.

Bereits die bisherigen Überlegungen im Kontext systemtheoretischer Biografiekonzepte belegen ja nachdrücklich, dass die Konstruktionsprozesse aufseiten der Subjekte „mehr" sind als festgelegte Reaktionen auf historisch-soziale Rahmenbedingungen einerseits oder Interakte „frei flottierender Konstrukteure" (Lindemann 1993a, b, 22 ff) in kontingenten Situationen andererseits. Es gilt, die relative Autonomie der handelnden Subjekte zu erfassen, die – unter konkreten historisch-gesellschaftlichen Rahmenbedingungen – durch wechselnde Situationen hindurch und in Interaktion mit anderen ihre je individuelle „Geschichte" des *Frau-* oder *Mann-Werdens* konstruieren. In diesem Sinne kann „doing gender" als eine *biografische Struktur* gedeutet werden, die jenem interaktiven Modus der „Herstellung" von Geschlecht eine temporale Tiefendimension und ein verbindendes Gestaltprinzip verleiht.

Diesem Gedanken ist mit dem bloßen Hinweis nicht Genüge getan, dass jener interaktive Gender-doing-Prozess „als Basis für die Identität der Person betrachtet" werden muss (Gildemeister und Wetterer 1992, S. 245). Er geht über herkömmliche Ansätze zur „geschlechtsspezifischen Sozialisation" hinaus.[13]

---

[12] Auf die Notwendigkeit einer historisch-gesellschaftlich Differenzierung der Kategorie Geschlecht weist besonders konsequent Becker-Schmidt hin (zuletzt 1996). Die Historizität des Geschlechterverhältnisses zeigt sich vor allem an den sich wandelnden Formen der Arbeitsteilung und den damit verbundenen Variationen gesellschaftlicher Geschlechtsrollenpräskripte und Handlungsspielräume. Ein anschauliches empirisches Beispiel für derartige Prozesse ist der „Geschlechtswechsel von Berufen", an dem sich die Herstellung und De-Konstruktion von Geschlecht auf *institutioneller* Ebene analysieren lässt (vgl. Wetterer 1992, 1995a, 1995b; Knapp 1995).

[13] Gerade sozialisationstheoretisches Konzepte (vgl. zusammenfassend Nunner-Winkler 1994) sind nämlich durch die (de-)konstruktivistische Kritik betroffen. Unabhängig davon, ob sie eher lerntheoretisch oder psychoanalytisch orientiert sind, unterliegen gerade sie der Gefahr einer essentialistischen Interpretation von Geschlecht (vgl. noch einmal das Beispiel „weiblichen Arbeitsvermögens" oder „weiblicher Moral"). Sie teilen die Stärken und Schwächen ihrer Herkunftstheorien und neigen entweder zu einer Überbetonung der gesellschaftlichen Prägung oder zur Annahme einer biologisch verankerten, inneren Triebdynamik.

Der Prozess des *Geschlecht-Werdens* erschöpft sich nicht in der ontogenetischen Aneignung interaktiver Regeln zur Darstellung des Geschlechts. Er kann als biografischer Prozess der Erfahrungsaufschichtung und -konstruktion begriffen werden (vgl. Dausien 1994, 1996a).

Diese Sichtweise verfolgt die individuellen „Wege"[14] durch die sich historisch verändernden „Handlungsumwelten", die ihrerseits immer geschlechtercodiert sind und spezifische Erfahrungsräume und -grenzen zur Verfügung stellen. So sind z.b. die Möglichkeiten, eine Biografie als Homosexueller zu leben, abhängig von historisch-kulturellen Rahmenbedingungen, vom konkreten sozialen Milieu, von familiären Konstellationen, von Beziehungsmöglichkeiten im sozialen Nahbereich, von der Zugänglichkeit „schwuler" Subkulturen etc. (vgl. Scheuermann 1996). Auch die Chancen, als Frau einen „normalen" Lebensentwurf zu verwirklichen, in dem Beruf und Familie nach den eigenen Vorstellungen miteinander verknüpft werden können (vgl. Dausien 1996a), sind nicht weniger limitiert als die Möglichkeit, ein Leben zu führen, das „aus der Rolle fällt". Ohne die Reflexion der konkreten biografischen Bedingungen ist der Schritt zur Pauschalisierung und damit zur Reifizierung sozialer Konstrukte nicht weit.

Die Analyse der biografischen Konstruktion von Geschlecht (vgl. Dausien 1996a) bleibt jedoch nicht dabei stehen, die individuelle „Route" zu rekonstruieren, die weibliche oder männliche Reisende in einer geschlechtercodierten Welt zurücklegen, um das Bild von Roth noch einmal aufzugreifen (s.o.). Es geht vor allem um die Rekonstruktion der jeweils eigenen biografischen Erfahrungsaufschichtung, die ein Individuum als Frau oder Mann auf diesem Weg herausgebildet hat und die ihrerseits die jeweils nächsten Schritte mitbestimmt. Empirische Rekonstruktionen biografischer Erzählungen zeigen, dass die Geschichte des „Geschlecht-Werdens" untrennbar in die einmalige biografische Erfahrungsgestalt hineinverwoben ist (Dausien 1996a). Auf diese Weise wird umgekehrt die soziale Konstruktion von Geschlecht durch alle individuellen und historischen Wandlungsprozesse hindurch rekonstruiert. Deshalb kann De-Konstruktion nicht die Abschaffung der Geschlechterkategorie bedeuten, sondern allenfalls deren Umgestaltung.

---

[14]Dass diese nicht als geschlossene autopoietische Strukturen, sondern immer als Interaktionsgeschichten zu denken sind, muss nach den vorstehenden Überlegungen nicht mehr begründet werden.

Die Ansätze zur sozialen Konstruktion von Geschlecht überzeugen zweifellos durch ihre konsequente Absage an essentialistische Theorien von Weiblichkeit und Männlichkeit. Sie zeigen darüber hinaus plausibel, dass die Idee strikter Autopoiese „personaler Systeme", wie sie die jüngere Systemtheorie vertritt, deutlich von der sozialen Wirklichkeit abweicht. Aber sie liefern noch kein konsistentes Gesamtkonzept dafür, wie die „Konstruktion von Geschlecht" theoretisch zu denken ist und wie die sozialen Akteurinnen und Akteure biografisch zu diesem Prozess beitragen. Genau das wäre freilich die Aufgabe einer soziologischen (und übrigens auch einer bildungswissenschaftlichen) Biografietheorie. Sie hätte einerseits den Einfluss sozialer Konstruktionen auf das individuelle Leben zu rekonstruieren, die Art und Weise, wie soziale Strukturen sich im Terrain der „Subjektivität" einnisten. Sie müsste andererseits transparent machen, wie Individuen auf jene Einflüsse von außen höchst eigensinnig reagieren. Diese „nach außen offene Selbstreferenzialität" biografischer Verarbeitung soll nun im folgenden Abschnitt exemplarisch entfaltet werden.

Biografizität als einzigartige „Grammatik des Sozialen"

Dass „Geschlecht" eben nicht auf intellektuellem Wege „dekonstruiert" werden kann, liegt nicht an seiner Unhintergehbarkeit als vorgeblich biologisches Faktum, sondern an der Tatsache, dass es im Laufe einer Biografie konkreter Frauen und Männer, ja, auch von Menschen, die sich intergeschlechtlich bewegen, erworben, angeeignet und immer neu „hergestellt" wird. Um eine Metapher aus der Sprachtheorie zu nutzen: Die „Semantik" des Geschlechtercodes mag in den sich historisch wandelnden institutionalisierten Interaktionsordnungen (klassisch: Goffman 1994) oder in den Routinen sozialer Praktiken (klassisch: Garfinkel 1967) verborgen sein, ihre *Grammatik* liegt in den biografischen Handlungsressourcen der Individuen, in ihrer *Biografizität*, selbst. Und diese Grammatik erzeugt Performanzen, die zum Konzept der Dekonstruktion nicht passen wollen, weil auf sie noch andere Semantiken einwirken: z.B. der in der klassischen soziologischen Diskussion lange ins Zentrum gestellte semantische Code der sozialen Ungleichheit („Klasse"), aber auch die im Zuge der postindustriellen Moderne mit ihren globalen Kolonisierungsprozessen und Migrationsbewegungen immer wichtiger werdende Semantik der Ethnizität („Rasse"). Auch die Weltregion, in der wir geboren werden, oder die historische Zeit, die uns prägt, können semantische Codierungen sein. In den betroffenen Individuen wirken diese Semantiken zusammen. Und die „mentale Grammatik", die jedes Individuum ausbilden muss, die zur Basis seiner Lebensführung wird und die Performanzen seines Alltagshandelns bestimmt, eben die *Biografizität,* ist nicht nur eine schlichte Addition jener semantischen Codes; sie ist eine einzigartige produktive Ressource des Umgangs mit sich selbst und der Welt – eine Art „*Erzeugungsprinzip*" der temporal abgeschichteten Performanzen einer konkreten Biografie.

Allerdings ist der großtheoretische Kontext, der durch diese Metapher assoziiert wird, keineswegs so eindeutig, wie es scheint. Weder die Beziehung von Semantik und Grammatik noch die Mehrdimensionalität des Grammatikbegriffs selbst sind geklärt. *Noam Chomsky,* dessen wichtige Studien zu einer „generativen Transformationsgrammatik" hier unmittelbar berührt sind (stellvertretend Chomsky 1965, 1969), ist – was seine „Grammatikidee" angeht – mehrdeutig geblieben. Was sein provokantes Konzept für die folgenden Überlegungen interessant macht, bleibt jedoch die Vorstellung, dass „Grammatik" eine *mentale Tiefenstruktur* darstellt, ein Erzeugungsprinzip, das durch bestimmte Transformationsregeln eine (in Chomskys Fall: *linguistische*) Performanzebene generiert (Chomsky 1977).

Konzeptionell wesentlich erscheint, dass diese Tiefenstruktur *syntaktisch,* als Regelsystem von Zeichen, und nicht – wie bei *George Lakoff,* seinem prominenten Gegner (stellvertretend Lakoff 1971) – *semantisch,* als Beziehung von Bedeutungen, angelegt ist. Wenn nämlich der enge Bereich der Linguistik verlassen wird, wenn die Frage nach einem generativen Erzeugungsprinzip nicht nur von Sprache, sondern von Verhaltensdispositionen, Routinen, Praktiken, Geschmackspräferenzen, impliziten Wissens- und Erfahrungsressourcen gestellt wird, ist Chomskys Modell überzeugender als Lakoffs „generative Semantik": Es erklärt, warum ein konkretes Individuum auf ganz unterschiedliche „gesellschaftliche Semantiken" – die Geschlechterproblematik, die soziale Ungleichheit, die ethnischen und religiösen Differenzen – auf eine „ureigene" Weise strukturähnlich reagiert, warum es offensichtlich einen „Erfahrungscode" zur Verarbeitung der verschiedenen sozialen Semantiken nutzt, dessen Transformationsregeln relativ stabil bleiben.

Was diese Übertragung des linguistischen Modells auf den komplexeren Bereich *biografischer Erfahrung* von Chomskys Grammatiktheorie unterscheidet, ist die Kritik der Tendenz, eine Art „nativistischer Kompetenz" anzunehmen, also einer Basisfähigkeit, die bei der Geburt bereits vorhanden ist. *Biografizität* als einzigartige soziale Grammatik des Individuums entsteht jedoch erst im biografischen Erfahrungsprozess. Durch selbstreferenzielle Verarbeitung externer Impulse, durch Umgang mit den verschiedenen Semantiken des konkreten sozialen Umfeldes wächst eine „*innere Logik",* die sich durch neue externe Impulse immer wieder auch verändern kann. Aber sie wandelt sich nicht nach einem, den Impulsen inhärenten Bestimmungsprinzip, sondern im Rahmen dieser inneren Logik selbst.[15]

Vielleicht ist deshalb eine andere theoretische Referenz als Ergänzung nützlich: das Konzept des *„Habitus"* in der Theorie Bourdieus (vgl. Bourdieu 1979, S. 139 ff; 1987, S. 277 ff). Auch dieses Konzept profitiert von Chomskys Grammatikidee (Bourdieu 1987; Krais und Gebauer 2002), aber in der Unterscheidung von *opus operatum,* als inkorporierter Form generativer Schemata, als „strukturierter Struktur", und *modus operandi,* als „strukturierender Struktur" (Bourdieu 1987, S. 282 f), entsteht die dialektische Vorstellung eines aktiven Erzeugungsprinzips, das auf eine vorgängige „soziale Syntax" verweist. Diese Tiefenstruktur wird durch die Praxis einverleibt. Sie ist keine „natürliche" Kompetenz (wie bei Chomsky), sondern „geronnene Lebensgeschichte" (Bourdieu 1987, S. 57 f).

Interessanterweise bezieht sich Bourdieu mit dieser Idee einer „zu Natur gewordenen Geschichte" (1979, S. 171) auf eine klassische Schrift der Bildungssoziologie, auf Emile Durkheims *L'évolution pédagogique en France* (1938):

„In jedem von uns steckt, entsprechend wechselnder Proportionen, der Mensch von gestern; er sogar ist es, der, durch die Macht der Dinge, in uns vorherrscht, ist das Gegenwärtige doch nur ein Geringes gegenüber jener langen Vergangenheit, in deren Verlauf wir Gestalt gewannen und aus der heraus wir kommen. Allein, wir spüren diesen Menschen der Vergangenheit nicht, da er tief in uns Wurzel gefaßt hat; er bildet den unbewußten Teil unserer selbst. Dessentwegen wird man auch dazu verleitet, ebensowenig von ihm wie von seinen legitimen Ansprüchen Rechenschaft abzulegen. Demgegenüber besitzen wir ein lebhaftes Gespür für die rezentesten Erwerbungen der Zivilisation, die, weil rezent, noch nicht die Zeit hatten, sich im Unbewußten zu organisieren." (ibid., S. 16)

Bourdieu interessiert an diesem Zitat nur das „Vergessen der Genesis" (1979, S. 171), die unbewusste Bereitschaft, die eigene (Lebens-)„Geschichte" als *fait accompli* zu verstehen und damit die eigensinnige Widerstandskraft und Trägheit des Habitus zu belegen. Bourdieus Konsequenzen aus dieser Deutung sind äußerst radikal und erinnern an Aussagen seines polemischen Essays über *Die biographische Illusion* (1990):

---

[15]Für die Art vergleichbarer Veränderung haben Maturana und Varela die überzeugende Metapher des „Driftens" vorgeschlagen (vgl. 1987, S. 14 f, 86 f, 119 ff), einer Bewegung, die nicht abrupt die Richtung verändert, sondern im Toleranzpegel eines vorgängig existenten dominanten Basisimpulses sehr allmähliche Verschiebungen erlaubt.

„Indem der Habitus als ein zwar subjektives, aber nicht individuelles System verinnerlichter Strukturen, als Schema der Wahrnehmung, des Denkens und Handelns angesehen wird, die allen Mitgliedern derselben Gruppe oder Klasse gemein sind und die die Voraussetzung jeder Objektivierung und Apperzeption bilden, wird derart die objektive Übereinstimmung der Praxisformen und die Einmaligkeit der Weltsicht auf der vollkommenen Unpersönlichkeit und Austauschbarkeit der singulären Praxisformen und Weltsichten gegründet. Das läuft allerdings darauf hinaus, alle nach identischen Schemata erzeugten Vorstellungen und Praxisformen für unpersönlich und austauschbar zu halten – nach Art der singulären Anschauungen des Raumes, die, wollte man Kant glauben, keine einzige Besonderheit des empirischen Ich reflektieren. [...] Da die Geschichte des Individuums nie etwas anderes als eine gewisse Spezifizierung der kollektiven Geschichte seiner Gruppe oder Klasse wiedergibt, können in den Systemen der individuellen Dispositionen *strukturelle Varianten* des Gruppen- oder Klassenhabitus gesehen werden, die systematisch gerade in den Unterschieden organisiert sind, die sie trennen und worin sich die Unterschiede der Laufbahnen und Positionen innerhalb und außerhalb der Klasse zum Ausdruck bringen: der ‚persönliche' Stil, dies besondere Kennzeichen, das alle Erzeugnisse ein und desselben Habitus, alle Handlungen und Werke, tragen, ist niemals mehr als eine selbst noch geregelte und zuweilen sogar kodifizierte *Abweichung* gegenüber dem einer Epoche oder einer Klasse eigentümlichen *Stil*, so daß er nicht nur durch die Konformität [...], sondern auch durch den Unterschied, der die Manier allererst macht, auf den gemeinsamen Stil verweist." (Bourdieu 1979, S. 187–189)

Aber geht es hier wirklich nur um den „persönlichen Stil"? Was ist mit den „wechselnden Proportionen", von denen Durkheim auch spricht? Was bedeutet die generative Kraft eines in der Zeit aufgeschichteten individuellen Erfahrungssystems, dessen Selbstreferenzialität im Laufe einer Lebensgeschichte relative Autonomie entwickelt? Lässt sich angesichts der in vorangegangenen Überlegungen entfalteten Bedeutung sozialkonstruktivistischer Einsichten eine solche „entindividualisierende" Perspektive auf den Habitus noch rechtfertigen?

Nehmen wir noch einmal die oben metaphorisch angesprochene dynamische Beziehung von „Semantik" und „Grammatik" auf. Semantiken sind objektivierte Bedeutungshorizonte wie etwa die *Klassenlage* von Individuen. Auch die *Geschlechterdimension* ist eine solche Semantik (s.o.) Es lässt sich empirisch kaum bestreiten, dass die prägende Kraft dieser „Meta-Semantiken" historisch variieren kann. Nimmt man etwa die US-Gesellschaft, so tritt die Klassenfrage schon im frühen 20. Jahrhundert hinter die Gender- und Rassenfrage zurück. Das hat sich kaum verändert. Es entstehen vielmehr Phänomene der „*Intersektionalität*" (stellvertretend Butler 1991), der Durchmischung objektivierter Semantiken, die auch neue Dimensionen von Grammatiken, also von Habitusformen, hervorbringen. Bourdieus Selbstgewissheit, was die Klassendimension angeht, ist womöglich ein zeitgeschichtliches und vielleicht auch ein europäisches Syndrom. Immerhin hat seine faszinierende Arbeit über die „männliche Herrschaft" (2005) der Gendersemantik einen zentralen Platz eingeräumt.

Unbestreitbar ist jedoch, dass sich die Funktion von *Grammatiken des Sozialen*, also des Erzeugungsprinzips bestimmter Verhaltensdispositionen, Weltdeutungen und Lebensstile der Subjekte, von kollektiven Basisorientierungen hin zum Individuum selbst verschoben hat. Die nicht zu Unrecht kritisch diskutierte „Individualisierungsthese" (stellvertretend Beck 1986, S. 205 ff; Reckwitz 2017) ist dafür ein oberflächliches Indiz. Erkenntnisse der jüngeren Neurowissenschaften (s. o.) sind womöglich nachhaltiger. Das kann bedeuten – und hier mögen Bourdieus frühe Arbeiten die Sensibilität schärfen –, dass zumal in Europa die „Klassensemantik" nach wie vor einen unübersehbaren Einfluss auf Habituskonfigurationen hat. Es heißt jedoch zugleich, dass die „Grammatik des Sozialen" im biografischen Erfahrungsprozess eines jeden und einer jeden Einzelnen entsteht: als „strukturierte Struktur" und als „strukturierende Struktur" – nur dass der Prozess der „Strukturierung" komplexer geworden ist. Es ist nicht mehr *eine* dominante Semantik allein, die die Struktur bestimmt; es geht um eine Melange externer Semantiken, womöglich um wechselnde Hegemonien in der Gemengelage. Was sich dann als „Grammatik des Sozialen" ausbildet, ist einzigartig und an den je biografischen Erfahrungsprozess eines Individuums gebunden. Es ist die *Biografizität* jedes und jeder Einzelnen – wenn man so will: sein/ihr *„biografischer* Habitus".

Wir haben es also in spät- oder „postmodernen" Gesellschaftsformationen mit figurationssoziologisch[16] neuen Konstellationen zu tun: Von der positionalen Fixierung ständischer Existenz in vormodernen Gesellschaften über gewisse Bewegungen im sozialen Raum bei relativer Stabilität sozialer Habitualisierungen in der Moderne geht der Trend in aktuellen Gesellschaften nun in Richtung einer Erosion sozialstruktureller Bindungen und Sicherheiten und zur Konzentration der (Über-)Lebensrisiken auf das Individuum selbst (vgl. dazu auch Reckwitz

---

[16] Eine „Figuration" ist nach Norbert Elias (1977), dem Begründer der Figurationssoziologie, ein *„Interdependenzgeflecht" von Machtbalancen und Affektökonomien*, das die sich wandelnde wechselseitige Durchdringung von Individuum und Gesellschaft im Prozess der Moderne beschreibt. Von sozialen Kleingruppen (etwa einer *Schulklasse*) über soziale Großgruppen (etwa die *„höfische Gesellschaft"*) bis zu Nationen (etwa die *deutsche Gesellschaft* im Vergleich zur englischen oder französischen) lassen sich nach Elias sehr spezifische Figurationen und ihre historischen Veränderungen identifizieren.

2006, 2017). Dies bedeutet keineswegs, dass soziale Beziehungsformen überflüssig würden; es heißt allerdings, dass sie nicht selbstverständlich als gleichsam „natürliche" Ressourcen zur Verfügung stehen, sondern immer wieder hergestellt werden müssen. Und die aktive Basiskompetenz für diesen Prozess ist die *Biografizität* der Individuen (vgl. dazu ausführlich Alheit 2019, S. 120–128).

Literatur

Alheit, Peter (2009): „Individuelle Modernisierung". Zur Logik biographischer Konstruktion in modernisierten modernen Gesellschaften. In: Stefan Hradil (Hg.): Differenz und Integration. Die Zukunft moderner Gesellschaften. Verhandlungen des 28. Kongresses für Soziologie 1996 in Dresden, Frankfurt a.M., New York: Campus, 941–952.

Alheit, Peter (2019): Biograficitat. Aspectes d'una nova teoria de l'aprenentatge social, Xàtiva: L'Ullal Edicions.

Alheit, Peter & Dausien, Bettina (2000): Die biographische Konstruktion der Wirklichkeit. Überlegungen zur Biographizität des Sozialen. In: Erika M. Hoerning (Hg.): Biographische Sozialisation, Stuttgart: Metzler, 257–283.

An der Heiden, Ulrich, Gerhard Roth & Hans Schwegler (1986): Die Organisation der Organismen: Selbstherstellung und Selbsterhaltung. In: Funkt. Biol. Med., Vol. 5, 330–346.

Beck, Ulrich (1986): Risikogesellschaft. Auf dem Weg in eine andere Moderne. Frankfurt am Main: Suhrkamp.

Becker-Schmidt, Regina (1996): Einheit – Zweiheit – Vielheit. Identitätslogische Implikationen in feministischen Emanzipationskonzepten. In: Zeitschrift für Frauenforschung, Vol. 14, 1/2, 5–18.

Bourdieu, Pierre (1979): Entwurf einer Theorie der Praxis. Frankfurt am Main: Suhrkamp.

Bourdieu, Pierre (1987): Die feinen Unterschiede. Kritik der gesellschaftlichen Urteilskraft. Frankfurt am Main: Suhrkamp.

Bourdieu, Pierre (1990): Die biographische Illusion. In: Bios, Vol. 3, H. 1, 75–81.

Butler, Judith (1991): Das Unbehagen der Geschlechter. Frankfurt am Main: Suhrkamp.

Chomsky, Noam (1965): Aspects of the Theory of Syntax. Cambridge, MA: MIT Press.

Chomsky, Noam (1969): Aspekte der Syntax-Theorie. Frankfurt am Main: Suhrkamp.

Chomsky, Noam (1977): Reflexionen über die Sprache. Frankfurt am Main: Suhrkamp.

Dausien, Bettina (1994): Auf der Suche nach dem „eigenen Leben"? Lernprozesse in weiblichen Biographien. In: Peter Alheit et al. (Hg.): Von der Arbeitsgesellschaft zur Bildungsgesellschaft? Perspektiven von Arbeit und Bildung im Prozeß europäischen Wandels. Bremen: Bremen University Press, 572–592.

Dausien, Bettina (1996): Biographie und Geschlecht. Zur biographischen Konstruktion sozialer Wirklichkeit in Frauenlebensgeschichten. Bremen: Donat.

Elias, Norbert (1977): Zur Grundlegung einer Theorie sozialer Prozesse. In: Zeitschrift für Soziologie, Vol. 6, 5, 127–149.

Garfinkel, Harold (1967): Studies in Ethnomethodology. Englewood Cliffs, N.J.: Prentice-Hall.

Gildemeister, Regine & Angelika Wetterer (1992): Wie Geschlechter gemacht werden. Die soziale Konstruktion der Zweigeschlechtlichkeit und ihre Reifizierung in der Frauenforschung. In: Gudrun-Axeli Knapp & Angelika Wetterer (Hg.): Traditionen Brüche. Entwicklungen feministischer Theorie. Freiburg: Kore, 201–254.

Goffman, Erving (1977): The arrangement between the sexes. In: Theory and Society, Vol. 4, 301–331.

Goffman, Erving (1994): Interaktion und Geschlecht. Herausgegeben und eingeleitet von Hubert A. Knoblauch. Mit einem Nachwort von Helga Kotthoff. Frankfurt am Main, New York: Campus.

Habermas, Jürgen (1992): Faktizität und Geltung. Beiträge zur Diskurstheorie des Rechts und des demokratischen Rechtsstaats. Frankfurt am Main: Suhrkamp.

Hirschauer, Stefan (1993a): Dekonstruktion und Rekonstruktion. Plädoyer für die Erforschung des Bekannten. In: Feministische Studien, Vol. 11, 2, 55–67.

Hirschauer, Stefan (1993b): Die soziale Konstruktion der Transsexualität. Über die Medizin und den Geschlechtswechsel. Frankfurt am Main: Suhrkamp.

Kessler, Suzanne J. & Wendy McKenna (1978): Gender: An Ethnomethodological Approach. New York: Wiley.

Knapp, Gudrun-Axeli (1995): Unterschiede machen: Zur Sozialpsychologie der Hierarchisierung im Geschlechterverhältnis. In: Regina Becker-Schmidt & Gudrun-Axeli Knapp (Hg.), Das Geschlechterverhältnis als Gegenstand der Sozialwissenschaften. Frankfurt am Main, New York: Campus, 163–194.

Kohli, Martin (1988): Normalbiographie und Individualität. Zur institutionellen Dynamik des gegenwärtigen Lebenslaufregimes. In: Hanns-Georg Brose & Bruno Hildenbrandt (Hg.): Vom Ende des Individuums zur Individualität ohne Ende, Opladen: Leske + Budrich, 33–53.

Krais, Beate & Gebauer, Gunter (2002): Habitus. Bielefeld: transcript.

Krappmann, Lothar (1982): Soziologische Dimensionen der Identität. Strukturelle Bedingungen für die Teilnehmer an Interaktionsprozessen. Stuttgart: Klett.

Lakoff, George (1971): Linguistik und natürliche Logik. Herausgegeben von Werner Abraham. Frankfurt am Main: Athenäum.

Lindemann, Gesa (1993a): Wider die Verdrängung des Leibes aus der Geschlechtskonstruktion. In: Feministische Studien, Vol. 11, 2, 44–54.

Lindemann, Gesa (1993b): Das paradoxe Geschlecht. Transsexualität im Spannungsfeld von Körper, Leib und Gefühl. Frankfurt am Main: Fischer.

Luhmann, Niklas (1980): Gesellschaftsstruktur und Semantik. Studien zur Wissenssoziologie der modernen Gesellschaft, Bd. 1. Frankfurt am Main: Suhrkamp.

Luhmann, Niklas (1984): Soziale Systeme. Grundriß einer allgemeinen Theorie. Frankfurt am Main: Suhrkamp.

Luhmann, Niklas (1985): Die Autopoiesis des Bewußtsein. In: Soziale Welt, Vol. 36, 402–446.

Luhmann, Niklas (1989): Individuum, Individualität, Individualismus. In: Niklas Luhmann, Gesellschaftsstruktur und Semantik. Studien zur Wissenssoziologie der modernen Gesellschaft, Bd. 3. Frankfurt am Main: Suhrkamp, 149–258.

Luhmann, Niklas & Karl-Eberhard Schorr (1982): Personale Identität und Möglichkeiten der Erziehung. In: Niklas Luhmann & Karl-Eberhard Schorr (Hg.), Zwischen Technologie und Selbstreferenz. Frankfurt am Main: Suhrkamp, 224–261.

Maturana, Humberto R. (1970): Neurophysiology of Cognition. In: Paul Garvin (ed.), Cognition: A multiple view. New York, Washington: Spartan Books, 3–23.

Maturana, Humberto R. (1978): The biology of language. In: George A. Miller & Elizabeth Lenneberg (eds.): The Biology and Psychology of Language and Thought: Essays in Honor of Eric Lenneberg. New York: Academic Press, 27–63.

Maturana, Humberto R. (1987a): Kognition. In: Siegfried Schmidt (Hg.), Der Diskurs des Radikalen Konstruktivis-mus. Frankfurt am Main: Suhrkamp, 89–118.

Maturana, Humberto R. (1987b): Biologie der Sozialität. In: Siegfried Schmidt (Hg.), Der Diskurs des Radikalen Konstruktivismus. Frankfurt am Main: Suhrkamp, 287–302.

Maturana, Humberto R. & Francisco J. Varela (1975): Autopoietic Systems. In: Biological Computer Laboratory. Report No. 9.4, Urbana: University of Illinois.

Maturana, Humberto R. & Francisco J. Varela (1987): Der Baum der Erkenntnis. Die biologischen Wurzeln des menschlichen Erkennens. Bern, München: Scherz.

Nassehi, Armin (1994a): Die Form der Biographie. Theoretische Überlegungen zur Biographieforschung in methodologischer Absicht. In: Bios, Vol. 7, H. 1, 46–63.

Nassehi, Armin (1994b): Differenz als Signum – Einheit als Horizont. Zur Zeitdiagnose posttraditionaler Vergesellschaftung. In: Sozialwissenschaftliche Literaturrundschau, Vol. 20, 81–90.

Nassehi, Armin & Georg Weber (1990): Zu einer Theorie biographischer Identität. Epistemologische und systemtheoretische Argumente. In: Bios, Vol. 3, 2, 153–187.

Nunner-Winkler, Gertrud (1994): Zur geschlechtsspezifischen Sozialisation. In: Sozialwissenschaftliche Frauenforschung in der Bundesrepublik Deutschland. Bestandsaufnahme und forschungspolitische Konsequenzen. Herausgegeben von der Senatskommission für Frauenforschung der Deutschen Forschungsgemeinschaft. Berlin: Akademie Verlag, 61–83.

Reckwitz, Andreas (2006): Das hybride Subjekt. Eine Theorie der Subjektkulturen von der bürgerlichen Moderne zur Postmoderne. Weilerswist: Velbrück Wissenschaft.

Reckwitz, Andreas (2017): Die Gesellschaft der Singularitäten. Zum Strukturwandel der Moderne. Berlin: Suhrkamp.

Roth, Gerhard (1985): Die Selbstreferentialität des Gehirns und die Prinzipien der Gestaltwahrnehmung. In: Gestalt Theory, Vol. 7, 4, 228–244.

Roth, Gerhard & Hans Schwegler (eds.) (1981): Self-organizing Systems. An Interdisciplinary Approach. Frankfurt am Main, New York: Campus.

Roth, Gerhard (1987a): Erkenntnis und Realität: Das reale Gehirn und seine Wirklichkeit. In: Siegfried Schmidt (Hg.), Der Diskurs des Radikalen Konstruktivismus. Frankfurt am Main: Suhrkamp, 229–255.

Roth, Gerhard (1987b): Autopoiese und Kognition: Die Theorie H.R. Maturanas und die Notwendigkeit ihrer Weiterentwicklung. In: Siegfried Schmidt (Hg.): Der Diskurs des Radikalen Konstruktivismus. Frankfurt am Main: Suhrkamp, 256–286.

Scheuermann, Antonius (1996): Sexualbiographien. Eine empirische Studie zur biographischen Konstruktion von Sexualität am Beispiel homosexueller Männer, Dissertation: Universität Bremen.

Schimank, Uwe (1988): Biographie als Autopoiesis – eine systemtheoretische Rekonstruktion von Individualität. In: Hanns-Georg Brose & Bruno Hildenbrand (Hg.): Vom Ende des Individuums zur Individualität ohne Ende. Opladen: Leske + Budrich, 55–72.

Schütz, Alfred & Thomas Luckmann (1979): Strukturen der Lebenswelt, Bd. 1. Frankfurt am Main: Suhrkamp.
Varela, Francisco J. (1979): Principles of Biographical Autonomy. New York, Oxford: Elsevier.
Varela, Francisco J. (1981): Autonomy and Autopoiesis. In: Gerhard Roth & Hans Schwegler (eds.), Self-organizing Systems. An Interdisciplinary Approach. Frankfurt am Main, New York: Campus, 14–23.
Varela, Francisco J. (1987): Autonomie und Autopoiese. In: Siegfried Schmidt (Hg.), Der Diskurs des Radikalen Konstruktivismus. Frankfurt am Main: Suhrkamp, 119–132.
Varela, Francisco J., Humberto R. Maturana & Ricardo B. Uribe (1974): Autopoiesis, the organization of living systems: its charaterization and a model. In: Biosystems, Vol. 5, 125 ff.
Varela, Francisco J., Evan Thompson & Eleanor Rosch (1991): The Embodied Mind: Cognitive Science and Human Experience. Cambridge, MA: MIT Press.
Wagner, Gerhard & Heinz Zipprian (1992): Identität oder Differenz? Bemerkungen zu einer Aporie in Niklas Luhmanns Theorie selbstreferentieller Systeme. In: Zeitschrift für Soziologie, Vol. 21, 6, 394–405.
West, Candace & Don H. Zimmerman (1987): Doing Gender. In: Gender and Society, Vol. 1, 2, 125–151.
Wetterer, Angelika (1992): Hierarchie und Differenz im Geschlechterverhältnis. Theoretische Ansätze zur Analyse der Marginalität von Frauen in hochqualifizierten Berufen. In: Angelika Wetterer (Hg.): Profession und Geschlecht. Über die Marginalität von Frauen in hochqualifizierten Berufen. Frankfurt am Main, New York: Campus, 13–44.
Wetterer, Angelika (1995a): Dekonstruktion und Alltagshandeln. Die (möglichen) Grenzen der Vergeschlechtlichung von Berufsarbeit. In: Angelika Wetterer (Hg.): Die soziale Konstruktion von Geschlecht in Professionalisierungsprozessen. Frankfurt am Main, New York: Campus, 223–246.
Wetterer, Angelika (1995b): Das Geschlecht (bei) der Arbeit. Zur Logik der Vergeschlechtlichung von Berufsarbeit. In: Ursula Pasero & Friederike Braun (Hg.), Konstruktion von Geschlecht. Pfaffenweiler: Centaurus, 199–223.

Prof. em. Dr. Dr. Peter Alheit, ehemaliger Lehrstuhl für Allgemeine Pädagogik am Pädagogischen Seminar der Georg-August-Universität Göttingen (jetzt: Institut für Erziehungswissenschaft).

Time and Education. Zeit und Bildung

Time, Power and Education. Zeit, Macht und Bildung

Matthew Krehl Edward Thomas and Ben Whitburn

Abstract

Situated at the intersection of time, power and education, we elaborate an argument for diffracting temporality to eschew the arrow of time, which promulgates pressure in modern societies. Risk adverse, neoliberal systems of education often invoke temporality as a reason not to provide genuine inclusive opportunities for diverse learners. Learning it would seem, comes at the cost of genuine inclusion. Drawing on the theoretical resources of chronopolitics, risk society and relational ontologies, we demonstrate that time is frequently put to work in the service of controlling and colonising education. Technology has come to dominate education—paradoxically saving time whilst permeating the membrane the professional and the personal for teachers and students. We deploy a methodological framework to diffract the temporal, fusing the past, together with present-future simultaneously, so as to re-imagine relational ontologies in the act of becoming. Temporality is demonstrably diffracted through the methodology, in an empirical project which is undertaken with pre-service teachers on a global education program in the South Pacific. The chapter concludes with a set of principles for explicitly drawing on time to inform wider applications of educational research.

M. K. E. Thomas (✉) · B. Whitburn
Deakin University, Melbourne, Australia
E-Mail: matthew.thomas@deakin.edu.au

B. Whitburn
E-Mail: b.whitburn@deakin.edu.au

© Springer Fachmedien Wiesbaden GmbH, ein Teil von Springer Nature 2020
E. Schilling und M. O'Neill (Hrsg.), *Frontiers in Time*
Research – Einführung in die interdisziplinäre Zeitforschung,
https://doi.org/10.1007/978-3-658-31252-7_9

> **Keywords**
>
> Temporality · relationality · risk · Inclusive education · teaching and learning · chronopolitics

Introduction

Modern western education systems position educators as self-policing units, deployed in post-panoptic discourses of risk, wherein both compliance and performance are simultaneously prioritised over inclusive practice. To put this another way, as an instrument of power, recurrent surveillance is exercised through a taken-for-granted understanding of temporality, which is implicated in the everyday practices of educators and is antithetical to enacting educational equity. This chapter advances a methodology of diffracting time in both educational research and teacher education, in ways that challenge what Slattery (1995, p. 614) calls 'the modern assumption that temporality is a linear series of events that can be broken down, isolated, segmented, and evaluated for the purpose of creating human progress over time'. Instead the basis of critique is chronopolitics (Virilio 2008), which takes as its starting point the uneven politics of time brought about through particular advancements to technology and the ways in which social relations are subsequently mediated.

The chapter proceeds through four sections. In the first we mount an argument for foregrounding chronopolitics to investigate the exercise of power in education. We examine speed as it is experienced in and through teaching and learning, which privileges a particular kind of knowledge production and producer. Through time, complex social dynamics are given over to algorithmic solutions, which foreground a dominant agenda of compliance and eschew the centrality of connection and institutional relationality. Concerned with both the control of teacher and student time, and the ways in which colonisation with time mediates educational practices (Whitburn and Thomas 2021), in the second section we develop a methodology that diffracts temporality in response to the exclusionary present. We employ this methodology in both research and teaching projects (the latter of which we exemplify in this chapter) in ways that facilitate alternative understandings about democratic practices in education. In the third section we demonstrate the type of work we have in mind through a recent project (Thomas et al. 2018), in which preservice teachers from an Australian university undertook an aspect of their practical training that diffracted the temporal and occasioned alternative ways of teaching and learning. In the fourth and final section, we submit ways in which the methodology might be put to work in other contexts of research, teaching and learning to support others concerned with the dominance of linear clock time in education.

In the Shadow of a Gnomon

In this chapter we establish an argument for drawing specifically on temporality as a means to investigate the exercise of power in education. Core to our argument is that temporality is too often employed lineally in education, specifically the capacity of educators to enact inclusive practices for the benefit of all students irrespective of their diversities (Thomas and Whitburn 2019). Simultaneously, student agency is threatened by the temporal; attributes of modern time privilege only that which can be quantified and commodified. In this section we set up our argument by examining the chronopolitics of education through teaching and learning. Our argument outlined herein is that speed leads temporality to privilege a particular kind of knowledge production and producer, in the paradox of neoliberal logic. In time, complex social dynamics are given over to algorithmic solutions, in the shadow of a gnomon, foregrounding a dominant agenda of compliance.

Significant to our inquiry is the inclusiveness of education, or more emphatically, the responsibility of all educational jurisdictions to ensure that equitable opportunities to both access and participate in learning are made available to all of their citizens. Inclusive education is both a shift in definitional intent, and an aspiration, that has occupied the global politics of education for little more than 30 years. As a point of departure, it draws a distinction between segregated special education provision and inclusive learning, one that ordinarily necessitates widespread cultural transformation. Though inclusion in education has held a place in educational provision in parts of Australia since the mid 1980s (Fulcher 1989) and other English-speaking countries not long thereafter (Mittler 2009), its international beginnings have been closely linked with the Jontien Declaration (UNESCO 1990), and the Salamanca Statement (UNESCO 1994). Though a landmark accord for the transformation of educational cultures, the principle focus for Salamanca was to establish that young people with disabilities, who are often diagnosed as having 'special educational needs', were afforded equal opportunities to learn alongside their peers in 'regular' schools.

At this time, temporality was used by researchers as a yardstick of success for inclusive education. As Allan (1996, p. 219) writes, '[r]esearch on the mainstreaming of children with special educational needs has tended to concentrate on the *amount* of integration taking place, seldom moving beyond crude notions of how much time a child spends in an ordinary school or classroom'. While the challenge to achieve inclusion of young people with disabilities in schools has certainly not gone away, inclusiveness more broadly in education has entered the debate. Equitable educational opportunities have proven wanting for any number of marginalised groups divided across invisible identity lines such as cultural and linguistic diversity (CALD), migrants and refugees, socially and economically disadvantaged, LGBTIQ++ students, and so forth. Developing inclusive opportunities for these and any number of other categorical differences begins with a conviction for democratic participation, and productive stakeholder relationships. We are, after all, shaped by the totality of our relationships. To this end, in attempting to explain further what inclusive education is, it seems almost as fruitful to explore what it is not, in a troubled present (Slee 2018). A resolve to provide conditions of inclusive possibility meet fierce opposition, made particularly salient through the growth of political strength that is undersigned by derision and fear. As Slee expresses, 'We could say that exclusion is an ontological given, a part of our social, and therein our educational, DNA or zeitgeist' (Slee 2018, p. 1). Fierce resistance to inclusion in education is often manifested through education traditions that favour diagnostic categories, ableist views of reduced expectations, disproportionately distributed resources, institutional rigidity, and limited transition opportunities, ensuring that the marginalised remain so.

We accept that educational inclusion is on the whole difficult to implement for globally dispersed education jurisdictions for a variety of reasons pertaining to the paradox that emerges between contextual situations and worldwide standardisation (Slee 2018). Pretexts for maintaining an exclusionary status quo can perhaps unexpectedly be found attributable to perceptions that it is excessively time consuming to implement. As we have argued elsewhere (Thomas et al. 2019), educators from schools to higher education providers are charged with contrary priorities of compliance, efficiency, and liability, and teaching situations that might present a challenge to ordered continuity present too much of a risk to their time. According to conventional wisdoms that impress upon a binary logic of special and regular or mainstream education, students are often diagnosed by clinical practitioners as having so-called special learning needs, which sets in motion a trajectory whereby teachers relinquish their responsibility for teaching them to specialist educators or teaching aides, in order to save valuable teaching time for the mainstream. This has become a 'biopolitical management of inclusion in the neoliberal present' (Done and Murphy 2016, p. 1). As we discuss further in the next section of this chapter, educators often consider time as a linear construct that is 'imbued with Marxist resonances of time and labour value' (Lingard and Thompson 2017, p. 1), wherein quick solutions win out to considered relational pedagogies and in doing so create a form of chronodystopia (Armitage and Roberts 2003).

Chronopolitics

Chronopolitics, according to Virilio (2008), epitomises the new frontier of political struggle in which we find ourselves. Virilio's thesis is that whereas cultures once concerned themselves with geopolitics—the surveying, occupying, and protection of land—the advance of both technology and disciplinary techniques after the second world war have led to the politics of time. This transformation has been principally concerned with vectors of pace: the ways in which actions are either slowed down or sped up, and as such, one of its principal affordances is a move from the primacy of space to the primacy of time in the everyday function of public and private institutions. Exploring the effect of temporality in education provides a way of understanding how rhythmicity in school-related undertakings is made plain suggesting the 'formal school hours and the content of lessons thus reinforce the prior socialization of children into clock times' (Glennie and Thrift 2009, p. 130)—grounding the principles of simple clock time and the value in speed for a later working life. Speed is the rhythmic metronome of the neoliberal order in liquid times (Bauman 2007). In this chapter we argue for examining how clock time has been utilised to affect how schooling is administrated in ways that refract classroom practices and obscure learning. This is critical because 'temporality is not something separate to activity but unfolds within it' (Eacott 2017, p. 121). We wonder what sort of learning happens when teaching is not subjected to the vicissitudes of temporal pressure.

Some educators and academics have forged a deliberative turn away from the culture of speed that has embraced modern education. They turn instead towards a culture of slow practice, in which a desire for sustained learning and deep thinking is valorized over fast production. Lau (2019) for example, argues that temporal regimes of modern universities are exclusionary for aspirant scholars who live with disabilities. The culture of speed produces conditions whereby failure is individualized, for those who cannot conform with a sped-up pace struggle to meet tight deadlines. Lau advocates for slowness: the deliberate turn to contemplation over acceleration and an accompanying revisioning of qualitative criteria over quantitative publication outcomes as measures for academic success. Lau's argument is that giving more than adequate time to academic practice, will ensure it can become more inclusive of diverse abilities, which in turn will add to the diversification of knowledge producers in academies. Whilst the exhalation to slow as a panacea to a culture of speed seems attractive, Sharma warns that a 'turn to slowness is a depoliticization of time' (Sharma 2014, p. 111). Slow pedagogy is defined by a privileging of the learner, at their temporal pace, through an invocation of reflective practices that are intertwined attuned to the interests of the student (Coxon 2012), whereas slow scholarship 'promotes the quality of relationships, grappling with ideas and recognising the importance of subjectivities, an anathema to the neoliberal academic enterprise'(Leibowitz and Bozalek 2018, p. 983). Slow practice invokes a privileging of one a particular experience of time, but in doing so it foregrounds that 'intellectual thought and the collaborative nature of teaching have been subject to various distortions, in part due to the depredations of neoliberalism and performativity'(Leibowitz and Bozalek 2018, p. 981).

We think, learn, love and exist in time. As Sharma suggests we 'exist in a grid of temporal power relations' (2014, p. 9). Yet, slow practice valorizes the designer, not the learner. It is an indulgence on the part of the curriculum creator to explore at will the shape and tenor of content and achievement outcomes, as if for the student. However, in application, time is not for the student as slow learning is never a possibility. Slow learning cannot be realized when our classrooms are predicated on notions of success and failure and regulatory practices that subsequently govern who is in and who is out. Such spectrums must be superimposed against a backdrop of something tangible, in this case time— a time that has a pre-set temporal measure by which to demonstrate learning (Thomas and Bellingham 2020).

A New Order

It seems certain that '[w]ishing for more time is a kind of collective fantasy' (Berg and Seeber 2016, p. 55), one that endangers us in a particular chronopolitical way. As Slattery (1995, p. 614) writes, '[a]nd so it is with the insatiable desire for more time, more data, more rigorous core curricula: our liberties are reduced and we actually become prisoners of time'. As such, in contrast to seeking to practice slowly, others seek to enhance time through speed. Compelled by competing pressures of the modern classroom, time poor classroom teachers are reaching for tools of speed to prolong interest drawing on tools like 'Internet, tablets, smartphones, apps' (Santos-Trigo and Reyes-Martínez 2019, p. 182). Yet, by simply increasing the pace with which teaching occurs we do not increase the rate of learning. Similar to a culture of slowness, 'a culture of speed is antithetical to democracy' (Sharma 2014, p. 6) because it 'is the commanding by-product of a mutually reinforcing complex that includes global capital, real-time communication technologies, military technologies, and scientific research on human bodies' (Sharma 2014, p. 6). To this end, we suggest that a chronopolitical understanding is necessary to make sense of the 'temporal perspectives of human groups [which] are fundamentally constitutive of political behaviors' (Stevens 2016, p. 44). Time is unwilling to be a commodity and yet, by politicizing the temporal we engage its capacity to be so. Put simply, we need to foreground time as a major constructive force in how teaching and learning happens.

Analysing Chronopolitics in Education

In this section we detail the methodological framework we draw on, which explores the chronopolitics at work that can impact educational inclusiveness. Chronopolitics, according to Virilio (Virilio 2008), epitomises the new frontier of political struggle in which we find ourselves, which has replaced a geopolitical past. Similarly attached to the contemporaneous turn to an ontology of relationality, both in educational research (Bozalek and Zembylas 2017), and as well in teacher education (Whitburn and Corcoran 2019), the methodology foregrounds time as a way of facilitating engagement with material and discourse to create collective meaning in educational contexts. Before detailing these aspects of the framework, it is first important to explore further how temporality has been taken up in the sociology of education, and how the temporal is understood to impact education.

Temporality and the Sociology of Education

In spite of a growing interest in the social time of education (Adam and Allan 1995; Slattery 1995) the sociology of education has persisted a limited, quantifiable understanding of temporal politics. In calling for an alternative engagement with temporality within educational inquiry, Lingard and Thompson

(Lingard and Thompson 2017) gesture at the constitutive power of lived time as it meets digital intervention in the globalised, educational present. Notwithstanding, western conceptions of regulatory time has dominated educational thought. As they express their lament:

> 'If we were to characterise the concept of time that has dominated the sociology of education, with some exceptions, we would suggest that it has been that of a linear and progressive, yet constitutive, time. In other words, just as education has inherited clock time and put this to work, so too has sociological inquiry into education'(Lingard and Thompson 2017, p. 5).

This seems indeed regrettable, if it were assured, although sociological inquiry has spurred both the impositions and complexities of the temporal in schooling for some time. Adam (1995), who is one of the pioneer sociologists of temporality, demonstrates that in spite of a domination of temporal linearity in education, through, for example, rigid timetabling and scheduled extra-curricular activities, predetermined milestones of learning and assessment, teacher labour and remuneration, temporality in education might best be understood as collective time—individuals and shared histories and futures which have consequential and simultaneous implications on any one moment generated by a group. While this latter conception of classroom time is suggestive of an equitable approach to recognising diverse chronological and relational powers, for Adam, the fixity of temporal dimensions, as well as the identities of teachers and learners, correspond with liberal traditions that emphasise unquestioned, normative approaches to quantifying social activity (culture) in the service of linear time (nature).

In this rigid, dualistic framework, we find that educational inclusion poses unmitigated risks to normative educational order (Thomas and Whitburn 2019; Whitburn and Thomas 2021). For Ulrich Beck (2003) and his colleagues, a central point of explanation of the origins of risks such as these can be found in their theory of reflexive modernisation. In contradistinction to simple modernisation, which relied on what might now be understood as contingent institutions of bordered nation states, stable welfare provision, class cultures and nuclear families through a stable industrial period, reflexive modernisation is characterised by the unintended consequences of technological advancement and global market expansion. Core to Beck's theory is that particular risks appear when relentless pursuits of industrial modernisation cannot be tempered, leading to contradictions that return to haunt systems. Reflexivity, then, emerges as a 'heightened awareness that mastery [over unassailable risks] is impossible' (2003, p. 3). As a result, scientific expertise is often foregrounded to minimise the magnitude of unintended consequences.

Beck's theory of reflexive modernisation has been critiqued for its emphasis on human agency (Bozalek and Zembylas 2017) and for its adherence to binary logics that pit nature against culture (Adam 1995). Nevertheless, its relationship with the temporal seems useful to us for explaining the extent to which industrial time has reached its limitations in education. As such, we pause here to consider the function of temporality in the midst of reflexive modernisation. For Adam (2003), reflexive modernisation signalled a discontinuity in time, which built on the ways that industrial temporality given to production, was already taken as fact, and embedded in cultural functions. Yet, the widespread acceptance of industrial time led to unintended consequences in which it was undermined by its own limitations. The way in which modern clock-driven time reaches its limits is discernible by way of what Adam terms 'The Enlightenment Project from a Temporal Perspective'(2003, p. 62). Consisting of five progressions that destabilise modern time, each of them starting with the letter C—creation, commodification, compression, control, and colonization—modern temporality has brought about marked discontinuities. For instance, time is a human creation that was designed as a regulatory socio-economic force in people's lives. It was not long before the economic value of time was linked to commodification, and could be traded for value as credit or interest. Saving money, then, led to the compression of time in production, of what Virilio (2008) calls the dromotological dimension of power, or the politics of speed. To this end, the control and colonisation of and with time refer to the mastery of time and the rhythms of life, in a complex, globalised present characterised by instantaneous digital information systems and data exchange, global displacement, and the expanse of western ideals through the enormous reach into both the past and the future simultaneously to shape the present.

In Whitburn and Thomas (2021), we draw on Adam's (2003) framework of modern temporality to explore this basis for theorising time with respect to education. Cautious not to rehearse our analysis here, our purpose is to demonstrate how education has been designed in a way that draws on the service of clock time in exclusionary ways, from design, commodification, compression and beyond, particularly as temporality is used to demarcate normative development, and increase particular risks. As Slattery (1995, p. 619) writes, 'School administrators know that randomness and chaos more accurately define their lives than predictability and stability, and yet modern schools remain organized around the modern conception of time as controllable and manageable'. The emphasis on financial resourcing for standardised achievement can perpetuate marginalisation (Slee 2018), further accentuated again through the control of time and global development. Conscious that '[t]he enslavement to time can only be appropriately addressed by first challenging the underlying modern assumptions about time itself' (Slattery 1995, p. 616), it is to an exploration of some of the risks associated with these latter Cs of modern temporality—control and colonisation—to which we now turn to consider the role of chronopolitics in forsaking marginalized students at the expensive of others, and hence rupturing the sensibilities of educational design in the service of time. Core to the presentation of these categories is that these are unintended consequences (Beck et al. 2003) of time (Adam 2003) in education.

Control: A Formulaic Education

The control of time refers to the regulation of rhythmic order to correspond with a desired pace (Adam 2003). Drawing on chronopolitics, Adam demonstrates that the control of time functions to either slow or speed time with particular use of technology. Bending time to either slow or speed up gives rise to new cultural imaginaries, and ways of working (Sharma 2014). In education, digital advancement is one way in which time has been brought into control, consequently framing both students and teachers and also shaping the social construction of experience and democratic possibility. Speed is enticing, especially for educators who trade in forty-five – ninety-minute allotments for the promise of learning, remade as a transactional arrangement naturalised in the liquid present. This has become the case through the evolution of technology and its easy integration into schooling. Evolutions in teaching and learning might enhance what schools do simultaneously, but they also mask their consequences: the 'boat was the invention of the shipwreck' (Virilio 2008, p. 46), and in schools, some students become collateral damage when a culture of speed is favoured over one of democratic participation in learning (Bellingham et al. 2019).

Our desire for rapid advancement, and progression in schools particularly over the later part of the twentieth century, was one of promise, efficiency and connection. For the most part computers have only begun to be integrated into secondary and primary classrooms over the last fifty years (Tatnall and Davey 2014). Digital transformation—and its comrade at arms speed—have been inseparable from the outset. To have a computer was to invest in education, for politicians' technology has been hailed as 'magical talisman for producing educational progress and excellence' (Martin 2014, p. 13). And why not? schools are under increasing pressure to perform and lift standards as they continue to fail, it is little wonder, then, that with only so much time in the day alongside finite resources, it is natural for school leaders to look for solutions to problems in clouds, databases and digital architecture.

Despite such manoeuvres the problems persist (Masters 2016) and the integration of technology into education continues. Such integration allows us as a species to 'process information at increasing speed, with increasing power, at decreasing cost' (Castells 2010, p. 32) prioritised locally and diffused almost globally (Santiago, Donaldson, Herman, & Shewbridge 2011). This undergirds a dissociative appetite that empowers a system encouraging a frantic assembly that simultaneously suspends human connection and encourages dehumanisation and disenchantment. As Zubhoff reminds us this formula is nothing new:

> 'Fragments of the formula had surfaced before—in meatpacking plants, flour-milling operations, sewing machine and bicycle factories, armories, canneries, and breweries. There was a growing body of practical knowledge about the interchangeability of parts and absolute standardization, precision machines, and continuous flow production. But no one had achieved the grand symphony that Ford heard in his imagination' (Zuboff 2019, p. 167).

Far from being unrelated to the control of time, Zuboff's thesis has a direct and significant correlation to the temporal in education. 'efficiency, calculability, predictability and control' (Ritzer 2013, p. 44), which together form the hallmarks of Ritzer's McDonaldization thesis, seem apt descriptors in what we now largely accept as fast education in which the end is privileged over the trajectory. Consider for example the ways in which teaching and learning occur under these hallmarks. Schools rely on processes of effective control of both staff and students through policy and practice. Consider the effect of the now infamous controlling technologies directed at minute detailing of student behaviour (Manolev et al. 2019) that have infiltrated schools globally. In addition, in a market economy, parents rely on the predictability that schools have come to offer. This is achieved through systemization, order and discipline – elements that are valorised throughout many primary and secondary schools (Judith 1981). Calculability is now rife within education, wherein all subjects, assessments and teacher time are held up for scrutiny and appraised by scores and results. Efficiency, too, is most keenly witnessed in our schools overreliance on policy to achieve pedagogical ends (Rivzi and Lingard 2010). This equates to a formula whereby attainment equals worth, or 'schools and teachers have been squeezed into the tunnel vision of test scores achievement targets and league tables of accountability' (Hargreaves 2003, p. 1).

Colonisation with Time: Educational Surveillance Workers

In chronopolitical times, colonisation with temporality takes place through global standardisation of chronological regulation. As established through the policy impositions of transnational organisations such as the OECD, UNESCO and the World Bank, globalised standards in education aspire to classes of learning mobilised in measurements of extracted clock time, temporally excreting learning into formative chunks based more on pay cycles than effective learning principles. The economic implications that this carries, Adam explains, favours clock time over deliberative practice. '[t]o be 'modern', 'progressive', even 'civilized' means to embrace the industrial approach to time' (2003, p. 73). Being modern and civilised also requires being self-surveillant (Page 2015).

As such, many teachers come to negotiate a professional identity that mirrors their local organisational needs. How learning is constructed within such as space actively blends the personal and the private lives of teachers. Among educators, overtime, or work taken home to be done after hours, is made possible through digital incursions that remove both time and space from their daily interactions (Slattery 1995; Thomas and Whitburn 2019). Surveillance schooling creates a false binary when the individual (teacher) is always suspect and fallible, but the organisation of the school is infallible and supported by data. Teachers become at fault for any failings, whilst the organisation (of the school) success is effectively guaranteed. A culture of speed excises teachers' personal identities, these are after all often not conducive to their role as part of the surveillant assemblages (Haggerty and Ericson 2000). Surveillant assemblages abstract the relational world from reflexive, messy and problematic classrooms, to a counterpoint of standards when we valorise testing, which 'privileges that which is simple and easy to measure over the more complex and untidy dimensions' (Mockler 2011, p. 518).

It is apparent that the construction of teacher professional identity in chronopolitical times is performative and illustrative of a culture of self-policed compliance. This occurs every time a teacher takes work home, comes in for another meeting or does anything under the banner of that's what you do as a teacher (Ball 2017), wherein the jailor becomes unnecessary, when teachers and students appreciate that they are forever being watched and instead undertake the practice of self-policing. This is becoming more and more evident in a culture of speed where we understand post-panoptic teachers are conditioned to live work and understand codes of compliance which became central to an understanding of who they are. The post panoptic teacher understands their environment to be defined by terms like a 'glass cage' (Page 2015, p. 1046), 'misrecognition' (Courtney 2016, p. 633) which leads to ontological instability and a focus on representation rather than 'information on the performance of the model, and not the event' (Bogard 2012, p. 35).

Diffracting the Temporal

Modern temporality, to which education is subjected, has left an enduring legacy. From a temporal perspective, the discontinuity that this imposes threatens the value that education can offer democracy. For Adam (2003), mastery over time leads to contradictory logics, or the creation of unanticipated risks. Paradoxically, speeding up educational practice has led to an emphasis on previously unanticipated risks that inclusive education poses to teacher time. To counter the potential of unjust socialisation that this foretells for education, we proffer a diffraction of time as a research and teaching methodology, with the objective of challenging uneven power structures that are exercised through the control and colonisation of linear temporality.

Before explaining a diffraction of time, it is appropriate to explore diffractive design. As an educational research methodology, many have utilised diffraction to examine alternative ways of addressing complex problems (Barad 2014; Bozalek and Zembylas 2017; Haraway 1997; Thomas 2020). Diffraction is predicated on the formation and effects of difference, and the co-constitution of material-discursive relations. Both human and non-human actors (matter) are entangled and congealed agents, and the differences thus created can inform the development of knowledge through research. The productive qualities of difference are key to diffractive methodologies:

> 'Difference here is not positioned as the opposition to sameness – but is also incorporated into the self as difference within and seen as a means of becoming. 'Diffractive patterns which reveal that there is light in darkness and dark in lightness are similarly fluid and provide an understanding of how binaries can be queered, and how differences exist both within and beyond boundaries' (Bozalek and Zembylas 2017, p. 4).

Variance, then, is accounted for as a strength of the methodology through a turn to the diffractive elements of ontology, epistemology and ethics of human and non-human agency. Threading the temporal to a diffractive methodological approach, we suggest, is to emphasise the ways that difference can reproduce becoming in time. It takes up what Slattery (1995, p. 616) calls '[t]he postmodern challenge … to integrate the past and the future into the existential present … allowing the process of becoming, rather than artificial demands of clocks and linear sequences, to dominate our personal and professional lives'. A diffraction of the temporal takes up the challenge of imagining alternative ontologies, through an emphasis on the relational. Virilio (2008) describes an examination of the chronological along these lines as a political incursion into speed, in which the consequences of pace is considered for its potential adversities to social development.

Virilio advocates for temporal breaks, or unregulated interruptions to chronopolitics, through which to explore alternative outcomes. An example of research that employs an inadvertent diffraction of time can be found by Humphry (2014), conducted with a group of teachers of an alternative school in the Australian State of New South Wales. Humphry observed research participants employing what she called 'the pause' (2014, p. 490) in interviews. Lengthy silences, she noted, became opportunities for participants to employ 'careful, deliberate and purposeful choice[s] in words and phrasing' (Humphry 2014, p. 491) that facilitated alternative ways of describing their students who might otherwise be labelled in deficit terms. Instead, by employing the pause, they focused on their relationships with the students, and their strengths therein. In the next section we put diffraction of time to work in teacher training in a recent project that purposefully foregrounded time.

The Global Experience Project

In seeking to subvert a culture of compliance, failure, and stress in teacher education, we draw here on a methodology of diffracted time. Through the Global Experience Project, in which preservice teachers from an Australian University undertook an aspect of their preservice teacher training in the Pacific nation of Vanuatu, we demonstrate how diffraction occasioned alternative ways of teaching and learning.

Background and Design of the Project

The Global Experience project runs yearly, however here we focus in particular on the 2018 iteration. In 2018, eighteen students were competitively selected from an initial pool of 46 applicants to participate in the Global Experience

Project (15 female, three males; 14 primary and four secondary education students). Two academic staff members with considerable classroom teaching experience accompanied the students for the duration of the 23 days and 22 nights spent on the island of Efate in Vanuatu. Vanuatu provides a significant cultural experience for a predominantly white middle-class group of students from Australia –the typical composition of teacher aspirants across the country (Lampert et al. 2015), offering many opportunities for contrasting and challenging the students' practicum teaching experiences with an island life where 'democracy was more or less imposed at the time of independence' (Prasad and Kausimae 2012, p. 1) in 1980.

The concept of the program is to build intercultural competence for preservice teachers, who are predicted to find themselves working across a rich diverse and multicultural Australian education system. Immersion in Ni-Van culture extends beyond mere classroom teaching, to a variety of aspects of that culture's approach to educational and social life. Significant to participation in an overseas program is reflective judgment, wherein intercultural competence is developed through iterative interrogation of ones' epistemological assumptions, with the objective of evaluating and reconstituting understanding as necessary. The Global Experience Project challenges pre-service teachers to think about, deal with, and appreciate the cultural, temporal and educational knowledges, practices and perspectives that differ from their own and to reflect on their daily experiences to inform their practice. To that end students where challenged in multiple ways confronting their own 'conflation of travel with an opportunity' that (McGloin and Georgeou 2016, p. 407) made them question their needs as professionals with a rhetoric of helping others, which over time became learning together.

The project draws on a deliberately diffractive methodology, whereby learning develops relationally. Tensions persist between reflexive and diffractive methodologies, in that reflection is understood as an individualised, inward-focused and agentic methodology that ignores the possibilities of collaborative production (Bozalek and Zembylas 2017). Yet, Bozalek and Zembylas demonstrate that reflection can become an apparatus of a diffractive methodology when 'entanglements of the ontological, epistemological and ethical dimensions of life and the entangled enlivening of being' (2017, p. 123) are accounted for by design. Through daily reflections and guiding questions, we posed ethical dilemmas for the students, continually asking forms of essential questions from diverse perspectives, broadening our understanding of ourselves (Deardorff and Arasaratnam-Smith 2017). In the following two vignettes we explain the diffractive methodology of the project further, in particular how it related to the temporal, specifically for this cohort of preservice teachers.

Relational Learning

In the first vignette we emphasise the relational approach of the Vanuatu Project that is premised on participatory encounters to support learning about working effectively with diversity (Whitburn and Corcoran 2019). In so doing we have utilised critical reflection in a way that dislocates sequential clock time by diffracting the past and future into the present, to facilitate the process of becoming, for the benefit of personal and professional development. Across the three weeks, the preservice teachers were arbitrarily arranged into groups on a day-to-day basis, within which they undertook daily reflection circles with the objective of interrogating each other's practices, to distil their reflections on the school day, and to plan ahead. This process was managed through a daily three step process that was explicitly structured to have the preservice teachers deliberate past actions and associated relational outcomes with their students, peers and mentors and the present to inform future practice. Reflection thus required cogitation on the following exemplar questions.

Past	What?	What happened, did you do/learn/ react today – what where the events, what was observed
Present	So What?	What are you going to do now, what matters as a result? What do these experiences mean for you? how do they affect your expectations/ reality? did you learn something new? What did you do that was effective? How has your understanding shifted, have your experiences today changed your understanding of what a teacher does? What does you being here at this time facilitate/foreclose?
Future	Now What?	What can you apply from this learning into the future, what do you now need to know, what has shifted for you as a result of this learning?

Within the larger group of 18, reflection time was used in a mixture of ways with participants recording themselves on computers using prompt questions, writing in diaries or talking through their responses in small 3-way conversations. To this end, evening reflection sessions created a safe space for participants to make sense of what it is to experience teaching and living in another culture, as well as participating in a variety of aspects of that culture's approach to educational and social life. Participants related how they had to help to push-start mini buses at 6.00am to get to school by means of the same transport as their students. Others discussed how they understood the world around them and if it would be culturally appropriate to say something to their mentor teachers who they witnessed physically engaging corporal punishment with students. Others discussed why so many young women in Vanuatu never have the opportunity to attend school after grade six.

what an educational system like that of Vanuatu might prepare a student for.

This simple but critically reflective structure coupled with a group management strategy of continual random collaboration allowed the preservice teachers to benefit from social learning. As one participant wrote about her experiences:

> 'I was expecting at least one falling out or for someone to feel like the odd one out but we have worked so well together – lesson planning, staying in pairs, days out, weekend plans—24/7 I knew if I needed anything I'd be supported'.

Over the three weeks, the experienced project convenors withdrew from the reflective circles, with the objective of providing increased autonomy to the preservice teachers. In difficult teaching and learning circumstances, this appeared to be fruitful, as one participant wrote:

> 'The group were amazingly supportive. The experience was so much better for it. Without the daily venting and stories, I would have really struggled mentally. I was very appreciative of how well the group worked together to support each other'.

Through this relational approach to work-integrated learning, it was clear that the participants were searching for what their roles were in such a place, as well as, more broadly, what it means to be a teacher. This occurred for them against a backdrop where they could find themselves in full control of a classroom as one student teacher reflected in his diary:

> 'On day two my school supervisor told me they were going to get some photocopying done, they came back three weeks later'

They were searching for answers while enacting practices with real students, and as such, their choices and decisions mattered. This engages the very essence of working with the temporal, where both students and teachers might operate at a particular speed that may seem at first difficult to align. We further explore this issue in the following vignette.

Learning with Island Time

The relationship that schools, their staff and students had with temporality troubled some of the preservice teachers who participated in the Vanuatu Project, whose understanding of time appeared to be much more uncompromising. Island time, as it is frequently referred to across Vanuatu, places clock time and written schedules as more of ambit claims than chronological structures, which was the cause of some consternation. As one preservice teacher noted:

> 'Island Time was a big challenge when it came to running a classroom- classes could start 30 mins [sic] late or go for an extra 45 minutes without any notice. I had to learn to adapt my teaching and be ready to wrap things up or come up with ways to keep the students engaged without warning'.

Adapting to island time, for participants, manifested in different ways. One participant who was particularly vexed by the perceived disorder of island time, described attempting to control and colonise time through the purchase of clocks.

Wednesday, 4th July

I just bought clocks for the school. But this is a place that is served by "Island Time". Then I started to think, is controlling time a westernised notion? So much of our lives are governed by time, but should it be? I'm starting to wonder whether my gift is thoughtful, or just creating the assumption that they should work more like the westernised-time system? Through the purchase of the clocks, this participant began to realise that the sequential nature of modern time was irrelevant in the Vanuatu context, an ethos she began to incorporate into her understanding of intercultural understanding in teaching and learning

Wednesday, 11th July

Moving past my initial frustration and reflecting on this incident helped me to gain a great deal of perspective that has helped me to begin to increase my cultural competence …, first through the disorienting event of experiencing the frustration of walking into school daily and having classes run consistently late. This led to a wealth of conversation and reflection with myself, my peers and mentors surrounding the notion of time and its cultural significance. Through this reflection I managed to capture my judgemental thinking and reconsider my perspectives on the appropriateness of giving clocks to the school as a gift.

This participant drew on her initial frustration and subsequent cultural faux pas to reflect on how teaching and learning can be mobilised in spite of the linear time spent on curriculum-based tasks.

Monday, 17th July

Maybe I need to remove my assumption that time is a thing to be grasped and governed. Focusing on the past or the future is the cause of anxiety for so many people, and there is something calming about focusing on the present moment. Maybe it is why the Ni-Vanuatu people are known for being so happy. Island time has allowed them to focus on the present moment, which is something that I know I personally need to do more. I think I need to embrace the Island time rather than fight against it. There is so much to learn from it!

As these vignettes have exemplified, Successful engagement in the Global Experience Project required the ability to negotiate different pedagogical styles, temporalities, approaches, and resources and to learn to self-manage carefully the ways that the preservice teachers interacted with students from differing cultural backgrounds in different settings. Teaching in Vanuatu therefore involved both cultural negotiation and understanding, and the development of new, and refinement of existing, pedagogical knowledge, skills and dispositions. This resulted in the development of a broader range of teaching and learning approaches contextualised in a global perspective on education. Through these examples, it is evident that The Vanuatu Project has had an insightful effect on the participants. These iterative reflections from the global experience program highlight the growth that trainee teachers can gain through the diffraction of time, and a marked concentration on shared experience and relational reflection.

Recommendations and Conclusions

In this chapter we have demonstrated that in modernist, speed-driven societies, temporality is squeezed in order for students to quantifiably justify the capabilities of teachers in circular motions of risk elimination. We argue that this does little for the project of inclusive education, which is often pitted against temporally strangled teachers as yet another challenge to implement in their daily practices (Done and Murphy 2016; Thomas and Whitburn 2019). It is integral that we keep a focus on the ways in which we remain trapped in the amber of time, ideologically positioned in transactional arrangements, as programs of learning have come to resemble commodity exchanges, whereby courses of learning more often begin and end with standard achievement outcomes measured through homogenous assessment practices. Virilio suggests 'speed is violence' (2008, p. 45) and there is indeed something in his assertion when schooling in modernity is a series of data extractions, whereby trust in teachers is constantly undermined and teaching and learning is compartmentalised into sped-up notions of demonstrated understanding. We exist in a chronopolitically counterproductive present in which a focus on outcomes, without the requisite time for consideration learning or development, means that inclusion is all but forgotten and learning is rendered farcical. In response, we have developed and demonstrated a methodology affecting temporal diffraction, and to conclude this chapter, we submit ways in which it might be put to work in other contexts of research, teaching and learning to support others concerned with the dominance of linear clock time in education and its effect on inclusive development.

1. The concept of modernised, industrial clock time and the violence of speed retains power over educators and students. How this is manifested in diverse contexts must be core to programs of teaching and learning in which fixity is disrupted to understand the 'becoming' of identity over time.
2. Technological incursions into education do more than saving time for educators. The power rendered over teachers must also be considered in training.
3. Recognition that learning takes time, and that it cannot be standardised for any one learner, is vital. Appealing to the 'slow' does not sufficiently disrupt imbalanced power relations, but rather plays into them. The process of learning needs to be understood in terms of temporal engagement as much as the development of curriculum knowledge and experience.
4. Effective relational ontologies recognise the diversity of the ways group members work in the service of time. This requires the acknowledgement of collective time, or the shared histories and futures that have constitutive implications on any one moment generated by a group, rather than a focus on risk posed through the involvement of any one individual.

As the politics of the spatial gives way to the political struggle of chronopolitics (Virilio 2008), the ways that global education is implicated in the culture of speed must come in for particular scrutiny. Technology has had a profound effect on the role of educators in their day-to-day jobs, however we are still yet to witness its capacity to eliminate risk of educational exclusion, and instead understand it to be utilised as instruments of control both to time and surveillance. Like others, (Bozalek and Zembylas 2017; Haraway 1997; Slattery 1995) we are drawn to the mechanics of the education system in which teachers and students form relational collectives. By exhuming the temporal, the risk avoidance strategies of schools, discrete technologies, implicit norms, professional expectations, local laws and self-policing coalesce to form chronopolitical tools for examination. Breaking continuity with diffraction creates opportunity for alternative understandings.

Acknowledgment We would like to extend our sincere gratitude to Ms. Helen Weston, successive Global Experience Cohorts and the students and teachers of Port Villa and Espiritu Santo, Vanuatu for their contributions to the research we have drawn on in this chapter.

References

Adam, B. (1995). *Timewatch: the social analysis of time*. Cambridge, UK: Polity Press.
Adam, B. (2003). Reflexive Modernization Temporalized. *Theory, Culture & Society, 20*(2), 59–78. https://doi.org/10.1177/0263276403020002004.
Adam, B., & Allan, S. (1995). *Theorizing culture: An interdisciplinary critique after postmodernism*. New York, NY: NYU Press.
Allan, J. (1996). Foucault and Special Educational Needs: A 'box of tools' for analysing children's experiences of mainstreaming. *Disability & Society, 11*(2), 219–234. https://doi.org/10.1080/09687599650023245.
Armitage, J., & Roberts, J. (2003). *Living with Cyberspace: Technology and Society in the 21st Century*. London, UK: Bloomsbury Publishing.
Ball, S. J. (2017). *Foucault as educator*. Cham, Switzerland: Springer.
Barad, K. (2014). Diffracting diffraction: Cutting together-apart. *Parallax, 20*(3), 168–187. https://doi.org/10.1080/13534645.2014.927623.
Bauman, Z. (2007). *Liquid times: living in an age of uncertainty*. Cambridge, UK: Polity Press.
Beck, U., Bonss, W., & Lau, C. (2003). The Theory of Reflexive Modernization: Problematic, Hypotheses and Research Programme. *Theory, Culture & Society, 20*(2), 1-33. https://doi.org/10.1177/0263276403020002001.
Bellingham, R., Thomas, M. K. E., Charman, K., Dixon, M., & Cooper, J. (2019). What Is Valued Knowledge and Where Does It Live? Educational Consciousness and the Democratisation of Education. In S. Riddle. & M. W. Apple (Eds.), *Re-imagining Education for Democracy* (pp. 77–91). London, United Kingdom: Routledge.
Berg, M., & Seeber, B. (2016). *Slow Professor: Challenging the Culture of Speed in the Academy*. Toronto, Buffalo: University of Toronto Press.

Bogard, W. (2012). Simulation and Post-Panopticism. In K. Ball, K. Haggerty, & D. Lyon (Eds.), *Routledge Handbook of Surveillance Studies* (pp. 30–37). London, UK: Routledge.

Bozalek, V., & Zembylas, M. (2017). Diffraction or reflection? Sketching the contours of two methodologies in educational research. *International Journal of Qualitative Studies in Education, 30*(2), 111–127. https://doi.org/10.1080/09518398.2016.1201166.

Castells, M. (2010). *The Rise of the Network Society*. Chichester, West Sussex: Wiley-Blackwell.

Courtney, S. J. (2016). Post-panopticism and school inspection in England. *British Journal of Sociology of Education, 37*(4), 623–642. https://doi.org/10.1080/01425692.2014.965806.

Coxon, S. (2012). Slow Bread, Slow Cities, Slow Pedagogy: Dale Primary School, Derby. In N. Owen (Ed.), *Placing Students at the Heart of Creative Learning*. Abingdon, Oxon: Routledge.

Deardorff, D. K., & Arasaratnam-Smith, L. A. (2017). *Intercultural Competence in Higher Education: International Approaches, Assessment and Application*. Abingdon, Oxon: Routledge.

Done, E. J., & Murphy, M. (2016). The responsibilisation of teachers: a neoliberal solution to the problem of inclusion. *Discourse: Studies in the Cultural Politics of Education, 39*(1), 142–155. https://doi.org/10.1080/01596306.2016.1243517.

Eacott, S. (2017). *Beyond Leadership: A Relational Approach to Organizational Theory in Education*. Singapore, Singapore: Springer.

Fulcher, G. (1989). *Disabling Policies?: A Comparative Approach to Education Policy and Disability*. London, UK: Falmer Press.

Glennie, P., & Thrift, N. (2009). *Shaping the Day: A History of Timekeeping in England and Wales 1300–1800*. Oxford, UK: Oxford University Press.

Haggerty, K. D., & Ericson, R. V. (2000). The surveillant assemblage. *The British Journal of Sociology*(4), 605.

Haraway, D. J. (1997). *Modest− Witness@ Second− Millennium. FemaleMan− Meets− OncoMouse: Feminism and Technoscience*. London, UK: Routledge.

Hargreaves, A. (2003). *Teaching in the Knowledge Society: Education in the Age of Insecurity*. New York, NY: Teachers College Press.

Humphry, N. (2014). Disrupting deficit: the power of 'the pause' in resisting the dominance of deficit knowledges in education. *International Journal of Inclusive Education, 18*(5), 484–499. https://doi.org/10.1080/13603116.2013.789087.

Judith, L. K. (1981). Socialization and the Symbolic Order of the School. *Anthropology & Education Quarterly, 12*(4), 258.

Lampert, J., Burnett, B., & Morse, K. (2015). Destabilising Privilege: disrupting deficit thinking in white pre-service teachers on field experience in culturally diverse, high-poverty schools. In Tania Ferfolja, C. J. Díaz, & J. Ullman (Eds.), *Understanding Sociological Theory for Educational Practices* (pp. 76–92). Melbourne, Australia: Cambridge University Press.

Lau, T. C. W. (2019). Slowness, disability, and academic productivity: The need to rethink academic culture. In C. McMaster & B. Whitburn. (Eds.), *Disability at the University: A Disabled Students' Manifesto*. New York, NY: Peter Lang.

Leibowitz, B., & Bozalek, V. (2018). Towards a Slow scholarship of teaching and learning in the South. *Teaching in Higher Education, 23*(8), 981–994. https://doi.org/10.1080/13562517.2018.1452730.

Lingard, B., & Thompson, G. (2017). Doing time in the sociology of education. *British Journal of Sociology of Education, 38*(1), 1-12. https://doi.org/10.1080/01425692.2016.1260854.

Manolev, J., Sullivan, A., & Slee, R. (2019). The datafication of discipline: ClassDojo, surveillance and a performative classroom culture. *Learning, Media and Technology, 44*(1), 36–51. https://doi.org/10.1080/17439884.2018.1558237.

Martin, S. (2014). Lessons from the Great Underground Empire: Pedagogy, Computers and False Dawn. In A. Tatnall & B. Davey (Eds.), *Reflections on the History of Computers in Education: Early Use of Computers and Teaching about Computing in Schools* (pp. 1-25). Berlin, Heidelberg: Springer.

Masters, G. N. (2016). *Five challenges in Australian school education*. Retrieved from.

McGloin, C., & Georgeou, N. (2016). 'Looks good on your CV': The sociology of voluntourism recruitment in higher education. *Journal of Sociology, 52*(2), 403–417. https://doi.org/10.1177/1440783314562416.

Mittler, P. (2009). The Global Context of Inclusive Education: The Role of the United Nations. In D. Mitchell (Ed.), *Contextualizing Inclusive Education: Evaluating Old and New International Paradigms* (pp. 22–36). London, UK: Routledge.

Mockler, N. (2011). Beyond 'what works': Understanding teacher identity as a practical and political tool. *Teachers and teaching: theory and practice, 17*(5), 517–528. https://doi.org/10.1080/13540602.2011.602059.

Page, D. (2015). The Visibility and Invisibility of Performance Management in Schools. *British Educational Research Journal, 41*(6), 1031–1049. https://doi.org/10.1002/berj.3185.

Prasad, B. C., & Kausimae, P. (2012). *Social Policies in Solomon Islands and Vanuatu*. United Nations Research Institute for Social Development: London: Commonwealth Secretariat.

Ritzer, G. (2013). *The McDonaldization of Society: 20th Anniversary Edition*. Los Angeles, Calif: SAGE Publications.

Rizvi, F., & Lingard, B. (2010). Globalizing Education Policy. London, UK: Routledge.

Santiago, P., Donaldson, G., Herman, J., & Shewbridge, C. (2011). OECD Reviews of Evaluation and Assessment in Education: Australia. *OECD Publishing (NJ1)*.

Santos-Trigo, M., & Reyes-Martínez, I. (2019). High school prospective teachers' problem-solving reasoning that involves the coordinated use of digital technologies. *International Journal of Mathematical Education in Science and Technology, 50*(2), 182–201. https://doi.org/10.1080/0020739x.2018.1489075.

Sharma, S. (2014). *In the Meantime: Temporality and Cultural Politics*. Durham, NC: Duke University Press.

Slattery, P. (1995). A postmodern vision of time and learning: a response to the National Education Commission Report Prisoners of Time. *Harvard Educational Review*(4), 612.

Slee, R. (2018). *Inclusive Education isn't Dead, it just Smells Funny*. Abingdon, Oxon: Routledge.

Stevens, T. (2016). *Cyber Security and the Politics of Time*. London, UK: Cambridge University Press.

Tatnall, A., & Davey, B. (2014). *Reflections on the History of Computers in Education: Early Use of Computers and Teaching about Computing in Schools*. Berlin, Heidelberg: Springer.

Thomas, M. K. E. (2020). Swarms and Murmurations. In M. K. E. Thomas & R. Bellingham (Eds.), *Post-Qualitative Research and Innovative Methodologies* (pp. 153–171). London, UK: Bloomsbury Academic.

Thomas, M. K. E., & Bellingham, R. (Eds.). (2020). Post-Qualitative Research and Innovative Methodologies. London, UK: Bloomsbury Academic.

Thomas, M. K. E, Weston, H, Whitburn, B, & McCandless, T. (2018). Global Experience for Pre-Service Teachers: Challenging settings, temporality and the AITSL standards. Vanuatu, South Pacific.

Thomas, M. K. E., & Whitburn, B. (2019). Time for inclusion? *British Journal of Sociology of Education, 40*(2), 159–173. doi:https://doi.org/10.1080/01425692.2018.1512848.

UNESCO. (1990). *World Declaration on Education for All*. Jomtien, Thailand: United Nations Educational Scientific Cultural Organization.

UNESCO. (1994). *The Salamanca Statement and Framework for action on special needs education: adopted by the World Conference on Special Needs Education; Access and Quality. Salamanca, Spain, 7–10 June 1994*. Salamanca, Spain: UNESCO.

Virilio, P. (2008). Pure war: Twenty-Five Years Later: (M. Polizzotti, Trans. S. Lotringer Ed.). Los Angeles, Calif.: Semiotexte.

Whitburn, B., & Corcoran, T. (2019). Ontologies of Inclusion and Teacher Education. In B. M. Rice (Ed.), *Global Perspectives on Inclusive Teacher Education* (pp. 1–15). Hershey, PA: IGI Global, Information Science Reference.

Whitburn, B., & Thomas, M. K. E. (2021). Risks in Time: To Inclusive Educational Rights. In Matthew Krehl Edward Thomas, Leechin Heng, & Peter Walker (Eds.), Inclusive Education is a Right, right? (Vol. 47, pp. 37–50). Brill.

Zuboff, S. (2019). *The Age of Surveillance Capitalism: The Fight for a Human Future at the New Frontier of Power*. New York, NY: PublicAffairs.

Erweiterte institutionalisierte Freizeit an Tagesschulen und ambivalente Bedeutsamkeit aus der Perspektive von Schülerinnen und Schülern, sozialpädagogischen Fachkräften, Lehrkräften und Eltern

Emanuela Chiapparini, Andrea Scholian, Christa Kappler und Patricia Schuler Braunschweig

Abstract

As part of the expansion of all-day schools in Switzerland, leisure time is being shifted to the school context. Pupils are increasingly present at school during lunchtime and in the afternoons. The extensive leisure time in the institutional context opens up the possibility of expanding the school's understanding of education (Chiapparini et al. 2018). Until now, this was almost exclusively focused on teaching and is now to be expanded to include political and moral personality development (Scherr 2008; Mansel und

E. Chiapparini (✉)
Berner Fachhochschule, Bern, Schweiz
E-Mail: Emanuela.Chiapparini@bfh.ch

A. Scholian
Zürcher Hochschule für Angewandte Wissenschaften, Zürich, Schweiz
E-Mail: Andrea.Scholian@zhaw.ch

C. Kappler · P. S. Braunschweig
Pädagogische Hochschule Zürich, Zürich, Schweiz
E-Mail: christa.kappler@phzh.ch

P. S. Braunschweig
E-Mail: patricia.schuler@phzh.ch

© Springer Fachmedien Wiesbaden GmbH, ein Teil von Springer Nature 2020
E. Schilling und M. O'Neill (Hrsg.), *Frontiers in Time Research – Einführung in die interdisziplinäre Zeitforschung*,
https://doi.org/10.1007/978-3-658-31252-7_10

Hurrelmann 2003). At the same time, fears of the scholarization of leisure time are growing (Fölling-Albers 2000) and doubts as to whether more time in school will actually lead to more formal education (Idel et al. 2009). In view of these contrasting contexts, the main question that arises is how pupils perceive and shape the extended school time and the institutionalized leisure time that takes place in it. Subsequently, the significance of extended leisure time at school must be clarified from the perspective of socio-educational specialists, teachers and parents. The research project on pedagogical responsibilities at all-day schools in Zurich, which is funded by the Swiss National Science Foundation (SNSF), provides a suitable data basis for this purpose. The contribution presents the methods and the methodological reflections on researching extended and institutionalized time as well as the concept and significance of "leisure" in the school context. Using the findings of the study, the paper discusses the research approach.

Zusammenfassung

Im Zuge des Ausbaus von Tagesschulen in der Schweiz findet eine Verlagerung der Freizeit in den Schulkontext statt. Schüler*innen sind während der Mittagszeit und im Anschluss an den Nachmittagsunterricht in der Schule vermehrt anwesend. Durch die ausgedehnte Freizeit im institutionellen Kontext eröffnet sich die Möglichkeit, das schulische Bildungsverständnis zu erweitern (Chiapparini et al. 2018). Dieses war bisher fast ausschließlich auf den Unterricht fokussiert und ist nun vermehrt auf politische und moralische Persönlichkeitsbildung (Scherr 2008; Mansel und Hurrelmann 2003) auszuweiten. Gleichzeitig nimmt die Befürchtung der Scholarisierung der Freizeit (Fölling-Albers 2000) zu und der Zweifel, ob mit mehr Zeit in der Schule tatsächlich „mehr" Bildung stattfindet (Idel et al. 2009). Vor dem Hintergrund dieses Spannungsfeldes stellt sich vorerst die Frage, inwiefern Schüler*innen die verlängerte Schulzeit und die darin stattfindende institutionalisierte Freizeit wahrnehmen und gestalten. Daran anschließend ist die Bedeutsamkeit einer erweiterten Freizeit in der Schule aus der Perspektive der sozialpädagogischen Fachkräfte, der Lehrkräfte und der Eltern zu klären. Hierzu bildet das im Rahmen des Schweizerischen Nationalfonds geförderte Forschungsprojekt zu pädagogischen Zuständigkeiten an Tagesschulen in Zürich die geeignete Datengrundlage. Es werden im Beitrag die methodologischen und methodischen Reflexionen zur Erfassung der erweiterten und institutionalisierten Zeit und des Freizeitbegriffs im Schulkontext und deren Bedeutsamkeit vorgestellt und anhand von Befunden der beteiligten Personengruppen in Tagesschulen diskutiert.

> **Keywords**
>
> All-day school · Institutionalized Leisure time · Leisure time · Teachers ·
> Social pedagogical specialists · Pupils · Parents · Education · Scholarization ·
> Switzerland · Tagesschule · Institutionalisierte Freizeit · Freizeit · Lehrkräfte ·
> Sozialpädagogische Fachkräfte · Schülerinnen und Schüler · Eltern · Bildung ·
> Scholarisierung · Schweiz

> **Schlüsselwörter**
>
> Tagesschule · Institutionalisierte Freizeit · Freizeit · Lehrkräfte ·
> Sozialpädagogische Fachkräfte · Schülerinnen und Schüler · Eltern · Bildung ·
> Scholarisierung · Schweiz

Ausdehnung der institutionellen Freizeit im Zuge des Ausbaus von Tagesschulen

Im Zuge des Ausbaus von Tagesschulen in Zürich und weiteren Städten in der Schweiz verbringen Kinder und Jugendliche mehr Zeit in der öffentlichen Schule. Dies betrifft insbesondere die Mittagszeit und die Zeit nach dem obligatorischen Unterricht am Nachmittag (Chiapparini et al. 2016). Dabei gibt es eine Verschiebung von Zeit, welche früher in der Familie und neu vermehrt als institutionalisierte Freizeit im Kontext Tagesschule verbracht wird. Zudem wird diese institutionalisierte Zeit aufgrund der zunehmenden Zahl an Schülerinnen und Schülern anders gestaltet.

Mit der Ausdehnung der Freizeit im Schulkontext eröffnen sich im deutschsprachigen Fachdiskurs zum einen Befürchtungen einer Scholarisierung der Freizeit (Fölling-Albers 2000), wobei ein Verwertungsdruck der außerschulischen Aktivitäten zur Erzielung besserer Schulleistungen zu beobachten ist (Heinz 2011). Zum anderen ergibt sich durch die vermehrte institutionalisierte Freizeit die Möglichkeit, das schulische Bildungsverständnis auszuweiten (Chiapparini 2019): Während im Unterricht vermehrt formales Lernen stattfindet, ermöglichen Freizeitangebote non-formale Lernsettings, die sich durch strukturierte sowie angeleitete Kursangebote oder durch nichtstrukturierte und nur punktuell begleitete Angebote, wie beispielsweise in Projekten der Offenen Kinder- und Jugendarbeit, auszeichnen (Züchner 2013). Außerdem wird informelles Lernen unter Peers vermehrt in Freizeitangeboten gefördert, wobei dieses ebenfalls im Unterricht stattfinden kann (Chiapparini et al. 2018). Im Schweizer Kontext wird die erwähnte Verzahnung von Unterricht und institutionalisierter Freizeit weniger vor dem Hintergrund eines Fachdiskurses reflektiert, sondern bisher vermehrt vor einem bildungspolitischen Hintergrund des Ausbaus von Tagesschulen. Zum Beispiel ist diese Verzahnung explizit als eines von drei Zielen der Stadt Zürich definiert, in der flächendeckend und sukzessiv Tagesschulen seit 2016 eingeführt werden (Schul- und Sportdepartement 2018). Ein zweites Ziel, die Vereinbarkeit von Familie und Beruf, ist mit der Verschiebung eines Teils der Freizeit von der Familie in die Schule verknüpft. Dies soll durch die verlängerte institutionalisierte Freizeit und der damit länger verbrachten Zeit in Tagesschulen als in Regelschulen, erreicht werden. Dieses Ziel ist insofern stark mit dem Ausbau verknüpft, da ohne die in den letzten Jahren stark nachgestiegene Nachfrage an außerfamiliärer Betreuung es keinen solchen Ausbau gegeben hätte (Neumann et al. 2015; Crotti 2015). Das dritte Ziel ist ebenfalls mit der Zeitverschiebung und der verlängerten institutionalisierten Freizeit verbunden: Indem Tagesschulen für alle Kinder einen Zugang zu Freizeitangeboten bieten und sie damit mehr und vielfältigere Lernmöglichkeiten erhalten, besteht die Erwartung, dass durch das Tagesschulmodell die Bildungsgleichheit erhöht wird. Allerdings liefern bisherige Forschungsbefunde aus Deutschland und der Schweiz hierzu ernüchternde Befunde (Sauerwein et al. 2019). Denn zwischen dem Besuch von Tagesschulen und Schulleistungen oder sozialem Verhalten bestehen keine bis nur gering nachgewiesene Zusammenhänge (Fischer 2018). Diese hängen wiederum mit dem dauerhaften und freiwilligen Besuch von Freizeitangeboten an Tagesschulen und deren Qualität zusammen (Sauerwein et al. 2019).

Die genannten bildungspolitischen Ziele, Vereinbarkeit von Familie und Beruf sowie Förderung der Bildungsgleichheit, sind folglich mit einer Zunahme der institutionalisierten Zeit von Schülerinnen und Schülern verbunden. Zudem geht das Ziel der Verzahnung von Unterricht und institutionalisierter Freizeit mit einer veränderten Zeitgestaltung einher. Im Rahmen dessen besteht die empirische Notwendigkeit, die Frage wissenschaftlich zu erkunden, welche zeitlichen Strukturveränderungen durch die Einführung von Tagesschulen zu beobachten sind und wie Schülerinnen und Schüler, die primären Adressatinnen und Adressaten des eingeführten Tagesschulmodells, die verlängerte und institutionalisierte Freizeit wahrnehmen und diese gestalten. Ergänzend dazu ist zu klären, wie die Erweiterung und veränderte Gestaltung der institutionalisierten Freizeit aus der Perspektive von Eltern, Fachkräften und Lehrkräften wahrgenommen werden. Die Stadt Zürich ist die erste Schweizer Gemeinde, welche Tagesschulen schrittweise und flächendeckend einführt (Chiapparini et al. 2016). Dieser Einführungsprozess wird vom schweizerischen Nationalfonds (SNF) unterstützten

Forschungsprojekt „AusTEr – pädagogische Zuständigkeiten an Tagesschulen" wissenschaftlich begleitet, auf dessen Datengrundlage sich dieser Beitrag stützt. In diesem wird zuerst die institutionalisierte Freizeit konzeptionell und theoretisch verortet. Dann wird die Datengrundlage zum besagten SNF-Projekt und der methodologische und methodische Zugang skizziert. Anschließend werden die Ergebnisse im vierten Kapitel vorgestellt und diskutiert, worauf das Fazit im fünften Kapitel folgt.

Theoretisch und empirisch basierte Reflexionen zur institutionalisierten Freizeit an Tagesschulen

Das Thema der institutionalisierten Freizeit an Tagesschulen verortet sich in einem breiteren theoretischen Rahmen in der Ausdehnung der Ausbildungszeit (Hurrelmann und Quenzel 2016) beziehungsweise einer Verschiebung der Zeit von einem familiären Kontext in einen schulischen Kontext. Mit dieser zusätzlichen Zeit im institutionalisierten Kontext geht ein ausgedehnter Schutz- und Sozialisationsraum (Bühler-Niederberger 2011) sowie ein theoretisches Verständnis von Kindheit als Bildungsmoratorium (Zinnecker 2000) und einer institutionalisierten Kindheit (Betz et al. 2018) einher. Dieser verlängerte zeitliche Bildungsraum bezieht sich sowohl auf den Unterricht, als auch auf die Freizeit im schulischen Kontext. Insbesondere seit den letzten 50 Jahren ist ein Ausbau der institutionalisierten Freizeit im deutschsprachigen Raum zu beobachten, wozu außerschulische Bildungsangebote, wie zum Beispiel Sportvereine, Musikschulen oder andere institutionalisierte Freizeitangebote zählen (Chiapparini und Skrobanek 2015; Fuhs 2002). An den ausgedehnten Bildungsraum in Schule und Freizeit knüpft die eingangs erwähnte „Scholarisierung von Freizeit" (Fölling-Albers 2000) an, die darüber hinaus mit einer „Scholarisierung von Familie" einhergeht (Fraij et al. 2015). Der Ansatz der Scholarisierung der Freizeit steht im deutschsprachigen Fachdiskurs in engem Zusammenhang mit dem Konzept der Verwertbarkeit von Freizeitgestaltung beziehungsweise der Verwertbarkeit von Zeit hinsichtlich der Schulleistungen von Kindern und Jugendlichen (Heinz 2011; Harring et al. 2010).

Aus der Perspektive der Eltern geht mit dem ausgedehnten Bildungsraum ein großer Planungs- und Organisationsbedarf in der Freizeitgestaltung der Heranwachsenden (Kränzl-Nagel und Mierendorff 2007) und eine damit verbundene Zeitnutzung der außerunterrichtlichen Zeit der Schülerinnen und Schüler einher. Tagesschulen entlasten die Eltern dabei, indem Freizeitangebote direkt und idealerweise mit einer breiten Auswahl an der Tagesschule angeboten werden.

Allerdings liegen zur Nutzung von Freizeitangeboten an Tagesschulen bisher wenige Studien in der Schweiz und Deutschland vor, wobei diese wenigen auf zahlreiche Einflussfaktoren hinweisen (Sauerwein et al. 2019). Zum Beispiel spielen die finanziellen Möglichkeiten der Eltern eine entscheidende Rolle (Fölling-Albers 2000), indem beispielsweise teure Sportkurse, Einzelunterricht und weit vom Wohnort entfernte Kurse nicht von allen Kindern und Jugendlichen besucht werden können. Grundsätzlich stellt sich im Zuge des Ausbaus von Tagesschulen die Frage, inwiefern die ausgedehnte Freizeit an Tagesschulen und damit die institutionalisierte Freizeit an Tagesschulen tatsächlich „mehr" formale Bildung fördert (Idel et al. 2009).

Nachgewiesen ist bisher eine geringe Wirkung der institutionalisierten Freizeit auf die Schulleistung (Sauerwein et al. 2019; Fischer et al. 2011; Thole und Höblich 2014). Ebenfalls geht aus den Studien hervor, dass die Kinder regelmäßig und freiwillig an den Freizeitangeboten teilzunehmen haben, wobei diese einem gewissen Qualitätsstandard entsprechen müssen. Dies ist der Fall, wenn sich beispielsweise die Kinder in den Angeboten „ernst genommen, motiviert und kognitiv herausgefordert [fühlen], so entwickelt sich auch die soziale Verantwortungsübernahme besser" (Fischer et al. 2011, S. 29). Zur Wirksamkeit der institutionalisierten Freizeit in der Schweiz liegen Längsschnittstudien vor (Schüpbach et al. 2018; Frei et al. 2016; Schüpbach 2014), allerdings mit keinem oder sehr geringem positiven Zusammenhang von Teilnahme an Tagessschulen und einzelnen Schulleistungen.

Jedoch besteht im deutschsprachigen Fachdiskurs zu Tagesschulen darüber Einigkeit, (Scherr 2008; Chiapparini et al. 2019; Andresen et al. 2011), dass Gestaltungsfreiräume innerhalb der institutionalisierten Freizeit Voraussetzung für ein gelingendes Aufwachsen „in öffentlicher Verantwortung" (Böllert 2008; Rauschenbach 2009) sind. Denn besonders durch eine selbstorganisierte Freizeitgestaltung an Tagesschulen kann die politische und moralische Persönlichkeits- und Identitätsbildung (Scherr 2008) gefördert werden. Dies geschieht, indem offene Freiräume in der institutionalisierten Freizeit „als attraktive Angebote für Eigenaktivität erfahren werden" können (Scherr 2008, S. 144) und Heranwachsende „zu einer selbstbewussten und selbstbestimmten Gestaltung ihrer Lebenspraxis" unterstützt werden (Scherr 2008, S. 139). Auch in Bezug auf das Wohlbefinden der Kinder belegen Befunde, dass selbstbestimmte Zeit von Schülerinnen und Schülern sowie Zeit in der Gleichaltrigengruppe für ihr gelingendes Aufwachsen zentral sind (Andresen et al. 2011; Soremski et al. 2011, 2015; Krüger 2008).

Hinsichtlich der Zeitgestaltung an Tagesschulen weisen Forschungsbefunde darauf hin, dass die institutionalisierte Freizeit eine Herausforderung für die

Schülerinnen und Schüler sein kann. Denn Tagesschulen stellen für sie eine Disziplinierungsleistung dar, weil es wenig Möglichkeiten des Rückzugs oder des Loslassens von Selbstkontrolle gibt (Deckert-Peaceman 2009; Chiapparini et al. 2018). Zudem wird von den Schülerinnen und Schülern eine hohe Leistung abverlangt aufgrund des „häufigen Wechselns ihrer Positionierung in der hybriden Struktur zwischen ‚Schule und Nicht- Schule'" (Deckert-Peaceman 2009, S. 100). Jedoch ist von Seiten der Lehrkräfte und sozialpädagogischen Fachkräfte, gemäß den Befunden des Bielefelder Forschungsprojekts „Familie als Akteure der Ganztagsschule", eine allgemeine Skepsis gegenüber der freien Zeitgestaltung von den Kindern feststellbar (Andresen et al. 2011). Sozialpädagogische Fachkräfte äußern die Sorge, dass in Ganztagsschulen wertvolle Zeit ungenutzt verstreicht und Potential, um die kindliche Entwicklung zu unterstützen, nicht ausgeschöpft wird (Andresen et al. 2011). Zudem versuchen sozialpädagogische Fachkräfte auf die Wahl der Freizeitangebote Einfluss zu nehmen, um die Kinder aus professioneller Perspektive zur „richtigen" Wahl zu ermuntern (Andresen et al. 2011).

Schweizer-Nationalfonds Studie zu pädagogischen Zuständigkeiten an Tagesschulen

Die Datengrundlagen des vorliegenden Beitrags beziehen sich auf das vom Schweizerischen Nationalfonds geförderte Projekt „AusTEr ". Darauf basierend werden die Deutungen von Schülerinnen und Schülern auf die institutionalisierte Freizeit und deren Gestaltung erkundet sowie die Perspektive von weiteren Beteiligten darauf erschlossen.

Der methodologische und methodische Zugang des Forschungsprojekts basiert auf das Verfahren der Grounded Theory (Glaser und Strauss 1967; Strauss und Corbin 1991), die sich auf die Wissenschaftstheorie des symbolischen Interaktionismus bezieht (Abels 2010). Diese besagt, dass Menschen den Gegenständen, Ereignissen und Erfahrungen Bedeutungen zuschreiben und dadurch diese „selbst schaffen" (Abels 2010, S. 46). Diese Sicht des Subjekts in Form subjektiver Theorien gilt es anhand der gewählten Forschungsmethode zu rekonstruieren. Dies ermöglicht einen Zugang, wie Menschen die Welt erklären, oder zumindest einen bestimmten Ausschnitt davon (Flick 2007).

Ein qualitativer Forschungszugang wurde zudem gewählt, weil eine „Theorie der Ganztagsbildung" (Coelen und Stecher 2014) bislang fehlt und weil es notwendig ist, die Deutungsmuster von verschiedenen Beteiligten an einer Ganztagsschule differenziert zu berücksichtigen. Der Forschungsfokus wird folglich auf die Erzählungen und nicht auf die Praxen gesetzt. Die Bedeutung der institutionalisierten Freizeit und deren Gestaltung, nach denen sich die Handlungen der Beteiligten in der Praxis orientieren, kommen in ihren Erzählungen zu Interaktionen mit Schülerinnen und Schülern zum Ausdruck. Der Schulalltag, mit Blick auf die Mittagszeit und nicht-unterrichtliche Zeit in der Schule, wurde mittels Einzel- und Gruppengesprächen mit narrativen Passagen (Schütze 1983; Bohnsack 2006) und mit möglichst aller an der Tagesschule tätigen Personen untersucht. Mittels der qualitativen Interviews und Gruppendiskussionen lassen sich aus den gewonnenen Erzählungen Deutungsmuster rekonstruieren, die wiederum Handlungsroutinen und Sichtweisen der handelnden Personen abbilden, die ihnen nicht als solche bewusst sind.

Das Forschungsprojekt ist als Cross-Case-Study konzipiert, indem vier Tagesschulen in der Stadt Zürich zu zwei Messzeitpunkten analysiert und miteinander verglichen wurden. Der erste Zeitpunkt verortet sich kurz vor der Einführung der Tagesschule im Sommer 2016 und der zweite Zeitpunkt etwas mehr als ein Jahr nach der Einführung im Herbst 2017. Da die institutionalisierte Freizeit erst in der eingeführten Tagesschule zum Tragen kam und erfasst werden kann, beziehen sich die hier analysierten Daten auf den zweiten Erhebungszeitpunkt. In diesem wurden insgesamt 51 Interviews und Gruppendiskussionen geführt. Für die Beantwortung der Forschungsfragen sind folgende Personengruppen zu berücksichtigen: 32 Schülerinnen und Schüler, 12 sozialpädagogische Fachkräfte[1], 14 Lehrkräfte der Unter-, Mittel- und Oberstufe, sowie 13 Eltern.

Die Gesprächsdauer betrug 45 bis 90 Minuten. Den Ort und die Zeit wählten die Teilnehmenden frei aus. Die aufgenommenen Gespräche wurden transkribiert und nach dem dreistufigen Verfahren der Grounded Theory (Strauss und Corbin 1991) ausgewertet. Während das offene Kodieren jeweils von einer Person vorgenommen wurde, fand die axiale und selektive Kodierung in der Forschungsgruppe statt. Da mit den letzten zwei Auswertungsschritten eine starke Kürzung der Materialfülle einhergeht und nur relevante Kategorien beizubehalten und irrelevante Kategorien auszuschließen sind, bietet sich ein intersubjektiver Prozess an.

Bezogen auf die Forschungsfrage, inwiefern in den erzählten Handlungen ein erweiterter Bildungsbegriff zum Ausdruck kommt, werden vorerst zentrale Hand-

---

[1]Während Lehrkräfte mehrheitlich denselben tertiären Bildungshintergrund haben, variiert dieser bei den sozialpädagogischen Fachkräften. Diese weisen einen berufsbezogenen Lehrabschluss oder eine Tertiärausbildung, die an einer Universität, einer Pädagogischen Hochschule, einer Fachhochschule oder einer Höheren Fachschule im Bereich Pädagogik stattfand.

lungsmuster anhand besonders aussagekräftiger Originalzitate der Teilnehmenden vorgestellt. Diese wurden aufgrund von gemeinsamen, ergänzenden oder kontrastierenden Aspekten jener Handlungsmuster ausgewählt. In einem zweiten Schritt werden diese mit den eingangs vorgestellten theoretischen Bezügen diskutiert.

Ergebnisse

Die Einführung von Tagesschulen führte zu einer verlängerten institutionalisierten Freizeit insbesondere über Mittag wie auch zu einer Umstrukturierung der Unterrichtszeiten in der Schule. Im Folgenden wird zuerst festgehalten, welche formale Zeitveränderung von der Regelschule zur Tagesschule stattgefunden hat (vgl. Abschn. „Zeitlich formale Veränderungen der Freizeit für Schülerinnen und Schüler an Tagesschulen") und anschließend dargelegt (vgl. Abschn. „Subjektive Wahrnehmung und Gestaltung der institutionalisierten Freizeit an Tagesschulen"), wie Schülerinnen und Schüler die verlängerte Schulzeit und damit die zusätzliche institutionalisierte Freizeit an Tagesschulen wahrnehmen und gestalten. Zusätzlich wird die Sichtweise von drei weiteren zentralen Beteiligten an Tagesschulen (sozialpädagogischen Fachkräften, Lehrkräften und Eltern) berücksichtigt, um Gemeinsamkeiten und Unterschiede in der Deutung der institutionalisierten Freizeit von Schülerinnen und Schülern aus den unterschiedlichen Perspektiven zu gewinnen.

Zeitlich formale Veränderungen der Freizeit für Schülerinnen und Schüler an Tagesschulen

Die größte Veränderung in der Zeit an der Schule von Schülerinnen und Schülern ist die Mittagszeit. Je nach Schulstufe gibt es zwei bis vier gebundene Mittage. Die Schülerinnen und Schüler sind für diese automatisch angemeldet. Die Eltern können ihre Kinder von diesen gebundenen Mittagen wieder abmelden, faktisch passiert dies kaum (Feller und Dietrich 2018). Die Mittage kosten inklusive Verpflegung sechs Franken für die Eltern. Früher war der Beitrag zwischen 4.50 und 33 Franken, abhängig vom steuerbaren Vermögen und Einkommen der Eltern (Schul- und Sportdepartement 2017). Außerdem wurde die Mittagszeit von 110 min auf 80 min verkürzt (Feller und Dietrich 2018) und der Schulschluss am Nachmittag ist etwas früher als in der Regelschule. Somit findet insbesondere während der Mittagszeit die verlängerte institutionalisierte Freizeit für alle

Schülerinnen und Schüler statt. Institutionalisierte Freizeit nach dem Unterricht kann bei Bedarf und für einen zusätzlichen Kostenbeitrag auch in Anspruch genommen werden. Die institutionalisierte Freizeit nach dem Nachmittagsunterricht ist in den seit 2016 eingeführten Tagesschulen in der Stadt Zürich wenig ausgebaut. Dies geht aus Vergleichen zu den bereits bestehenden öffentlichen und privaten Tagesschulen in der Stadt Zürich (Chiapparini et al. 2016) oder zu den Tagesschulen in Deutschland und USA (Sauerwein et al. 2019) hervor.

In den meisten Schulen wurde, aufgrund der gestiegenen Anzahl an Schülerinnen und Schülern über Mittag, die Gestaltung der Mittagszeit angepasst und ein Open Restaurant Betrieb eingeführt, wobei die Schüler und Schülerinnen oft das Essen selbst ausgeben. Die Ausgestaltung der Freizeit über Mittag hat sich insofern verändert, dass die Schülerinnen und Schüler über Mittag selbst entscheiden können, wann und wie lange sie zu Mittag essen wollen. Zudem können sie oft vor und nach dem Mittag zwischen unterschiedlichen Angeboten auswählen (Turnhalle, draußen spielen, Bibliothek, etc.).

Für die Schülerinnen und Schüler, welche in der Regelschule bereits im „Hort" zu Mittag gegessen haben, hat sich mit der Tagesschule die Zeit über Mittag verkürzt und die Gestaltung des Mittags geändert. Für Schülerinnen und Schüler, welche zuvor jeweils über Mittag nach Hause gegangen sind, hat sich die Zeit über Mittag in der Schule verlängert. Eine Schülerin der dritten Klasse verbringt beispielsweise dreimal 80 min mehr Zeit in einer Tagesschule.

Eine weitere organisatorische Veränderung ist, dass nun Tagesschulen unentgeltliche und freiwillige Aufgabenstunden anbieten (Schulamt Stadt Zürich 2018). Diese werden mehrheitlich von Lehrkräften und vereinzelt von sozialpädagogischen Fachkräften betreut, wie aus dem erhobenen Datenmaterial hervorgeht.

Zusätzlich werden nun teils unentgeltliche, teils kostenpflichtige Freizeitangebote über Mittag und nach dem Nachmittagsunterricht von den Schulen organisiert. Die Schulen informieren die Eltern über die Möglichkeiten und erleichtern deren Kindern den Zugang zu Freizeitangeboten. Die Organisation, um solche Freizeitangebote zu besuchen wird so vereinfacht, zudem fällt die Organisation des Weges weg, da die Angebote an den Schulen stattfinden. Der Besuch solcher Angebote ist freiwillig (Schulamt Stadt Zürich 2018).

Da die jeweils verbindlichen Mittagszeiten von fast allen Schülerinnen und Schülern besucht werden (Feller und Dietrich 2018) und Aufgabenstunden und Freizeitangebote nur von einigen Schülerinnen und Schülern genutzt werden, wird im folgenden Artikel ausschließlich auf die Mittagszeit eingegangen.

Vollständigkeitshalber ist festzuhalten, dass die Anzahl der Unterrichtslektionen kantonal geregelt ist und sich durch die Einführung von Tagesschulen nicht verändert hat (Volksschulamt Kanton Zürich 2017). Jedoch wird der Unterricht an Tagesschulen gestaffelter durchgeführt (Feller und Dietrich 2018). Zum Beispiel hatte ein Schüler der vierten Klasse zuvor vier Unterrichtslektionen am Morgen und an vier Nachmittagen pro Woche Unterricht. In der Tagesschule hat er nun jeweils fünf Unterrichtslektionen am Morgen und an drei Nachmittagen Unterricht (Volksschulamt Kanton Zürich 2018).

Die Unterrichtszeit und die Freizeit findet somit konzentrierter statt: längere Unterrichtszeit am Morgen oder auch am Nachmittag und mehr freie Nachmittage sowie verkürzte Mittagszeit und früherer Schulschluss. Wie dies von Beteiligten an Tagesschulen beurteilt wird, wird im darauffolgenden Kapitel thematisiert.

Subjektive Wahrnehmung und Gestaltung der institutionalisierten Freizeit an Tagesschulen

Im folgenden Kapitel wird zuerst darauf eingegangen, wie Schülerinnen und Schüler die verlängerte institutionalisierte Freizeit wahrnehmen und diese gestalten. Ergänzend dazu wird anschließend auf die Sichtweise der sozialpädagogischen Fachkräfte, der Lehrkräfte sowie der Eltern hinsichtlich der Erweiterung und veränderten Gestaltung der institutionalisierten Freizeit eingegangen.

Sichtweise der Schülerinnen und Schüler

Die Schülerinnen und Schüler thematisieren explizit weder die veränderte Länge der Mittagspause an der Schule noch die verbindlichen Mittage, die neu an der Schule zu verbringen sind. Durchgehend positiv deuten sie die zusätzliche Zeit mit Kolleginnen und Kollegen der ganzen Klasse insbesondere während der Mittagszeit. Früher gingen einige Schülerinnen und Schüler in den Hort und andere nach Hause. In der Tagesschule sind alle Schülerinnen und Schüler an den verbindlichen Mittagen anwesend, was mit dem früheren Hortsystem nicht garantiert werden konnte. Einige Schülerinnen und Schüler berichten retrospektiv, dass sie in der Regelschule teilweise alleine Zuhause über Mittag waren und beurteilen dies als langweilig. Demgegenüber sind sie mit der Tagesschule zumindest an den verbindlichen Mittagen „zusammen" und so „können wir uns besser kennenlernen". In der Tagesschule ist somit durch die konstante Zusammensetzung der Schülerinnen und Schüler die Voraussetzung gegeben, damit peer-group-Effekte gefördert werden können.

Die Schülerinnen und Schüler schätzen die Auswahlmöglichkeiten unterschiedlicher Aktivitäten, aus welchen sie über Mittag auswählen können. Dazu zählen unter anderem freies Spiel, draußen oder in der Turnhalle, wie auch Bastelraum oder Leseecke in der Bibliothek. Besonders beliebt sind „Auszeiten" unter Peers, in welchen sie für sich sein können. Dazu gibt es zum Beispiel in einem Schulhaus mit rund 200 Schülerinnen und Schüler zwei kleine Räume, welche sie reservieren können. Das Zusammensein in diesen Räumen schätzen sie sehr, auch wenn Regeln einzuhalten sind. So dürfen sie nicht zu laut sein, denn sonst interveniert diskussionslos die sozialpädagogische Fachkraft: „wenn irgendjemand von der Gruppe sehr laut ist und herumschreit, dann kommt halt der Hortleiter". Die Knappheit jener Räume, die Regeln der Reservation der Räume und des schulkonformen Verhaltens der Schülerinnen und Schüler („Laut sein gehört nicht in die Schule, auch wenn es hier um Freizeit handelt") verweist auf ein Deutungsmuster der institutionalisierten Freizeit, in der lediglich ein eingeschränkter Ausbruch aus der schulischen Normalität möglich ist.

Sichtweise der sozialpädagogischen Fachkräfte

Die sozialpädagogischen Fachkräfte vergleichen die Länge der Mittagszeit mit derjenigen Zeit, welche sie in der Regelschule im Hort zu gestalten hatten und eine halbe Stunde länger dauerte (bis 13:40 Uhr) im Vergleich zur Mittagszeit in der Tagesschule (bis 13.10 Uhr). Mit Bezug auf die Schülerinnen und Schüler wird diese allerdings nur auf der Oberstufe thematisiert und als positiv für die Jugendlichen erachtet. Eine sozialpädagogische Fachkraft berichtet folgendes: „Von 13:10 bis 13:40 haben die Schlägereien angefangen. Dann ist es wirklich mühsam geworden. Sie wissen nicht mehr, was mit sich anzufangen-, also sie sind sich gewöhnt, ich werde da gefüttert. Zuerst mit Schulinhalten und nachher mit Food und nachher mit Schulinhalten, nachher mit Spielen. Und ja. Also wir haben sie zu dem erzogen."

Wann das nicht schulkonforme Verhalten, z. B. „Schlägereien" beginnt, definiert die sozialpädagogische Fachkraft auf die Minute genau und stereotypisch. Die durch die Zeit bestimmte Denkstruktur ist aus ihrer Sicht stark verankert. Zudem begründet die sozialpädagogische Fachkraft das nicht schulkonforme Verhalten einseitig und mit der Unfähigkeit der Schülerinnen und Schüler, Freiräume in der Freizeit konstruktiv zu gestalten. Hierbei schiebt sie eine mögliche personenspezifische Verantwortung weg von sich auf die anonymisierte Institution Schule, welche zum einseitigen schulfachspezifischen Lernen konditioniert und selbstorganisiertes Lernen kaum fördert.

Kontrastierend dazu nehmen sozialpädagogische Fachkräfte der Primarstufe die Mittagszeit an Tagesschulen, mit Blick auf die Schülerinnen und Schüler, anders wahr, indem sie die veränderte Ausgestaltung der Zeit über Mittag thematisieren. In der Regelschule war der Mittag zeitlich länger, damit die Kinder die Möglichkeit hatten, für das Mittagessen nach Hause zu gehen. Allerdings hatten die Schülerinnen und Schüler im Hort aufgrund der festen Organisation des Mittagessens an vorbestimmten Tischen länger zu warten, beispielsweise bis alle Kinder am Tisch saßen oder bis alle Kinder am Tisch fertig gegessen hatten. Diese Essensorganisation an Horten der Regelschule beurteilen die sozialpädagogischen Fachkräfte als negativ für die Schülerinnen und Schüler. Demgegenüber orientieren sich Tagesschulen bei der Essensorganisation oft am Prinzip des Open Restaurants.

Die Kinder und Jugendlichen wählen selber den Zeitpunkt innerhalb eines Zeitfensters, wann und wie lang sie zu Mittag essen wollen. Diese zeitliche Wahlfreiheit beurteilen die sozialpädagogischen Fachkräfte positiv, denn die Kinder und Jugendlichen hätten nun mehr Erholungszeit in der Tagesschule im Vergleich zu zuvor im Hort. Dies geht aus folgender Textstelle besonders klar hervor:

Ähm, also wir haben einfach plötzlich realisiert, dass die Kinder bei einem normalen Ablauf [des Hortes], so wie's früher gewesen ist, einfach so viel Zeit nur am Warten waren. Also sie kommen, sie warten bis irgendwie alle da sind, sie warten bis sie können anfangen essen, sie warten bis sie Zähne putzen, bis. Also (1), und und die Zeit, wo sie effektiv dann noch können spielen ist eigentlich wirklich kurz. Und wo wir dann gemerkt haben, wir haben dazumal dann auch noch längere Mittage gehabt. Mit der Tagesschule ist es jetzt eine halbe Stunde. Und wo wir gemerkt haben, mit dem Open Restaurant, ist einfach die Zeit plötzlich so lang geworden, wo die Kinder einfach sich auch haben erholen können.

Die Kürzung der Mittagszeit und damit die Neuorganisation des Mittags nach dem Prinzip des Open Restaurants, eröffnet Lernmöglichkeiten für Kinder und Jugendliche sowie ihre Zeiteinteilung und Freizeitgestaltung am Mittag selber zu bestimmen. Diesen Raum zur Selbstorganisation beurteilen die sozialpädagogischen Fachkräfte als positiv und wirksam, damit Schülerinnen und Schüler selbstbestimmt und gezielt auf eigene Bedürfnisse eingehen können.

Denn gemäß der sozialpädagogischen Fachkraft war dies im Hort an der Regelschule nicht möglich, weil die festen Gruppen („Masse") von den Fachpersonen quasi „fremdgeleitet" wurden und wenig Freiraum für Selbstentscheidung zur Verfügung stand.

In dieser Argumentationsrichtung ermöglicht die selbstbestimmte Essenszeit und Freizeit über Mittag die Förderung der Persönlichkeitsbildung, was sozialpädagogische Fachpersonen im Fokus haben und sich von Erwartungen abgrenzen, Kindern das „ordentlich zu essen" beizubringen. Damit orientiert sich die Ausgestaltung der Freizeit, aus Sicht der sozialpädagogischen Fachkräfte, vielmehr an der Förderung der Persönlichkeitsbildung, statt auf das Erlernen von Tischmanieren. Diese sozialpädagogische Orientierung geht aus folgender Textpassage besonders klar hervor:

Es gibt, hat rechte Bedenken gegeben, „Habt ihr schon gehört, dass die Kinder dann [in der Tagesschule] nicht lernen ordentlich zu essen?". (3) Und äh, was ich halt spannend finde, an unserem System ist, sie lernen dafür, Entscheidungen zu treffen. Sie kommen nämlich hinein und stehen vor dieser Magnetwand und müssen überlegen, wo sie hingehen. „Und was mache ich jetzt zuerst?", oder? Und, ich weiß nicht, ich glaube unter dem Strich, bringt einem das mehr wie das schöne Essen. Das lernt man ja dann schon irgendwann.

Bei dieser sozialpädagogischen Fachkraft findet sich das Deutungsmuster, dass die Persönlichkeitsbildung (Scherr 2008) über die Tischmanieren steht und letzteres sich mit der Zeit einstellt. Auf dies weisen sozialpädagogische Fachkräfte auch in anderen Kontexten insofern hin, dass sie der Meinung sind, die Schülerinnen und Schüler sollen in ihrer Freizeit ihren Interessen nachgehen können, welche nicht immer einen bestimmten Zweck erfüllen müssen.

Gleichzeitig äußern weitere sozialpädagogische Fachkräfte, dass das Prinzip über Mittag, welches selbstorganisierte Tätigkeiten fördert, ebenso Schülerinnen und Schüler überfordern kann und eine „fremdbestimmte Tätigkeitsstrukturierung" nötig wird. Dies geht zum Beispiel aus folgender Aussage hervor:

Aber jetzt mit der Tagesschule haben wir einfach gemerkt, es gibt Kinder, wo, wo das wie zu viel wird. Also, wo einfach die völlige Freiheit, äh, wo das eine Ü- Überforderung ist, die verlieren sich. Und wo wir wieder angefangen haben, denen zu sagen, wann sie wo sind.

Sozialpädagogische Fachpersonen beobachten zudem, wie die institutionalisierte Freizeit dazu führt, dass Schülerinnen und Schüler sich mehr mit der Schule identifizieren und dass ihnen diese vertrauter ist, was durchaus positiv konnotiert wird. Sie teilen die Befürchtung einer Scholarisierung der Freizeit an Tagesschulen nicht, sondern erkennen eine Chance in der Gestaltung von zeitlichen- und räumlichen Freiräumen in der Tagesschule.

Sichtweise der Lehrkräfte

Interessanterweise thematisieren Lehrkräfte die Zeitdauer und die Gestaltung der Mittagszeit von Schülerinnen und Schülern an Tagesschulen kaum. Hingegen verweisen einige Lehrkräfte darauf, dass die verkürzte Mittagszeit für sie selbst eine Kürzung der Erholungszeit darstellt.

Bezogen auf die Gestaltung der institutionalisierten Freizeit an Tagesschulen stellen einige Lehrkräfte, eine stärkere „Überwachung" der Schülerinnen und Schüler fest, welche die institutionalisierte Freizeit über Mittag an Tagesschulen mit sich führt. Die Schülerinnen und Schüler haben keine räumlichen Freiräume mehr in dem Sinne, dass „überall" eine pädagogische Aufsichtsperson ist, wie in folgender Textstelle etwas zugespitzt zum Ausdruck kommt:

Ah, sicher die, oder der Raum für die Kinder, wo sie niemand um sich herum haben. Weil sie sind konstant vom Morgen bis abends unter Begleitung von irgendwelchen Erwachsenen, die das Gefühl haben, die müssen sie halt irgendwo auf den Zahn fühlen. (1) Also auch über den Mittag, wenn Freizeit ist. Dann haben sie schon ihre Bereiche, die verschiedenen Stufen. Aber da ist immer irgendeine Person da, die halt da zuschauen muss (1) Dass eben alles halt gerecht geregelt ist. Außer sie gehen, die Kinder gehen nach draußen, aber auch draussen sind halt Aufsichtspersonen. Also es ist wirklich so völlig überwachtes System eigentlich. Tagesschule.

Aus dieser Textstelle geht ein kontrollierender Aspekt der institutionalisierten Freizeit an Tagesschulen hervor, welche die Lehrkraft festhält. Dieses Deutungsmuster zeigt Parallelen auf zum impliziten Deutungsmuster der Schülerinnen und Schüler „eines eingeschränkten Ausbruchs aus der schulischen Normalität", wie eingangs erläutert wurde.

Zudem erhärtet diese Textstelle das einseitige Tätigkeitsverständnis, welches die Lehrkraft den sozialpädagogischen Fachkräften über Mittag zuschreibt. Dieses bezieht sich mehr auf eine eher kontrollierende Tätigkeit („„zuschauen muss") als auf eine persönlichkeitsfördernde Tätigkeit, wie aus dem weiter oben bereits erwähnten Selbstverständnis der sozialpädagogischen Fachpersonen hervorgeht.

Aus der Sicht der Lehrkräfte geht mit der zeitlich veränderten Mittagszeit, während der am Montag und Freitag fast alle an der Tagesschule teilnehmen, ebenfalls eine verlängerte institutionalisierte Freizeit an Tagesschulen einher. Dadurch sind Lehrkräfte zusätzlich herausgefordert, weil der Beginn des Nachmittagsunterrichts durch die institutionalisierte Freizeitbeschäftigung der Schülerinnen und Schüler teilweise verschoben wird. So erwähnt eine Lehrkraft mit einer negativen Konnotation, dass „oft die ersten 10 Minuten" des Nachmittagsunterrichts für Konfliktlösungen unter den Schülerinnen und Schülern einzusetzen sind, die während der Mittagszeit entstanden seien. Somit beeinflusst die verlängerte institutionalisierte Freizeit und die damit zusammenhängenden Konfliktlösungen einen zeitlichen Raum im beginnenden Nachmittagsunterricht an Tagesschulen. Diese sozialpädagogische Tätigkeit könnte, im Sinne eines erweiterten Bildungsbegriffs (Chiapparini et al. 2018), ebenfalls als zeitliche, personelle und inhaltliche Verzahnung der sozialpädagogischen Tätigkeiten über Mittag und den schulstoffvermittelnden Tätigkeiten im Unterricht erachtet werden, was ein explizites Ziel des Konzept Tagesschule ist (Schulamt Stadt Zürich 2018). In unterschiedlichen Passagen geht eher das Deutungsmuster von Lehrkräften hervor, dass eine personelle, zeitliche und inhaltliche Trennung von institutionalisierter Freizeit und Unterricht an Tagesschulen sinnvoll scheint. Dieses Deutungsmuster verweist auf eine Mehrbelastung der Lehrkräfte, was eine Folge der zeitlichen Veränderungen an Tagesschulen ist. An anderen Gesprächsstellen werden die verdichtete Unterrichtszeit oder die Verfügbarkeit, sowie weniger Rückzugsräume für Lehrkräfte im Vergleich zur Regelschule genannt.

Hinsichtlich der Schülerinnen und Schüler wird die Gestaltung der institutionalisierten Freizeit dennoch von den meisten Lehrkräften, als positiv bewertet. Über Mittag sind beispielsweise die Unterrichtsräume offen und die Schülerinnen können sich somit frei im Schulhaus bewegen. Zudem haben die Schülerinnen und Schüler die Möglichkeit, Lehrkräfte auch außerhalb des Unterrichts anzusprechen. Eine Lehrkraft beschreibt dies exemplarisch folgendermaßen:

Ja und man muss dann halt-, oder auch im Gang ist halt viel ein Herumgelaufe. Die Kinder sind da und auch im Team sind wir, also wir haben die Tür immer auf. Nein, also wir sind sehr ein offenes Teamzimmer, dann geht die Türe auf und die Kinder kommen herein und heraus. Was ja eigentlich mega schön ist, sehr familiär. Aber man ist einfach-, eben Tagesschule, man ist immer präsent und man wird ja nicht bezahlt für das.

Dies weist auf ein Spannungsfeld hin, in welchem sich Lehrkräfte zu verorten haben: Zwischen der eigenen Mehrbelastung, indem sie („unbezahlte") Ansprechpersonen in der unterrichtsfreien Zeit sind und der Möglichkeit für die Schülerinnen und Schüler ungezwungene Begegnungen und Gespräche außerhalb des Unterrichts zu ermöglichen, wodurch ein vertrauensvolles Schulklima gefördert werden kann.

Ebenso wird in weiteren Aussagen der Lehrkräfte ein positives Deutungsmuster der veränderten Zeitgestaltung über Mittag für die Schülerinnen und Schüler mit Bezug auf die Peer-Thematik sichtbar. Die meisten Lehrkräfte erachten es als positiv für die Schülerinnen und Schüler, dass sich durch die zusätzliche gemeinsame Mittagszeit unter Schulfreunden an einzelnen Tagen Freundschaften festigen können und dass sie zwischen unterschiedlichen Freizeitangeboten über Mittag aussuchen können.

Wie auch bei den sozialpädagogischen Fachkräften ist bei den Lehrkräften das Denken in Zeiteinheiten stark verankert, was sich in der minutengenauen Zeitangabe in selbstlaufenden Erzählpassagen abbildet.

Sicht der Eltern

Aus den Interviewgesprächen wird diese zeitliche Veränderung positiv eingeschätzt. Viele Eltern merken jedoch an, dass für sie als Eltern die Tagesschule keine große Veränderung brachte in Bezug auf die institutionalisierte Freizeit. Möglicherweise liegt dies daran, dass bereits viele Kinder der interviewten Eltern vor der Einführung der Tagesschule den Mittag im Hort und damit bereits in der Schule verbracht haben.

In Bezug auf die Gestaltung der institutionalisierten Freizeit ist für die Eltern insbesondere wichtig, dass sich die institutionalisierte Freizeit einfach organisieren lässt. Beispielsweise ist den Eltern wichtig, dass die Freizeitangebote anschließend an die Schule stattfinden oder sie sind froh, dass die Kinder über Mittag „versorgt" sind.

In Bezug auf die Ausgestaltung der erweiterten institutionalisierten Freizeit steht für die Eltern nicht die pädagogische Förderung im Fokus, sondern vielmehr der Freiraum. Dies äußert eine Mutter in folgender Textstelle:

Und, ja, gut es ga-, also es ist natürlich ein riesen, äh, was finde ich wichtig? Ähm (4), schon so ein vielseitiges Freizeitangebot. Ich finde es auch wichtig, dass in der Freizeit nicht alles immer irgendwie pädagogisch gefärbt ist, also es, also dass wirklich das Spiel im Vordergrund steht. Und nicht immer noch irgendwie ein, irgendetwas erreicht werden, oder geförde-, also nicht, also nicht, dass die Tagesschule. Dass es wirklich so diesen Schulbereich gibt und, und das andere nicht auch noch immer Förderung, Förderung, Förderung. Weil ich mei-, ich bin da ein bisschen kritisch.

Diese Mutter kritisiert etwas zugespitzt explizit eine Verwertbarkeit der Freizeitgestaltung, die implizit aber gezielt beispielsweise die Schulleistungen fördern soll oder andere pädagogische Ziele beabsichtigt. Damit lehnt diese Mutter implizit eine Verzahnung von Unterricht und Freizeit ab, in der schulische Leistung gefördert wird. Der Ausdruck „wirklich das Spiel im Vordergrund stehen" bezieht sich implizit auf eine Persönlichkeitsbildung (Scherr 2008), die auf „pädagogischen" Freiräumen für selbstorganisierte Freizeitgestaltung von

Kindern basiert. Dies umfasst Erholungsmomente und im ersten Moment für die Schulleistung zwecklose Tätigkeiten. Sie spricht sich folglich implizit gegen eine Scholarisierung der Freizeit aus.

Fazit und Perspektiven

Aus den Ergebnissen wird ersichtlich, dass aus formaler Sicht Schülerinnen und Schüler durch die Einführung der Tagesschule mehr Zeit an der Schule verbringen und somit die institutionalisierte Freizeit an Tagesschulen zugenommen hat. Die zusätzliche institutionalisierte Freizeit für alle Schülerinnen und Schüler ist die Mittagszeit, wobei durch die Tagesschule nun alle Schülerinnen und Schüler auf der Primarstufe mindestens drei Mittage in der Schule verbringen (Schulamt Stadt Zürich 2018). Die Ergebnisse bestätigen somit die zeitliche Zunahme des Aufwachsens in öffentlicher Verantwortung (Böllert 2008; Rauschenbach 2009). Interessanterweise kann diese Zeitzunahme kaum als explizites oder implizites Deutungsmuster der Schülerinnen, Schüler, sozialpädagogischen Fachkräfte, Lehrkräfte und Eltern in der durchgeführten Studie nachgewiesen werden. Vielmehr stehen in den Interviews die Chancen und Herausforderungen verbunden mit der Gestaltung der zugenommenen institutionalisierten Zeit im Mittelpunkt. Der in der Fachliteratur diskutierte theoretische Ansatz der Scholarisierung in der allgemeinen Freizeit (Fölling-Albers 2000) und bezogen auf die institutionalisierte Freizeit in den Tagesschulen (Deckert-Peaceman 2009), bestätigt sich durch die Befunde nur bedingt. So geht aus den Handlungsorientierungen von einigen sozialpädagogischen Fachkräften explizit hervor, wie sie Aspekte der Persönlichkeitsbildung (Scherr 2008) fokussieren und sich von schulleistungsrelevanten Inhalten abgrenzen. Damit positionieren sich diese Deutungsmuster entgegen des Ansatzes der Scholarisierung von institutionalisierten Freizeitangeboten an Tagesschulen. Parallel dazu geht aus den Deutungsmustern einiger Eltern explizit hervor, dass die institutionalisierte Freizeit über Mittag an Tagesschulen zur Erholung und nicht für Schulleistungen direkt verwertbare Angebote, zur Verfügung stehen soll. Diese Sichtweise ist in zukünftigen Untersuchungen auf die Leistungsstärke und die tatsächliche Freizeitgestaltung der Kinder dieser Eltern außerhalb des Mittags zu überprüfen, um mögliche soziale Erwünschtheit und einseitige Deutungen auszuschließen. Allerdings zeichnen sich in den Befunden zum anderen Tendenzen der Pädagogisierung der Freizeit ab, indem Freiräume ohne pädagogische Aufsicht knapp sind oder dass Schülerinnen und Schüler lernen müssen mit Freiräumen umzugehen. Dies geht mit der thematisierten zunehmenden institutionalisierten Freizeit mit ausbaufähigen Gestaltungsfreiräumen mit wenig pädagogischer Aufsicht einher (Rauschenbach

2009; Chiapparini et al. 2019; Deckert-Peaceman 2009). Die vorliegenden Befunde legen eine Differenzierung des theoretischen Ansatzes der Scholarisierung nahe, indem die Schulleistungsförderung und die Gestaltungsfreiräume ohne pädagogische Aufsicht in der Freizeit zu unterscheiden sind.

Mit Blick auf die Primarschülerinnen und -schüler gehen aus dem Datenmaterial die bereits zugenommenen Wahl- und Gestaltungsfreiheiten der institutionalisierten Freizeit an Tagesschulen, im Vergleich zur Regelschule, als ein positiv gedeutetes und aktiv wahrgenommenes Handlungsmuster hervor. Dies trifft sowohl auf die Perspektive der Schülerinnen und Schüler selbst, als auch auf die Perspektive der sozialpädagogischen Fachkräfte zu. Diese Befunde stehen im Widerspruch zu den Befunden des Bielefelder Forschungsprojekts (Andresen et al. 2011) die besagen, dass Lehrkräfte wie auch sozialpädagogische Fachkräfte hinsichtlich der freien Zeitgestaltung der Schülerinnen und Schüler skeptisch sind. Denn gewisse Kinder könnten überfordert sein (Deckert-Peaceman 2009), wozu in der vorliegenden Studie altersspezifische und implizite Hinweise zu finden sind. So ist die institutionalisierte Freizeit von Kindergartenkindern stärker geleitet und ritualisiert, wie ebenfalls andere Studien belegen (Chiapparini 2017). Oder sozialpädagogische Fachkräfte und Lehrkräfte erwähnen „unscheinbare" Kinder, deren Sichtweise stärker im Mittelpunkt zukünftiger Forschungsprojekte stehen soll. Erst dann kann ebenfalls erkundet werden, wie sie mit der erweiterten institutionalisierten Freizeit und den Wahl- und Gestaltungsfreiheiten umgehen.

Mit Blick auf die drei eingangs erwähnten bildungspolitischen Konzepte in der Stadt Zürich und die damit zusammenhängende Bedeutung der Ausdehnung der institutionalisierten Freizeit an den eingeführten Tagesschulen, ist Folgendes festzuhalten:

Das Konzept der Tagesschulen sieht unter anderem vor, Unterricht und Freizeit stärker zu verzahnen. In der Beurteilung dieser Verzahnung geht aus den Befunden zum einen ein positives Beurteilungsmuster der Lehrkräfte mit Blick auf die Kinder und zum anderen ein negatives Beurteilungsmuster für ihren professionellen Handlungsspielraum hervor. Bei den sozialpädagogischen Fachkräften ist die Verzahnung von Unterricht und Freizeit kaum Thema. Dies stimmt mit den Forschungsbefunden überein, dass Lehrkräfte eher auf ihre Profession berufen, wohingegen sozialpädagogische Fachkräfte eher kooperationsbereit sind (Szczyrba 2003; Kappler et al. 2016).

Hinsichtlich des Ziels der „Vereinbarkeit von Familie und Beruf" belegen die Befunde, dass durch die Tagesschule beziehungsweise die Ausdehnung der institutionalisierten Freizeit eine Verschiebung der Zeit in der Familie zu Zeit in der Schule stattgefunden hat, was zu einer Vereinbarkeit beiträgt. Die Zeit beschränkt sich bisher auf den Mittag. Aus Sicht der Eltern wird mit der Tagesschule die Vereinbarkeit nur geringfügig erhöht und ein weiterer Ausbau wird als wichtig erachtet. Dies spiegelt sich auch darin, dass in einer Abstimmung der Stadt Zürich im Juni 2018 über 77 % der Stimmbevölkerung die Überführung von Regelschulen in weitere Tagesschulen unterstützen (Stadt Zürich 2018). Ein Ausbau an institutionalisierter Freizeit im Kontext Schule war laut Crotti (2015) möglich, weil die Bevölkerung auch eine Vereinbarkeit wünscht. Wenn folglich die Nachfrage weiter steigt, ist auch eine Verlängerung der institutionalisierten Freizeit im Rahmen der Tagesschule zu erwarten.

Ob mit den eingeführten Tagesschulen und der verlängerten institutionalisierten Freizeit mehr Bildungsgleichheit hergestellt wird (drittes bildungspolitisches Ziel), ist nur bedingt zu beantworten. Zum einen stehen gemäß den Befunden durch die verlängerte institutionalisierte Freizeit in der Schule allen Kindern verschiedene Angebote offen, wie auch einzelne Freizeitangebote nach dem Unterricht. Zum andern bleibt offen inwiefern ressourcenstarke Eltern aufgrund der ungenügenden Freizeitangebote an Tagesschulen die Freizeit der Kinder außerhalb der Tagesschule privat gestalten (Andresen et al. 2011). In diesem Zusammenhang ist zudem die Qualität der Freizeitangebote an Tagesschulen in der Schweiz zu klären, was bisher eine Forschungslücke bildet.

Zusammenfassend lässt sich in Bezug auf die erweiterte institutionalisierte Freizeit sagen, dass diese durch die Tagesschulen hinsichtlich des Mittags verlängert und ausgebaut wurde. Das Angebot aus „formaler" zeitlicher Perspektive ist mit dem Ziel der Vereinbarkeit von Familie und Beruf und dem Ziel der Bildungsgleichheit weiter auszubauen, wobei gewisse Qualitätsstandards zu beachten sind. Das dritte Ziel, die Verzahnung von Unterricht und Freizeit, ist insbesondere hinsichtlich der Gestaltung der verlängerten institutionalisierten Freizeit weiter zu thematisieren und die Rollen der jeweiligen Berufsfelder sind zu klären.

Hinsichtlich der Frage, ob mit der zusätzlichen Zeit in der Schule auch „mehr" Bildung stattfindet (Idel et al. 2009), ist abschließend und basierend auf den vorgestellten Befunden festzuhalten, dass diese jeweils differenziert und aus den unterschiedlichen Perspektiven der beteiligten Personen zu beantworten ist.

Literatur

Abels, H. (2010). *Interaktion, Identität, Präsentation: Kleine Einführung in interpretative Theorien der Soziologie* (5. Aufl.). Wiesbaden, Germany: VS Verlag für Sozialwissenschaften.
Andresen, S., Richter, M. & Otto, H.-U. (2011). Familie als Akteure der Ganztagsschule. Zusammenhänge und Passungsverhältnisse. *Zeitschrift für Erziehungswissenschaft 14*, S. 205–219.

Betz, T., Bollig, S., Joos, M., & Neumann, S. (Hrsg.). (2018). *Institutionalisierungen von Kindheit: Childhood Studies zwischen Soziologie und Erziehungswissenschaft*. Weinheim, Basel: Beltz Juventa.

Böllert, K. (2008). Aufwachsen in öffentlicher Verantwortung. Zur Bildungsidee des 11. Kinder- und Jugendberichts. In: H.-U. Otto & T. Rauschenbach (Hrsg.), *Die andere Seite der Bildung. Zum Verhältnis von formellen und informellen Bildungsprozessen* (S. 209–222). 2. Aufl. Wiesbaden: Verlag für Sozialwissenschaften.

Bohnsack, R. (Hrsg.) (2006). Das Gruppendiskussionsverfahren in der Forschungspraxis. Opladen: Budrich.

Bühler-Niederberger, D. (2011). *Lebensphase Kindheit. Theoretische Ansätze, Akteure und Handlungsräume*. Weinheim, München: Juventa Verlag. doi:https://doi.org/10.21256/zhaw-1271.

Chiapparini, E. (2019). Erweiterte Lernzeiten und ambivalente Förderung des Wohlbefindens der Kinder an Tagesschulen in Basel-Stadt. In S. Maschke, G. Schulz-Gade & L. Stecher (Hrsg.), *Lernzeit-Hausaufgaben. Jahrbuch Ganztagsschule 2019* (S. 200–210). Schwalbach am Taunus: Debus Pädagogik Verlag.

Chiapparini, E. (2017). *Förderung des Wohlbefindens von Kindern durch die pädagogische Arbeit der Lehrkräfte und Fachpersonen Tagesstrukturen. Zwei Literaturarbeiten und eine empirische Untersuchung auf Kindergartenstufe in der Stadt Basel*. Zürich: Zürcher Hochschule für Angewandte Wissenschaften. https://www.zhaw.ch/de/sozialearbeit/forschung/kindheit-jugend-und-familie/soziale-arbeit-und-schule/wohlbefinden-von-kindern-in-der-ganztagesbildung/. Zugegriffen am 05. April 2019.

Chiapparini, E., Kappler, Ch., & Schuler, P. (2018). Ambivalenzen eines erweiterten Bildungsbegriffs an Tagesschulen. Befunde aus einer qualitativen Untersuchung mit Lehrkräften und sozialpädagogischen Fachkräften an Tagesschulen in Zürich. *Discourse. Journal of Childhood and Adolescence Research. Diskurs Kindheits- und Jugendforschung. 13*(3), S. 321–335. https://budrich-journals.de/index.php/diskurs/article/view/32001. Zugegriffen: 05. April 2019.

Chiapparini, E., Schuler Braunschweig, P., & Kappler, Ch. (2016). Pädagogische Zuständigkeiten in Tagesschulen. *Diskurs Kindheits- und Jugendforschung 11*(3), S. 355–361.

Chiapparini, E., & Skrobanek, J. (2015). Alles eine Frage der Lebenslage? – Vereinsaktivitäten von Jugendlichen im Kanton Zürich. Just a Matter of Life Circumstances? – Association Activity of Young People in the Canton of Zurich. *Schweizerische Zeitschrift für Soziologie 41*(1), S. 119–144. doi: https://doi.org/10.21256/zhaw-1193.

Chiapparini, E.; Thieme, N., & Sauerwein, M. (2019). Tagesschulen in der Schweiz. Ein neues und herausforderndes Handlungsfeld der Sozialen Arbeit. *Schweizerische Zeitschrift für Soziale Arbeit* (1).

Coelen, T., & Stecher, L. (2014). *Grundlagentexte Pädagogik. Die Ganztagsschule: Eine Einführung*. Weinheim, Germany: Beltz Juventa.

Crotti, C. (2015). Die Zeitpolitik von Kindergarten, Vor- und Grundschule in der Schweiz. In K. Hagemann & K. Jarausch (Hrsg.), *Halbtags oder Ganztags? Zeitpolitiken von Kinderbetreuung und Schule nach 1945 im europäischen Vergleich* (S. 371–391). 1. Aufl. Weinheim, Basel: Beltz Juventa.

Deckert-Peaceman, H. (2009). Zwischen Unterricht, Hausaufgaben und Freizeit. Über das Verhältnis von Peerkultur und schulischer Ordnung in der Ganztagsschule. In H. Boer,

H. Deckert-Peaceman (Hrsg.), *Kinder in der Schule. Zwischen Gleichaltrigenkultur und schulischer Ordnung* (S. 85–117). 1. Aufl. Wiesbaden: VS Verlag für Sozialwissenschaften/GWV Fachverlage GmbH Wiesbaden.

Feller, R., & Dietrich, F. (2018). Evaluation der Pilotphase I des Projekts Tagesschule 2025. Schlussbericht zuhanden der Schulpflege der Stadt Zürich, Luzern: Interface Politikstudien, Forschung, Beratung. https://www.stadt-zuerich.ch/content/dam/stzh/ssd/Deutsch/Volksschule/dokumente/stadtzuercher_volksschule/tagesschule/tagesschulen2025_schlussbericht_pilotphase1.pdf. Zugegriffen: 05. April 2019.

Fischer, N. (2018). Ganztagsschule als Bildungsraum (für alle?!) – Erkenntnisse aus 10 Jahren „Studie zur Entwicklung von Ganztagsschulen" (StEG). In E. Glaser, H.-C. Koller, W. Thole & S. Krumme (Hrsg.), *Räume für Bildung – Räume der Bildung. Beiträge zum 25. Kongress der Deutschen Gesellschaft für Erziehungswissenschaft* (S. 214–225). Opladen, Berlin & Toronto: Budrich.

Fischer, N., Kuhn, H-P., & Züchner, I. (2011). Entwicklung von Sozialverhalten in der Ganztagsschule. In N. Fischer, H.-G. Holtappels, E. Klieme, T. Rauschenbach, L. Stecher & I. Zürcher (Hrsg.), *Ganztagsschule: Entwicklung, Qualität, Wirkungen. Längsschnittliche Befunde der Studie zur Entwicklung von Ganztagsschulen (StEG)* (S. 246–266). Weinheim: Beltz Juventa.

Flick, U. (2007). *Qualitative Sozialforschung: Eine Einführung* (Rev. ed.). *Rowohlts Enzyklopädie*. Reinbek bei Hamburg, Germany: Rowohlt Taschenbuch Verlag.

Fölling-Albers, M. (2000). Entscholarisierung von Schule und Scholarisierung von Freizeit? Überlegungen zu Formen der Entgrenzung von Schule und Kindheit. In: *Zeitschrift für Soziologie der Erziehung und Sozialisation 20*(2), S. 118–131.

Fraij, A., Maschke, S., & Stecher, L. (2015): Die Scholarisierung der Jugendphase – ein Zeitvergleich. In *Diskurs Kindheits- und Jugendforschung 10* (2), S. 167–182.

Frei, L., Schüpbach, M., Allmen, B. v., & Nieuwenboom, W. (2016). Bildungsbezogene Erwartungen an Tagesschulen: Förderangebote an offenen Tagesschulen in der Deutschschweiz. *Schweizerische Zeitschrift für Bildungswissenschaft 38* (3), S. 549–568.

Fuhs, B. (2002). Kindheit, Freizeit und Medien in Krüger, H.-H.; Grunert, C. (Hrsg.), *Handbuch Kindheits- und Jugendforschung* (S. 637–651). Opladen: Leske + Budrich.

Glaser, B. G., & Straus, A. L. (1967). The Discovery of Grounded Theory. Strategies for Qualitative Research. New Brunswick, NJ: Aldine transaction.

Harring, M., Böhm-Kasper, O., Rohlfs, C., & Palentien, Ch. (Hrsg.). (2010). *Freundschaften, Cliquen und Jugendkulturen. Peers als Bildungs- und Sozialisationsinstanzen.* Wiesbaden: Verlag für Sozialwissenschaften

Heinz, W. R. (2011). Jugend im gesellschaftlichen Wandel: soziale Ungleichheiten von Lebenslagen und Lebensperspektiven. In Elisabeth M. Krekel (Hrsg.), *Neue Jugend, neue Ausbildung? Beiträge aus der Jugend- und Bildungsforschung* (S. 115–126). Bielefeld: Bertelsmann.

Hurrelmann, K., & Quenzel, G. (2016). *Lebensphase Jugend. Eine Einführung in die sozialwissenschaftliche Jugendforschung.* 13., überarbeitete Aufl. Weinheim: Beltz Juventa.

Idel, T.-S., Reh, S., & Fritzsche, B. (2009). Freizeit – Zum Verhältnis von Schule, Leben und Lernen. In F.-U. Kolbe, B. Fritzsche, T.-S. Idel, K. Rabenstein & S. Reh (Hrsg.), *Ganztagsschule als symbolische Konstruktion. Fallanalysen zu Legitimationsdiskursen in schultheoretischer Perspektive* (S. 179–193). Wiesbaden: Verlag für Sozialwissenschaften.

Kappler, Ch., Chiapparini, E., & Schuler Braunschweig, P. (2016). Die gute neue Tagesschule in der Schweiz. Der Erziehungs- und Bildungsauftrag aus der Sicht der Professionen. In N. Fischer, H. P. Kuhn und C. Tillack (Hrsg.). *Was sind gute Schulen? Teil 4: Theorie, Praxis und Forschung zur Qualität von Ganztagsschulen.* (S. 216–230). Immenhausen: Prolog-Verlags.

Kränzl-Nagel, R., & Mierendorff, J. (2007). Kindheit im Wandel. Annäherung an ein komplexes Phänomen. *SWS-Rundschau 47*(1), S. 3–25. https://www.kindergartenpaedagogik.de/1613.pdf. Zugegriffen: 05. April 2019.

Krüger, H.-H. (2008). Family, school, youth culture. International perspectives of pupil research. Frankfurt am Main: Peter Lang Pub. Inc.

Neumann, S., Tinguely, L., Hekel, N., & Brandenberg, K. (2015). *Machbarkeitsstudie Betreuungsatlas Schweiz. Die Geographie betreuter Kindheit.* Fribourg: Universitäres Zentrum für Frühkindliche Bildung Fribourg (ZeFF). Online verfügbar unter https://www.unifr.ch/pedg/zeff/de/pdf/machbarkeitsstudie_betreuungsatlas_ch.pdf. Zugegriffen: 05. April 2019.

Rauschenbach, T. (2009). Bildung – eine ambivalente Herausforderung für die Soziale Arbeit? *Soziale Passagen* 1, S. 209–225.

Sauerwein, M., Thieme, N., & Chiapparini, E. (2019). Wie steht es mit der Ganztagsschule? Ein Forschungsreview mit sozialpädagogischer Kommentierung. *Soziale Passagen.* Manuskript eingereicht zur Publikation.

Scherr, A. (2008). Subjekt- und Identitätsbildung. In T. Coelen & H.-U. Otto (Hrsg.), *Grundbegriffe Ganztagsbildung. Das Handbuch* (S. 137–145). 1. Aufl. Wiesbaden: Verlag für Sozialwissenschaften.

Schul- und Sportdepartement. (2018). Tagesschule 2025. https://www.stadt-zuerich.ch/ssd/de/index/volksschule/tageschule2025.html. Zugegriffen: 05. April 2019.

Schul- und Sportdepartement (2017). *Tarifübersicht.* https://www.stadt-zuerich.ch/content/dam/stzh/ssd/Deutsch/Volksschule/dokumente/betreuung/tarifuebersicht_neue_verordnung.pdf. Zugegriffen: 05. April 2019.

Schulamt Stadt Zürich (2018). *Tagesschule 2025. Pilotprojekt der Stadt Zürich.* https://www.stadt-zuerich.ch/content/dam/stzh/ssd/Deutsch/Volksschule/dokumente/stadtzuercher_volksschule/tageschule/sam_tageschule_2025.pdf. Zugegriffen: 05. April 2019.

Schüpbach, M. (2014). Effects of extracurricular activities and their quality on primary school-age students' achievement in mathematics in Switzerland. *School Effectiveness and School Improvement* 26 (2), S. 279–295. doi: https://doi.org/10.1080/09243453.2014.929153.

Schüpbach, M, Frei, L., & Nieuwenboom, W. (Hrsg.). (2018). *Tagesschulen. Ein Überblick.* 1. Aufl. 2018. Wiesbaden: Springer Fachmedien.

Schütze, F. (1983). Biographieforschung und narratives Interview. *Neue Praxis, 13*(3), 283–293.

Soremski, R. (2015). Ganztagsschule als Formalisierung jugendlicher Freizeit? Zur individuellen Aneignung schulischer Freizeiträume. In S. Maschke, G. Schulz-Gade & Ludwig Stecher (Hrsg.), *Jahrbuch Ganztagsschule 2016. Wie sozial ist die Ganztagsschule?* (S. 119–126). Schwalbach/Ts.: Debus Pädagogik Verlag.

Soremski, R., Urban, M., & Lange, A. (Hrsg.). (2011). *Familie, Peers und Ganztagsschule.* Weinheim, München: Juventa.

Stadt Zürich. (2018). Tagesschule 2025: Abstimmung vom 10. Juni 2018. *Medienmitteilung*. https://www.stadt-zuerich.ch/ssd/de/index/volksschule/aktuell/news/tagesschule_2025_abstimmung_10_juni_18.html. Zugegriffen: 05. April 2019.

Strauss, A. L., & Corbin, J. M. (1991). *Basics of qualitative research. Grounded theory procedures and techniques*. 3. Aufl. Newbury Park, California: Sage.

Szczyrba, B. (2003). *Rollenkonstellationen in der pädagogischen Beziehungsarbeit. Neue Ansätze zur professionellen Kooperation am Beispiel von Schule und Jugendhilfe*. Bad Heilbrunn: Klinkhardt.

Thole, W., & Höblich, D. (Hrsg.). (2014). *„Freizeit" und „Kultur" als Bildungsorte – Kompetenzerwerb über non-formale und informelle Praxen von Kindern und Jugendlichen. Bildung ist mehr als Schule*. Wiesbaden: Springer Fachmedien.

Volksschulamt Kanton Zürich (2018). *Stundenplanbeispiele*. https://vsa.zh.ch/content/dam/bildungsdirektion/vsa/projekte/lehrplan_21/projekt_lp_21/stundenplanbeispiele_ps.pdf. Zugegriffen: 05. April 2019.

Volksschulamt Kanton Zürich (2017). *Neue Lektionentafel Kindergarten- und Primarstufe*. Online verfügbar unter https://vsa.zh.ch/internet/bildungsdirektion/vsa/de/projekte/zuercher_lehrplan21/zuercher_lehrplan21_lehrplan_lektionentafel/_jcr_content/contentPar/downloadlist/downloaditems/1041_1481098264482.spooler.download.1534166343211.pdf/lektionentafel_ps_kg.pdf. Zugegriffen: 05. April 2019.

Zinnecker, J. (2000). Selbstsozialisation. Essay über ein aktuelles Konzept. *Zeitschrift für Soziologie der Erziehung & Sozialisation 20*(3), S. 272–290.

Züchner, I. (2013). Formale, non-formale und informelle Bildung in der Ganztagsschule. *Jugendhilfe 51*(1), S. 26–35.

„Das muss am Gymnasium schneller gehen": Eine praxeologisch-wissenssoziologische Rekonstruktion von „Zeit" im Kontext von Differenzierungspraktiken im Gymnasialunterricht

Marcus Syring, Lena Brinkmann, Sabine Weiß und Ewald Kiel

Abstract

Time can be considered as an element of social structure as well as an instrument of control and power. Transferring this to the micro level of teaching interactions at the High School time (and tempo) can be reconstructed in the context of the (re-)production of inequality between students, and thus as an instrument for fulfilling the social functions of school. The article therefore examines time structures in the High School and answers the following questions: How and why do teachers use the aspect of time to create inequality? How do teachers handle this inequality?

M. Syring (✉) · L. Brinkmann
Abteilung Schulpädagogik, Eberhard Karls Universität Tübingen,
Tübingen, Deutschland
E-Mail: marcus.syring@uni-tuebingen.de

L. Brinkmann
E-Mail: lena.brinkmann@uni-tuebingen.de

S. Weiß · E. Kiel
Lehrstuhl für Schulpädagogik, Ludwig-Maximilians-Universität München,
München, Deutschland
E-Mail: sabine.weiss@edu.lmu.de

E. Kiel
E-Mail: kiel@lmu.de

© Springer Fachmedien Wiesbaden GmbH, ein Teil von Springer Nature 2020
E. Schilling und M. O'Neill (Hrsg.), *Frontiers in Time Research – Einführung in die interdisziplinäre Zeitforschung*,
https://doi.org/10.1007/978-3-658-31252-7_11

To answer these questions, we will apply praxeological-sociological knowledge using the Documentary Method: Based on two cases (two teachers in each class over four lessons, AV recorded) the results show two different practices in dealing with time in the context of inequality and two orientation patterns in the same orientation framework.

Zusammenfassung

Zeit kann als Element sozialer Ordnungen sowie als ein Instrument von Kontrolle und Macht betrachtet werdet. Überträgt man dies auf die Mikroebene unterrichtlicher Interaktionen am Gymnasium, können Zeit (und Tempo) im Kontext der Herstellung von Differenz und somit als ein Instrument zur Erfüllung der gesellschaftlichen Funktionen von Schule rekonstruiert werden. Der vorliegende Beitrag untersucht daher Zeitstrukturen im gymnasialen Unterricht und beantwortet folgende Fragen: Wie und warum nutzen Lehrkräfte den Aspekt Zeit, um Differenz herzustellen? Wie gehen Lehrkräfte mit dieser Differenz um? Zur Beantwortung dieser Fragen bedient sich der Beitrag eines praxeologisch-wissenssoziolgischen Zugangs unter Nutzung der Dokumentarischen Methode: Anhand von Videographien gymnasialen Unterrichts werden zwei Fälle (zwei Lehrkräfte in je einer Klasse über vier Unterrichtsstunde) und der gemeinsame Orientierungsrahmen rekonstruiert. Die Ergebnisse zeigen unterschiedliche Praktiken im Umgang mit Zeit im Kontext von Differenzierung sowie zwei Orientierungsmuster beim gleichen Orientierungsrahmen. Die Ergebnisse werden abschließend diskutiert.

Keywords

Time · High School · Inequality · Teachers · Homogenity · Zeit · Gymnasium · Differenzierung · Lehrkräfte · Homogenität

Schlüsselwörter

Zeit · Gymnasium · Differenzierung · Lehrkräfte · Homogenität

Einleitung

Das in der Überschrift gewählte Zitat aus einem Interview mit einer Lehrkraft im Rahmen der hier berichteten Studie steht stellvertretend für den exklusiven und elitären Charakter des Gymnasiums (Helsper et al. 2018), seinen selektiven

Zugang sowie den in ihm vorherrschendem Primat des Kognitiven. Diese Strukturmerkmale können als Belege für die Affinität des Gymnasiums bzw. der in ihm handelnden Akteurinnen und Akteure zur Homogenität verstanden werden (Trautwein et al. 2011). Das Zitat steht aber auch für den Aspekt der Zeit, der nicht nur die institutionelle Rahmung von Unterricht stark normiert, sondern den die Lehrkraft im Unterricht selbst prozessiert, aushandelt und mit Bedeutung versieht. Bisher ist wenig darüber bekannt, wie Gymnasiallehrkräfte auf interaktionaler Ebene im Unterricht die genannten Strukturmerkmale aushandeln. Dabei bedienen sie sich – so die These des Beitrags – verschiedener Kategorien, um Differenzierungen in der Klasse vorzunehmen. Differenz wird dabei nicht als ontologisches Prinzip verstanden, sondern das Gymnasium als gesellschaftliche Institution betrachtet, dass an der Konstruktion und Re-Produktion von Unterschiedlichkeit beteiligt ist (Budde und Rißler 2017). „Zeit" stellt sich als ein im Kontext von Differenzierungspraktiken relevanter Aspekt dar, der sowohl als Element sozialer Ordnungen (Burzan und Schöneck 2014) sowie als ein Instrument von Kontrolle und Macht (Foucault 1982) betrachtet werden kann.

Der vorliegende Beitrag untersucht den Aspekt „Zeit" im Kontext von Differenzierungspraktiken im gymnasialen Unterricht und beantwortet folgende Frage: Wie nutzen Lehrkräfte den Aspekt „Zeit" in Differenzierungspraktiken und welche Orientierungen liegen dem zugrunde? Zur Beantwortung dieser Frage bedient sich der Beitrag eines praxeologisch-wissenssoziologischen Zugangs (Sturm 2018a) unter Nutzung der dokumentarischen Methode.

Theoretischer Hintergrund

Differenz und Differenzierung (im gymnasialen Unterricht)

Circa seit Mitte der 1990er Jahre wird das Themenfeld „Differenz" in der deutschsprachigen Erziehungswissenschaft verstärkt diskutiert. Insbesondere die Schulpädagogik führt diesen Diskurs seit der Jahrtausendwende auch entlang des Begriffs „Heterogenität". Trotz begrifflicher Unterschiede lässt sich zwischen den Begriffen der Differenz und Heterogenität eine Grundgemeinsamkeit finden: So werden beide jeweils in Relation zu Gleichheit bzw. Homogenität konzeptualisiert (Sturm und Wagner-Willi 2015b).

Beschäftigt man sich mit Differenz, so lassen sich grob zwei Sichtweisen unterscheiden: eine essentialistische und eine sozialwissenschaftliche Perspektive (Weisser 2005). Unterschieden wird dabei, ob Differenz bzw. „Abweichung von einer Norm" in einer Person selbst verortet und ihr zugeschrieben wird oder ob diese als sozial, situativ oder überdauernd hervorgebracht (Budde 2017; Derrida 1990; Sturm 2018a) bzw. in kulturellen Zusammenhängen entstanden

(Bohnsack und Nohl 2001) konzeptualisiert wird. Daraus ergibt sich auch die Frage, ob Differenz etwas ist, was an Schule und Unterricht herangetragen oder in ihr hervorgebracht wird. Vor allem im öffentlichen Diskurs werden Heterogenität bzw. Differenzen (z. B. Geschlecht, soziale Herkunft oder Migrationshintergrund) als etwas betrachtet, was an Schule herangetragen wird. In der erziehungswissenschaftlichen Differenzforschung dominiert hingegen über die unterschiedlichen Konzepte und theoretischen wie methodologischen Zugänge hinweg eher eine sozialwissenschaftliche Perspektive: Dies gilt für ethnografische (z. B. Diehm et al. 2013), anerkennungstheoretische (z. B. Fritzsche 2014), sozial-konstruktivistische sowie dekonstruktivistische (z. B. Wrana 2014) oder aber auch rekonstruktiv-praxeologische (z. B. Sturm 2015) Zugangsweisen. Folglich werden Differenzen als „sozial hergestellte Phänomene [betrachtet], die in interaktiven Praktiken innerhalb von Bildungsorganisationen selbst (auch) hervorgebracht, bearbeitet bzw. (re)produziert werden" (Sturm und Wagner-Willi 2015b, S. 165; siehe auch Tervooren 2000). Differenzen werden folglich in der Schule und im Unterricht selbst hergestellt. Trotzdem können diese Praktiken der Differenzierung – zumindest zum Teil – nicht losgelöst von gesellschaftlichen Kontexten betrachteten werden: So orientierten sie sich im Sinne einer Reproduktion von Gesellschaft in Schule auch an sozialen Differenzkategorien wie Geschlecht, Milieuzugehörigkeit, Migrationshintergrund, Behinderung etc. (vgl. zusammenfassend Budde 2017). Dennoch ist über diese (und weitere) etablierten Differenzkategorien hinaus in den letzten Jahren verstärkt die Frage aufkommen, welche Differenzierungen für Lehrkräfte im Unterricht überhaupt von Bedeutung sind und vorgenommen werden (z. B. Sturm 2012) sowie ob und wenn ja, wie diese mit den genannten soziologischen Großkategorien zusammenfallen (Emmerich und Hormel 2013).

Dieser Position folgend erzeugt das pädagogische Handeln von Lehrkräften– wie jede menschliche Interaktion – immer auch Differenzen (Göhlich et al. 2013). Somit sind Lehrpersonen nicht nur maßgeblich an der Herstellung und Bearbeitung von Differenz beteiligt, sondern dadurch auch an der (Re-)Produktion von (Bildungs-)Ungleichheit (z. B. Ainscow 2008). Die Produktion von Differenz steht wesentlich im Zusammenhang zu formal gesetzten Normen, Rollen und Erwartungen sowie Handlungsweisen von Lehrkräften (Sturm 2018a). In den letzten Jahren wurden Praktiken der Herstellung von und des Umgangs mit Differenz im Unterricht im qualitativ-rekonstruktiven Paradigma beforscht: Zu nennen sind beispielsweise die ethnografischen Studien von Budde (2014), Kalthoff (2006) oder auch Rabenstein und Kolleginnen und Kollegen (2013). Ebenso wurde verstärkt auf Grundlage des praxeologisch-wissenssoziologischen

Paradigmas geforscht (z. B. Martens et al. 2015; Sturm 2012; Sturm und Wagner-Willi 2015a). Oftmals werden in diesen Studien Grundschulen, Schulen der Sekundarstufe oder inklusive Schulen beforscht. Explizite Untersuchungen zu Gymnasien stellen hier eine Seltenheit dar und können daher als Forschungsdesiderat beschrieben werden.

Über die genannten empirischen Studien hinweg zeigt sich, dass vor allem der Prozess der Herstellung von Leistungsdifferenzen beforscht wird. Dies geschieht entweder als zentrale supercodierte Differenzkategorie in der Schule und zwar nicht als Produkt von Lehr-Lern-Prozessen, sondern als soziales Konstrukt (Sturm 2013a, b) oder in dem Sinne, dass Leistung als soziale Ordnung im Unterricht, als „zentrale schulische Währung" (Rabenstein et al. 2013), verhandelt wird. Hierzu identifizieren Zaborowski und Kollegen (2011) Schulartenunterschiede: Am Gymnasium wird Leistung als zentraler Kern schulischer Differenzordnung als selbstverständlich anerkannt, während dies in anderen Schularten erst noch zum Thema gemacht wird. Gellert (2013) kommt in seinen Rekonstruktionen unterrichtlichen Handelns an Hauptschulen und Gymnasien zu dem interessanten Ergebnis, dass „Leistungshierarchien in beiden Schulformen wesentlich von der Kompetenz der Schülerinnen, sich in die impliziten unterrichtlichen Strukturen einzufügen, abhängen und fachlich-kognitive Aspekte der Wissensaneignung in beiden Schulformen nachgeordnet werden" (Sturm 2018a, S. 259).

Im Zusammenhang mit Leistung steht als eine weitere zentrale Differenzkategorie die Erfüllung unterrichtlicher Verhaltenserwartungen im Mittelpunkt; Sturm (2018a) spricht hierbei von „sozialen Leistungen" der Schülerinnen und Schüler. „Diese unterrichtshabituellen Erwartungen stellen eine Differenzdimension dar, anhand derer Schüler/-innen analog zu fachlichen Erwartungen unterschieden werden" (Sturm 2018a, S. 62). Über Studien zu unterschiedlichen Kategorien von Differenzen (z. B. zu sozial-ökonomischer Benachteiligung, zu interkultureller Pädagogik, zu Gender bzw. Geschlecht) hinweg erkennt Sturm (2018a) ein weiteres wesentliches Muster: Unterschiede zwischen Schülerinnen und Schülern bzw. „Abweichungen von einer Norm" werden über die situativ gesetzte Differenz hinaus generalisiert und auf die gesamte Person übertragen. Garfinkel (1956) benennt dieses Phänomen als „totale Zuschreibung".

Die Hervorbringung von Differenzen erfolgt über Praktiken (zum Praktiken-Begriff siehe auch die Anmerkungen im methodischen Teil), die nicht nur auf sprachlichen Ebene, sondern auch in nonverbaler sowie körperlich-räumlicher Hinsicht zu finden sind (Reckwitz 2003; Wagner-Willi 2004). In den Analyseprozessen unterrichtlichen Handelns werden diese Perspektiven folglich mit einbezogen.

Zeit im Kontext von Differenzierungspraktiken

Zeit ist eine zentrale Kategorie, die sich mit Blick auf unterrichtliche Verhaltenserwartungen von Lehrkräften und Differenzierungspraktiken als relevant darstellt. Dabei versteht man im soziologischen Sinne Zeit als ein von Menschen geschaffenes Konstrukt, welches auch veränderbar ist (Sorokin und Merton 1937). So ist z. B. das Empfinden, ob etwas lang oder kurz dauert, nicht objektiv bestimmbar. In der hier vorliegenden empirischen Analyse wird Zeit als „soziale Zeit" begriffen: Dabei stehen „Aspekte zeitlicher Regelungen, die die Formen des Zusammenlebens von Menschen betreffen […] im Mittelpunkt" (Burzan und Schöneck 2014, S. 638). Betrachtet werden Zeitnormen und Zeitfunktionen, wie beispielsweise Synchronisation, Koordination, Orientierung oder die Herstellung und Aufrechterhaltung von Ordnung. Gerade in der Schule stellt Zeit ein stark strukturierendes Moment dar (Meseth et al. 2011). So ist z. B. der traditionelle, lehrerzentrierte Unterricht durch die Synchronität von Lernprozessen gekennzeichnet (Breidenstein et al. 2017). Eine gewissermaßen „Kehrseite" dieser Synchronität sind Zeitknappheit und Langeweile: „Beides […] sind unter anderem sicherlich ein Produkt der tradierten Zeitstrukturen von Schule und Unterricht, also innerhalb des Schulwesens ‚hausgemacht'" (Fölling-Albers 2008, S. 140). Die Betrachtung von „sozialer Zeit" lässt sich auch im Kontext von Normen und Herrschaft fassen: Zeit ist damit ein Ausdruck von Herrschaftsverhältnissen, z. B. wann man bestimmte Dinge tun darf (zeitliche Koordination), wer mehr freie Zeit hat, wer über die Zeit anderer bestimmt. All dies trifft auch auf Zeit im Unterricht zu. Zeitvorgaben müssen dabei nicht von konkret handelnden Personen, sondern können auch von Institutionen, wie zum Beispiel der Schule, kommen (Burzan und Schöneck 2014). Breidenstein und Kollegen (2017) sprechen in diesem Kontext auch von Zeitregimen.

Zeit als Aspekt im Kontext von Differenzierungspraktiken steht laut Sturm (2013b) im engen Zusammenhang mit Leistung, die Schülerinnen und Schüler individualisierend und oftmals hierarchisierend zugeschrieben werden: „Differenzen werden dabei meist als ‚Defizite' den Schülerinnen zugeschrieben und die ‚Schwachen' von den ‚Starken' unterschieden. Zu letztgenannten zählen die Lehrpersonen solche, die die unterrichtlichen, vielfach implizit bleibenden Ziele in einem vorgesehenen Zeitfenster nicht ohne zusätzliche Erklärungen und/oder anderweitige (außer)unterrichtliche Formen kompensatorischer Unterstützung erreichen" (Sturm 2018a, S. 259). Breidenstein und Kolleginnen und Kollegen (2017) verglichen drei Schulen mit unterschiedlichen Konzepten individualisierten Unterrichts. Zusammenfassend kamen sie zu dem Schluss, dass an allen Schulen Unterricht „als eine vordefinierte Zeitspanne gefasst [wird], in der bestimmte Tätigkeiten legitim sind und andere nicht" (Breidenstein et al. 2017, S. 49). Somit kommt im individualisierten Unterricht ein kollektives und institutionalisiertes Verständnis von Zeit zur Geltung und es finden Zeitstrukturen der schulischen Organisation Anwendung, die Vorrang vor möglichen differenzierten fachlichen Inhalten haben. Die „zur Verfügung stehende Zeit dominiert inhaltliche Relevanzen" (Breidenstein et al. 2017, S. 51).

Für den gymnasialen Unterricht liegen Untersuchungen, die Zeit als Aspekt im Kontext von Differenzierungen betrachten, bisher nicht vor.

Erkenntnisinteresse und Forschungsfragen

Wie bisher gezeigt wurde, kann in Schule und Unterricht nicht nicht-differenziert werden. „Leistung" lässt sich als ein Supercode benennen, der hinter vielen anderen Kategorien rekonstruiert werden kann. „Zeit" stellt in unserem Verständnis – nach Analyse des empirischen Materials – keine eigene Kategorie der Differenzierung dar, sondern ist ein Aspekt im Kontext von Differenzierungspraktiken im Unterricht. Der vorliegende Beitrag untersucht daher „Zeit" im gymnasialen Unterricht und beantwortet folgende Fragen:

- Wie wird der Aspekt „Zeit" im Kontext von Differenzierungspraktiken durch Lehrkräfte thematisiert und genutzt?
- Welche Orientierungsschema und Orientierungsrahmen liegen diesen Praktiken zugrunde und bilden damit Orientierungsmuster?

Methodologische Grundlagen und methodisches Vorgehen

Die für die vorliegende Studie genutzten Fälle stammen aus dem Projekt „Heterogenität, Exklusivität, Professionalität: Eine Videostudie zum Lehrer/innenhandeln am Gymnasium", welche das Ziel verfolgt, Prozesse der Herstellung von und des Umgangs mit Differenz mittels Videoaufzeichnungen sowie das handlungspraktische Wissen der Lehrkräfte mittels Interviews (jeweils vor und nach der Videographie) zu untersuchen und somit das routinierte Handeln der Lehrkräfte zu erfassen. In der Studie wird demnach gefragt, wie Lehrkräfte am Gymnasium Differenz herstellen und welche Deutungen diesen Praktiken zugrunde liegen. Mittels Triangulation der Daten und Perspektiven sollen auf Grundlage der Dokumentarischen Methode (Bohnsack 2010a; Nohl 2009; Asbrand und Martens

2018) sowohl Praktiken als auch (implizites) Wissen rekonstruiert und aufeinander bezogen werden. Für die kontextuelle Einordnung wurden zudem öffentliche schulische Dokumente (Homepage, Leitbild, Schulprogramm bzw. -profil) gesammelt und mittels Dokumentenanalyse ausgewertet. Im vorliegenden Beitrag werden jedoch nur aus den Videodaten Praktiken exemplarisch rekonstruiert.

Datenerhebung, Sample und Fälle

Die Erhebung der Daten fand im zweiten Halbjahr des Schuljahrs 2017/2018 an zwei Gymnasien einer Großstadt statt. Insgesamt wurden 43 Unterrichtsstunden von sechs Lehrkräften in neun Klassen videographiert (siehe Tab. 1).

Innerhalb der Unterrichtsvideos wurden anschließend Sequenzen mit analytischer Dichte identifiziert, in denen Differenzen durch die Lehrkraft interaktiv hergestellt wurden. Dies bezog sich auf Kategorien unterschiedlicher Abstraktionsniveaus, wie z. B. Leistung, Macht und Partizipation oder auch Sprache, Ordnung/Sauberkeit, Aufrufeverhalten, Gruppenzusammensetzung und bilingualen Unterricht. Daraufhin wurden zwei Fälle (Fall=Lehrkraft in einer Klasse in einem Fach über mehrere Stunden) ausgewählt, in denen das Thema Zeit virulent (gemacht) wurde und die zunächst auf sprachlicher bzw. Sichtebene ähnlich erschienen (siehe graue Hinterlegung in Tab. 1).

Tab. 1 Gesamtsampling in der Studie und Fälle in diesem Beitrag (grau hinterlegt). Die Namen der Schulen und Lehrkräfte sowie Schülerinnen und Schüler sind anonymisiert

Thomas-Müntzer-Gymnasium					Karl-Liebknecht-Gymnasium					
Schulleitungs-Interview & Dokumentenanalyse										
videographierter Unterricht & Lehrkräfte-Interviews (vor und nach der Aufnahme)										
Fr. Fiedler		Hr. Karl		Fr. Wolf	Hr. Kukal		Fr. Leißler		Fr. Korb	
10/1	10/2	10/1	5/1	7/1	5/2	8/1	5/1	10/1	10/1	10/2
10/1	10/2	10/1	5/1	7/1	5/2	8/1	5/1	10/1	10/1	10/2
10/1	10/2	10/1	5/1	7/1	5/2	8/1	5/1	10/1	10/1	10/2
10/1	10/2	10/1	5/1	-	5/2	8/1	5/1	10/1	10/1	10/2

Dokumentarische Methode und Videographieanalyse

Die vorliegende Studie basiert auf den Annahmen der praxeologischen Wissenssoziologie, wie sie Bohnsack (2010a, 2017) in Anlehnung an Mannheim (1980, 1995) entwickelt hat. Bohnsack hob besonders die praxeologische Relevanz hervor (Sturm 2018b). Hierbei geht es vor allem um Fragen nach dem Verhältnis von sprachlichem und nicht-sprachlichem Wissen (Reckwitz 2003; Sturm 2018a). Gerade das nicht-sprachliche Wissen führt in „habitualisierten Praktiken, die auf den handlungsleitenden und zum Teil inkorporierten Erfahrungswissen der Akteure basieren" (Bohnsack 2007, S. 182 f.), zur handlungspraktischen Herstellung von Realität. Diese meta-theoretischen Überlegungen schlagen sich methodologisch wie methodisch in der Dokumentarischen Methoden nieder. Beobachtete Erscheinungen werden als Dokumente von Mustern bezeichnet, die den jeweiligen Handlungspraktiken zugrunde liegen (Bohnsack 2010a). Unter Praktiken werden „wiederholte bzw. wiederholbare, d. h. iterative, aber nicht identische Aufführungen von Aktivitäten verstanden, die über ein implizites Wissen zusammengehalten werden" (Reh et al. 2015, S. 37). Die Analyse des Datenmaterials (der Dokumente) soll folglich kollektive Wissensordnungen, die sich in sprachlicher, ikonischer sowie körperlich-räumlicher (also auch performativer) Hinsicht ausdrücken (Wagner-Willi 2004), also das implizite, konjunktive Wissen explizieren.

Die Dokumentarische Methode greift die von Mannheim (1980) getroffene wissenssoziologische Differenzierung der „Doppelstruktur alltäglichen Wissens" (Bohnsack 2007, S. 183) auf, indem zwischen theoretisch-kommunikativen und atheoretisch-konjunktiven Wissen respektive zwischen immanentem und dokumentarischem Sinngehalt einer Handlung bzw. einer Aussage unterschieden wird (siehe Tab. 2). In der Praxis der Methode findet sich die Unterscheidung der Wissens- bzw. Sinnformen in den beiden Schritten der Interpretation wieder: der formulierenden und der reflektierenden Interpretation (Bohnsack 2010a). Die formulierende Interpretation arbeitet das *Was* der sozialen Wirklichkeit aus der Perspektive der handelnden Lehrkräfte heraus (Martens 2015), indem untersucht wird, was die Akteurinnen und Akteure gesagt und getan haben. Für die Videographie bedeutet dies, die körperlichen und sprachlichen Handlungen sowie Interaktionen deskriptiv zu beschreiben. Die reflektierende Interpretation fragt danach, *wie* „Themen verhandelt und gerahmt sowie Handlungen ausgeführt" (Martens 2015, S. 216) werden. Hier erfolgt die Rekonstruktion der Prozesse der Herstellung von Wirklichkeit und der zugrunde liegenden Wissensbestände, in diesem Beitrag also die Frage der Herstellung von Differenz. Für die Videographie bedeutet dies wiederum, dass implizites Handlungswissen und Muster der inter-

Tab. 2 Interpretationsschritte der Dokumentarischen Methode nach Sinngehalt und Wissen(-sbeschaffenheit). (Eigene Darstellung)

Interpretation	Formulierend	Reflektierend
Sinngehalt	Immanent	Dokumentarisch
Wissen	Theoretisch-kommunikativ	Atheoretisch-konjunktiv
	Kommunikativ-generalisiert	Konjunktiv
	Explizite, reflexiv	Implizit, in sozialen Erfahrungen und Beziehungen fundiert
	Wissen über etwas: „Theorien der Erforschten über ihr eigenes Handeln, über ihre eigene Praxis" (Bohnsack 2012, S. 120)	Wissen „um und innerhalb von etwas" (Bohnsack 2009, S. 323)
	Common sense	Praktisch, habituell
	Meist sprachlich	Nicht zwingend explizierbar

aktiven Praktiken rekonstruiert werden. Während und nach beiden Interpretationsschritten erfolgt konsequent die komparative Analyse innerhalb und zwischen Fällen mittels Abstraktion und Generalisierung, um mögliche Homologien und Strukturidentitäten zu identifizieren (Fritzsche und Wagner-Willi 2015).

Die in dieser Studie verwendete Videographieanalyse greift die Aspekte der Dokumentarischen Methode auf und besteht aus der dokumentarischen Gesprächsanalyse, der Analyse von Körperlichkeit und Materialität sowie der Analyse von Interaktionen Die Betrachtung dieser unterschiedlichen Aspekte ist relevant, da Unterricht eine komplexe Simultanstruktur darstellt (Wagner-Willi 2004) und nur so Differenzierungsprozesse in der Vielschichtigkeit kommunikativer, materieller und körperlicher Interaktionen rekonstruiert werden können.

Die Auswahl der zu rekonstruierenden Sequenzen innerhalb der beiden ausgewählten Fälle erfolgte nach den Kriterien der Relevanz, der Fokussierung und der interaktiven Dichte (Bohnsack 2010a). Um die Situation intersubjektiv nachvollziehbar zu präsentieren, werden diese Sequenzen bei den Interpretationen in eine Verlaufsbeschreibung des Unterrichts eingebettet. Da beide ausgewählten Fälle deutlich durch Sprache strukturiert sind, steht diese auch im Fokus der Rekonstruktionen. Hinzu kommt die Darstellung von Fotogrammen zu den gewählten Sequenzen, die nach den Kriterien der Fokussierung, der Repräsentanz und des Kontrasts ausgewählt wurden (Fritzsche und Wagner-Willi 2015). Hier konnten Aspekte der Materialität und Körperlichkeit sowie der Einbettung in den

Raum analysiert werden. Die Rekonstruktionen erfolgten im Rahmen mehrerer Sitzungen einer Forschungswerkstatt.

Rekonstruiert wird der Aspekt von Zeit im Kontext von Differenzierungen. Dabei orientieren wir uns am Vokabular der Dokumentarischen Methode (Bohnsack 2012), wie es auch von Asbrand und Martens (2018) verwendet wird: Unter Orientierungsmustern wird die Gleichzeitigkeit von kommunikativen und konjunktiven Wissen gefasst. Damit stellen sie den Zusammenhang von Orientierungsschema (kommunikatives Wissen der Erforschten) und Orientierungsrahmen (konjunktives bzw. implizites Wissen) dar.

Interpretationen: Praktiken im Umgang mit Zeit als Differenzierung

Im Folgenden werden zwei Fälle und die darin eingebetteten Sequenzen näher beschrieben und um Fotogramme angereichert. Der Beschreibung der Sequenzen folgt die reflektierende Interpretation, in der der dokumentarische Sinngehalt respektive das konjunktive Wissen herausgearbeitet wird. Auf die formulierende Interpretation wird nur an ausgewählten Stellen eingegangen.

Frau Fiedler (Fall 1): Verlagerung und Kollektivierung von Zeit im Orientierungsrahmen Synchronität und Homogenität

Im vorliegenden Fall handelt es sich um zwei Doppelstunden der Klasse 10/1 im Fach Biologie bei Frau Fiedler. Sie unterrichtet parallel die Klassen 10/1 und 10/2 in Biologie am Thomas-Müntzer-Gymnasium. Die Stunde findet in einem Fachraum für Biologie mit festmontierten Tischreihen (Frontalausrichtung) und einem Mittelgang statt. Das Lehrerpult mit Experimentiertisch ist hoch, so dass man als Lehrkraft hier nicht sitzen kann. Auf dem Pult stehen eine Dokumentenkamera sowie eine von Frau Fiedler mitgebrachte Uhr, die von der Klasse zu erkennen ist.

Bereits in der Beschreibung der Eingangssequenz des Videos (des Settings) fällt auf, dass die Lehrerin eine eigene Uhr mit in den Unterricht bringt, die sie für alle sichtbar auf dem Lehrerpult positioniert (siehe auch Fotogramm 1). Sie dient möglicherweise als Ersatz für eine nicht vorhandene Wanduhr. Damit wird das Thema Zeit in der Dinglichkeit bzw. der Materialität der mitgebrachten Digitaluhr virulent. Im ersten Fotogramm wird auch sichtbar, dass Frau Fiedler eine eigene Armbanduhr am linken Handgelenk trägt. Die zur Klasse hin ausgerichtete Uhr auf dem Pult dient folglich nicht der eigenen, individuellen Zeitorientierung, sondern der der Klasse bzw. der Gesamtheit aus Klasse und ihr.

Im ersten Teil der ersten Doppelstunde begrüßt die Lehrkraft die Schülerinnen und Schüler nach den Ferien zur ersten Biologiestunde. Das Thema der Stunde ist Genetik und es geht um die Vererbung beim Menschen (Humangenetik). Nach einer fast 25-minütigen Wiederholung des bekannten Stoffes zu Kreuzungsschemata im Pflanzen- und Tierreich erarbeitet die Klasse im Plenum einen genetischen Stammbaum zum Thema „Daumenknicken" (genetische Veranlagung bei ca. 25% der Menschen für eine besondere Daumenstellung, die man „Anhalterdaumen" nennt), der auch gleich von Frau Fiedler an der Tafel

Fotogramm 1: Minute 11:27

festgehalten wird. Anschließend sollen die Schülerinnen und Schüler in Einzelarbeit oder Partnerarbeit einen weiteren genetischen Stammbaum zum Thema „Zungenrollen" entwickeln. Die Aufgabe hierfür wird von der Lehrerin diktiert, die Schülerinnen und Schüler schreiben mit. Während die Aufgabe durch die Schülerinnen und Schüler bearbeitet wird, geht Frau Fiedler durch die Klasse. Nach circa sechs Minuten fragt die Lehrkraft ins Plenum, jedoch mit Blick auf die Bankreihe, in der Michael, Fabricio und Mareike sitzen (2. Std., Minute 11:26-11:31):

L: „Kann ich eure Diskussionen deuten, dass ihr fertig seid?"
(L fasst sich an den Hinterkopf)
Grummeln in der Gruppe.
L: „Nicht? ((betonend)) Aha."

Danach wendet sie sich kurz von der Gruppe ab, geht aber gleich wieder auf diese zu:
L: „Kann man euch irgendwie unterstützen?"

Frau Fiedler gibt in dieser Sequenz zunächst den Freiraum, selbst zu entscheiden, in welcher Arbeitsform die Schülerinnen und Schüler die Aufgabe lösen wollen. Trotzdem scheint ihr das Gespräch in der Gruppe nicht recht zu sein. Hier zeigt sich Diskrepanz zwischen dem explizit Genannten und der Art und Weise wie das Thema kommuniziert wird. Sprachlich ermöglicht sie Freiheiten, bei einer Gruppe scheint sie dies jedoch zu stören. Indirekt unterstellt sie der Gruppe auch, dass diese sich nicht mit dem Thema der Stunde beschäftige. Sie fragt in der Sequenz eher rhetorisch, was durch das Stehen in Entfernung zur Gruppe verstärkt wird, ob sie die Gespräche so interpretieren solle, dass die Gruppe fertig sei. Damit adressiert sie zwar direkt die Gruppe (verbal), tut dies aber öffentlich im Plenum, sogar über eine Bankreihe hinweg (siehe Fotogramm 1). Frau Fiedler verhandelt demnach das scheinbare Fehlverhalten der Schülergruppe auf der Bühne. Das zeitliche „fertig sein" drückt sprachlich die Frage nach dem Ende der Lerneinheit aus, dient jedoch auf der nicht-sprachlichen Ebene eher der Disziplinierung. Hier wird eine Differenz zwischen Klassenkollektiv und bestrafter Gruppe hergestellt, die durch die Adressierung mit dem Personalpronomen „ihr" kommunikativ expliziert wird. Nachdem die Gruppe signalisiert, dass sie noch nicht fertig ist – die Gespräche also eventuell doch inhaltlicher Natur waren –, macht die Lehrkraft nochmals eine Differenz zwischen der Gruppe und den übrigen Mitschülerinnen und Mitschülern deutlich, indem sie fragt, ob man „euch" helfen könne. Damit adressiert sie die Gruppe als hilfebedürftig aufgrund der zeitlich noch nicht erledigten Aufgabe.

Der Aspekt der Zeit („fertig sein") dient im Kontext der hier durch die Lehrkraft vollzogenen Differenzierungspraktik der Aufrechterhaltung der sozialen Ordnung im Unterricht. Zeitaspekte im messbaren Sinne spielen eine untergeordnete Rolle.

Nachdem Frau Fiedler in der Gruppe eine Frage beantwortet hat, wird die Arbeit der ganzen Klasse ziemlich rasch beendet und die Aufgabe im Plenum besprochen. Frau Fiedler hält den Stammbaum und einige Merksätze an der Tafel fest. Die Schülerinnen und Schüler beginnen eigenständig, das Tafelbild zu übernehmen, ohne dass Frau Fiedler einen Auftrag dazu erteilt hat. Anschließend lösen die Schülerinnen und Schüler eine weitere Aufgabe in Einzelarbeit, Frau Fiedler geht dabei durch die Klasse. Beim Vergleichen der Lösungen einer weiteren Aufgabe ruft die Lehrerin nacheinander die Schülerinnen und Schüler auf. Auch Fabricio soll eine Aufgabe lösen, nachdem er bei der Beantwortung der vorherigen Aufgabe dazwischengeredet hat (2. Std., Minute 35:00 – 35:53):

L: „Fabricio, ich an deiner Stelle würde da nicht ganz so laut das raushauen."
F: „Because?"
L: ((nickt zögerlich und zieht die Schultern nach oben)) (…) „Mach das nächste bitte."
F: (unverständlich)
L: „Lies bitte die Aufgabe vor und beantworte die Aufgabe 2."
F: „Ach so. Ich?"
L: „Ja."
F: „Ah. Welche Begründungen (unverständlich) finden sich in Abbildung 1. Also in Abbildung 1 sind verschiedene Blutgruppen. ((zögerlich aber lächelnd)) Und ähm, da hat man natürlich auch verschiedene Genotypen, ja. ((Gelächter in der Bankreihe)).
L: „Da die Zeit begrenzt ist, und drei von euch heute noch nach England wollen, würde ich die Beantwortung der Aufgabe gerne an Robert weitergeben."
R: „Also ich […]"

Nach dem Vergleichen der restlichen zwei Aufgaben beendet die Lehrkraft die Stunde.

Nach anfänglichen Hin und Her kommt Fabricio der Aufforderung von Frau Fiedler nach, liest die Aufgabe vor und beginnt diese stockend zu beantworten. Dies erscheint der Lehrkraft jedoch nicht weiter zielführend, da sie Fabricio in seiner Beantwortung unterbricht. Das zeigt sich auch in ihrem Einstieg „Da die Zeit begrenzt ist". In dieser Aussage expliziert sie, dass sie in der Folge einen spezifischen Schüler (hier: R) aufrufen möchte, um den zeitlichen Ablauf der von ihr geplanten Stunde nicht zu gefährden (Kounin 1976/2006). Interessant erscheint dabei, dass Frau Fiedler nicht etwa mit der zögerlichen, vielleicht falschen oder wenig durchdachten Antwort – und damit mit der Kategorie der

Leistung – argumentiert, sondern den zeitlichen Aspekt in den Vordergrund stellt. Sie begründet zudem die Zeitknappheit nicht etwa mit ihrer Unterrichtsplanung oder ihrem Willen, einen reibungslosen Stundenablauf zu garantieren, sondern verlagert die Begründung von sich weg nach außen (weil „drei von euch heute noch nach England wollen").

Die zweite Doppelstunde findet eine Woche später statt und beginnt mit einem Lückentext zum Stoff der letzten Stunde, der gemeinsam im Plenum „ausgefüllt" wird. Anschließend kontrolliert Frau Fiedler in den Heftern, ob die Hausaufgaben gemacht wurden und bespricht diese Aufgaben im Plenum. Für die nächste Partnerarbeit legt sie eine Folie mit einem Text in altdeutscher Schrift mit der Dokumentenkamera auf. Michael liest den Text vor, danach erläutert Frau Fiedler die Aufgabe und fragt (3. Std., Minute: 38:31-38:33):

L: „Schafft ihr das in fünf Minuten?" (dabei hat sie ihre rechte Hand am linken Handgelenk)
Sc: (..) „Jaaa."
L: „Ach so, ich muss gucken wie viel Uhr es ist." (geht zum Lehrerpult, auf dem die Uhr steht)

Die Lehrerin fragt hier die Klasse, ob die von ihr vorgegeben Zeit ausreichend ist. Dabei berührt sie ihre eigene Uhr. Als die Klasse dies bestätigt, geht sie zu der Uhr, die sie selbst mitgebracht hat und die auf dem Lehrerpult steht (siehe auch Fotogramm 1). Anstatt auf ihre eigene Armbanduhr zu gucken – was zu erwarten wäre, denn sie sagt „ich muss gucken..." –, welche Zeit zur Verfügung steht bzw. bis wann die Aufgabe abgeschlossen werden muss, wählt sie die für alle sichtbare Uhr im Klassenzimmer. Diese fungiert als Artefakt im Klassenzimmer (Asbrand et al. 2013): Frau Fiedler versucht mittels dieses Artefakts die eigentlich soziale Zeit (siehe Abschn. „Zeit im Kontext von Differenzierungspraktiken") zu objektivieren. Dies zeigt sich auch in der Diskrepanz zwischen dem von der Lehrkraft ausgesprochenen „... ich muss gucken ..." und dem – durch das Zugehen auf die Uhr – gemeinten „ihr müsst gucken".

Mit Blick auch auf die vorherigen Sequenzen könnte sich eine Praktik der Differenzen zwischen unterschiedlichen Formaten von Zeit hier manifestieren: Frau Fiedler unterscheidet zwischen „ihrer Uhr" für die Versicherung der (sozialen) Zeit und ihrer Unterrichtsplanung und der „Klassenuhr" als Wächter und objektiven Zeitgeber.

Anschließend geht sie durch die Klasse und beantwortet einzelne Fragen bzw. gibt Hinweise. Nach sieben Minuten steht die Lehrerin gerade zwischen zwei Bankreihen hinter der Schülergruppe von Thomas, Marcel und Igor (3. Std., Minute: 45:18-45:27):

Fotogramm 2: Minute 45:19

L: „Wie weit seid ihr? (blickt dabei auf die Aufgaben der drei Schüler, richtet anschließend den Blick wieder auf und setzt ihre Brille auf den Kopf) Sollen wir schon mal eine, möchte jemand seine Lösung präsentieren?"

M (aus einer anderen Bankreihe): „Noch zwei Minuten?"
L: „Zwei Minuten willst du Mika, wir haben schon eine mehr."

In der Sequenz überprüft die Lehrerin, wie weit die Schülerinnen und Schüler mit der Bearbeitung der Aufgabe fortgeschritten sind. Im Vergleich zur ersten Sequenz nähert sie sich diesmal der Gruppe räumlich an (siehe Fotogramm 2). Die Situation ist damit durch eine andere Raum-Körper-Konstellation gekennzeichnet. Die Lehrkraft erfragt den Bearbeitungsfortschritt in der Gruppe, will aber eigentlich im Unterricht fortfahren. Dies deutet sich sprachlich durch die Frage an, ob jemand aus der Klasse bereits die erste Aufgabe lösen will. Die Lehrkraft scheint hier bemüht zu sein, Scheinsynchronität herzustellen und macht damit auch den drei Schülern der Gruppe deutlich, dass sie eigentlich schon fertig sein müssten. Hier zeigt sich eine Differenz nicht zwischen der Gruppe und dem Rest der Klasse, sondern eher noch zwischen der Gruppe und dem geplanten synchronen Zeitverlauf. Die Differenz wird auch hier durch Konstitution des Körpersubjekts verstärkt: Trotz Nähe zu der Gruppe bleibt Frau Fiedler außenstehend und nicht zum Lernprozess gehörend.

Im zweiten Teil der Sequenz fordert die Schülerin Mika noch zwei Minuten Bearbeitungszeit ein. Sie passt sich dem sprachlichen Habitus der Lehrerin an, in dem sie lexikalisch im Zeitbereich bleibt und damit argumentiert. In der darauffolgenden Äußerung der Lehrkraft zeigt sich erneut die Koordinationsfunktion von Zeit: Es kann keine weitere Zeit gegeben werden, da bereits eine Minute mehr zur Verfügung stand. Hier steht also nicht das Lösen der fachlichen Aufgabe im Vordergrund. Gleichzeitig äußert sich hierin aber auch, dass die (zeitliche) Ordnung des

Unterrichts gefährdet ist, da bereits mehr Zeit gegeben wurde, als von der Lehrkraft veranschlagt. Hier greift Frau Fiedler die von Mika gemachte allgemeine Aussage auf und praktiziert eine Differenz zwischen der Schülerin, die noch Zeit einfordert („willst du Mika"), und dem Rest der Klasse („wir haben"), der stellvertretend für die einzuhaltende Ordnung und Synchronität steht. Nimmt man die vorherige Sequenz dazu („Schafft ihr das in fünf Minuten"), wird diese Differenzierung noch mal umso stärker: Alle haben zugestimmt, dass die Zeit ausreichend ist. Auch hier weist die Lehrerin – wie zuvor bei den England-Fahrern – die Verantwortung für die Zeit wieder von sich, indem sie das „wir" in die Verantwortung nimmt.

Frau Fiedler fordert daraufhin Mareike auf, ihre Lösung an der Dokumentenkamera zu präsentieren. Frau Fiedler unterbricht die Schülerin dabei immer wieder und die Klasse ergänzt. Anschließend beginnt die Lehrerin das Thema Vererbung des Geschlechts und teilt hierfür ein weiteres Arbeitsblatt aus. Sie diktiert noch einen Satz, der beim Kopieren „abgeschnitten" wurde, blickt kurz auf ihre Uhr und tritt vom Lehrerpult vor die erste Reihe (3. Std., Minute: 56:39-56:50)

Fotogramm 3: Minute 56:44

L: „In eurer, eure Parallelklasse musst das auch in

sieben Minuten schaffen. Also 40. 12:40 Uhr würde ich gerne mit euch das ganze besprechen." (blickt dabei auf die Uhr auf dem Pult)

Betrachtet man in dieser folgenden Sequenz zunächst die Raum-Körper-Konstellation, so rückt die „Klassenuhr" deutlich in den Fokus des Unterrichtsgesprächs (siehe Fotogramm 3). Es lässt sich ein Dreieck zwischen dieser, der Lehrerin und der Klasse ausmachen. Die Uhr stellt somit einen gemeinsamen Bezugspunkt dar und fungiert als Co-Lehrerin, die das „objektive Zeiteinhalten" bestimmt. Die hier für die Schülerinnen und Schüler zur Verfügung stehende Zeit (sieben Minuten) scheint zunächst arbiträr gesetzt zu sein, wird jedoch dadurch begründet, dass die Parallelklasse es auch in diesem Zeitfenster schaffen musste. Wieder erscheint hier die Praxis der Verlagerung der Zeitvorgabe weg von Frau Fiedler, diesmal sogar nach außerhalb des Klassenraums. Zudem wird erneut die

Funktionalisierung der Zeit zur Synchronisation und Homogenisierung ersichtlich, in dem eine Differenz zwischen der Klasse und der Parallelklasse, die damit zur Idealklasse wird, erzeugt wird: Die Parallelklasse hat die Aufgabe in sieben Minuten geschafft, also muss diese Klasse das auch schaffen. Hier scheint auch ein Orientierungsrahmen hinter dem Handeln von Frau Fiedler zu stecken, dass die Klassen eines Jahrgangs homogen zu laufen haben bzw. unter gleiche Bedingungen unterrichtet werden.

Frau Fiedler sagt noch, dass alle leise sein und aufhören sollen zu schwatzen. Die ersten Minuten der Arbeitsphase sind dann auch ruhig, die Schülerinnen und Schüler lesen das Arbeitsblatt. Anschließend wird leise getuschelt beim Lösen der Aufgaben. Frau Fiedler geht wieder durch die Klasse und verweilt länger an einigen Tischen, ohne etwas zu sagen. Nach circa sechs Minuten blickt sie auf die ersten Hefteinträge. Sie geht zu Fabricio, spricht ihn darauf an, warum er nicht arbeitet und unterstellt ihm, dass er wartet, bis jemand anderes seine Lösungen präsentiert. Danach tritt sie vor die erste Bankreihe (Amalia, Cansu, Marlene und Cécile) und fragt (4. Std., 6:36-7:25):

Fotogramm 4: Minute 7:18

L: „Wie weit seid ihr?"
Ca: „Ich habe die Aufgabe 2 gemacht und die Aufgabe 1 nicht verstanden."
L: „Versuch mit einem Kreuzungsschema, versuch dir zu überlegen, wie würdest du jemandem erklären, wie das Geschlecht vererbt wird […]."

Sie geht weiter zur Fensterreihe und spricht dabei im Gehen ins Plenum:

L: „Für alle, die sich da noch schwertun, manche sind schon fertig, es ist nicht immer so, dass das Geschlecht so vererbt wird, wie beim Menschen […]."

Nach ein paar weiteren Minuten werden die Aufgaben im Plenum gelöst. Mit dieser Aufgabe beschließt die Lehrkraft das Thema „Genetik" und verabschiedet sich von den Schülerinnen und Schülern.

Trotz der direkten Äußerung einer Schülerin, dass sie diese eine Aufgabe nicht verstanden habe, verweilt die Lehrerin nicht bei ihr, um zu helfen, sondern geht im Sprechen ein Stück durch das Klassenzimmer. Sie verhandelt das Unwissen der Schülerin auf offener Bühne. Die Differenz wird hier zwischen den nicht so leistungsfähigen Schülerinnen und Schülern, „die sich da noch schwertun", und denen, die „schon fertig sind" aufgemacht. Dabei wird die Schnelligkeit der Schülerinnen und Schüler mit der kognitiven Leistungsfähigkeit supercodiert. Eine denkbare Differenz hätte hier auch die Korrektheit der bearbeiteten Aufgabe darstellen können. Die fachliche Auseinandersetzung wird hier der zeitlichen Ordnungsstruktur vorgezogen.

Herr Kukal (Fall 2): Tempo und Personalisierung von Zeit im Orientierungsrahmen Synchronität und Homogenität

Es handelt sich im Folgenden um zwei Mathematikdoppelstunden bei Herrn Kukal in der Klasse 5/2 am Karl-Liebknecht-Gymnasium.

In der ersten Doppelstunde werden zunächst die Hausaufgaben kontrolliert. Herr Kukal geht dafür durch die Klasse, schaut in die Hefte und verteilt Sticker für die gemachten Aufgaben. Anschließend führt er in das neue Thema „Ausmultiplizieren und Ausklammern" zunächst mit einem kurzen Videoclip, dann erklärend ein, und die Schülerinnen und Schüler bekommen Übungsaufgaben. Diese werden dann zusammen im Plenum besprochen und an der Tafel festgehalten. Anschließend werden Regeln und Merksätze gemeinsam erarbeitet. Um das Gelernte anzuwenden, vergibt Herr Kukal weitere Übungsaufgaben (1. Std., Minute 39:51-40:06).

Fotogramm 1: Minute 40:00

L: „Okay, wir wollen das noch ein bisschen üben. Ich glaube, ihr seid da schon ganz schön fit. Das (zeigt auf Tafel) war schon ein Beispiel aus der ersten Aufgabe. Ihr kriegt von mir noch weitere, die ich anschreibe. Wie immer gibt es auch eine kleine Bonusaufgabe für die Schnellen. Ähm, die erste Aufgabe ist dabei noch relativ leicht […]"

In der vorliegenden Sequenz der Mathematikstunde soll nach dem Erlernen neuen Stoffes eine Übungseinheit beginnen. In der Ankündigung der Aufgabe nimmt Herr Kukal auf sprachlicher Ebene eine Differenzierung anhand von Zeitattributionen vor: Es gibt die Schnellen und den Rest der Klasse. Dabei wird, wie schon im vorherigen Fall bei Frau Fiedler, scheinbar „schnell" mit „richtig" oder „gut" gleichgesetzt. Zudem wird die schnelle Erledigung der Aufgabe mit einem positiven Anreiz – einer Bonusaufgabe – versehen. Diese Bonusaufgabe wird durch den Sprachmodus als erstrebenswert angepriesen. Sprachlich bleibt zudem festzuhalten, dass sich Herr Kukal Worten bedient, die Tempo – als die Erledigung einer Aufgabe in einer bestimmten Zeit – ausdrücken, wie „schnell".

Die Schülerinnen und Schüler beginnen in Einzelarbeit die Aufgaben zu lösen, Herr Kukal befestigt Hinweiszettel an der Tafel und geht dann durch die Klasse, um Meldungen zu beantworten. Im zweiten Teil der Doppelstunden werden die Aufgaben dann an der Tafel besprochen. Anschließend werden erneut Übungsaufgaben vergeben. Die Schülerinnen und Schüler beginnen zu rechnen, Herr Kukal gibt an einzelnen Plätzen Hinweise und geht dann auf Celine und Mathias in der letzten Bankreihe zu und adressiert noch im Laufen Celine (2. Std., Minute 41:10-41:21):

Fotogramm 2: Minute 41:13

L: „Celine ist fertig ((lacht)).
Ce: „Ja."
L: „Ja (lachend). Habe ich mir gedacht. Hast du sechs und sieben schon gemacht?"
Ce: „Mh."
L: „Okay, dann hast du noch ein bisschen Pause jetzt."
Ce: „Okay."

Dieses kurze Gespräch findet quasi im Vorbeigehen statt, der Lehrer widmet sich nicht weiter den Aufgaben von Celine. Die Schülerinnen und Schüler rechnen noch bis zum Klingelzeichen, der Rest der Aufgaben wird als Hausaufgabe gegeben.

Herr Kukal geht während der Erledigung der Aufgaben durch die Klasse, gibt Hilfestellungen und beantwortet Fragen. Dabei scheint er zu registrieren, dass Celine fertig mit ihren Aufgaben ist. Dabei fragt er bereits im Zugehen bzw. im Vorbeigehen mit einem Lächeln, ob Celine „sechs und sieben schon gemacht" habe. Damit evaluiert er den Lernprozess nicht etwa anhand der Kategorien „richtig" oder „gut", sondern anhand des zeitlichen „Fertig seins". Dies verdeutlicht sich auch – wie auch im Fotogramm 2 ersichtlich – an der Bewegung im Vorbeigehen, die selbst auch die Praxis des Tempos ersichtlich werden lässt. Die von der Lehrkraft ermöglichte Pause erscheint zunächst als Belohnung für die Schülerin bzw. als etwas individuell Zugestandenes. Möglich wäre auch eine Bonusaufgabe gewesen, wie zuvor in der Sequenz angekündigt. Mit der so gewählten Handlung (Schülerin muss „warten") wird versucht, die Synchronität der Klasse aufrecht zu erhalten. In dieser kurzen Sequenz wird eine Differenz zwischen Celine (die zeitlich schnell war, was bewundernd und lächelnd anerkannt wird) und dem Rest der Klasse markiert.

In der zweiten Doppelstunde eine Woche später wird das Gelernte wiederholt und geübt. Anschließend wird ein Tafelbild entwickelt. Bevor auf einem Arbeitsblatt gerechnet werden soll, wird das Vorgehen noch geklärt (3. Std., Minute 55:14-55:49):

Fotogramm 3: Minute 45:46

L: „Okay, noch eine Frage?"
Ha: „Kommt jetzt ein neues Thema?"
L: „Nein, wir machen rucki zucki die Rückseite des Blattes. Ähm, macht ihr alleine. Wer fertig ist mit einer Aufgabe, darf zu mir hier vorkommen (läuft zum Lehrerpult) und sich eine Folie holen (nimmt leere Folie und zeigt sie in die Luft) und ihr schreibt die Lösungsfolie auf. Okay? Also wer fertig ist, kommt nach vorne, holt sich dann eine Lösungsfolie ab und schreibt die Lösung hier einmal auf Folie für die anderen.

Na: „Ähm kann man auch in einer anderen Reihenfolge die Aufgaben machen?"
L: (schüttelt zunächst den Kopf) ((zögerlich)) „Okay."
Ha: „Herr Kukal, sollen wir die ganze Seite machen?"
L: „Ja schaffen wir, wir schaffen die ganze Seite, das geht ziemlich schnell. (schaut dabei auf das Arbeitsblatt)"

Bevor – wie von einem Schüler erfragt – ein neues Thema beginnt, soll noch geübt werden. Dies soll nach Herrn Kukal schnell geschehen. Er verwendet die Worte „rucki zucki". Wiederholt bedient er sich einer Lexik, die auf Schnelligkeit und Beschleunigung ausgerichtet ist. Dies wird in der Sequenz noch verstärkt, als von einem Schüler die Nachfrage kommt, ob alle Aufgaben gemacht werden sollen. Herr Kukal reagiert mit „Ja, das geht ziemlich schnell" und argumentiert auch hier mit der Komponente Zeit. Er hätte auch auf die Fähigkeit der Schülerinnen und Schüler verweisen können. Durch das vorausgehende „Ja schaffen wir, wir schaffen", was im Zusammengang mit dem „schnell" jedoch als zeitliches „Schaffen" zu lesen ist, manifestiert sich der Gedanke der Synchronizität in der Gemeinschaft nochmals. Dabei orientiert er sich an der Klasse und nicht auf eine objektiv gesetzte Zeit. Durch die Referenz auf das „wir" schafft Herr Kukal auch eine Norm von Homogenität, von der eine Abweichung (die sich ja in der vorausgehenden Äußerung des Schülers andeutet) nicht zulässig erscheint oder zumindest zunächst nicht sprachlich in Erwägung gezogen wird.

Die Schülerinnen und Schüler rechnen anschließend auf den Arbeitsblättern, gestalten die Lösungsfolien und tauschen sich untereinander aus. Mit einem Signal (Klangschale) beendet Herr Kukal die Arbeitsphase (4. Std., Minute 19:20-19:57):

Fotogramm 4: Minute 19:39

L: „Okay (langgezogen). Pssst. (…) Also wir haben (…) Da jetzt sehr viele schon fertig waren, breche ich das an der Stelle ab. Ihr habt die Lösung hier vorne aufgeschrieben. Ich würde gerne, dass die oder der- oder diejenige, der die Lösung aufgeschrieben hat, kurz erklärt, wie ihr die Aufgabe gemacht habt, für die
anderen dann zum Vergleichen […]."

Nach dem gemeinsamen Vergleichen endet die Stunde.

Da ein Großteil der Schülerinnen und Schüler mit der Erledigung der Arbeitsaufträge fertig zu sein scheinen, beendet Herr Kukal die Arbeitsphase. Dadurch vollzieht er am zeitlichen „Fertig sein" erneut eine Differenzierung zwischen denjenigen, die mit der Aufgabe fertig sind und den (scheinbar kleineren) Rest. Damit legitimiert er auch den Abbruch der Lerneinheit und die Herstellung einer Synchronität. Dabei orientiert er sich erneut an der Klasse bzw. der Mehrheit in dieser und nicht etwa an „objektiven" Kriterien, wie dem nahenden Stundenende oder ähnlichem, worin sich ebenso erneut ein gewisser Grad an Individualisierung mit Blick auf Zeit zeigt.

Zusammenfassung, Diskussion und Ausblick

In dem Beitrag wurde anhand von zwei ähnlichen Fällen eine empirische Rekonstruktion von Handlungspraktiken der Differenzherstellung im Kontext des Aspektes „Zeit" vorgenommen. Zentral schien dabei nochmals der bereits theoretisch postulierte Sachverhalt, Differenz als sozial gefasstes Phänomen (Scharenberg 2013) zu betrachten: Differenzierung vollzieht sich durch Praktiken in sozialen Zusammenhängen und erschafft diese gleichzeitig, wie in beiden Klassen sichtbar wurde. Differenzierung beinhaltet– wie ebenfalls gezeigt werden konnte – eine normative Setzung. Nimmt man beides zusammen, so können individuelle oder kollektive Abweichungen von einer subjektiv wie objektiv gewonnenen Norm beschrieben werden. Ein großer Mehrwert konnte in den Interpretationen aus der Auswertung der Fotogramme, die in die Analyse der visuellen und körperlichen Praktiken einbezogen wurden, gezogen werden. Hierin wurde vor allem die Materialität von Unterricht deutlich.

In Tab. 3 sind die zentralen Ergebnisse der Rekonstruktionen nochmals strukturiert zusammengefasst. Es zeigt sich, dass unterschiedliche Praktiken im Modus der Differenzierung genutzt werden, um unterschiedliche Funktionen von Zeit zu erfüllen, die den Lehrkräften als relevante Kategorien erschienen.

Es zeigte sich zwischen beiden Fällen ein gemeinsamer Orientierungsrahmen im Kontext von Zeit, der durch die Vorstellung von Homogenität und Synchronität und damit einer Zeitnorm des Homogenen charakterisiert werden kann. Dies erscheint besonders in Schule und Unterricht von hoher Relevanz, da hier institutionell Lernmöglichkeiten zeitlich koordiniert werden (Meseth et al. 2011). Die Frage, die zunächst offenbleibt, ist dabei, inwiefern dies ein spezifisches Charakteristikum von Schule im Allgemeinen oder doch ein Charakteristikum des Gymnasiums im Besonderen ist. Innerhalb der genannten Orientierungsrahmen werden einzelne Schülerinnen und Schüler, Gruppen von Lernenden oder sogar die gesamte Klasse mittels unterschiedlicher Praktiken (siehe Tab. 3)

Tab. 3 Zeitfunktionen, rekonstruierte Praktiken (der Differenzierung) und Lehrkräfte

Zeitfunktion	Praktiken
(Wieder-)Herstellung und Aufrechterhaltung von Ordnung	Herstellung der Differenz zwischen Schülerinnen und Schülern bzw. Gruppen und der Klasse
	Herstellung der Differenz zwischen Klasse und Parallelklasse
	Herstellung der Differenz zwischen „Fertig sein" und Rest
Synchronität	Enge Führung durch Lehrkraft
	Scheinsynchronität durch Scheinfragen
	Herstellung der Differenz zwischen Klasse und Parallelklasse
	Herstellung von Differenz zwischen Einzelschülerin und Rest mittels Pause
	Herstellung von Differenz zwischen Gruppe und dem eigentlich verfolgten Unterrichtsverlauf
	Herstellung von Differenz in Schnelle und Rest mit Bonusaufgaben
Koordination	Unter- und Abbrechen von Schülerinnen- und Schülerantworten
	Herstellung der Differenz zwischen Schülerinnen und Schülern bzw. Gruppen und der Klasse
	Fragen nach Zeit

in Beziehung gesetzt, woraus sich unterschiedliche Orientierungsmuster ergeben. Die hierbei angewandten genannten Praktiken lassen sich grob in vier Gruppen einteilen:

- Praktiken der Verlagerung von Zeit,
- Praktiken der Kollektivierung von Zeit,
- Praktiken der Beschleunigung/des Tempos,
- Praktiken der Personalisierung von Zeit.

Die Praktiken der Differenzierung orientierten sich mit Blick auf den Aspekt „Zeit" im Unterricht nur teilweise an den Leistungen der Schülerinnen und Schüler (als ein Art Supercode), sondern eher daran, inwiefern unterrichtshabituelle Erwartungen (Sturm) erfüllt wurden bzw. inwiefern einzelne Schülerinnen und Schüler oder Gruppen sich in unterrichtliche Hierarchien einfügen konnten (Gellert 2013).

Ein nächster Schritt liegt in der Auswertung weiterer Fälle. Anschließend soll – wie bereits anhand der beiden Fälle von Frau Fiedler und Herrn Kukal angedeutet – über Homologien eine relationale Typenbildung erfolgen. Dies ist vor allem mit Blick auf die Frage der Gymnasialität bzw. des Gymnasialen interessant. Es ist zu erwarten, dass sich am Gymnasium ein bestimmtes, charakteristisches Organisationsmilieu herausbildet, „wenn formale Regeln in ihrer konkreten Umsetzung (in informellen Regeln) kollektiv getragen werden" (Sturm und Wagner-Willi 2015a, S. 234;). Inwiefern also die rekonstruierten Praktiken und der Orientierungsrahmen Ausdruck einer gymnasial geteilten Vorstellung sind, wäre zu prüfen.

Literatur

Ainscow, M. (2008). Teaching for diversity. The Next Big Challenge. In F.M. Connelly, M. Fang He & J.A. Phillion (Hrsg.), *The Sage Handbook of Curriculum and Instruction* (S. 240–258). Los Angeles u. a.: SAGE Publications.

Asbrand, B. & Martens, M. (2018). *Dokumentarische Unterrichtsforschung*. Wiesbaden: Springer VS.

Asbrand, B., Martens, M. & Petersen, D. (2013). Die Rolle der Dinge in schulischen Lehr-Lernprozessen. In Nohl, A.-M./Wulf, C. (Hrsg.), *Mensch und Ding. Die Materialität pädagogischer Prozesse. Beiheft der Zeitschrift für Erziehungswissenschaft, 16*(2), 171–188

Bohnsack, R. (2007). Dokumentarische Methode und praxeologische Wissenssoziologie. In R. Schützeichel (Hrsg.), *Handbuch Wissenssoziologie und Wissensforschung* (S. 180–190). Konstanz: UVK Verlagsgesellschaft.

Bohnsack, R. (2009). Dokumentarische Methode. In R. Buber & H. Holzmüller (Hrsg.), *Qualitative Marktforschung. Konzepte – Methoden – Analysen* (S. 321– 330). Wiesbaden: Springer.

Bohnsack, R. (2010a). *Rekonstruktive Sozialforschung. Einführung in qualitative Methoden*. Opladen: Leske + Budrich.

Bohnsack, R. (2010b). Zugänge zur Eigenlogik des Visuellen und die dokumentarische Videointerpretation. In M. Corsten, M. Krug & C. Moritz (Hrsg.), *Videographie praktizieren. Herangehensweisen, Möglichkeiten und Grenzen* (S. 271–294). Wiesbaden: VS Verlag/Springer Fachmedien.

Bohnsack, R. (2012). Orientierungsschemata, Orientierungsrahmen und Habitus. Elementare Kategorien der Dokumentarischen Methode mit Beispielen aus der Bildungsmilieuforschung. In K. Schittenhelm (Hrsg.), *Qualitative Bildungs- und Arbeitsmarktforschung. Grundlagen, Perspektiven, Methoden* (S. 119–153). Wiesbaden: Springer VS.

Bohnsack, R. (2017). *Praxeologische Wissenssoziologie*. Opladen: Verlag Barbara Budrich.

Bohnsack, R. & Nohl, A.-M. (2001). Ethnisierung und Differenzerfahrung. *Zeitschrift für Qualitative Forschung* 2(1), 15–36.

Breidenstein, G., Dorow, S., Menzel, C. & Rademacher, S. (2017). Die Organisation individualisierten Unterrichts. In G. Breidenstein & S. Rademacher (Hrsg.), *Individualisierung und Kontrolle. Empirische Studien zum geöffneten Unterricht in der Grundschule* (S. 17–74). Wiesbaden: Springer VS.

Budde, J. (2014). Differenz beobachten? In A. Tervooren, N. Engel, M. Göhlich, I. Miethe & S. Reh (Hrsg.), *Ethnographie und Differenz in pädagogischen Feldern. Internationale Entwicklungen erziehungswissenschaftlicher Forschung* (S. 133–148). Bielefeld: transcript.

Budde, J. (2017). Differenzierungspraktiken im Unterricht. In M. Proske & K. Rabenstein (Hrsg.), *Unterricht beobachten – beschreiben – rekonstruieren. Kompendium qualitativer Unterrichtsforschung* (S. 137–152). Bad Heilbrunn: Klinkhardt.

Budde, J. & Rißler, G. (2017). Exklusion aus dem schulischen Anspruch. In I. Diehm, M. Kuhn & C. Machold (Hrsg.), *Differenz – Ungleichheit – Erziehungswissenschaft. Verhältnisbestimmungen im (Inter-)Disziplinären* (S. 179–199). Wiesbaden: Springer VS.

Burzan, N. & Schöneck, N. M. (2014). Zeit. In G. Endruweit, G. Trommsdorff & N. Burzan (Hrsg.), *Wörterbuch der Soziologie* (S. 638–639). Konstanz: UVK.

Derrida, J. (1990). La differance. In P. Engelmann (Hrsg.), *Postmoderne und Dekonscruktion* (S. 76–113). Stuttgart: Reclam.

Diehm, I., Kuhn, M., Machold, C., Mai, M. (2013). Ethnische Differenz und Ungleichheit. *Zeitschrift für Pädagogik 59*(5), 644–656.

Emmerich, M. & Hormel, U. (2013). *Heterogenität – Diversity – Intersektionalität. Zur Logik sozialer Unterscheidungen in pädagogischen Semantiken der Differenz*. Wiesbaden: Springer VS.

Fölling-Albers, M. (2008). Alte und neue Rhythmen schulischer Zeit. In S. Schroeder & H. Zeiher (Hrsg.), *Schulzeiten, Lernzeiten, Lebenszeiten: Pädagogische Konsequenzen und zeitpolitische Perspektiven schulischer Zeitordnungen* (S. 133–142). Weinheim: Juventa.

Foucault, M. (1982). The subject and power. *Critical inquiry, 8*(4), 777–795.

Fritzsche, B. & Wagner-Willi, M. (2015). Dokumentarische Interpretation von Unterrichtsvideografien. In R. Bohnsack, B. Fritzsche & M. Wagner-Willi (Hrsg.), *Dokumentarische Video- und Filminterpretation* (S. 131–152). Opladen, Berlin & Toronto: Barbara Budrich.

Fritzsche, B. (2014). Inklusion als Exklusion. Differenzproduktionen im Rahmen des schulischen Anerkennungsgeschehens. In A. Tervooren, N. Engel, M. Göhlich, I. Miethe & S. Reh (Hrsg.), *Ethnographie und Differenz in pädagogischen Feldern. Internationale Entwicklungen erziehungswissenschaftlicher Forschung* (S. 329–345). Bielefeld: transcript.

Garfinkel, H. (1956). Conditions of Successful Degregation Ceremonies. *American Journal of Sociology, 61*(5), 420–424.

Gellert, U. (2013). Heterogen oder hierarchisch? Zur Konstruktion von Leistung im Unterricht. In J. Budde (Hrsg.), *Unscharfe Einsätze. (Re-)Produktion von Heterogenität im schulischen Feld* (S. 211–227). Wiesbaden: Springer VS.

Göhlich, M., Reh, S. & Tervooren, A. (2013). Ethnographie der Differenz. *Zeitschrift für Pädagogik, 59*(5), 639–643.

Helsper, W., Dreier, L., Gibson, A., Kotzyba, K., & Niemann, M. (2018). Exklusive Gymnasien und ihre Schüler: Passungsverhältnisse zwischen institutionellem und individuellem Schülerhabitus. Studien zur Schul- und Bildungsforschung: Vol. 64. Wiesbaden: Springer VS.

Kalthoff, H. (2006). Doing/undoing dass in exklusiven Internatsschulen. Ein Beitrag zur empirischen Bildungssoziologie. In W. Georg (Hrsg.), *Soziale Ungleichheit im Bildungssystem. Eine empirisch-theoretische Bestandsaufnahme* (S. 93–122). Konstanz: UVK Verlagsgesellschaft.

Kounin, J. S. (1976/2006). *Techniken der Klassenführung*. Stuttgart: UTB.
Mannheim, K. (1980). *Strukturen des Denkens*. Frankfurt a. M.: Suhrkamp.
Mannheim, K. (1995). *Ideologie und Utopie* (8. Aufl.). Frankfurt a. M.: Vittorio Klostermann.
Martens, M. (2015). Differenz und Passung: Differenzkonstruktionen im individualisierenden Unterricht der Sekundarstufe. *Zeitschrift für Qualitative Forschung, 16*(2), 211–229.
Martens, M., Petersen, D. & Asbrand, B. (2015). Die Materialität von Lernkultur. Methodische Überlegungen zur dokumentarischen Analyse von Unterrichtsvideografien. In R. Bohnsack, B. Fritzsche, M. Wagner-Willi (Hrsg.), *Dokumentarische Video- und Filminterpretation* (S. 179–206). Opladen, Berlin & Toronto: Barbara Budrich.
Meseth, W., Proske, M. & Radtke, F.-O. (2011). Was leistet eine kommunikationstheoretische Modellierung des Gegenstandes „Unterricht"? In dies. (Hrsg.), *Unterrichtstheorien in Forschung und Lehre* (S. 223–240). Bad Heilbrunn: Klinkhardt.
Nohl, A.-M. (2009). *Interview und dokumentarische Methode. Anleitungen für die Forschungspraxis*. Wiesbaden: Springer VS.
Rabenstein, K., Reh, S., Ricken, N. & Idel, T.-S. (2013). Ethnographie pädagogischer Differenzordnungen. *Zeitschrift für Pädagogik, 59*(5), 668–690.
Reckwitz, A. (2003). Grundelemente einer Theorie sozialer Praktiken. Eine sozialtheoretische Perspektive. *Zeitschrift für Soziologie 32*(4), 282–301.
Reh, S., Fritzsche, B., Idel, T.-S. & Rabenstein, K. (2015). *Lernkulturen. Rekonstruktion pädagogischer Praktiken an Ganztagsschulen*. Wiesbaden: Springer.
Scharenberg, K. (2013). Heterogenität in der Schule. Definitionen, Forschungsbefunde, Konzeptionen und Perspektiven für die empirische Bildungsforschung. In N. McElvany, M. M. Gebauer, W. Bos & H. G. Holtappels (Hrsg.), Jahrbuch der Schulentwicklung, Band 17. Sprachliche, kulturelle und soziale Heterogenität in der Schule als Herausforderung und Chance der Schulentwicklung (S. 10–49). Weinheim: Juventa.
Sorokin, P. A. & Merton, R. K. (1937). Social Time. A Methodological and Functional Analysis. *American Journal of Sociology, 42*, 615–629.
Sturm, T. (2012). Praxeologische Unterrichtsforschung und ihr Beitrag zu inklusivem Unterricht. *Inklusion online, 1–2*. Abgerufen am 19.03.2019 von https://www.inklusion-online.net/index.php/inklusion-online/article/view/65/65
Sturm, T. (2013a). Orientierungen unterrichtlicher Praktiken: lerntheoretische Vorstellungen und schulischer Kontext. In J. Budde (Hrsg.), *Unscharfe Einsätze. (Re-)Produktion von Heterogenität im schulischen Feld* (S. 276–294). Wiesbaden: Springer VS.
Sturm, T. (2013b). (Re-)Produktion von Differenzen in unterrichtlichen Praktiken. *Schweizerische Zeitschrift für Bildungswissenschaften, 35*(1), 131–146.
Sturm, T. (2015). Rekonstruktiv-praxeologische Schul- und Unterrichtsforschung im Kontext von Inklusion. *Inklusion online, 4*. Abgerufen von https://www.inklusion-online.net/index.php/inklusion-online/article/view/321/27 [Zugriff: 19.03.2019].
Sturm, T. (2018a). Lehrpersonen: Differenzkonstruktionen im Unterricht. In T. Sturm & M. Wagner-Willi (Hrsg.), *Handbuch schulische Inklusion* (S. 251–265). Opladen: Barbara Budrich.
Sturm, T. (2018b). (Leistungs-)Differenz in Schule und Unterricht aus praxeologisch-wissenssoziologischer Perspektive. In J. Budde, M. Dittrich, A. Bossen & G. Rißler (Hrsg.), *Konturen praxistheoretischer Erziehungswissenschaft* (S. 51–66). Weinheim u. a.: Beltz Juventa.

Sturm, T. & Wagner-Willi, M. (2015a). 'Leistungsdifferenzen' im Unterrichtsmilieu einer inklusiven Schule der Sekundarstufe I in der Schweiz. *Zeitschrift für Qualitative Forschung, 16*(2), 231–248.

Sturm, T. & Wagner-Willi, M. (2015b). Videografien schulischer Praktiken der Differenzbearbeitung und –herstellung. Einleitung in den Themenschwerpunkt. *Zeitschrift für Qualitative Forschung, 16*(2), 163–171.

Tervooren, A. (2000). Differenz anders gesehen: Studien zu Behinderung. *Vierteljahreszeitschrift für Heilpädagogik und ihre Nachbargebiete, 69*(3), 316–319.

Trautwein, U., Neumann, M., & Baumert, J. (2011). Das Gymnasium. In S. Hellekamps, W. Plöger, & W. Wittenbruch (Eds.), Utb-studi-e-book: Vol. 8438. Schule: Handbuch der Erziehungswissenschaft 3 (1st ed., pp. 177–182). Stuttgart: UTB GmbH.

Wagner-Willi, M. (2004). Videointerpretation als mehrdimensionale Mikroanalyse am Beispiel schulischer Alltagsszenen. *Zeitschrift für qualitative Bildungs- Beratungs- und Sozialforschung, 5*(1), 59–66.

Wagner-Willi, M. & Sturm, T. (2012). Inklusion und Milieus in schulischen Organisationen. *Inklusion online, 4*. Abgerufen am 19.03.2019 von https://www.inklusion-online.net/index.php/inklusionlarticle/view/185/173

Weisser, J. (2005). *Behinderung, Ungleichheit und Bildung. Eine Theorie der Behinderung.* Bielefeld: transcript.

Wrana, D. (2014). Praktiken des Differenzierens. Zu einem Instrumentarium der poststrukturalistischen Analyse von Praktiken der Differenzierung. In A. Tervooren, N. Engel, M. Göhlich, I. Miethe & S. Reh (Hrsg.), *Ethnographie und Differenz in pädagogischen Feldern. Internationale Entwicklungen erziehungswissenschaftlicher Forschung* (S. 79–96). Bielefeld: transcript,

Zaborowski, K. U., Meier, M. & Breidenstein, G. (2011): *Leistungsbewertung und Unterricht. Ethnographische Studien zur Bewertungspraxis in Gymnasium und Sekundarschule.* Wiesbaden: VS Verlag für Sozialwissenschaften.

Individueller Lernanspruch als temporaler Einflussfaktor – Konzeptionell-methodische Reflexionen zur Erfassung wissenschaftlicher Weiterbildungslernzeit mittels Leitfadeninterviews

Ramona Kahl

> **Abstract**
>
> Time is a substantial study condition for the successful participation of adults in an on the job continuing education. The paper focusses on the conceptual and methodical analysis of a qualitative research project how to reconcile continuing education, work and private life. The main question is how the learning time for continuing education is conceptualized and collected in the project. The analysis of implicit time-attached assumptions within the project, the conception of the interview questions and selected interview material show that the interviews generate additional time-attached results aside the expected ones like the importance of the learners education aspiration for the time investment in learning.

> **Zusammenfassung**
>
> Für die erfolgreiche Teilnahme Erwachsener an berufsbegleitender wissenschaftlicher Weiterbildung stellt Zeit eine maßgebliche Lernbedingung dar. Der Beitrag fokussiert die konzeptionell-methodische Auseinandersetzung mit einer

---

R. Kahl (✉)
Philipps-Universität Marburg, Marburg, Deutschland
E-Mail: kahl@uni-marburg.de

© Springer Fachmedien Wiesbaden GmbH, ein Teil von Springer Nature 2020
E. Schilling und M. O'Neill (Hrsg.), *Frontiers in Time*
Research – Einführung in die interdisziplinäre Zeitforschung,
https://doi.org/10.1007/978-3-658-31252-7_12

qualitativen Studie zur Vereinbarkeit von wissenschaftlicher Weiterbildung mit dem Arbeits- und Privatleben der Teilnehmenden. Zentrale Frage ist, wie Weiterbildungslernzeit (Präsenzphasen und Selbstlernphasen) in der leitfadengestützten Interviewstudie konzipiert und erfasst wird. Über die Analyse impliziter zeitbezogener Prämissen der Studie, der Leitfadenkonzeption und ausgewähltem Interviewmaterial wird deutlich, dass die Interviews über den Erwartungshorizont hinaus weitere zeitbezogene Befunde, wie die Bedeutung des Weiterbildungsanspruchs der Teilnehmende für ihre Lernzeitinvestition, aufzeigen.

Keywords

Time quality · Learning · Continuing education participants · Interview method · Time scale

Schlüsselwörter

Zeitqualität · Lernen · Weiterbildungsteilnehmer · Interviewmethode · Zeitumfang

Einführung

Der Einsatz von Zeit stellt eine Grundbedingung des Lernens dar. Obschon es eine kontroverse Debatte um „die Bedeutung des Zeitbegriffs für die Pädagogik" (Lüders 1995) und den Stellenwert der Zeit als „pädagogisches Grundproblem" (Lüders 1995, S. 161) gibt, ist zumindest eine pragmatische Bedeutung von Zeit als einer Ressource für die Lernaktivität unstrittig. Denn „Bildung und Lernen vollziehen sich in der Zeit, sind zeitbezogen, verbrauchen Zeit" (Seitter 2017, S. 10). Besonders für die Erwachsenenbildung stellt Zeit „eine Schlüsselkategorie" (Schmidt-Lauff 2018, S. 319) dar. Zur Bildung Heranwachsender haben sich in den vergangenen Jahrhunderten gesellschaftlich legitimierte Lernzeiten etabliert, während „die Lebenslaufbedeutsamkeit des Lernens über das Kinder- und Jugendalter hinaus erst in der jüngsten Gegenwart als gesellschaftliche Normalität und Erwartungshaltung akzeptiert und kommuniziert wird" (Seitter 2010, S. 305). Obgleich es (noch) „keine kollektiven, expliziten Lernzeitfenster" (Schmidt-Lauff 2018, S. 320) für das Erwachsenenalter gibt und Zeit demzufolge eine „(individuelle) Weiterbildungsbarriere" (Schmidt-Lauff 2008, S. 237) darstellt, gewinnen Weiterbildung und lebenslanges Lernen an Bedeutung.

Die verstärkte Notwendigkeit einer wissenschaftlichen Weiterbildung hängt mit gesellschaftlichen Veränderungen „wie demographischer Wandel, Fachkräftemangel, Akademisierung, Lebenslanges Lernen" (Seitter et al. 2018, S. 1) und beschleunigten Veränderungen des Arbeitsmarkts zusammen. Vor diesem Hintergrund hat die wissenschaftliche Weiterbildung an Hochschulen – ein berufsbegleitendes, kostenpflichtiges, akademisches Weiterbildungsformat für Erwachsene – in den letzten Jahren einen (bildungspolitisch gezielt beförderten)[1] Aufschwung erfahren.[2] Als abschlussbezogenes, mehrsemestriges Bildungsformat (Zertifikatskurse, Masterstudiengänge) und „berufs- oder familienbegleitendes Arrangement hat (wissenschaftliche Weiterbildung) Zeitknappheit als Ausgangsprämisse" (Seitter 2017, S. 11) und ist maßgeblich auf die individuelle Umstrukturierung bzw. Freisetzung von Zeitressourcen angewiesen (vgl. Wonneberger et al. 2015, S. 78; Schirmer 2017). Wie dies geschieht und wie viele temporale Ressourcen die wissenschaftlichen Weiterbildungsteilnehmenden aufbringen, bildet jedoch ein Desiderat.

Fragen des Zeitbudgets und der zeitlichen Vereinbarkeit einer wissenschaftlichen Weiterbildungsteilnahme hat sich das Forschungsprojekt „Individuumsbezogene Zeitbudgetstudie" (2015–2017) gewidmet. Die Studie ist im Rahmen des Verbundprojekts „WM³ Weiterbildung Mittelhessen" (2011–2017), das sich der Entwicklung und Erforschung wissenschaftlicher Weiterbildungsangebote gewidmet hat, durchgeführt worden.[3] Anlass für die Studie waren Befunde der

---

[1] „In diesem Zusammenhang ist insbesondere der Wettbewerb ‚Aufstieg durch Bildung: offene Hochschule' zu nennen, der durch seine lange Laufzeit (2011 bis 2020) und sein finanzielles Fördervolumen (250 Mio. EUR) zu einem gezielten, kontinuierlichen und breit gestreuten Innovationsschub beigetragen hat – und noch immer beiträgt" (Seitter et al. 2018, S. 1).

[2] Wissenschaftliche Weiterbildung wird definiert als eine „Fortsetzung oder Wiederaufnahme organisierten Lernens nach Abschluss einer ersten Bildungsphase und in der Regel nach Aufnahme einer Erwerbs- oder Familientätigkeit, wobei das wahrgenommene Weiterbildungsangebot dem fachlichen und didaktischen Niveau der Hochschule entspricht" (KMK 2001, S. 2).

[3] Die Justus-Liebig-Universität Gießen, Philipps-Universität Marburg und Technische Hochschule Mittelhessen haben sich mittels des BMBF-Wettbewerbs „Aufstieg durch Bildung: offene Hochschulen" zum Verbundprojekt „WM³ Weiterbildung Mittelhessen" zusammengeschlossen, um wissenschaftliche Weiterbildungsangebote an ihren Hochschulen zu befördern und zu erforschen. Das Projekt ist in der ersten Förderphase (2011–2015) aus Mitteln des BMBF und aus dem ESF der EU (Förderkennzeichen 16OH11008, 16OH11009, 16OH11010), in der zweiten Förderphase (2015–2017) aus Mitteln des BMBF (Förderkennzeichen 16OH12008, 16OH12009, 16OH12010) gefördert worden. Weitere Informationen: www.wmhoch3.de.

ersten Projektphase (2011–2015) (vgl. Präßler 2015, S. 174 ff.; Kahl et al. 2015, S. 402 f.), denen zufolge Zeit von den potentiellen Weiterbildungsteilnehmenden „als äußerst knappe Ressource behandelt (wird), die (häufig) schwieriger bereitzustellen ist als monetäre Ressourcen" (Seitter 2017, S. 10 f.). Die „Individuumsbezogene Zeitbudgetstudie" umfasst eine qualitative und eine quantitative Teilstudie (vgl. Abschn. „Forschungsdesign").

Der Beitrag setzt den Schwerpunkt auf die konzeptionelle-methodische Auseinandersetzung mit der qualitativen Interviewstudie zur Vereinbarkeit von wissenschaftlicher Weiterbildung mit dem Arbeits- und Privatleben der Teilnehmenden. Die Auseinandersetzung mit der Interviewstudie erfolgt aufgrund der weiten Verbreitung dieser qualitativen Erhebungsmethode in der sozialwissenschaftlichen Forschung (vgl. Hopf 2008, S. 349).[4] Die betrachteten „Interviews (repräsentieren) den „Durchschnittstypus" des qualitativen Interviews: nämlich das von der entsprechenden Forschergruppe selbst durchgeführte, wenig strukturierte Interview, das von lockeren Hypothesen angeleitet, der Exploration eines bestimmten, wissenschaftlich wenig erschlossenen Forschungsfeldes dienen soll und das – zumindest der Intention nach – den Befragten einen breiten Spielraum der Strukturierung und Äußerung subjektiver Deutungen einräumt" (Hopf 1978, S. 99). Anhand der „Individuumsbezogenen Zeitbudgetstudie" und ihrer qualitativen Teilstudie, der „Zeitvereinbarkeitsstudie" werden die „lockeren" temporalen Prämissen, der daraufhin konzipierte teilstandardisierte Interviewleitfaden und ein exemplarischer Befund (jenseits der Vorannahmen) zum wenig erforschten Feld der zeitlichen Vereinbarkeit einer wissenschaftlichen Weiterbildungsteilnahme betrachtet. Zentrale Frage des Beitrags ist, wie die Vereinbarkeit der Lernzeit für die wissenschaftliche Weiterbildung mit beruflichen und privaten Verpflichtungen in der leitfadengestützten Interviewstudie konzipiert und erfasst wird. Als Weiterbildungslernzeiten gelten sowohl die Teilnahme an Präsenzveranstaltungen der Studienangebote, als auch die Selbstlernphasen der wissenschaftlichen Weiterbildungsteilnehmenden.[5]

---

[4]In den letzten Jahrzehnten hat sich ein breites Spektrum an Interviewmethoden herausgebildet, das von klinischen Interviews (Argelander 1970) bis zu offenen, erzählgenerierenden Formen wie dem narrativen Interview (Schütze 1983) reicht. Die Literatur zu Interviewmethoden und -techniken ist entsprechend mannigfaltig und vielfältig (als Übersichtsbeiträge vgl. Friebertshäuser und Langer 2013; Hopf 2008).

[5]Zum Verhältnis von Präsenz- und Selbstlernphasen in zeitlicher und räumlicher Hinsicht in der wissenschaftlichen Weiterbildungsstudie vgl. Kahl 2019, zur raumbezogenen Lernzeitverausgabung für das Selbststudium vgl. Denninger et al. 2019.

Im ersten Teil des Beitrags wird das konzeptionelle und methodische Design der „Zeitvereinbarkeitsstudie" dargelegt. Dafür wird zunächst das Forschungsdesign der Gesamtstudie („Individuumsbezogene Zeitbudgetstudie") dargestellt. Im Anschluss werden die zeitbezogenen Vorannahmen der Studie und ihre methodische Umsetzung mittels eines teilstandardisierten Interviewleitfadens, seinen Hauptthemen und Fragestellungen verdeutlicht. Anhand von Interviewmaterial wird im zweiten Teil dargelegt, dass die Leitfadeninterviews weiterführende Zusammenhänge, wie den Einfluss des individuellen (Lern-) Anspruchs auf die Zeitinvestition, aufzeigen. Zum Abschluss wird dieser Befund konzeptionell und methodisch reflektiert.

Konzeptionell-methodisches Design der Zeitvereinbarkeitsstudie

Im Rahmen der Zeitbudgetforschung kommen vielfältige, eigens entwickelte Erhebungsinstrumente zum Einsatz. „In der Forschung vielfach erprobt wurden u. a. Time-Use-Studies, aktivitätsorientierte Befragungen, Yesterday-Interviews und Tagebücher" (Denninger et al. 2017, S. 69).[6] Im Bereich der für den Beitrag relevanten (Hochschul-)Weiterbildungsforschung zur Vereinbarkeit von Lernzeiten kommt das vielfältige Spektrum sozialwissenschaftlicher Verfahren zur Anwendung. So untersuchten Nahrstedt et al. „Neue Zeitfenster für Weiterbildung" (1998) mittels Programmheftanalysen, Straßenbefragungen mit Fragebögen und Einzelinterviews. Schmidt-Lauff setzte eine standardisierte Fragebogenerhebung und eine Gruppenbefragung ein, um „organisatorische und instrumentelle Zugriffe auf Zeit (Zeitstrukturierung) (und) (…) das Zeiterleben" (2008, S. 272) in der beruflichen Weiterbildung zu untersuchen. Präßler führte eine OMNIBUS-Befragung[7], eine Fragebogenerhebung sowie leitfadengestützte Experteninterviews durch, um die Bedarfe potentieller wissenschaftlicher Weiterbildungszielgruppen zu erheben. Im Ergebnis erwies sich Zeit als eine zentrale Voraussetzung (vgl. 2015, S. 174 ff.). Lobe untersuchte mittels problemzentrierter Interviews das berufsbegleitende Studium als bewusste biografische Transition (vgl. 2015, S. 7).

---

[6]Erläuterungen der einzelnen Verfahren siehe Denninger et al. 2017, S. 68 ff.
[7]„Der repräsentative OMNIBUS ist eine Form der Primärerhebung in der Marktforschung, welcher neben allgemeinen sozio-demographischen Merkmalen mehrere Fragen verschiedener Auftraggeber erhebt" (Präßler 2015, S. 89).

Die exemplarische Studienauswahl aus verschiedenen Feldern der Weiterbildungsforschung verdeutlicht, dass qualitative Verfahren als alleiniger methodischer Zugang oder im Kontext von Mixed-Methods-Designs eingesetzt werden.

Forschungsdesign

Die „Individuumsbezogene Zeitbudgetstudie" verwendet ebenfalls ein Mixed-Methods-Forschungsdesign. Sie hat sich im Kontext des Verbundprojekts „WM^3 Weiterbildung Mittelhessen" (2011–2017) im Rahmen der zweiten Förderphase (2015–2017) der Untersuchung der Lernzeiten von Teilnehmenden wissenschaftlicher Weiterbildung gewidmet. Die explorative Studie untersucht die zeitliche Vereinbarkeit der Weiterbildungsteilnahme mittels einer qualitativen Interviewstudie („Zeitvereinbarkeitsstudie") und die Lernzeitverausgabung der Weiterbildungsteilnehmenden mittels einer quantitativen Zeitprotokollstudie („Lernzeitbudgetstudie"). Damit trägt die Studie konzeptionell-methodisch dem Doppelcharakter von Zeit als „interner Erlebniszeit und äußerer Parameterzeit" (Müller 2002, S. V) Rechnung, indem sie in der „Zeitvereinbarkeitsstudie" das subjektive Zeiterleben und „die individuellen Bewertungen von Zeitkapazitäten und Vereinbarkeitsoptionen" (Denninger et al. 2020, S. 10) betrachtet, während der messbare Aspekt der Lernzeitverausgabung „mit der quantifizierenden Darstellung der Zeitorganisation insbesondere der Selbstlernzeiten" (ebd.) in den Blick genommen wird.

Die qualitative und die quantitative Studie stellen zwei gleichrangige Erhebungen mit komplementärem Charakter dar, deren Resultate zusammengeführt worden sind (vgl. Denninger et al. 2020, S. 203 ff.).[8] Abbildung 1 zeigt eine Übersicht des Studiendesigns mit den Stichprobengrößen und den Auswertungsdimensionen.[9]

Die im vorliegenden Beitrag analysierte „Zeitvereinbarkeitsstudie" umfasst 26 leitfadengestützte Interviews mit Teilnehmenden von wissenschaftlichen Weiterbildungsangeboten und weiteren Weiterbildungsformaten der drei mittelhessischen Hochschulen des Verbundprojekts WM^3, die im Zeitraum von September 2015 bis Juni 2016 geführt wurden. Die Interviews sind zwischen 20 und 60 min lang und wurden kategorienbasiert nach dem inhaltsanalytischen Ver-

---

[8]Nähere Erläuterungen zu Mixed-Methods-Designs vgl. Kuckartz 2014, S. 57 ff.
[9]Weitere Informationen zum Sample und zur Auswertung vgl. Denninger et al. 2020, S. 11 ff.

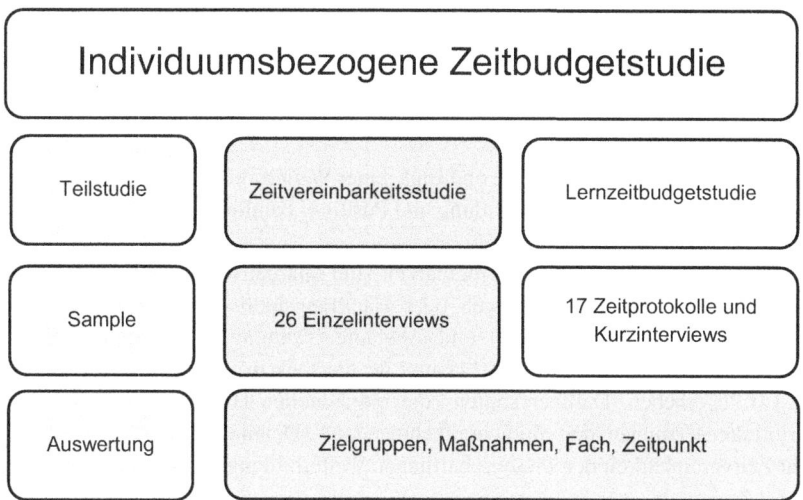

Abb. 1 Forschungsdesign der „Individuumsbezogenen Zeitbudgetstudie". (Nach Denninger et al. (2017, S. 81), leicht verändert)

fahren von Mayring (2016) ausgewertet (vgl. Denninger et al. 2020, S. 16 ff.).[10] Die übergeordneten Auswertungsdimensionen für die Zeitvereinbarkeits- und Lernzeitbudgetstudie sind bereits bei der Konzeption des Samples berücksichtigt worden (vgl. Denninger et al. 2020, S. 11 f.).[11] Entsprechend liegen der „gezielte(n) Stichprobenauswahl" (Friebertshäuser 2003, S. 391) vier Auswahlkriterien mit folgenden Ausprägungen zugrunde:

---

[10]Bei der Auswertung ist die strukturierte Inhaltsanalyse eingesetzt worden (vgl. Mayring 2016, S. 114 f.; Denninger et al. 2020, S. 16 ff.).

[11]Die übergeordneten Auswertungsdimensionen sind im Drittmittelantrag für das Projekt ausgewiesen (vgl. Philipps-Universität Marburg et al. 2014, S. 4 und 7). Nach Kade sind sie Teil der „Gründung des Projekts im Medium des Antrags" (2007, S. 332) und gelten aus „(Perspektive des Projektes) als gesichertes Gründungswissen ( ), an dem das Projekt Halt findet, und auf das es auch wieder Bezug nehmen muss, spätestens dann, wenn die Projektergebnisse vor der Förderinstitution zu verantworten sind" (2007, S. 332 f.). Sie basieren auch auf Wissensbeständen, Forschungserfahrungen und Erwartungen der Antragstellenden.

- Weiterbildungsformat (Masterstudiengänge und Zertifikatskurse der wissenschaftlichen Weiterbildung, ein konsekutiv-dualer Masterstudiengang und ein hochschulisch-postgraduales Weiterbildungsangebot),
- Weiterbildungsfach (Medizin, Wirtschafts-, Ingenieurs- und Sozialwissenschaften),
- Studienphase (Anfang, Mitte und Ende einer Weiterbildungsmaßnahme),
- Lebenslage (berufliche Vorbildung und Position, Familienstand, Wohnort).

Für die Studie zur zeitlichen Vereinbarkeit sind qualitative Interviews eingesetzt worden, um „Situationsdeutungen oder Handlungsmotive in offener Form zu erfragen" (Hopf 2008, S. 350) und „Abläufe, Deutungsmuster und Strukturmerkmale" (Flick et al. 2015, S. 14) aus „der Perspektive der Betroffenen" (ebd., S. 17) zu erheben. Darüber sollten „die individuellen Handlungsstrategien und Prioritätensetzungen der Studienteilnehmenden" (Denninger et al. 2020, S. 13) zur Zeitvereinbarkeit der wissenschaftlichen Weiterbildung untersucht werden.

Zeitbezogene Vorannahmen der Zeitvereinbarkeitsstudie

Die Anlage der Zeitvereinbarkeitsstudie enthält implizite zeitbezogene Vorannahmen, die sich an drei Schlüsselstellen des Forschungsprojekts veranschaulichen lassen: der Fragestellung, der Zielsetzung und den übergeordneten Auswertungsdimensionen.

Die erste Prämisse betrifft den Stellenwert der wissenschaftlichen Weiterbildung für die Teilnehmenden in zeitlicher Hinsicht. Sie lässt sich an der *Leitfrage* der Interviewstudie erkennen, „wie eine Teilnahme an den Angeboten wissenschaftlicher Weiterbildung unter zeitlichen Gesichtspunkten mit den anderen Lebensbereichen der Teilnehmenden kompatibel ist" (Denninger et al. 2020, S. 12). Dabei sollten vor allem „die individuellen zeitlichen Vereinbarkeitsstrategien der Teilnehmenden wissenschaftlicher Weiterbildung im Kontext ihres beruflichen, sozialen und familiären Umfeldes" (ebd.) betrachtet werden. Hinsichtlich der Zeitkonzeption wurde davon ausgegangen, dass es verschiedene Lebensbereiche gibt, die zeitlich miteinander in Konflikt geraten können und auszubalancieren sind.[12] Wissenschaft-

---

[12]In Studien zur Vereinbarkeit von Beruf und Familie bzw. Privatleben kommt eine solche Perspektive zum Tragen (vgl. Böhm 2015, Keller und Haustein 2012, Weßler-Poßberg 2014, Brinkmann 2014).

liche Weiterbildung stellt demnach einen zeitweiligen zusätzlichen Lebensbereich neben dem Berufs- und Privatleben dar, der zu vermehrten temporalen Spannungen zwischen Lebensbereichen führen kann und den es zeitlich zu integrieren gilt. Diese Annahme wurde aus Studien zur Work-Lern-Life-Balance (Antoni et al. 2014, S. 109 ff.), zum weiterbildenden Studium (Lobe 2015, S. 211 ff.) und zur beruflichen Weiterbildung (Schmidt-Lauff 2011) abgeleitet.

Eine zweite zeitbezogene Vorannahme ist in der *Zielsetzung* der Untersuchung enthalten, „zentrale Gelingens- und Optimierungsfaktoren wissenschaftlicher Weiterbildung – wie etwa Zeitstrukturierung und Zeitverausgabung" (Denninger et al. 2020, S. 10) zu erforschen, um eine „Anpassung und Optimierung der zeitlichen Organisation und Strukturierung von Studiengängen" (Denninger et al. 2020, S. 13) vorzunehmen. Das Erkenntnisinteresse bezieht sich auf die „Individuumsbezogene Zeitbudgetstudie" insgesamt und bildet folglich auch eine Zielsetzung der hier betrachteten qualitativen Teilstudie zur Zeitvereinbarkeit. Dieses Forschungs- und Entwicklungsziel der Studie enthält die temporale Prämisse, dass der Umgang mit und Einsatz von Zeit eine wichtige Teilnahmebedingung für die Weiterbildung darstellt, die zu optimieren ist und sich auch optimieren lässt. Die Annahme, dass Zeit eine zentrale Teilnahmebedingung darstellt, basiert auf Befunden der ersten Förderphase des Projekts WM^3 (2011–2015). Erhebungen von potentiellen Weiterbildungsbedarfen von Adressat*innen und (möglichen) Weiterbildungsbereitschaften seitens der Hochschulangehörigen haben ergeben, dass zeitliche Ressourcen eine zentrale Rolle bei der Entscheidung für eine wissenschaftliche Weiterbildungsaktivität spielen (vgl. Präßler 2015, S. 112 f., 174 f.; Kahl et al. 2015, S. 330 ff.). Ein geeignetes Weiterbildungsangebot für die gewünschten Zielgruppen zu entwickeln, ist nicht zuletzt eine Frage der zeitlichen Passung (vgl. Seitter et al. 2015, S. 51). Zu vergleichbaren Ergebnissen sind auch andere Studien im Bereich der wissenschaftlichen Weiterbildung gelangt (vgl. Wonneberger et al. 2015, S. 75; Rahnfeld und Schiller 2015, S. 32, 46). Dementsprechend wurde die zeitliche Vereinbarkeit als verbesserungsbedürftig und verbesserungsfähig angesehen und von einem positiven Einfluss einer Anpassung des wissenschaftlichen Weiterbildungsangebots an die Zeitfenster und -ressourcen der Teilnehmenden ausgegangen.

Die dritte zentrale temporale Vorannahme ist in den vier übergeordneten *Auswertungsdimensionen* zielgruppen-, maßnahmen-, fach- und zeitpunktspezifisch erkennbar. Zum einen rekurrieren die Dimensionen auf die fächerbezogenen Profile der drei untersuchten Hochschulen des Projektverbunds WM^3. Zum anderen sind damit temporale Überlegungen der „Individuumsbezogenen Zeitbudgetstudie" und ihrer „Zeitvereinbarkeitsstudie" verbunden, die sich auf den Forschungsstand beziehen:

- *Zielgruppenbezug:*
  Mit dieser Dimension soll betrachtet werden, inwiefern sich einzelne Faktoren der (berufs-)biographischen Lebenslage der Teilnehmenden – von der Vorbildung über den Familienstand bis zur beruflichen Position – auf die zeitliche Vereinbarkeit auswirken. Denn Untersuchungen zur Bedarfserschließung und zur Akzeptanz wissenschaftlicher Weiterbildung unter Hochschulangehörigen in der ersten Förderphase des Verbundprojekts WM^3 haben gezeigt, dass (potentielle) Teilnehmende eine heterogene Zielgruppe mit besonderen zeitlichen Bedarfen darstellen (vgl. Präßler 2015, S. 174 ff.; Kahl et al. 2015, S. 402 f.). Andere Studien im Bereich der wissenschaftlichen Weiterbildung, (vgl. Wonneberger et al. 2015, S. 75, 78; Rahnfeld und Schiller 2015, S. 27, 32) wie auch im Bereich des grundständigen Studiums, (vgl. Mertens 2013, S. 34) kommen zu analogen Befunden.
- *Maßnahmenbezug:*
  „Im Rahmen der maßnahmenspezifischen Betrachtung wird eruiert, ob sich die Vereinbarkeit je nach Studienformat bzw. Abschlussform des Angebots unterschiedlich aufwendig gestaltet und ob je nach Maßnahme besondere zeitliche Belastungen existieren" (Denninger et al. 2020, S. 11). Es wird betrachtet, ob kürzere Weiterbildungsformate – wie ein zweisemestriger Zertifikatskurs – andere zeitliche Belastungen aufweisen als ein viersemestriger Masterstudiengang. Bisherige Befunde verweisen darauf, dass die zeitliche Vereinbarkeit umso herausfordernder ist, je länger und umfangreicher die berufs- bzw. familienpflichtenbegleitende Weiterbildungsmaßnahme ist (Präßler 2015; S. 111).
- *Fachbezug:*
  Mit dieser Dimension wird der mögliche Einfluss der fachdisziplinären Verortung des Weiterbildungsangebots auf die Zeitverausgabung der Teilnehmenden (für Präsenz- und Selbstlernzeiten) in den Blick genommen. Das Kriterium basiert auf empirischen Befunden zur unterschiedlichen Lernzeitverausgabung im grundständigen Studium, denen zufolge Studierende der Medizin, Natur- und Ingenieurswissenschaften mehr wöchentliche Lernzeit in ihr Studium investieren als Studierende der Geistes- und Sozialwissenschaften (vgl. Middendorff et al. 2013, S. 318; Ramm et al. 2014, S. 30; Projektgruppe Studierbarkeit 2007, S. 32; Übersicht der Befunde vgl. Denninger et al. 2017, S. 70 ff.).
- *Zeitpunktbezug:*
  Die Betrachtung des Studienzeitpunkts soll den möglichen unterschiedlichen Arbeitsaufwand in verschiedenen Phasen des Weiterbildungsangebots – zum Beispiel Arbeitsverdichtungen aufgrund von Prüfungszeiten – ein-

beziehen. Denn Befunde zum grundständigen Studium zeigen, dass die Lernzeitinvestition im Semesterverlauf ungleich verteilt ist und sich vor allem auf Prüfungsphasen konzentriert, während sie in der vorlesungsfreien Zeit sehr gering ausfällt (vgl. Schulmeister und Metzger 2011, S. 57 f.; Projektgruppe Studierbarkeit 2007, S. 208). Aufgrund der eigenständigen Studienstruktur der wissenschaftlichen Weiterbildung sollte untersucht werden, ob es zu einer ähnlichen Verteilung der zeitlichen Arbeitsbelastung kommt wie beim Fernstudium (vgl. Sommerfeldt und Höllermann 2016, S. 8, 22 f.).

Die vier Sample- und Auswertungsdimensionen lassen sich in der zeitbezogenen Prämisse zusammenführen, dass sowohl personenbezogene Faktoren (heterogene Teilnehmerschaft) als auch angebotsbezogene Faktoren (Studienphase, Studienfach und Studiengangformat) für die zeitliche Vereinbarkeit und somit die Lernzeitinvestition der Weiterbildungsteilnahme relevant sein können. Eine thesenhafte Zusammenfassung der drei zentralen zeitbezogenen Prämissen, die in die Konzeption der „Zeitvereinbarkeitsstudie" Eingang gefunden haben, zeigt Abbildung 2.

Methodische Operationalisierung im Interviewleitfaden

Die qualitative Befragung der wissenschaftlichen Weiterbildungsteilnehmenden ist mithilfe eines teilstandardisierten Interviewleitfadens erfolgt. Teilstandardisiert bedeutet, dass zwar Fragen vorformuliert wurden, die in einer sinnhaften Abfolge angeordnet sind, die Reihenfolge und Formulierung jedoch dem Gesprächsverlauf, insbesondere den Antwortgehalten der Befragten, angepasst worden ist (vgl. Hopf 2008, S. 358;

Prämisse I	Es existieren verschiedene Lebensbereiche (beruflich, sozial, familiär), die zeitlich miteinander kollidieren können und vermehrt ausbalanciert werden müssen, wenn die wissenschaftliche Weiterbildung (zeitweilig) als weiterer Lebensbereich hinzutritt.
Prämisse II	Der Zeiteinsatz ist ein zu verändernder und zu optimierender Faktor für eine gelungene Weiterbildungsteilnahme und kann durch die Angebotsgestaltung verbessert werden.
Prämisse III	Die individuellen Lebenslagen der Teilnehmenden und die Angebotsgestaltung beeinflussen die Lernzeitinvestition.

Abb. 2 Zeitbezogene Prämissen der Zeitvereinbarkeitsstudie. (Eigene Darstellung)

Friebertshäuser 2003, S. 375 f.; Flick 1999, S. 94 ff.). Diese Interviewform ist in der vorliegenden Studie auch aufgrund der Verbundstruktur des Forschungsprojekts gewählt worden: Denn die Interviews sind von den Mitarbeiterinnen der drei Verbundhochschulen durchgeführt worden. Durch den gemeinsam erarbeiteten Fragen- und Themenkorpus, der flexibel gehandhabt werden konnte, gewährleistete ein teilstandardisierter Leitfaden „eine gewisse Vergleichbarkeit der Ergebnisse verschiedener Einzelinterviews" (Friebertshäuser 2003, S. 375).

Der Leitfaden umfasst im Kern fünf Themenfelder mit entsprechenden Hauptfragen, wie Abbildung 3 zeigt.[13] Hinzu kommt eine Einführungsphase in das Interview, in der vor allem formale Aspekte geklärt wurden (Gesprächsdauer, Datenschutz etc.) und eine Abschlussphase für Ergänzungen der Befragten sowie einen Kurzfragebogen zu demographischen und studienangebotsbezogenen Daten für die Auswertung nach den übergeordneten Dimensionen (vgl. Denninger et al. 2020, S. 243 f.).[14]

Die dargelegten temporalen Vorannahmen der „Zeitvereinbarkeitsstudie" mit dem darin eingegangenen Forschungsstand liefern die gegenstandstheoretische Basis für die Konzeption des Leitfadens der teilstandardisierten Interviews.[15] „Dazu gehören Vereinbarkeitsherausforderungen (Nahrstedt et al. 1998), hinderliche und förderliche Teilnahmefaktoren, Zeitkonkurrenzen zwischen Lebensbereichen oder (Lern)Zeitwünsche (Schmidt-Lauff 2011) sowie (zeitliche) Anforderungen an wissenschaftliche Weiterbildungsformate (Präßler 2015)" (Denninger et al. 2020, S. 15). Darüber hinaus sollen sowohl „das individuelle Zeitmanagement und Vereinbarkeitsstrategien, betriebliche wie private Unterstützungsstrukturen, die zeitliche Gestaltung des Weiterbildungsangebots als auch die Zufriedenheit mit dem persönlichen Zeitbudget" (Denninger et al. 2020, S. 12) in den Blick genommen werden.

Obgleich die impliziten zeitbezogenen Vorannahmen der Interviewstudie für diesen Beitrag erarbeitet worden sind, lassen sich die einzelnen Leitfragen den drei Prämissen zuweisen.

---

[13]Dazu sind noch mögliche Unterfragen formuliert worden, die Teilaspekte der Hauptfragen abbilden und bei Bedarf zum Tragen kommen konnten – vor allem wenn die Teilaspekte nicht von der befragten Person selbst zur Hauptfrage benannt wurden (vgl. Denninger et al. 2020, S. 241 f.).

[14]Insofern stellt die Zeitvereinbarkeitsstudie in sich bereits ein Mixed-Methods-Design dar, in dem die Fragebögen Informationen zur Einteilung der Befragten in bestimmte Merkmalsgruppen für die qualitative Auswertung liefern (vgl. Auswertungsdimensionen).

[15]In die Formulierungen und die Anzahl der Hauptfragen des Leitfadens sind die Vorerfahrungen der Forscherinnen aus der ersten Förderphase des Projekts WM³ eingegangen (vgl. Präßler 2015, S. 96 ff., 409 ff.; Habeck und Denninger 2015, S. 193, 432; Kahl et al. 2015, S. 297 ff., 434 ff.).

Nr.	Themenfeld	Leitfrage	Prämisse
-	Einführung/Vorrede	(Dank für Teilnahme Aufzeichnung, Anonymität)	-
1	Einstieg: Motivation zur wissenschaftlichen Weiterbildungsteilnahme	Was hat Sie persönlich veranlasst, [das Angebot] zu besuchen?	I
2	Zeitumfang wissenschaftlicher Weiterbildung (wWB)/ Lernverhalten	Wie gestaltet sich der zeitliche Aufwand für ihr Weiterbildungsstudium gerade?	II
3	Vereinbarkeit der wWB mit anderen Lebensbereichen	Wie vereinbaren Sie das Weiterbildungsstudium zeitlich mit Ihrem Arbeits- und Privatleben? Gibt es besondere Absprachen mit dem Arbeitgeber, dem privaten Umfeld – etwa dem Partner/der Partnerin und der Familie?	III
4	Vereinbarkeitskonflikte & Lösungsformen	Fallen Ihnen Situationen ein, in denen Ihr Studium mit anderen Bereichen kollidiert?	III
5	(Individuelle) Handlungskonzepte und Bewältigungsstrategien	Was sind für Sie generell erfolgreiche Strategien, mit zeitlichen Konflikten umzugehen?	I
6	Zufriedenheit mit Zeitbudget/ Zeitwünsche	Entspricht der Zeitaufwand für die Weiterbildung Ihren Erwartungen?	II
7	Abschluss	(a) Welche Tipps würden Sie anderen Teilnehmenden zur Vereinbarkeit von Weiterbildung mit Arbeit, Freizeit, Familie geben?	I
		(b) Rückblickend auf das Gespräch: Möchten Sie noch etwas ergänzen?	-
-	Kurzfragebogen	(Fragebogen ausfüllen lassen)	-

Abb. 3 Leitfaden „Individuumsbezogene Zeitvereinbarkeitsstudie". Veränderte, ergänzte Fassung nach Denninger et al. (2020, S. 14)

- Prämisse I: Fragen nach der Motivation für die wissenschaftliche Weiterbildungsteilnahme (Nr. 1), den (erfolgreichen) Strategien zum Umgang mit zeitbezogenen Konflikten (Nr. 5) und den Empfehlungen für andere Teilnehmende (Nr. 7a) können Hinweise zum Zusammenspiel der verschiedenen Lebensbereiche (beruflich, sozial, familiär) liefern. Insbesondere können sie die Vereinbarkeitsanforderungen beim (zeitweiligen) Hinzutreten der wissenschaftlichen Weiterbildung als weiterer Lebensbereich verdeutlichen.[16]
- Prämisse II: Auskünfte zur Optimierung der Zeitinvestition sollen die Fragen zum Zeitaufwand der wissenschaftlichen Weiterbildungsaktivität (Nr. 2) und zur erwarteten und tatsächlichen Zeitinvestition (Nr. 6) erbringen.
- Prämisse III: Inwiefern die individuellen Lebenslagen der Teilnehmenden und die Angebotsgestaltung die Lernzeitinvestition beeinflussen, sollen die Fragen zur Vereinbarkeit der wissenschaftlichen Weiterbildung mit dem beruflichen und privaten Lebensbereich (Nr. 3) und zu Konflikten zwischen Weiterbildungsaufgaben bzw. Weiterbildungszeiten und anderen Lebensbereichen und deren Lösungen (Nr. 4) aufzeigen.

Als Erhebungsinstrument zur Erfassung der zeitlichen Vereinbarkeit stellt das Interview eine Form der „nachträglichen Sinnstiftung" (Weick 1995, S. 25) der Lernzeitgestaltung und Lernzeitinvestition dar, da es eine rückblickende Einschätzung von Zeitinvestitionen und temporalen Vereinbarkeitsleistungen aus der subjektiven Perspektive erhebt. Damit ermöglicht es zwar eine eingeschränkte Einschätzung des Lernzeitbudgets, eröffnet jedoch den Zugang zu einer subjektiven Bewertung der Lernzeitverausgabung und zu individuellen Vereinbarkeitsherausforderungen und -strategien.

Lernanspruch als temporaler Einflussfaktor – ein Erhebungsbefund der Leitfadeninterviews

Im Folgenden wird anhand von Interviewmaterial exemplarisch eine individuelle Vereinbarkeitsherausforderung der Lernzeitinvestition für die wissenschaftliche Weiterbildung dargelegt, die als Befund über die zeitbezogenen Vorannahmen der

---

[16]Der Fragebogen zu den demographischen und studienangebotsbezogenen Angaben liefert weitere Informationen zu Prämisse I.

Studie hinausweist. Die inhaltsanalytische Auswertung des Interviewmaterials hat ergeben, dass jenseits der individuellen Lebenslagen ein weiterer personenbezogener Faktor, aus Sicht der Teilnehmenden, Einfluss auf die Vereinbarkeit der wissenschaftlichen Weiterbildung mit den anderen Lebensbereichen und folglich auf die Lernzeitinvestition nimmt: der individuelle Anspruch.

Der weiterführende Zeitbefund im Interviewmaterial

Aus der Perspektive der wissenschaftlichen Weiterbildungsteilnehmenden stellt sich „die Frage (…): Welchen Anspruch hat man ja auch daran?" (Teilnehmende/r 21, Abs. 37). Die eigenen Ambitionen und Einstellungen drücken sich in Bezug auf die wissenschaftliche Weiterbildung in dem zeitlichen Umfang und dem Aufwand für das Lernen aus und schließen die Ziele hinsichtlich der gewünschten Lern- und Prüfungsergebnisse mit ein. Daneben kann sich der eigene Anspruch jedoch auch auf die Erfüllung von Aufgaben aus dem beruflichen oder privaten Lebensbereich beziehen, die dann zuweilen auf Kosten der Weiterbildungslernzeiten priorisiert werden. „Allerdings finden sich auch Befragte, die ihren beruflichen Leistungsanspruch zugunsten der wissenschaftlichen Weiterbildung zeitweilig verringert bzw. mittels Aufgabenverlagerungen bearbeitet haben" (Denninger et al. 2020, S. 67). Die „Querschnittsdimension" (ebd.) des individuellen Anspruchs wird bei unterschiedlichen Fragestellungen und in verschiedenen Phasen des Interviews thematisiert.

„I: Und gibt es da Absprachen mit dem Partner, der Partnerin, Familie, Freunden, die Sie da irgendwie getroffen haben?
B: Die Absprache ist, ich muss wieder eine Hausarbeit schreiben, Du machst für eine Woche die Kinder, Punkt. Ja, also muss man halt, also so platt ist es nicht, es geht schon wieder in die Richtung. Und wenn klar ist, ich sage mal, die Veranstaltungen selber, die lassen sich relativ gut organisieren. Also für mich jetzt dann vom Management her Donnerstag, Freitag, Samstag, wenn es nur ein Block ist, wenn sich da meine Frau drauf einstellen kann und wir das langfristig planen und die Termine stehen ja langfristig, dann ist das managebar. Was wirklich anstrengend ist, ist die, ist das Schreiben der Hausarbeiten. Weil es einfach vom zeitlichen Umfang her sehr, es ist umfangreich, ich hab da auch einen ganz klaren Anspruch. Also ich mache jetzt diesen Studiengang nicht, um danach das Zertifikat in den Händen zu halten, sondern weil mich die Sache interessiert. Deswegen habe ich einen Anspruch an meine Leistung und das, was ich da abgebe. Und ja, und in diesen Zeiten ist es zum Teil, wie gesagt, schon grenzwertig" (Teilnehmende/r 01, Abs. 16 f.).

Auf die Nachfrage zur Vereinbarkeit der wissenschaftlichen Weiterbildung durch Regelungen mit dem beruflichen und privaten Umfeld (Themenfeld Nr. 3) äußert der Befragte, dass schriftliche Prüfungsleistungen (Hausarbeiten) schwieriger zu vereinbaren sind als langfristig planbare Termine von Präsenzveranstaltungen und eine Entlastung bzw. Unterstützung durch die Partnerin erfordern (z. B. Übernahme von Betreuungspflichten). Das hängt nach Sicht des Befragten nicht allein an der geringeren zeitlich-räumlichen Festlegung von Selbstlernphasen und ihren Anforderungen an die Selbstorganisation und das individuelle Zeitmanagement,[17] sondern insbesondere an dem eigenen Anspruch an das (Prüfungs-)Ergebnis. Auf die später im Interview gestellte Frage, ob der Zeitumfang für die wissenschaftliche Weiterbildung den Erwartungen entspricht (Themenfeld Nr. 6), wird explizit ein temporaler Konflikt benannt, der aus den eigenen Leistungszielen erwächst.

„Ich meine, ich wusste, dass Arbeiten auf mich zukommen, aber das ist vom zeitlichen Umfang her schon mehr, als ich so mir vielleicht erhofft hatte, auch, weil ich wie ich vorhin gesagt habe, einen bestimmten Anspruch habe und nicht Arbeiten schreibe, um sie geschrieben zu haben, sondern Arbeiten, wenn ich sie schon schreibe, schreibe, um die wirklich auch sehr gut zu machen. Und das ist auch so ein innerer Konflikt zwischen meinem Anspruch an mich selber und einem anderen Teil, der in mir sagt: „Du hast auch noch Familie und jetzt gebe dieses Ding halt so ab und nimm halt mal eine 3 in Kauf." Bis jetzt hat die Seite noch nie gewonnen, aber den Konflikt gibt es" (Teilnehmende/r 01, Abs. 28 f.).

Bei mehreren Befragten geraten das Lerninteresse und der Leistungs- bzw. Qualitätsanspruch an die wissenschaftliche Weiterbildungstätigkeit in einen Konflikt mit dem Anliegen, Zeit mit dem privaten Umfeld (Familie, Freunden) zu verbringen. Solche Vereinbarkeitskonflikte lösen manche der Befragten zugunsten des Lernerfolgs in der wissenschaftlichen Weiterbildung, andere zugunsten ihrer Betreuungspflichten und Familienzeiten.

„Und ich denke, am schwierigsten ist es halt, Menschen deswegen zurückzustellen. Also meine Mutter wird nicht zurückgestellt, basta. Wenn jetzt jemand ist, der kleine Kinder hat und so weiter, das kann man auch nicht wirklich zurückstellen" (Teilnehmende/r 12, Abs. 91).[18]

---

[17]Ausführlich zu den Vereinbarkeitsherausforderungen von Selbstlernphasen aus Sicht der wissenschaftlichen Weiterbildungsteilnehmenden vgl. Denninger et al. 2019; Kahl 2019, S. 191 ff.

[18]Antwort zu Themenfeld Nr. 7a (Empfehlungen für andere Teilnehmende).

Neben einer grundlegenden, individuellen Prioritätensetzung spielen zudem situative Bedarfe und Verpflichtungen eine wichtige Rolle, wenn es um die persönlichen Relevanzsetzungen geht.

„Jetzt am Wochenende als kleines Beispiel wollte ich eigentlich eben meine eine Hausarbeit zu Ende schreiben und dafür hätte ich zwei Tage eingeplant und meine Frau wollte eigentlich zu ihren Eltern fahren. Ja aber nun war sie krank und ich saß mit beiden Kindern alleine da. Eine kranke Frau und zwei schreiende Kinder, da war nicht eine Minute für die Hausarbeit" (Teilnehmende/r 02, Abs. 09).[19]

Hinsichtlich der Vereinbarkeit von wissenschaftlicher Weiterbildung und beruflichem Lebensbereich zeigt sich ein vergleichbares Bild.[20] Bei manchen Teilnehmenden liegt die Priorität auf der Weiterbildungsaktivität, bei anderen auf der Erwerbstätigkeit, wobei es kurzfristig oder phasenweise zu Verschiebungen der Schwerpunktsetzung kommen kann – abhängig davon, welcher Lebensbereich besondere Aufmerksamkeit erfordert und Anforderungen stellt (im Beruf z. B. Stoßzeiten, Krankheitsvertretungen, Aufgabenerweiterung, in der Weiterbildung v. a. Prüfungsphasen, Blockveranstaltungen).

„Also, ich sage, okay, ich muss nicht immer so viel machen, also das ist jetzt 1,5 Jahre, da ist es halt so und zwar, dass ich, also in dem Sinne im Geschäft Abstriche gemacht habe, mich da anders organisiert habe, nicht alles selber gemacht habe, sondern auch delegiert habe" (Teilnehmende/r 18, Abs. 51).[21]

„(…) auch wenn ich weiß, ich muss morgen eine Arbeit abgeben, sitze ich trotzdem abends da und mache noch drei Stunden meinen [Arbeitgeber-]kram oder so, weil ich halt meine, dass ich das auch erledigen muss" (Teilnehmende/r 03, Abs. 13).[22]

---

[19]Antwort zu Themenfeld Nr. 3 (Vereinbarkeit der wissenschaftlichen Weiterbildung).

[20]Personen mit Familienpflichten sind von zeitlichen Vereinbarkeitsherausforderungen in besonderem Maße betroffen (vgl. Schulmeister und Metzger 2011; Nahrstedt et al. 1998; Schmidt-Lauff 2008; Präßler 2015). Es lassen sich nach wie vor geschlechtsbezogene Differenzen in der Zeitinvestition für Betreuungs- und Haushaltstätigkeiten finden, denen zufolge weibliche Personen mehr Zeit für diese Tätigkeiten aufwenden, selbst wenn sie (vollzeit-)erwerbstätig sind (vgl. Anger und Kottwitz 2009; Grunow 2014; Keller 2014). Die Kategorie Geschlecht ist in dieser Studie und Auswertung nicht gesondert berücksichtigt worden, da zunächst andere Auswertungsdimensionen wie vorhandene und nicht-vorhandene Familienpflichten bearbeitet wurden (vgl. Denninger et. al. 2017, S. 188 ff.). Darauf aufbauend sollten geschlechtsbezogene Untersuchungen zur Weiterbildungsentscheidung und -teilnahme erfolgen.

[21]Antwort zu Leitfrage 4 (Vereinbarkeitskonflikte und Lösungsformen).
[22]Antwort zu Leitfrage 4 (Vereinbarkeitskonflikte und Lösungsformen).

Insgesamt lässt sich mittels der qualitativen „Zeitvereinbarkeitsstudie" feststellen, dass „der eigene Anspruch der Weiterbildungsteilnehmenden (…) als selbstständiger konfliktfördernder Faktor" (Denninger et al. 2020, S. 58) in Erscheinung tritt und insofern bedeutsam für die Lernzeitverausgabung sein kann.

Erweiterung der dritten zeitbezogenen Prämisse

In Bezug auf die methodisch-konzeptionelle Analyse der Interviews ist festzustellen, dass der individuelle Anspruch an die eigenen Tätigkeiten – besonders an die wissenschaftliche Weiterbildung – weder Bestandteil der zeitbezogenen Vorannahmen noch der Haupt- und Nachfragen des Leitfadens und der Interviewdurchführung gewesen ist. Hinsichtlich der Positionierung im Interviewverlauf zeigt sich zudem, dass der individuelle Qualitäts- und Leistungsanspruch gegenüber den eigenen Aufgaben in den Antworten zu verschiedenen (Leit-)Fragen thematisiert worden ist. Dazu gehören (Nach-)Fragen zum erwarteten Zeitaufwand, zur Vereinbarkeit der wissenschaftlichen Weiterbildung mit den anderen Lebensbereichen, zu Vereinbarkeitskonflikten zwischen den Lebensbereichen bis hin zu den Empfehlungen für andere Teilnehmende in der Abschlussphase der Interviews.

Der Befund zum eigenen wissenschaftlichen Weiterbildungsanspruch verweist auf die Möglichkeiten eigener Themensetzungen seitens der Befragten in den teilstandardisierten Interviews der „Zeitvereinbarkeitsstudie". Damit hat die Leitfadenerhebung (und ihre inhaltsanalytische Auswertung) ein Ergebnis zur Lernzeitinvestition von wissenschaftlichen Weiterbildungsteilnehmenden erbracht, das die dargelegten zeitbezogenen Prämissen erweitert.[23] Es lässt sich dahin gehend zusammenfassen, dass ein hoher Qualitäts- und Leistungsanspruch an die wissenschaftliche Weiterbildungsaktivität mit einer höheren Lernzeitinvestition und folglich vermehrten Zeitkonflikten mit anderen Lebensbereichen einhergeht; umgedreht kann ein hoher Anspruch an andere Tätigkeitsfelder dazu führen, die Zeitressourcen für die wissenschaftliche Weiterbildung zu verringern. Mit seinem Einfluss auf die zeitliche Vereinbarkeit der verschiedenen Lebensbereiche stellt der Befund eine Ergänzung der dritten zeitbezogenen Prämisse dar. Die überarbeitete und erweiterte zeitbezogene These lautet : Die individuellen

---

[23]Die Thematik ist bisher im Rahmen der „Vereinbarkeitskonflikte" behandelt worden (vgl. Denninger et al. 2017, S. 14, 58 ff.).

Lernansprüche und Lebenslagen der Teilnehmenden sowie die Angebotsgestaltung können die Lernzeitinvestition in der wissenschaftlichen Weiterbildung beeinflussen.

Fazit

Die methodisch-konzeptionelle Reflexion der „Zeitvereinbarkeitsstudie" zeigt, wie mittels einer qualitativen Interviewbefragung individuelle Handlungsweisen zur Zeitverausgabung und subjektive Einschätzungen der temporalen Vereinbarkeitsherausforderungen in den Blick genommen werden können. Das Forschungsprojekt lässt anhand der Fragestellung, Zielsetzung und Auswertungsdimensionen drei implizite zeitbezogene Prämissen erkennen, die sich auch im Erhebungsinstrument des Interviewleitfadens wiederfinden. Es konnte gezeigt werden, dass die Studie dennoch ein Material generiert hat, das jenseits der gegenstandstheoretisch gestützten, zeitbezogenen Vorannahmen, der Leitfragen und dem (zunächst deduktiv gebildeten) Kategoriensystem in der Auswertung zusätzliche zeitbezogene Querschnittsthemen eröffnet hat.

Der exemplarisch aufgezeigte Zeitbefund zur Bedeutung des eigenen Lernanspruchs für die Weiterbildungszeitverausgabung kann mit der Interviewführung – den offenen Fragestellungen und einer flexiblen Handhabung des Leitfadens – zusammenhängen, die den Befragten Gelegenheiten eröffnet hat, eigene Themen einzubringen. Die Relevanzsetzungen konnten mit der kategorienbasierten, strukturierten Inhaltsanalyse in einer induktiven Kategorienbildung (vgl. Mayring 2016, S. 115) herausgearbeitet werden. Demnach waren die impliziten „lockeren Hypothesen" (Hopf 1978, S. 99) der „Zeitvereinbarkeitsstudie" im Forschungsprozess nicht „so dominant (…), dass das Material stromlinienförmig interpretiert" (Schmidt 2013, S. 485) worden ist. Vielmehr konnte mittels der Interviews über den Erwartungshorizont hinaus eine inhaltliche Erweiterung der zeitbezogenen Prämissen aus der individuellen Perspektive der Befragten erfolgen (siehe „Erweiterung der dritten zeitbezogenen Prämisse"). Zur qualitativen Erforschung von Zeitinvestitionen in der wissenschaftlichen Weiterbildung zeigt die Studie auf, dass mit der Erfassung von subjektiven Einstellungen und Situationsdeutungen relevante Zusammenhänge der Lernzeitinvestition in den Blick genommen werden, die zu einer Erweiterung und Ergänzung vorhandener zeitbezogener Weiterbildungsbefunde beitragen können. Daneben liefert die „Individuumsbezogene Zeitbudgetstudie" durch das Mixed-Methods-Design einen eigenen Mehrwert. Die Verbindung der qualitativen und quantitativen Ergebnisse der Studien zeigt unter anderem, dass die zeitliche Vereinbarkeit während der Weiterbildungsteilnahme beständig auszuhandeln ist (vgl. Denninger et al. 2020, S. 211) und die Qualität der Lernzeiten bedeutsam ist (vgl. Kahl 2019, S. 195 f.; Denninger et al. 2019, S. 121).

Konkret leistet der dargelegte Befund der „Zeitvereinbarkeitsstudie" einen Beitrag zur hochschulischen Weiterbildungsforschung im Sinne einer „Partizipationsforschung über Zeitstunden und Weiterbildungsteilnahme" (Schmidt-Lauff 2018, S. 335), insbesondere zur wissenschaftlichen Weiterbildungsforschung im Bereich der „‚Blackbox' Selbststudium" (vgl. Behm und Beditsch 2013, S. 25). Die Überschneidungen mit Befunden aus anderen Weiterbildungsformaten (vgl. Schmidt-Lauff 2008, S. 406 ff.; Kade und Seitter 1996, S. 215 ff.) verweisen auf vergleichbare zeitbezogene Vereinbarkeitsherausforderungen und „Konstitutionsleistungen" (Kade und Seitter 1996, S. 157) erwachsener Weiterbildungsteilnehmender, die sich berufsbegleitend weiterqualifizieren. In zukünftigen Studien ist zu untersuchen, welche Gemeinsamkeiten und Eigenheiten verschiedene Weiterbildungsformate bezüglich zeitlicher Konstitutionsbedingungen aufweisen, beispielsweise welchen Stellenwert der eigene Lernanspruch bei verschiedenen wissenschaftlichen Weiterbildungsformaten (Master, Zertifikatskurse) einnimmt.

Literatur

Anger, S., Kottwitz, A. (2009). Mehr Hausarbeit, weniger Verdienst. *Wochenbericht des Deutschen Instituts für Wirtschaftsforschung DIW Berlin 6*, 102–109. https://www.diw.de/documents/publikationen/73/diw_01.c.94527.de/09-6-1.pdf. Zugegriffen: 20.09.2019.

Antoni, C. H., Friedrich, P., Haunschild, A., Josten, M., Meyer, R. (Hrsg.) (2014). *Work-Learn-Life-Balance in der Wissensarbeit. Herausforderungen, Erfolgsfaktoren und Gestaltungshilfen für die betriebliche Praxis*. Wiesbaden: Springer VS.

Argelander, H. (1970). Das Erstinterview in der Psychotherapie. Darmstadt: Wiss. Buchges.

Behm, W. & Beditsch, C. (2013). Workloaderfassung im berufsbegleitenden Fernstudium. *Hochschule und Weiterbildung 1*, 23–29. https://www.pedocs.de/volltexte/2014/8897/pdf/HuW_2013_1_Behm_Beditsch.pdf. Zugegriffen: 24. Juni 2019.

Böhm, S. (2015). Beruf und Privatleben. Ein Vereinbarkeitsproblem? Entstehungsfaktoren von erwerbsarbeitsbedingten Abstimmungsproblemen und Konflikten im Privatleben von Beschäftigten in Deutschland. Wiesbaden: Springer VS.

Brinkmann, T. (2014). Seiltanz zwischen Privat- und Erwerbsleben. Anspruchsdiskrepanzen und Selbstsorgedilemmata Kinderloser im Gesundheitsdienstleistungsbereich. Baden-Baden: Nomos.

Denninger, A., Kahl, R., & Präßler, S. (2017). Individuumsbezogene Zeitbudgetstudie – Konzeptionen zur Erhebung der Zeitverausgabung von Teilnehmenden wissenschaftlicher Weiterbildung. In: W. Seitter (Hrsg.), *Zeit in der wissenschaftlichen Weiterbildung* (S. 59–93). Wiesbaden: Springer VS.

Denninger, A., Döring, A., & Kahl, R. (2019). Räumliche Lernzeitverausgabung des Selbststudiums in der wissenschaftlichen Weiterbildung. In: W. Seitter (Hrsg.), *Räume in der wissenschaftlichen Weiterbildung* (S. 99–125). Wiesbaden: Springer VS.

Denninger, A., Kahl, R., & Präßler, S. (2020). Individuumsbezogene Zeitbudgetstudie. Zeitvereinbarkeit und Lernzeitbudget in der wissenschaftlichen Weiterbildung. Wiesbaden: Springer VS.

Flick, Uwe (1999). *Qualitative Forschung. Theorie, Methoden, Anwendung in Psychologie und Sozialwissenschaften*. 4. Aufl. Hamburg: Rowohlt.

Flick, U., Kardorff, E. & Steinke, I. (2015). Was ist qualitative Forschung? Einleitung und Überblick. In: Dies. (Hrsg.), *Qualitative Forschung. Ein Handbuch* (S. 13–29). 11. Aufl., Hamburg: Rowohlt.

Friebertshäuser, B. (2003). Interviewtechniken – ein Überblick. In: B. Friebertshäuser & Prengel, A. (Hrsg.), *Handbuch qualitative Forschungsmethoden in der Erziehungswissenschaft* (S. 371–396). Weinheim u. München: Juventa.

Friebertshäuser, B., & Langer, A. (2013). Interviewformen und Interviewpraxis. In: B. Friebertshäuser, Langer, A. & Prengel, A. (Hrsg.), *Handbuch qualitative Forschungsmethoden in der Erziehungswissenschaft* (S. 437–457). Weinheim u. Basel: Beltz Juventa

Grunow, D. (2014). Die Korrespondenz von normativen Vorstellungen und Handeln: das Beispiel männlicher Hausarbeit. *Comparative Population Studies – Zeitschrift für Bevölkerungswissenschaft 39*, 479–520.

Habeck, S., & Denninger, A. (2015). Potentialanalyse. Forschungsbericht zu Potentialen institutioneller Zielgruppen. In: W. Seitter, Schemmann, M., & Vossebein, U. (Hrsg.), *Zielgruppen in der wissenschaftlichen Weiterbildung. Empirische Studien zu Bedarf, Potential und Akzeptanz* (S. 189–290). Wiesbaden: Springer VS.

Hopf, C. (1978). Die Pseudo-Exploration. Überlegungen zur Technik qualitativer Interviews in der Sozialforschung. *Zeitschrift für Soziologie 2*, 97–115.

Hopf, C. (2008). Qualitative Interviews. Ein Überblick. In: Flick, U., Kardorff, E. v., & Steinke, I. (Hrsg.), *Qualitative Forschung. Ein Handbuch* (S. 349–360). 6. Aufl., Hamburg: Rowohlt.

Kade, J. (2007). Der Umgang mit der Unwahrscheinlichkeit des Wissens: (Selbst-)Beobachtung in der Forschungskommunikation. In: J. Kade & Seitter, W. (Hrsg.), *Umgang mit Wissen: Recherchen zur Empirie des Pädagogischen* (S. 329–345). Leverkusen: Budrich.

Kade, J. & Seitter, W. (1996). *Lebenslanges Lernen. Mögliche Bildungswelten. Erwachsenenbildung, Biographie und Alltag*. Opladen: Leske & Budrich.

Kahl, R., Lengler, A., & Präßler, S. (2015). Akzeptanzanalyse. Forschungsbericht zur Akzeptanz innerhochschulischer Zielgruppen. In: W. Seitter, Schemmann, M., & Vossebein, U. (Hrsg.), *Zielgruppen in der wissenschaftlichen Weiterbildung. Empirische Studien zu Bedarf, Potential und Akzeptanz* (S. 291–444). Wiesbaden: Springer VS.

Kahl, R. (2019). Lernzeiten und Lernräume etablieren. Gelingensbedingungen zur Teilnahme an wissenschaftlicher Weiterbildung. *Zeitschrift für Weiterbildungsforschung*. 42(2), 183–199. doi: https://doi.org/10.1007/s40955-019-0139-7

Keller, M. (2014). Vereinbarkeit von Familie und Beruf. Ergebnisse des Mikrozensus 2013. Statistisches Bundesamt, Wirtschaft und Statistik. https://www.destatis.de/

DE/Methoden/WISTA-Wirtschaft-und-Statistik/2014/12/vereinbarkeit-familie-beruf-122014.pdf?__blob=publicationFile. Zugegriffen: 20.09.2019.
Keller, M., Haustein, T. (2012). Vereinbarkeit von Familie und Beruf. Ergebnisse des Mikrozensus 2010. Hg. v. Statistisches Bundesamt (Wirtschaft und Statistik). https://www.destatis.de/DE/Publikationen/WirtschaftStatistik/Bevoelkerung/VereinbarkeitFamilieBeruf_112.pdf?__blob=publicationFile. Zugegriffen: 07.01.2016.
KMK (2001). Sachstands- und Problembericht zur „Wahrnehmung wissenschaftlicher Weiterbildung an Hochschulen" (Beschluss der Kultusministerkonferenz vom 21.09.2001). https://www.kmk.org/fileadmin/Dateien/veroeffentlichungen_beschluesse/2001/2001_09_21-Problembericht-wiss-Weiterbildung-HS.pdf. Zugegriffen: 26. Juni 2019.
Kuckartz, U. (2014). *Mixed-Methods. Methodologie, Forschungsdesign und Analyseverfahren.* Wiesbaden: Springer VS.
Lüders, M. (1995). *Zeit, Subjektivität und Bildung: die Bedeutung des Zeitbegriffs für die Pädagogik.* Weinheim: Dt. Studien-Verl.
Lobe, C. (2015). *Hochschulweiterbildung als biografische Transition. Teilnehmerperspektiven auf berufsbegleitende Studienangebote.* Wiesbaden: Springer VS.
Mayring, P. (2016). *Einführung in die qualitative Sozialforschung. Eine Anleitung zu qualitativem Denken.* 6. Aufl. Weinheim: Beltz.
Mertens, A. (2013). Studium und Erwerbstätigkeit. *Beiträge zur Hochschulforschung 4*, 34–53. https://www.bzh.bayern.de/uploads/media/4-2013-gesamt.pdf. Zugegriffen: 26. Juni 2019.
Middendorff, E., Apolinarski, B., Poskowsky, J., Kandulla, M. (2013). Die wirtschaftliche und soziale Lage der Studierenden in Deutschland 2012. 20. Sozialerhebung des Deutschen Studentenwerks durchgeführt durch das HIS-Institut für Hochschulforschung. Hrsg. v. Bundesministerium für Bildung und Forschung. Bonn, Berlin. https://www.sozialerhebung.de/sozialerhebung/archiv/soz_19_haupt. Zugegriffen: 29. März 2019.
Müller, A. (2002). Die Zeit als implizite Kategorie der pädagogischen Anthropologie. Eine pädagogische Anthropologie der Zeit. Hamburg: Kovač.
Nahrstedt, W., Brinkmann, D., Kadel, V., Kuper, K., Schmidt, M. (1998). *Neue Zeitfenster für Weiterbildung. Temporale Muster der Angebotsgestaltung und Zeitpräferenzen der Teilnehmer im Wandel.* Abschlussbericht des Forschungsprojektes: Entwicklung und begleitende Untersuchung von neuen Konzepten der Erwachsenenbildung unter besonderer Berücksichtigung des Aspekts des lebenslangen Lernens und des institutionellen Umgangs mit veränderten temporalen Mustern der Angebotsnutzung; mit Beiträgen der Fachtagung „Zeit für Weiterbildung" am 10.9.1998 in der VHS Rheine. (Dokumentation/IFKA, Bd. 20), Bielefeld: IFKA.
Philipps-Universität Marburg, Justus-Liebig-Universität Gießen, Technische Hochschule Mittelhessen (2014). *Verbundprojekt WM³ – Weiterbildung Mittelhessen.* Projektantrag.
Präßler, S. (2015). Bedarfsanalyse. Forschungsbericht zu Bedarfen individueller Zielgruppen. In: W. Seitter, Schemmann, M., & Vossebein, U. (Hrsg.), *Zielgruppen in der wissenschaftlichen Weiterbildung. Empirische Studien zu Bedarf, Potential und Akzeptanz* (S. 61–187). Wiesbaden: Springer VS.
Projektgruppe Studierbarkeit (2007). Studierbarkeit an der Humboldt-Universität. Wie läuft das Experiment „Studienreform"? Ergebnisse der Umfrage aus dem Sommersemester

2006. Berlin. https://www.studierbarkeit.de/fileadmin/studierbarkeit/pdf/HU_Studie/Studierbarkeit_2007_color.pdf. Zugegriffen: 21. März 2019.

Rahnfeld, R. & Schiller, J. (2015). Der Zugang nicht-traditioneller Studierender zur wissenschaftlichen Weiterbildung. Erfordernisse an die Didaktik in der Studiengangsentwicklung. *Beiträge zur Hochschulforschung 37*, 26–50.

Ramm, M., Multrus, F., Bargel, T., Schmidt, M. (2014). Studiensituation und studentische Orientierungen. 12. Studierendensurvey an Universitäten und Fachhochschulen. Kurzfassung. Hrsg. v. Bundesministerium für Bildung und Forschung. Bonn, Berlin. https://www.bmbf.de/pub/Studierendensurvey_Ausgabe_12_Kurzfassung.pdf. Zugegriffen: 21. März 2019.

Schirmer, K. (2017). Work-Learn-Life-Balance. Temporale Vereinbarkeitsstrategien von berufsbegleitenden Studierenden in der wissenschaftlichen Weiterbildung. In: W. Seitter (Hrsg.), *Zeit in der wissenschaftlichen Weiterbildung* (S. 21–46). Wiesbaden: Springer VS.

Schmidt, C. (2013). Auswertungstechniken für Leitfadeninterviews. In: B. Friebertshäuser, Langer, A. & A. Prengel (Hrsg.), *Handbuch qualitative Forschungsmethoden in der Erziehungswissenschaft* (S. 473–486). Weinheim, München: Juventa.

Schmidt-Lauff, S. (2008). *Zeit für Bildung im Erwachsenenalter. Interdisziplinäre und empirische Zugänge*. Münster, New York, München, Berlin: Waxmann.

Schmidt-Lauff, S. (2011). Zeitfragen und Temporalität in der Erwachsenenbildung. In: R. Tippelt (Hrsg.), *Handbuch Erwachsenenbildung/Weiterbildung* (S. 213–228). 5. Aufl. Wiesbaden: Springer VS.

Schmidt-Lauff, S. (2018). Zeittheoretische Implikationen in der Erwachsenenbildung. In: R. Tippelt & A. von Hippel (Hrsg.). *Handbuch Erwachsenenbildung/Weiterbildung* (S. 319–338). Wiesbaden: Springer VS.

Schulmeister, R., & Metzger, C. (2011). Die Workload im Bachelor: Ein empirisches Forschungsprojekt. In: R. Schulmeister & Metzger, C. (Hrsg.). *Die Workload im Bachelor: Zeitbudget und Studierverhalten. Eine empirische Studie* (S. 13–128). Münster: Waxmann.

Schütze, F. (1983). Biographieforschung und narratives Interview. *Neue Praxis 13*, 283–293.

Seitter, W. (2010). Zeitformen (in) der Erwachsenenbildung. Eine historische Skizze. *Zeitschrift für Pädagogik 56*, 305–316.

Seitter, W., Schemmann, M., & U. Vossebein (2015). Einleitung. In: W. Seitter, Schemmann, M., & Vossebein, U. (Hrsg.), *Zielgruppen in der wissenschaftlichen Weiterbildung. Empirische Studien zu Bedarf, Potential und Akzeptanz* (S. 15–23). Wiesbaden: Springer VS.

Seitter, W. (2017). Zeit in der wissenschaftlichen Weiterbildung. Eine Einleitung. In: W. Seitter (Hrsg.), *Zeit in der wissenschaftlichen Weiterbildung* (S. 9–18). Wiesbaden: Springer VS.

Seitter, W., Friese, M. & P. Robinson (2018). Wissenschaftliche Weiterbildung zwischen Implementierung und Optimierung. Eine Einleitung. In: Dies. (Hrsg.). *Wissenschaftliche Weiterbildung zwischen Implementierung und Optimierung* (S. 1–3). Wiesbaden: Springer VS.

Sommerfeldt, H., & Höllermann, P. (2016). Trendstudie Fernstudium 2016. Ergebnisse der Fernstudienumfrage 2014 zu aktuellen Trends und Entwicklungen in deutschsprachigen

Fernstudienprogrammen. Hrsg. v. Internationale Hochschule Bad Honnef: Bad Honnef. https://static1.squarespace.com/static/57286de5e707ebe0b4240685/t/57bda8233e00bea28d5d9759/1472579194462/2016+-+Trendstudie+Fernstudium+2016+-+HQ.pdf. Zugegriffen: 21. März 2019.

Weick, K. (1995). *Sensemaking in Organizations*. Thousand Oaks, London, New Delhi: Sage.

Weßler-Poßberg, D. (2014). *Betriebliche Angebote zur Vereinbarkeit von Familie und Beruf im Spannungsverhältnis von Geschlecht und Qualifikation. Fallstudien zur Umsetzung, Nutzung und Wirkung der Instrumente betrieblicher Familienpolitik in Organisationen der privaten Wirtschaft und des öffentlichen Sektors.* Duisburg: Universitätsbibliothek Duisburg-Essen.

Wonneberger, A., Weidtmann, K., Hoffmann, K., & Draheim, S. (2015). Die Öffnung von Hochschulen durch flexible Studienformate am Beispiel zweier neuer weiterbildender Masterstudiengänge. *Beiträge zur Hochschulforschung 37*, 70–91.

Construction of Schooling Time as Part of Mothers' Identities

Lyudmila Nurse

Abstract

The chapter approaches the nature of time associated with the school routine as part of mothers' identities and their distinctive parenting styles. The mothers' narratives are analysed from the perspective of their personal experiences that are embedded in biographical reflections of their own schooling in the past and expectations for their children's future. The time of schooling is understood as exploratory, family time, a time of strengthening emotional bonds between mother and child and mothers' identities and parenting. The analysis contributes to understanding of structuring (constructing) of schooling time as deeply rooted in mothers' biographical experience and their meaning of "family time". Analysis in this chapter is based on a set of auto-biographical interviews with mothers with pre-school and primary school age children conducted by the author in the ISOTIS project (ISOTIS-"Inclusive Education and Social Support to tackle Inequalities in Society" EC Horizon -2020 project, grant agreement No.727069.) in the North West of England in 2018.

Keywords

Identities · Mothers · Parenting styles · Schooling time · Family time · Biographical

L. Nurse (✉)
Oxford XXI think tank, Thame, Oxfordshire, UK
E-Mail: lyudmilanurse@oxford-xxi.org

© Springer Fachmedien Wiesbaden GmbH, ein Teil von Springer Nature 2020
E. Schilling und M. O'Neill (Hrsg.), *Frontiers in Time*
Research – Einführung in die interdisziplinäre Zeitforschung,
https://doi.org/10.1007/978-3-658-31252-7_13

This chapter examines relativistic time from the perspective of mothers' everyday life routine associated with parenting of their primary school age children. Although schooling time is more traditionally associated with a time of learning, part of educational institution's time, and as 'a resource that directly translates into student learning' (Compton-Lilly 2016, p. 589), schooling time is also an integral part of family daily routine (getting ready for school, getting to school by walking or driving, doing homework). It is both positivistic and socially constructed: positivistic in the Newtonian understanding of time measurable by clocks, calendars (Wingard 2007, p. 76), school terms and holidays, and socially constructed time constituted through the interaction of individuals (Mead 1932). For example, a mother and a child interaction during their walk to school explains it this way: "How long does it take you to walk your children to school?"—"... *it depends how many spiders' webs they see, because if they see a spider web we have to stop and hunt for the spider...*".

In education and human development studies, biographical methods have been long used to understand accounts of life experience of individuals within the education system, teachers, students, learners (Roberts 2002; Wright 2011; Waller 2010), but less so the life experiences of those who are not directly involved in teaching or studying, but whose involvement in the education system is crucial. Scholars of parenting cultures argue that parenting styles are crucial for understanding the children's educational and life perspectives (Hayes 1996; Lee et al. 2014; Furedi 2007); and types of interactions in children's immediate environment-family, in which children grow up (Bronfenbrenner and Ceci 1994; Bronfenbrenner and Morris 2006). The Bronfenbrenner's theoretical model of bio-ecological systems of personal development was an overarching conceptual framework of the ISOTIS project in the development of its empirical studies and of the analysis of children's close environment (microsystems) in which they grow up. The model identifies the importance of recurrent interactions of persons within their immediate environment across the entire lifespan. These individual-level interactions within the immediate environment are referred to as proximal processes. The type of interactions between parents and their children in relation to the children's schooling time is a reflection on the ways parents foresee their parental roles as 'co-educators', how schooling time is engrained in their identities and views about their children's future.

The importance to appreciate the identities of parents as parents and as co-'educators' is a relatively new area of educational research (Furedi 2008; Lee et al. 2014). The importance of understanding the identities of parents by the schools has become part of major educational studies, but mostly from the perspective of schools and education. For example, research into parents involvement in their children's schooling, as demonstrated in a series of studies (Hornby 2011; Hornby and Blackwell 2018), has identified a number of factors that negatively affect parents' relationship with their children's schooling, including those parents' own negative experience of school, parents' personal issues (divorce, illiteracy etc.) and parents' difficulties over the course of their lives. Factors such as lack of time, experience of education or confidence also play a significant role along with the personal experience, demographic and social class factors (Hornby and Blackwell 2018; Jackson 2013). The other studies on women's biographical experiences of education, for example Waller's study of educational biographies of women who are returning to Higher Education programmes as mature students, demonstrate strong connection between biographical life circumstances and changing identities through "re-engagement with education", due to their own re-entering the education systems (Waller 2010).

In this context the meaning of schooling time could be explained through the type of parenting and the phenomenon of "intensive parenting" (Hayes 1996; Furedi 2007; Faircloth 2014) which assumes that parents spend significant amount of time with their children. Furedi in particular refers to "parenting on demand", as a new concept in child rearing, due to the changing expectations of society by observing that "the roles of the modern parent stretch from that of a chauffeur, who transports the kids from one activity to another, to an educator, who supplements formal schooling" (Furedi 2008, p. 71). It has also been observed by recent research that especially middle-class parents spend more time with their children than their own parents did (Hochschild 2003). Both working and stay at home mothers spend more time caring for their children than their own mothers did (Furedi 2008, p. 94).

However, research into parenting of working class mothers, lone mothers have also shown that they are also intensively involved in their children schooling (Reay 2007; May 2010), but are not so often a prime attention of the research as regards their experiences in arranging and managing their children's schooling time within their own daily routine. The main issues addressed within the scope of this chapter are challenges and opportunities of interpreting biographical data on "schooling time" and identities of mothers of primary school age children from the native-born population (without immigrant background) from a low income, disadvantaged families.

Methodology

The biographical data used in the analysis are biographical narratives of British, white, native-born mothers from low-income families who have pre-school and primary school age children. The interviews were conducted by the author in 2018 in Greater London and North-West England as part of the ISOTIS qualitative study of parents (www.isotis.org). Use of the biographical approach in the ISOTIS qualitative study of native born, low social and economic status background families enabled the research team to understand huge variety and "the changing experiences and outlooks of individuals in their daily lives, what they see as important, and how to provide interpretations of the accounts they give of their past, present and future" (Roberts 2002). We looked at how mothers' biographies and own educational experiences intersect with their children's schooling and how their children's schooling time interacts with mothers' own time. Analysis of the qualitative biographical interviews in England was focused on a number of research questions: How do women adjust and perceive their time and space when they have young children? How do their children's learning and educational needs fit in their daily routine? How do they spend time when they are on "school duties" and 'off school duties"? Qualitative in-depth interviews were conceptualised and designed to examine resources (both financial and cultural capital) and experiences of parents from socially and economically disadvantaged groups, related to the preschool and primary school system. Qualitative interviews were conducted with mothers who had participated in the preceding quantitative study, by applying strict selection criteria as regards their socio-economic and ethnic origin (Nurse and Melhuish 2018).

The interview structure was developed by the author and was drawn upon a method of an (auto) biographical interview (Schuetze 2008) which incorporates in its structure time and space for clarification of spontaneous narration about mothers' biographical circumstances, school experiences, families and children (Nurse and Melhuish 2018). The topics and prompts for the semi-structured part of the interview were designed to specifically address issues of parenting and the environment in which children are brought up. One of the crucial points in the interviewing technique was that the qualitative biographical interview was the second interview with each of the selected mothers; the first was a structured interview, a part of the quantitative survey, which preceded the qualitative study. Each interview started by inviting the interviewee to speak about their own life in their own words, their families and their own children. Mothers were also keen to talk about issues related to their children's schooling. Although mothers were asked to talk about the children, whom the research project identified as "target" child to maintain the comparative perspective of children of the two age groups

(3–5 and 6–11 years old) across the project, mothers were also reflecting on the other children in their family (their own or step children).

Individual interview files were transcribed and coded using NVivo 11/12 software. Individual coding trees were gradually merged for comparative analysis, and analysed by the emerging themes from the spontaneous narration. These were subsequently merged with responses to the semi-structured part of the interviews.

Case Study

For the case study, two types of narrative data were used: analysis of the biographical account of each mother, which created a time-line of their lives and led to the creation of their biographical profiles. The second type of data were coded data which relates to their daily routine and schooling time of their children within their daily routine. This coded data covers both parts of the interview spontaneous narration and the semi-structured part.

For the case study, narratives of two British, white, native-born mothers were selected. They both live in North-West England, where they were born and went to school. They also have similar working-class backgrounds and experienced some traumatic family events due to death of a parent or broken between parents' relationship. Although 'Maria[1]' and 'Linda' (not real names of the informants) are not contemporaries, Maria is ten years older than Linda, their lives and everyday life routine seems to be organised around the school time of their children: however the social construction of parenting time differs significantly.

Maria is in her late 30's; she is married with three children. Maria's husband lives in the same house, but due to his recent serious illness, he is now mostly confined to the house. Maria is the only carer for her children and her husband which at the present (at the time of interview) is her full-time occupation. The second mother—Linda is in her late 20's and a single mother who lives with her two children on her own while also running a makeshift beauty services business from home, to save on paying a rent at a beauty salon, but mainly to be able to organise her time around the schooling time of her children. Her relationship with her ex-partner broke down some time ago; she admitted that she keeps in touch with her ex-partner "for the sake of her own children". However his

---

[1]Here and throughout the text only pseudonyms are used. The author does not use any demographic or geographical names to protect identities of the interviewed and their families.

rather intensive involvement in their children's life is thoroughly presented in their family diary: the children spend weekends with their father in his house and he visits them on Wednesdays, which seems to be part of Linda's very well organised family routine and time.

Perception of schooling time through the prism of own schooling
Both mothers' daily routines time are split between home (work and family) and time with children around their school routine.

Reflection on their childhood from the perspective of their current position and daily routines present are now viewed and interpreted "from a standpoint of a different time system" and they interpret those "situations with an awareness of social expectations" (Mead 1932, p. 176, 47).

Maria described her childhood as both 'difficult' and happy. Maria's father's illness overshadowed her happy time at school and her father's death from cancer, just before she took her GCSE[2] exams made a big impact on her emotionally, which she refers to while talking about her husband's current illness which for her created a clear parallel between the past, present and future worries, when she spoke about her son's response to his father's illness. Back to school time, Maria completed GCSEs and A-Levels at the local college and went to University. She was the first who went to the University in her family. Her father was a lorry driver and her mother was a cleaner and then worked as a receptionist in the local garage and then at the newsagent. Maria recollects with a sense of pride that her mother was very proud of her and she was of herself. But Maria did not enjoy the University life. She studied Biomedical Sciences and wanted to become a Forensic Scientist, but she found it a shock moving from a close-knit community in school and having her family around and could not adjust to the atmosphere and way of life at University.

Maria: <...>*Yes, I was the first one* [she means the first member of her family who went to the university LN]. *My Mum was very proud of me going, but she was proud of me giving it up, because I was brave enough to say: 'this isn't for me' rather than forcing me to go through it because I kept thinking 'I got to do this for my Dad, I got to do this for my Mum'. I just couldn't do it. Didn't enjoy one little bit of University et all. It is a shame, but (...)*<...>

---

[2]GCSE – General Certificate of Secondary Education. This level is normally achieved at the age 16.

Maria is fully aware of the family and social expectations about a working-class girl going to University, but is more aware of that situation now when it is time to consider how to support her older daughter, when she decided to go to university. Significantly, her most vivid memories of the past University life were lengthy lectures, which lasted up to three hours! The time seemed to run very slowly for Maria at that point. She badly missed her family and after one and a half years she left University to move back home.

Linda's present time perspective on her schooling experience in the past is also clearly perceived from the present time position of a parent. Linda was an only child in her family. Before she turned one year old, her parents split up and her father kicked her mother out of their family home. Linda only reflected on the fact that her father wanted to keep her in his family and her mother had to put up a big fight to keep her. Linda and her mother lived with her grandmother, then her grandfather, and then moved to a house close to the street where Linda has been living since. Linda describes her childhood as unhappy, as she changed homes and schools several times. After doing her GCSEs she went to the local college and qualified as a physio-therapist.

She was brought up by a single mother, who did not have enough money to get Linda '... *all the new stuff that all the kids were having or the top of the range stuff*'. Linda was bullied at school for her appearance, *'for being poor, for being this, for being that. But that* [she means bullying LN] *went through, that went through primary school and high school'*.

However it is her mother that Linda is now "blaming" for giving her bad advice:

Linda: <...>*Oh, my Mum, my Mum* [Uhm] *to be fair, I am not gonna blame my Mum, but my Mum made it a little bit worse, because she told me to, basically run away and go and tell the teacher. And you know that's what you suppose to do, but it makes the situation ten times worse. 'Cause then you get even more bullied for being a grass, for being a snitch'.*

Her past time childhood experience keeps haunting her in the present through her children's experience of school, she keeps reminding herself of that unhappy past as she described one of her son's experience at school, repeating: *'but as you* [she refers to the interviewer LN] *know my past, I don't want him to be (...). I want him to be as happy as he possibly can'*.

When Linda started working she kept changing jobs as well, as she kept changing schools when she was younger. She worked in bars, eating places and salons. However most of the time she was 'on the dole'. She has had a few jobs, although mostly her income came from government welfare.

Despite some similarities in both mothers' backgrounds and complicated family circumstances, their own school experiences could not be more different. Maria has very happy memories from childhood of there always being people in the house—she describes it as like having an extended family. She loved school, both primary and secondary, and never had any problems. Her children now go to the same school that she went to herself when she was a child.

Linda on the contrary has very bad school memories. She describes her childhood as unhappy, as she changed schools several times, was bullied for being poor and overweight, and had no friends or local family. Despite her claims that she did not have any friends at school: ' *I was always on me own*', she recollects that she has a friend whom she has known for 13 years, her best friend who lives locally—she became close with this woman, because she stuck up for her when Linda was getting bullied in school.

Families and children: 'reconnecting' the time-line
Mothers' reflections on their now own families' and the children's constantly swing between "then", "now" and the "future". The important key moments in both women's lives that have shaped their identities as mothers, have also been reflected upon from the perspective of their current situations.

Both Maria and Linda had their first children in their 20's. Maria met the father of her first child at work. When she was still at the University, in order to support herself financially she worked at the fast food chain restaurant, when she dropped out of University and moved back home, she went to work at the local restaurant at her home town and met her now ex-boyfriend there. Maria and her then partner were together for two years before he left upon the birth of their daughter. Her ex-partner still lives locally but has not seen her since, nor does his daughter (now a teenager) want to see him. Maria's husband adopted her daughter from her earlier relationship. She had a son and a daughter with her husband, but they could not have more children. Maria now feels this was ultimately for the best, as her husband is now very ill with a heart condition and she is now his full-time carer. Ironically, before Maria met her husband who was previously married, but didn't have children, her husband did not want to have children at all. His attitude to children changed when he met Maria and they both wanted to have more children together. And now Maria is seeing her unfortunate and traumatic events of the past, such as 'miscarriages" as: *'it was for the best having the miscarriages, in a strange way, because he wouldn't* [means her husband LN] *have been able to cope with the baby, being ill'*.

Due to his current illness her husband can also no longer cope with visitors, he doesn't get out of bed for more than an hour to two hours a day. *'If you are lucky* three [Uhm], *but he doesn't go out, he doesn't go out, you know, to do, help me with the shopping, or to take the kids to school, he doesn't do that'<...>*. From 'Maria's perspective the time is now 'reversed': her husband's illness makes her again feeling like a 'lone' mother, who does everything on her own. The future of her family is also not clear, because of her husband's health condition.

Linda met her then partner and father of her two children at a job centre. Linda and her partner had two children together and she described her family life with him as very happy, despite the fact that she doesn't like her ex-partner's family, who she describes as not nice people and she doesn't have them around her boys. Despite splitting from her partner after a drink-related accident, she maintains a good 'working', calendar-planned relationship with him for the sake of the children. Her now ex-partner is supporting her with the children, and she appreciates and feels she needs the time she gets to herself when her ex-partner looks after their children at weekends. She does not want a new partner, as she is scared of breaking the relationship, Linda also feels well supported by her family and one of her old friends.

Types of schooling time
"Plodding along"- Maria

There is a certain similarity of education-related daily routine of both mothers: children of both women go to primary school and they have two children of primary school age (however Maria has also an older daughter from her first relationship).

Planning schooling and family time lies on 'Maria's own shoulders. Although her husband is at home, he is not involved in the family daily routine:

Maria: *<...>No. No. He doesn't know half of what goes on* (laughs). *In fact he doesn't know 90 % of what goes on. He lives in (...) his world so I don't tell him. He knows bits, but (...) he doesn't deal with stress very well and then (...) when you're stressed (...) and you've gotta then deal with him in a mood (...), it doesn't help you, so I just don't tell him and he just doesn't know and I deal with it all. So it does take its toll sometimes. There's- there's times where I can deal with everything everyone throws at me and then it'll just, you know, it'll all build up and build up to the one day where you are thinking 'I can't cope with this today'. But you- you have to get on with it, you have carry on. But there is times where I have (...) thought I could just do with a little break a day please (laughs). But you can't, you know. Plod along<...>.*

There is feeling of two parallel time systems in their home: one—the children-schooling time which is moving fast. The other one is her husband, where everything goes and feels much slower.

Walking to school is considered part of a child's healthy life style approach. However, it is the parents that decide on the way the children go to school. The decision is primarily based on concerns about children's safety, as well as proximity to school. Maria's family neighbourhood now is very similar to how it was when she was a child, very close knit. There are more cars around than when she was little so she doesn't let her children play out at the front because it's too dangerous due to this. Kids would always play out at the front and parents would watch but it's no longer considered to be appropriate to go and pick up someone else's child when they're crying, as times have changed. She used to go to the shop on her own when she was 6 years old, but she wouldn't let her own daughter go until she was about 11. Maria regretfully acknowledged that community spirit has gone, not everyone knows everyone.

However, Maria's different approaches to the way the children go to school are nothing to do with the type of neighbourhood or changed community spirit. She prefers to walk her daughter to school, but to drive her son to school, because of his autism. Concern for her son's unexpected behaviour make her to construct school walks in a very unusual way, taking into consideration the nature of their school walks and an estimated time to reach the destination.

When Maria walks her children to school and from school which is at the end of the road—the walk takes a long time depending on how many spiders webs they see, as the children have to count them all! Actual walking to school could take a long time, but it "flies" for Maria, because she is helping her children to explore the natural world on the way to school.

Maria: <...>*Er if we're walkin' with the two little ones, it depends how many spider webs they see, because if they see a spider web we have to stop and hunt for the spider. So it usually takes them about- if they just walkin' straight and concentrating, about 30 min. It has been known to take me an hour to walk home with them but that's, like I say, we've got to stop at every spider web and 'oooh a ladybird... oooh a ladybird, yes we've just seen four of them'. So it is quite a walk, so I drive<...>.*

But she prefers to drive her son to school. She is pre-occupied with his assessment for autism, which is a painful experience for Maria. Her son's speech problems create a very challenging situation at home. Nobody knows how to handle him at school either and this makes it very difficult; the school aren't very understanding and supporting. He didn't do nursery because of the speech problems, he is also in the class which is a year below his peer group. However she is not sharing this news with anybody. She feels people often make their own judgements about what is wrong with a child and she doesn't like this as she would rather the doctor just told her. Her best friend is very helpful though, they help each other taking each other's children to clubs and having them round for tea sometimes. However, she is concerned about her son, due to his condition and timing of her children's school routine changes:

Maria: <...>*No, I drive, I drive him. 'Cause it's a long way, I think. I have walked, if the weather is nice I try to walk. But I don't walk there because it's a long way, they're gonna be tired all day, and I think, you know, it's not fair. We walk home when we can take it slow, we can stop at everything, they can- they love animals so we have to stop at every dog, we need to for them to stroke it, every bird that flies past we have to look, we have to watch them. So it takes a good hour.* <...>

Interviewer: An hour?

Maria: <...>*Yeah. They walk so slow. We do, we have to stop at every little bug, every spider web, everything. And then it's a long walk and* [Daughter] *walks so slowly anyway, 'cause she only got little legs. But they do, they have to stop, they have to look, they have to (...) every car.*[Son] *likes writing registration numbers down, so if he sees an interesting one, we have to stop. So yeah, it is quite a walk away. I can do it by myself, I can walk to their school from here 15–20 min. But them, no, no chance. It takes ages.* <...>

It is clear that Maria's perception of distance from home to school in terms of time changes depending whether she is taking her daughter or son to school, or whether it is a walk to or from school. Her perception of physical/positivistic time changes due to her social awareness of her son's unpredictable behaviour during the walk to avoid any unwanted social impressions, she drives her son to school, thus constructing a school "walking" time according to her son's condition. She recollected one incident with her son on the shopping walk with the family friends, when her son lost a temper and started kicking her. She was shocked by that and is now trying to adjust walking to school practices of her son accordingly. 'Maria's' self-consciousness is maximized when she 'confronts problematic circumstances—an observation that is derived from Mead's writings' (Flaherty and Fine 2001, p. 148). This social awareness is very much part of 'Maria's identity.

Calendar-like—Linda

Like Maria, Linda also plans her children's schooling time and after school routine by herself. The description of her children's before and after school daily routine sounds very calendar-like:

Interviewer: And what does their normal week look like? What do they do?

Linda: <...>*So they go school on Monday, home, kickboxing 'til- se-kickboxing 'til half 7, home, bath, bed. Same on Tuesday. Wednesday it's their perk thing, when they- they go to school and when they go home I say 'What do you wanna do? We can go to the park, go to the play area...' anything they wanna do, we'll do it on a Wednesday. Thursday kickboxing, so it's the same as the Monday and Tuesday and then Friday they come home, have tea with me and then they go to the* [their] *dad's for 5. And then I get them back on Sunday at 5 o'clock. And on Sunday we watch a film, then it's bath and bed*<...>

Linda's time management of her children's schooling is clear and structured. She is arranging it around her kids. She said; *'I can work around me kids, I can work when me kids are in bed'*. She has always dreaded the idea for children to be with baby sitters or nurseries. Linda is a busy working mother, but she wants to see her children grow up. At the same time there is a degree of contradiction in what she says. First, she prefers to see her children around, but at the same time, she is arranging their time to be out (at least on weekends with their father) and she is also keen to delegate her children's homework to their dad, as well, because she is very busy.

Linda: <...> *'Cause **I just haven't got time** (...) **I just haven't** know, like obviously, 'cause I'm so busy doing everything in the day, **I just haven't got time** to sit down with them of a night and do their homework and stuff so their dad does it*<...>.

Interviewer: Do you go out to eat with the children?

Linda: *(Erm), well, because **I haven't really got much time with them** through the week and like I don't have them at the weekend, so I don't like tend to take them out places*<...>.[Emphasis is mine LN]

Linda also walks her two children to school, but in her case it is not a matter choice. The school walks are described as a mere routine of the day, which she takes without attaching much value, or significance to. Linda does not drive, as she cannot afford to have a driving licence, so she has to walk her children to and from school. But the school walks were not significant to her, as she only described them as factual time, a daily routine without much to add. Linda describes the neighbourhood as completely different from the time she was a child, kids used to play out even though she did not herself, and now they cannot do that, the community has gone and instead no one speaks to each other and it's now considered dangerous—dangerous drivers. Whilst she did not play in the neighbourhood herself as a child, she has noticed a huge change in the area—children no longer play outside and there are dangerous drivers about. She likes her rented house, although ideally would live closer to her mother—it is not far away and there it is safer for children to play without parents worrying.

However, it is the safety of the roads in the neighbourhood that concerns her most about the school walks.

Linda: *'So it's literally that at the bottom of the road* [She means her children's school LN]. *And even when they are in year 6*[3]*, even when they are old enough to walk themselves, I shall still be walkin' them. 'Cause it's just (…), it's more the road, there's like, the amount of lunatics there on the road, they are speedin' and stuff. So* [Uhm] *not a lot, a few years ago there was a drunk driver in the middle of the day, in the middle of the afternoon and literally crashed into someone's living room.<…>…so I am thinking to me* [my] *self, if I let my kids out there and some idiot driving up the road and swerves onto the kerb (…), not a chance'.*

Linda's reflection on the school walk is also very much part of her identity. Her memories about her own school walks were also 'linear'/calendar-like:

Linda: *'I'd come ho(…), go to school, come home from school, sit in the house and stay in the house, wouldn't go out and play'.*

And also from her experience of a lot of dangerous situations in her early life (e.g. bullying) and the relationship with her ex-partner, that she is taking on extra planning when it concerns the safety of her children.

Time to play
Children of both mothers are engaged in a number of after school activities: run by the local school, local churches, but their approach to the activities is

---

[3]School children normally reach year 6 at the age of 10.

very different. Maria's children attend a variety of after school clubs and those which are run by the church, the children also attend Sunday school. On the other hand Linda's children's choice of afterschool activities is rather limited by the walking distance to the activities, as she does not drive. Apart from the organised activities, the children spend time at home; both mothers are not keen for them to play on the street, because of safety reasons (careless driving).

Linda talks quite a lot about how the children are busy with their activities, yet they still have time to watch films together on a Sunday night and choose an activity (whatever they want) on a Wednesday afternoon. She appears to let them choose what they want to eat, although she values sitting together at a table they have laid. It doesn't appear that she has to give in to her children's demands, or that her children are difficult so she gives them what she wants, instead family life seems like a well-oiled machine. 'Linda's' children after school get their tablets, telly and *'ridiculous amount of toys"* according to how she describes their time space after they get back home from school. Whereas Maria is specifically emphasising that her children do not have any *'gadgets et all'* and feels sorry for the children who spend all the time indoors, as their parents do not take them to the local parks.

Linda gets on well with the other parents at school, but had a few issues at school to start with—feisty response to her son getting his head flushed down the toilet. That incident suddenly reminded of her own tough time at school, however, she is not shy to confront the school, as compared to her own children, when she was young and had been bullied at school. She is also involved in her children's school-organised activities, such school fetes, where she can contribute her talent and skills of a beauty therapist (eg. face painting) of which she is talks with a great enthusiasm.

Being a good mother for Linda first of all means: telling her children she loves them several times a day. Whilst she doesn't get on with her ex-partner, they get on for the sake of the children; they support each other a lot. She was discriminated for the way she looks and she has found that her son has been too when he was wearing a pair of scruffy trainers. She has taught him to deal with things in the same way she does, being confident and not caring what others think—she is proud of him for this.

Time off schooling duties
Although being a very outgoing person, who likes being with people, as Maria remarked about herself: *'Always with people'* speaks she about herself. Maria describes herself as a very proud person and does not like asking people for help, especially financially. She would ask for a couple of pounds and pay back the following day, but she would never ask her friends for more than that. She feels that

she has to cope and should not ask for help, even though she knows she should be able to ask—she is surprised that her mother does not offer her help, and believes she is too proud to do this. She does not tell her husband about these issues because she does not want to worry him. Some days she feels fine, others she feels she cannot cope, but she knows she has to, so she just keeps going on her own.

An hour break feels like the time Maria needs in order to have some rest and to carry on with her numerous tasks. Maria desperately needs this time to have some rest. In Maria's case one hour means a long time.

Maria: <...>*I find it- I do get stressed a lot because of everything that goes on. Erm there is [are] times where I have had to say 'I just need to go out, **just need to go and have an hour's break'** erm (...) I- it is- I do- I don't personally have a stressful life but because of everything around me (...) I am stressed and things do stress me out.*<...>

Maria doesn't have much help from her family—her mother doesn't come to the house, Maria visits her occasionally and she looks after the kids if she needs her, especially her eldest daughter, who spends a lot of time with her grandmother, but she wouldn't offer any help with the younger children in order to give Maria time off. Her husband's mother doesn't visit more than once every two weeks, as her husband has a short temper now so cannot cope with visitors, they're not enjoyable visits. However, even when she has got a free holiday from the Mothers' Union, she also took her mother on holiday:

Maria <...>*We were given a holiday last year from the Mother's Union, they gave us a free holiday because we haven't had one since [husband] being ill. And, you know, with everything going on, they gave- they said that we deserved it, so we had a week away, me and the children. I took my mum. 'Cause I did, you know, I felt that (...) I could- I would have liked to have gone with just me and the children but I felt bad 'cause she hadn't been away*<...>.

When an opportunity to have free time became available, Maria preferred to spend it with her extended family.

Linda enjoys arts and crafts and film nights. She wants to take them to Disney because she went herself and she wants them to have the same great memories that she has. Construction of the family time and "me " time comes in the narratives from the types of activities that time contains to the clarifying question about what does Linda normally do during her own time, she replies: "... *but I don't actually do anything...*"

Linda: <...>*No, not really. I just sit, I just, I just sit, I mean I'll go over to me friends or we'll go out for a few drinks or whatever **but I don't actually do anything** [emphasis mine LN] 'cause I like being in the quiet. Because me house is full of noise all day through the week, I like to just sit and be quiet*<...>.<...>*Oh yeah, I have people over, but that's what I mean, I tend-I like- I prefer to have people in the house rather than me going out anywhere. 'Cause if people come to me, I can stay in me jammies, I don't have to get dressed*<...>

Analysis and discussion
The significance of mothers' identities in relation to the construction of schooling time originates from the role of mothers in forming early identities of their children. Arendell (2000) in her review of a decade of scholarship on motherhood observed that; 'Mothering is particularly significant it is 'the main vehicle through which people first form their identities and learn their place in society'. Arendell also highlight the 'multifaceted and complex nature of mothering, symbolically laden, representing what often is characterized as the ultimate in relational devotion' (Arendell 2000, p. 1192). The analysis of the process of constructing of two mothers' identities in time perspective based on their reflection of their own schooling time through becoming part of the children's schooling time and planning for their future.

Socially constructed daily routines and activities: Maria walks her younger daughter to school and enjoys interacting with her in exploring of the natural worlds of the school route (spiders, birds, dogs, etc.), whereas her son, who has all the signs of autism is normally driven to school in a car. Maria is constantly aware of protecting him from being labelled as a 'nasty' boy, when he is not. Maria is constantly 'putting herself in her son's shoes' trying to explain the situation from his point of view, compares it with her own biographical experience of as a child who grew up in a family with a terminally ill father; she constantly creates parallels with what her children now feel, especially her son, who she describes as very emotional, sensitive about his father's illness. It is worth mentioning here how Frank Furedi reflected on Cassidy's point regarding intertwined identities of parents and children that for some parents children's childhood is used as a vehicle to discover adult identity; for adults' own psychic transformation (Furedi 2008, p. 106).

Whereas Linda's mothering approach is less 'exclusive, wholly child centred, emotionally involving and time-consuming' (Hays 1996), she is not even intending to share her identities with her two sons, by first, happily 'delegating' some of parenting duties to their father, who as she describes him ' takes them everywhere', when they spend their time with him. Even the home work is 'delegated' to the father of her two children, because Linda recognises the reality of her own dyslexia and the fact, that she might not be able to help her boys with their school subjects. Thus she has already considered a strategy for getting this sorted out: *'I am gonna be like, phoning his dad and go: 'Right, you need to help with homework now'*.

The analysis of the time spend with their children by two mothers in the case study provided two different understandings/meanings on what schooling time means and how it fits around mothers' daily routine. It could be defined as "they time" and 'me' time.

Maria's 'me' time is a continuation of her family time, whereas Linda enjoys "me" time in real terms (including days of the week and perfectly planned time/hours), as the time she gets when her children spend time with their father over weekends, as it gives her time to herself, which she feels she needs. She uses this time to socialise and relax. The irony of 'Maria's situation is that even her 'me' time in the past, when she left her family and went to University did not result in completion of her studies and getting independence in her life. She was missing her family and returned home, however she now does not get any help from her family with the children, when she needs it the most. She referred to the situation when there was a fire in the next road and the fireman came round to install fire alarms, and saw their situation and suggested she needs help and occupational health. They told her there are various things she is entitled to claim for, but she hasn't heard since and the services she has been to haven't been very helpful in advising her, so they haven't made any progress in getting her any help. She feels she just has to cope with it and get on with it, because it's what she has to do since she has children. To her, putting her children's needs above your own, means being a good mother. The children's time for Maria is part of her own identity. She thinks it's important to enjoy your children, enjoy spending time with them and seeing them grow up. She does get stressed and it all gets a bit much so she knows she's not always the best parent to them, but she tries very hard. She doesn't discuss any of this with her husband though.

Linda's 'me' time is means that it is just her personal time; her children and her family are not counted in. The family time and "me" time are clearly defined and separated:

Linda: <...>*No, I find it better that I get on- I- I seem to deal with them* [she means her children] *better because I get that break. I mean, I don't even do nothing in- in- at the weekend, most of the time I lock me door and I don't come out until the Sunday. I lie on me couch with loads of crisps and sweets and* *chockies* [chocolates] *and just watch the telly for the whole entire weekend. But it's- it's a break, it's a **me*** [highlight mine LN] *time, so if I wanted to go out and do something, I've still got the time there to do it<…>*

Linda's need of personal time, just 'me' time also expands to her attitude to personal relationship, as she describes it:

Linda: *<…>No. (…) I haven't got time. I can't be bothered. To be perfectly honest with you erm I'm jus- I- I'm scared of ha*-[having] *something like that happening again. So it's easier to just keep me self to me self<…>*

Analysis of the two narratives suggest that definition of the parenting time is socially constructed and is more connected with mothers' identities than the nature of everyday school routine and family circumstances. Availability of support from own family and ex-partner who looks after the children during weekend does not expand Linda's schooling time. Maria on the contrary psychologically "stretching" the schooling time to fit in more activities with her children. Maria's perception of time means that it is much longer than the physical, real time (Flaherty 1991). It equals one hour for a rest, where as Linda free time is the whole weekend.

The importance of understanding schooling time as mothers' identity work is crucial in terms of battling with the stigmatization of disadvantaged families and providing an in-sight into parents-school engagement which is important factor in children's development and success in life. Mothers from the low-income families also experience pressure of society and schools expectations regarding their parenting, but their family circumstances are much more complex and have to be examined without any prejudice or generalisations. The biographical data used in the analysis allowed us to identify some rather significant aspects in schooling time construction by mothers from low-income families: their own biographical circumstances and also the mothers' educational backgrounds.

More detailed analysis on the temporality of mothers' identity changes since they became mothers is beyond the scope of this chapter, however their narratives regarding their children and their references to what does it mean to be a good mother throughout the interview indicate that motherhood modified several areas of their identities. Motherhood indeed made impact on their "autonomy, physical appearance, sexuality and occupations" (Laney et al. 2015, p. 127). Maria had her first child when she was 22, after she returned from one and half years at the University. Despite the fact that first relationship didn't last long because her first partner couldn't cope with the family and left her and their daughter and that her new husband was also not keen on having children, when they just married, motherhood made Maria a very devoted mother. Maria co-shares, fuses her emotional experiences or sense of value with her children and can be defined by her children's experiences and time. Maria fully "incorporated" her children and their time into her identities, through "a process of self- loss, identity fracturing and redefinition" (Laney et al. 2015, p. 139).

Linda on the contrary demonstrates a "high level of differentiation" and doesn't "incorporate her children "into the boundaries" of herself. (Laney et al. 2015, p. 139). This explains the strict time schedule/boundaries in her relationship with her children and their father. After this experience she is protective of her children—she encourages them to stick up for themselves and is proud when they respond well to any discrimination.

There is also a social class and marital situation differences obvious from the mothers' biographical background. Maria was the first in her family who went to the University and also did well at school. Linda struggled at school and although she reached the level of vocational education college, schooling wasn't among her strengths; she only referred to her school time in negative terms. Both mothers at some point shared a status of lone mothers, however, Maria got married, whereas Linda factually accepted her position of lone mother and is not in a hurry to change it (Reay 2007; May 2010). However the main difference lies in the type parenting time and their construction of that time. Researchers in parenting culture observe that raising children now encompasses a growing range of activities that were not previously seen as an obligatory dimension of their social role (Furedi 2008, Lee et al. 2014; Faircloth and Murray 2015). Maria would be more aware of this public discourse and more concerned that despite all odds, she has to add these challenges to her daily routine.

Linda's response on what her children do when they come back from school first recollects that they [her children] *"they've got their tablets, they've got game consoles, got telly, we've got books and ridiculous amount of toys in the room"*, however she also mentions that her eldest child does kickboxing. Her time with the children is arranged around their "homely" home. Linda doesn't drive, which is another factor which makes it difficult for her to take her children around.

"Lack of time" is a concern for many families and this is evident in both popular media and scholarly writing which refer to "time scarcity" (Provonost 1989) or the time bind when the borders between time for work and time for family are gradually disappearing (Hochschild 2003). Viewing time as socially constructed is particularly relevant here since this perspective underscores the link between activity and experience time (Wingard 2007).

However, our analysis demonstrates that socially constructed meaning of time is directly connected with the types of parenting and mothers' perception of their roles in bringing up their children. Both mothers are spending their entire life bound to home; one due to family circumstances (husband illness) the other one by choice (running a small business from home).

However their parenting time is a reflection of their approach to parenting and also the way they feel about being mothers.

Acknowledgements The data used in the analysis was generated in the qualitative study of parents, which was conducted by the author in England as part of her work at the Department of Education of the University of Oxford which was a partner organisation in the ISOTIS-"Inclusive Education and Social Support to tackle Inequalities in Society" EC Horizon -2020 project, grant agreement No.727069

References

Arendell, T. (2000). Conceiving and Investigating Motherhood: The Decade's scholarship. In: Journal of Marriage and family, 62 (November 2000): 1192–1207.

Bronfenbrenner, U., & Ceci, S. J. (1994). Nature-Nurture Reconceptualized in Developmental Perspectives: A Bioecological Model. In: *Psychological Review*, 101, 568–586. https://doi.org/10.1037/0033-295X.101.4.568

Bronfenbrenner, U., & Morris, P. A. (2006). The Bioecological Model of Human Development. In: R. M. Lerner & W. Damon (Eds.), *Handbook of child psychology: Theoretical models of human development* (pp. 793–828). Hoboken, NJ, US: John Wiley & Sons Inc.

Compton-Lilly, C., (2016). Time in education: Intertwined dimensions and theoretical possibilities. In: Time and Society, 2016, Vol. 25(3). Sage. Pp. 575–593

Faircloth, C. (2014). Intensive parenting and the Expansion of Parenting. In: Lee et al. Parenting Cultures Studies. Palgrave Macmillan

Faircloth, C., & Murray, M. (2015). *Parenting: Kinship, Expertise, and Anxiety*. In: Journal of Family Issues, 2015, Vol. 36(9), pp. 1115–1129

Flaherty, M.G. (1991) The Perception of Time and Situated Engrossment. In: Social Psychology Quarterly, 1991, Vol. 54, No1, PP. 76–85

Flaherty, M.G. & G.A. Fine (2001). Present, Past and Future. Conjugating George Herbert Mead's perspective on time. In: Time and Society, Volume 10 (2/3): 147–161. London, Thousand Oaks, CA and New Delhi: Sage.

Furedi, F., (2008) Paranoid parenting. Why Ignoring the experts may be best for your child. London, New Delhi: Bloomsbury Publishing Plc

Hays, S. (1996). The cultural contradictions of motherhood. New haven, CT: Yale University Press.

Hochschild, A. (2003). The Time Bind: When Work Becomes Home and Home Becomes Work. New York: Henry Holt and Company LLC.

Hornby, G. (2011) Parental Involvement in Childhood Education. Building Effective School-Family Partnerships. Springer.

Hornby, G. & Blackwell, I. (2018). Barriers to parental involvement in education: an update. Educational Review. 70. 109–119. DOI: 10.1080/00131911.2018.138861210.1 080/00131911.2018.1388612

Jackson, M. (2013). Determined to Succeed? Performance versus Choice in Educational Attainment. Stanford: Stanford University Press.

Laney, E.K., Hall, E.L., Anderson, T.L.& M.M. Willingham. (2015) Becoming a Mother: the Influence of motherhood on Women's Identity Development. In: Identity. An International Journal of Theory and Research, 15:2, pp 126—145, DOI: https://doi.org/10.10 80/15283488.2015.1023440 Routledge.

Lee, E., Bristow, J., Faircloth, C.& J. Macvarish (editors) (2014). Parenting Culture Studies. Palgrave Macmillan.

May, V. (2010) Lone Motherhood as a category of practice. In: Sociological review (2010), 58:3.

Mead, H. 1932. (Edited by A. E. Murphy). The Philosophy of the present. Chicago and London: The University of Chicago Press. Phoenix edition. Published in 1980.

Nurse, L. & E. Melhuish (2018). Parent in-depth interview study. Technical report https://www.isotis.org/en/publications/parent-in-depth-interview-study-technical-report

Reay, D., (2007). Doing Dirty Work of Social Class? Mothers' Work in Support of Their Children's Schooling. In: Sociological Review, January 2006 DOI https://doi.org/10.1111/j.1467-954X.2005.00575x

Roberts, B. (2002). Biographical research. Buckingham, Philadelphia: Open University press.

Schütze, F. (2008). Biography analysis on the empirical base of autobiographical narratives. How to analyze autobiographical narrative interviews- Part one and two, in: European studies on Inequalities and Social cohesion, N01/2, p.153–242; No 3/4, p. 5–77

Provonost, G. (1989). *The Sociology of Time*. London: Sage publications.

Waller, R. Changing identities through re-engagement with Education: Narrative accounts from two women learners (2010). In: Bathmaker, A-M & P. Harnett (editors) (2010). Exploring Learning, Identity and Power through Life History and Narrative Research. London: Routledge. https://doi.org/10.4324/9780203858370

Wingard, L., (2007). Constructing time and prioritizing activities in parent–child Interaction. In: Discourse & Society https://doi.org/10.1177/0957926507069458 2007; 18; 75

Wright, H., (2011) Using biographical approaches to explore student views on learning and teaching, Enhancing Learning in the Social Sciences, 3:3, 1–22, DOI: https://doi.org/10.11120/elss.2011.03030005 To link to this article: https://doi.org/10.11120/elss.2011.03030005.

Time, Future and Innovation. Zeit, Zukunft und Innovationen

Wie denkt die Verwaltung über die Zukunft? Dokumentenanalyse von Strategiepapieren zur Digitalisierung der öffentlichen Verwaltung

How Public Administrations Think About the Future. Analysis of Policy Papers on the Digital Transformation of Public Administrations

Malte Schophaus

Abstract

Public administrations, like other organizations, depend on assumptions about the future. These assumptions give orientation to political decisions and actions. The planning periods of public administrations are traditionally based on election periods and are therefore short. How do public administrations think about the future in medium and longer time periods? This question will be examined using the future trend of digital transformation as an example. Based on a document analysis of policy papers at the federal, state and municipal level, patterns of interpretation for the future of the digital transformation are reconstructed. Particular attention is paid to digitalized human resources management. It becomes clear that future thinking is guided by two contradictory poles of interpretation: on the one hand, digital transformation is perceived as a threat and as an inherently dynamic process, over which control

M. Schophaus (✉)
Hochschule für Polizei und öffentliche Verwaltung NRW, Bielefeld, Deutschland
E-Mail: malte.schophaus@hspv.nrw.de

must be gained. On the other hand, digital transformation is described as a process of reform and innovation that has enormous potential for improvement in almost all administrative areas.

Zusammenfassung

Öffentliche Verwaltungen sind wie andere Organisationen darauf angewiesen, Annahmen über die Zukunft zu entwickeln, um ihr Handeln an diesen auszurichten. Die Planungszeiträume von Verwaltungen orientieren sich traditionell an Legislaturperioden und sind kurz. Wie denken öffentliche Verwaltungen aber in mittleren und längeren Zeiträumen über die Zukunft? Diese Frage wird exemplarisch anhand des Zukunftstrends Digitalisierung untersucht. Anhand einer Dokumentenanalyse von Strategiepapieren zur Digitalisierung der öffentlichen Verwaltung auf Bundes-, Landes- und kommunaler Ebene, werden Deutungsmuster zur Zukunft der digitalen Verwaltung rekonstruiert. Besonderes Augenmerk wird dabei auf die digitalisierte Personalarbeit gelegt. Es wird deutlich, dass zwei widerstrebende Deutungspole das Feld der Zukunftsvorausschau aufspannen: einerseits die Wahrnehmung der Digitalisierung als Bedrohung und als eigendynamischer Prozess, über den dringend Kontrolle gewonnen werden muss. Andererseits wird Digitalisierung als Reform- und Innovationsprozess beschrieben, der enormes Verbesserungspotenzial für nahezu alle Handlungsbereiche der Verwaltung in sich trägt.

Keywords

Future · Future research · Future thinking · Public administration · Digitalization · Digital transformation · Human resources management · Municipality

Schlüsselwörter

Zukunft · Zukunftsforschung · Zukunftsdenken · öffentliche Verwaltung · Digitalisierung · Personalmanagement · Kommune

Einleitung und Fragestellung

Die Zukunft ist die Zeitdimension, die eng verknüpft mit den großen aktuellen Herausforderungen besprochen wird. Diese Herausforderungen können alle politischen und alltagsweltlichen Handlungsfelder betreffen. Dazu gehören etwa die Zukunft der natürlichen Lebensgrundlagen, die Zukunft der weltweiten Migrationsbewegungen, oder die Zukunft der technologischen Entwicklung und damit verbunden auch immer die Zukunft der öffentlichen Verwaltungen. In diesem Beitrag werden Zukunftsdeutungen der öffentlichen Verwaltungen zum Megatrend Digitalisierung analysiert.

Die enorme Bedeutung von Zukunftsvorstellungen für gesellschaftliche Veränderungsprozesse lässt sich gut am Trend des Klimawandels und der nachhaltigen Entwicklung veranschaulichen, da dieser derzeit wohl die umfassendste Herausforderung ist, die wir mit der Zukunft verbinden. Die Art und Weise, wie Zukunft konzipiert wird, zieht dann entsprechenden gesellschaftlichen Wandel nach sich. Der Wandel ist meist durch abwechselnde Phasen von Gestaltung und von Verdrängung geprägt. So hat die Prognose der Umweltkrise einerseits eine Schar an verwaltungsorganisatorischen Innovationen (z. B. Umweltministerien und Umweltämter), politischen Parteien und Steuerungsinstrumenten (z. B. Bündnis 90/Die Grünen, Umweltsteuern, Emissionsschutzrichtlinien), wissenschaftlichen Entwicklungen (transdisziplinäre sozial-ökologische Forschung), kulturellen Neuerungen (Bildung für Nachhaltige Entwicklung) und zahlreichen technischen Innovationen (vom Katalysator bis zur Photovoltaikanlage) angeregt. Zugleich vollziehen sich mit dem Aufkommen einer solchen Zukunftsherausforderung Gegenbewegungen und Machtkämpfe, die aktiv oder aus Gewohnheit die Zukunftsannahmen infrage und andere Annahmen dagegen stellen. Auch diese lassen sich in allen gesellschaftlichen Subsystemen identifizieren, wenngleich sie dort oftmals subtiler auftreten und die Nennung hier sicher nicht unumstritten sein dürfte: so treten politische Parteien an, die programmatisch mit der Verleugnung des menschengemachten Klimawandels werben (z. B. Alternative für Deutschland), politische Steuerungsinstrumente werden entwickelt, um ökonomische Ziele vor den Anforderungen und Kosten der Umweltschutzziele zu schützen (z. B. Subvention von nicht-regenerativen Energieträgern, etwa Kohle, oder Steuerausnahmen für energieintensive Industrien oder für Kerosin), technische Innovationen etwa bemühen sich um die Umgehung politischer Steuerungsinstrumente (vgl. die Debatte zum sogenannten ‚VW-Skandal', aber auch die Forschung zur ‚geplanten Obsoleszenz', also zur gezielten technischen Verkürzung von Produktlebenszyklen, um den Konsum anzuregen).

Die Zukunft ist offenbar ein streitbarer und hoch politisierter Deutungsraum. Die Dynamik von Zukunftsdiskursen lässt sich anhand solcher langfristig und stark debattierten Bereiche, wie der Umweltkrise, besonders pointiert nachzeichnen. Sie finden aber natürlich ebenso in anderen Politikfeldern statt. Im Folgenden werden Zukunftsdiskurse in der öffentlichen Verwaltung am Beispiel der Digitalisierung untersucht. Dieser Diskurs ist im Vergleich zum o.g. Nachhaltigkeitsdiskurs noch recht neu und die Deutungsmuster sind bislang weniger zutage getreten und wurden seltener reflektiert.

Digitalisierung ist der Zukunftstrend, der aktuell als Referenz für nahezu alle Veränderungsprozesse in der öffentlichen Verwaltung angeführt wird. Egal ob Herausforderungen im Bereich Personal, Organisation, Umwelt, Verkehr, Wirtschaft oder Bildung, ihre Lösungen werden ausnahmslos mit Digitalisierung verknüpft. Anhand von strategischen Zukunftspapieren des politisch-administrativen Systems[1] auf Bundes-, Landes- und kommunaler Ebene wird hier dem Zukunftsdenken zur digitalen Verwaltung nachgegangen. Dazu befasst sich der Beitrag mit zwei aufeinander aufbauenden Fragen:

Im ersten Schritt wird für unterschiedliche Verwaltungsebenen nach dem Zukunftsdenken gefragt: Wie denken öffentliche Verwaltungen über Zukunft? Die öffentliche Verwaltung wird somit als Kollektiv mit geteilten sozialen Deutungsmustern verstanden. Welche Deutungsmuster lassen sich aus den in die Zukunft gerichteten Strategiepapieren der Bundes-, Landes- und Kommunalverwaltungen rekonstruieren? Das Zukunftsdenken wird hier auf die Digitalisierung von Verwaltungen bezogen.

In einem zweiten Schritt werden diese Deutungen auf das Interessengebiet des Personalmanagements fokussiert: Lassen sich aus obigen Beobachtungen Rückschlüsse ableiten, die zum besseren Verständnis der Zukunftsplanung in der digitalisierten Personalarbeit aufschlussreich sind? Welche Deutungsmuster finden sich darüber, wie die Personalarbeit der Zukunft aussehen sollte, an welche Herausforderungen zukünftiges Personal angepasst sein muss und wie es entsprechend ausgewählt und qualifiziert wird?

Um die Fragestellungen für einen empirischen Zugang einzugrenzen, wird die Betrachtung exemplarisch auf nur einen Zukunftstrend bezogen, den der Digitalisierung. Dieser eignet sich besonders, da Digitalisierung in Politik und Verwaltung auf allen Ebenen aktuell sehr hohe Priorität hat und als Querschnittsthema nahezu alle Handlungsbereich der Verwaltung – in hohem Maße auch das Personalmanagement – betrifft. Weitere Zukunftstrends, die in aktuellen Zukunftsstudien identifiziert wurden, können hier nicht berücksichtigt werden: Demographischer Wandel, Neue Arbeit, Nachhaltige Entwicklung, Migration und

---

[1]Für die vorliegende Fragestellung kann die genaue Abgrenzung von Politik und Verwaltung vernachlässigt werden. Wenn hier von öffentlicher Verwaltung gesprochen wird, ist genauer das politisch-administrative System (Mayntz 1982, S. 33 f.) gemeint. Dadurch kommt zum Ausdruck, dass die untersuchten Zukunftsdokumente keine reinen Produkte von Verwaltungsbehörden sind, sondern auch durch vorstaatliche Prozesse der politischen Willensbildung (etwa durch die Einbeziehung von Parteien oder direkt von Bürger*innen) geprägt sind.

Diversität, Neue Formen der Mobilität (Schophaus 2018; Bundesministerium für Bildung und Forschung 2015).

Der Beitrag ist wie folgt gegliedert: zunächst werden sozialwissenschaftliche Zukunftskonzepte erörtert und das Nachdenken über die Zukunft in der Personalarbeit beschrieben (2). Das methodische Vorgehen der Dokumentenanalyse (3) und die Ergebnisse der Analyse (4) werden dargestellt. Der Beitrag schließt mit einer Zusammenfassung und einer Diskussion der Ergebnisse zum Zukunftsdenken in der öffentlichen Verwaltung (5).

Nachdenken über Zukunft

Die Zukunftsorientierung ist historisch recht neu. Der Historiker Reinhart Koselleck identifizierte für die Zeit um 1800 eine Wende im Zukunftsdenken. Hatten die Menschen bis dahin in einem Kreislauf des Gleichen gelebt, wurde Zukunft nun als etwas Neues gedacht (Koselleck 1979), was es relevant machte, über die Gegenwart hinaus zu denken und die Zukunft zu planen. Noch bis heute lässt sich eine „allseits praktizierte Kurzfristigkeitsorientierung" (Druyen 2016, S. 233) beobachten, die von Quartalsabschlüssen, Innovationszyklen oder der Dauer von Legislaturperioden verfestigt wird. Hinsichtlich einer langfristigen Vorausschau besteht ein Vakuum, das psychologisch, politisch und gesellschaftlich aufrechterhalten wird. Im 20. Jahrhundert, insbesondere seit den 1960-er Jahren, entwickelte die Zukunftsforschung Methoden und Strategien, sich systematisch mit zukünftigen Entwicklungen zu befassen und Zukunftsszenarien in die Planung von Organisationen mit einzubeziehen (Steinmüller 2012).

Doch die Zukunft ist immer unsicher. Sie ist a priori abwesend und kann daher nur in der Gegenwart als gemachte, imaginierte Zukunft gedacht werden (Bühler und Willer 2016, S. 9). Frühe Ansätze der Futurologie legten nahe (Flechtheim 1980), dass die Zukunft im Sinne einer „Science of Probability" vorausbestimmt werden könne. Der Zukunftsforscher Bertrand De Jouvenel kritisierte diesen Determinismus und es muss heute von der Gemachtheit und demzufolge auch von Pluralität der Zukunft ausgegangen werden. Wenn wir hier also über die Zukunft nachdenken, denken wir im Plural an „mögliche Zukünfte" (de Jouvenel 1967). In diesem Verständnis handelt es sich also um einen aktiven Konstruktionsprozess von Zukunftsvoraussagen.

Armin Grunwald weist darauf hin, dass Zukunftsprognostik eigentlich Gegenwartsdenken ist, da sie sich mit „in der Gegenwart erzeugten und zu begründenden Zukunftsannahmen" (Grunwald 2009, S. 31) befasst. Die Entwürfe der Zukunft basieren immer auf dem gegenwärtigen Wissen.

Zukunftsentwürfe wirken in der Gegenwart wie Interventionen. „Prognosen wirken appelativ und persuasiv, als szientifische Ermunterungen, Aufforderungen, Mahnungen, Drohungen, Versprechungen, Verheißungen" (Bühler und Willer 2016, S. 15). Sie können auf unintendierte und unvorhergesehene Weise die zukünftigen Entwicklungen verändern, wodurch sich wiederum die Bedingungen für die Voraussagen wandeln. Zukunftsdenken erzeugt also eine Veränderungsdynamik, die die Zukunftsentwürfe überholt, sobald sie kommuniziert werden.

Für das Verständnis der Zukunftsvorausschau sind somit zwei Prämissen festzuhalten: a) die Erkenntnisse über Zukünfte werden immer in der Gegenwart erzeugt und b) das Zukunftswissen interveniert in der Gegenwart, d. h. das Wissen verändert die zukünftige Entwicklung und verändert damit bereits die Voraussetzungen für die Voraussage.

Zukunftsprognostik liefert somit keine Sicherheit. Dennoch kommt keine Gesellschaft, auch keine Verwaltung, ohne den Bezug auf die Zukunft aus. Die Zukunftsvorausschau „gibt Orientierung, ermöglicht Planung, organisiert Erwartungen, spendet Hoffnung oder erzeugt Ängste" (Bühler und Willer 2016, S. 9). Für die öffentliche Verwaltung dürfte insbesondere die Vorstellung von Sicherheit und Planbarkeit der Zukunft ein Anreiz sein.

Von besonderem Interesse ist hier das Zukunftsdenken öffentlicher Verwaltungen, das exemplarisch am Bereich der Personalarbeit betrachtet wird. Personalplanung in Kommunalverwaltungen bezieht bislang in der Regel keine Methoden der langfristigen Vorausschau ein. Auch wenn die Personalbedarfsplanung als „… die zukunftsgerichtete Bestimmung der personellen Kapazitäten" (Nicolai 2018, S. 47) verstanden werden kann, so orientiert sich diese Zukunftsgerichtetheit meist an den üblichen drei- bis fünfjährigen Ausbildungszyklen (Ausbildungsdauer zzgl. Ausschreibungs- und Bewerbungsphase). Neben den Fragen nach der Anzahl der benötigten Beschäftigten und der Qualifikationen und Kompetenzen dieser Beschäftigten, muss die zeitliche Frage stärker und sorgfältiger berücksichtigt werden: wann und für welche Dauer werden die Personalressourcen benötigt?

Im Zuge der demografischen Entwicklung und der daraus folgenden personellen Engpässe wurde diese Fokussierung bereits vor mehreren Jahren angemahnt. So ist im Bericht der Kommunalen Gemeinschaftsstelle für Verwaltungsmanagement (KGSt) zum Demografischen Wandel von 2010 bereits zu lesen: „Da sich die kommunalen Leistungen und damit der quantitative sowie qualitative Stellenbestand und der Stellenbedarf im Zuge des demografischen Wandels in allen kommunalen Handlungsfeldern verändern werden, ist es zwingend erforderlich, die Personalbedarfsplanung zu verbinden mit: […] einer Entscheidung darüber, welche Fähigkeiten und Fertigkeiten die Beschäftigten in

Zukunft brauchen." (KGSt – Kommunale Gemeinschaftsstelle für Verwaltungsmanagement 2010, S. 24) Dafür werden fachbereichsbezogene Zukunftsszenarien empfohlen.

Angesichts vielfältiger und rascher gesellschaftlicher Veränderungen begründet sich der Bedarf nach Zukunftsvorausschau nicht nur aus dem demografischen Wandel, sondern aus einer Vielzahl von Trends. Eine zunehmende Beschleunigung von sozialem und technischem Wandel und der Steigerung von Produktion und Konsumtion führen zu immer kürzeren Zyklen, in denen sich Bekanntes verändert oder Neues hinzukommt (Rosa 2018, S. 13 f.). Die Zukunftsdynamik ist geprägt durch Beschleunigung und Unsicherheit. Die Arbeit in Kommunalverwaltungen ist hingegen charakterisiert durch eine Kultur der Verlässlichkeit, Sicherheit und Planbarkeit. Dieser Widerspruch könnte hinsichtlich der Personalplanung durch Methoden der langfristigen Zukunftsvorausschau überbrückt werden.

Zukunftsdeutungen in Strategiepapieren des politisch-administrativen Systems –methodisches Vorgehen

Die Untersuchung geht der Frage nach, wie die Zukunft in Strategiepapieren des politisch-administrativen Systems auf Bundes-, Landes- und kommunaler Ebene besprochen wird. Hintergrund des Forschungsinteresses ist ein Projekt an der Hochschule für Polizei und öffentliche Verwaltung Nordrhein-Westfalen, in dem betrachtet wird, wie Kommunen in der Personalplanung und -entwicklung Zukunftsvorausschau betreiben (Schophaus 2018; Schophaus et al. 2019). Dort ist zu ersehen, dass eine langfristige Prognose zukünftiger Entwicklungen in der Regel nicht systematisch vorgenommen wird. Die Perspektive etwa der kommunalen Personalarbeit beschränkt sich meist auf die Zeitdauer von drei bis fünf Jahren. Da aber Zukunftstrends erhebliche Auswirkungen auf die Personalsituation in Kommunen haben, rückt die längerfristige Prognostik in den Blickpunkt. Insbesondere Trends wie der demografische Wandel, aber auch technologische Entwicklungen wie die Digitalisierung, haben enorme langfristige Auswirkungen auf die Personalsituation. Einerseits kommt es zu mehr Wettbewerb und zu Personalengpässen durch den demografischen Wandel. Ein zunehmender Fachkräftemangel ist ein Element von Zukunftsstudien. Andererseits werden andere Kompetenzen erforderlich. Annahmen über die Zukunft verändern die Aufgaben der Kommunen.

Um dieses auf Personalarbeit fokussierte Forschungsprojekt zu zukünftigen Kompetenzanforderungen von Verwaltungsmitarbeiter*innen in einem weiteren

Kontext des Zukunftsdenkens besser verstehen zu können, wird in dem vorliegenden Beitrag auf abstrakterer Ebene das Zukunftsdenken von Verwaltungen hinsichtlich des Trends Digitalisierung betrachtet. Um einen ersten Zugang dazu zu erlangen, bietet sich die Analyse von Dokumenten der Politik und der Verwaltungen an, die den Anspruch haben, sich mit der mittelfristigen Zukunftsperspektive der digitalen Verwaltungen zu befassen. Dafür wurden auf den drei politisch-administrativen Ebenen – Bund, Länder, Kommunen – einzelne Dokumente exemplarisch ausgewählt und auf das Zukunftsverständnis hin analysiert. Das Vorgehen und die ausgewählten Dokumente werden im Folgenden erläutert.

Rekonstruktion von Deutungsmustern aus Strategiedokumenten öffentlicher Verwaltungen

Die Dokumentenanalyse basiert auf der inhaltsanalytischen Auswertung von Konzept- und Strategiepapieren unterschiedlicher öffentlicher Verwaltungen. Das Ziel der Auswertung der Dokumente ist die Rekonstruktion von sozialen Deutungsmustern zur Zukunft der digitalen Verwaltung. Deutungsmuster können allgemein als „die von einem Kollektiv geteilten Vorstellungen über vergleichsweise komplexe Phänomene bezeichnet werden." (Ullrich 2019, S. 7)[2] Beispiele für diese Phänomene sind etwa Armut, Demokratie, Nationalität, soziale Ungleichheit, Familie oder Protest. Dazu gehören aber auch die sozial geteilten Annahmen über die Zukunft sowie über die Digitalisierung. Diese werden aus den genannten Strategiedokumenten rekonstruiert.

Die Auswahl der Dokumente zielt auf Texte, die sich explizit auf die Digitalisierung der öffentlichen Verwaltungen beziehen oder implizit Digitalisierung im Rahmen von breiteren Zukunftsdebatten behandeln (z. B. Leitbilder). Die ausgewerteten Dokumente sind in Tab. 1 als Übersicht dargestellt. Bei unten stehenden Zitaten aus den Dokumenten werden jeweils die Kennzeichnung des Dokumentes (s. Tab. 1) sowie die Seitenzahl im Dokument angegeben (z. B.: „D1, S. 19").

Die Auswahl der Landes- und kommunalen Dokumente aus Nordrhein-Westfalen ist pragmatisch mit der Verortung des Forschungsprojektes an einer

---

[2]Für die genauere Bestimmung der Konzeptionen sozialer Deutungsmuster vgl. Meuser und Sackmann (1991) und aktuell Ullrich (2019, Kap. 1).

Tab. 1 Analysierte Dokumente

Politisch-administrative Ebene	Dokument	Kennzeichnung für Zitation
Bund	Die Bundesregierung (2019). Digitalisierung Gestalten – Umsetzungsstrategie der Bundesregierung. Aktualisierung März 2019 (4. überarbeitete Auflage). Berlin	D1
Land	Die Landesregierung Nordrhein-Westfalen (2019). Strategie für das digitale Nordrhein-Westfalen. Teilhabe ermöglichen – Chancen eröffnen. April 2019 (MWIDE WI-0032). Düsseldorf	D2
Kommune	Stadt Tecklenburg (2015). Tecklenburg 2023: Die Festspielstadt! Leitbild und strategische Ausrichtung. Tecklenburg. Online: https://www.tecklenburg.de/wp-content/uploads/Leitbild-Tecklenburg-2023.pdf [Abgerufen: 01.08.2019]	D3
Kommune	Stadt Münster (2017). Digitale Stadt Münster – Digitalisierungsstrategie der Stadtverwaltung. Münster. Online: https://www.stadt-muenster.de/sessionnet/sessionnetbi/getfile.php?id=414343&type=do [Abgerufen: 01.08.2019]	D4

nordrhein-westfälischen Hochschule zu erklären. Die Auswahl der beiden kommunalen Dokumente berücksichtigt das Ziel, Digitalisierung einmal als Querschnittsthema zu beobachten, das in bestehende Strategiepapiere integriert wird und andererseits eine explizite Digitalisierungsstrategie zu analysieren. Eine Untersuchung von Digitalisierungsstrategien in Kommunen in NRW zeigt, dass von den untersuchten Kommunen 55 % eine separate Digitalisierungsstrategie entwickeln und 45 % der Kommunen sich dazu entscheidet, das Thema Digitalisierung als Querschnittsthema in bestehende Strategiedokumente (z. B. Leitbild, Stadtentwicklungsplan oder Nachhaltigkeitsstrategie) zu integrieren (Niehaves et al. 2018, S. 40).

Die Dokumentenanalyse ist ein nicht-reaktives Verfahren, d. h. die Daten mussten nicht für den vorliegenden Zweck extra erhoben werden und sind nicht durch eine Erhebung verzerrt. Dafür erfordert es allerdings die Betrachtung des Entstehungs- und Nutzungskontextes der Dokumente. Die Betrachtung muss klären, zu welchem Zweck und wie die Daten produziert, genutzt und überliefert wurden (Salheiser 2014, S. 816 f.). Der Kontext der analysierten Dokumente wird im Folgenden betrachtet.

Beschreibung der Dokumente und ihres Entstehungs- und Nutzungskontextes

Der Entstehungszusammenhang der beiden Dokumente auf Bundes- (Die Bundesregierung 2019) und auf Landesebene (Die Landesregierung Nordrhein-Westfalen 2019) ist hier nur allgemein rekonstruierbar, da keine Möglichkeit zur Befragung der handelnden Akteure bestand. Strategiepapiere auf Bundes- oder auf Landesebene haben einen langen Vorlauf, sie sind geprägt von Kompromissen zwischen den jeweils beteiligten Ressorts und letztendlich auch politischen Parteien. Weiter muss in solchen Strategiepapieren ein hoher Abstraktionsgrad gewählt werden, um die Übertragbarkeit auf einen breiten Anwendungskontext für Gesamtdeutschland bzw. im Bundesland zu gewährleisten. Es handelt sich weiter um Expertenpapiere, die also nicht – wie etwa im Fall eines kommunalen Leitbildes (s. u.) – durch die Beteiligung von Bürger*innen oder Betroffenen geprägt sind, sondern im ministeriellen Expertensystem entstanden sind.

Die Umsetzungsstrategie der Bundesregierung knüpft an vorhergehende Programmpapiere zur Digitalisierung an, insbesondere an die Digitale Agenda 2014–2017 (Die Bundesregierung 2014), womit die Bundesregierung erste Antworten zur Gestaltung des digitalen Wandels vorlegen wollte, sowie an die Berichte der Enquete-Kommission „Internet und digitale Gesellschaft" des Deutschen Bundestages (2010–2013)[3], die die Digitalpolitik der Bundesregierung beriet. Das vorliegende Dokument hat also den Charakter einer handlungspraktischen Fortschreibung, mit dem eine neue Phase der Auseinandersetzung mit Digitalisierung angekündigt wird, nämlich die Umsetzung und Gestaltung zuvor erarbeiteter Konzepte.

Strategiepapiere auf Landesebene sind zwar unabhängig von anderen Bundesländern, aber doch eng verknüpft mit dem entsprechenden Diskurs auf Bundesebene. Von einer engen Abstimmung mit bundesweiten Strategien, insbesondere der Digitalisierungsstrategie der Bundesregierung, ist auszugehen. Das wird durch interne Verweise auf die Dokumente der Bundesebene bestätigt.

Die Informationslage zur Entstehung des Leitbildes der Stadt Tecklenburg ist deutlich expliziter, als in den Fällen der beiden oben genannten Dokumente. Es liegen Meta-Bemerkungen und Prozessbeschreibungen zum Leitbildprozess in Tecklenburg vor (Stadt Tecklenburg 2015). Der Leitbild-

---

[3]Vgl. https://www.bundestag.de/internetenquete/ [Abgerufen 01.08.2019].

prozess ist aufgrund von finanziellen Engpässen begonnen worden. Um Lösungen für diese zu finden und dabei Akzeptanz in der Öffentlichkeit für Konsolidierungsmaßnahmen zu erlangen, wurde das Leitbild in einem partizipativen Prozess mit den Bürger*innen der Stadt vorgenommen. In mehreren Beteiligungsworkshops wurden Ideen zum Leitbild gesammelt, priorisiert und dann auf die wichtigsten Eckpunkte und Ziele reduziert. Das Ergebnis wurde vom Stadtrat im Juni 2015 verabschiedet und anschließend im Internet frei zugänglich veröffentlicht.[4]

Die Stadt Münster stellt ihr Digitalisierungskonzept in den größeren Kontext der Stadtentwicklung. Digitalisierung ist damit im Kontext zu sehen mit längerfristigen Zukunftsstrategieprozessen („MünsterZukünfte 20/30/50"[5]), wie auch der „Nachhaltigkeitsstrategie Münster 2030" (Stadt Münster 2018). Die Einordnung in vorangehende Zukunftspapiere wird besonders betont: „Eine Digitalisierungsstrategie der Stadt Münster muss sich einordnen in die strategischen Entwicklungsziele, die mit den genannten übergeordneten Handlungskonzepten formuliert werden." (Stadt Münster 2017, S. 4).

Die Digitalisierungsaktivitäten der Kommunen sind zudem von rechtlichen Vorgaben getrieben, die durch das E-Governmentgesetz des Bundes (EGovG) aus dem Jahr 2013 und darauf aufbauend einem vergleichbaren Gesetz des Landes NRW (EGovG NRW) im Jahr 2016 geprägt sind. Das Gesetz verpflichtet die Kommunen zu bestimmten E-Governmentfunktionen, wird aber von der Stadt Münster überwiegend als Ermöglichungsgesetz mit „Motorfunktion" begriffen (Stadt Münster 2017, S. 6).

Auswertung

Die Dokumente sind zunächst sorgfältig durchgesehen und auf besondere Abschnitte zu den im Interesse stehenden Inhalten überprüft worden. Eine sorgfältige sequentielle Analyse der jeweiligen Einleitung wurde bei allen Texten vorgenommen, um den Sinnkontext einordnen und deuten zu können. Anschließend wurde – insbesondere wegen des Umfangs der zwei langen Dokumente (Bund, Land NRW) – eine Auswahl entsprechender inhaltlicher Passagen auf Grundlage a) der Kapitelüberschriften sowie b) einer Stichwortsuche vorgenommen.

---

[4]Zum Leitbildprozess vgl. https://www.tecklenburg.de/leitbild-2023/ [Abgerufen: 01.08.2019].
[5]https://www.stadt-muenster.de/zukuenfte/ [Abgerufen 01.08.2019].

So wurden Abschnitte identifiziert, die sich mit Zukunft, Digitalisierung und Personalmanagement befassen. Diese wurden inhaltlich kodiert und entsprechende Kodes miteinander verglichen (Mayring 2000). Zur Unterstützung der Analyse wurde die Software für qualitative Datenanalyse MAXQDA (Verbi Software 2013) genutzt.

Aus dem Abgleich der Sequenzen wurden Deutungsmuster zur Zukunft und Zukunftsvorausschau sowie zur Digitalisierung im politisch-administrativen System rekonstruiert.

Ergebnisse

Die Ergebnisse werden in einer Reihe von Deutungen zusammengefasst und im Folgenden komprimiert dargestellt.

Entwicklung entlang vorgegebener ‚Schienen' – Extrapolation des Bestehenden

Eine dominante Denkweise, die sich in den Dokumenten widerspiegelt, ist die Idee von Zukunft als Extrapolation des Bekannten und Bestehenden. Die in den Dokumenten beschriebene Zukunft orientiert sich am Status Quo. Das Bestehende wird auf Kontinua fortgeschrieben, unter der Annahme, dass die Voraussetzungen über den zeitlichen Verlauf gleich bleiben.

Im Leitbild der Stadt Tecklenburg mit einem Zeithorizont bis 2023 werden Ziele formuliert, die genau diese Konzeption von Zukunft zeigen. Zwei Beispiele beschreiben das: „Wir wollen erreichen, dass die Zahl der sozialversicherungspflichtig Beschäftigten in Tecklenburger Betrieben in den nächsten 10 Jahren um 20 % steigt." (D3, S. 6) und „Wir wollen erreichen, dass die Gewerbesteuereinnahmen in Tecklenburg in den nächsten 10 Jahren real um 20 % steigen." (D3, S. 6) Von dem aktuellen Ist-Zustand ausgehend, wird hier Zukunft anhand der Regelung einzelner Veränderungsvariablen konstruiert. Eine Veränderung der Rahmenbedingungen und Voraussetzungen, in denen die Orientierung am Bestehenden nicht möglich oder nicht wünschenswert wäre, wird nicht in Erwägung gezogen. Dieses wäre etwa denkbar unter der Beachtung anderer Zukunftstrends, wie beispielsweise die Konzepte Postwachstum oder Schrumpfung im Rahmen der Debatte zur nachhaltigen Entwicklung. In dem Leitbild werden solche Zukunftstrends aber nicht miteinander in Verbindung gebracht.

Dieselbe Denkweise findet sich ebenso auf anderen politischen Ebenen: „Wir wollen Arbeitsplätze und Wertschöpfung sichern und mehren, indem wir neue Technologien einsetzen." (D2, S. 4) und „Alle Menschen müssen Zugang zu modernen Technologien haben." (D2, S. 4) Die digitalen Technologien sollen zu Wachstum im Bereich Arbeitsplätze und Wohlstand führen. Die Anzahl der Menschen, die über neue Technologien verfügen, soll auf das Maximum erhöht werden. Das Bestehende wird fortgesetzt und gesteigert.

Diese Form der Zukunftskonstruktion impliziert Vorhersehbarkeit und Kontrolle. Es handelt sich um Planungsdenken in Kontinua. Andere Konstruktionen, die etwa in der Zukunftsvorausschau – wie in der Szenarientechnik oder der Visionsarbeit – stattfindet, bemühen sich um die Einbeziehung vielfältiger Änderungsfaktoren und kalkulieren aktiv den Umgang mit Unsicherheit ein. Hier findet sich eher ein binäres Entwicklungskonzept, vergleichbar mit einer Bewegung auf Schienen. Es geht voran, oder zurück. Eine Richtungsänderung wird nicht in Betracht gezogen.

Mehr desselben – Beschleunigte Steigerung von Bestehendem

Eine spezifizierende Qualität des extrapolierenden Zukunftsdenkens ist die Steigerung des Bestehenden. Das oben Gesagte wird hinsichtlich der technischen Erneuerung quantitativ erhöht. Dieses Deutungsmuster des Wachstums ist nicht neu und wird auch für den Trend der Digitalisierung weitergeführt. Neu im Diskurs der Digitalisierung ist allenfalls die Beschleunigung der Steigerung. Die Erwartung an die Digitalisierung ist es, Verbesserungen in noch kürzeren Zeiträumen zu erlangen. Interessant ist, dass diese Steigerungen in der Regel ohne Verweis auf ein gesichertes Wissen über den Ausgangspunkt – etwa in Form von Evaluationsergebnissen – formuliert werden. Wenn also die Zukunft als „schneller", „besser", „effizienter", „flexibler" und „transparenter" vorgestellt wird, wird die Gegenwart implizit als zu langsam, unflexibel, intransparent etc. beschrieben. Ob überhaupt Wissen darüber vorliegt, wie langsam, unflexibel etc. die gegenwärtigen Prozesse ablaufen, bleibt aber offen.

Die Dokumente sind geprägt von Steigerungsformen. Es geht etwa um „schnellere Innovation" (D1, S. 44), um „Schnelleres Erreichen der Einsatzreife neuer Systeme" (D1, S. 79), Berichtpflichten „sollen zukünftig schneller und deutlich effizienter erfüllt werden" (D1, S. 1138), der „Datenaustausch zwischen Bund, Länder und der EU soll flexiblere und schnellere Übermittlungen und Auswertungen ermöglichen, um auf Ereignisse und krisenhafte Geschehnisse noch schneller und adäquat reagieren zu können." (D1, S. 138) In NRW sollen „Echtzeitinformationen zur Verkehrslage [...] leichter und schneller verfügbar sein." (D2, S. 30) Die Digitalisierung bietet das Potenzial, die „Verwaltungsabläufe schneller und unkomplizierter zu machen" (D2, S. 41) und „erlaubt, Informationen und Daten den Bürgerinnen und Bürgern schneller und besser aufbereitet zur Verfügung zu stellen." (D2, S. 41) „Transparentere Verwaltungsprozesse" (D1, S. 43), „Zugang zu effizienteren [...] digitalen Verwaltungssystemen" (D1, S. 120) sowie „bessere Beteiligungsmöglichkeiten" (D1, S. 120) werden durch die Digitalisierung erwartet. Auf kommunaler Ebene wurden oben bereits die quantitativen Wachstumsziele benannt, etwa die Steigerung von Einwohnerzahlen, Beschäftigungszahlen oder der Gewerbesteuer (D3, S. 6). Zukunft wird konstruiert als ‚mehr desselben'.

Digitalisierung der Vergangenheit – Überlagerung bekannter Diskurse mit neuen Zukunftstrends

Die Zukunftsgestaltung orientiert sich an stabilen Zielen, die durch neue technologische Diskurse überlagert werden. Insbesondere wird hier der Entbürokratisierungsdiskurs mit neuen Begriffen und neuer Technologie überlagert. Diese Deutung zeigt sich in folgendem Zitat zum Verwaltungshandeln: „Wir werden das Recht für die Digitalisierung anpassen und teilweise vollständig auf Anträge verzichten. Wir können uns dann aktiv um die Anliegen der Menschen kümmern. So könnte beispielsweise Eltern nach der Geburt ihres Kindes ohne weitere Antragstellung die Geburtsurkunde übersandt und Kindergeld ausgezahlt werden." (D1, S. 131)

Als Beispiele für die Digitalisierungsvorteile werden hier zwei Beispiele für Dienstleistungen herangezogen, die genauso auch unter dem Stichwort des Bürokratieabbaus ohne neue Technologie hätten genannt werden können. Auf eine separate Antragstellung für die Übersendung der Geburtsurkunde sowie für die Auszahlung des Kindergeldes, könnte auch unabhängig von Digitalisierungsprozessen verzichtet werden. Bereits bekannte aber nicht umgesetzte Forderungen (Bürokratieabbau) werden unter dem Titel der Digitalisierung neu aufgelegt. Daraus darf gefolgert werden, dass Defizite in der Umsetzung von vergangenen Reformversprechen nun in ein neu formuliertes Versprechen übernommen werden. Digitalisierung wird in bestehende Reformprozesse integriert: „Digitalisierung ist Teil von Verwaltungsmodernisierung." (D4, S. 7)

Ob das Versprechen durch Digitalisierung bessere Umsetzungschancen hat, wird durch Widersprüche in den Zielbeschreibungen infrage gestellt. So wird die

Antragsfreiheit im gleichen Text später wieder negiert, aus ‚ohne Antrag' wird ‚online-Beantragung': „Wir wollen vereinfachte und komfortable datenschutzkonforme Online-Beantragung und Bearbeitung von Elterngeld." (D1, S. 132)

Kommunaler Flaschenhals – Diskrepanzen zwischen den Politikebenen

Mit abnehmender politisch-administrativer Ebene wandelt sich die Auseinandersetzung mit der Zukunft von abstrakten zu konkreten Vorstellungen. Die Digitalisierung, die sich aus nationaler oder Landesperspektive als unbedingt notwendig und allumfassend darstellt, wird in Einzelmaßnahmen auf der kommunalen Ebene auf praktische Umsetzbarkeit hin kritisch überprüft.

So heißt es im Strategiepapier der Bundesregierung: „Moderne Verwaltung braucht eine moderne Ausstattung. Ausstattung alleine genügt jedoch nicht. Es müssen auch die notwendigen Kompetenzen vorhanden sein. Wir wollen eine digital kompetente Verwaltung in einer digitalen Gesellschaft." (D1, S. 131) Hier wird Wandel weitreichend für die Verwaltung und Gesellschaft gefordert. Auf kommunaler Ebene geht es dann um konkrete kommunal finanzierte Umsetzungen. In der Stadt Münster wird deutlich gemacht, dass Vorteile nicht umsonst zu haben sind: „Die zukünftigen Chancen und Potentiale der Digitalisierung sind gewaltig. Ihre Erschließung ist aber nur mit einem deutlich erweiterten Finanz- und Personalrahmen möglich." (D4, S. 21) Im Zusammenhang mit Effizienzsteigerungen durch mehr Zusammenarbeit heißt es im Leitbild Tecklenburg sehr viel zurückhaltender: „Weitere Möglichkeiten zur Effizienzsteigerung sind unter Umständen durch eine stärkere Nutzung von Online-Verfahren im Rahmen des e-Government zu erschließen. Hierfür sind jedoch zunächst Investitionen zu veranschlagen, sodass Einsparungen erst längerfristig erwartet werden können." (D3, S. 5).

Die Darstellungsform des „brauchen" und „müssen" in dem Bundesdokument wird auf kommunaler Umsetzungsebene relativiert durch Begrifflichkeiten wie „unter Umständen", „längerfristig" und „können erwartet werden". Die Notwendigkeit der Entwicklungen und Veränderungen nimmt in Politik und Verwaltung offenbar von oben nach unten hin ab.

Im Maßnahmenprogramm der Bundesregierung werden Veränderungslinien großzügig vorgezeichnet und dann in Form von (Pilot-)Projekten konkretisiert. Auf kommunaler Ebene hingegen müssen die Zukunftsziele in die Fläche gebracht werden, was – wie hier am Beispiel der Haushaltskonsolidierung gezeigt – mit sehr viel mehr Vorbehalten vorstellbar wird.

Zukunft als „Aufholjagd" – Defensives Zukunftsdenken als Reaktion auf Defizite

Wir finden in den Dokumenten ein weiteres Muster in der Art der Auseinandersetzung mit der Zukunft, das ich als „Defensives Zukunftsdenken" bezeichnen möchte: Politik und Verwaltung reagieren auf Defizite in der Vergangenheit und Gegenwart. Zukunftsdenken und strategische Vorausschau findet offenbar besonders dann statt, wenn Defizite im Status Quo wahrgenommen werden. Das zeigt sich im Digitalisierungsdiskurs deutlich auf allen drei Verwaltungsebenen.

Auf Landesebene in NRW wird von einer „Aufholjagd" gesprochen. Zukunftsdenken orientiert sich am Vergleich mit anderen Bundesländern und anderen Nationen. So beschreibt das Land NRW seine Ausgangslage im Digitalisierungsprozess so: „Eine Aufholjagd, auch im internationalen Vergleich, ist bei Infrastruktur, Bildung, Mobilität, Gesundheit und E-Government notwendig. Wir benötigen sie, um unser Bundesland fit zu machen für die digitale Zukunft." (D2, S. 9)

Die Entwicklungsdefizite sollen durch eine „Jagd" ausgeglichen werden. Der kämpferische Jagdbegriff verweist dabei auf die zeitliche Zukunftsdynamik: Geschwindigkeit ist existentiell. Kann der Standort nicht mit anderen Standorten gleichziehen oder überholen, so wäre die Jagd verloren, was existentielle Folgen hat. Die Jagd ist ein starkes Bild für diesen Prozess: misslingt eine Jagd, so mangelt es an Nahrungsmitteln. Das ist die gravierende Bedeutung, die der Digitalisierung zugeschrieben wird. Scheitert die Digitalisierung in der Zukunft, so werden existentielle Probleme im zukünftigen Leben und Wirtschaften erwartet.

Im kommunalen Beispiel zeigt sich die gleiche Dynamik. Die Notwendigkeit der Leitbildentwicklung und der strategischen Planung wird mit einem massiven Mangel begründet. Verschuldung und Konsolidierungsdruck zwingen zur strategischen Auseinandersetzung mit der Zukunft: „Die Stadt Tecklenburg steht vor der Notwendigkeit einer nachhaltigen und substanziellen Konsolidierung und Entschuldung des städtischen Haushalts." (D3, S. 1)

Die Stadt Münster beschreibt den Prozess gar als technologisch determiniert: „Digitalisierung ist kein Projekt! Sie ist eine nicht mehr umkehrbare laufende technische Weiterentwicklung ohne Enddatum. Daher ist die Digitalisierung als nachhaltiger Prozess zu organisieren, damit die Stadtverwaltung, der Stadtkonzern und die gesamte Stadt Münster auch morgen und übermorgen noch up to date sind." (D4, S. 8)

Die Zukunft wird durch die technologische Entwicklung getrieben. Digitalisierung wird als unabhängiger und unaufhaltsamer Prozess beschrieben.

Dieser kann zwar ausgestaltet, nicht aber gestoppt werden. Nur wenn die Aufholjagd gewonnen wird, kann Politik und Verwaltung wieder Steuerungsmöglichkeiten zurückgewinnen: „Hierzu müssen die citeq [städtischer IT-Dienstleister der Stadt Münster, Anm. des Autors] und die städtischen Ämter und Einrichtungen sich neu positionieren […] und so gemeinsam zum Treiber der Digitalisierung werden." (D4, S. 8)

Andere Städte formulieren dies noch expliziter in ihren Digitalisierungsstrategien, so etwa die Stadt Wuppertal: „Die technischen Möglichkeiten sind aber mittlerweile so weit, dass die Digitalisierung vom Werkzeug zum Motor wird und die Arbeitsweise und die Struktur der Verwaltung selbst grundlegend verändert." (Stadt Wuppertal/Amt für Informationstechnik und Digitalisierung 2018, S. 3) Die Technologie verändert die Arbeitsweise und die Struktur der Verwaltung. Nicht etwa die Politik – also gewählte Vertreter des Volkes – verändern die Verwaltung, sondern ein technologischer Digitalisierungsprozess ist der Motor. Politik und Verwaltung sind in der Defensive.

Das Strategiedokument der Bundesregierung betont durch aktive Formulierungen die proaktiven Möglichkeiten des Gestaltens im digitalen Wandel. Bereits der Titel des Dokumentes ist „Digitalisierung gestalten" (D1, S. 1). Das Muster des defensiven Zukunftsdenkens prägt aber auch dieses Dokument, sogar noch grundlegender als zuvor gesehen. Denn auch das Gestalten wird als eine Reaktion auf einen unaufhaltsamen technischen Wandlungsprozess beschrieben. Die Zukunft wird als vorgegeben konstruiert, lediglich die Ausgestaltung und das „beherrschbar machen" (D1, S. 4) der Risiken sind noch variabel. So heißt es einleitend am Beginn des Dokumentes:

„Der digitale Wandel verändert unsere Art zu leben, zu arbeiten und zu lernen fundamental und mit rasanter Geschwindigkeit. Wir, die Bundesregierung, wollen diesen Wandel gestalten und unser Land auf die Zukunft bestmöglich vorbereiten. Im Mittelpunkt steht: Was bringt die Digitalisierung dem Einzelnen? Und: Wie erhalten und stärken wir die Werte unserer freiheitlich demokratischen Grundordnung im digitalen Zeitalter?" (D1, S. 4)

Der digitale Wandel verändert das gesamte Leben, er verändert es fundamental und rasant. Die Bundesregierung möchte „unser Land auf die Zukunft bestmöglich vorbereiten". Es geht um die digitalisierte Zukunft. Dieser Aspekt von Zukunft wird als unveränderbar gedeutet. Ob Digitalisierung nicht aufhaltbar ist – geradezu wie eine naturgegebene Entwicklung – oder nicht aufgehalten werden soll, wird nicht explizit. Sicher sind aber die fundamentalen und riskanten Veränderungen, auf die keine ideale Vorbereitung denkbar ist, lediglich „bestmöglich" kann die Bundesregierung ihr Land vorbereiten. Hier greift die Deutung des defensiven Zukunftsdenkens: so gut wie eben möglich wird auf eigendynamische

Veränderungen reagiert. Und diese Veränderungen – bis hierhin zwar möglichst neutral formuliert – werden als Bedrohung gedeutet. Es geht um den Erhalt der freiheitlich demokratischen Grundordnung im digitalen Zeitalter. Hier wird eine Zukunft konstruiert, in der ein unabwendbarer Wandel die freiheitlich demokratische Grundordnung infrage stellt, ja angreift. Auf diese Bedrohung reagiert die Bundesregierung mit dem vorgelegten Maßnahmenkatalog.

Personalarbeit in den Zukunftsstrategien

Deutungsmuster der Zukunft im Kontext der Digitalisierung der öffentlichen Verwaltungen sind oben rekonstruiert worden. Wie verhalten sich diese nun für die Zukunft des Personalmanagements in öffentlichen Verwaltungen? Die Dokumente werden im Folgenden spezifischer hinsichtlich der Deutungen zum Personal analysiert.

Die Bedeutung von Personal ist im Digitalisierungsdiskurs immer präsent, da die sich verändernden Wissens- und Kompetenzanforderungen durch Digitalisierungsprozesse als bedeutsam eingeschätzt werden. Der Kompetenzerwerb zu den Herausforderungen der Digitalisierung wird als Grundlage zur Bewältigung der als fundamental eingeschätzten Digitalisierungsrisiken benannt. Diese Einschätzung gilt für den Beruf, aber auch für alle anderen Lebensbereiche: „Kompetenzen sind entscheidend für Teilhabe – an Wissen und Kommunikation, für gelingendes Aufwachsen, für gesellschaftliche und betriebliche Partizipation, für berufliche wie persönliche Entwicklung sowie für lebensbegleitendes und generationenübergreifendes Lernen." (D2, S. 22)

Auf gesellschaftlicher Ebene gelten Kompetenzen als grundlegend für die Wirtschaft: „Die Sicherstellung von ‚Kompetenzen in einer digital geprägten Welt' ist Basis für die Innovationsfähigkeit unserer Gesellschaft und unserer Wirtschaft." (D2, S. 22)

Ein höherer Stellenwert könnte den digitalen Kompetenzen nicht eingeräumt werden. Das bestätigt auch die Auswahl „Digitale Kompetenz" als erstes der fünf Handlungsfelder in der Umsetzungsstrategie zur Digitalisierung der Bundesregierung (D1, S. 6). Dieses wird auch für die öffentliche Verwaltung bestätigt: „Wir wollen eine digital kompetente Verwaltung in einer digitalen Gesellschaft." (D1, S. 131)

Der Handlungsdruck in der Personalarbeit wird darin erkennbar, dass eine ganz neue Art der Verwaltung nahegelegt wird: „Personalentwicklung und -gewinnung in der digitalen Verwaltung" (D1, S. 158). Personalmanagement muss sich verändern, da erwartet wird, dass der Gegenstand sich ändert. Aus der (analogen) Verwaltung wird die digitale Verwaltung. Das umfasst Materielles wie Immaterielles. Hinsichtlich der Kompetenzen in der Verwaltung wird die Besonderheit hervorgehoben, dass die technische Entwicklung der Ausstattung und der digitalen Kompetenzen immer einhergehen müssen: „Moderne Verwaltung braucht eine moderne Ausstattung. Ausstattung alleine genügt jedoch nicht. Es müssen auch die notwendigen Kompetenzen vorhanden sein." (D1, S. 131)

Die Bundesverwaltung setzt sich zum Ziel: „Wir schaffen eine behördenübergreifende Personalentwicklung von Führungskräften (insbesondere zukünftig benötigte Kompetenzen und Maßnahmen zur Qualifizierung) und eine Verbesserung von Personalgewinnungsprozessen, insbesondere für IT-Fachkräfte." (D1, S. 137) Die Kooperation zwischen Organisationseinheiten, Behörden und Ressorts soll intensiviert werden. Ziel ist „die ressortübergreifende Personalentwicklung von Führungskräften." (D1, S. 158) Das gilt auch für die Kooperation innerhalb und zwischen Kommunen: „Es ist davon auszugehen, dass in Zukunft interkommunale Kooperationen und die Entwicklung kooperativer Formen mobiler oder stationärer Verwaltungs- und privater Dienstleistungen als Mittel der Kostensenkung und Möglichkeit zur Erhaltung von Angeboten an Bedeutung gewinnen werden. Kooperationen bieten sich dabei vor allem im Bereich der inneren Verwaltung an (Personal, Buchhaltung, Logistik, Datenverarbeitung) […]." (D3, S. 5)

Flexibilisierungsbedarf wird auch in der Definition und Messung von Kompetenzen erwartet, was insbesondere die Personalauswahl vor neue Aufgaben stellen dürfte: „Die Arbeitsgesellschaft ist durchlässiger geworden. […] Das Können zählt mehr als Dienstjahre, Position oder Zeugnisse. Informell erworbene Kompetenzen erfahren mehr Wertschätzung, Aufstiegschancen sind nicht nur von zertifizierter Bildung abhängig." (D2, S. 8) Um dieses Verständnis von Kompetenz mit dem Leistungs- und Laufbahnprinzip im öffentlichen Dienst konform zu gestalten, bedarf es einen umfangreichen Wandel im Selbstverständnis des Personalwesens.

Flexibilität reagiert einerseits auf die raschen Veränderungen von Aufgaben in der digitalisierten Verwaltung, zugleich kann darin aber auch die Vorbereitung auf einen Fachkräftemangel oder aber die Reaktion auf Effizienzsteigerung unter Konsolidierungsdruck erkannt werden. Letzteres gilt für die untersuchte Stadt Tecklenburg. Hier ist ein direkter Zusammenhang zu Kosteneinsparungen zu sehen. Tecklenburg ist laut Leitbild entschlossen, „[…] alle Möglichkeiten zur Entlastung des städtischen Haushalts durch Reduzierung der Aufwendungen und Steigerung der Erträge zu nutzen." (D3, S. 6) Für das Personal heißt das: „Daher fördern wir die Flexibilität und Leistungsbereitschaft unserer Mitarbeiterinnen und Mitarbeiter, um sie auf künftige Anforderungen besser vorzubereiten." (D3, S. 6)

Lebenslange Kompetenzentwicklung, Flexibilität und organisations- und disziplinenübergreifende Kooperation werden als zentrale Entwicklungsziele für das Personal in der digitalen Verwaltung bestimmt.

Zusammenfassung und Fazit

Zukunftsvorstellungen von öffentlichen Verwaltungen wurden hinsichtlich des Digitalisierungstrends analysiert. Dazu wurden die Deutungsmuster über zukünftige Entwicklungen aus Strategiedokumenten der Bundes-, Landes- und kommunalen Verwaltungsebene rekonstruiert. Folgende Deutungen bestimmen das Zukunftsdenken der Verwaltungen:

- *Entwicklung auf Schienen.*

Zukunft wird als Extrapolation des Bekannten und Bestehenden gedacht. Bestehendes wird – wie eine Vor- oder Rückwärtsbewegung auf Schienen – unter der Annahme fortgeschrieben, dass die Voraussetzungen über den zeitlichen Verlauf gleich bleiben.

- *Mehr desselben.*

Das extrapolierende Zukunftsdenken ist durch eine Steigerungsannahme geprägt. Bekannte Deutungsmuster des Wachstums werden auch für den Trend der Digitalisierung weitergeführt. Neu im Diskurs der Digitalisierung ist die Beschleunigung der Steigerung.

- *Digitalisierung der Vergangenheit.*

Die Zukunftsgestaltung orientiert sich an stabilen Zielen, die durch neue technologische Diskurse überlagert werden. Insbesondere wird in der Auseinandersetzung mit Digitalisierung der Diskurs zum Bürokratieabbau fortgeführt.

- *Kommunaler Flaschenhals.*

Weitreichende Vorstellungen zur zukünftigen Gestaltung der Digitalisierung aus nationaler oder Landesperspektive werden auf kommunaler Ebene sehr kritisch auf praktische Umsetzbarkeit überprüft.

- *Zukunft als „Aufholjagd"*

Defensives Zukunftsdenken prägt die Auseinandersetzung von Politik und Verwaltung mit der Zukunft. Es reagiert auf Defizite der Vergangenheit, die Defizite ergeben sich aus dem Vergleich mit konkurrierenden Standorten. Zukunft wird als „Aufholjagd" in diesem Wettbewerb gedacht.

In Bezug auf das Personalwesen im öffentlichen Dienst wird deutlich, dass die Digitalisierung alle Bereiche der Personalarbeit betrifft und verändert. Im Vordergrund steht dabei der Wandel der Verwaltungsaufgaben durch Digitalisierung, was neue Kompetenzen bei den Mitarbeiter*innen erfordert. Als zentral gilt die Flexibilität der Mitarbeiter*innen, um sich auf die sich immer rascher ändernden Aufgaben einstellen zu können. Der Anspruch des Kompetenzerwerbs in der Digitalisierung geht aber weit darüber hinaus, da er nicht nur für berufliche Aufgaben als wichtig gedeutet wird, sondern über alle Lebensbereiche und Lebens- und Arbeitsphasen hinweg für die gesellschaftliche Teilhabe sowie für die berufliche und persönliche Entwicklung wichtig erscheint. Daraus dürfte seitens der Verwaltungen der dringende Bedarf abgeleitet werden, Personalentwicklung, berufliche Ausbildung sowie lebenslange Bildungsprozesse außerhalb des Berufs stärker aufeinander zu beziehen und als Einheit zu betrachten. Diese Deutung hätte enorme Auswirkungen auf das Verständnis und die Ausgangsbedingungen der Personalauswahl und -entwicklung.

Abschließend kann festgehalten werden, dass sich erwartbarer Weise kein einheitliches Bild des Zukunftsdenkens von Verwaltungen hinsichtlich der Digitalisierung ergibt. Vielmehr weisen die Deutungsmuster der Verwaltungen auf die Bearbeitung eines Widerspruchs hin. Der Diskurs ist durch zwei auseinander strebende Deutungspole geprägt. Einerseits gibt es den Versuch, Kontrolle über einen technischen Entwicklungsprozess zu gewinnen, der den Verwaltungen durch seine beschleunigte Eigendynamik aufgezwungen wird. Andererseits wird die technische Entwicklung als sehr hoch gewichtetes Potenzial gedeutet, das Reformen der Verwaltungen voranbringen kann und Flexibilität und Kreativität in der Verwaltungsarbeit und im Angebot ihrer Dienstleistungen zu erzeugen vermag.

Beide Pole werden zum Teil drastisch formuliert. Zukunft wird in der heutigen Sozialforschung mit folgenden Merkmalen beschrieben: prozesshaft, unsicher, konstruiert, offen. Das Zukunftsdenken von Politik und Verwaltung ist geprägt durch den Versuch, diese Merkmale zu negieren und durch den (Wieder-)Gewinn von Kontrolle aufzuheben. Es wird versucht, den Prozess statisch beschreibbar zu machen: statt prozesshaft werden Entwicklungen ‚zukunftsfest' gemacht. Die Offenheit wird auf das Voranschreiten und Steigern bekannter Dimensionen – wie auf festgelegten ‚Schienen' – begrenzt. Der Konstruktionsprozess, der das Performative des Veränderns – also die Veränderung der Randbedingungen durch jede Intervention – beinhaltet, wird auf ein Fortschreiben und Steigern des Bekannten reduziert. Zukunftsdenken in Bezug auf Digitalisierung wird auf dieser Seite des Widerspruchs nicht als kreativer offener Prozess der Gestaltung von neuen Entwicklungen beschrieben. Die digitalisierte Zukunft wird als Bedrohung gedacht, die als Motor der gesellschaftlichen Entwicklung der Politik und Verwaltung die Steuerung aus der Hand genommen hat. Diesen Kontrollverlust gilt es nun rückgängig zu machen und anschließend in Potenziale und Chancen umzuformen.

Auf der anderen Seite werden diese Potenziale durchaus gesehen und in den Dokumenten bereits beschreibbar gemacht. Kompetenzerwerb von Verwaltungspersonal und Bürger*innen werden zusammengedacht, die Ausweitung der Teilhabe von Menschen an unterschiedlichen gesellschaftlichen Teilbereichen wird als möglich erachtet. Das Verhältnis von Bürger*innen und Verwaltung soll durch die neuen technischen Kommunikationsmodi neu bestimmt und kooperativ werden.

Das Zukunftsdenken der digitalisierten Verwaltungen muss innerhalb dieses Spannungsfeldes aus Defensive und Kontrollbedürfnis sowie Veränderungswunsch und Innovationspotenzial gedeutet werden.

Literatur

Bühler, B., & Willer, S. (2016). Einleitung. In B. Bühler & S. Willer (Hrsg.), *Futurologien: Ordnungen des Zukunftswissens* (S. 9–21). Paderborn: Wilhelm Fink.
Bundesministerium für Bildung und Forschung – BMBF (Hrsg.) (2015). *Zukunft verstehen, Zukunft gestalten. Deutschland 2030: Ergebnisse des zweiten Foresight-Zyklus*. Online: https://www.bmbf.de/pub/Zukunft_verstehen_Zukunft_gestalten.pdf *[Abgerufen 01.08.2019]*.
de Jouvenel, B. (1967). *Die Kunst der Vorausschau*. Neuwied: Luchterhand.
Die Bundesregierung (2014). *Digitale Agenda 2014–2017*. Berlin.
Die Bundesregierung (2019). *Digitalisierung Gestalten – Umsetzungsstrategie der Bundesregierung. (Aktualisierung März 2019, 4. Überarbeitete Auflage)*. Berlin.
Die Landesregierung Nordrhein-Westfalen (2019). *Strategie für das digitale Nordrhein-Westfalen. Teilhabe ermöglichen – Chancen eröffnen. April 2019 (MWIDE WI-0032)*. Düsseldorf.
Druyen, T. (2016). *Drei Generationen im Gespräch: Eine Studie zum intergenerativen Zukunftsmanagement*. Wiesbaden: Springer.

Flechtheim, O. K. (1980). *Der Kampf um die Zukunft. Grundlagen der Futurologie.* Bonn: Dietz.
Grunwald, A. (2009). Wovon ist die Zukunftsforschung eine Wissenschaft? In R. Popp & E. Schüll (Hrsg.), *Zukunftsforschung und Zukunftsgestaltung: Beiträge aus Wissenschaft und Praxis* (S. 25–35). Berlin: Springer.
KGSt – Kommunale Gemeinschaftsstelle für Verwaltungsmanagement (Hrsg.) (2010). *Der demografische Wandel in Kommunalverwaltungen. Strategische Ausrichtung und Handlungsansätze des Personalmanagements. KGSt-Bericht 3/2010.* Köln.
Koselleck, R. (1979). *Vergangene Zukunft: Zur Semantik geschichtlicher Zeiten.* Frankfurt a. M.: Suhrkamp.
Mayntz, R. (1982). *Soziologie der öffentlichen Verwaltung* (2. Aufl.). Heidelberg: UTB.
Mayring, P. (2000). *Qualitative Inhaltsanalyse. Grundlagen und Techniken.* Weinheim: Deutscher Studien Verlag.
Meuser, M., & Sackmann, R. (1991). *Zur Einführung—Deutungsmusteransatz und empirische Wissenssoziologie.* Pfaffenweiler: Centaurus.
Nicolai, C. (2018). *Personalmanagement* (5., überarbeitete und erweiterte Auflage). Konstanz: UVK.
Niehaves, B., Röding, K., Oschinsky, F., Klein, H. C., Weigel, H., & Hoffmann, J. (2018). *Digitalisierungsstrategien für Kommunen—Studie im Rahmen des Projekts „Digitale Modellkommunen" in Nordrhein-Westfalen.* Siegen.
Rosa, H. (2018). *Resonanz: Eine Soziologie der Weltbeziehung.* Berlin: Suhrkamp.
Salheiser, A. (2014). Natürliche Daten: Dokumente. In N. Baur & J. Blasius (Hrsg.), *Handbuch Methoden der empirischen Sozialforschung* (S. 813–827). Wiesbaden: Springer.
Schophaus, M. (2018). Digitalisierung, Demographie, Neue Arbeit – Zukunftstrends und ihre Auswirkungen auf Kompetenzanforderungen an Verwaltungspersonal. In A. Gourmelon (Hrsg.), *Personalauswahl – Ein Blick in die Zukunft* (S. 5–24). Heidelberg: Rehm.
Schophaus, M., Gourmelon, A., & Winschuh, T. (2019). Verwaltung 2030 – Zukünftige Kompetenzanforderungen an das Personal in Kommunalverwaltungen. *Der öffentliche Dienst, 09/2019,* 1–8.
Stadt Münster (2017). *Digitale Stadt Münster – Digitalisierungsstrategie der Stadtverwaltung.* Münster.
Stadt Münster (2018). *Nachhaltigkeitsstrategie Münster 2030 – Entwurfsfassung.* Münster. Online: https://www.stadt-muenster.de/fileadmin/user_upload/stadt-muenster/67_umwelt/pdf/gnk_nachhaltigkeitsstrategie-muenster2030_entwurf.pdf *[Abgerufen: 01.08.2019].*
Stadt Tecklenburg (2015). *Tecklenburg 2023: Die Festspielstadt! Leitbild und strategische Ausrichtung.* Tecklenburg. Online: https://www.tecklenburg.de/wp-content/uploads/Leitbild-Tecklenburg-2023.pdf *[Abgerufen: 01.08.2019].*
Stadt Wuppertal/Amt für Informationstechnik und Digitalisierung (Hrsg.) (2018). *digiTal 2023. IT- und Digitalisierungsstrategie der Stadtverwaltung Wuppertal 2018–2023.* Wuppertal.
Steinmüller, K. (2012). Zukunftsforschung in Deutschland – Versuch eines historischen Abrisses (Teil 1). *Zeitschrift für Zukunftsforschung, 1*(1), 6–19.
Ullrich, C. G. (2019). *Das Diskursive Interview: Methodische und methodologische Grundlagen.* Wiesbaden: Springer.
Verbi Software. (2013). *MAXQDA 11 [computer software].* Berlin: Verbi.

Time and Futures. Zeit und Zukünfte in der Vorausschau – Konzepte in den Zukunftswissenschaften

Kerstin Cuhls

Abstract

This contribution about time and futures is from Foresight. It introduces Foresight as the long-term view into the future or different futures, defined as the more action-oriented "structured debate about complex futures". The academic counterpart is Futures Research dealing with possible, probable and desirable future developments. Since we regard the future as open, we talk about Futures and have different time concepts in mind when we talk about the future. Methods are available to work with the different time horizons (e.g. Delphi surveys), to prepare for "the future" with different long-term scenarios, to support decision making or even to travel as thought experiments in time. But although investments in new infrastructures, technologies or changes in people's behaviour must take into account periods of up to 30, 40 or even more years, decisions today are often made ad hoc. Many do not take the time to think about the (long-term) consequences of what we are doing now. This article provides an overview of the possibilities for dealing with the future – and which methods can be used to scale future times.

K. Cuhls (✉)
Fraunhofer-Institut für System- und Innovationsforschung (ISI), Karlsruhe, Deutschland
E-Mail: kerstin.cuhls@isi.fraunhofer.de

Zusammenfassung

Dieser Beitrag über Zeit und Zukunft stammt aus dem Konzept der Vorausschau (Foresight) bzw. der Zukunftsforschung. Er stellt Foresight als den langfristigen Blick in die Zukunft oder unterschiedliche Zukünfte, definiert als die handlungsorientierte „strukturierte Debatte über komplexe Zukünfte", vor. Das akademische Pendant ist die Zukunftsforschung, die sich mit möglichen, wahrscheinlichen und wünschenswerten zukünftigen Entwicklungen (Zukünften) beschäftigt. Da wir die Zukunft als offen betrachten, sprechen wir über Zukünfte und haben unterschiedliche Zeitkonzepte im Blick, wenn wir über die Zukunft sprechen. Es stehen Methoden zur Verfügung, um mit den verschiedenen Zeithorizonten zu arbeiten (z. B. Delphi-Befragungen, Szenarien), um sich mit verschiedenen Langzeitszenarien auf „die Zukunft" vorzubereiten, die Entscheidungsfindung zu unterstützen oder sogar als Gedankenexperimente in der Zeit zu reisen. Aber obwohl bei Investitionen in neue Infrastrukturen, Technologie oder zur Veränderung des Verhaltens von Menschen Zeiträume von bis zu 30, 40 oder noch mehr Jahren berücksichtigt werden müssen, werden Entscheidungen heute oft noch ad hoc getroffen. Viele nehmen sich nicht die Zeit, über die (langfristigen) Folgen des jetzigen Tuns nachzudenken. Dieser Beitrag gibt einen Überblick über die Möglichkeiten, sich mit Zukünften bzw. mit „der Zukunft" wissenschaftlich und praktisch auseinanderzusetzen – und welche Methoden zur Skalierung zukünftiger Zeiten einsetzbar sind.

Schlüsselwörter

Foresight · Time · Zukunftsforschung · Zukünfte · Reiwa · Szenarien · Delphi-Studien · Wild Cards · Roadmaps

Einleitung

Foresight (der deutsche Begriff ist „Vorausschau") und Zukunftsforschung sind zwei Seiten einer Medaille. Die Zukunftsforschung ist die Wissenschaft, die sich mit der Zukunft und damit der Zeit, die vor uns liegt und damit noch unbestimmt ist, auseinandersetzt. Sie entwickelt Methoden und Methodenkombinationen sowie die theoretischen Grundlagen für eine fundierte, universitäre Wissenschaft, die das Wissen unterschiedlicher Wissenschaftszweige aufgreift, also interdisziplinär aufgestellt ist. An deutschen Universitäten und

Hochschulen ist die Zukunftsforschung noch nicht sehr weit verbreitet, ihre Methoden werden aber in unterschiedlichen Wissenschaftszweigen angewandt. Der wissenschaftliche Umgang mit Zukunft bzw. Zukünften (siehe unten) wird daher unter sehr verschiedenen Titeln geführt. Diese reichen von „Nachhaltigkeit" bis zu Infrastrukturen, einige Projekte verbergen sich in der Mobilität oder den Kommunikationswissenschaften.

Alle Ansätze beschäftigen sich mit Zeit und mit dem menschlichen Handeln unter Unsicherheit. Alle Ansätze gehen von einem linearen Zeitkonzept aus.

„Foresight" ist in der praktischen Anwendung und aus der Notwendigkeit heraus entstanden, (strategisch) denken und unter Unsicherheit dessen, was die Zukunft bringen mag, planen zu müssen. Dabei ist Foresight tatsächlich der möglichst weitreichende Blick voraus. Foresight ist keine Vorschau, keine Vorhersage und auch keine Prognose.

Unter Foresight (Vorausschau) verstehen wir die *systematische Auseinandersetzung über komplexe Zukünfte.* Foresight ist ein systematischer Ansatz, der sich aller Methoden der Zukunftsforschung bedient (Coates 1985; Cuhls 2008a; Martin 1995a; Technology Futures Analysis Methods Working Group 2004). Foresight nutzt nachvollziehbare Methoden unterschiedlicher Disziplinen. Es werden für die Vorausschau aber auch eigenständige Verfahren, Vorgehensweisen und Methodenkombinationen entwickelt. Oftmals wird Vorausschau eher als eine „Kunst" betrachtet (de Jouvenel 1967). Die Wissenschaftlichkeit von Foresight und Zukunftsforschung ist bereits früh diskutiert worden, wobei man zu dem Ergebnis kam, Wissenschaft sei nicht nur auf Erklärung und Prognose empirischer Phänomene beschränkt, sondern umfasse auch Beschreibungen, Klassifikationen, „nichterklärende wissenschaftliche Informationen" und Erfassen der Gesetzeshypothesen.

Vorausschau ist prospektiv, kann jedoch keine deterministischen Voraussagen treffen, sondern trägt sowohl normative als auch explorative Züge in sich. Das heißt, in der Vorausschau treffen Menschen Annahmen über lange Zeithorizonte, mit denen sie weiterarbeiten. Sie sagen jedoch nicht, wie die Zukunft werden wird (Vorhersage). Daher wurde gezielt der Begriff „Vorausschau" (im Englischen „Foresight", zur Entstehung siehe Martin 2010) im Sinne von „einen offenen Blick in die Zukunft werfen" gewählt. Die Pioniere der amerikanischen Vorausschau sprachen anfangs sogar von einem Vorauswissen, „foreknowledge". Prognosen werden in der Vorausschau daher als „Arbeitsmaterial" bzw. Annahmen angesehen, nicht als Determinante im Sinne von „so wird die Zukunft werden".

*Technik*vorausschau deckt nur einen Teil der Zukunftsforschung ab, insbesondere, wenn sich diese als holistischer Ansatz betrachtet. Foresight hat immer auch Grenzen, die von Themen, Komplexität und Dynamik des jeweiligen Feldes abhängen: Einige Felder sind so komplex oder entwickeln sich so dynamisch, dass zu viele Annahmen oder keine begründbaren Ableitungen getroffen werden können. In anderen dagegen sind die Entwicklungen sehr klar, sodass fast schon Vorhersagen möglich erscheinen.

In Foresight-Ansätzen geht es immer auch um die Interaktion der relevanten Akteure und ihre Auseinandersetzung mit Zukünften. Im Zentrum steht die aktive Vorbereitung auf die auch langfristige Zukunft und die Gestaltung der Zukunft. Foresight versucht dabei, den systemischen Kontext einzubeziehen. Deshalb ist der Blick in die Zukunft immer breit und umfassend, einschließlich multipler Perspektiven (Linstone 1999).

Der vorliegende Beitrag beschreibt, wie Zeit in den Zukunftswissenschaften betrachtet wird und welche Methoden dabei genutzt werden. Die Autorin möchte ihre Leserinnen und Leser ein wenig dafür sensibilisieren, dass Zukunftsforschung und Foresight manchmal weniger mit dem Alltagsverständnis von Zukunft und Zeit zu tun haben, als die Begrifflichkeiten zu suggerieren scheinen. Zukünftige Zeit und vergangene Zeit unterscheiden sich hier. Betrachtet man Zeit mit dem Konzept eines Zeitpfeils, dann können Zukunftswissenschaften als Pendant zu den Geschichtswissenschaften angesehen werden. Problematisch wird diese Sichtweise, wenn Zeit emotional betrachtet, rhythmisiert gesehen oder sogar zyklisch betrachtet wird. Es stellt sich die Frage, ob „die Zukunft" als Zeitangabe überhaupt existiert, wie sie skaliert werden kann und wann wir es mit „Zukünften" zu tun haben.

Zeit und das Denken in Zukünften

In der genannten Logik erscheinen die Begriffe „Vorhersage" oder „Prognose" (Forecast) nicht mehr geeignet, da sie eine deterministische, fixe Sichtweise suggerieren – Zeit ist festgelegt und auch Zeitspannen stehen fest. Dem ist aber nicht so, denn wir können durch unser Handeln im Jetzt die Zukunft beeinflussen.

Zukunftsforschung beschäftigt sich nicht nur dem Namen nach mit der Zeitkomponente. Wir wissen: Was „Zeit" ist, können bisher weder Philosophen noch Physiker erklären. Zeit ist relativ – seit Albert Einstein gibt es da nur wenig Genaues. In den Regionen der Erde geht man mit dem Begriff „Zeit" daher auch sehr unterschiedlich um (Adam 1990, 1994, 1995; Levine 2003). In einigen Ländern der Erde gibt es den Zeitbegriff erst seit Einführung der Uhren aus „dem Westen" (Gendolla 1992) – manchmal sogar als politisches oder Herrschaftsinstrument eingeführt (Lenz 2005). In manchen Kulturen gibt es zyklische Zeitkonzepte, in denen das „Werden" an den Jahreszeiten, den Ernten, der Wiederkehr der Blumen und Vögel oder der Veränderung der Landschaft etc. fest-gemacht wird. Rhythmik findet sich sogar in Lebewesen – hier sind alle Abläufe im Körper aufeinander abgestimmt, rhythmisiert, eingetaktet – dies ist das Untersuchungsfeld der Chronobiologie (siehe z. B. Roenneberg 2010; Roenneberg et al. 2012; Rönneberg 2000).

Neben den zyklischen Konzepten sind in den westlichen Kulturen bereits früh lineare Zeitkonzepte entstanden, die davon ausgehen, dass es eine Vergangenheit gibt, d. h. Dinge oder Vorgänge, die vorbei sind, eine Gegenwart, d. h. das Jetzt, dieser eine kurze Augenblick, diese Stunde, mein Leben. Und es gibt eine Zukunft im Sinne von gleich, in einer Stunde, morgen, nächstes Jahr oder „nach meinem Tod". Genau ist auch hier die Wahrnehmung nicht: Die Gegenwart kann ein Zeitraum sein oder nur der Trennstrich zwischen Vergangenheit und Zukunft. Die Zukunftsforschung benutzt eben diese lineare Zeitvorstellung basierend auf dem „Zeitpfeil", d. h. die Zeit ist nach „vorn" in Richtung Zukunft gerichtet. Sie kann nicht umgekehrt werden. Sie kann auch nicht eingespart werden (Erdmann und Cuhls 2019). Roadmaps (siehe unten) sind auf Basis des Zeitpfeils aufgebaut.

Hinzu kommt die individuelle Zeitwahrnehmung des Menschen. Diese ist persönlich und selbst bei einer einzigen Person kann sie unterschiedlich wahrgenommen werden – wenn man warten muss, vergeht die Zeit gefühlt langsamer, als wenn man gut beschäftigt ist. Zeit ist relativ, weil sie an den Raum gekoppelt ist. Zunehmend sind z. B. Entfernungen und die Zeit zur Überwindung von Entfernungen einer anderen Wahrnehmung unterworfen. Und auch hier sind neue Relativitäten entstanden: In einer Stunde mit dem ICE legt man andere Entfernungen zurück als in einer Stunde mit der S-Bahn.

Inmitten dieses schwierigen Konzeptes „Zeit" sind Science-Fiction-Autoren, Physiker und Filmemacher auf die Idee gekommen, man könne in der Zeit „reisen", also von der Gegenwart aus in die Vergangenheit oder Zukunft gelangen. Einer der ersten, die Zeitreisen in die Zukunft in einem Roman beschrieben haben, war Herbert George Wells mit seinem Werk „The Time Machine" von 1895. Physiker wie Werner Heisenberg, Max Planck, Albert Einstein oder Erwin Schrödinger haben sich über Zeit und Zeitreisen aus physikalischer Sicht Gedanken gemacht. Nicht so tiefschürfend sind etliche Kinofilme, in denen Zeitreisen das Thema sind. Die bekannteste Reihe unter ihnen ist sicherlich „Zurück in die Zukunft" (Back to the Future) von Regisseur Robert Zemeckis. In den meisten Fällen reisen die Helden (selten Heldinnen) dabei in die Vergangenheit – und es geht darum, in der Vergangenheit etwas zu „reparieren" oder „richtigzustellen".

Diesen Fällen liegt die Annahme zugrunde, dass es auf dem Zeitpfeil vom jeweiligen Standpunkt aus nur eine Vergangenheit, eine Zukunft zu einer bestimmten Zeit und damit auch eine Gegenwart gibt, die chronologisch aufeinander aufbauen. Diese gängige Hypothese ist bisher nicht widerlegt. Es gibt allerdings weitere Zeitkonzepte, z. B. gibt es Wissenschaftler, die von Paralleluniversen ausgehen und damit unterschiedlichen Vergangenheiten und Zukünften (siehe Gribbin 2002, S. 250 ff.; Blask und Windhorst 2011 auch Projekt „Illustris" des MIT (https://www.illustris-project.org/, Blask und Windhorst 2011; Kaku 2005, 2014).

Was in der Zukunftsforschung benötigt und generiert wird, sind „Informationen" über die Zukunft oder über unterschiedliche Zukünfte. Menschen wollen und müssen planen, wollen sich auf Zukünfte (die verschiedenen Möglichkeiten) einstellen oder sich auf sie vorbereiten. Menschen wollen auch wissen, wie realistische Zukünfte aussehen könnten, und bestimmte Zukünfte, nämlich die mit Chancen für uns, Wirklichkeit werden lassen und gleichzeitig diejenigen Zukünfte verhindern, die mit Gefahren oder Unannehmlichkeiten verbunden sind. Deshalb gibt es die unterschiedlichen Methoden und Methodenkombinationen und deshalb auch die mentalen Zeitreisen (siehe unten) in unterschiedliche Zukünfte (Cuhls 2016; Markley 2008). In allen Fällen lernen wir oft mehr über die Gegenwart als über „die" Zukunft.

Deshalb wird in Europa zwischen dem Konzept „Foresight" (Vorausschau) und „Forecast"/„Forecasting" (Cuhls 2003) unterschieden. Die Zukunftsforschung als Wissenschaft „beschäftigt sich mit möglichen, wahrscheinlichen und wünschbaren zukünftigen Entwicklungen. Denn auch wenn sich die Zukunft nicht vorhersehen lässt, zeichnen sich doch schon heute wichtige Entwicklungsstrukturen in ihren Grundzügen ab. Die Leitplanken des Möglichen, Wahrscheinlichen und Wünschenswerten sind in diesem Sinn durch wissenschaftliche Verfahren und im gesellschaftlichen Diskurs bestimmbar."[1] Gleichzeitig ist die Vorausschau offen für unterschiedliche Pfade in die Zukunft und das Denken in Alternativen (Abb. 1 und 2).

Für heutige Entscheidungen muss ich eine Zukunft auswählen (Abb. 2), damit ich mich auf diese vorbereiten bzw. sie ermöglichen kann. Diese Option kann auch ein „Business as Usual" oder „Weiter wie bisher"-Szenario (zur Methodik siehe unten) sein. Dabei ist wichtig, sich zu verdeutlichen, welche Zukunft und welchen Zeitraum oder Zeitpunkt ich gerade untersuche, die

---

[1]Aus dem ersten Flyer des Masterstudienganges Zukunftsforschung der Freien Universität Berlin. Dies ist die einzige Einrichtung, an der in Deutschland explizit Zukunftsforschung studiert werden kann.

Unterschiedliche Zukünfte – systematische Exploration

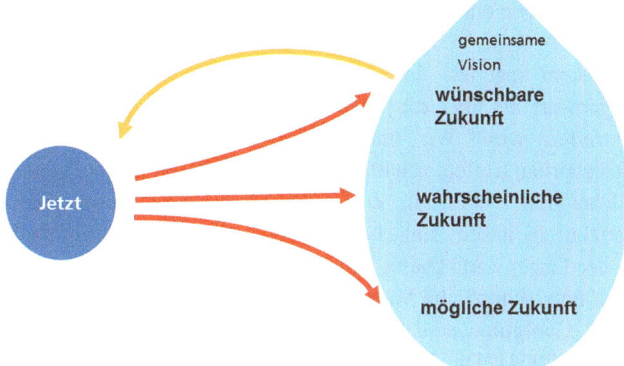

Abb. 1 Alternative Zukünfte sind möglich

Unterschiedliche Zukünfte – systematische Exploration

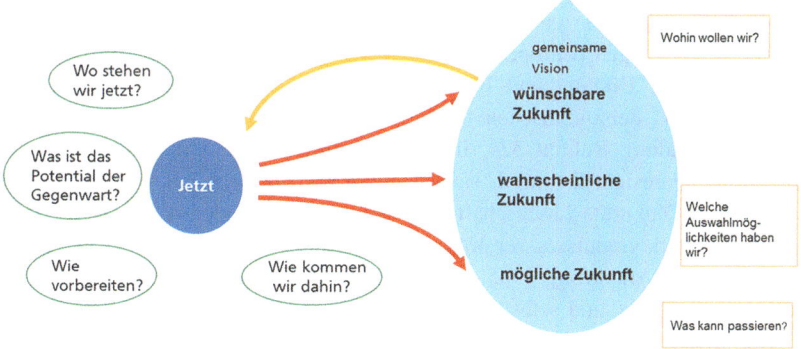

Abb. 2 Fragen der Zukunftsforschung

- mögliche Zukunft (Was liegt vor uns? Welche Möglichkeiten gibt es? Wann? realistische Einschätzung),
- wahrscheinliche Zukunft (Welche dieser möglichen Zukünfte ist am wahrscheinlichsten? Wann? Wahrscheinlichkeitseinschätzung),

- wünschbare oder wünschenswerte Zukunft (Was wollen wir? Wohin wollen wir? Wann sind wir dort angelangt? Wünschbarkeit) oder
- Visionen (Wie sieht die Vision aus? Eine Vision ist eine kurze, prägnant formulierte und wünschbare Zukunft, langfristig, meistens zeitlich unbestimmt).

Insgesamt sagt uns damit der Blick in die Zukunft sehr viel mehr über die Gegenwart als über die (zeitliche) Zukunft, von der wir nicht wissen, welche eintreffen wird. Wir müssen also unsere Entscheidungen weiterhin unter Unsicherheit treffen, schaffen es aber, die Möglichkeiten einzugrenzen und damit Informationen über „die Zukunft" bzw. „Zukünfte" mit einem bestimmten Zeithorizont in unsere Entscheidungen einzubeziehen. Entscheidungen treffen wir in der Gegenwart. Damit beschäftigt sich „Foresight" (Martin 2010) und nutzt dazu unterschiedliche Vorgehensweisen und Methoden (Cuhls 2008; Cuhls et al. 2015; Georghiou et al. 2008; Harper et al. 2008; Kuusi et al. 2015; Cuhls und Jaspers 2004). Die Wirkungen unserer Entscheidungen in der Gegenwart sind genauso unterschiedlich (Cuhls und Georghiou 2004), insbesondere im Bereich der Politikgestaltung (Cuhls 2015; Cuhls et al. 2015; European Commission/European Union 2018a; Havas et al. 2010).

„Gutes" Foresight lässt sich nicht daran festmachen, ob etwas richtig vorhergesagt wurde, sondern daran, *ob* etwas angestoßen wurde – gleiches gilt für Entscheidungen. So sind zum Beispiel Zukunftsthemen aus Foresight-Projekten in die Planung des europäischen Forschungsrahmenprogramms „Horizon Europe" eingegangen (European Commission 2017) oder im deutschen Bundesministerium für Bildung und Forschung wurde ein neues Referat gegründet, das sich mit demografischem Wandel und Mensch-Technik-Interaktionen befasst (Gründung Referat 524, inzwischen Referat 522, Gründung als Folge des BMBF Foresight Zyklus I, siehe Cuhls et al. 2009). Auch wenn Foresight und andere Zukunftswissenschaften keine Prognose oder Vorhersage eines einzelnen Vorkommnisses ermöglichen, besteht ein Zusammenhang zum „Forecasting" (Armstrong 1985; Coates 1985; Coates et al. 1994; Coates et al. 2001; Cuhls 2003), und selbstverständlich hat Foresight einen strategischen Teil (Martin 1995): „(technology) foresight is the process involved in systematically attempting to look into the longer-term future of science, technology, the economy and society with the aim of identifying the areas of strategic research and the emerging of generic technologies likely to yield the greatest economic and social benefits". In diesem Kontext fällt häufig sogar der Begriff „Strategic Foresight" (Coates et al. 2010; European Commission 2017; Godet 1997; Godet et al. 2011). Damit wird sehr zielgerichtet und mit einem bestimmten Zweck in die Zukunft geschaut und Planung vorbereitet.

Wenn allerdings der Blick offen und kreativ bleiben soll, dann passt „strategische Vorausschau" nicht. Gerade in Fällen, in denen die Vorausschau betrieben wird, um sich die Umwelt oder das „Umfeld" und seine zukünftigen Entwicklungen anzusehen, ist ihr Zweck einer Vorausschau die Vorbereitung auf wichtige Entwicklungen, Diskontinuitäten oder mögliche „Überraschungen". Dann dient Foresight der Erarbeitung der Ziele, der Strategie und der (Zukunfts-) Fragen, die noch ungelöst sind, und einem Denken auf Vorrat. Hier kann man noch einen Schritt weitergehen (Nelson 2010 mit „Foresight 2.0"): Nicht nur über den Tellerrand hinaus denken, sondern weiter, über alle Tellerränder, Boxen und Biases[2] in unseren Köpfen hinaus, weiter in Richtung Gesellschaft, die Zukunft der Menschheit und der Kulturen. In der Zukunftsforschung und im Foresight geht es immer um den Umgang mit Unsicherheit und das Entscheiden unter Unsicherheit. Dafür gibt es sehr unterschiedliche Methoden.

Vorausschau-Methoden

Es gibt sehr unterschiedliche Methoden der Vorausschau, die kombiniert werden können, um die gesetzten Ziele zu erreichen. Jede Methode hat eigene Einsatzzwecke. Manche sind zeitlich eher langfristig, andere eher kurzfristig orientiert (Abb. 3). Manche beziehen mehr Personen ein, andere nur wenige.

Szenarien sind der Klassiker, um in Alternativen zu denken. Wie kann die Zukunft zu einem bestimmten Zeitpunkt aussehen? Wie sieht sie 2025, 2040 oder 2100 aus? Typisch für Szenarien ist die Darstellung in einem Trichter (siehe Abb. 4). Dabei gehen die Betrachtenden von der Gegenwart aus, legen ein bestimmtes Thema und damit einen Systemrahmen fest und projizieren unterschiedliche Annahmen auf einen bestimmten Zeithorizont in der Zukunft. So entstehen unterschiedliche Zukunftsbilder und unterschiedliche Pfade dorthin. Es gibt einige Varianten, Szenarien zu erstellen (Kosow et al. 2008) sowie unterschiedliche „Schulen" bzw. Herangehensweisen (für einen Überblick siehe z. B. Fink und Siebe 2016).

---

[2]Biases sind hier Neigungen des Menschen, bestimmte Dinge zu über- oder zu unterschätzen (z. B. Overestimation Bias: das eigene Forschungsfeld ist immer das wichtigste; Optimisten schätzen Zeithorizonte zur Realisierung ihrer Innovationen immer früher ein als die Pessimisten usw.).

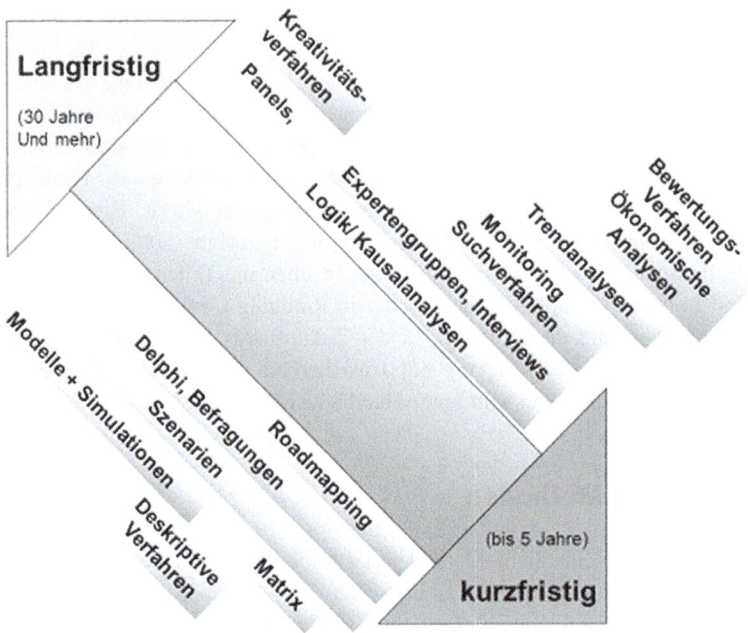

Abb. 3 Lang- und kurzfristig ausgerichtete Methoden. (Nach Cuhls 2008)

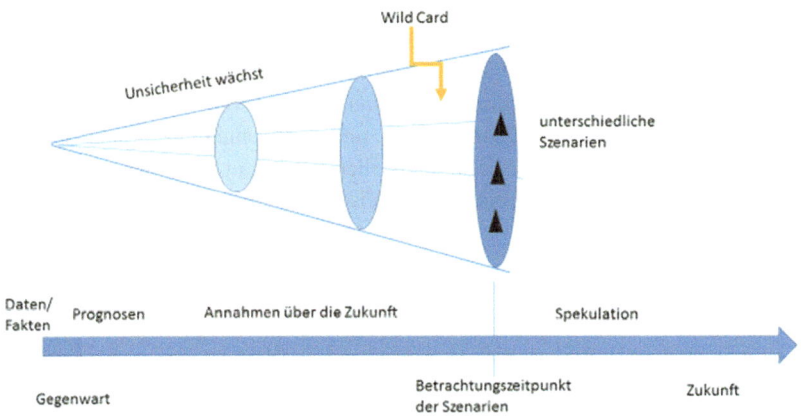

Abb. 4 Szenario-Trichter. (Eigene Darstellung)

Moderne Szenarien erarbeiten insbesondere plausible und in sich konsistente Zukünfte, vielfach über Konsistenzanalysen und mit Software-Unterstützung (ein Beispiel ist Opiela et al. 2018). In Szenarien und besonders Szenario-Workshops finden dann auch sogenannte „Wild Cards" Verwendung (Steinmüller und Steinmüller 2004). Das sind einzelne Ereignisse und damit eine Art von Extremsignalen, die insgesamt gar nicht so unwahrscheinlich sind, aber bei denen es unwahrscheinlich ist, dass sie gerade zu dem bestimmten Zeitpunkt eintreffen. Typische Beispiele sind der Asteroid, der mit der Erde kollidiert, eine neue sehr plötzliche Eiszeit, eine Pandemie oder für eine einzelne Person ein hoher Lotteriegewinn. Mit einer derartigen Wild Card testen wir, ob die Szenarien „robust" sind oder ob sie sich unter seinem Einfluss verändern. Wenn wir beispielsweise ein Szenario zur Entwicklung im Energiebereich haben, das uns aufzeigt, wie unser Energiebedarf im Jahr 2040 aussieht und wie er durch neue Technologie bis dann gestiegen ist, was im Jahr 2040 alles möglich ist, wie mobil wir sind und wie wir wohnen, dann wird dieses durch eine Wild Card wie das „Aufkommen einer neuen Eiszeit durch das Umkippen des Golfstroms" (zu einer bestimmten angenommenen Zeit, z. B. im Jahr 2035) innerhalb von fünf Jahren zu einem komplett anderen Zukunftsbild führen. Unser Szenario verändert sich dann: viele Techniken sind nicht mehr nutzbar, weil es zu kalt ist (z. B. E-Autos), wir müssen mehr heizen, Pflanzen wachsen nicht mehr, Gebiete werden unbewohnbar, und wir benötigen insgesamt noch mehr Energie.

Auch farbige Darstellungen, die in die Diskussion der Szenaren mit eingebunden und später für die Veröffentlichungen verwendet werden können, sind inzwischen beliebt, um die unterschiedlichen Zukünfte zu bebildern. Dabei darf aber nicht vergessen werden: dies sind Optionen, die eigentliche, einzige Zukunft, die der Mensch erleben wird, wird anders sein als alle Darstellungen. Sprich: auch die Zukünfte der Szenarien sind nichts als Arbeitsmaterial in den Zukunftswissenschaften.

Workshops: Die Arbeit in interdisziplinären Gruppen mit sehr unterschiedlichen Formaten (von sogenannten Zukunftswerkstätten über Design Thinking bis zu Szenario-Workshops oder einfachen kreativen Verfahren) gehört mit als Baustein in die Methodik von Foresight. Sie dienen dazu, Menschen in einer anderen Umgebung einmal unvoreingenommen, langfristig und kreativ denken zu lassen und ggf. auch einmal ungewöhnliche Ideen bewerten zu lassen. Neben den Szenarien gibt es offene und **kreative Methoden,** über Zukünfte nachzudenken. Insbesondere, wenn Partizipation gewünscht ist, sind Panels, Expertengruppen oder kreative Verfahren für sehr heterogene Gruppen beliebt. Diese reichen von einfachen Brainstormings bis zu mentalen **Zeitreisen** (Cuhls 2016; Markley

2008) und können helfen, sehr offen in die Zukunft hinein zu denken, sich verschiedene Zukünfte auszudenken, auszumalen (ggf. im wahren Sinne des Wortes) oder beispielsweise über Design Thinking herzustellen (designen, modellieren, basteln, bauen).

Suche nach „Signalen": Die Suche nach Signalen für neue Entwicklungen wird mit den Begrifflichkeiten Horizon Scanning (Cuhls 2019) oder Früherkennung beschrieben. In jedem Foresight gibt es eine Form der Signalsuche in unterschiedlichen Quellen (Publikationen, Patenten, Internet, den Köpfen von Experten, teilweise sogar über Algorithmen). Dieses **Horizon Scanning** ist eine Bestandsaufnahme dessen, was man schon weiß oder „am Horizont" feststellen kann. Verwendet werden dafür Bibliometrie und Patentanalysen, Datenbank-Scanning und Screening, Internet-Recherchen, Mustererkennung in Big Data (also großen, bis dato unstrukturierten Datensätzen), Kausalanalysen oder Trendanalysen. In Szenarien werden dann die Signale verarbeitet.

Daneben gibt es **wissenschaftliche Modelle,** die in die Zukunft verlängert – extrapoliert – werden können. Sie folgen strikten Verfahren, können auf unterschiedliche Weisen Variablen verarbeiten und so Zukünfte simulieren, indem sie Annahmen berechnen.

Delphi- und andere Befragungen: Um die gefundenen starken oder schwachen Signale einzuschätzen, werden zum Beispiel Befragungen eingesetzt, in denen Experten (oft auch in zwei Runden mit Feedback, dann heißen sie Delphi-Befragungen) bewerten, wann eine bestimmte Situation eintreffen könnte oder zum Beispiel eine bestimmte Technologie im praktischen Einsatz sein kann. Experten, die wissen sollten, wann ihre Projekte enden und Resultate erbracht haben sollten, werden in klassische Interviews, Delphi-Umfragen oder einfache Zukunftsbefragungen einbezogen, es können aber auch andere Personen teilnehmen.

Delphi ist ein spezieller Typ von Befragung, von der es inzwischen ebenfalls viele Varianten gibt (siehe Cuhls 2019 bzw. Niederberger und Renn 2019). Hier werden einzelne Thesen über Zukunftsannahmen im Präsens formuliert und dann über einen (Online-) Fragebogen bewertet. Die Befragung ist (bis auf Ausnahme des Gruppen-Delphi) anonym. Niemand verliert sein Gesicht oder muss sich bei einer Meinungsänderung in der zweiten Befragungsrunde rechtfertigen. Diese Studien liefern uns – insbesondere in ihrer neuesten Form mit Argumenten – Einschätzungen und Inhalte zu einzelnen Zukunftsthemen, die wie Hypothesen formuliert werden (Einfache Beispiele: Krebs kann geheilt werden. Oder: Salzwasser-resistente Pflanzen werden in großem Maßstab zur Begrünung von Wüsten eingesetzt.). An den Ergebnissen orientieren sich dann Forscher oder die Politik mit ihren Maßnahmen, um das Thema tatsächlich zu realisieren, schneller zu realisieren oder sogar – wenn zum Beispiel von sehr vielen Befragten der Studie als nicht wünschbar eingestuft – um es zu verhindern oder einzuschränken.

Visioning: Foresight kann als lernender Prozess betrachtet werden, in dem das wichtigste Ziel das Vorausdenken, die Kommunikation und die Teilhabe an der Gestaltung der Zukunft ist. Man kann z. B. „Visionen" (im Sinne eines wünschbaren Zukunftsbildes, keine Utopie) bilden (sogenanntes „Visioning"). Dies geschieht in der Regel in einem strukturierten Gruppenprozess. Wenn Foresight als visionsbildender Prozess angesehen wird, ist die normative Komponente (Beeinflussung in Richtung einer wünschenswerten Zukunft) im Vordergrund. Die Vision ist dann eine erwünschte, möglichst in gemeinsamem Konsens angestrebte Zukunft, die möglichst prägnant formuliert wird. Wir finden Visionen häufig in Unternehmenskontexten, in denen die Unternehmensziele und „Missionen" von Visionen abgeleitet werden. Trotzdem ist eine klare Unterscheidung zwischen „Foresight" (offener Blick) und „Strategie" (fokussiert, Ziel ist festgelegt) in den einzelnen Schritten des Prozesses sehr wichtig. In diesem Zusammenhang kann Foresight die Rolle eines „strategischen Dialogs" einnehmen, um die gewünschte Zukunft möglich zu machen.

Die Entscheidung in der Gegenwart kann auf der Basis der Ergebnisse dann lauten, etwas zu ändern, um bestimmte Dinge zu ermöglichen – so entstehen neue Forschung, Technologie und Innovationen, die auf den Markt kommen, aber auch soziale Innovationen oder andere gesellschaftliche Veränderungen. Die Entscheidung kann lauten, etwas nicht zu tun oder mit etwas aufzuhören (z. B. ein Forschungsprojekt abzubrechen, weil es Widerstand gibt oder es technisch unmöglich erscheint oder es zu teuer wird etc.). Eine Entscheidung der Gegenwart kann aber auch lauten, nichts zu tun, etwas „auszusitzen" oder „Business as usual" zu betreiben. Auch dies ist eine Entscheidung, die vielen nicht bewusst ist, aber Auswirkungen auf die Zukunft und die zukünftige Zeit, möglicherweise sogar zukünftige Zeitverfügbarkeiten hat.

Roadmaps – Übergang zur Planung: In allen Fällen gibt es eine wichtige Beziehung – aber auch einen Unterschied (Cuhls 2003) – zur Planung, um Coates (1985, S. 30) zu zitieren:

> „Foresight is the overall process of creating an understanding and appreciation of information generated by looking ahead. Foresight includes qualitative and quantitative means for monitoring clues and indicators of evolving trends and developments and is best and most useful when directly linked to the analysis of policy implications. Foresight prepares us to meet the needs and opportunities of the future. Foresight in government cannot define policy, but it can help condition policies to be more appropriate, more flexible, and more robust in their implementation, as times and circumstances change. Foresight is, therefore, closely tied to planning. It is not planning – merely a step in planning."

Das Roadmapping ist zwischen Foresight (langfristig) und Planung (Bezug zur Gegenwart) angesiedelt. Es kann sicherlich auch in die langfristige Zukunft fortgesetzt werden, bedeutet in der Regel aber einen kurzfristigen Ansatz und ein Rückwärtsdenken aus der Zukunft (Backcasting). Für eine Roadmap wird meistens eine Vision oder ein Ziel erarbeitet und man arbeitet auf der Zeitschiene abwechselnd mit und entgegengesetzt dem Zeitpfeil. Eine Roadmap hat oft mehrere Ebenen (Layer), auf denen man unterschiedliche Entwicklungen eintragen kann, z. B. Märkte, neue Techniken oder welche neuen Techniken die Konkurrenz wann entwickeln könnte.

Roadmaps werden oft im Unternehmenskontext erstellt (Möhrle und Isenmann 2017), werden inzwischen aber auch in politischen Kontexten (z. B. Außenpolitik) eingesetzt. Um die Roadmap zu füllen, müssen sehr unterschiedliche Daten vorhanden sein (in der Abb. 5 sind das die unterschiedlich farbigen und unterschiedlich großen Formen), die in den o. g. Scanning Methoden, Befragungen oder gemeinsamen Workshops erhoben werden. Roadmaps sind daher einfache Visualisierungen dessen, was man über zeitliche Zusammenhänge weiß und eine Bestandsaufnahme der Informationen. Weiße Stellen oder fehlende Pfeile/Zusammenhänge zeigen dann auf, was man noch einschätzen muss.

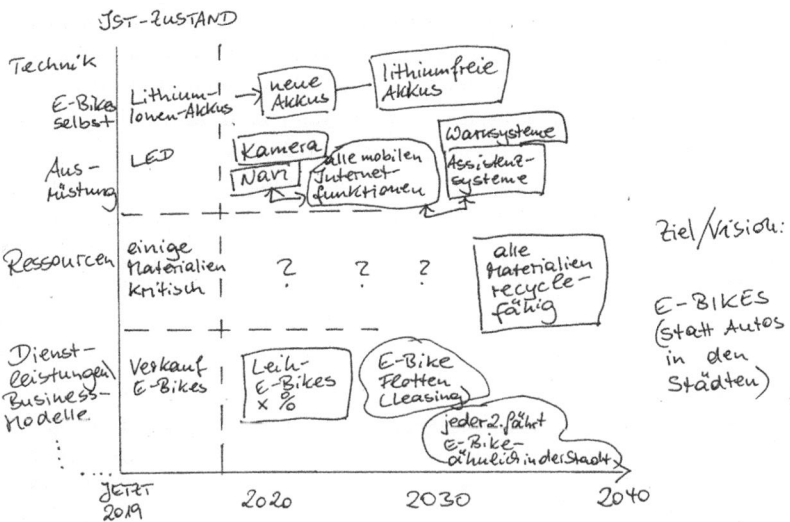

Abb. 5 Roadmap E-Bikes 2019 – 2040. (Daten aus unterschiedlichen Workshop-Roadmaps)

Besonders Delphi-Studien und Roadmapping nutzen daher den Zeitbegriff explizit (siehe Abb. 5, hier am vereinfachten Beispiel E-Bikes), allerdings in unterschiedlicher Art. Bei einer Delphi-Studie wird häufig nach dem Zeitraum oder sogar Zeitpunkt der Realisierung gefragt (Cuhls 1998, 2012; Cuhls et al. 2002), manchmal sogar mit Argumenten für einen frühen oder späten Zeitraum (European Commission 2018a, b). Roadmaps dagegen arbeiten mit zeitlichen Bezügen auf dem Zeitpfeil, d. h. es wird eingetragen, was wann realisiert werden kann und was unbedingt *vor* einer anderen Entwicklung realisiert werden muss, um diese erst zu ermöglichen.

In der Vorausschau werden einige Ansätze leicht zu *self-fulfilling* bzw. *self-destroying prophecies* (letzteres bei ungewünschten Entwicklungen), was die hohe Erfolgsrate einzelner Studien erklären kann. Sie arbeiten also mit „Zeit" als Mittel, sich in die Zukunft zu versetzen, und danach in der Gegenwart die Weichen zu stellen und entsprechende Entscheidungen zu treffen. Wenn wir aber nur mit Annahmen über die Zukunft arbeiten können, wie gehen wir mit Zeit in der Zukunft um?

Wie skaliert man Zeit in Foresight und Zukunftsforschung?

Wie skalieren wir zum Beispiel „Zukunft"? In westlichen Kulturkreisen zentriert man sich um die Berechnung vor und nach Christus, sodass alles, was nach Erscheinen dieses Beitrags (er ist von 2019) folgt, logischerweise in den Folgejahren 2020, 2021 usw. stattfindet. Soweit, so einfach. Was aber, wenn wir hier eine andere Zeitskala haben. In Japan erlebt man mit dem 1.5.2019 den Anbruch einer neuen Zeitrechnung. Am 30.4.2019 war der letzte Tag der Ära (Nengo) Heisei 平成. Diese währte seit 1989 unserer westlichen Zeitrechnung, dem Zeitpunkt, als ein damals neuer Tennô („Kaiser") inthronisiert wurde. Dem Tennô wurde erlaubt, im Jahr 2019 abdanken zu dürfen, um seinem Sohn Platz zu machen. Für den Thronfolger wurde der neue Ära-Name 令和 Reiwa bestimmt[3]. Über die Bedeutung des

---

[3]REI – Anweisung des Herrschers, WA – Harmonie, ein Zeichen, das auch in Heiwa – Friede steht, angeblich aus einer „rein" japanischen Anthologie, dem Manyôshu, eine ähnliche Textzeile wurde aber auch in chinesischen Quellen aufgefunden. Ein erster Überblick findet sich zum Beispiel von Reinhard Zöllner: https://kotoba.japankunde.de/?p=6654 (Zugriff 30.4.2019) oder von Steffi Richter: https://geschichtedergegenwart.ch/reiwa-in-japan-wechselt-mit-dem-thron-auch-diezeit/ (Zugriff 1.5.2019).

Namens gibt es immer noch unterschiedliche Auffassungen, die uns hier aber nicht weiter beschäftigen sollen. Wir befinden uns also seit dem 1.5.2019 in Reiwa 1. Das ist für Zeitbestimmungen in den Zukunftswissenschaften ein echtes Problem: Wir wissen nicht, wie lange Reiwa in die Zukunft reichen wird. Wir wussten am Beginn der Ära auch nicht, dass Heisei im Äquivalent des Jahres 2019 enden würde. Wie planen wir also, wenn wir keine allgemeingültige Skala haben bzw. eine Skala, von der wir nicht wissen, ob sie nicht schon in Kürze wieder zu Ende ist? Pragmatisch, wie man in Japan häufig ist, benutzt man deshalb bei Zukunftseinschätzungen die „nach Christus"-Zählung, z. B. in den japanischen Delphi-Studien (für die letzte nationale Studie siehe NISTEP 2016), was allerdings auch schon zu Konfusionen in der Berechnung bei internationalen Vergleichen von Zukunftsthemen geführt hat (Cuhls 1998).

Häufig werden die Zeithorizonte einfach in kurz-, mittel- und langfristig eingeteilt oder in now – transition – future (Curry und Hodgson 2008), wohl wissend, dass diese Einteilung sehr subjektiv geprägt ist. Aber auch die frühen Vorausschau-Studien aller Art taten sich mit den Zeiteinteilungen der Zukunft sehr schwer, einen guten Überblick hierzu gibt Nordlund (2012). Es soll auch Kulturen geben oder gegeben haben, die keine Zukunft kennen. Für diese machen Zukunftswissenschaften mit Zeitskalen keinen Sinn.

Conclusio: Wozu brauchen wir Zeitbetrachtungen im Foresight?

Wir kennen die Zukunft nicht und können sie nicht vorhersagen. Warum also brauchen wir zukunftsorientierte Zeitbetrachtungen?

Menschen werden häufig als vorausschauende Lebewesen kategorisiert. Wir Menschen sind kulturell so weit gekommen, weil wir gelernt haben, uns vorausschauend zu verhalten. Viele Tiere können dies nicht. Menschen haben in der Steinzeit überlebt, wenn sie sich auf Gefahren eingestellt haben, wenn sie damit gerechnet haben, dass ein gefährliches Tier gleich um die Ecke kommen könnte. Menschen haben später überlebt, weil sie geplant haben, insbesondere in der Landwirtschaft. Heute tun wir Menschen fast nichts mehr ungeplant: wir schauen den Wetterbericht im Fernsehen oder auf der WetterApp an und ziehen uns entsprechend an, nehmen den Regenschirm mit oder nicht, wählen das Auto oder das Fahrrad. Für langfristige, große Infrastrukturprojekte brauchen wir Planung. Wir brauchen Planung, um ein Haus zu erstellen. Wir müssen uns überlegen, woher wir Energie bekommen, um unser Heim zu versorgen – oder woher unser Essen kommt. Wir planen unsere Wasserversorgung – und für einige ist die Planung der Internetversorgung das Wichtigste im Leben geworden.

Für all dies und unser persönliches Leben betreiben wir sowieso Vorausschau. Um aber auch in der Forschung oder Politik langfristig Planung betreiben zu können und Informationen zu generieren, brauchen wir auch den langfristigen Blick in unterschiedliche Zukünfte und unterschiedliche Zeiten, die in der Zukunft liegen. Wir müssen Eventualitäten einplanen, Risiken kalkulieren und mit nicht geplanten Hindernissen (Wild Cards) oder Ereignissen rechnen. Wir müssen unsere (langfristigen) Szenarien auf ihre Robustheit testen. Und wahrscheinlich befinden wir uns gerade in einer Umbruchsphase, für die ein geweiteter Blick auf die Zukunft der gesamten Menschheit notwendig ist – ein langfristiger Blick, der alle Boxen sprengt und uns über die für das Überleben der Menschheit notwendigen Dinge und Taten nachdenken lässt – ein Foresight 3.0 bzw. eine Zukunftsforschung 3.0, die unterschiedliche Zeitdimensionen einbezieht, den Blick auch auf emotionale Zeit, Zeitwohlstand (Rinderspacher 2017a), Zeitpolitik (im Sinne der Deutschen Gesellschaft für Zeitpolitik (Deutsche Gesellschaft für Zeitpolitik 2007; Rinderspacher 2017) und andere den Menschen betreffende Komponenten richtet.

Für all dies lohnt sich ein Blick in die Zukunft – nur ist einer nicht genug, denn wenn man Alternativen in Betracht ziehen möchte, braucht man auch einen zweiten und dritten Blick. Ohne eine – wenn auch niemals 100 % genaue – Zeiteinschätzung hilft die beste Planung oder strategische Ausrichtung nicht.

Literatur

Adam, B. (1990). *Time and Social Theory*. Cambridge: Polity Press.
Adam, B. (1994). Perceptions of Time. In T. Ingold (Hrsg.), *Humanity, Culture and Social Life, Companion Encyclopaedia of Anthropology* (S. 503-526). London: Routledge.
Adam, B. (1995). *Timewatch. The Social Analysis of Time*. Cambridge: Polity Press.
Armstrong, J. S. (1985). *Long-Range Forecasting. Internet version* (2nd Edition). https://hops.wharton.upenn.edu/forecast/Long-Range%20Forecasting/. Zugegriffen: 8. Februar 2002.
Blask, F., & Windhorst, A. (2011). *Zeitreisen – Die Erfüllung eines Menschheitstraumes*. Reinbek bei Hamburg: rowohlt digitalbuch.
Coates, J., Durance, P. & Godet, M. (2010). Strategic Foresight Issue. Introduction. *Technological Forecasting and Social Change, 77* (9), 1423–1425.
Coates, J. F. (1985). Foresight in Federal Government Policymaking. *Futures Research Quarterly* (1), 29–53.
Coates, J.F, Mahaffie, J.B. & Hines, A. (1994). Technological Forecasting: 1970-1993. *Technological Forecasting and Social Change* (47), 23–33.

Coates, V., Farooque, M., Klavans, R., Lapid, K., Linstone, H.A., Pistorius, C. & Porter, A.L. (2001). On the Future of Technological Forecasting. *Technological Forecasting and Social Change* (67), 1–17.
Cuhls, K. (1998). *Technikvorausschau in Japan. Ein Rückblick auf 30 Jahre Delphi-Expertenbefragungen.* Heidelberg: Physica Verlag.
Cuhls, K. (2003). From Forecasting to Foresight processes – New participative Foresight Activities in Germany. *Cuhls, Kerstin und Salo, Ahti (Guest Editors): Journal of Forecasting* (Special Issue, no. 22), 93–111. Wiley Interscience.
Cuhls, K. (2008a). Foresight in Germany. In L. Georghiou, J. C. Harper, M. Keenan, I. Miles & R. Popper (Eds.), *The Handbook of Technology Foresight. Concepts and Practice* (PRIME Series on Research and Innovation Policy, pp. 131–153). Cheltenham, UK: Edward Elgar Publishing Ltd.
Cuhls, K. (2008b). *Methoden der Technikvorausschau – eine internationale Übersicht.* Stuttgart: Fraunhofer IRB Verlag.
Cuhls, K. (2012). Zu den Unterschieden zwischen Delphi-Befragungen und „einfachen" Zukunftsbefragungen. In R. (H.) Popp (Hrsg.), *Zukunft und Wissenschaft. Wege und Irrwege der Zukunftsforschung* (Wissenschaftliche Schriftenreihe Zukunft und Forschung des Zentrums für Zukunftsstudien Salzburg, Bd. 2, Bd. 2, S. 139–159). Berlin: Springer. Verfügbar unter DOI 978-3-642-28954-5_7. Zugegriffen: 12. September 2019.
Cuhls, K. (2015). *Bringing Foresight to decision-making – lessons for policy-making from selected non-European countries. Policy Brief by the Research, Innovation, and Science Policy Experts (RISE)*, Brussels. https://ec.europa.eu/research/innovation-union/index_en.cfm?pg=expert-groups. Zugegriffen: 12. September 2019.
Cuhls, K., Blind, K. & Grupp, H. (2002). *Innovations for our Future. Delphi '98: New Foresight on Science and Technology. Technology, Innovation and Policy. Series of the Fraunhofer Institute for Systems and Innovation Research ISI* (13. Aufl.). Heidelberg: Physica-Verlag.
Cuhls, K. & Georghiou, L. (2004). Evaluating a participative foresight process: ‚Futur – the German research dialogue'. *Research Evaluation, 13* (3), 143–153.
Cuhls, K. (2019). Horizon Scanning in Foresight – Why Horizon Scanning is only a part of the game, *Futures and Foresight Science*. DOI: 10.1002/ffo2.23. Zugegriffen 12.03.2020.
Cuhls, K. E. (2016). Mental Time Travel in Foresight Processes—Cases and Applications. *Futures.* DOI: 10.1016/j.futures.2016.05.008. Zugegriffen 12.03.2020.
Cuhls, K. & Jaspers, M. (2004). *Participatory Priority Setting for Research and Innovation Policy.* Stuttgart: IRB Verlag.
Curry, A. & Hodgson, A. (2008). Seeing in Multiple Horizons: Connecting Futures to Strategy. *Journal of Futures Studies, 13* (1), 1–20.
Deutsche Gesellschaft für Zeitpolitik (Hrsg.). (2007). *Lokale Zeitpolitik* (Zeitpolitisches Magazin, Bd. 10).
Erdmann, L. & Cuhls, K. (2019). *Der Zeit-Rebound Effekt. unveröffentlichtes Papier im Rahmen des Projektes ReZeitKon*, Karlsruhe.
European Commission. (2017). *Strategic Foresight in EU R&I Policy. Wider Use – More Impact. Report of the Expert Group 'Strategic Foresight for R&I Policy in Horizon 2020'*, Brüssel. https://ec.europa.eu/research/foresight/index.cfm?pg=fb_policy. Zugegriffen: 12. September 2019.

European Commission/European Union. (2018a). *New Horizons: Data from a Delphi Survey in Support of European Union Future Policies in Research and Innovation. Report KI-06–17–345-EN-N*. Brussels. Verfügbar unter https://publications.europa.eu/en/publication-detail/-/publication/d1ea6c83-e538-11e7-9749-01aa75ed71a1/language-en/format-PDF/source-60761593; doi:https://doi.org/10.2777/654172 or https://ec.europa.eu/research/foresight/index.cfm. Zugegriffen: 12. September 2019.

European Commission/European Union. (2018b). *Transitions at the Horizon: Perspectives for the European Union's future research- and innovation-related policies.*, Brussels. https://ec.europa.eu/info/research-and-innovation/strategy/support-policy-making/support-eu-research-and-innovation-policy-making/foresight/activities/current/bohemia_en. Zugegriffen: 12. September 2019.

Fink, A. & Siebe, A. (2016). *Szenario Management. Von strategischem Vorausdenken zu zukunftsrobusten Entscheidungen.* Frankfurt/New York: Campus.

Gendolla, P. (1992). *Zeit – Zur Geschichte der Zeiterfahrung.* Köln: DuMont.

Georghiou, L., Harper, J. C., Keenan, M., Miles, I. & Popper, R. (Hrsg.). (2008). *The Handbook of Technology Foresight. Concepts and Practice* (PRIME Series on Research and Innovation Policy). Cheltenham, UK: Edward Elgar Publishing Ltd.

Godet, M. (1997). *Scenarios and Strategies. A Toolbox for Problem Solving.* Paris: Cahiers du LIPS, Special Issue.

Godet, Michel and Durance, Philippe. (2011). STRATEGIC FORESIGHT. https://www.laprospective.fr/dyn/traductions/2dunod-unesco-strategic-foresight-ext-veng.pdf. Zugegriffen: 27. Juni 2016.

Gribbin, J. (2002). *Auf der Suche nach Schrödingers Katze. Quantenphysik und Wirklichkeit* (Serie Piper, Bd. 1353, Ungekürzte Taschenbuchausg., 8. Aufl.). München: Piper.

Harper, J. C., Cuhls, K. & Georghiou, Luke und Johnston, Ron. (2008). Future-Oriented Technology analysis as a Driver of Strategy and Policy. *Technology Analysis & Strategic Management, 20* (1), 78–83.

Havas, A., Schartinger, D., Weber, M. (2010). The impact of foresight on innovation policy making: recent experiences and future perspectives. *Research Evaluation, 19* (2), 91–104.

Jouvenel, B. d. (1967). *Die Kunst der Vorausschau, (original: L'Art de Conjecture).* Neuwied, Berlin.

Kaku, M. (2005). *Parallel Worlds. A Journey Through Creation, Higher Dimensions, And the Future of the Cosmos.* New York: Doubleday.

Kaku, M. (2014). *The Future of the Mind. The Scientific Quest To Understand, Enhance and Empower the Mind.* London: Penguin.

Kosow, H., Gaßner, R., Erdmann, L. & Luber, B.-J. (2008). *Methoden der Zukunfts- und Szenarioanalyse. Überblick, Bewertung und Auswahlkriterien* (WerkstattBericht/IZT, Institut für Zukunftsstudien und Technologiebewertung, Bd. 103). Berlin: IZT.

Kuusi, O., Cuhls, K. & Steinmüller, K. (2015). Quality criteria for scientific futures research. *Futura* (1), 60–77.

Lenz, H. (2005). *Universalgeschichte der Zeit.* Wiesbaden: Marix-Verlag.

Levine, R. (2003). *Eine Landkarte der Zeit. Wie Kulturen mit Zeit umgehen.* Sonderausgabe. München: Piper Verlag.

Linstone, H. A. (1999). *Decision Making for Technology Executives. Using Multiple Perspectives to Iimprove Performance.* Boston/London: Artech House.

Markley, O. W. (2008). Mental time travel. A practical business and personal research tool for looking ahead. *Futures, 40* (1), 17–24.

Martin, B. R. (1995a). Foresight in Science and Technology. *Technology Analysis & Strategic Management, 7* (2), 139–168.

Martin, B. R. (1995b). *Technology Foresight 6: A Review of Recent Overseas Programmes. London.* London: HMSO.

Martin, B. R. (2010). The origins of the concept of 'foresight' in science and technology. An insider's perspective. *Technological Forecasting and Social Change, 77* (9), 1438–1447. https://ac.els-cdn.com/S0040162510001307/1-s2.0-S0040162510001307-main.pdf?_tid=1c937db6-5953-11e6-9e3c-00000aab0f02&acdnat=1470212597_7abfa005a9bcf64ae6b24300afaaa3b. Zugegriffen: 03. August 2016.

Möhrle, M. G. & Isenmann, R. (H.) (Hrsg.). (2017). *Technologie-Roadmapping. Zukunftsstrategien für Technologieunternehmen* (4. Aufl.). Berlin: Springer Vieweg.

Nelson, R. (2010). Extending foresight. The case for and nature of Foresight 2.0. *Futures, 42* (4), 282–294. https://foresightcanada.com/wp-content/uploads/2015/09/Extending-Foresight-The-Case-for-Foresight-2.0-R.-Nelson-2007.pdf. Zugegriffen: 29. April 2019.

NISTEP. (2016). *10th Foresight – summary*, Tōkyō. https://data.nistep.go.jp/dspace/bitstream/11035/3079/2537/NISTEP-NR164-SummaryE.pdf. Zugegriffen: 16. Oktober 2017.

Nordlund, G. (2012). Time-scales in futures research and forecasting. *Futures, 44* (4), 408-414.

Opiela, N., Mohabbat Kar, R. & Thapa, Basanta, Weber, Mike unter methodischer Mitarbeit von Cuhls, Kerstin und Meissner, Svetlana. (2018). *Exekutive KI 2030 – Vier Zukunftsszenarien für Künstliche Intelligenz in der öffentlichen Verwaltung* (Fraunhofer FOKUS, Hrsg.), Berlin. Verfügbar unter https://publica.fraunhofer.de/documents/N-515298.html; https://www.isi.fraunhofer.de/content/dam/isi/dokumente/ccv/2018/2018_Exekutive_KI_2030.pdf. Zugegriffen: 12. September 2019.

Rinderspacher, J. P. (2017a). Arbeitszeitpolitik und die Nullwachstumsgesellschaft – Möglichkeiten und Grenzen. In H. Diefenbacher, B. Held & D. Rodenhäuser (Hrsg.), *Ende des Wachstums Arbeit ohne Ende* (S. 71–102). Metropolis verlag.

Rinderspacher, J. P. (2017b). *Mehr Zeitwohlstand! Für den besseren Umgang mit einem knappen Gut* (HERDER spektrum, Bd. 6833, 1. Auflage). Freiburg: Verlag Herder.

Rönneberg, T. (2010). *Wie wir ticken. Die Bedeutung der inneren Uhr für unser Leben* (1. Aufl.). Köln: DuMont.

Roenneberg, T., Allebrandt, K. V., Merrow, M. & Vetter, C. (2012). Social jetlag and obesity. *Current biology: CB, 22* (10), 939–943. Zugriff am 18.12.2018. Verfügbar unter https://ac.els-cdn.com/S0960982212003259/1-s2.0-S0960982212003259-main.pdf?_tid=9345d0b4-3511-4a82-9d0b-71799817aa9c&acdnat=1545131421_2565b91d295bdf5a798545947010c4eb.

Rönneberg, T. (2000). Zeit als Lebensraum. In M. Held, K. A. Geißler & R. Kirchhof-Stahlmann (Hrsg.), *Ökologie der Zeit. Vom Finden der rechten Zeitmaße* (Edition Universitas, 2. Aufl., S. 41–51). Stuttgart: Hirzel.

Steinmüller A. & Steinmüller, K. (2004). Wild Cards – Wenn das Unwahrscheinliche eintritt. (aktualisierte und erweiterte Ausgabe von „Ungezähmte Zukunft") Hamburg: Murmann Verlag Hamburg.

Technology Futures Analysis Methods Working Group. (2004). Technology futures analysis: Toward integration of the field and new methods. *Technological Forecasting & Social Change* (71), 287–303.

Zeit-Rebounds im Arbeitsleben – Transformative Forschung zu zeitpolitischen Innovationen

Gerrit von Jorck und Sonja Geiger

Abstract

In corporate life, the logic that time is money dominates. The aim is to budget working hours as efficiently as possible. However, it turns out that time rebound effects often occur when trying to "save" time. Such an effect is characterized by the fact that the demand for time-efficient activities increases. Such time-rebound effects are often accompanied by negative effects on sustainability, since the increased number of actions alone usually requires more resources. In this paper, we show what transformative research can do to develop time-policy innovations that reduce such time-rebound effects.

Zusammenfassung

Im Arbeitsleben dominiert die Logik, dass Zeit Geld ist. Ziel ist es, möglichst effizient mit der Arbeitszeit zu haushalten. Doch zeigt sich, dass gerade beim Versuch Zeit zu „sparen" vielfach Zeit-Rebound-Effekte auftreten. Ein solcher Effekt zeichnet sich dadurch aus, dass die Nachfrage nach zeiteffizienten Tätigkeiten steigt. Solche Zeit-Rebound-Effekte gehen vielfach mit negativen Nachhaltigkeitseffekten einher, da allein schon die gesteigerte Handlungsanzahl in der Regel mehr Ressourcen in Anspruch nimmt. In diesem Beitrag

G. von Jorck (✉) · S. Geiger
Technische Universität Berlin, Berlin, Deutschland
E-Mail: gerrit.vonjorck@tu-berlin.de

S. Geiger
E-Mail: sonja.m.geiger@tu-berlin.de

zeigen wir auf, welchen Beitrag transformative Forschung leisten kann, um zeitpolitische Innovationen zu entwickeln, die solche Zeit-Rebound-Effekte reduzieren.

Keywords

Design Thinking · Field Experiment · Innovation · Living Lab · Transdisciplinarity · Transformative research · Time-rebound effect · Time use · Time wealth · Working Time

Schlüsselwörter

Arbeitszeit · Betriebliche Experimentierräume · Design Thinking · Innovation · Reallabor · Transdisziplinarität · Transformative Forschung · Zeit-Rebound-Effekt · Zeitverwendung · Zeitwohlstand

Einleitung

Stetig effizientere Techniken, Praktiken und Prozesse gehen mit dem Versprechen einher, Zeit einzusparen. Stattdessen mehren sich jedoch die Anzeichen, dass diese Entwicklungen zu einer Steigerung der Zeitnot führen. Dieses Paradox bezeichnen wir als Zeit-Rebound-Effekt: Die zeiteffizienten Techniken und Praktiken führen tendenziell dazu, mehr Tätigkeiten in derselben Zeit zu verrichten. Dabei geht die veränderte Zeitnutzung häufig mit ökologisch negativen Effekten einher (Buhl 2016). In unserem Beitrag diskutieren wir am Beispiel des Forschungsdesigns des vom Bundesministerium für Bildung und Forschung (BMBF) im Rahmen der Sozial-ökologischen Forschung geförderten Verbundprojekts „Zeit-Rebound, Zeitwohlstand und nachhaltiger Konsum" (ReZeitKon), wie gemeinsam mit unterschiedlichen Arbeitgebern (Unternehmen verschiedener Größe und mit verschiedenen Arbeitszeitmodellen) zeitpolitische Innovationen entwickelt werden können, um solche Zeit-Rebound-Effekte abzuschwächen und den Zeitwohlstand der Beschäftigten zu fördern. Dazu werden wir insbesondere herausarbeiten, welchen Beitrag ein transformativer Forschungszugang (WBGU 2011) zur Erprobung solcher zeitpolitischen Innovationen leisten kann. Wir werden aufzeigen, wie Treiber von Zeit-Rebound-Effekten in einem Mixed-Method-Ansatz erfasst werden können. Aufbauend auf diesen Methoden werden Möglichkeiten zur partizipativen Entwicklung zeitpolitischer Innovationen dargestellt. Im Gesamten zeigt der Beitrag Möglichkeiten transformativer Forschungsmethoden auf, die Wechselwirkungen zwischen institutionellen Zeitordnungen unterschiedlicher Arbeitszeitmodelle und individuellem Zeiterleben zu verstehen und gegebenenfalls zu ändern. Die leitenden Fragestellungen dieses Beitrags lauten:

- Wie können Treiber von Zeit-Rebound-Effekten im Rahmen eines Mixed-Method Ansatzes beforscht werden?
- Welchen Beitrag kann transformative Forschung zur Be- und Erforschung zeitpolitischer Innovationen leisten?
- Welchen Beitrag können betriebliche Experimentierräume zur Erforschung der Wechselwirkungen zwischen institutionellen Zeitordnungen unterschiedlicher Arbeitszeitmodelle und individuellem Zeiterleben leisten?

Erkenntnisinteresse: Zeit-Rebound-Effekte in der Arbeitswelt

Keynes (2016) attestierte in den 1930-er Jahren seinen Enkelkindern, dass der technologische Fortschritt zu einer radikalen Verkürzung der Arbeitszeit führen würde. Das Bild, welches sich uns heute zeigt, ist jedoch ein anderes: zwar haben sich die Arbeitszeiten pro Arbeitnehmer/in im Vergleich zu den 1930-er Jahren tatsächlich reduziert, zugleich ist jedoch auch die Erwerbsquote deutlich gestiegen, insgesamt hat die Erwerbsarbeitszeit in der Bevölkerung demnach zugenommen. Auch wird trotz rückgängiger Arbeitszeiten pro Person eine zunehmende Zeitnot unter den Beschäftigten wahrgenommen (DGB 2015). Modernere, flexible Arbeitsformen, in denen die Beschäftigten mehr Souveränität über ihre Zeit haben, haben zudem häufig eine Intensivierung und Extensivierung der Arbeitszeit zur Folge (Matta 2015). Die Arbeitnehmer/innen verinnerlichen in diesen Arbeitsformen teilweise die unternehmerische Logik als Arbeitskraftunternehmer/innen (Pongratz und Voß 1998). Indem sie die unternehmerische Logik verinnerlichen, werden für Arbeitskraftunternehmer/innen auch die Opportunitätskosten nichteffizienter Handlungen relevant. Jede nicht effizient ausgeführte Handlung verlängert die Arbeitszeit und reduziert damit den relativen Stundenlohn. Dadurch wird es ökonomisch rational die Arbeitszeit zu intensivieren (Jorck 2019). Diese individuell rationale Handlung kann jedoch kollektiv zu einer „Tyrannei der Workaholics" (Claassen 2012) führen, indem jede/r einzelne die zeitlichen Anforderungen erhöht.

Nach Rosa (2005) ist diese Entwicklung in eine **Beschleunigungsspirale** eingebettet. Der technologische Fortschritt, zum Beispiel im Übergang vom Brief auf die E-Mail, führt dann nicht wie von Keynes attestiert zu einer Zeitersparnis, sondern zu einer „Steigerung der Zahl an Handlungs- oder Erlebnisepisoden pro Zeiteinheit" (Rosa 2014): aus einem Brief werden schließlich zehn E-Mails. Liegt die Beschleunigungsrate dabei unterhalb der Wachstumsrate, kommt es zu Zeitnot. Im Zuge technologischer Beschleunigung beschleunigt sich auch der soziale Wandel: Berufe verschwinden und neue entstehen, wie es sich gerade auch im Zuge der digitalen Transformation zeigt. Dies macht stetige Anpassungen an sich verändernde Rahmen- und Wettbewerbsbedingungen der Beschäftigten notwendig, wodurch sich deren Lebenstempo beschleunigen kann: um auf dem sich verändernden Arbeitsmarkt mithalten zu können, müssen zunehmend größere Anstrengungen unternommen werden. Dabei wird zur Entlastung des Lebenstempos wiederum auf weitere Formen technologischer Beschleunigung zurückgegriffen (z. B. das Auto oder das Flugzeug zum Reisen), wodurch die Beschleunigungsspirale weiter angetrieben wird. Einher geht diese Beschleunigung nach Rosa (2016) mit dem Verlust von **Resonanzbeziehungen,** also gegenseitigen Beziehungen des Berührtwerdens, unter anderem auch zu den Kolleg/innen und der Arbeit selbst, da diese Beziehungen Zeit benötigen. Dieser Verlust wird dann teilweise durch Resonanzsimulationen in der Konsum- und Warenwelt kompensiert. Schor (1993) beschreibt diese Kompensation des Arbeitsleids durch Konsum auch als **Work-and-Spend Cycle:** während das Arbeitsleid durch Konsum kompensiert wird, bildet der Konsum zugleich die Motivation zu arbeiten, sodass Produktivitätsgewinne technischen Fortschritts nicht in freie Zeit übersetzt werden.

Arbeitszeitregimes scheinen somit auf verschiedenen Wegen die Konsumpraktiken der Beschäftigten zu prägen. Zunächst fehlt in beschleunigten Arbeitszeitregimen vielfach die freie Zeit für zeitintensive Konsumpraktiken wie Reparieren und Selbermachen (Schor 2016). Weiterhin werden mangelnde Resonanzerfahrungen teilweise durch Kompensationskonsum (z. B. Kurztrip mit dem Flugzeug als Belohnung für eine stressige Arbeitswoche) ausgeglichen. Dann wird auch instrumentell auf zeiteffiziente Konsumpraktiken wie das Auto oder Fast Food zurückgegriffen, um in der Beschleunigungsspirale mithalten zu können. Schließlich zeichnet sich die Beschleunigung direkt durch eine Steigerung der Konsumhandlungen aus. Viele dieser veränderten Konsumpraktiken gehen mit einem verstärkten Ressourcenverbrauch einher, weshalb eine veränderte Zeitpolitik auch als ein Schlüssel für eine nachhaltige Lebensweise gilt (Deutscher Bundestag 2013; Gorz 1989; Rosa et al. 2017).

Im Rahmen des Forschungsprojektes wird insbesondere der Einfluss verschiedener Arbeitszeitmodelle und zeitpolitischer Innovationen auf den Zeitwohlstand der Beschäftigten untersucht. **Zeitwohlstand** umfasst dabei in Anlehnung an Rinderspacher (2012) sowohl einen quantitativen als auch einen qualitativen

Begriff von Zeit. Zeitwohlstand ist ein angemessener Umfang frei zur Verfügung stehender Zeit (freie Zeit) mit genügend Zeit pro Zeitverwendung (Tempo) bei ausreichend stabilen Erwartungshorizonten (Planbarkeit) und zufriedenstellender Abstimmung unterschiedlicher zeitlicher Anforderungen (Synchronisierung) unter hinreichend selbst bestimmten Bedingungen (Zeitsouveränität) (Jorck et al. 2019). Zeitwohlstand wird dabei bewusst einem materiellen Wohlstandsbegriff gegenübergestellt. Goodin et al. (2008) zeigen dabei auf, dass der Umfang frei zur Verfügung stehender Zeit ebenso eine Frage der Verteilungsgerechtigkeit sein kann wie dies bei materiellem Wohlstand der Fall ist. Während bei Goodin et al. jedoch sozialstaatliche Maßnahmen im Fokus stehen, fokussiert sich dieses Forschungsprojekt auf Maßnahmen auf der betrieblichen Ebene. Prinzipiell lassen sich drei Formen **zeitpolitischer Instrumente** auf betrieblicher Ebene unterscheiden: Arbeitszeitflexibilisierung, innere und äußere Arbeitszeitverkürzung (Jorck und Schrader 2019). Arbeitszeitflexibilisierung umfasst dabei Maßnahmen, welche die Flexibilität der Beschäftigten erhöht. Davon zu unterscheiden sich solche Maßnahmen, welche die Flexibilität des Arbeitgebers auf Kosten der Arbeitnehmenden erhöht (z. B. Arbeit auf Abruf). Es zeigt sich, dass es insbesondere Frauen schwer fällt nach der Arbeit abzuschalten, wenn die Flexibilisierung sich an den Interessen des Unternehmens orientiert. Wiederum tendieren Väter dazu ihre Arbeitszeiten auszuweiten und Sorgetätigkeiten zurückzufahren, wenn sich die Flexibilisierung an den Interessen der Beschäftigten orientiert (Lott 2018, 2019). Instrumente einer **inneren Arbeitszeitverkürzung** bleiben im Rahmen der vorgegebenen Erwerbsarbeitszeit, eröffnen jedoch innerhalb dieses Rahmens Auszeiten, die nicht der Verwertungslogik unterstehen. Hier stehen qualitative Aspekte von Zeit im Fokus. Eine klassische Form der inneren Arbeitszeitverkürzung stellt der Bildungsurlaub dar. Weitere Formen lassen sich als „Zeitinvestitionen in die Umwelt" (Rinderspacher 1996) beschreiben: Wenn beispielsweise die längeren Fahrzeiten als Arbeitszeit anerkannt werden, die Arbeitnehmer/innen mit dem Fahrrad anstatt dem Auto zurücklegen (Doiber 2018). Auch eine Mindestpersonalbemessung, welche beispielsweise die Anzahl der Patient/innen je Krankenpfleger/in reduziert und darüber zeitliche Freiräume während der Arbeitszeit schafft, stellt eine Form innerer Arbeitszeitverkürzung dar (Jorck 2019). Maßnahmen äußerer Arbeitszeitverkürzung sind wiederum solche, welche die Arbeitszeit verkürzen, also die quantitative Dimension der für Arbeit verwendeten Zeit adressieren.

Zeiteffiziente Innovationen, die auf die Einsparung von Zeit ausgerichtet sind, können dabei zu Zeit-Rebound-Effekten führen. Ein **Zeit-Rebound-Effekt** liegt dann vor, wenn der Einsatz zeiteffizienter Techniken und Praktiken die Zeitressourcen verknappt und den Zeitwohlstand einschränkt. Es lässt sich zwischen einem Zeit-Rebound-Effekt erster und zweiter Ordnung unterscheiden: Ein

Zeit-Rebound-Effekt erster Ordnung liegt in Anlehnung an Binswanger (2001) dann vor, wenn der Einsatz zeiteffizienter Techniken und Praktiken zu einer gesteigerten Nachfrage nach diesen zeiteffizienten Techniken und Praktiken führt. Ein Zeit-Rebound-Effekt zweiter Ordnung (Backfire-Effekt) liegt dann vor, wenn der Einsatz zeiteffizienter Techniken und Praktiken den Zeitwohlstand negativ beeinflusst, sprich zu Zeitnot führt, indem sich beispielsweise das allgemeine Lebenstempo steigert (Jorck 2019). Ziel des Forschungsprojektes ist es Maßnahmen zu entwickeln, mit denen sich Zeit-Rebound-Effekte reduzieren lassen und zugleich der Zeitwohlstand der Beschäftigten erhöht wird. Daraus ergeben sich die folgenden Forschungsziele:

- Forschungsziel 1: Bestandsaufnahme zu hinderlichen und fördernden Faktoren für Zeitwohlstand.
- Forschungsziel 2: Entwicklung spezifischer Maßnahmen zur Reduktion von Zeit-Rebound-Effekten und zur Förderung von Zeitwohlstand.
- Forschungsziel 3: Evaluation von Maßnahmen am Arbeitsplatz, die Zeit-Rebound-Effekte reduzieren und Zeitwohlstand fördern.

Methodologische Positionierung: Transformative Forschung

Der deutschsprachige Diskurs um transformative Forschung wurde im Wesentlichen im Zuge des Gutachtens des Wissenschaftlichen Beirats Globale Umweltveränderungen „Welt im Wandel. Gesellschaftsvertrag für eine große Transformation" (WBGU 2011) angestoßen und bewegt sich seit seinen Anfängen im Feld der Nachhaltigkeitsforschung. Der WBGU unterscheidet zwischen transformativer Forschung und Transformationsforschung. Während **Transformationsforschung** den gesellschaftlichen Umbau selbst sowie seine Ermöglichungsbedingungen zum Gegenstand hat, befördert **transformative Forschung** diesen Umbau durch geeignete Methoden und Prozesse. Transformationsforschung zieht Lehren aus erfolgreichen Transformationsprozessen für die nachhaltige Transformation spätindustrieller Gesellschaften. Durch interdisziplinäre Zusammenarbeit werden dabei insbesondere Wechselwirkungen zwischen Technik, Mensch und Natur identifiziert. Transformative Forschung ist hingegen anwendungsorientiert und dient der Entwicklung klimaverträglicher und nachhaltiger Innovationen, welche sowohl technischer, betriebswirtschaftlicher oder auch sozialer Natur sein können. So wird die Konsumforschung im WBGU-Gutachten explizit als ein Teil transformativer Forschung erwähnt.

Dabei sind interkulturelle Übertragbarkeit der Innovationen sowie mögliche Rebound-Effekte, also eine unbeabsichtigte Steigerung des Outputs in Folge einer Effizienzsteigerung beim Input (Santarius 2015), stets mit zu untersuchen.

In der Debatte um transformative Forschung (Schneidewind und Wissel 2015; Strohschneider 2014) wird transformative Forschung sowohl als interdisziplinäre als auch transdisziplinäre Forschung definiert, womit sie sich auch an den Forschungsleitlinien der Sozial-ökologischen Forschung (Bundesministerium für Bildung und Forschung (BMBF) 2015) orientiert. **Transdisziplinäre Forschung** meint dabei zunächst die Anerkennung des Wissens von Nicht-Wissenschaftler/innen als gleichberechtigtes Erfahrungswissen. Sie umfasst darüber hinaus die Integration von Nicht-Wissenschaftler/innen in den Forschungsprozess, was auch die gemeinsame Aushandlung der Forschungsfragen umfasst. In der **Reallaborforschung** wird die transdisziplinäre Forschung insofern weiter gefasst, als dass Innovationen direkt in realen, lebensweltlichen Kontexten getestet werden (Schneidewind und Singer-Brodowski 2015). Reallabore dienen zum einen der Erforschung von Transformationswissen, führen zugleich aber auch zu konkreten Nachhaltigkeitsinterventionen, womit sie in die Nähe der Interventionsforschung rücken. Zur Beforschung von Rebound-Effekten von Nachhaltigkeitsinnovationen bieten sich nach Buhl et al. (2017) Reallabore an. Diese zeichnen sich nach Liedtke et al. (2015) durch vier Eigenschaften aus: Erstens werden die kulturellen, rechtlichen, technischen und marktwirtschaftlichen Rahmenbedingungen des Kontextes erfasst, in welchen die Innovation eingeführt wird. Zweitens werden die Innovationen gemeinsam mit den späteren Anwender/innen entwickelt. Drittens werden Innovationen bereits in einem frühen Stadium in Experimenten mit den Anwender/innen getestet und viertens findet die Bewertung der Innovationen in realweltlicher Umgebung statt. Hierbei stehen Aktivitäten und Handlungen der Anwender/innen im Fokus, wodurch insbesondere der Verwendung der Zeit und Zeit-Rebound-Effekten eine besondere Aufmerksamkeit zukommt (Buhl et al. 2017).

Die Reallaborforschung orientiert sich am **Transformationszyklus** (Loorbach 2010). Dieser unterscheidet vier Phasen einer Transformation: Strategie, Taktik, Operation und Reflexion. In der **strategischen Phase** wird die Transformationsarena gebildet. Diese besteht aus systematisch ausgewählten Akteuren, die offen für innovative Prozesse und neue Visionen sind. Die Akteure sollten zudem möglichst unterschiedliche Interessensgruppen repräsentieren. Zentrale Aufgabe dieser Transformationsarena ist es schließlich eine gemeinsame Vision zu entwickeln. Diese bildet die Grundlage für die **taktische Phase**. In dieser liegt der Fokus darauf, zentrale Hindernisse für die Realisierung der Vision ausfindig zu machen. Dazu wird die Transformationsvision in konkrete Transformationspfade übersetzt, welche sich an die konkreten Gegebenheiten anpassen. Diese Transformationspfade werden schließlich in der **operativen Phase** in Experimenten getestet. Die Experimente gehen entweder direkt aus dem Innovationsprozess der beiden vorherigen Phasen hervor oder knüpfen an bestehende Innovationsexperimente an, sofern sie sich in die Transformationsvision und den Transformationspfad einfügen. Abschließend werden die Experimente, ebenso wie der vorangegangene Innovationsprozess als solcher, in der **reflexiven Phase** evaluiert. Dieser kontinuierliche Reflexionsprozess wird gemeinsam mit den Praxisakteuren vollzogen und soll soziales Lernen ermöglichen, um einen neuen Transformationszyklus anzustoßen.

Schneidewind und andere (vgl. u. a. Schneidewind und Singer-Brodowski 2015) ergänzen diesen Zyklus um eine einleitende Phase der **Problemanalyse**. In dieser wird die Problemstellung des Transformationsvorhabens systematisch herausgearbeitet. Das Ergebnis ist eine wissenschaftlich fundierte Bestandaufnahme des bei den betroffenen Akteursgruppen vorhandenen **Systemwissens**. Angelehnt an die strategische Phase wird in der Phase **Visionsentwicklung** die normative Zielsetzung des Transformationsprozesses in transdisziplinärer Zusammenarbeit entwickelt. Das konkrete Ziel des Forschungsvorhabens wird demnach nicht extern vorgegeben, sondern erst partizipativ im Prozess bestimmt. Dabei entsteht **Zielwissen** über wünschenswerte Zukünfte und ein „**Boundary Object**" (Star und Griesemer 1989) wird entworfen. Dieses bildet im weiteren transdisziplinären Prozess die gemeinsame Bezugsgröße der beteiligten Akteure. Ein solches Boundary Object kann beispielsweise eine Stadt darstellen, die sich zum Ziel gesetzt hat 100 % CO_2-frei zu werden (Schneidewind und Scheck 2013). Die räumliche Abgrenzung der Stadt sowie das gemeinsame Ziel schaffen damit einen Rahmen, innerhalb dessen Innovationen entwickelt und getestet werden können. Die taktische und operative Phase des Transformationszyklus werden bei Schneidewind in der Phase **Experimente** zusammengefasst. In Realexperimenten wird auf Basis der entwickelten Vision eine konkrete Innovation von Praxispartnern umgesetzt und dabei wissenschaftlich begleitet. Dadurch soll **Transformationswissen** über die konkrete Gestaltung der Transformation erlangt werden, welches das konkrete Alltagswissen der beteiligten Akteure umfasst. Abschließend werden die Erfahrungen aus diesen Experimenten in der Phase **Diffusion und Lernen** systematisch evaluiert und fließen als sozialer Lernprozess in die Problemanalyse eines erneuten Zyklusdurchlaufs ein. Die Evaluation umfasst dabei sowohl den konkreten Output als auch den Outcome, Prozess und Input des Experiments (Luederitz et al. 2017).

Liedtke et al. (2015) übertragen diesen Transformationszyklus auf die angewandte Innovationsforschung. In ihrer Konzeption **nachhaltiger Reallabore** integrieren sie Aspekte transformativer Forschung, der Strukturationstheorie, der Theorie sozialer Praktiken sowie des Normen-Aktivations-Modells und stellen damit eine Methodologie sozio-technischer Realexperimente in Transformationsprozessen auf. Sie unterscheiden wiederum drei Phasen der nutzerzentrierten Innovationsforschung in nachhaltigen Reallaboren: Insight Research, Prototyping und Field Testing. In der Phase **Insight Research** steht das Problemverständnis und das Verständnis des Status Quo im Fokus. In der zweiten Phase **Prototyping** werden gemeinsam mit den späteren Nutzer/innen sowie weiteren relevanten Stakeholdern Prototypen nachhaltiger Innovationen entwickelt. Die dritte Phase **Field Test** umfasst schließlich die Phasen Experimente sowie Diffusion und Lernen des Transformationszyklus nach Schneidewind. In diesem werden die Prototypen im Rahmen eines Reallabors getestet und systematisch evaluiert. Die erste und dritte Phase ergeben dabei ein **Prä-/Post-Design** zur Evaluation der Innovationen.

Unser Forschungsvorhaben, Maßnahmen zur Reduktion von Zeit-Rebound-Effekten und zur Erhöhung des Zeitwohlstandes im betrieblichen Kontext zu entwickeln, verortet sich innerhalb der transformativen Forschung und fokussiert dabei auf die anwendungsorientierte Innovationsforschung. In Anlehnung an Liedtke et al. unterteilt sich das Forschungsvorhaben in die drei Phasen Problemanalyse, Innovationsentwicklung und betriebliche Experimentierräume, welche den drei Wissensarten Systemwissen, Zielwissen und Transformationswissen zugeordnet sind. Das Boundary Object bildet der betriebliche Experimentierraum, in welchem die partizipativ entwickelte zeitpolitische Innovation getestet wird. Das Bundesministerium für Arbeit und Soziales empfiehlt zur Erprobung neuer Arbeitszeit- und Organisationsmodelle die Einrichtung solcher **betrieblicher Experimentierräume,** auf die sich die Sozialpartner gemeinsam einigen und in denen neue Arbeitsformen unter Realbedingungen getestet werden können (Bundesministerium für Arbeit und Soziales (BMAS) 2016). Betriebliche Experimentierräume können als Reallabore im betrieblichen Kontext verstanden werden. In ihnen werden zeitpolitische Innovationen eingebettet in tarifvertragliche, gesetzliche und marktwirtschaftliche Rahmenbedingungen getestet.

Forschungsfeld und Sampling: Kurzdarstellung der Praxispartner

Zur Entwicklung von Maßnahmen zur Förderung von Zeitwohlstand und Reduktion von Zeit-Rebound-Effekten im Arbeitsleben werden insgesamt fünf Betriebe als betriebliche Experimentierräume ausgewählt. Es werden nur solche Betriebe in Betracht gezogen, in denen Personal abhängig beschäftigt ist. Selbstständige oder ehrenamtlich arbeitende Vereine und Organisationen werden nicht berücksichtigt, um eine gewisse Ähnlichkeit der Grundbedingungen zu gewährleisten. Ziel bei der Auswahl der Praxispartner ist es, die Vielfalt innerhalb des Forschungsfeldes „**Betriebe mit abhängig Beschäftigten**" zu erfassen und die Unterschiede, die sich innerhalb dieses Feldes ergeben, explorativ herauszuarbeiten. Dazu werden Betriebe mit möglichst unterschiedlicher Arbeitszeitgestaltung ausgewählt, um über den Vergleich der Fälle zu einem besseren Verständnis der unterschiedlichen Rahmenbedingungen und Konstellationen für Zeitwohlstand auf betrieblicher Ebene zu kommen.

Eine zentrale Herausforderung bei der Auswahl der Betriebe ist die Bereitschaft an der partizipativen Entwicklung sowie Umsetzung zeitpolitischer Innovationen mitzuwirken. Da sowohl die Entwicklung als auch die Umsetzung zeitpolitischer Innovationen recht umfängliche Zeitressourcen seitens der Praxispartner erfordern, konnten überwiegend solche Betriebe als Praxispartner gewonnen werden, in denen zentrale Akteure bereits ein intrinsisches Interesse an den Forschungsfragen des Forschungsprojektes hatten. Die erfolgreiche Auswahl der Praxispartner erfolgte daher überwiegend über direkte Kontakte auf themenspezifischen Fachtagungen[1]. Im Folgenden werden die Praxispartner des ReZeitKon-Projekts kurz vorgestellt:

Praxispartner 1 (PP1): Im Bundesverband evangelischer Ausbildungsstätten für Sozialpädagogik (BeA) sind über 50 Mitgliedschulen zusammengeschlossen, an denen rund 10.000 Erzieherinnen und Erzieher pro Jahr ausgebildet werden. PP1 ist eine dieser Mitgliedschulen und beschäftigt 18 Lehrer/innen. Die Arbeitszeitgestaltung zeichnet sich zum einen durch fixe Stundenpläne für den Unterricht, zum anderen durch einen hohen Grad an Zeitsouveränität für Vor- und Nachbereitung des Lehrstoffs aus (z. B. in den Schulferien, am Nachmittag oder an unterrichtsfreien Tagen). Der Arbeitsalltag ist insbesondere durch einen vergleichsweise hohen Anteil an Beziehungsarbeit zwischen Lehrer/innen und Schüler/innen geprägt.

Praxispartner 2 (PP2): PP2 ist ein Kollektivunternehmen und über den Verkauf eines Markengetränks bekannt geworden. Das Unternehmen existiert rein digital und organisiert sich überwiegend über ein gemeinsam genutztes Forum. Es besteht aus einem Organisationskreis mit neun Mitgliedern, die vom Kollektiv finanziert werden. Das Kollektivverständnis geht jedoch über diesen

---

[1] 5. Internationale Degrowth-Konferenz, Tagung „Gute Arbeit ohne Wachstum" der evangelischen Akademie Tutzing, Fachtagung „Zeitkompetenz und Zeitmanagement" der Deutschen Gesellschaft für Zeitpolitik.

Organisationskreis hinaus und umfasst alle involvierten Partner entlang der gesamten Wertschöpfungskette vom Rohstoffproduzenten bis zum Gastronomiepartner. In der Fallstudie wird sich jedoch auf die abhängig Beschäftigten des Organisationskreises konzentriert. PP2 ist längst mehr als ein Getränkekollektiv und verkauft sein „Betriebssystem" auch an Großkonzerne, indem es aus den eigenen Erfahrungen heraus Unternehmensberatung anbietet. Die Kollektivist/innen erfassen ihre Arbeitszeiten selbst und entscheiden eigenständig über den Umfang ihrer Arbeitszeit. Dafür erhalten sie einen sozial gestaffelten Einheitslohn je Stunde. Dieser ist zunächst für alle Kollektivist/innen des Organisationskreises identisch, kann aber bei erhöhten Bedarfen, zum Beispiel durch Kinder oder körperlichen Beeinträchtigungen, erhöht werden.

Praxispartner 3 (PP3): PP3 ist ein Co-Working Space, der sich selbst auch als „Slow-Working Space" beschreibt. Er entstand 2013 mit dem Anspruch, die Arbeit an sozial-ökologischen Projekten mit einer Arbeitsweise zu verbinden, die selbst nachhaltigkeitsorientiert ist. Unter diesem gemeinsamen Dach arbeiten Unternehmen und Vereine wie zum Beispiel ein Bildungsdienstleister oder eine Onlineplattform. Die Grenze zwischen Arbeit und Engagement ist bei PP3 fließend.

Praxispartner 4 (PP4): PP4 ist ein führendes deutsches Unternehmen für Outdoor-Ausrüstung. Am Hauptsitz sind im Jahr 2017 529 Mitarbeiter/innen beschäftigt. Als nachhaltigkeitsorientiertes Unternehmen unterzieht sich PP4 einer Gemeinwohlökonomie-Bilanzierung. Diese bewertet Arbeitszeitreduktion, den Abbau von Überstunden und Teilzeitstellen als positiv. Derzeit beschäftigt sich PP4 mit dem Übergang in die komplette Vertrauensarbeitszeit, mit Mobilem Arbeiten sowie mit Modellen für Arbeitszeitkonten, die Flexibilität schaffen und lebensphasenorientiert sind.

Praxispartner 5 (PP5): Bei diesem Betrieb handelt es sich um einen weltweit führenden Technologiekonzern in der Antriebs- und Fahrwerktechnik sowie der aktiven und passiven Sicherheitstechnik. Er ist mit 146.000 Mitarbeiter/innen an rund 230 Standorten in nahezu 40 Ländern vertreten und zählt zu den weltweit größten Automobilzulieferern. An einem Standort soll ein 4-Gruppen-Schichtsystem eingeführt werden, welches Überstunden deutlich abbauen würde. Vergangene Erfahrungen haben gezeigt, dass solche potenziell entlastenden Arbeitszeitmodelle bei einem Teil der Beschäftigten auf Widerstände stoßen können (Gerold et al. 2017). Im Fall von PP5 dürften diese insbesondere damit zusammenhängen, dass durch den Entfall von gut bezahlten Überstunden Einkommensverluste befürchtet werden. Zudem würde ein solches Schichtsystem zwar längere Freizeitblöcke ermöglichen, allerdings auch mehr Wochenendschichten beinhalten.

Die beiden Praxispartner 2 und 3 zeichnen sich dadurch aus, dass sie sowohl direkt zum Zeitwohlstand ihrer Beschäftigten beitragen wollen als auch zu einer sozial-ökologischen Lebensweise. Gemeinsam ist den beiden Betrieben zudem, dass sie regelmäßig Auszeiten wählen, um ihre Arbeitsweise gemeinsam zu reflektieren. Zugleich unterscheiden sie sich in der Art ihrer Organisation. Als Co-Working Space stellt PP3 insbesondere einen gemeinsamen Arbeitsort bereit, während eben ein solcher bei PP2 nicht existiert.

PP4 und PP5 gleichen sich darin, dass es sich um etablierte, gewinnorientiert wirtschaftende Unternehmen mit einer eigenen Personalpolitik handelt. Während PP5 am untersuchten Standort jedoch überwiegend männliche Mitarbeiter im Schichtarbeitsbetrieb beschäftigt, sind am Standort von PP4 überwiegend weibliche Beschäftigte in flexiblen Arbeitsverhältnissen angestellt.

Methodisches Verfahren: Transformative Zeitforschung

Das methodische Vorgehen orientiert sich am Transformationszyklus nach Loorbach (2010), Schneidewind und Singer-Brodowski (2015) und Liedtke et al. (2015). Es unterteilt sich in die drei Phasen Problemanalyse, Innovationsentwicklung sowie betriebliche Experimentierräume (siehe Abb. 1). Im Folgenden

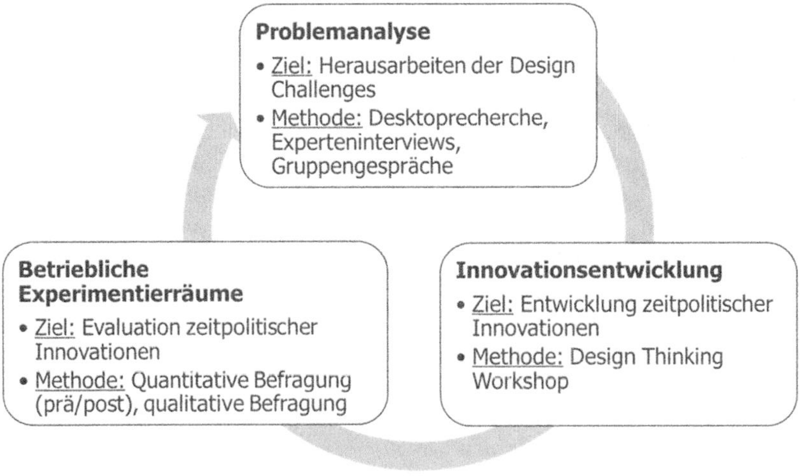

Problemanalyse
- Ziel: Herausarbeiten der Design Challenges
- Methode: Desktoprecherche, Experteninterviews, Gruppengespräche

Innovationsentwicklung
- Ziel: Entwicklung zeitpolitischer Innovationen
- Methode: Design Thinking Workshop

Betriebliche Experimentierräume
- Ziel: Evaluation zeitpolitischer Innovationen
- Methode: Quantitative Befragung (prä/post), qualitative Befragung

Abb. 1 Transformative Forschung zu zeitpolitischen Innovationen in Anlehnung an Loorbach 2010; Schneidewind & Singer-Brodowski 2015 und Liedtke et al. 2015

werden das Erkenntnisinteresse, das Sampling und insbesondere das methodische Vorgehen in diesen jeweiligen Phasen dargestellt.

Problemanalyse

Im Rahmen der Problemanalyse wird Systemwissen über die Arbeitszeitsysteme der jeweiligen Praxispartner generiert. Über qualitative Forschungsmethoden werden die spezifischen Herausforderungen für Zeitwohlstand in den jeweiligen Fallstudien herausgearbeitet. Die Untersuchungsphase führt dabei zu einem gemeinsamen Problemverständnis, welches die Grundlage für die weiteren Untersuchungsphasen bildet.

Erkenntnisinteresse

Ziel der Problemanalyse ist es, in den jeweiligen Fallstudien ein fundiertes Wissen bezüglich der aktuell angewendeten Arbeitszeitmodelle zu schaffen. Spezifische Barrieren, welche die Realisierung von Zeitwohlstand bei den Arbeitnehmenden erschweren, sowie bereits diskutierte Strategien zu deren Überwindung, werden hier identifiziert. Generell wird ein besseres Verständnis für kulturelle, organisationale und soziale Schwellen zur Entfaltung von Zeitwohlstand entwickelt. Zudem wird in dieser Projektphase ein gemeinsames Problemverständnis der beteiligten Wissenschaftler/innen und des Praxispartners entstehen. Im Ergebnis dieser Arbeitsphase werden zwei zentrale Herausforderungen (sog. **„Design Challenges"**) für Zeitwohlstand herausgearbeitet. Gemeinsam mit den Praxispartnern wird anschließend eine dieser Design Challenges für die Innovationsentwicklung in der zweiten Untersuchungsphase ausgewählt.

Methodisches Vorgehen

Zunächst erfolgen eine **Desktoprecherche** und eine inhaltliche Analyse relevanter Dokumente (z. B. Betriebsvereinbarungen zu Arbeitszeiten) zu aktuellen, geplanten und bereits gescheiterten Arbeitszeitmodellen. In leitfadengestützten Experteninterviews werden Motive, Erfahrungen, Hindernisse und günstige Rahmenbedingungen für einen veränderten Umgang mit Zeit ausfindig gemacht. Es handelt sich dabei um ein **problemzentriertes Interview** nach Witzel (2000), welches mit zwei offenen Fragen zu den Hemmnissen für Zeitwohlstand auf betrieblicher Ebene und möglichen Maßnahmen zur Förderung von Zeitwohlstand beginnt. Im zweiten Teil des Interviews wird mit der ReZeitKon-Definition von Zeitwohlstand (siehe Abschn. 2) ein Stimulus gesetzt, um weitere Dimensionen von Zeitwohlstand zu eröffnen. Um die Expertenmeinungen zu validieren und die Gruppenmeinung losgelöst von Einzelmeinungen zu erheben, wird ein **Gruppengespräch** mit Beschäftigten durchgeführt. Im Fokus steht dabei die Interaktion der Gruppenmitglieder. Ziel dieser Gruppengespräche ist es, vorherrschende Argumentationsmuster innerhalb der möglichst natürlichen Gruppenzusammensetzung herauszufiltern. Dazu werden wie beim Experteninterview nacheinander zwei Fragen zu den Hemmnissen und förderlichen Bedingungen für Zeitwohlstand im Betrieb gestellt.

Sampling

Je Unternehmen werden zwei Experteninterviews mit einer Vertretung des Personalwesens sowie des Betriebsrats beziehungsweise einer Mitarbeitervertretung geführt. Dies ermöglicht ein kontrastreiches Bild der Arbeitszeitgestaltung in den jeweiligen Betrieben. Die Interviewten zeichnen sich dadurch als Expert/innen aus, dass sie „über ein spezifisches Rollenwissen verfügen, solches zugeschrieben bekommen und eine darauf basierende besondere Kompetenz für sich selbst in Anspruch nehmen" (Przyborski und Wohlrab-Sahr 2008). In den kleineren Betrieben, in denen keine formelle Mitarbeitervertretung bestimmt ist, werden zwei zufällig ausgewählte Mitarbeiter/innen interviewt. Zudem findet ein Gruppengespräch je Betrieb statt. Dabei handelt es sich um regelmäßig stattfindende Teambesprechungen in möglichst natürlicher Besetzung. Die Gruppengespräche werden in den Teilen des Betriebes geführt, in denen der betriebliche Experimentierraum etabliert wird.

Innovationsentwicklung

In der Phase Innovationsentwicklung werden auf Basis der Design Challenge aus der Problemanalyse gemeinsam mit ausgewählten Stakeholdern spezifische Maßnahmen zur Reduktion von Zeit-Rebound-Effekten sowie zur Förderung von Zeitwohlstand entwickelt. Auf diese Weise entsteht Zielwissen darüber, welche zeitlichen Bedarfe die Beschäftigten haben. Mit der **Design Thinking Methode für Nachhaltigkeit** (DT^N) (Schrader et al. 2018) wird das konkrete Erfahrungswissen der Beschäftigten zu zeitlichen Infrastrukturen ihres Arbeitsumfeldes sowie ihrem subjektiven Zeitempfinden in einen kreativen Innovationsprozess überführt, an dessen Ende Prototypen für die Verbesserung des konkreten Arbeitszeitmodells entstehen. Dabei spiegelt sich die Gesamt-Methodologie der transformativen Forschung im Teil-Ablauf des Design Thinking Prozesses wider. Dieser besteht ebenfalls aus den vergleichbaren vier Phasen: Problembeschreibung, Lösungsentwicklung, Test und kritische Reflexion (Maher et al. 2018).

Erkenntnisinteresse

Design Thinking ist ein abduktiver Erkenntnisprozess (Dorst 2011). Was und wie etwas designt wird, ist nicht im Vorfeld bestimmt, sondern Ergebnis des Prozesses. Hingegen ist das grobe Ergebnis – in diesem Projekt die Steigerung des Zeitwohlstandes der Beschäftigten und die Vermeidung von Zeit-Rebound-Effekten – durch die Design Challenge festgelegt. Im weiteren Sinne ist das Ziel der Phase Innovationsentwicklung, *eine* mögliche zeitpolitische Innovation zu generieren, die als Prototyp getestet wird.

Methodisches Vorgehen

Eine Woche vor dem DT^N-Workshop werden die Teilnehmenden aufgefordert **Cultural Probes** in Vorbereitung auf den Workshop zu sammeln. Diese umfassen vier Aspekte: ein Zeittagebuch über einen typischen Arbeitstag, eine kurze Einschätzung zu ihrem Zeitwohlstand sowie Zeit-Rebound-Effekten auf Basis eines kurzen Befragungsbogens mit acht Items, die Benennung von Situationen, in denen Zeitwohlstand geschaffen wird und solchen, in denen Zeitwohlstand verhindert wird, sowie das Fotografieren von Situationen des Alltags, die mit Zeitwohlstand in Verbindung gesetzt werden. Auf Basis dieser Vorarbeiten sowie der weiteren Auseinandersetzung mit der Design Challenge aus der Problemanalyse (z. B: „Wie können wir den Schichtbetrieb optimal auf flexible, betriebliche Anforderungen einstellen und dabei zugleich den Zeitwohlstand der Beschäftigten erhöhen?") wird dann im Rahmen des DT^N-Workshops durch die Teilnehmenden die **Persona** definiert, also ein/e stellvertretende/r Nutzer/in, deren Zeitwohlstand gefördert werden soll. In der zweiten Phase des Workshops werden dann in einem Kreativprozess **Prototypen** zeitpolitischer Innovationen erstellt. Die Visualisierung der Prototypen dient dazu, die zeitpolitische Innovation bereits recht konkret werden zu lassen, um darüber auf mögliche Probleme aufmerksam zu werden. Hieran schließt sich sogleich eine dritte Workshopphase an. In dieser wird der Prototyp mittels eines **Time Wealth Innovation Cube** (TWICE) durch die Workshopteilnehmer/innen getestet. Dieser bezieht die fünf Zeitwohlstandsdimensionen (siehe Abschn. 2) auf die Beschäftigten sowie die Arbeitsabläufe. Anhand des Würfels werden Vor- und Nachteile der Prototypen für Zeitwohlstand und mögliche Zeit-Rebound-Effekte überprüft. Das Testverfahren findet innerhalb des Workshops statt, indem die Prototypen den anderen Gruppen vorgestellt werden. Das Feedback fließt anschließend in eine Überarbeitung des Prototypens ein. Der vielversprechendste Prototyp wird daraufhin ausgewählt und weiter ausgearbeitet. Dazu wird das Potenzial des Prototypens durch **Experteninterviews** mit Expert/innen aus Arbeitszeitberatungsagenturen und Stakeholdern des Betriebes systematisch beurteilt. Auf Grundlage dieser

Beurteilungen werden schließlich konkrete Umsetzungspläne der zeitpolitischen Innovationen erstellt, welche die betrieblichen Experimentierräume vorbereiten.

Sampling

Für den DT^N-Workshop werden zwischen sechs und 24 Personen ausgewählt, die innerhalb des Workshops auf ein bis drei Arbeitsgruppen aufgeteilt werden. Die Erfahrung zeigt, dass heterogene Gruppen innovativere Ergebnisse produzieren (Paulus 2001). Jede Arbeitsgruppe setzt sich, sofern vorhanden, aus mindestens einer Vertretung des Managements und der Mitarbeitervertretung zusammen. Zudem zeichnet sich mindestens eine Person durch einen höheren Zeitwohlstand aus, eine andere Person durch einen niedrigeren Zeitwohlstand. Die Zuordnung erfolgt auf Basis einer Selbsteinschätzung zu Beginn des Workshops. Weitere Personen repräsentieren je nach Fallstudie unterschiedliche relevante Rollenträger/innen des Betriebes (z. B. Halbtagsbeschäftigte, ältere Mitarbeiter/innen, Vertreter/innen unterschiedlicher Arbeitszeitsysteme etc.).

Betriebliche Experimentierräume

In der Phase betriebliche Experimentierräume werden die Praxispartner bei der Implementierung zeitpolitischer Innovationen wissenschaftlich begleitet und die zeitpolitischen Innovationen hinsichtlich ihrer Auswirkungen systematisch evaluiert. Dabei entsteht Transformationswissen über die konkreten Auswirkungen einer Veränderung von Arbeitszeitmodellen auf die alltägliche Lebensführung. Nachhaltigkeitsinnovationen stoßen in der Praxis häufig auf zwei wesentliche Probleme: Zum einen werden sie auf dem Markt beziehungsweise von den Anwender/innen nicht akzeptiert. Zum anderen kommt es nicht zu den erwarteten Nachhaltigkeitseffekten, da sich Konsumpraktiken in Folge der Einführung einer Nachhaltigkeitsinnovation so verändern können, dass das Einsparpotenzial nicht völlig zur Geltung kommt (Buhl et al. 2017). Die eingesparten Ressourcen werden dann für erneuten Konsum verwendet, folglich liegt ein Rebound-Effekt vor. Neben monetären Einspareffekten sind hierbei ebenso Zeitersparnisse sowie psychologische Effekte relevante Treiber eines solchen Rebound-Effektes (Buhl et al. 2017). Da neue Produkte und Dienstleistungen immer auch in einen sozialen Kontext eingebettet sind und soziale Praktiken, also institutionalisierte alltägliche Handlungen, verändern, ist es wichtig, dass bei der Entwicklung von Innovationen der jeweilige Kontext und die jeweiligen sozialen Praktiken berücksichtigt werden, um darüber Rebound-Effekte in Folge sich verändernder Konsumpraktiken und Verhaltensweisen einzudämmen.

Erkenntnisinteresse

Es wird untersucht, welche Zeit-Rebound-Effekte sich im realweltlichen Kontext durch die Einführung einer zeitpolitischen Innovation ergeben. Zudem werden mögliche Hürden bei der Implementierung erfasst.

Methodisches Vorgehen

Die Einführung der zeitpolitischen Innovation (z. B. eines 4-Gruppen-Schichtsystems, um Überstunden zu reduzieren und Planbarkeit zu erhöhen) findet über einen Zeitraum von sechs Monaten statt. Der Zeitraum wird so gelegt, dass er einen typischen Arbeitsalltag abbildet, also keine längeren Urlaubszeiten von Großteilen der Belegschaft oder ungewöhnliche Auftragsspitzen umfasst. Die Einführung der zeitpolitischen Innovation erfolgt eigenständig durch die Betriebe. Sie werden dabei durch Wissenschaftler/innen sowie eine Arbeitszeitberatungsagentur unterstützt. Die Betriebe benennen eine Person, die den Prozess der Innovationseinführung begleitet und im engen Austausch mit einer konkret benannten Person aus dem Forschungsteam steht. Dieser regelmäßige Austausch dient zum einen der erfolgreichen Durchführung des Feldtests. Dabei wird sichergestellt, dass keine anderen neuen Maßnahmen zeitgleich implementiert werden. Zugleich sind Veränderungen der sozialen Praktiken gerade Teil des Erkenntnisinteresses. Zum anderen dient der regelmäßige Austausch auch der Dokumentation von Herausforderungen bei der Einführung der zeitpolitischen Innovation.

Die Wirkung der zeitpolitischen Innovation auf die alltägliche Lebensführung wird in einem **sequentiellen quantitativ-qualitativen Design** beziehungsweise **explanativem Design** (Creswell und Plano Clark 2011) systematisch evaluiert. Ein solches Design zeichnet sich dadurch aus, dass die quantitativen Ergebnisse durch qualitative Methoden erklärt werden. Zunächst wird die zeitpolitische Innovation quantitativ in einem **Prä-/Post-Design** evaluiert. Dazu werden die Mitarbeitenden in jenem Teil des Betriebs, in dem die zeitpolitische Innovation eingeführt wird, vor und nach der Einführung der Innovation befragt. Für die Evaluation stehen Wirkungen auf die folgenden Lebensbereiche im Vordergrund: Beschleunigung der Lebensführung, Zeitwohlstand, subjektives Wohlbefinden und nachhaltiger Konsum. Die Postbefragung der Beschäftigten erfolgt sechs Monate nach Einführung der zeitpolitischen Innovation. Dabei sollen Veränderungen im Zeitwohlstand nach Einführung des neuen Arbeitszeitmodells festgestellt werden.

Auf Basis der quantitativen Befragung werden Interviews mit ausgewählten Beschäftigten durchgeführt. Die Auswahl basiert auf den Ergebnissen der Befragung und umfasst je betrieblichen Experimentierraum je eine Person, bei der sich eine Verbesserung beziehungsweise Verschlechterung ihres Zeitwohlstands feststellen lässt. Diese Interviews werden durch weitere Interviews mit Beschäftigten ergänzt, sofern eine Sättigung des Erkenntnisgewinns noch nicht erreicht ist. Die Interviews dienen der Ergründung von Erklärungsmustern für unterschiedliche Effekte der zeitpolitischen Innovation auf Zeitwohlstand, individuelle Zeitverwendung, subjektives Wohlbefinden und nachhaltige Konsumweisen. Hierüber sollen mögliche Treiber von Zeit-Rebound-Effekten ausfindig gemacht werden, die sich in der Veränderung sozialer Praktiken manifestieren. Im Rahmen eines **Stakeholder-Workshops** mit den Beteiligten des Innovationsworkshops (siehe Abschn. 5.2.3) werden die Ergebnisse dieser Evaluation abschließend gemeinsam interpretiert.

Über den **Vergleich** der insgesamt fünf betrieblichen Experimentierräume wird das Verständnis über Zeit-Rebound-Effekte in Abhängigkeit von Arbeitszeitmodellen vertieft. Sämtliche Betriebe haben sich der Herausforderung angenommen den Zeitwohlstand ihrer Beschäftigten zu steigern, entwickeln jedoch angepasst an ihre spezifischen Herausforderungen unterschiedliche zeitpolitische Innovationen, um diesem Ziel näher zu kommen. Die Kontrastierung der einzelnen Fälle legt dabei offen, welche spezifischen Zeit-Rebound-Effekte sich durch die Einführung zeitpolitischer Innovationen ergeben und welche Dimensionen von Zeitwohlstand jeweils als zentral erachtet werden. Durch einen Wechsel von Fallvergleich und Fallkontrastierung können so empirische Typen zeitpolitischer Innovationen gebildet werden (Kelle und Kluge 2010). Die Ergebnisse dieses Vergleichs werden anschließend dem wissenschaftlichen Beirat mit Vertreter/innen aus Wissenschaft und Zivilgesellschaft präsentiert und hinsichtlich ihrer Verallgemeinerbarkeit diskutiert. Auf Basis dieser Reflexion werden Handlungsempfehlungen einer betrieblichen Zeitpolitik entwickelt.

Sampling

Voraussetzung für betriebliche Experimentierräume ist zunächst die Bereitschaft des Betriebes und der Belegschaft sich auf das Experiment mit einer spezifischen zeitpolitischen Innovation einzulassen. Der betriebliche Experimentierraum wird je nach Betriebsgröße zunächst in einem klar abgrenzbaren Bereich (z. B. Abteilungen, Projektgruppen) etabliert, um die Vermischung unterschiedlicher Arbeitszeitmodelle möglichst gering zu halten. Im Rahmen weiterer iterativer Schleifen kann der betriebliche Experimentierraum dann ausgeweitet und vergrößert werden. Dies ist jedoch in diesem Projekt nicht vorgesehen. Die betrieblichen Experimentierräume werden danach ausgewählt, dass sie möglichst repräsentativ in der Zusammensetzung der Belegschaft sowie des Tätigkeitsprofils des jeweiligen Betriebes sind. In kleineren Betrieben kann es sich dabei bereits um den kompletten Betrieb handeln.

Reflexion des Forschungsdesigns

Zur Zeit der Verfassung des Beitrags steht das transdisziplinäre Forschungsprojekt bei den verschiedenen Praxispartnern in unterschiedlichen Projektphasen. Bei PP5 ist die Innovationsentwicklung abgeschlossen und die Durchführung des betrieblichen Experimentierraums steht unmittelbar bevor, die anderen Praxispartner befinden sich noch mitten in der Innovationsentwicklung, sodass Vor- und Nachteile des Forschungsdesigns im Folgenden ohne konkrete Evaluationsergebnisse reflektiert werden. Im Vergleich zu klassischeren Methoden der empirischen Sozialforschung ist in der transformativen Zeitforschung, wie sie hier entwickelt wurde, die starke partizipative Einbettung von Betroffenen als hauptsächliches Novum zu nennen. Im Gegensatz zu zum Beispiel reinen Experteninterviews stehen von der Problemanalyse über die Innovationsentwicklung hin zur Phase betrieblicher Experimentierräume die Offenlegung und Nutzung der Repräsentationen, Wissensbestände und Wünsche der Betroffenen im Vordergrund, die dadurch zu aktiven Mitgestalter/innen des Prozesses werden. Die Vorteile der **partizipativen Herangehensweise** entfalten vor allen in der Phase der Innovationsentwicklung ihre Bedeutung. Die Design Thinking Methode birgt das Potenzial, eine (gegebenenfalls neue) gemeinsame Vision für mehr Zeitwohlstand im Betrieb zu entwickeln, indem sie die Ideen und Bedarfe ganz unterschiedlicher Beschäftigter in den Mittelpunkt rückt. Dies verspricht zum einen, die Akzeptanz der zeitpolitischen Maßnahmen in der Test- und späteren Umsetzungsphase für eine breitere Zielgruppe zu steigern. Erfahrungen mit dieser Methode zeigen, dass interne Mitarbeiter/innen dabei häufig passgenauere Innovationen entwickeln als externe Berater/innen (Jorck und Schrader 2019). Gleichzeitig kann die Legitimation der entstandenen Lösungen darunter leiden, dass nur ausgewählte Beschäftigte am Prozess des Innovationsdesigns beteiligt sind. Daher kommt dem Auswahlprozess der Teilnehmenden in dieser Phase eine wesentliche Bedeutung für den Erfolg zu. Zum anderen wird bei der lösungszentrierten, kreativen Auseinandersetzung mit der Design Challenge ein **implizites Handlungs- und Erfahrungswissen** der Beschäftigten angesprochen, das sich von einer expliziten, verbalisierbaren Problemrepräsentation drastisch unterscheiden kann und somit eine neue Erkenntnisquelle birgt. So haben zum Beispiel Beschäftigte eines Praxispartners während der Problemanalyse vor allem mangelnde freie Zeit als zeitliche Herausforderung benannt, im Rahmen der Innovationsentwicklung jedoch vor allem Lösungen zur Planbarkeit des Arbeitsalltags entworfen. Hier kann von einer impliziten Bedeutung dieser Zeitwohlstandsdimension ausgegangen werden, die bei der reflexiven Betrachtung eines Themas, wie sie zum Beispiel in einem qualitativen Interview erfolgt, nicht in Erscheinung tritt.

Eine Herausforderung dieses Innovationsprozesses ist die **prinzipielle Offenheit**. Denkbar sind Änderungen der Gestaltung von Arbeitszeit, Arbeitsort und/oder Arbeitsinhalt. Ebenso könnte das Ergebnis dieses Prozesses sein, das bestehende Arbeitszeitmodell komplett zu ersetzen. Gerade diese Offenheit birgt interessante Erkenntnispotenziale, da die Design Thinking Methode nicht bei der Ablehnung einer Innovation stehen bleibt, sondern stets nach neuen Verbesserungsvorschlägen fragt, um darüber dem eigentlichen Bedürfnis der Beschäftigten möglichst nahe zu kommen. Diese Offenheit des Design Thinking Prozesses ist auch dazu geeignet neue Hypothesen über den Forschungsgegenstand zu bilden.

Eine weitere Herausforderung besteht in der Explizierung von Kriterien, wonach eine gewählte Lösung beurteilt werden soll. Wann ist eine partizipativ entwickelte zeitpolitische Innovation als erfolgreich einzustufen? Für die Beantwortung dieser Frage sollte bei transformativen Zeitforschungsdesigns ein starker Fokus auf eine systematische Evaluation der Testphase in der realweltlichen Umgebung gelegt werden (Luederitz et al. 2017). Als Vorteil ist hier die große Alltagsnähe der Umsetzungsphase zu nennen, wie sie in einem echten **Feldexperiment** zu erwarten ist: die Innovationen werden am realen Arbeitsplatz getestet und evaluiert. Die sequentielle Kombination von quantitativen und qualitativen Methoden erlaubt hier zum einen den quantitativen Nachweis von Veränderungen in den verschiedenen Bewertungskriterien und deren Ausmaß (Hat sich das Tempo der Lebensführung, der Zeitwohlstand und die Lebenszufriedenheit der Beschäftigten erhöht bzw. reduziert? Wie stark?) als auch die Identifikation von Gründen für deren Eintreten oder Ausbleiben in einem qualitativen Zugang (Gab es hinderliche Umstände? Besonders gelungene Aspekte?). Ebenso werden Interviews als Quelle für unerwartet eingetretene Konsequenzen (Haben sich neue soziale Praktiken als Folge der Innovation entwickelt?) eingesetzt. Eine Mixed-Method Auswertung der Daten erlaubt zudem die Identifikation von Moderatoren, die Einfluss auf den Erfolg der zeitpolitischen Innovation haben. Dies kann in eine Typologie überführt werden, für welche Beschäftigten die zeitpolitischen Innovationen besonders begünstigend wirken (z. B. könnte ein Tool zur Planbarkeit vor allem für Eltern wichtig sein, Schichtflexibilität hingegen für kinderlose Beschäftigte?).

Wie bei allen echten Realexperimenten ist die **experimentelle Kontrolle** im Feld eine der Haupterausforderungen (Geiger et al. 2017). In der betrieblichen Innovationsforschung sollten deshalb bei großen Betrieben vergleichbare Abteilungen mitevaluiert werden, in der die zeitpolitische Innovation nicht oder später eingeführt wird. Für kleinere Betriebe, in denen eine teilweise Einführung der Innovation nicht möglich ist, bleibt die Frage nach der Kausalität der Effekte offen. Zu den weiteren Herausforderungen des Forschungsdesigns zählt der im Gesamten hohe Aufwand für die beteiligten Praxispartner, so ist für die Durchführung des Design Thinking Workshops allein ein recht hoher Zeitaufwand von zumindest einem vollen Arbeitstag für eine ganze Gruppe der Beschäftigten einzuplanen. Zur Evaluation der ausgewählten zeitpolitischen Innovation im Feldtest sollte zudem ein möglichst langer Zeitrahmen gewählt werden (hier ein halbes Jahr), um zu erlauben, dass sich auch schleichende Folgen eines veränderten Zeitregimes entfalten können.

Fazit

In diesem transformativen Zeitforschungsdesign wird der Einfluss verschiedener Arbeitszeitmodelle auf Zeit-Rebound-Effekte und Zeitwohlstand und damit indirekt auch auf Wohlbefinden und nachhaltigen Konsum von Beschäftigten untersucht. Dieser Zugang zeichnet sich durch eine starke inter- und transdisziplinäre Zusammenarbeit aus. Es werden verschiedene Wissensbestände untersucht: Systemwissen, Zielwissen und Transformationswissen. Entsprechend unterteilt sich das methodische Vorgehen in drei Phasen: Problemanalyse, Innovationsentwicklung sowie betriebliche Experimentierräume. In den verschiedenen Phasen werden jeweils verschiedene Forschungsmethoden angewandt: quantitative, qualitative und partizipativ-kreative. Dieser Forschungsansatz verspricht neue Erkenntnisse über den Zusammenhang zwischen Zeitstrukturen und individueller Zeitverwendung. Zugleich profitieren Praxispartner direkt von einer wissenschaftlichen Begleitung der Etablierung innovativer Arbeitszeitmodelle, die im Idealfall eine höhere Erfolgswahrscheinlichkeit im Sinne von Akzeptanz und nachhaltigeren, erwünschten Wirkungen gewährleistet.

Literatur

Binswanger, M. 2001. Technological progress and sustainable development: What about the rebound effect? *Ecological Economics* 36/1: 119–132.

Buhl, J. 2016. *Rebound-Effekte im Steigerungsspiel: Zeit- und Einkommenseffekte in Deutschland*. 1. Auflage. Umweltsoziologie. Baden-Baden: Nomos.

Buhl, J., J. v. Geibler, L. Echternacht, M. Linder. 2017. Rebound effects in Living Labs: Opportunities for monitoring and mitigating re-spending and time use effects in user integrated innovation design. *Journal of Cleaner Production* 151: 592–602.

Bundesministerium für Arbeit und Soziales (BMAS). 2016. *Weißbuch Arbeiten 4.0.*
Bundesministerium für Bildung und Forschung (BMBF). 2015. *Sozial-ökologische Forschung: Förderkonzept für eine gesellschaftsbezogene Nachhaltigkeitsforschung 2015–2020*, Bonn.
Claassen, R. 2012. Temporal Autonomy in a Laboring Society. *Inquiry* 55/5: 543–562.
Creswell, J. W., V. L. Plano Clark. 2011. *Designing and conducting mixed methods research.* 2nd edition. Los Angeles, London, New Dehli, Singapore, Washington DC: SAGE.
Deutscher Bundestag. 2013. *Schlussbericht der Enquete-Kommission „Wachstum, Wohlstand, Lebensqualität – Wege zu nachhaltigem Wirtschaften und gesellschaftlichem Fortschritt in der Sozialen Marktwirtschaft"*, Berlin.
DGB. 2015. *DGB Index Gute Arbeit: Der Report 2015: Mit dem Themenschwerpunkt Profilmerkmale der Arbeitshetze*, Berlin.
Doiber, M. 2018. *Arbeits- und Mobilitätszeit neu gedacht.* Graz.
Dorst, K. 2011. The core of 'design thinking' and its application. *Design Studies* 32/6: 521–532.
Geiger, S., A. Hirscher, M. Müller. 2017. Maßnahmenevaluation im transdisziplinären Forschungssetting. *GAIA – Ecological Perspectives for Science and Society* 26/2: 147–148.
Gerold, S., M. Soder, M. Schwendinger. 2017. Arbeitszeitverkürzung in der Praxis: Innovative Modelle in österreichischen Betrieben. *Wirtschaft und Gesellschaft* 43/2: 177–204.
Goodin, R. E., J. Rice, A. Parpo, L. Eriksson. 2008. *Discretionary time: A new measure of freedom.* 1. publ. Cambridge: Cambridge University Press.
Gorz, A. 1989. *Kritik der ökonomischen Vernunft: Sinnfragen am Ende der Arbeitsgesellschaft.* 1. Aufl. Rotbuch-Rationen. Berlin: Rotbuch.
Jorck, G. von. 2019. Flexibilisierung der Arbeit, Zeitwohlstand und nachhaltige Lebensführung. In: *Gute Arbeit und ökologische Innovationen: Perspektiven nachhaltiger Arbeit in Unternehmen und Wertschöpfungsketten.* Herausgegeben von G. Becke. München: oekom. 101–116.
Jorck, G. von, S. Gerold, S. Geiger, U. Schrader. 2019. *Zeitwohlstand: Arbeitspapier zur Definition von Zeitwohlstand im Forschungsprojekt ReZeitKon*, Berlin.
Jorck, G. von, U. Schrader. 2019. Unternehmen als Gestalter nachhaltiger Arbeit. In: *Tätigsein in der Postwachstumsgesellschaft.* Herausgegeben von I. Seidl, A. Zahrnt. Marburg: Metropolis. 95–109.
Kelle, U., S. Kluge. 2010. *Vom Einzelfall zum Typus: Fallvergleich und Fallkontrastierung in der qualitativen Sozialforschung.* 2., überarb. Aufl. Wiesbaden: VS Verlag für Sozialwissenschaften.
Keynes, J. M. 2016. Economic Possibilities for Our Grandchildren. In: *Essays in Persuasion.* Herausgegeben von J. Keynes. 3rd ed. London: Palgrave Macmillan UK. 321–332.
Liedtke, C., C. Baedeker, M. Hasselkuß, H. Rohn, V. Grinewitschus. 2015. User-integrated innovation in Sustainable LivingLabs: An experimental infrastructure for researching and developing sustainable product service systems. *Journal of Cleaner Production* 97: 106–116.
Loorbach, D. 2010. Transition Management for Sustainable Development: A Prescriptive, Complexity-Based Governance Framework. *Governance* 23/1: 161–183.
Lott, Y. 2018. Does Flexibility Help Employees Switch Off from Work?: Flexible Working-Time Arrangements and Cognitive Work-to-Home Spillover for Women and Men in Germany. *Social Indicators Research*.

Lott, Y. 2019. Weniger Arbeit, mehr Freizeit?: Wofür Mütter und Väter flexible Arbeitszeitarrangements nutzen. *WSI Report*/47.
Luederitz, C. et al. 2017. Learning through evaluation – A tentative evaluative scheme for sustainability transition experiments. *Journal of Cleaner Production* 169: 61–76.
Maher, R., M. Maher, S. Mann, C. A. McAlpine. 2018. Integrating design thinking with sustainability science: A Research through Design approach. *Sustainability science* 13/6: 1565–1587.
Matta, V. 2015. Führen selbstgesteuerte Arbeitszeiten zu einer Ausweitung der Arbeitsstunden?: Eine Längsschnittanalyse auf der Basis des Sozio-oekonomischen Panels. *Zeitschrift für Soziologie* 44/4: 253–271.
Paulus, P. 2001. Groups, Teams, and Creativity: The Creative Potential of Idea-generating Groups. *Applied Psychology* 49/2: 237–262.
Pongratz, H. J., G. G. Voß. 1998. Der Arbeitskraftunternehmer: Auf dem Weg zu einer neuen Grundform der Ware Arbeitskraft. *Kölner Zeitschrift für Soziologie und Sozialpsychologie* 50/1: 131–158.
Przyborski, A., M. Wohlrab-Sahr. 2008. *Qualitative Sozialforschung: Ein Arbeitsbuch*. 1. Aufl. München: Oldenbourg.
Rinderspacher, J. P. 1996. Zeitinvestitionen in die Umwelt: Annäherung an ein ökologisches Handlungskonzept. In: *Zeit für die Umwelt: Handlungskonzepte für eine ökologische Zeitverwendung*. Herausgegeben von J. P. Rinderspacher. Berlin: Ed. Sigma. 69–129.
Rinderspacher, J. P. 2012. Zeitwohlstand – Kriterien für einen anderen Maßstab von Lebensqualität. *WISO – Wirtschafts- und Sozialpolitische Zeitschrift des ISW* 35/1: 11–26.
Rosa, H. 2005. *Beschleunigung: Die Veränderung der Zeitstrukturen in der Moderne*. Orig.-Ausg. Suhrkamp Taschenbuch Wissenschaft 1760. Frankfurt am Main: Suhrkamp.
Rosa, H. 2014. *Beschleunigung und Entfremdung: Entwurf einer kritischen Theorie spätmoderner Zeitlichkeit*. 4. Auflage. Berlin: Suhrkamp.
Rosa, H. 2016. *Resonanz: Eine Soziologie der Weltbeziehung*. Erste Auflage. Berlin: Suhrkamp.
Rosa, H., K. Dörre, S. Lessenich. 2017. Appropriation, Activation and Acceleration: The Escalatory Logics of Capitalist Modernity and the Crises of Dynamic Stabilization. *Theory, Culture & Society* 34/1: 53–73.
Santarius, T. 2015. *Der Rebound-Effekt: Ökonomische, psychische und soziale Herausforderungen für die Entkopplung von Wirtschaftswachstum und Energieverbrauch*. Wirtschaftswissenschaftliche Nachhaltigkeitsforschung Band 18. Marburg: Metropolis.
Schneidewind, U., H. Scheck. 2013. Die Stadt als „Reallabor" für Systeminnovationen. In: *Soziale Innovation und Nachhaltigkeit: Perspektiven sozialen Wandels*. Herausgegeben von J. Rückert-John. Research. Wiesbaden: Springer VS. 229–248.
Schneidewind, U., M. Singer-Brodowski. 2015. Vom experimentellen Lernen zum transformativen Experimentieren: Reallabore als Katalysator für eine lernende Gesellschaft auf dem Weg zu einer Nachhaltigen Entwicklung. *Zeitschrift für Wirtschafts- und Unternehmensethik* 16/1: 10–23.
Schneidewind, U., C. von Wissel. 2015. Transformative Wissenschaft: Warum Wissenschaft neue Formen der Demokratisierung braucht. *Forum Wissenschaft*/4: 4–8.
Schor, J. B. 1993. *The overworked American: The unexpected decline of leisure*. 1. [print.]. New York: Basic Books.

Schor, J. B. 2016. *Wahrer Wohlstand: Mit weniger Arbeit besser leben.* Deutsche Erstausgabe. München: oekom.

Schrader, U. et al. 2018. Design Thinking für Nachhaltigkeit. https://www.nachhaltigkeitsinnovation.de/ (abgerufen 30.07.2019).

Star, S., J. Griesemer. 1989. Institutional Ecology, `Translations' and Boundary Objects: Amateurs and Professionals in Berkeley's Museum of Vertebrate Zoology, 1907-39. *Social Studies of Science* 19/3: 387–420.

Strohschneider, P. 2014. Zur Politik der Transformativen Wissenschaft. In: *Die Verfassung des Politischen: Festschrift für Hans Vorländer.* Herausgegeben von A. Brodocz. Wiesbaden: Springer. 175–192.

WBGU. 2011. *Welt im Wandel: Gesellschaftsvertrag für eine Große Transformation.* Hauptgutachten, Berlin.

Witzel, A. 2000. The Problem-centered Interview. Forum Qualitative Sozialforschung/ Forum: Qualitative Social Research, Vol 1, No 1 (2000): Qualitative Research: National, Disciplinary, Methodical and Empirical Examples.

Methodology for the Study of Time.
Methodologien der Zeitforschung

Zeitforschung als vergleichende Prozessanalyse. Die Verbindung von Qualitative Comparative Analysis und Einzelfallstudien für die Untersuchung zeitlicher Dynamiken

Comparative Process Analysis as a Method for Time Research. Combining Qualitative Comparative Analysis and Within-Case Analysis for Inquiring Temporal Dynamics

Simon Gordt und Thomas Laux

Abstract

The comparative analysis of temporal dynamics is a challenge for qualitative social research. Whereas within-case studies capture temporal dynamics and patterns for single cases, Qualitative Comparative Analysis (QCA) as a comparative approach mostly neglects time as an important factor. Therefore, the combination of QCA and within-case analysis offers a promising approach to analyse temporal processes in comparative perspective. While QCA identifies

---

S. Gordt (✉)
Institut für Sozialwissenschaften, Universität Hildesheim, Hildesheim, Deutschland
E-Mail: simon.gordt@uni-hildesheim.de

T. Laux
Institut für Europäische Studien und Geschichtswissenschaften (IESG), TU Chemnitz, Chemnitz, Deutschland
E-Mail: thomas.laux@phil.tu-chemnitz.de

equifinal solutions for different combinations of conditions, within-case analysis focuses on causal mechanisms in order to explain the process in question. We present here two possibilities of how to combine QCA and within-case analysis: 1) The so-called step principle describes a combination that begins with one method followed by the other one, either to analyse a typical case further or to proof a mechanism for other cases. 2) The so-called parallel principle uses within-case methods for calibration to directly implement time in QCA.

Zusammenfassung

Die vergleichende Analyse von zeitlichen Dynamiken und Prozessen stellt eine Herausforderung für die qualitative Sozialforschung dar. Die Analyse von Prozessen fokussiert sich zumeist auf Einzelfälle, um zeitliche Dynamiken und Muster zu ermitteln. Hingegen zielt die Qualitative Comparative Analysis (QCA) auf die Untersuchung sozialer Phänomene ab, indem die logischen Beziehungen der dafür relevanten Bedingungen für eine mittlere Fallzahl verglichen werden. Der Aspekt Zeit wird hierbei zumeist nicht näher berücksichtigt. Ausgehend davon ermöglicht es die Kombination beider Ansätze, zeitliche Dynamiken und Prozesse vergleichend zu untersuchen. Während QCA die Möglichkeit des strukturierten Fallvergleichs bietet und äquifinale Bedingungskombinationen zur Erklärung sozialer Phänomene ermittelt, erlaubt die Prozessanalyse, den kausalen Prozess zwischen Erklärungsbedingungen und Outcome anhand der Identifizierung sozialer Mechanismen in Fällen zu beschreiben. Dieser Beitrag diskutiert zwei Kombinationsmöglichkeiten: 1) das sogenannte Stufenprinzip, bei dem die einzelnen Methoden aufeinander aufbauen, um entweder typische Fälle einer Lösung näher zu betrachten oder um zu überprüfen, ob in einem Fall entdeckte Mechanismen auch auf andere Fälle zutreffen. 2) Das sogenannte Parallelprinzip nutzt hingegen die Prozessanalyse als Kalibrierungsmethode für QCA, um zeitliche Dynamiken direkt in die vergleichende Analyse zu implementieren.

Keywords

Qualitative Comparative Analysis · Process Tracing · Mixed-Methods · Case-Oriented Research · Within-Case Analysis

Schlüsselwörter

Qualitative Comparative Analysis · Prozessanalyse · Process Tracing · Mixed-methods · Fallorientierte Forschung · Fallstudien

Einleitung

Die Dimension Zeit wohnt allen Phänomenen des Sozialen inne: So ist soziales Handeln an der Vergangenheit oder der Zukunft orientiert, Institutionen sind zeitlich gebunden oder die Rede vom gesellschaftlichen Wandel verweist auf die grundlegende Bedeutung der temporalen Dimension (Baur 2005, S. 13–14; Rosa 2005, S. 19; Mayntz 2002, S. 27). Diese Omnipräsenz der Zeit weist zum einen auf die Notwendigkeit hin, temporale Dynamiken theoretisch zu bestimmen, um soziales Handeln und gesellschaftliche Strukturen zu erfassen (siehe etwa Nassehi 2008; Rosa 2005; Abbott 2001). Zum anderen fordert die Vielfalt und Verschiedenheit der Zeit-Bezüge im Sozialen das methodische Vorgehen in den Sozialwissenschaften heraus (Baur 2005, S. 16; Abbott 1995, S. 94), um, gemäß der Forderung Max Webers, soziales Handeln und gesellschaftliche Ordnung „deutend verstehen und dadurch in seinem Ablauf und seinen Wirkungen ursächlich erklären" (Weber 2014, S. 1) zu können. Hierzu ist je nach Fragestellung oder Analysefokus ein angemessenes methodisches Vorgehen notwendig, um die spezifische Relevanz der zeitlichen Dimension für das zu untersuchende Phänomen zu ermitteln.

Vor diesem Hintergrund gehen die folgenden Ausführungen auf die vergleichende Prozessanalyse als eine Kombination von Qualitative Comparative Analysis (QCA) und Einzelfallstudien („within-case analysis" (Goertz und Mahoney 2012, S. 87–99)) ein.[1] Kombinationen von QCA und Einzelfallstudien sind bislang vor allem in der Politikwissenschaft und der Soziologie vorzufinden, wobei sie ein neueres Phänomen darstellen und vornehmlich im Kontext einer sich auf Basis von mengentheoretischen Annahmen entwickelnden Multimethodenforschung („set-theoretic multimethod research" (Rohlfing und Schneider 2018)) diskutiert werden (siehe etwa Beach und Rohlfing 2018; Rohlfing und Schneider 2018; Schneider und Rohlfing 2013, 2016; Schneider und Wagemann 2012, S. 305–312). Die im Folgenden diskutierten Kombinationen von QCA und Einzelfallstudien bezeichnen wir als vergleichende Prozessanalyse

---

[1]Die Einzelfallstudie ist keine konkrete Analysemethode, sondern vielmehr ein „Forschungsansatz" (Lamnek 2016, S. 285). Dieser beschreibt eine Perspektive, die auf Basis umfassender Informationen über einzelne Fälle Erklärungen für ebendiese ermittelt (Lamnek 2016, S. 286; Goertz und Mahoney 2012, S. 10). Hierbei können unterschiedliche Analysemethoden verwendet und kombiniert werden.

und sie eröffnen, so unsere These, ein passendes methodisches Vorgehen für die Erfassung und Analyse zeitlicher Dynamiken. Als Ansatz für die Zeitforschung stehen hierfür die Besonderheiten der vergleichenden Prozessanalyse im Fokus des Beitrags, um die Zeitgebundenheit von Handeln und Strukturen, die Historizität von Ereignissen, Handeln und Strukturen sowie das zeitliche Zusammenwirken zwischen Bedingungen und Ereignissen zu erfassen. Die vergleichende Prozessanalyse ermöglicht es, mittlere Fallzahlen aus synchroner und diachroner Perspektive zu untersuchen. QCA bietet dabei die Möglichkeit des strukturierten Vergleichs und ermittelt äquifinale Bedingungskombinationen zur Erklärung sozialer Phänomene (Schneider und Wagemann 2012, S. 8, 12). Der Fallvergleich mittels QCA erfüllt damit eine „Basisoperation" (Raab 2018, S. 33) der empirischen Sozialforschung, die es erlaubt, Gemeinsamkeiten und Unterschiede zwischen Fällen zu identifizieren, Regelmäßigkeiten festzustellen oder auf deren Basis Typen zu bilden (Raab 2018, S. 33; Ragin 1987, S. 1). Komplementär dazu liefern die Fallanalysen zum einen umfassende Kenntnisse über einzelne Fälle und ihren Kontext (Lamnek 2016, S. 286; Hering und Schmidt 2014, S. 529). Zum anderen können auch auf Basis von Einzelfallstudien Handlungs- bzw. Strukturmuster und Kausalbeziehungen ermittelt werden (Lamnek 2016, S. 298; Beach und Pedersen 2013, S. 1–2).

Die Analyse einzelner Fälle geht von einer Prozessperspektive aus, die auf Basis von Informationen über einen Fall Rückschlüsse über das zu untersuchende Phänomen ermittelt (Lamnek 2016, S. 286; Goertz und Mahoney 2012, S. 10). Hierbei spielt auch die zeitliche Dimension eine zentrale Rolle, woraus wichtige Erkenntnisse für sozialwissenschaftliche Analysen gewonnen werden können. Denn schließlich verweisen eine Vielzahl soziologischer Theorien und Erklärungskonzepte auf die Bedeutung prägender Ereignisse oder zeitlicher Dynamiken, wie etwa der Prozess der Institutionalisierung (Berger und Luckmann 2009, S. 56–72), Formen der Pfadabhängigkeit (Mahoney 2000) oder „critical junctures"[2] (Collier und Collier 1991, S. 29). Das zeitliche und – damit oftmals zusammenhängend – kausale Zusammenwirken von Bedingungen wird darin hervorgehoben, was die soziale Wirkmächtigkeit des Faktors Zeit in seiner nachhaltig-prägenden Wirkung auf das soziale Handeln oder auf institutionelle Ordnungen verdeutlicht.

---

[2] Am ehesten mit „kritischen Phasen" respektive auch „kritischen Ereignissen" zu übersetzen. Siehe dazu auch Fußnote 7.

Der Begriff der vergleichenden Prozessanalyse bezeichnet also ein fallorientiertes Vorgehen, das einen Vergleich von Analyseeinheiten mit der Untersuchung der darin ablaufenden Prozesse systematisch verbindet. Bei den Fällen kann es sich entweder um Akteure (Individuen, Gruppen, soziale Bewegungen, Organisationen, Staaten, etc.) oder andere Analyseeinheiten, wie etwa spezifische Ereignisse (z. B. Formen des institutionellen Wandels), handeln, die anhand räumlicher oder anderer Merkmale unterschieden werden können. Damit wird auch deutlich, dass sich die vergleichende Prozessanalyse für Untersuchungen auf der Mikro-, Meso- und Makroebene eignet.

Ziel des folgenden Beitrags ist es, verschiedene Kombinationsmöglichkeiten von QCA und Fallstudien vorzustellen und zu diskutieren: Einerseits können Einzelfallstudien zur Konkretisierung der QCA-Ergebnisse dienen, indem die zeitlichen Dynamiken und kausalen Beziehungen der Bedingungen untersucht werden (Schneider und Rohlfing 2013, S. 588; 2016, S. 527). Andererseits können Einzelfallstudien ebenfalls zur Kalibrierung der zu untersuchenden Bedingungen genutzt werden. Dies ermöglicht die zeitliche Differenzierung der betrachteten Analyseeinheiten, wodurch die relevanten Ereignisse und Veränderungen innerhalb der einzelnen Fälle bestimmt werden, um den prozesshaften Wandel des zu erklärenden Phänomens sowie der Erklärungsbedingungen in eine einzige QCA einzubinden. Diese Formen der vergleichenden Prozessanalyse stellen dabei innovative Verbindungen im Sinne eines „mixed methods"-Forschungsdesigns dar, indem verschiedene Methoden ergänzend kombiniert werden, um das zu untersuchende Phänomen „aus unterschiedlichen Perspektiven heraus empirisch zu erfassen" (Burzan 2016, S. 9; vgl. Rohlfing und Schneider 2018; Kelle 2014; Schneider Rohlfing 2013; Kelle und Erzberger 2010, S. 305–306).

Im folgenden Abschnitt diskutieren wir die Eigenschaften und die Chancen der vergleichenden Prozessanalyse für die Untersuchung zeitlicher Dynamiken. Danach folgt die Vorstellung der Methoden, um anschließend schließlich ihre Kombinationsmöglichkeiten vorzustellen.

Der Mehrwert der vergleichenden Prozessanalyse für die Zeitforschung

Der methodische Ausgangspunkt der vergleichenden Prozessanalyse bildet die Zugehörigkeit von QCA und Einzelfallstudien zu der von Goertz und Mahoney (2012; Mahoney und Goertz 2006) identifizierten qualitativen „Kultur" der empirischen Sozialforschung (Goertz und Mahoney 2012, S. 1). Jener liegt ein „causes-of-effects"-Ansatz zugrunde, der Forschungsperspektiven zusammenfasst, die spezifische Ausprägungen von Fällen („outcomes") umfassend untersuchen und erklären wollen (Goertz und Mahoney 2012: 42; Mahoney und Goertz 2006, S. 230), z. B. die Entstehung von Protestbewegungen oder die Institutionalisierung von rechtlichen Regelungen.[3] Der Ansatz folgt einem holistischen Verständnis von Fällen als Konstellationen verschiedener Merkmale mit unterschiedlichen Ausprägungen (Ragin 1987, S. 3). Damit sollen die Fälle als „Ganzes" und nicht bloß als Merkmalsträger für spezifische Ausprägungen der untersuchten Variablen erfasst werden (Lamnek 2016, S. 286). Die Analyse verfolgt das Ziel, die relevanten Bedingungen sowie ihr Zusammenwirken für das zu erklärende Phänomen zu ermitteln (Mahoney und Goertz 2006, S. 241). Insofern stehen die Fälle, gemäß dem holistischen Verständnis, mit ihren Ausprägungen im zu erklärenden Phänomen im Zentrum des Erkenntnisinteresses. Die Fallorientierung zeigt sich insbesondere darin, dass die Fälle bewusst anhand des Vorhandenseins der Ausprägung ausgewählt werden (Mahoney und Goertz 2006, S. 239).

Für die Erklärung des untersuchten Phänomens der Fälle wird nach dem kausalen Zusammenwirken verschiedener Bedingungen gesucht, wobei Kausalität als „a generative process in which a cause yields an effect by triggering the operation of certain mechanisms and processes" (Goertz und Mahoney 2012, S. 100) verstanden wird. Demgemäß liegt der Analysefokus darauf, das Zusammenwirken von Bedingungen zu erfassen. Hierbei sind die einzelnen Bedingungen nicht allein hinreichend für die Erklärung des Phänomens, wohl aber ein notwendiger Bestandteil der erklärenden Bedingungskonstellation (Mahoney und Goertz 2006, S. 234–236).[4] Das Verstehen der Zusammenhänge der Bedingungen und ihre Rekonstruktion bilden stattdessen die Grundlage für die Erklärung des zu untersuchenden Phänomens (Lamnek 2016, S. 298; Lange 2013,

---

[3]Der „effects-of-causes"-Ansatz ist dagegen typisch für quantitative Methoden der empirischen Sozialforschung. Der Fokus dieses Ansatzes liegt auf der Analyse der *„average effects* of particular variables within populations or samples" (Goertz und Mahoney 2012, S. 41, Hervorhebung im Original). Eine knappe Zusammenfassung der Unterschiede zwischen der qualitativen und quantitativen Kultur in der empirischen Sozialforschung findet sich in Mahoney und Goertz (2006, S. 229).

[4]Es handelt sich somit um sogenannte INUS-Bedingungen, die in Bezug auf ein zu erklärendes Phänomen definiert sind als „*insufficient* but *non-redundant* part of an *unnecessary* but *sufficient* condition" (Mackie 1974, S. 62, Hervorhebung im Original).

S. 21).⁵ Ein weiteres konstitutives Merkmal der qualitativen Forschungskultur ist ihre Diversitätsorientierung („diversity-oriented research" (Ragin 2000)), die sich in der Annahme der Äquifinalität von Erklärungen zeigt. Demnach wird davon ausgegangen, dass verschiedene Bedingungskonstellationen ein und dasselbe Phänomen verursachen (Mahoney und Goertz 2006, S. 236; Ragin 2000, S. 119). Die Ursachen für die verschiedenen Erklärungen liegen sowohl in der Unterschiedlichkeit der Fälle selbst als auch ihres sozialen, zeitlichen und geographischen Kontexts begründet (siehe etwa Moore 1969).

Die vergleichende Prozessanalyse, wie wir sie hier vorstellen, kombiniert im Sinne eines „mixed methods"-Vorgehens QCA und Fallstudien auf Basis der skizzierten geteilten Grundannahmen der qualitativen Kultur der empirischen Sozialforschung. QCA und Fallstudien ergänzen sich komplementär (Kelle und Erzberger 2010, S. 305), indem mittels QCA auf Basis des Fallvergleichs (zumeist im Querschnitt) verschiedene Bedingungskonstellationen für ein zu erklärendes Phänomen ermittelt werden (Ragin 2000, S. 13). Diese Bedingungskonstellationen lassen jedoch nicht ohne Weiteres Rückschlüsse auf das kausale und zeitliche Zusammenwirken ebenjener Bedingungen zu, sondern bedürfen der weiteren Untersuchung (Beach und Rohlfing 2018, S. 5; Schneider und Rohlfing 2016, S. 527). Dementsprechend ist das jeweilige Zusammenwirken der Bedingungen mittels Fallstudien im Sinne einer „fallbezogene[n] Auswertung" (Döring und Bortz 2016, S. 603) näher zu ermitteln. Fallstudien und Fallvergleiche identifizieren so geteilte Strukturmerkmale der Fälle sowie entscheidende Ereignisse oder Sequenzen für die Erklärung eines spezifischen Phänomens (Lange 2013, S. 4; McAdam et al. 2001, S. 24).

Die Kombination von QCA und Fallstudien bietet damit auf Basis fallvergleichender *und* fallbezogener Erkenntnisse die Möglichkeit zur Analyse sozialer Mechanismen als „Sequenzen kausal verknüpfter Ereignisse, die in der Wirklichkeit wiederholt auftreten, wenn bestimmte Bedingungen gegeben sind" (Mayntz 2009, S. 101).⁶ Erklärungen mittels sozialer Mechanismen sind dabei „weniger

---

⁵Dies stellt einen grundlegenden Unterschied zur quantitativen „Kultur" in der empirischen Sozialforschung dar, die ihren Fokus auf die statistische Analyse von Korrelationen zwischen Variablen und deren Wahrscheinlichkeiten legt (Mahoney und Goertz 2006, S. 232).

⁶„Substanziell gesprochen stellen Mechanismen fest, *wie,* also durch welche Zwischenschritte, ein bestimmtes Ergebnis aus einem bestimmten Satz von Anfangsbedingungen hervorgeht" (Mayntz 2009, S. 101, Hervorhebung im Original).

allgemein" als „nomologisch-deduktive Erklärungen" und legen den Fokus zunächst darauf, Prozesse zu rekonstruieren (Mayntz 2009, S. 100). Soziale Mechanismen basieren auch wesentlich auf Informationen und Aussagen über zeitliche Zusammenhänge und Dynamiken, die bedeutsam für die Erklärung sozialer Phänomene sind, denn „[w]hen things happen within a sequence affects how they happen" (Tilly 1984, S. 14).

Um den Mehrwert der vergleichenden Prozessanalyse für die Zeitforschung deutlich zu machen, soll nun präzisiert werden, welche zeitlichen Dimensionen damit überhaupt erfasst werden können. Aus unserer Sicht lassen sich drei verschiedene Aspekte von Zeit für die Erklärung sozialer Phänomene unterscheiden: 1) Handeln und Strukturen sind zeitgebunden, sodass ihre *Zeitlichkeit* als Basis des Vergleichens zu erfassen ist, um ihren Wandel sowie auch ihre Wirkung für gesellschaftliche oder politische Veränderungen bestimmen zu können (Tilly 2008, S. 202). So untersucht etwa Tilly (1993, S. 270–276) den Wandel von Protestformen in Großbritannien zwischen dem 18. und 19. Jahrhundert und zeigt, dass Demonstrationen, Streiks oder öffentliche Versammlungen die Zerstörung symbolischer Objekte zur Artikulation von Ansprüchen an die Herrschenden abgelöst hat. Die unterschiedlichen Protestformen wurden, je nach zeitlichen Kontexten, zur Artikulation ähnlicher Ansprüche eingesetzt und können aufgrund dessen im Quer- und/oder Längsschnitt untersucht werden. Die Zeitlichkeit von Handeln und Strukturen kann sowohl im Zuge der Kalibrierung von Bedingungen im Rahmen einer QCA als auch durch Fallstudien erfasst werden. 2) Die *Historizität* von Strukturen und Ereignissen in Form „der prägenden Bedeutung der Vergangenheit für die Gegenwart" (Mayntz 2002, S. 27) stellt eine weitere zeitliche Dimension dar, die mit der vergleichenden Prozessanalyse bearbeitet werden kann, um die Art des gesellschaftlichen Wandels bzw. die Persistenz institutioneller Ordnungen zu verstehen. Nur auf Basis des Wissens um die Historizität von Strukturen, z. B. in Form von „critical junctures" (Collier und Collier 1991, S. 29) oder Pfadabhängigkeiten, lässt sich erklären, warum institutionelle Ordnungen, wie etwa das Rentensystem, über lange Zeiträume hinweg stabil bleiben und nicht im Zuge von Reformen grundlegend verändert werden (Neumann und Schaper 2008, S. 208–209).[7] Die Historizität wird zunächst über die Prozessperspektive der Fallstudie erfasst. Mittels des Fallvergleichs von QCA lässt sich dazu ergänzend untersuchen, ob und inwieweit weitere Bedingungen für die Stabilität der Ordnung

---

[7] „Critical junctures" beschreiben eine spezifische Art von Pfadabhängigkeit (Mahoney 2000: 513). Pfadabhängigkeiten sind dabei „historical sequences in which contingent events set into motion institutional patterns or event chains that have deterministic properties" (Mahoney

bedeutsam sind oder durch welche Aspekte sich Fälle unterscheiden. 3) Das *zeitliche Zusammenwirken von Bedingungen und Ereignissen* wurde bereits in der Definition sozialer Mechanismen von Mayntz (2009, S. 101) betont. Der Begriff der Sequenzen verweist schließlich auf die zeitliche Ordnung von Ereignissen (Abbott 1995, S. 94), die im Hinblick auf fallbezogene und/oder fallübergreifende Regelmäßigkeiten zu untersuchen sind. So unterliegt etwa der Prozess der Institutionalisierung nach Berger und Luckmann (2009, S. 57) einer zeitlichen Ordnung nach der „Habitualisierungsprozesse […] jeder Institutionalisierung" vorausgehen. Darüber hinaus wirft die zeitliche Ordnung von Bedingungen und Ereignissen nach Aljets und Hoebel (2017, S. 12–13) auch Fragen bezüglich ihres „Timings" auf, d. h. die *„Abfolge"* der Bedingungen und Ereignisse, der spezifische *„Zeitpunkt"* von Ereignissen im Hinblick auf ihre Auswirkungen, der zeitliche *„Abstand"* von Ereignissen zueinander sowie ihr *„Treffpunkt"* bzw. die Art ihres zeitlichen Zusammentreffens sind von Interesse (Aljets und Hoebbel 2017, S. 13, Hervorhebungen im Original). Anhand des zeitlichen Ablaufs ist die sequenzielle Logik zu untersuchen und zu ermitteln, ob und inwieweit sich daraus Rückschlüsse für die Erklärung sozialer Phänomen ziehen lassen. Um die Fragen bezüglich des Timings zu beantworten, bedarf es der Prozessperspektive der Fallstudien, um die Sequenzen und ihre Ordnung näher zu bestimmen (Beach und Rohlfing 2018, S. 18; Aljets und Hoebbel 2017, S. 17; Baur 2005, S. 268).

Diese drei Aspekte von Zeit erfassen keineswegs alle bestehenden temporalen Dynamiken, wohl aber die wichtigsten im Hinblick auf die vergleichende Prozessanalyse. Des Weiteren möchten wir betonen, dass der jeweilige Analysefokus bei vergleichenden Prozessanalysen primär vom Forschungsinteresse und der Fragestellung abhängen sollten.

Methoden

Wie bereits angesprochen, ist es unser Ziel, QCA als vergleichende Methode mit Einzelfallstudien zu verbinden, um zeitliche Dynamiken historisch-vergleichend zu analysieren. Im Folgenden werden daher die einzelnen Methoden mit ihren grundlegenden Prinzipien in gegebener Kürze vorgestellt.

2000: 507). Hierzu unterscheidet Beyer (2005: 18) sieben Ursachen für die Entstehung von Pfadabhängigkeiten. „Critical junctures" bezeichnen „a period of significant change, which typically occurs in distinct ways in different countries (or in other units of analysis) and which is hypothesized to produce distinct legacies" (Collier und Collier 1991, S. 29).

Fallvergleich mittels Qualitative Comparative Analysis

QCA stellt sowohl ein „methodological tool" (Schneider und Wagemann 2012, S. 8) als auch einen Forschungsansatz dar (Schneider und Wagemann 2012, S. 8–13).[8] Als Analysewerkzeug zielt QCA auf die Erklärung sozialer Phänomene auf Basis mittlerer Fallzahlen ab und nutzt mengentheoretische Annahmen. Für die Analyse werden sogenannte Wahrheitstafeln verwendet, die die verschiedenen empirischen Regelmäßigkeiten und Zusammenhänge zwischen Bedingungen und einem zu erklärenden Phänomen visualisieren und diese im Hinblick auf seine kausale Komplexität untersuchen.[9] Dabei werden die Gemeinsamkeiten und Unterschiede der betrachteten Fälle miteinander verglichen und mittels logischer Minimierung wird die empirische Komplexität reduziert, ohne die Unterschiede zwischen den Fällen außer Acht zu lassen (Schneider und Wagemann 2012, S. 8–9). Das Ziel ist, vorhandene Muster und Kausalbeziehungen zwischen mehreren Bedingungen und dem zu erklärenden Phänomen logisch zu ermitteln (Schneider und Wagemann 2012, S. 11–12). Dabei ermöglicht es die mengentheoretische Basis von QCA, zwischen hinreichenden und notwendigen Bedingungen in den Lösungen zu unterscheiden (Ragin 1987, S. 99–101): Als hinreichend gilt eine Bedingung, wenn sie zum interessierenden Phänomen führt. Hingegen folgt eine notwendige Bedingung dem spiegelverkehrten Muster. Das heißt, eine Bedingung ist dann notwendig, wenn bei Fällen mit dem interessierenden Outcome immer auch die Bedingung vorhanden ist (Ragin 2000, S. 94–96). Statt also die Beziehung zwischen einzelnen Variablen und dem Erklärungsphänomen zu untersuchen, fokussiert QCA auf die Konfigurationen von Bedingungen und ihrer Beziehung zum Outcome (Lange 2013, S. 90).

Drei Merkmale kennzeichnen Erklärungen von QCA: 1) QCA ermittelt *äquifinale* Erklärungen für ein gegebenes Phänomen (Ragin 1987: 25). 2) QCA zeigt *multikausale* Erklärungen aus einer Kombination mehrerer Erklärungsbedingungen auf, die auf ihr zeitliches und kausales Zusammenwirken hin zu überprüfen sind (Ragin 1987, S. 24–26). 3) Die Erklärungen sind *asym-*

---

[8]Zum grundlegenden Verständnis von QCA sei auf die Bücher von Ragin (1987, 2000) verwiesen sowie auf das Lehrbuch von Schneider und Wagemann (2012).

[9]In einer Wahrheitstafel werden alle logisch-möglichen Kombinationen der zu untersuchenden Bedingungen aufgeführt und die Fälle werden den Kombinationen zugeordnet. Die Wahrheitstafel bildet damit das zentrale Analysewerkzeug von QCA (Ragin 1987, S. 87–89).

metrisch, was bedeutet, dass eine Erklärung eines gegebenen Phänomens nicht auch umgekehrt für dessen Gegenteil gilt. Dahinter steht die Annahme, dass eine kausale Bedingung nicht auch die Information enthält, dass das Gegenteil der Bedingung ebenfalls kausal für das zu erklärende Phänomen ist. Mengentheoretische Erklärungen sind daher nicht linear und sowohl ihre Präsenz als auch ihre Absenz in Kombination mit anderen Bedingungen kann ursächlich für das zu erklärende Phänomen sein (Buche und Siewert 2015, S. 389; Schneider und Wagemann 2012, S. 6).

QCA als Forschungsansatz kennzeichnet ein spezifisches Vorgehen in der Datenerhebung und im Umgang mit den Analyseergebnissen. Als solcher folgt QCA dem im qualitativen Forschungsparadigma vorzufindenden zirkulären Modell, das sowohl die Rückbindung der Ergebnisse an die Analyse vorsieht als auch ggf. eine erneute Datensammlung und Umkodierung (Schneider und Wagemann 2012, S. 11; Ragin 1987, S. 164–171). Die gezielte Auswahl der Fälle sowie der zu untersuchenden Bedingungen stellt den ersten Schritt einer QCA dar (Schneider und Rohlfing 2013, S. 561). Im Sinne des holistischen Verständnisses gelten Fälle dabei als Konfigurationen (Ragin 1987, S. 3). Entsprechend untersucht QCA die relationalen Konstellationen und berücksichtigt die Unterschiede zwischen den Fällen, um die relevanten Bedingungen für das Entstehen eines Phänomens zu bestimmen (Ragin 2000, S. 38–39).

Gemäß dem holistischen Verständnis dienen die Mitgliedschaften der ausgewählten Fälle in der Menge der zu untersuchenden Bedingungen als Grundlage der Analyse mit der Wahrheitstafel (Ragin 1987, S. 3). Die Kalibrierung der Bedingungen sowie des Outcomes stellt den nächsten Schritt einer QCA dar und bezeichnet den Prozess der Zuordnung der empirischen Informationen zum Grad der Mitgliedschaft in den jeweiligen Bedingungen sowie im zu untersuchenden Outcome, z. B. die Mitgliedschaft eines Staates in der Menge von Staaten mit starken Lohngleichheitsrechten (siehe Laux 2016a, S. 398–400) oder eines Schulsystems zur Menge der Schulsysteme mit starker institutioneller Regelung der Bildungsinhalte (siehe von Below 2002). Grundsätzlich werden dazu die Daten binär kodiert, das heißt, sie werden in eine Dichotomie zwischen Mitgliedschaft (kodiert mit 1) und Nicht-Mitgliedschaft (kodiert mit 0) überführt (Schneider und Wagemann 2012, S. 32). Mit der Verwendung von fuzzy sets (fs) können auch Mitgliedschaften zwischen den Polen 0 und 1 vergeben werden (Ragin 2000, S. 6). Fuzzy sets ermöglichen es, Teilmitgliedschaften von Fällen in Bedingungen für die Analyse zu berücksichtigen (Ragin 2000, S. 265). Dies ist im Hinblick auf die komplexe Realität geboten und beispielsweise dann sinnvoll, wenn es sich um nicht eindeutig zuordenbare Informationen handelt, so erhalten etwa Staaten mit einer mittelstarken Sicherung des Lohngleichheitsrechts nur einen fs-Wert von 0,75 anstatt eines fs-Werts von 1 für Staaten mit einer starken Sicherung (Laux 2016a, S. 399). Mit der Verwendung von fuzzy sets bei der Kalibrierung ist außerdem gewährleistet, dass qualitative Unterschiede zwischen den Fällen im Abgleich mit den theoretischen Konzepten ebenfalls abgebildet werden (Schneider und Wagemann 2012, S. 32). Im Zuge der Kalibrierung sind drei Ankerwerte zu bestimmen, um die Nachvollziehbarkeit des Kalibrierens zu gewährleisten: die vollständige Nichtmitgliedschaft in der Menge (0), die vollständige Mitgliedschaft (1) und der Indifferenzpunkt (0,5) (Ragin 2000, S. 270). Um die Plausibilität der Kalibrierung zu sichern, sollten sowohl theoretisches Wissen über den jeweiligen Analysegegenstand als auch Fallwissen und qualitative Unterschiede zwischen den Fällen berücksichtigt werden (Ragin 2000, S. 150). Die Kalibrierung ist damit immer auch ein interpretativer Prozess (Lange 2013, S. 91).

Neben der Mitgliedschaft der Fälle in der Menge von Bedingungen sind weitere Mengenbeziehungen für eine QCA bedeutsam, wobei die Operatoren der Booleschen Algebra Verwendung finden. Im Gegensatz zur Mitgliedschaft beschreibt die Negation (~) die Nichtmitgliedschaft eines Falles in einer Menge. Die in Abschn. 2 vorgestellten Prinzipien der Äquifinalität und des Zusammenwirkens von Bedingungen (INUS-Bedingungen) verweisen auf zwei weitere Mengenbeziehungen: Die Verbindung mehrerer Bedingungen wird mittels einer Und-Verbindung (*) erfasst, die eine Schnittmenge der Mitgliedschaft in mehreren Mengen beschreibt. Zur Abbildung von Äquifinalität ist dagegen eine Oder-Verbindung (+) notwendig, die ein Äquivalenzverhältnis der Mitgliedschaft in mehreren Mengen anzeigt (Schneider und Wagemann 2012, S. 54–55, 78).

Im Anschluss an die Kalibrierung erfolgt die eigentliche Analyse, wobei zuerst notwendige und dann hinreichende Bedingungen separat untersucht werden (Schneider und Wagemann 2012, S. 278). Hinreichende Bedingungen werden mit Hilfe der Wahrheitstafel als Analyseinstrument ermittelt, wobei jede logisch-mögliche Kombination der Bedingungen aufgeführt wird. Abweichend von der klassischen Datenmatrix der quantitativen Methodologie, stellen die Zeilen in einer Wahrheitstafel somit keine einzelnen Fälle dar und umfasst auch logisch-mögliche Kombinationen, die empirisch nicht auffindbar sind (Schneider und Wagemann 2012, S. 92–93). Zur Überprüfung wird dann jede Zeile der Wahrheitstafel danach geprüft, ob die betrachtete Bedingungskombination hinreichend ist. Um die Wahrheitstafel zu vereinfachen, wird sie bei der Analyse mit dem Ziel, redundante Bedingungen zu ermitteln und zu kürzen, minimiert. Das Ergebnis besteht dann aus der Kombination der Bedingungen, wobei die ermittelten Lösungsformeln den Informationsgehalt der Wahrheitstafel in komprimierter Form wiedergeben. Die von QCA ermittelten Lösungen bezeichnen somit eine

Schnittmenge von Bedingungen, in der die korrekt erklärten Fälle (mit einer Mitgliedschaft im Outcome>0,5) eine Mitgliedschaft>0,5 aufweisen (Buche und Siewert 2015, S. 394–395; Schneider und Wagemann 2012, S. 104–115).

Prozessanalyse mittels Fallstudien und Einzelfallmethoden

Wie bereits ausgeführt, handelt es sich bei Fallstudien weniger um eine konkrete Analysemethode, sondern eher um einen „Forschungsansatz" (Lamnek 2016, S. 285). Im Unterschied zu QCA ermöglichen Einzelfalluntersuchungen Erkenntnisse über einen spezifischen Fall, indem alle „relevanten Dimensionen" erfasst und untersucht werden (Lamnek 2016, S. 286). Fallstudien können mit unterschiedlichen Methoden durchgeführt werden, die sich im Vorgehen unterscheiden und die verschiedene Ziele verfolgen. Im Folgenden konzentrieren wir uns gemäß des temporalen Fokus ausschließlich auf die Prozessanalyse, welche allerdings innerhalb der Literatur auf verschiedene Art und Weise beschrieben und zugleich mit verschiedenen Labeln benannt wird, wie beispielsweise „Process Tracing" oder „Causal Narrative" (vgl. u. a. Bennett und Checkel 2014; Beach und Pedersen 2013; Lange 2013; George und Bennett 2005).[10]

Hierzu werden unabhängig vom konkreten Vorgehen grundsätzlich Prozesse beschrieben und ihre kausalen Ursachen untersucht, teilweise durch Ermittlung sozialer Mechanismen, die eine kausale Beziehung erklären (Lange 2013, S. 4). Mit Bezug auf Mahoney (2012, S. 571) lassen sich dabei basale Gemeinsamkeiten einer jeden Prozessanalyse festhalten: Die Prozessanalyse zielt auf den Nachweis, 1) dass ein bestimmtes Ereignis oder ein bestimmter Prozess stattfand, 2) dass ein weiterer Prozess oder ein weiteres Ereignis nach diesem anfänglichen Ereignis oder Prozess auftrat und 3) dass ersteres oder ersterer die Ursache des nachfolgenden Ereignisses oder Prozesses gewesen ist. Mit einer solchen Herangehensweise soll der Verlauf des Prozesses veranschaulicht werden, um ihn anschließend zu erklären. Dafür steht die Betrachtung der Dynamik und der Ursachen umfassender sozialer Prozesse im Mittelpunkt der Analyse, die in der Regel anhand eines Narratives veranschaulicht werden (Lange 2013, S. 43–45). Entsprechend konzentriert sich die Analyse auf die Identifikation kausaler Mechanismen, welche die kausale Beziehung bzw. Sequenz zwischen

---

[10]Im Folgenden sprechen wir für ein besseres Verständnis ausschließlich von Prozessanalyse.

Bedingungen und Outcome erklären (Beach und Pedersen 2013, S. 1–2; George und Bennett 2005, S. 206). Folglich ist ein Mechanismus auch als transformative Aktion zu verstehen, durch welche die Ursache den kausalen Effekt erst erzeugt (Lange 2013, S. 49).

In diesem Sinne bezeichnet eine Prozessanalyse ein systematisches, bei welchem die empirischen Informationen und Daten in eine chronologische Reihenfolge hinsichtlich des theoretisch zu erwartenden Zusammenhangs gebracht und evaluiert werden (Collier 2011, S. 823). Je nach Forschungsstand und Fallwissen umfassen die Methoden sowohl induktive als auch deduktive Elemente. Bestehen vielfältige theoretische Ansätze, die konkurrierende Erklärungen für das infrage kommende Outcome anbieten, dann können diese im Sinne eines deduktiven Theorietests an einem Fall überprüft werden. Gibt es hingegen für die betrachtete Beziehung keine ausgearbeitete Theorie oder stellt der betrachtete Fall einen abweichenden Fall dar, erfolgt die Prozessanalyse eher induktiv (Bennett 2008, S. 705). Darüber hinaus kann grundsätzlich danach differenziert werden, ob die Prozessanalyse eher theorie- oder fallorientiert vorgeht. Während die theorieorientierte Variante das Ziel verfolgt, entweder generalisierbare Mechanismen an einem bestimmten Fall zu überprüfen oder anhand empirischer Beobachtungen zu entwickeln, zielt die fallorientierte Variante vielmehr darauf ab, ein bestimmtes historisches Phänomen mittels einer minimalhinreichenden Erklärung zu begründen, die allerdings ausschließlich für den betrachteten Fall gilt und insofern auf keine generalisierbaren Aussagen innerhalb des betrachteten Forschungsprozesses zielt (Beach und Pedersen 2013, S. 2–3, 9–22).

Bei der Prozessanalyse geht es also darum, einen oder mehrere soziale Mechanismen zu rekonstruieren, um die kausale Beziehung zwischen bestimmten Ereignissen zu verstehen. Dafür werden für einen bestimmten Fall empirische Daten gesammelt und hinsichtlich der angenommenen kausalen Beziehung detailliert analysiert. Aufgrund dessen sind sowohl ein umfangreiches Fallwissen als auch ausgeprägte Kenntnisse des Forschungskontextes unabdingbar (Lange 2013, S. 48–53, 69). Dazu werden empirische Befunde gesucht, die einen beweiskräftigen Wert für die Verifizierung oder Falsifizierung der beschreibenden und erklärenden Hypothesen besitzen (Mahoney 2012, S. 571). Collier et al. (2010, S. 187) nennen diese Form der Evidenz „causal-process observations" und definieren sie als empirische Daten, die Informationen über den Kontext, die Sequenz und/oder den Mechanismus liefern. Damit aus jenen Rohdaten empirische Evidenzen werden können, müssen sie fallspezifisch bewertet werden.

Nur dann ist eine logische Schlussfolgerung überhaupt möglich.[11] Entsprechend müssen mitunter unterschiedliche Arten empirischer Daten herangezogen werden, die wiederum unterschiedlicher Erhebungs- und Auswertungsmethoden bedürfen (Beach und Pedersen 2013, S. 73). Die hier dargelegte Prozessanalyse ist insofern zu allererst eine Analysestrategie und beinhaltet „searching for within-case data to carry out strong tests of hypotheses and using knowledge of existing generalizations to design such tests" (Mahoney 2012, S. 587).

Varianten der vergleichenden Prozessanalyse

Im Folgenden werden verschiedene Kombinationsmöglichkeiten von Einzelfallstudien und QCA vorgestellt, mit denen unterschiedliche Aspekte von Zeit berücksichtigt werden können. Das *Stufenprinzip* beschreibt, dass die Fallstudien vor oder nach der QCA stattfinden und sich so das fallbezogene und fallvergleichende Vorgehen auf verschiedene Weise ergänzen. Hingegen zielt das *Parallelprinzip* auf eine synergetische Verbindung beider Methoden, indem die Prozessanalyse als Kalibrierungsmethode für QCA genutzt wird.

Stufenprinzip

QCA und anschließende Fallstudien
Wie bereits ausgeführt, ermittelt QCA Konstellationen von notwendigen und hinreichenden Bedingungen in Bezug auf ein zu erklärendes Phänomen. Anschließend können die Lösungen mittels Fallstudien auf die Plausibilität sowie auf das kausale und zeitliche Zusammenwirken der jeweiligen Bedingungen hin überprüft werden. Dieses Vorgehen entspricht auch den Standards einer guten QCA (Schneider und Wagemann 2012, S. 280–281). Das Ziel besteht darin, die sozialen Mechanismen zu verstehen und, in Bezug auf zeitliche Aspekte, die Historizität von Handeln und Strukturen sowie das zeitliche Zusammenwirken der Bedingungen und Ereignisse adäquat zu erfassen (Beach und Rohlfing 2018, S. 18; Schneider und Rohlfing 2013, S. 561).

---

[11]Formell kann dieser Evaluationsprozess folgendermaßen erfasst werden: Wenn b = Beobachtung, k = Kontextwissen, e = Evidenz, dann gilt: b + k → e (Beach & Pedersen 2013, S. 73).

Um dies zu erreichen, sind typische Fälle der äquifinalen Lösungen der QCA auszuwählen und diese in Fallstudien näher zu untersuchen (Schneider und Rohlfing 2013). Die Auswahl solch typischer Fälle orientiert sich an den Mitgliedschaftswerten der Fälle in den Lösungsformeln, so dass Fälle mit einem hohen Mitgliedschaftswert in der Menge der Lösungsformeln ($> 0{,}5$) und des Ergebnisses ($> 0{,}5$) ausgewählt werden (Schneider und Rohlfing 2013, S. 563; Schneider und Wagemann 2012, S. 311). Komplementär dazu sind auch abweichende Fälle zu untersuchen. Damit kann erklärt werden, warum Fälle entweder von keiner Lösungsformel erfasst werden, obwohl ihre Mitgliedschaft in der Menge des Ergebnisses bei $> 0{,}5$ liegt, oder warum die Fälle trotz einer Mitgliedschaft von $> 0{,}5$ in einer der Lösungsformeln keine Mitgliedschaft in der Menge des Ergebnisses $> 0{,}5$ aufweisen (Schneider und Wagemann 2012, S. 308).[12]

Die Kombinationen eines zunächst vergleichenden und dann rekonstruktiven Vorgehens bietet einige Vorteile für die Analyse zeitlicher Dynamiken (siehe Laux 2016b, S. 116–119): Die QCA ermittelt die notwendigen und hinreichenden Bedingungen und reduziert damit die Komplexität der Fälle. Dies bietet die Grundlage, um die Plausibilität sowie das zeitliche und kausale Zusammenwirken der Bedingungen in Form sozialer Mechanismen zu rekonstruieren (Mayntz 2002: 13). Zudem können die unterschiedlichen Formen des zeitlichen Zusammenwirkens im Sinne des Timings näher bestimmt werden (Aljets und Hoebbel 2017, S. 12–13). Die Fallrekonstruktionen haben damit das Ziel, die „inhaltliche[n] Sinnzusammenhänge" bzw. die „Sinnadäquanz" der Bedingungskonstellationen auf Basis ihrer „Kausaladäquanz", das heißt aufgrund der „empirische[n] Regelmäßigkeiten" zu erfassen und zu rekonstruieren (Kluge 2000: Absatz 2). Dies kann als Grundlage dafür dienen, Mechanismen zu bilden, die ein höheres Maß an Verallgemeinerung beanspruchen und die in Folgestudien weiterführend untersucht werden (Kluge 2000: Absatz 9).

Diese Kombination von QCA und Fallstudien kehrt damit den zumeist vorherrschenden Ablauf qualitativer Prozessanalysen um, da die Lösungsformeln von QCA die Fallstudien vorab strukturieren und auf bestimmte Bedingungen hin fokussieren (Laux 2016b, S. 118; Baur 2005, S. 268; Abbott 1995, S. 105–106).

---

[12]Eine detaillierte Erklärung und Diskussion unterschiedlicher Techniken der Fallauswahl nach einer QCA finden sich in Schneider und Rohlfing (2013, S. 565–588) und Schneider und Wagemann (2012, S. 305–312).

Die mit QCA ermittelten Lösungen bilden dabei sowohl einen theoretisch- als auch empirisch-fundierten Rahmen für die Fallrekonstruktionen und damit einhergehend für die Erfassung sozialer Mechanismen (Schneider und Rohlfing 2013, S. 588).

Fallstudien und anschließende QCA

Die Kombination von QCA und Fallstudien im vorherigen Abschnitt beruht auf fundiertem Fallwissen, das für die Kalibrierung der Bedingungen notwendig ist, aber das kausale und zeitliche Zusammenwirken der Bedingungen wird wesentlich durch das vergleichende Vorgehen herausgearbeitet und erst in Fallstudien erfasst.

Die Kombination von Fallstudien und anschließender QCA geht den umgekehrten Weg und startet mit der Analyse einzelner, als zunächst „typisch" klassifizierter Fälle. Ziel hierbei ist es, einen sozialen Mechanismus für ein spezifisches Phänomen, z. B. für einen Regimewechsel in einem Staat (siehe etwa Kern und Laux 2017), anhand einzelner Fälle herauszuarbeiten, wobei der Fokus gerade auf der Erfassung spezifischer Verlaufsmuster und Kausalbeziehungen liegt (Beach und Rohlfing 2018, S. 12–15; Lamnek 2016, S. 298; Baur 2005, S. 268). Hierzu ist der jeweils ausgewählte Fall umfassend zu untersuchen (Lamnek 2016, S. 286). Dies bildet zudem die Grundlage für die Fallauswahl für den anschließenden Fallvergleich mit QCA (Schneider und Rohlfing 2013, S. 561; Rihoux und Lobe 2009, S. 230) sowie ebenso für die Wahl und die Kalibrierung der dabei zu untersuchenden Bedingungen (Rihoux und Lobe 2009, S. 228; Ragin 2000, S. 309).

Um soziale Mechanismen zu erfassen und zu erarbeiten, kann eine Prozessanalyse durchgeführt werden. Damit können die Historizität von Bedingungen sowie auch ihr zeitliches Zusammenwirken näher bestimmt werden. Falls sich soziale Mechanismen in einem Fall entdecken lassen, dann kann mittels QCA untersucht werden, ob der Mechanismus auch für andere Fälle zutrifft (Rohlfing und Schneider 2018, S. 44). Die identifizierten Bedingungen des Mechanismus leiten dabei die Auswahl der Bedingungen für QCA an. Dieses Vorgehen ist einerseits gegenüber einer Vielzahl von Fallstudien weniger aufwendig, gerade für die Analyse mittlerer Fallzahlen (Beach und Rohlfing 2018, S. 14). Denn der Vergleich mittels QCA reduziert die beobachtbare Komplexität der Fälle und systematisiert diese, wobei jedoch die Fülle der qualitativen Informationen zu einem gewissen Grad verloren geht (Rihoux und Lobe 2009, S. 228). Andererseits kann durch den anschließenden Vergleich das Ausmaß der Geltung des sozialen Mechanismus bzw. dessen Generalisierungsniveau näher bestimmt werden, also auf wie viele und auf welche Fälle der beobachtete Mechanismus zutrifft (Beach und Rohlfing 2018, S. 14; Mayntz 2002, S. 23–24).

Lässt sich als Ergebnis der QCA der identifizierte Mechanismus aus den Fallstudien nicht auf andere Fälle übertragen, dann ist zumindest davon auszugehen, dass kein typischer Fall untersucht wurde. Des Weiteren stellt sich die Frage, ob die beobachtete Kausalbeziehung nun verworfen werden sollte, oder ob es sich lediglich um eine äquifinale Erklärung handelt, die ein Merkmal der qualitativen Kultur der Sozialforschung darstellt (Beach und Rohlfing 2018, S. 14–15). Um dies zu klären, ist der jeweilige Fall erneut zu untersuchen.

Parallelprinzip

Prozessanalyse als Kalibrierungsmethode

Von ihrer Grundidee ist jede QCA mehr an Ereignissen und weniger an Prozessen interessiert. Entsprechend lassen sich zeitliche Entwicklungen in QCA bisher lediglich umständlich integrieren (vgl. Schneider und Wagemann 2012, S. 269).[13] Hier setzt nun unser zweiter Vorschlag an. Anstatt dass, wie im Stufenprinzip, die einzelnen methodischen Ansätze aufeinander aufbauen, zielt das Parallelprinzip darauf ab, Einzelfallmethoden in QCA zu integrieren, um Prozesse so direkt in die vergleichende Analyse zu implementieren. Entscheidend dabei ist, dass Zeit nicht als Ursache betrachtet wird, sondern vielmehr werden zeitliche Dynamiken über die Kalibrierung direkt aufgenommen (Ragin 1987, S. 162–163). Das heißt, dass das Parallelprinzip, wie auch das Stufenprinzip, auf eine komplementäre Verwendung der verschiedenen Analysestrategien abzielt.

Die Kalibrierung innerhalb jeder QCA ist ein entscheidender Schritt, deren Ergebnis letztlich eine qualitative Abwägung unter Berücksichtigung des Forschungskontextes darstellt. Die qualitative Dimension wird durch das relationale Vorgehen noch verstärkt, denn da sich die Werte aufeinander beziehen, ist ihre Bedeutung stets vom gegebenen Kontext abhängig. Beispielsweise bedeutet die wirtschaftliche Entwicklung eines Landes im europäischen etwas anderes als im globalen Kontext, während ein Staat innerhalb von Europa vergleichsweise schwach entwickelt ist, kann der gleiche Staat im Weltmaßstab als

---

[13]So weisen Schneider und Wagemann (2012, S. 269) auf eine Variante hin, die „temporal QCA", mit der die „causally relevant role of time" in QCA integriert werden soll. Zugleich sind hier jedoch mehrere Bedingungen zu erfüllen.

verhältnismäßig fortschrittlich gelten. Damit ist jede Kalibrierung letztlich das Resultat einer qualitativen Interpretation der vorhandenen Daten in Abhängigkeit vom Forschungsstand, der gewählten Theorie(n) und des gegebenen Vergleichskontextes. Da für QCA eine bestimmte Mindestfallanzahl gegeben sein muss, um überhaupt angewandt werden zu können (Hammersley und Cooper 2012, S. 134 f.), werden üblicherweise Daten aus Einzelfallstudien herangezogen, um diese dann weitestgehend im Sinne einer qualitativen Inhaltsanalyse zu analysieren (vgl. Flick 2016). Oder es finden sogenannte „primary within-case methods" Verwendung, womit Methoden bezeichnet sind, die benutzt werden „to generate evidence for within-case analysis", wie zum Beispiel Werkzeuge der Geschichtswissenschaften, Methoden der Netzwerkanalyse, ethnographische oder linguistische Methoden (Lange 2013, S. 55–69).

Unser Implementierungsvorschlag setzt am Ziel einer jeden Kalibrierung an, der möglichst validen Bestimmung der Mitgliedschaft des Falles in den betreffenden Bedingungen und des Outcomes. Normalerweise werden die Daten dafür im Querschnitt verwendet; wenn also zum Beispiel die Bedingung Urbanisierung kalibriert wird, dann gilt das Urbanisierungsniveau für den erhobenen Zeitpunkt und nicht für eine zeitliche Periode. Allerdings kann sich der Urbanisierungsgrad über die Zeit wandeln, mit der Folge, dass diese Information für die Analyse verloren geht. Lediglich in Relation zu den anderen Fällen können mitunter längere Zeiträume aufgenommen werden. Beispielsweise betrachtet Mahoney (2003) in seiner Studie die unterschiedlichen sozialen und ökonomischen Entwicklungen lateinamerikanischer Länder und untersucht, welchen Einfluss die spanische Kolonialgeschichte auf deren Modernisierung genommen hat. Die Länder, die das ehemalige Zentrum des spanischen Kolonialreichs darstellten, gehören heutzutage zu den am wenigsten entwickelten Staaten des lateinamerikanischen Kontinents, während die Länder, die damals zur Peripherie gehörten, heute sowohl sozial als auch ökonomisch am weitesten fortgeschritten sind. Um dieses Paradox zu ergründen, vergleicht er die nationalen Entwicklungen miteinander und kalibriert die jeweiligen Bedingungen sowie die beiden Outcomes in Relation zueinander, das heißt, die Fälle werden in eine Rangfolge gebracht. Ihre Mitgliedschaft wird dann anhand der Platzierung in einen eindeutigen Wert übertragen. So verfügen zum Beispiel die Länder, die ökonomisch am weitesten entwickelt sind, über eine volle Mitgliedschaft im Outcome ‚ökonomische Entwicklung', während die zurückliegenden Länder hier keine Mitgliedschaft aufweisen. Wie die meisten historisch arbeitenden Sozialforscher/innen nutzt auch Mahoney (2003) für die Kalibrierung historische Einzelfallstudien (vgl. Skocpol 1984), schließlich ist ein umfangreiches „tracing" (Siewert 2017, S. 240) für eine größere Fallzahl in der Regel nicht zu leisten.

Die Verwendung des Parallelprinzips impliziert also, dass anstatt sich auf bestehende Studien zu verlassen, für alle betrachteten Fälle kleine(re) Einzelfallstudien durchgeführt und diese zur Kalibrierung verwendet werden. Denn so lassen sich Prozesse direkt verfolgen und mittels der relationalen Kalibrierung in Mitgliedschaftswerte umwandeln. Dies ermöglicht es auch, die Zeitlichkeit von Handeln, Strukturen und Ereignissen näher zu bestimmen und die Informationen darüber in die Kalibrierung einfließen zu lassen. Zugleich kann QCA auch so bei einer kleinen Fallzahl durchgeführt werden, denn mit dem Parallelprinzip können zentrale Sequenzen der Fälle ermittelt werden, in denen sich die Fälle qualitativ wandeln. Jene Sequenzen, etwa „kritische Ereignisse", bezeichnen Wendepunkte des Entwicklungsprozesses, die gemäß dem Konzept der Pfadabhängigkeit den Ausgangspunkt eines neuen Verlaufs darstellen (Collier und Collier 1991, S. 29). Dadurch kann schließlich die Fallzahl erhöht werden, denn der ermittelte Zeitpunkt dient zugleich auch als Endpunkt des vorherigen Prozesses. Insofern begründet jede neue Sequenz einen neuen Fall.

Die Kalibrierung erfolgt also relational anhand der einzelnen Prozessanalysen aller betrachteten Fälle. Wird beispielsweise die Regierungsform eines Staates als Bedingung verwendet, gilt es für die interessierende Epoche die vorhandenen Formen zu beleuchten und die Zeitpunkte zu erarbeiten, an denen sich die Form drastisch wandelt, wie beispielsweise nach einer Revolution oder einem Staatsstreich. Zur Ermittlung der kritischen Ereignisse sind dabei grundsätzlich zwei Vorgehensweisen denkbar: Entweder sind kritische Ereignisse zu identifizieren, die für alle betrachteten Fälle gelten und so global bei allen Fällen eine neue Sequenz begründen. Dazu zählen beispielsweise historische Ereignisse mit (fast) universaler Wirkung, wie die Französische Revolution oder die Reformation. Ebenso sind interne kritische Ereignisse als Ausgangspunkt für eine neue Sequenz denkbar, wie beispielsweise der Wandel zur konstitutionellen Monarchie in Österreich 1867, womit die absolutistische Regierungsform ihr Ende fand (Gordt 2019, S. 29–30). Auf ähnliche Weise können damit auch Mechanismen als Erklärungsbedingungen in QCA eingebaut werden. Für die betrachteten Fälle erfolgt dazu beispielsweise ein Process Tracing, um die interessierenden Mechanismen zu gewinnen, die anschließend als Erklärungsbedingungen fungieren. Mittels eines Vergleichs der Mechanismen aus den Einzelfallstudien können anschließend ihre Mitgliedschaftswerte entsprechend kalibriert werden.

Die Prozessanalyse ergänzt QCA demnach komplementär, weil ersteres zur Kalibrierung des letzteren benutzt wird. So können mit QCA auch Prozesse analysiert, Mechanismen miteinander verglichen sowie, unter Umständen, QCA auch für kleine Fallzahlen verwendet werden. Allerdings ist letzteres für all jene Bedingungen ungeeignet, die sich über die Zeit nicht weiter wandeln, da ansonsten keine Varianz zwischen dem neuen und ursprünglichen Fall besteht und sich diese nicht voneinander trennen lassen. Zudem steht außer Frage, dass dieses Vorgehen nur für eine verhältnismäßig kleine Fallanzahl aufgrund der sehr zeitaufwendigen Kalibrierung geleistet werden kann.

Fazit

Dass Zeit als Dimension Teil aller sozialen Phänomene ist, diente als Ausgangspunkt unseres Beitrags, der das Ziel hatte, verschiedene Vorgehensweisen einer vergleichenden Prozessanalyse zu skizzieren, um die temporale Dimension näher zu untersuchen. Dazu wurden zwei Herangehensweisen für die Verbindung von QCA und Einzelfallstudien unterschieden: Bei dem *Stufenprinzip* bauen die einzelnen Methoden aufeinander auf, um entweder soziale Mechanismen hinsichtlich ihrer zeitlichen Aspekte besser zu verstehen oder um soziale Mechanismen an weiteren Fällen und hinsichtlich ihres Generalisierungsniveaus zu überprüfen. Damit können vor allem die Historizität von Handeln und Strukturen sowie das zeitliche Zusammenwirken von Bedingungen erfasst werden, wobei der Fallvergleich darüber informiert, ob und, wenn ja, inwieweit dieselben Mechanismen bei anderen Fällen auch vorzufinden sind. Hingegen beschreibt das *Parallelprinzip* ein Vorgehen, bei der die Prozessanalyse für die Kalibrierung verwendet wird, um Zeit, vorzugsweise in Form von Prozessen, direkt in QCA zu implementieren. Vor allem beim letzteren spielt das relationale Prinzip einer jeden QCA eine entscheidende Rolle, denn die Kalibrierung wird erst durch den Vergleich der Ergebnisse der einzelnen Fallstudien abgeschlossen. Dieses Vorgehen ermöglicht vor allem, die Zeitlichkeit von Handeln, Strukturen und Ereignissen auf Basis von detailliertem Fallwissen zu erfassen. Während also beim Stufenprinzip die verwendeten Methoden nacheinander erfolgen, wie Stufen einer Treppe, ist beim Parallelprinzip die Einzelfallstudie Teil des Kalibrierungsprozesses, weswegen die Methoden im übertragenen Sinne gleichzeitig genutzt werden.

Beiden Herangehensweisen ist gemein, dass durch die Kombinationen der verschiedenen Analysestrategien die temporale Dimension – in Form der Zeitgebundenheit von Handeln und Strukturen, die Historizität von Ereignissen und Institutionen sowie das zeitliche Zusammenwirken zwischen Bedingungen und Ereignissen – systematisch für kleine bis mittlere Fallzahlen erfasst werden können. Damit verbindet die vergleichende Prozessanalyse die Vorteile der Einzelfallstudie, die im detaillierten Verstehen und Erklären eines Falls liegen, wozu insbesondere die Identifizierung kausaler Mechanismen gehört, mit denen von QCA, die wiederum in der Darlegung von Regelmäßigkeiten zwischen mehreren Fällen und schließlich in der Typenbildung liegen. Je nach Forschungsinteresse und Fragestellung bietet die vergleichende Prozessanalyse damit eine sinnvolle Herangehensweise, zeitliche Prozesse empirisch zu untersuchen.

Literatur

Abbott, A., 1995: Sequence Analysis: New Methods for Old Ideas. Annual Review of Sociology 21: 93–113.
Abbott, A., 2001: Time Matters. On theory and method. Chicago/London: Chicago University Press.
Aljets, E., und T. Hoebbel. 2017: Prozessuales Erklären. Gründzüge einer primär temporalen Methodologie empirischer Sozialforschung. Zeitschrift für Soziologie 46: 4–21.
Baur, N., 2005: Verlaufsmusteranalyse. Methodische Konsequenzen der Zeitlichkeit sozialen Handelns. Wiesbaden: VS Verlag.
Beach, D., und I. Rohlfing. 2018: Integrating Cross-case Analyses and Process Tracing in Set-Theoretic Research: Strategies and Parameters of Debate. Sociological Methods and Research 47: 3–36.
Beach, D., und R. B. Pedersen. 2013: Process-Tracing Methods. Ann Arbor: The University of Michigan Press.
Below, S. v., 2002: Bildungssysteme und soziale Ungleichheit. Das Beispiel der neuen Bundesländer. Opladen: Leske+ Budrich.
Bennett, A., und J. T. Checkel. 2014: Process tracing: from metaphor to analytic tool. Cambridge: Cambridge University Press.
Bennett, A., 2008: Process Tracing: A Bayesian Perspective. S. 702–721 In: Box-Steffensmeier, J. M., H. E. Brady, und D. Collier (Hrsg.): The Oxford Handbook of Political Methodology. Oxford u.a.: Oxford University Press.
Berger, P. L., und T. Luckmann. 2009: Die gesellschaftliche Konstruktion der Wirklichkeit. Frankfurt: Fischer.
Beyer, J., 2005: Pfadabhängigkeit ist nicht gleich Pfadabhängigkeit! Wider den impliziten Konservatismus eines gängigen Konzepts. Zeitschrift für Soziologie 34: 5–21.
Buche, J., und M. B. Siewert. 2015. Qualitative Comparative Analysis (QCA) in der Soziologie – Perspektiven, Potentiale und Anwendungsbereiche. Zeitschrift für Soziologie 44 (6): 386–406.
Burzan, N., 2016: Methodenplurale Forschung. Weinheim/Basel: Beltz Juventa.
Collier, D., H. E. Brady, und J. Seawright. 2010: Sources of leverage in causal inference: Toward an alternative view of methodology. S. 161–199. In: Brady, H. E., und D. Collier (Hrsg.): Rethinking social inquiry: Diverse tools, shared standards. Lanham: Rowman & Littlefield Publishers.
Collier, D., 2011: Teaching Process Tracing. PS: Political Science & Politics 44 (4): 823–30.
Collier, R. B., und D. Collier. 1991: Shaping the Political Arena. Critical Junctures, the Labor Movement, and Regime Dynamics in Latin America. Princeton: Princeton University Press.

Döring, N., und J. Bortz. 2016: Forschungsmethoden und Evaluation in den Sozial- und Humanwissenschaften. Berlin/Heidelberg: Springer.

Flick, U., 2016: Qualitative Sozialforschung. Eine Einführung. Reinbeck bei Hamburg: Rowohlt.

George, A. L., und A. Bennett. 2005: Case Studies and Theory Development in the Social Sciences. Cambridge/London: MIT Press.

Goertz, G., und J. Mahoney. 2012: A Tale of Two Cultures. Princeton/Oxford: Princeton University Press.

Gordt, S., 2019: Die Säkularisierung der katholischen Schulsysteme. Eine historisch-vergleichende Analyse der Schulsysteme in Frankreich und Österreich. SWS-Rundschau 59 (2): 17–37.

Hammersley, M., und B. Cooper. 2012: Analytic induction versus qualitative comparative analysis. S. 129–169. In: Cooper, B., J. Glaeser, R. Gomm, und M. Hammersley (Hrsg.): Challenging the qualitative-quantitative divide: explorations in case-focused causal analysis. London: Continuum.

Hering, L., und R. J. Schmidt. 2014: Einzelfallanalyse. S. 529–541. In. Baur, N., und J. Blasius (Hrsg.): Handbuch Methoden der empirischen Sozialforschung. Wiesbaden: VS Verlag.

Kelle, U., 2014: Mixed Methods. S. 153–166. In. N. Baur und J. Blasius (Hrsg.): Handbuch Methoden der empirischen Sozialforschung. Wiesbaden: Springer.

Kelle, U., und C. Erzberger. 2010: Qualitative und quantitative Methoden: Kein Gegensatz. S. 299–308. In. Flick, U.,E. V. Kardorff und I. Steinke (Hrsg.): Qualitative Forschung: Ein Handbuch. Reinbek bei Hamburg: Rowohlt.

Kern, T., und T. Laux. 2017: Revolution or Negotiated Regime Change? Structural Dynamics in the Process of Democratization. The Case of South Korea in the 1980s. Historical Social Research 42: 245–274.

Kluge, S., 2000: Empirisch begründete Typenbildung in der qualitativen Sozialforschung [14 Absätze]. Forum Qualitative Sozialforschung/Forum: Qualitative Social Research 1: https://nbn-resolving.de/urn:nbn:de:0114-fqs0001145.

Lamnek, S., 2016: Qualitative Sozialforschung. Weinheim/Basel: Beltz.

Lange, M., 2013: Comparative-historical methods Los Angeles/London/New Delhi/Singapore: SAGE.

Laux, T., 2016a: Die Institutionalisierung von Lohngleichheitsrechten. Eine vergleichende Analyse von OECD Staaten. Zeitschrift für Soziologie 45: 393–409.

Laux, T., 2016b: Erkämpfte Gleichstellung. Eine Qualitative Comparative Analysis von OECD Staaten. Wiesbaden: Springer VS.

Mackie, J. L., 1974: The Cement of the Universe. Oxford: Oxford University Press.

Mahoney, J., 2000: Path Dependence in Historical Sociology. Theory and Society 29: 507–548.

Mahoney, J., 2003: Long-run development and the legacy of colonialism in Spanish America. American Journal of Sociology 109 (1): 50–106.

Mahoney, J., 2012: The logic of process tracing tests in the social sciences. Sociological Methods & Research 41 (4): 570–97.

Mahoney, J., und G. Goertz. 2006: A Tale of Two Cultures: Contrasting Quantitative and Qualitative Research. Political Analysis 14: 227–249.

Mayntz, R., 2002: Zur Theoriefähigkeit makro-sozialer Analysen. S. 7–43. In. Mayntz, R. (Hrsg.): Akteure – Mechanismen – Modelle. Zur Theoriefähigkeit makro-sozialer Analysen. Frankfurt/New York: Campus.

Mayntz, R., 2009: Soziale Mechanismen in der Analyse gesellschatflicher Makrophänomene. S. 97–121. In. Mayntz, R. (Hrsg.): Sozialwissenschaftliches Erklären. Frankfurt/New York: Campus.

McAdam, D., S. Tarrow und C. Tilly. 2001: Dynamics of contention. Cambridge: Cambridge University Press.

Moore, B., 1969: Soziale Ursprünge von Diktatur und Demokratie. Frankfurt: Suhrkamp.

Nassehi, A., 2008: Die Zeit der Gesellschaft. Wiesbaden: VS Verlag.

Neumann, L. F., und K. Schaper. 2008: Die Sozialordnung der Bunderepublik Deutschland. Bonn: Bundeszentrale für politische Bildung.

Raab, J., 2018: Die Unverzichtbarkeit des Vergleichens. S. 33–60. In. Burzan, N. , und R. Hitzler (Hrsg.): Typologische Konstruktionen. Wiesbaden: Springer VS.

Ragin, C. C., 1987: The Comparative Method. Moving beyond qualitative and quantitative strategies. Berkeley/Los Angeles/London: University of California Press.

Ragin, C. C., 2000: Fuzzy-Set Social Science. Chicago/London: The University of Chicago Press.

Rihoux, B., und B. Lobe. 2009: The Case for Qualitative Comparative Analysis (QCA): Adding Leverage for Thick Cross-Case Comparison. S. 222–242. In. Byrne, D., und C. C. Ragin (Hrsg.): The SAGE Handbook of Case-Based Methods. Los Angeles/London/ New Delhi/Singapore/Washington D.C.: SAGE.

Rohlfing, I., und C. Q. Schneider. 2018: A Unifying Framework for Causal Analysis in Set-Theoretic Multimethod Research. Sociological Methods and Research 47: 37–63.

Rosa, H., 2005: Beschleunigung. Frankfurt: Suhrkamp.

Schneider, C. Q., und C. Wagemann. 2012: Set Theoretic Methods for the Social Sciences. Cambridge: Cambridge University Press.

Schneider, C. Q., und I. Rohlfing. 2013: Combining QCA and Process Tracing in Set-Theoretic Multi-Method Research. Sociological Methods and Research 42: 559–597.

Schneider, C. Q., und I. Rohlfing. 2016: Case studies nested in fuzzy-set QCA on sufficiency: Formalizing case selection and causal inference. Sociological Methods and Research 45: 526–568.

Siewert, M. B., 2017: Process Tracing. S. 239–271. In. Jäckle, S. (Hrsg.): Neue Trends in den Sozialwissenschaften. Wiesbaden: Springer.

Skocpol, T., 1984: Vision and method in historical sociology. Cambridge [u.a.]: Cambridge University Press.

Tilly, C., 1984: Big Structures, Large Processes, Huge Comparisons. New York: Russel Sage Foundation.

Tilly, C., 1993: Contentious Repertoires in Great Britain, 1758–1834. Social Science History 17: 253 280.

Tilly, C., 2008: Explaining Social Processes. Boulder: Paradigm Publishers.

Weber, M., 2014: Wirtschaft und Gesellschaft: Soziologie. Tübingen: J.C.B. Mohr (Paul Siebeck).

Verfahren zur Analyse von Alltagshandlungen

Doris Cornils

Abstract

Studying everyday routines and actions presents a challenge for qualitative social research. Therefore, within the framework of the dissertation „Families' everyday conduct of life: workers with blurred work boundaries and their children" a method for the analysis of everyday actions has been devised. This method, called VAA, is a subject-scientific and ethnographically oriented system of self-documentation for Everyday Life Sociology. The VAA enables micro-sociological analyses of everyday actions within a temporal perspective. It focuses on analysing the protagonists' daily routines and which actions are being performed at what time during the day. This article first outlines the VAA's theoretical and methodological basis. Building on these principles, the development, structure and use of the VAA will be described. The article closes with an overview of the VAA's possible applications and a research pragmatic reflection on the chances and limitations of this qualitative method.

Zusammenfassung

Die Untersuchung von Alltagshandlungen stellt die qualitative Sozialforschung vor Herausforderungen. Im Rahmen der Dissertation „Alltägliche Lebensführung von Familie: zeitlich entgrenzt Erwerbstätige und ihre Kinder" wurde

---

D. Cornils (✉)
Bendestorf, Deutschland
E-Mail: info@doriscornils.de

© Springer Fachmedien Wiesbaden GmbH, ein Teil von Springer Nature 2020
E. Schilling und M. O'Neill (Hrsg.), *Frontiers in Time*
Research – Einführung in die interdisziplinäre Zeitforschung,
https://doi.org/10.1007/978-3-658-31252-7_18

deshalb das „Verfahren zur Analyse von Alltagshandlungen" (VAA) entwickelt. Hierbei handelt es sich um ein subjektwissenschaftlich-ethnografisch orientiertes Selbstdokumentationsverfahren für die Alltagsforschung. Das VAA dient der mikrosoziologischen Analyse von Alltagshandlungen in zeitlicher Perspektive. Es fokussiert auf die Analyse von dem was Akteur*innen tagtäglich tun, welche Handlungen von ihnen zu welcher Tageszeit vollzogen werden. In diesem Beitrag erfolgt im ersten Teil die theoretische und methodologische Grundlegung vom VAA. Auf Basis dieser Explikationen wird die Entwicklung, der Aufbau und die Anwendung vom VAA dargelegt. Der Beitrag schließt mit Einsatzmöglichkeiten vom VAA und einer forschungspragmatischen Reflexion der Chancen und Begrenzungen des qualitativen Verfahrens ab.

Einleitung und Übersicht

Die sozialwissenschaftliche Untersuchung des Alltags ist ein komplexes Unterfangen. Um das alltägliche Handeln von sozialen Akteur*innen sowie das Zusammenspiel von Alltagshandlungen in den Blick zu nehmen, bedarf es theoretischer und methodischer Ansätze, die dieser Komplexität gerecht werden. Der Impuls, das „Verfahren zur Analyse von Alltagshandlungen" (VAA) zu entwickeln, entsprang aus der Forschungspraxis im Rahmen der Dissertation „Alltägliche Lebensführung von Familien: zeitlich entgrenzt Beschäftigten und ihren Kindern" (Universität Hamburg).[1] Im Zentrum steht die Frage, was Menschen

---

[1]Der Begriff „Alltägliche Lebensführung von Familien" bezeichnet die im Rahmen der Dissertation weiterentwickelte Konzeption von den Ansätzen „Alltägliche Lebensführung" (Projektgruppe Alltäglicher Lebensführung 1995), „familiale Lebensführung" (Jürgens 2001) mit weiteren Lebensführungsansätzen aus der Kindheits- und Jugendsoziologie. Das Konzept „Alltägliche Lebensführung" wurde von der Münchner „Projektgruppe Alltäglicher Lebensführung" (1995) entwickelt. Im Forschungsfokus stand die Untersuchung der Auswirkungen des strukturellen Wandels der Arbeitswelt, genauer der Entgrenzungsprozesse in der Erwerbsarbeit auf das alltägliche Leben zu untersuchen (vgl. auch Kudera und Voß 2000 und weiterführend Alleweldt et al. 2016). Unter Entgrenzung wird ein „sozialer Prozess, in dem unter bestimmten historischen Bedingungen entstandene soziale

„Tag für Tag" (Weihrich 2002; vgl. auch Voß und Weihrich 2001) tun, um alltagspraktisch alles „unter einen Hut" zu bekommen. Globale Umbrüche der Arbeitswelt haben zur Folge, dass Zeit eine zunehmend bedeutsame und kostbare Ressource für die Gestaltung des Alltags darstellt. Die Flexibilisierung und Digitalisierung der Arbeits- und Lebenswelt bedingen zeitliche und räumliche Entgrenzungsprozesse, die sich in einer sukzessiven Auflösung der Grenzen zwischen privater und beruflicher Sphäre widerspiegeln. Damit einhergehend sind die zeitlichen Anforderungen an die Alltagsgestaltung und -koordination enorm angestiegen. Eine zentrale These der Lebensführungsforschung lautet, dass mit der „Entgrenzung von Arbeit" (Voß und Pongratz 1998; Minssen 2000; Kratzer 2003, 2013; Kratzer et al. 2004), der „Entgrenzung von Arbeit und Leben" (Voß 2000; Gottschall und Voß 2003; Bundeszentrale für politische Bildung 2004; Kratzer und Lange 2006; Janczyk 2009) und einer Entgrenzung von Arbeit, Familie und Geschlechterverhältnissen (Jurczyk et al. 2009)[2] „nicht nur kognitiv-rational zu lösende Herausforderungen an Individuen und Familien" verbunden sind, „sondern [...] [auch] handlungspraktisch zu bewältigende Aufgaben in der alltäglichen Lebensführung" (Jurczyk et al. 2005, S. 13). Da Handlungen und Zeit in einem unmittelbaren Zusammenhang stehen, sind Familien tagtäglich mit der zeitlichen Organisation und Koordination des Familienalltag befasst, der aus der Erwerbs-, Haus-, Sorge- und Pflegearbeit, sozialen Kontakten, Schul- und Öffnungszeiten, Freizeitaktivitäten etc. der Familienmitglieder besteht. Vor dem Hintergrund der skizzierten gesellschaftlichen Wandlungsprozesse wird Zeit, auch im Sinne gemeinsam im Alltag geteilter Familienzeit, zu einer immer voraussetzungsvolleren Ressource,

---

Strukturen der regulierenden Begrenzung von sozialen Vorgängen ganz oder partiell erodieren bzw. bewusst aufgelöst werden" gefasst. Jurczyk et al. (2009) differenzieren zwischen Entgrenzung der Erwerbsarbeit, Entgrenzung der Familie und zu beiden Sphären quer, die Entgrenzung der Geschlechterverhältnisse (S. 31 ff.). Bezogen auf die Dimension Zeit zeigt sich die Entgrenzung in Form flexibler Arbeitszeiten; bzgl. der räumlichen Dimension hinsichtlich flexibler Arbeitsorte.

[2]Zeitliche Vereinbarkeitsschwierigkeiten von Familien wurden in zahlreichen Studien untersucht (vgl. Ludwig et al. 2002; Heitkötter et al. 2009; Klenner und Pfahl 2009; Zartler et al. 2009; Lange 2011; Jurczyk 2015; Birken 2015). Das „Zeit für Familien" gesellschaftlich von zunehmender Bedeutung ist, verdeutlicht der achte gleichnamige Familienbericht (BMFSFJ 2012). Besonders Zeitknappheit und Zeitstress belasten Familien bei der Gestaltung ihres Alltagslebens (Bundeszentrale für politische Bildung 2004).

damit das Projekt „Familie" gelingt (vgl. BMFSFJ 2012, S. 208; vgl. Jurczyk und Lange 2006). Denn „Familie ist ein Ort, an dem unterschiedliche Zeiten der unterschiedlichen Mitglieder aufeinander treffen. Dabei werden neben der Organisation der Zeiten der einzelnen auch gemeinsame Zeiten geschaffen, denn es geht in Familie nicht primär um ein reibungsloses zeitliches Nebeneinander [...], sondern um die Herstellung einer Balance individueller und gemeinsamer Zeiten" (BMFSFJ 2012, S. 208). Die handlungspraktische Ebene alltäglicher Lebensführung steht folglich im engen Zusammenhang mit der zeitlichen Alltagsgestaltung. Erkenntnistheoretisch relevante Fragen für die Untersuchung alltäglicher Lebensführung von Familien lauten: Wer geht wann der Erwerbsarbeit nach, zu welchen Zeiten besuchen Kinder Bildungs- und Betreuungseinrichtungen, wie wird die Betreuung der Kinder inner- und außerhäusig organisiert, wer investiert welche Zeit in die tagtäglich anfallenden Hausarbeitstätigkeiten oder wie und wann werden Familienzeiten gestaltet?[3]

In den zahlreichen vorliegenden Studien der alltäglichen Lebensführungsforschung wird zwecks Beantwortung der skizzierten handlungs- und zeittheoretischen Fragestellungen i. d. R. auf qualitative Interviewverfahren zurückgegriffen (u. a. Projektgruppe alltägliche Lebensführung 1995; Behnke und Meuser 2003; Kleemann 2005; Jurczyk et al. 2009; Wörmer 2016; Egbringhoff 2007; Streit von 2011). Qualitative Interviewbefragungen begründen sich methodologisch jedoch „durch die Möglichkeit, Situationsdeutungen und Handlungsmotive in offener Form zu erfragen" (Hopf 2004, S. 350). Je nach Forschungsinteresse werden „Deutungsmuster" (Lüders und Meuser 1997), „soziale Konstruktionen", „Alltagstheorien" (Flick 1991) oder die „subjektive Problemsicht" (Witzel 1985) erfragt. Qualitative Interviews zielen somit auf die Reflexionen von erinnerten Handlungen ab, können aber nicht die Handlungen selbst abbilden (vgl. Lamnek 1989, S. 237 f.). „Man braucht, anders gesagt, eine Kontrastfolie, etwas, mit dem sich das Gesagte vergleichend in Beziehung setzen lässt, damit erkennbar wird, was im Reden stecken bleibt" (Wetterer 2003, S. 292). Werden Handlungs- und Sinndeutungsebene erkenntnistheoretisch differenziert, kann nicht ein- und dasselbe methodische Instrument herangezogen werden. Denn, „prinzipielle Maßgabe für die Wahl der Methodik ist ihre Gegenstandsangemessenheit, d. h. das Verfahren muss geeignet sein, für den spezifischen Forschungsgegenstand angemessene Daten zu liefern" (Helfferich 2004, S. 26; vgl. auch Flick 2002, S. 16).

---

[3]Vgl. zur Praxisdimension alltäglicher Lebensführung Hagen-Demszky (2006).

Ein bislang noch wenig beschrittener Weg stellt bei der Erforschung der alltäglichen Lebensführung zeitlich entgrenzt Beschäftigter und ihrer Kinder demnach die methodisch basierte Untersuchung der Handlungsebene dar. Darüber hinaus liegen zum Untersuchungsgegenstand kaum Studien vor, die Handlungs- und Sinndeutungsebene theorie- und methodenbasiert differenzieren und die mittels unterschiedlicher qualitativer Forschungsmethoden erhobenen Daten miteinander verbinden. Ein zentrales Forschungsanliegen bestand deshalb darin, eine Differenzierung zwischen Handlungs- und Sinndeutungsebene theoretisch und methodisch umzusetzen. Konkret galt es, angelehnt an die Dimensionierungen im Konzept alltäglicher Lebensführungsforschung,[4] zu erforschen, welche Alltagshandlungen von wem (personelle, generationale und geschlechtliche Dimension) mit welchen weiteren Personen (soziale Dimension) zu welchen Zeiten (zeitliche Dimension) praktiziert werden. Die Frauen- und Geschlechterforschung sowie quantitative Zeitbudgetstudien belegen, dass zwischen den Dimensionen Zeit und Geschlecht ein enger Zusammenhang bzgl. der Zeitverwendung für Erwerbs-, Haus- und Sorgearbeit (Krüger und Born 2000; Hewener 2004; Statistisches Bundesamt 2015) und im Bereich unbezahlter Arbeit eine zeitliche Entgrenzung (im Sinne von Verdichtung und Beschleunigung) zu Lasten von Frauen zu beobachten ist (Ludwig et al. 2002; Winker und Carstensen 2004).[5]

Während die handlungs- und zeitsoziologischen Fragen mittels des VAA untersucht wurden, erfolgte die Beantwortung der Fragestellung, die sich auf die Sinndeutungen von Alltagshandlungen bezogen, mittels qualitativer Interviewverfahren.[6] Zwecks Eruierung eines geeigneten Methodeninstruments zur Erfassung

---

[4] Zur Dimensionierung im Konzept alltägliche Lebensführung vgl. u. a. Voß (2001, S. 206); Kudera (2000, S. 113).

[5] Während im Gesamtkontext der Dissertation dieser Zusammenhang herausgearbeitet wird, kann eine Vertiefung in diesem Beitrag nicht erfolgen.

[6] In der vorliegenden Studie wurden am Ende des gesamten Erhebungsprozesses, die mit dem VAA erhobenen Daten (Handlungsebene) mit denen mittels qualitativer Interviewverfahren gewonnenen Daten (Sinndeutungsebene) trianguliert (vgl. Flick 2004, S. 314). Als Interviewmethoden der qualitativen Sozialforschung zur Befragung der Sinndeutungen kamen das leitfadengestützte problemzentrierte Interview (vgl. Witzel 1985, 2006; Mayring 2002, S. 67 ff.) für Erwachsene und Jugendliche sowie das lebensweltliche Interview für Kinder (vgl. Fuhs 2000) zum Einsatz. Methodisch an der Grounded Theory angelehnt, wird davon ausgegangen: „Je mehr Datenmaterial vorliegt, desto mehr Beweiskraft wird sich anhäufen, desto mehr Variationen werden gefunden und eine desto größere Dichte wird erreicht" (Strauss und Corbin 1996, S. 161).

der Handlungsebene und zeitlichen Dimension von Alltagshandlungen, wurden zahlreiche qualitative Methoden einer intensiven Prüfung unterzogen, aber aus Gründen fehlender Gegenstandsangemessenheit ausgeschlossen.[7] Am Ende dieses Prozesses stand die Entscheidung zur Entwicklung des „Verfahrens zur Analyse von Alltagshandlungen" (VAA).

Das VAA ist als ein qualitatives Selbstdokumentationsverfahren einzuordnen. Es handelt sich um einen Feldforschungsansatz, der sowohl ethnographische als auch soziologische Züge trägt, im Sinne einer „Ethnographie als Alltagssoziologie" (Breidenstein et al. 2013, S. 26). „Eine ethnografische Untersuchung zielt in der Regel darauf ab, Menschen über einen längeren Zeitraum in ihrem alltäglichen Leben zu erforschen" (Seel und Hanke 2015, S. 804). Qualitative Feldforschung bedeutet, „überschaubare und unterscheidbare Einheiten des menschlichen Zusammenlebens ganzheitlich zu erfassen, sie hinsichtlich ihrer Strukturen und zeitlichen Zustandekommens zu analysieren und zu dokumentieren" (ebd.). Gleichzeitig ist das VAA als ein Instrument der Soziologie zu verorten, einer „Wissenschaft, welches soziales Handeln deutend verstehen und dadurch in seinem Ablauf und seinen Wirkungen ursächlich erklären will" (Weber 1980, S. 1). Im Fokus stehen Alltagshandlungen im Raum-Zeit-Zusammenhang, wobei der Schwerpunkt des eigenen Forschungsinteresses auf der zeitlichen Dimensionierung liegt. Die Entwicklung des VAA orientierte sich im Wesentlichen an theoretischen und methodischen Aspekten von quantitativen und qualitativen Zeittagebüchern (Ehling und Schäfer 1988; Ehling 1991; Ehling et al. 2001; Jahoda et al. 1975) sowie Log- und Tagebüchern (Wilz und Brähler 1997; Kunz 2015), die das Ziel verfolgen, Zeitbudgets, Tätigkeitssequenzen oder Tagesabläufe zu rekonstruieren. Mit dem VAA wird folglich nicht methodisches Neuland betreten. Vielmehr stellt das VAA einen Beitrag zur Fortschreibung und Weiterentwicklung der Selbstdokumentationsverfahren sozialwissenschaftlich-ethnographischer Alltagsforschung dar. Das VAA basiert auf einer handlungs- und zeitsoziologischen Grundlegung. Das Kernstück des Verfahrens bildet das qualitative Erhebungsinstrument, das „Protokoll zur Erhebung von Alltagshandlungen" (PEA). Abgerundet wird es mit dem für das VAA entwickelte Auswertungsvorgehen.

---

[7]Geprüft wurden: 1. Die teilnehmende Beobachtung (Lamnek 1989), 2. das „Prozessmodell zur Erforschung der Handlungsgenese" (Zeiher 2017) geprüft sowie 3. das „Verfahren zur Analyse von Arbeit im Haushalt (AVAH-Verfahren) (Resch 1999a, b).

In diesem Beitrag wird der theoretische und methodische Entwicklungsprozess des VAA wie auch dessen Anwendung im Rahmen des Dissertationsprojektes dargestellt und reflektiert. Handlungs- und zeitsoziologische Vorüberlegungen bilden die theoretische Grundlegung. Darauf aufbauend folgt die Darlegung jener quantitativen und qualitativen Methoden, von denen Impulse für die Entwicklung des VAA ausgingen. Zentrales Element der VAA ist das „Protokoll zur Erhebung von Alltagshandlungen" (PEA), das in Entwicklung, Aufbau und Anwendung skizziert wird. Es folgen Beschreibungen zur Datenauswertung sowie Vorschläge zu Einsatzmöglichkeiten des VAA. Forschungspragmatische Reflexionen zu Chancen und Begrenzungen des Verfahrens schließen den Beitrag ab.

Theoretische Vorüberlegungen und Grundlegungen für die Entwicklung des VAA

Um den Zusammenhang von Alltagshandeln und Zeit empirisch zu erfassen, braucht es zunächst die begriffliche Klärung. Ausgehend von der Handlungstheorie nach Max Weber (1980) werden die Begriffe „Handeln", „soziales Handeln", „soziale Beziehungen" sowie der Begriff „Alltagshandlungen" (Schütz 1971; Esser 1991) expliziert. Auf Basis dieser theoretischen Vorüberlegungen erfolgt eine zeit- und handlungstheoretische Grundlegung, die der Entwicklung des VAA zugrunde liegt.

Handlungstheoretische Grundlegung

Nach Max Weber ist die Soziologie „eine Wissenschaft, welche soziales Handeln deutend verstehen und dadurch in seinem Ablauf und seinen Wirkungen ursächlich erklären will" (Weber 1980, S. 1). Im Mittelpunkt des soziologischen Forschungsinteresses steht „das Einzelindividuum und sein Handeln als unterste Einheit, als ihr ‚Atom'" (Weber 1985, S. 439). „‚Handeln' soll dabei ein menschliches Verhalten […] heißen, wenn und insofern als der oder die Handelnde mit ihm einen subjektiven Sinn verbinden" (Weber 1980, S. 1). In der Weberschen Interpretation gilt es zu unterscheiden, ob eine Handlung mit einer Absicht oder unbeabsichtigt zustande kam. Wird eine Tür bewusst geöffnet, mit der Absicht diese zu öffnen und durch sie hindurchzutreten, wird dem Handeln ein subjektiver Sinn zugeschrieben. Erfolgt hingegen das Türöffnen unbeabsichtigt, weil die Person sich beispielsweise auf die Türklinke abstützte, dann ist das Öffnen der

Tür „ohne jede Verknüpfung mit einem subjektiven Sinn zustande" (Schneider 2008, S. 22) gekommen. Handeln wird erst dann zum „sozialen Handeln", wenn es dem „gemeinten Sinn nach auf das Verhalten *anderer* bezogen wird und daran in seinem Ablauf orientiert ist" (Weber 1980, S. 1, kursiv im Original). Dabei unterscheidet Weber nicht, ob das soziale Handeln der Akteur*innen sich auf Handeln von Einzelnen, von Gruppen, von bekannten oder unbekannten Personen bezieht, sich an gegenwärtigen, zurückliegenden oder zukünftigen Handlungen orientiert. Alleine ein Buch zu lesen zählt ebenso als soziale Handlung wie das Kochen für die Familie. „Soziales Handeln verlangt also weder die Anwesenheit anderer Personen noch deren Wissen vom Tun des Akteurs" (Schneider 2008, S. 58). Werden soziale Handlungen wechselhaft aufeinander bezogen, wie wir es im Alltag von Familien beobachten können, stellt die „soziale Beziehung" (Weber 1980, S. 13) eine weitere zentrale Begrifflichkeit dar. „'Soziale Beziehung' soll ein seinem Sinngehalt nach aufeinander gegenseitig *eingestelltes* und dadurch orientiertes Sichverhalten mehrerer heißen. Die soziale Beziehung besteht also durchaus und ganz ausschließlich: in der *Chance,* daß in einer (sinnhaft) angebbaren Art sozial gehandelt wird" (Weber 1980, S. 13). Eine soziale Beziehung, deren Grundlage des sozialen Handelns „auf subjektiv *gefühlter* (affektueller oder traditionaler) *Zusammengehörigkeit* der Beteiligten beruht" bezeichnet Weber als „Vergemeinschaftung" (ebd., S. 21, kursiv im Original).

Die Vergemeinschaftung in Familien erfolgt vorzugsweise über Alltagshandlungen sowie gemeinsam geteilter Zeiten, die sich durch Routinen auszeichnen. Alltägliches Handeln basiert auf „selbstverständlichem" Alltagswissen und -erfahrungen. „Es enthält eine begrenzte Anzahl an [...] ,Rezepten' für typisches Handeln in typisch wiederkehrenden Situationen." Alltagshandlungen ist eine „Fraglosigkeit" des Alltagswissens inhärent. Sie zeichnen sich durch „Habitualisierung, Automatismus und Halbbewußtsein" (Esser 1991, S. 436) aus. Habitualisiertes und von Routinen geprägtes Handeln besteht aus der Anwendung von „Rezepten und Faustregeln [...], die die Probe bis dahin bestanden haben" (Schütz 1971, S. 24). Dieses „Wissen von vertrauenswerten Rezepten, um damit die soziale Welt auszulegen und um mit Dingen und Menschen umzugehen, damit die besten Resultate in jeder Situation mit einem Minimum an Anstrengung und bei Vermeidung unerwünschter Konsequenzen erlangt werden können" (Schütz 1972, S. 58), stellt die Grundlage für alltägliches Handeln dar. Die von zahlreichen Routinen geprägten Alltagshandlungen sind an Zeitrhythmen und zeitliche Ordnungssysteme – wie z. B. Öffnungs- und Schließzeiten von Betreuungs- und Bildungseinrichtungen, Schlafenszeiten, Familienzeiten, Erwerbsarbeitszeiten, Termine etc. gebunden (vgl. Morgenroth 2008, S. 58).

Zeit und Handeln

Zeit spielt eine wichtige Rolle für das Verstehen von sozialen Handlungen, denn die menschliche Befähigung mit Zeit umzugehen bildet die Basis für die Organisation sozialen Handelns (vgl. Muri 2004, S. 247). „Handeln und Zeit sind nicht trennbar" (Jürgens 2003, S. 53), denn jede Handlung erfolgt in der Zeit, bedarf Zeit und jede Handlung nimmt in irgendeiner Form Bezug auf Zeit (vgl. Schöneck 2009, S. 68). Durch ihre Körperlichkeit sind Individuen „Teil der Raumwelt und deren Gesetzen unterworfen"; die dem „Menschen inhärente Zeit" (Zeiher und Zeiher 1993, S. 397) ist ihr Tun.[8] Indem Akteur*innen in Abhängigkeit zu den bestehenden Bedingungen in ihrer sozialen Umwelt selbst bestimmen was sie tun, werden sie zu aktiv Handelnden (vgl. Dunckel 1999, S. 234). Die bestehenden sozialen und physisch-räumlichen Bedingungen zur Zeit des Handelns bestimmen die Möglichkeiten des Handelns. Gleichsam werden diese durch die Bedingungen der Akteur*innen determiniert, die mit ihnen selbst verbunden sind. D. h. an ihre zum jeweiligen Zeitpunkt existierenden Fähigkeiten, an ihre Beweggründe, ihre Bedürfnisse und Einstellungen, die sie zum Handeln bewegen könnten (vgl. Zeiher und Zeiher 1993, S. 397).

Handeln ist ohne Zeit nicht denkbar. Aber: Was ist Zeit?[9] Während aus der Perspektive der Physik Zeit als eine objektiv messbare Größe aufgefasst wird, betont die soziologische Perspektive nach Elias (1982) den sozialen Charakter von Zeit, dem ein konstruktivistisches Verständnis zugrunde liegt. Gesellschaftliche Erscheinungsformen von Zeit werden als soziale Zeitvorstellungen aufgefasst, „denn die Wahrnehmung, Beobachtung, Analyse und Funktionalisierung verschiedener Aspekte von Zeit geschieht stets vor sozialem Hintergrund und mit gesellschaftlicher Rückwirkung" (Hungerland 2002, S. 37). Die physikalische Zeitmessung und astronomische Zeit erhalten so die Relevanz einer Orientierungsfunktion zur Koordination von Handlungen und dienen dazu, Zeit greif- und

---

[8]Handeln von Individuen ist stets in einem Raum-Zeit-Gefüge eingebettet, denn „Raum und Zeit sind ein konstitutives Prinzip sozialer Praktiken" (Hielscher 2006, S. 29). Giddens (1988) folgend wird jede gesellschaftliche Praxis über Raum-Zeit-Aspekte geregelt und durch soziale Handlungen der Akteur*innen permanent (re-)produziert. Der Raum-Aspekt wird, da es sich um ein qualitatives Instrument mit der Schwerpunktlegung auf Zeit handelt, nicht weiter ausgeführt; findet sich aber im PEA wieder (s. .).

[9]Dieser großen Frage haben sich zahlreiche Wissenschaftlerinnen verschiedener Disziplinen gewidmet. Vgl. vertiefend z. B. Schöneck (2009, S. 19 ff.); bezogen auf die lange Tradition einer soziologischen Perspektive auf Zeit.

berechenbar zu machen. Ebenso zählen zyklische Abläufe der Natur (wie z. B. Jahreszeiten) als gesellschaftliche Orientierungsmarker für menschliches Handeln. Zeit als sozial hergestellte Kategorie macht es sozialen Akteur*innen möglich, sich in der bzw. ihrer (Um-)Welt zu orientieren. Standardisierte Messinstrumente (Uhren, Kalender) sind von ihnen erschaffene Symbole, mit deren Hilfe sie Zeit darstellen und instrumentalisieren können – Zeit kann als soziales Orientierungsschema erst durch diese Instrumente entstehen (vgl. Elias 2004). Gleichsam erhalten sie die Funktion eines Bezugsrahmens, um (den relativen Anfang und das relative Ende) von Erfahrungen und Handlungen einordnen, festlegen, miteinander vergleichen, aufeinander abstimmen und in Beziehung setzen zu können. Die von Menschen hingegen geteilte, naturhafte Auffassung von Zeit als objektivierbare Größe verweist auf ihre Einbindung in die soziale Welt, welche durch verbindliche Zeitnormen und -regeln den Umgang mit Zeit bereithält. Die Wissensaneignung durch die Einzelnen setzt gesellschaftlich-kulturell geteilte Zeitsymboliken voraus, denn nur wenn eine Gesellschaft eine gemeinsame Vorstellung von Zeit teilt, kann diese ihre Funktion erfüllen (vgl. Elias 1982, S. 849).

Zeit stellt ein Verbindungsglied zwischen Gesellschaft und den handelnden Akteur*innen dar (vgl. Zeiher 1996, S. 158). Reflexiv betrachtet: „Der Mensch prägt seine Zeit und seine Gesellschaft – und wird dann von beiden weitergeprägt" (Wendorff 1993, S. 8). Akteur*innen betreiben aktiv Zeitorganisation, gleichzeitig werden sie durch zeitliche Rahmenbedingungen beeinflusst und erleben „zeitliche Zwänge, Handlungseinschränkungen und Begrenzungen"[10] (Schöneck 2009, S. 56). Das alltägliche Handeln orientiert sich an kulturellen Zeitordnungen, d. h. „der Standarisierung der Zeit, die Ausformung von Zeitinstitutionen und die Herausbildung von Zeitnormen" (Schöneck 2009, S. 31 ff.). Ein typisches Beispiel ist die Sieben-Tage-Woche, bestehend aus „Alltagszeit (Montag bis Freitag) und Wochenendzeit (Samstag und Sonntag)" (ebd., S. 36).[11]

---

[10]Im Ansatz der Zeitgeographie nach Hägerstrand (1975), der sog. Lund-Schule, sind diese Einschränkungen und Begrenzungen in der „contrains theory" (Parker und Thrift 1980, S. 248 f.) beschrieben.

[11]Den Werktagen wird eher ein sachbezogener, den Wochenendtagen hingegen primär ein sozialbezogener Charakter zugeschrieben (vgl. Rinderspracher 1987, S. 37). Der für einen Teil der Erwerbstätigen arbeitsfreie Samstag, wird seit geraumer Zeit für Arbeiten und Aufgaben genutzt, die unter der Erwerbsarbeitswoche nicht erledigt werden konnten (vgl. Maurer 1992, S. 291 f.). Der Sonntag behält hingegen seinen Sozialfunktionscharakter. Wie sich später in diesem Beitrag im Kontext der Beschreibung des „Protokolls zur Analyse von Alltagshandlungen" (PEA) zeigt, wurde dieser Aspekt bei der Entwicklung des methodischen Instruments berücksichtigt.

Durch das Handeln der Akteur*innen werden Zeitinstitutionen reproduziert und verstetigt. „Ihre zeitlichen Handlungen und ihr ‚Wissen' von Zeit, ihre Zeitkonzepte, ihre Interessen an Zeit [...], ihre Zeitstile [...], die selber immer bereits durch die Gestalt der Gesellschaft geprägt sind, konstituieren schließlich wiederum soziale Zeitstrukturen" (vgl. Lange und Heitkötter 2006, S. 1). Akteur*innen beziehen sich nicht passiv auf Zeitordnungen, sondern aus der zeitlichen Gestaltung und Organisation ihrer Handlungen resultieren wiederum Routinen, „die den Alltag zeitlich strukturieren. Umgang mit Zeit bedeutet also auch, aktiv an der Entstehung von temporalen Mustern mitzuwirken" (Morgenroth 2008, S. 59).

Gemeinsam geteilte Zeit ist für die Bildung und Reproduktion von Gemeinschaft, für die sog. „Sozialzeit" (Hielscher 2006, S. 19) Voraussetzung. Soziale Zeit kann sich nur auf Basis einer gemeinschaftlich geteilten Auffassung von Zeit entwickeln, und es kommt erst durch gemeinsam geteilte und aufeinander abgestimmte Zeit(en) zur Handlungsinteraktionen der Akteur*innen. Beziehen sie sich in ihren Handlungen nicht aufeinander, bleibt es bei einem losen Nebeneinander. D. h. soziale Zeit von Familien entsteht nicht von allein, sie ist an ein gemeinsames „doing time" (Jurczyk 1997, S. 180) innerhalb der kollektiven Zeitordnung und Zeitinstitutionen gebunden.[12]

Methodische Vorüberlegungen und Grundlegungen für die Entwicklung des VAA

Die Entwicklung des VAA stellt eine Fortschreibung der Tradition von Selbstdokumentationsmethoden in Form von Zeittagebüchern dar. Theoretische Impulse gingen von den Log- und Tagebüchern der ethnografischen Feldforschung sowie von den Zeittagebüchern der quantitativen Zeitbudgetforschung aus. Insbesondere die zeittheoretische Grundlegung der quantitativen Zeitbudgetforschung waren für

---

[12] „Zeitinstitutionen verlieren zugunsten von individuell bestimmten Routinen, Ritualen und Regeln an Bedeutung. Für [...] Familien bzw. deren Mitglieder (Erwachsene und Kinder) ergibt sich hiermit die Aufgabe, verstärkt das Alltagsleben aufeinander abzustimmen und zeitlich zu steuern" (Lange und Heitkötter 2006, S. 1). Je flexibler und unplanbarer die Erwerbsarbeitszeit ist, desto schwieriger wird es diese Öffnungs- und Schließzeiten der Erziehungs- und Bildungsinstitutionen in Einklang zu bringen, da sie zeitlich noch (weitestgehend) entlang industrieller Zeittaktungen organisiert sind (Jurczyk und Lange 2005; Klenner und Pfahl 2005).

die Entwicklung des Erhebungsinstruments „Protokoll zur Erhebung von Alltagshandlungen" (PEA) hilfreich.

Log- und Tagebücher gelten in der ethnografischen Feldforschung als recht spezifische Datenerhebungsinstrumente. Ihr Einsatz macht das Tun im Alltag und die alltäglichen Routinen der Befragten aus der Selbstbeschreibungsperspektive sichtbar. Die sog. „Selbstreport-Verfahren" (Kunz 2015, S. 147) zeichnet aus, dass die Beforschten zu Beobachtenden ihres Alltags werden. Obgleich zwischen Beobachtung und Selbstreflexion deutlich zu unterscheiden ist, können dadurch Selbstreflexionsprozesse angeregt werden.[13] Wenn die Dokumentationen in zeitlicher Nähe zum Erlebten erfolgen, können Erinnerungslücken überwunden werden, die insbesondere bei der Erforschung von Alltagsroutinen eine große Herausforderung darstellen. Darüber hinaus wird davon ausgegangen, dass nur die Handelnden selbst in der Lage sind, den Anfang und das Ende ihres Handelns zu bestimmen (Schütz 1971, S. 27). Hier knüpft das bereits explizierte methodisch kontrollierte Fremdverstehen an, nämlich die Aufgabe der Forschenden, die subjektive Perspektive der Handelnden verstehen und erklären zu wollen.

Angelehnt an die Log- und Tagebücher der Ethnographie lässt sich das VAA methodologisch „als sozialwissenschaftliches Instrument der Datenerhebung vor allem sozialkonstruktivistisch-handlungstheoretisch begründen" (Kunz 2015, S. 148). Wie diesen Verfahren liegt auch dem VAA die Annahme zugrunde, dass „die Konstruktion von Wirklichkeit ihren Ausgang an menschlichen Handlungen und dem damit verbundenen subjektiven Sinn nimmt" (ebd.). Mit dem VAA wird die subjektive Perspektive hinsichtlich alltäglicher Handlungen in zeitlichem Zusammenhang abgebildet. Außerdem ist es möglich die verschiedenen Subjektperspektiven der Familienakteur*innen auf das gleiche Ereignis (wie z. B. gemeinsame Mahlzeiten) zu rekonstruieren und vergleichend ins Verhältnis zu setzen.

---

[13]Zu einem Kriterium qualitativer Sozialforschung zählt die Reflexivität der Forschenden (diese und weitere Grundannahmen vgl. Flick et al. 2004, S. 20 ff.). Während der Erhebungsphase wurde ein Forschungstagebuch geführt und Prozesse, Beobachtungen und die eigene Forschungspraxis reflektiert und dokumentiert (s. weiterführend.). In diesen wurde festgehalten, dass einige der an der Untersuchung Teilnehmenden von Selbstreflexionsprozessen berichteten, die aus den regelmäßig wiederkehrenden Selbstdokumentationsphasen ihrer Alltagshandlungen mit dem VAA resultierten. Aus diesen Rückmeldungen wurde deutlich, dass der Einsatz des VAA zur Bewusstwerdung von Routinen und Handlungsabläufen führte, aus denen seitens der Befragten Veränderungsentscheidungen bezogen auf ihre Alltagsroutinen und die Organisation des Alltags resultierten.

Das Erhebungsinstrument „Protokoll zur Erhebung von Alltagshandlungen" (PEA) (s. Abschn. 4.1.) wurde in Anlehnung an das „selbstgeführte Tagebuch" aus der quantitativen Zeitbudgetforschung entwickelt (Ehling und Schäfer 1988, S. 459; Ehling et al. 2001, S. 428; vgl. Ehling 1991, S. 33 ff.). Während die Methode der quantitativen Zeitbudgetforschung die Erfassung von Zeitaufwendungen (statistischer Bevölkerungsgruppen) im Verlauf bestimmter Zeiträume in Form von Zeitmessungen zu ihrem Gegenstand erhebt (vgl. Blass 1980; Schweitzer et. al. 1990; Tietze und Rossbach 1991, S. 12 ff.), beruht eine qualitative Verfahrensweise, wie das VAA, auf dem Fremdverstehen von Alltagshandlungen und Zeit aus einer subjekt- und sozialkonstruktivistischen Perspektive. Wie bereits in Abschn. 2.2 verdeutlicht, wird Zeit im sozialen Handeln als Mengenmaß wirksam, jedoch im geschilderten Sinne, als von Menschen erschaffene und gesellschaftlich-kulturell geteilte symbolische Ordnung zur Strukturierung ihrer alltäglichen Lebensführung (vgl. Voß 1991, S. 7 f.). Orientiert an symbolisch geteilten standardisierten Messinstrumenten sind fünf Stunden für jede Person gleich lang. Zeit entwickelt ihren qualitativen Charakter jedoch erst durch die spezifischen Handlungen, in den jeweilig verschiedenen Handlungssituationen und sozialen Kontexten. Dementsprechend sind „z. B. 5 h Berufstätigkeit etwas völlig anderes als 5 h Familienarbeit, Spiel oder Schlaf" (Voß 1991, S. 76). Während also innerhalb der quantitativen Zeitbudgetforschung Zeit als Instrument zur Messung der Dauer und Häufigkeit von Tätigkeiten dient, wird Zeit im VAA als Moment der Strukturierung von Alltagshandlungen aufgefasst. In dieser Hinsicht unterscheidet sich auch das Erkenntnisinteresse beider Verfahrensweisen. Ziel der quantitativen Zeitbudgetforschung ist es, „die Aktivitäten von Personen [...] in ihrer ‚linearen' zeitlichen Reihenfolge [...] zu erheben"; das qualitative Verfahren zur Analyse von Alltagshandlungen hingegen beabsichtigt über die Erfassung von Handlungen zu einer „Rekonstruktion realer Tagesabläufe" (ebd., S. 69) zu gelangen. Es wird damit der Versuch unternommen, „die wissenschaftliche Aufklärung von Struktur, Logik und Qualität der realen Lebensweise von Personen mit Hilfe eines zeitbezogenen Instruments" (ebd., S. 70) zu verfolgen.

Das quantitative selbstgeführte Tagebuch wurde für die qualitative Verfahrensweise, konkret für das „Protokoll zur Erhebung von Alltagshandlungen" (PEA) modifiziert. So knüpft beispielsweise die Einsatzhäufigkeit des Erhebungsinstruments PEA an die quantitative Zeitbudgetforschung an. Demnach ist davon auszugehen, dass eine einmalige Erhebungswelle (z. B. von einigen Tagen im Jahr) zu Ergebnisverzerrungen führt, da Handlungen nicht nur im engen Zusammenhang mit den Wochentagen stehen, sondern auch mit der jeweiligen Jahreszeit bzw. den klimatischen Bedingungen (vgl. Ehling et al. 2001, S. 433).

Darüber hinaus sind bei Untersuchungen von Familien Ferien- und Urlaubszeiten zu berücksichtigen, da die Handlungen in diesen Zeiträumen von der Gestaltung des sonstigen Alltags abweichen. Zur Vermeidung saisonaler Verzerrungen haben diese Faktoren erheblichen Einfluss auf die Einsatzhäufigkeit des Erhebungsinstruments sowie auf die Anzahl und Auswahl der Wochentage, an denen erhoben wird. Vor diesem Hintergrund erfolgt der Einsatz vom PEA zu den vier Jahreszeiten, d. h. pro Jahreszeit erfolgt jeweils eine Erhebungswelle. Da innerhalb der quantitativen Zeitbudgetforschungen Erfahrungen darüber vorliegen, dass eine optimale Erhebungswelle drei bis fünf Tage umfasst (davon sollte ein Tag ein Wochenendtag sein) und die bereits skizzierten Wandlungsprozesse von Zeitinstitutionen berücksichtigt werden sollten, wurden die folgenden fünf Wochentage als Erhebungstage im Rahmen der VAA ausgewählt: Montag, Dienstag, Donnerstag, Freitag und Sonntag.[14] An allen Tagen erfolgte eine Erhebung im 24-h-Umfang, um eine möglichst detaillierte und „dichte" Abbildung der Alltagshandlungen zu erreichen. An folgende Kriterien des selbstgeführten Tagesbuchs lehnte die Konzeption des Erhebungsinstruments PEA im Verfahren VAA an:

- Es können Informationen über mehrere Tage erhoben werden (vgl. Ehling und Schäfer 1988, S. 459).
- Die Handlungen werden von den Untersuchungsteilnehmenden bei dem VAA mit eigenen Worten beschrieben. Zur Verfahrensweise des VAA zählen keine Vorgaben durch eine sog. Tätigkeitsliste oder eine Vereinheitlichung der erhobenen Aktivitäten anhand von Listen postum, wie in der quantitativen Sozialforschung angewandt (vgl. Ehling et al. 2001, S. 430).
- Die Vorgabe einer Zeitdimension (24-h-Grenze) „führt zu geringen Verzerrungen durch Effekte der sozialen Erwünschtheit von Aktivitäten" (Ehling et al. 2001, S. 430).
- Es lässt sich ermitteln, zu welchen Tageszeiten welchen Handlungen von den Untersuchungsteilnehmenden nachgegangen wird (vgl. ebd., S. 429 f.).
- Das selbstgeführte, schriftliche Tagebuch verursacht geringe Kosten und es können alle Haushaltsmitglieder in die Befragung einbezogen werden (Ehling und Schäfer 1988, S. 459).

---

[14]Da sich im Kontext der Flexibilisierung der Erwerbsarbeit zunehmend abzeichnet, dass Sonntage eine hohe soziale Funktion zukommt (Stichwort: Sonntagsmorgenfrühstück, vgl. Jurczyk et al. 2005; S. 26), wurde der Sonntag, statt der Samstag als Erhebungstag ausgewählt. Vgl. theoretische Grundlegung Fußnote 10.

- Kinder ab dem Alter von zehn Jahren können ihren Tagesablauf selbstständig protokollieren (vgl. ebd., S. 430).[15] Bei Kindern unter zehn Jahren bzw. jener Altersgruppe, die noch nicht in der Lage ist, Tagebuchnotizen alleine vorzunehmen (wie z. B. im Kindergartenbetreuungs- und Vorschulalter), wird ein „fremdgeführtes Tagebuchprotokoll" (Ehling 1991, S. 36) eingesetzt. Dieses wird von den jeweiligen Betreuungspersonen, d. h. den Eltern, den Erzieher*innen, den Großeltern usw. geführt (vgl. Tietze und Peek 1991, S. 131 ff.).

Verfahren zur Analyse von Alltagshandlungen (VAA)

Das VAA wurde mit der Zielsetzung entwickelt, einen theoretisch fundierten und in der Forschungspraxis erprobten Zugang zur „Rekonstruktion realer Tagesabläufe" (Voß 1991, S. 69) zu entwickeln, mittels dessen die sozialen Alltagshandlungen von einzelnen Akteur*innen und kollektiven Akteursgruppen erfassbar und analysierbar sind. Zur Erhebung von Alltagshandlungen wurde für das VAA das Erhebungsinstrument „Protokoll zur Erhebung von Alltagshandlungen" (PEA) entwickelt und empirisch erprobt. Nach der Beschreibung des Erhebungsinstruments PEA wird das Auswertungsvorgehen skizziert. Auf der Grundlage der vorliegenden Forschungserfahrungen schließt die Darstellung mit der Reflexion von Chancen und Begrenzungen des VAA ab.

Protokoll zur Erhebung von Alltagshandlungen (PEA)

Beim PEA handelt es sich um ein Erhebungsinstrument in Form eines Handlungs- und Zeittagebuchs, das die Studienteilnehmenden in ihrem Alltag begleitet. Der Protokollbogen setzt sich aus vier senkrechten Spalten mit folgenden Kategorien zusammen: Uhrzeit, Ort(e), Handlungen/Tätigkeiten und sonstige Anmerkungen. Jeder Protokollbogen ist mit dem jeweiligen Namen der Untersuchungsteilnehmenden sowie dem Tag und Datum des Erhebungstages beschriftet. Für alle ausgewählten Erhebungstage werden Protokollbögen

---

[15]Die Anwendung des Verfahrens VAA zeigte, dass bereits Kinder im Alter von acht Jahren selbstständig die Protokollnotizen vornehmen konnten.

erstellt, auf denen in einstündigen Zeitintervallen[16] im Umfang von 24 h die Zeiträume (z. B. 12:00 Uhr bis 13:00 Uhr) abgebildet sind. Mit der rechts daneben liegenden Kategorie Ort(e) wird die räumliche Dimension erfasst.[17] Im nächsten Aufzeichnungsfeld „Handlungen/Tätigkeiten" werden die innerhalb der einstündigen Intervalle vollzogenen Alltagshandlungen notiert. Das Feld „sonstige Anmerkungen" eröffnet die Möglichkeit für persönliche Erläuterungen oder Bemerkungen, („heute war ich müde, aus dem Bett gequält"), für Nebentätigkeiten („während Waschmaschine einräumen telefoniert") oder sonstige freie Assoziationen.

Die Teilnehmenden erhalten für jede Erhebungswelle eine individuell erstellte Mappe mit den vorbereiteten Protokollbögen. Für Kinder, die zwischen zwei Orten (z. B. Kita und Zuhause oder zwei Wohnorten) pendeln, werden zwei Mappen angefertigt. Für die Protokollierung ihrer Handlungen wird auf erwachsene Bezugspersonen (Eltern, Erzieher*innen, Großeltern u. a.) zurückgegriffen. Um eine lückenlose Dokumentation zu gewährleisten und um für die Eltern den Organisations- und Logistikaufwand so gering wie möglich zu halten, verbleibt eine Mappe in der betreuenden Institution und die andere im Familienhaushalt. Kinder im schulfähigen Alter benötigen wie auch die Erwachsenen i. d. R. lediglich eine Untersuchungsmappe je Erhebungswelle. Die Protokollierung ihrer Alltagshandlungen erfolgt von ihnen persönlich bzw. bei jüngeren Schüler*innen mit Unterstützung eines Elternteils.

Die Einweisung in das Erhebungsinstrument findet im persönlichen Gespräch sowie in schriftlicher Form statt. Die schriftlichen Informationen werden der Protokollmappe beigefügt. Diese enthalten Angaben zum jeweiligen Erhebungszeitraum und zu den Protokollierungstagen, Unterweisungen zum Erhebungs-

---

[16]Die Zeitskala im Rahmen der quantitativen Verfahrensweise weist i. d. R. Zehn-Minuten-Schritte auf (vgl. Ehling et al. 2001, S. 430). Gegen eine solche Vorgehensweise wurde sich u. a. deshalb entschieden, weil die Anforderungen, die an die Studienteilnehmenden mit dem Einsatz eines Erhebungsverfahrens gestellt werden, von ihnen im Alltag realisierbar sein müssen und kein weiteres Belastungsmoment darstellen dürfen. Zwecks Vermeidung von Aufzeichnungslücken sowie mit Blick auf eine zeitlich langfristig gesicherte Studienteilnahme wurde auf eine Protokollierung der Alltagshandlungen in einstündigen Zeitintervallen zurückgegriffen. Erfahrungen zu einstündigen Erhebungszeiträumen liegen mit der Marienthal-Studie (Jahoda et al. 1975) vor.

[17]Der Ort der Handlungen wurde in der vorliegenden Studie mit erfragt, um kopräsente und soziale Zeiten der Familienmitglieder identifizieren zu können. Für Untersuchungen, die den Fokus auf die Analyse von räumlichem Handeln oder Raum-Zeit-Handeln legen, eignet sich das VAA ebenfalls.

bogen sowie zwei Protokoll-Musterbeispiele, eines für Erwachsene, eines für Kinder. Alle dokumentierenden Personen (darunter auch Erzieherinnen, die die Kinder betreuen) erhalten eine Einführung in das PEA und werden vor jeder Erhebungswelle mündlich und schriftlich darauf hingewiesen, dass die Dokumentation in zeitlicher Nähe zum Erlebten erfolgen sollte. In der Regel fand die Übergabe der Mappen vor und nach jeder Erhebungswelle bei den Befragten Zuhause statt. Das Erhebungsinstrument PEA wird idealtypisch innerhalb von einem Kalenderjahr zu allen vier Jahreszeiten, d. h. in vier Erhebungswellen, eingesetzt.

Aufbereitung und Auswertung des Datenmaterials

Die Aufbereitung der Daten erfolgt computergestützt, indem die handschriftlichen Aufzeichnungen in einer Tabelle gesammelt werden (die Programme Excel von Microsoft und alternativ Numbers von Apple bieten sich dafür an). Parallel erfolgt die Anonymisierung der Personendaten und anderer sensibler Informationen. Im ersten Auswertungsschritt werden aus dem Datenmaterial induktiv soziologische Kategorien (wie z. B. Erwerbsarbeit, Essen/Mahlzeiten, Schlaf, Arztbesuche, Krankheit usw.) gebildet.[18] Angewandt wird dieser Analyseschritt zunächst auf alle Daten der ersten Erhebungswelle, dann auf die zweite und fortlaufend weiter. Derart verfahrend, liegt nach der vierten und letzten Erhebungswelle, für alle vier Wellen das Datenmaterial nach soziologischen Kategorien strukturiert für jede Person vor. Um das Datenmaterial einer Feinanalyse unterziehen zu können, bedarf es abschließend der Zusammenführung des gesamten Datenmaterials. Diese erfolgt nunmehr entlang der soziologischen Kategorien. Verdeutlicht werden soll dieses an einem Beispiel: Alle Datensätze, die für die Kategorie Mahlzeiten/Essen vorliegen, werden für jede Person pro Erhebungswelle auf einem Datenblatt erfasst. Dadurch ist es möglich, nach jeder Erhebungswelle die Essenshandlungen von jeder Einzelperson sowie von allen Familienmitgliedern interaktiv zu rekonstruieren und Vergleiche zwischen den Erhebungswellen zu erstellen. Zum Beispiel lässt sich aus den Datensätzen der ersten drei Erhebungswellen ablesen, dass die gemeinsam im Familienverband

---

[18]Bei der Auswertung der VAA-Daten kann auf das Auswertungsverfahren für Problemzentrierte Interviews nach Witzel (1996) zurückgegriffen werden (vgl. auch Kühn und Witzel 2000). Diese Vorgehensweise bietet sich hinsichtlich der Vergleichbarkeit mit den Interviewdaten aus problemzentrierten Interviews an.

eingenommene Mahlzeit am frühen Abend lag, aber in der vierten Erhebungswelle zeigt sich, dass das Abendessen nicht mehr gemeinsam eingenommen wird. Diese ersten, rekonstruktiven empirischen Erkenntnisse, sollten in Form von Memos festgehalten werden. „Schriftliche Analyseprotokolle, die sich auf das Ausarbeiten der Theorie beziehen" (Strauss und Corbin 1996, S. 169), Memos genannt, begleiten den gesamten Auswertungsprozess: Sie sind Ergebnisse des induktiven und deduktiven Analysierens über Kategorien(-bildungen), Dimensionen, Einzelfällen, Fallvergleichen, empirisch-theoretischen Verknüpfungen, Zitaten und bieten Raum zur Selbstreflexion im Untersuchungs- und Auswertungsprozess.[19] Zusätzlich erweist sich das Anlegen von Ideendateien (vgl. Kühn und Witzel 2000) als hilfreich: In ihnen können offene Fragen und analytische Ideen festgehalten und stets herangezogen werden.

Die Datensätze der vier Wellen für jede ermittelte Kategorie in einer Übersicht zusammengefasst, können nun einer Feinanalyse unterzogen werden. Den übergeordneten Kategorien (z. B. Care/Fürsorge) gilt es nun gemäß Kühn und Witzel (2000) einzelne Handlungskodes zuzuordnen (z. B. Care/Fürsorge mit zu Bett bringen Kind(er)). Anhand dieser Kodes wird deutlich, welche Relevanzsetzungen von den Befragten erfolgen. Bei einem generationsgemischten Sample (wie bei einer Untersuchung von Familien gegeben) gilt es, bei der Kategorienbildung die unterschiedlichen generationalen Perspektiven der Erwachsenen und der Kinder zu berücksichtigen. Daraus resultiert, dass sich einige Kategorien ausschließlich auf die Perspektive der Kinder, andere auf die der Erwachsenen beziehen (Kategorien aus der vorliegenden Studie sind z. B. „Handlungen in Zeiten mit Erwachsenen – Kinderperspektive " oder „Handlungen in Zeiten mit Kindern – Erwachsenenperspektive"). Durch die Gesamtschau auf alle Daten bzw. auf die mit Datensätzen gefüllten Kategorien ist es nun möglich, Fallbeschreibungen nach der qualitativen Inhaltsanalyse (vgl. Mayring 1993) zu erstellen. Mittels dieser fast detektivisch anmutenden Arbeit werden per Rekonstruktion aller Alltagshandlungen einer Person in Verbindung mit den Handlungen anderer Personen (Familienmitglieder), Schritt für Schritt sowohl individuelle als auch kollektive Handlungsmuster in zeitlicher Perspektive identifizierbar. Da der Analyseweg zu den Ergebnissen also zunächst

---

[19]Auch die auf das Untersuchungsinteresse bezogenen Beobachtungen und Erfahrungen, die während der Feldbesuchen durch die Mappenübergabe gemacht werden, sollten notiert und die Auswertung einbezogen werden.

über die Betrachtung der Aufzeichnungen von einer Person führt, wird innerhalb dieses ersten Auswertungsprozesses der individuelle Fall zum Einzelfall. Aus der Gesamtschau der Einzelfälle einer Familie können mittels Fokus auf die Verwobenheit und Verschränkungen der Alltagshandlungen aller Akteur*innen, Rückschlüsse über die Handlungsmuster bezogen auf die alltägliche Lebensführung von Familie gezogen werden.

Chancen und Begrenzungen des VAA

Vor dem empirischen Einsatz des VAA gilt es, Chancen wie auch Begrenzungen des Verfahrens im Kontext des jeweiligen Untersuchungsinteresses zu reflektieren. Folgende Erkenntnisse über die Einsatzmöglichkeiten, die Untersuchungsgegenstände und Strukturkategorien liegen vor. Eine deutliche Chance des VAA liegt in dem Untersuchungsgegenstand selbst begründet, nämlich der Möglichkeit individuelle und kollektive Alltagshandlungen aus qualitativer Zeitforschungsperspektive zu erfassen. Mit dem VAA sind Untersuchungen der individuellen Akteur*innenebene, in Bezug auf verschiedene soziale Bedingungsfaktoren bzw. strukturelle Handlungsbereiche (wie Erwerbsarbeit, Haus- und Sorgearbeit, Schule etc.) möglich. Mit dem VAA eröffnet sich die Chance, Analysen der kollektiven Akteur*innenebene, wie z. B. Familien, Lebensgemeinschaften, Organisationsgruppen, ebenfalls in Bezug auf strukturelle Handlungsbereiche etc., zu untersuchen. Durch die Verschränkung individueller zu kollektiven Handlungsmustern ist die Analyse alltäglicher Lebensführung von Familien möglich. Das VAA ermöglicht Erkenntnisgewinne über institutionalisierte, komplexe Handlungs-Modi alltäglicher Lebensführung. Darüber hinaus öffnet es Dimensionierungen von Lebensführung zu erfassen und abzubilden. Aus zeitlicher Dimensionierung kann untersucht werden, wie, wann und mit wem die einzelnen Mitglieder welchen Handlungen nachgehen, wie ihre Alltagshandlungen von Routinen und Zeitinstitutionen geprägt sind, wann Familienzeiten stattfinden und vieles mehr. Darüber hinaus bietet sich das Verfahren dafür an, generationale Perspektiven zu berücksichtigen und sowohl die Alltagshandlungen von Erwachsenen, als auch die von Kindern und Jugendlichen getrennt sowie in Verbindung miteinander in den Blick zu nehmen. Für die folgenden Untersuchungsgegenstände ist der Einsatz des VAA ebenfalls möglich: Kollektive Alltagshandlungen im Kontext von Organisationen, qualitative Erforschungen zu Zeit-Raum-Handeln im Alltag, jahreszeitbedingtes Alltagshandeln, Langzeituntersuchungen bezogen auf die Prozesse von Alltagshandlungen u. v. m. Doch es bietet nicht nur die Chance einer differenzierten Analyse von Handlungsdimensionen alltäglicher Lebensführung, sondern auch von sozialen Strukturkategorien wie z. B. Klasse/Milieu, Geschlecht, Ethnie, Generation(en), Alter, Kultur, Nord-Süd/Ost-West, Stadt/Land u. a.m.[20] Das VAA bietet damit zahlreiche Anknüpfungspunkte z. B. mit dem Konzept und der Methode Intersektionalität (Winker und Degele 2009).

Der in der VAA erfolgte Fokus auf die Erhebung von Haupthandlungen und nicht explizit auf Nebenhandlungen (wie im standardisierten quantitativen Verfahren) ist aus forschungspragmatischer Perspektive zu diskutieren. Ohne Zweifel ginge von der systematischen Erhebung von Nebentätigkeiten, für die im VAA das Feld „sonstige Anmerkungen" von den Studienteilnehmenden genutzt werden kann, ein erkenntnistheoretischer Mehrwert aus.[21] Andererseits würde es zu einem erhöhten Belastungsaufwand der Befragten führen, weshalb es abzuwägen gilt, ob durch weitere Anforderungen eine kontinuierliche Studienteilnahme über einen langen Zeitraum weiterhin gewährleistet wäre.

Das VAA beinhaltet die Chance große Untersuchungsgruppen gleichzeitig zu befragen, da die Forscher*innen sich nicht zum gleichen Zeitpunkt an verschiedenen Orten aufhalten müssen. Außerdem sind die Forschenden nicht im Forschungsfeld präsent, wodurch die Effekte sozialer Erwünschtheit minimiert werden. Die lange Erhebungszeitdauer von einem Jahr birgt Chancen und Hindernisse gleichermaßen. Auf der einen Seite können aufgrund der reichhaltigen Datenlage (jahreszeitliche) Schwankungen, Urlaubs- und Ferienzeiten sowie Wandlungsprozesse im Alltagsleben der Untersuchungsteilnehmenden (z. B. Geburten, Trennungen) erfasst werden. Auf der anderen Seite bindet die Erhebungszeit Forschungsressourcen, und der Erfolg der Studie steht in starker Abhängigkeit zur verbindlichen Teilnahmebereitschaft der an der Untersuchung Teilnehmenden. Vor Einsatz vom VAA sollte deshalb sichergestellt sein, dass diese willens sind, an einer langfristigen und durchaus zeitintensiven Befragung teilzunehmen. Die Durchführung der Protokollierung stellt, außer einer gewissen Aufzeichnungsdisziplin, keine erhöhten Anforderungen an die Teilnehmenden. Mit dem Erhebungsinstrument PEA, als ein Kernelement des Verfahrens zur

---

[20]Siehe weitere Differenzierungsdimensionen bei Lutz und Wennig (2001, S. 20).

[21]Z.B. „Während Waschmaschine einräumen, telefoniert" oder „gerade stressig, Hetze zwischen Schreibtisch und Kindern hin und her." Unter der Kategorie „sonstige Anmerkungen" Nebentätigkeiten, Emotionen etc. zu notieren, ist für die Teilnehmenden optional.

Analyse von Alltagshandlungen (VAA), liegt nun ein methodisches Werkzeug vor, das die Erfassung und Analyse alltäglicher Handlungen von Erwachsenen, Jugendlichen und Kindern ermöglicht.

Zusammenfassung

Mit dem hier dargestellten Verfahren zur Analyse von Alltagshandlungen erfolgt ein Beitrag zur Fortschreibung und Weiterentwicklung von Selbstdokumentationsverfahren subjektwissenschaftlich-ethnographisch verfahrender Alltags- und Feldforschung. Darüber hinaus können vom VAA Impulse zur Widerbelebung des Methodendiskurses von Selbstdokumentationsmethoden, Log- und Tagebüchern aus handlungs- und zeitsoziologischer Perspektive ausgehen. Das VAA dient der mikrosoziologischen subjektwissenschaftlichen Analyse der Alltagshandlungen von Akteur*innen. Das Verfahren fokussiert auf die Erfassung und Analyse dessen, was Akteur*innen tun, welche Handlungen von ihnen zu welcher Tageszeit vollzogen werden. Das VAA widmet sich Alltagshandlungen im Max Weberschen Sinne: Um diese deutend zu verstehen und zu erklären (Weber 1980), indem das, was Menschen täglich tun, ihre Routinen und Handlungsmuster aus zeitlicher Perspektive rekonstruiert werden. So ermöglicht das Verfahren, unterschiedliche Strukturdimensionen von Alltagshandlungen – und somit von Lebensführung – zu erfassen und abzubilden. Entwickelt wurde das VAA, um Erkenntnisse über institutionalisierte, komplexe Handlungs-Modi der alltäglichen Lebensführung von Familien zu gewinnen. Das VAA lässt sich mit anderen qualitativen Methoden hervorragend triangulieren, wodurch im Sinne der Grounded Theory (Strauss und Corbin 1996) eine dichte und detaillierte Beschreibung des Untersuchungsgegenstands erfolgen kann.

Zusammenfassend lässt sich festhalten, dass es sich bei dem VAA um ein Forschungsinstrument handelt, das sich durch Anwendungsfreundlichkeit für die Forschenden und die Untersuchungsteilnehmenden auszeichnet. Herausforderungen liegen aus der Perspektive der Forschenden in erster Linie im Bereich der Auswertung umfassender Datenmengen sowie der langen Erhebungsphase. Zudem sind sie gefordert Strategien zu entwickeln, um die Studienteilnehmenden langfristig an die Studie zu binden. Insgesamt weist das Verfahren ausreichend Flexibilität auf, um einer Modifizierung für unterschiedliche Forschungsanliegen Stand zu halten. Abschließend sei noch angemerkt, dass das Instrument sich in der Forschungs- und Anwendungspraxis hinsichtlich der Erfassung des Untersuchungsgegenstandes und -interesses bewährt hat. Das Verfahren zur Analyse von Alltagshandlungen eröffnet damit einen weiteren methodischen Zugang zur qualitativen Erforschung der Alltagshandlungen sozialer Akteur*innen.

Literatur

Adam B (1990) Time and Social Theory. Temple University Press, Philadelphia
Alleweldt E, Röcke A, Steinbicker J (Hrsg) (2016) Lebensführung heute. Klasse, Bildung, Individualität. Beltz Juventa, Weinheim, Basel
Arbeitsgruppe Bielefelder Soziologen (1976) Alltagswissen, Interaktion und gesellschaftliche Wirklichkeit – Teil 2 – Ethnotheorie und Ethnographie des Sprechens. Rowohlt, Reinbek
Behnke C, Meuser M (2003) Modernisierte Geschlechterverhältnisse? Entgrenzung von Beruf und Familie bei Doppelkarrierepaaren. In: Gottschall K, Voß GG (Hrsg) Entgrenzung von Arbeit und Leben: zum Wandel der Beziehung von Erwerbstätigkeit und Privatsphäre im Alltag. Hampp, München, S 285–306
Bergmann JR (2004) Ethnomethodologie. In: Flick U, Kardorff E v, Steinke I (Hg) Qualitative Forschung. Ein Handbuch. 8. Aufl, Rowohlt, Reinbek bei Hamburg, S 118–135
Birken T (2015) Avantgarde im Kreuzfeuer? Vereinbarkeitsarrangements weiblicher Führungskräfte. In: Kratzer N, Menz W, Pangert B (2015) Work-Life-Balance – eine Frage der Leistungspolitik. Analysen und Gestaltungsansätze. Springer VS, Wiesbaden, S 123–140
Blass W (1980) Zeitbudgetforschung. Eine kritische Einführung in Grundlagen und Methoden. Campus, Frankfurt a. M.
BMFSFJ (2012) Zeit für Familie. Familienzeitpolitik als Chance einer nachhaltigen Familienpolitik. Achter Familienbericht. BMFSFJ, Berlin
Breidenstein G, Hirschauer S, Kalthoff H, Nieswand B (2013) Ethnographie: die Praxis der Feldforschung. UTB, Konstanz
Bundeszentrale für politische Bildung (Hrsg) (2004) Aus Politik und Zeitgeschichte (APuZ), 31–32/2004
Bundeszentrale für politische Bildung (Hrsg) (2007) Entgrenzung von Arbeit und Leben. Aus Politik und Zeitgeschichte (APuZ), 34/2007, Beilage Wochenzeitung. Das Parlament
Dunckel H (1999) Leitfaden zur Kontrastiven Aufgabenanalyse (KABA). In: Dunckel H (Hrsg) Handbuch psychologischer Arbeitsanalyseverfahren. Verlag der Fachvereine, Zürich, S 231–254
Durkheim E (1998) [1912] Die elementaren Formen des religiösen Lebens. 2. Aufl, Suhrkamp, Frankfurt am Main
Egbringhoff J (2007) Ständig selbst: eine Untersuchung der alltäglichen Lebensführung von Ein-Personen-Selbständigen. Hampp, München
Ehling M (1991) Formen der Tagebuchmethode zur Erhebung von Zeitbudgets. In: Tietze W, Rossbach HG (Hrsg) Mediennutzung und Zeitbudget. Ansätze, Methoden, Probleme. Deutscher Universitätsverlag, Wiesbaden, S 33–48
Ehling M, Holz E, Kahle I (2001) Erhebungsdesign der Zeitbudgeterhebung 2001/2002. In: Wirtschaft und Statistik: WISTA. Statistisches Bundesamt, Wiesbaden, 6, S 427–436
Ehling M, Schäfer D (1988) Internationale Erfahrungen mit Zeitbudgeterhebungen im Rahmen der amtlichen Statistik. In: Wirtschaft und Statistik: WISTA, Statistisches Bundesamt, Wiesbaden, 7, S 451–461
Eichholz D, Kunz AM (2012) „My Campus Karlsruhe" – Zur Rekonstruktion studentischer Raumnutzungsmuster mittels Logbuch-Verfahren. In: Schröteler-von Brandt H, Coelen T, Zeising A, Ziesche A (Hrsg) Raum für Bildung. Ästhetik und Architektur von Lern- und Lebensorten. Transcript, Bielefeld, S 61–71
Elias N (1982) Über die Zeit. In: Merkur, Jg 36, H 9 und 10, S 841–856 und S 998–1016

Elias N (Hrsg Schröter M) (2004) Über die Zeit. Frankfurt a. M, Suhrkamp
Esser H (1991) Die Rationalität des Alltagshandelns. Eine Rekonstruktion der Handlungstheorie von Alfred Schütz. In: Zeitschrift für Soziologie, Jg 20, H 6, Dezember 1991, S 430–445
Flick U (1991) Alltagswissen über Gesundheit und Krankheit. Subjektive Theorien und soziale Repräsentationen. Asanger, Heidelberg
Flick U (2002) Qualitative Sozialforschung. Eine Einführung. 6. Aufl. Rowohlt, Reinbek
Flick U, Kardorff E von, Steinke I (Hg) (2004) Qualitative Forschung. Ein Handbuch. 3. Aufl. Rowohlt, Reinbek
Fuhs B (2000) Qualitative Interviews mit Kindern. Überlegungen zu einer schwierigen Methode. In: Heinzel F (Hrsg) Methoden der Kindheitsforschung. Ein Überblick über Forschungszugänge zur kindlichen Perspektive. Juventa, Weinheim, S 87–103
Giddens A (1988): Die Konstitution der Gesellschaft. Grundzüge einer Theorie der Strukturierung. Campus, Frankfurt a M
Gottschall K, Voß GG (Hrsg) (2003) Entgrenzung von Arbeit und Leben: zum Wandel der Beziehung von Erwerbsarbeit und Privatsphäre im Alltag. Hampp, München
Hagen-Demszky A von der (2006) Familiale Bildungswelten. Theoretische Perspektiven und empirische Explorationen. Deutsches Jugendinstitut, München
Hägerstrand T (1975) Space, Time and Human Conditions. In: Karlqvist A, Snickars F (Hrsg) Dynamic Allocation of Urban Space. Saxon House, Lexington, S 3–14
Heitkötter M, Jurczyk K, Lange A, Maier-Gräwe U (Hrsg) (2009) Zeit für Beziehungen? Zeit und Zeitpolitik für Familien. Budrich, Opladen
Helfferich C (2004) Die Qualität qualitativer Daten. Manual für die Durchführung qualitativer Interviews. VS, Wiesbaden
Hewener V (2004) Geschlechtsspezifische Unterschiede im Umgang mit der Zeit. In: Bundeszentrale für politische Bildung. Aus Politik und Zeitgeschichte (APuZ), 31–32/2004:26–32
Hielscher V (2006) Verflüssigte Rhythmen. Flexible Arbeitszeitstrukturen und soziale Integration. Edition sigma, Berlin
Hopf C (2004) Qualitative Interviews – ein Überblick. In: Flick U, Kardorff E v, Steinke I (Hg) Qualitative Forschung. Ein Handbuch. Rowohlt, Reinbek, S 349–360
Hungerland B (2002) Wie viel Zeit für´s Kind? Zur gesellschaftlichen Produktion generationaler Ordnung durch elterliche Zeitinvestition. Dissertation, Universität Wuppertal
Jahoda Mm Lzarsfeld PF, Zeisel H (1975) Die Arbeitslosen von Marienthal: ein soziographischer Versuch über die Wirkungen langdauernder Arbeitslosigkeit. Suhrkamp, Frankfurt a M
Janczyk S (2009) Arbeit und Leben: eine spannungsreiche Ko-Konstitution; zur Revision zeitgenössischer Konzepte der Arbeitsforschung. Westfälisches Dampfboot, Münster
Jürgens K (2001) Familiale Lebensführung. In: Voß GG, Weihrich M (Hrsg) Tagaus tagein. Neue Beiträge zur Soziologie alltäglicher Lebensführung. Hampp, München, S 33–60
Jürgens K (2003) Zeithandeln – eine neue Kategorie der Arbeitssoziologie. In: Gottschall K, Voß GG (Hrsg) Entgrenzung von Arbeit und Leben. Zum Wandel der Beziehung von Erwerbstätigkeit und Privatssphäre im Alltag. Hampp, München, S 37–58
Jurczyk K (1997) Ein subjektorientierter Blick auf die „Zeit". Wider unbrauchbare Dualismen. In: Voß GG, Pongratz HJ (Hrsg) Subjektorientierte Soziologie. Leske und Budrich, Opladen, S 169–182

Jurczyk K (2015) Zeit für Care: Fürsorgliche Praxis in „atmenden Lebensverläufen". In: Hoffmann R, Bogedan C (Hrsg) Arbeit der Zukunft. Campus, Frankfurt a M, S 260–288

Jurczyk K, Lange A (2005) ArbeitskraftunternehmerInnen und Familie. Herausforderungen an das Management. In: Forum Wissenschaft, 1/2005, S 15–19

Jurczyk K, Lange A (2006) Familienzeit – ein wertvolles und prekäres Gut. In: DJI Bulletin 74, Heft 1, S 18–21

Jurczyk K, Lange A, Pzymenderski P (2005) Zwiespältige Entgrenzungen: Chancen und Risiken neuer Konstellationen zwischen Familien- und Erwerbstätigkeit. In: Mischau A, Oechsle M (Hrsg) Arbeitszeit – Familienzeit – Lebenszeit: Verlieren wir die Balance? VS, Wiesbaden, S 13–33

Jurczyk K, Schier M, Szymenderski P, Lange A, Voß GG (2009) Entgrenzte Arbeit – Entgrenzte Familie. Grenzmanagement im Alltag als neue Herausforderung. Edition sigma, Berlin

Kleemann F (2005) Die Wirklichkeit der Teleheimarbeit: eine arbeitssoziologische Untersuchung. Edition sigma, Berlin

Klenner C, Pfahl S (2005) Stabilität und Flexibilität. Ungleichmäßige Arbeitsmuster und familiale Arrangements. In: Seifert H (Hrgs) Flexible Zeiten in der Arbeitswelt. Campus, Frankfurt a M, S 244–259

Klenner C, Pfahl S (2009) Jenseits von Zeitnot und Karriereverzicht – Wege aus dem Arbeitszeitdilemma. In: Heitkötter M, Jurczyk K, Lange A, Maier-Gräwe U (Hrsg): Zeit für Beziehungen? Zeit und Zeitpolitik für Familien. Budrich, Opladen, S 259–290

Kratzer N (2003) Arbeitskraft in Entgrenzung. Grenzenlose Anforderungen, erweiterte Spielräume, begrenzte Ressourcen. Edition sigma, Berlin

Kratzer N (2013) Entgrenzung. In: Hirsch-Kreinsen H, Minssen H (Hrsg) Lexikon der Arbeits- und Industriesoziologie. Edition sigma, Berlin, S 186–191

Kratzer N, Boes A, Marrs K, Sauer D (2004) Entgrenzung von Unternehmen und Arbeit – Grenzen der Entgrenzung. In: Beck U, Lau C (Hrsg) Entgrenzung und Entscheidung – Was ist neu an der Theorie reflexiver Modernisierung? Suhrkamp, Frankfurt a M, S 329–359

Kratzer N, Lange A (2006) Entgrenzung von Arbeit und Leben: Verschiebung, Pluralisierung, Verschränkung. In: Dunkel W, Sauer D (Hrsg) Von der Allgegenwart der verschwindenden Arbeit. Neue Herausforderungen für die Arbeitsforschung. Edition sigma, Berlin, S 171–202

Krüger H, Born C (2000) Vom patriarchalen Diktat zur Aushandlung – Facetten des Wandels der Geschlechterrollen im familialen Generationenverbund. In: Kohli M, Szydlik M (Hg) Generationen in Familie und Gesellschaft. Budrich, Opladen, S 203–221

Kudera W (2000) Lebenslauf, Biographie und Lebensführung. In: Kudera W, Voß GG (Hrsg) Lebensführung und Gesellschaft: Beiträge zu Konzept und Empirie alltäglicher Lebensführung. VS, Wiesbaden, S 109–130

Kudera W, Voß GG (Hrsg) (2000) Lebensführung und Gesellschaft: Beiträge zu Konzept und Empirie alltäglicher Lebensführung. VS, Wiesbaden

Kühm T, Witzel A (2000) Der Gebrauch einer Textdatenbank im Auswertungsprozess problemzentrierter Interviews. Forum Qualitative Sozialforschung, 1(3), DOI: http://dx.doi.org/https://doi.org/10.17169/fqs-1.3.1035

Kunz AM (2015) Log- und Tagebücher als Erhebungsmethode in ethnographischen Forschungsdesigns. In: Hitzler R, Gothe M (Hrsg) Ethnographische Erkundungen. Methodische Aspekte aktueller Forschungsprojekte. Springer VS, Wiesbaden, S 141–161

Lamnek S (1988) Qualitative Sozialforschung. Bd 1. Methodologie. Verlags Union, München

Lamnek S (1989) Qualitative Sozialforschung. Bd 2. Methoden und Techniken. Verlags Union, München

Lange A (2011) Gesellschaftliche Bedingungen der „Vereinbarkeit" – soziologische Perspektiven unter besonderer Berücksichtigung der Konsequenzen mangelnder gesellschaftlicher Unterstützung. In: Becker-Stoll F, Klös HP, Rainer H, Thüsing G (Hrsg) Expertisen zum Achten Familienbericht „Zeit für Familie". Ifo Institut, München, S 49–88

Lange A, Heitkötter M (2006) DJI Bulletin 74 Plus. Zeitpolitik für Familien. Ein kleiner Kompass im Meer der Zeitbegriffe. In: DJI Bulletin 74, 1/2006:1–4

Ludwig, I, Schlevogt V, Klammer U, Gerhard U (2002) Managerinnen des Alltags. Strategien erwerbstätiger Mütter in Ost- und Westdeutschland. Edition sigma, Berlin

Lüders C, Meuser M (1997) Deutungsmusteranalyse. In: Hitzler R, Honer A (Hg) Sozialwissenschaftliche Hermeneutik. Leske, Budrich, Opladen, S 57–79

Lutz H, Wenning N (2001) Differenz über Differenz – Einführung in die Debatten. In: Lutz H, Wenning N (Hg) Unterschiedlich verschieden. Differenz in der Erziehungswissenschaft. Leske, Budrich, Opladen, S 11–24

Maurer A (1992) Das Zeitgerüst der Arbeitswelt: Arbeitstag – Arbeitswoche – Arbeitsjahr. In: Zeitschrift für Arbeitsforschung, Arbeitsgestaltung und Arbeitspolitik. J 1, H 3:282–298

Mayring P (1993) Qualitative Inhaltsanalyse: Grundlagen und Techniken. Dt. Studien-Verlag, Weinheim

Mayring P (2002) Einführung in die qualitative Sozialforschung. 5. Aufl. Beltz, Weinheim

Menz W (2013) Entgrenzte Arbeit(sverhältnisse). Zum Wandel des Verhältnisses von Arbeit und Leben. In: Wagner U (Hrsg) Familienleben: Entgrenzt und vernetzt?! Kessler Druck u Medien, Koblingen, S 23–38

Minssen H (Hrsg) (2000) Begrenzte Entgrenzung – Wandlungen von Organisation und Arbeit. Edition sigma, Berlin

Morgenroth O (2008) Zeit und Handeln. Psychologie der Zeitbewältigung. Kohlhammer, Stuttgart

Muri G (2004) Pause! Zeitordnung und Auszeiten aus alltagskultureller Sicht. Campus, Frankfurt a M

Parker D, Thrift N (1980) Putting Time in its Place. In: Carlstein T, Parker D, Thrift N (Hrsg) Timing Space and Spacing Time. Edward Arnold, London, S 119–129

Projektgruppe „Alltägliche Lebensführung" (1995) (Hrsg) Alltägliche Lebensführung. Arrangements zwischen Traditionalität und Modernisierung. Leske u Budrich, Opladen

Resch M (1999a) Verfahren zur Analyse von Arbeit im Haushalt (AVAH). In: Dunckel H (Hrsg) Handbuch psychologischer Arbeitsanalyseverfahren. Verlag der Fachvereine, Zürich, S 55–81

Resch M (1999b) Arbeitsanalyse im Haushalt. Erhebung und Bewertung von Tätigkeiten außerhalb der Erwerbsarbeit mit dem AVAH-Verfahren. Verlag der Fachvereine, Zürich

Rindersprachner JP (1987) Am Ende der Woche. Die soziale und kulturelle Bedeutung des Wochenendes. Verlag Neue Gesellschaft, Bonn

Schneider, Wolfgang Ludwig (2008): Grundlagen der soziologischen Theorie. Band 1. VS: Wiesbaden.

Schöneck NM (2009) Zeiterleben und Zeithandeln Erwerbstätiger. Eine methodenintegrative Studie. VS, Wiesbaden

Schütz A (1971) Gesammelte Aufsätze I. Das Problem der sozialen Wirklichkeit. Nijhoff, Den Haag

Schütz A (1972) Gesammelte Aufsätze. Bd 2: Studien zur soziologischen Theorie. Nijhoff, Den Haag

Schweitzer R v, Ehling M, Schäfer D (1990) Zeitbudgeterhebungen. Ziele, Methoden und neue Konzepte. Metzler-Poeschel, Stuttgart

Seel NM, Hanke U (2015) Erziehungswissenschaft. Lehrbuch für Bachelor-, Master- und Lehramtsstudierende. Springer VS, Wiesbaden

Statistisches Bundesamt (2015) Wie die Zeit vergeht. Ergebnisse zur Zeitverwendung in Deutschland 2012/2013. Statistisches Bundesamt, Wiesbaden

Strauss A, Corbin J (1996) Grounded Theory: Grundlagen Qualitativer Sozialforschung. Psychologie Union, Weinheim

Streit A v (2011) Entgrenzter Alltag – Arbeiten ohne Grenzen?: das Internet und die raumzeitlichen Organisationsstrategien von Wissensarbeitern. Transcript, Bielefeld

Tietze W, Rossbach HG (Hrsg) (1991) Mediennutzung und Zeitbudget. Ansätze, Methoden, Probleme. Dtsch. Universitäts-Verlag, Wiesbaden

Voß GG (1991) Lebensführung als Arbeit. Über die Autonomie der Person im Alltag der Gesellschaft. Enke, Stuttgart

Voß, GG (1995) Alltägliche Lebensführung. Entwicklung und Eckpunkte des theoretischen Konzepts. In: Projektgruppe „Alltägliche Lebensführung" (Hrsg) Alltägliche Lebensführung. Arrangements zwischen Traditionalität und Modernisierung. Leske u Budrich, Opladen, S 23–43

Voß G (2000) Das Ende der Teilung von „Arbeit und Leben"? An der Schwelle zu einem neuen gesellschaftlichen Verhältnis von Betriebs- und Lebensführung. In: Kudera W, Voß GG (Hrsg) Lebensführung und Gesellschaft. Leske u Budrich, Opladen, S 309–342

Voß GG (2001) Der eigene und der fremde Alltag. In: Voß GG, Weihrich M. (Hrsg): tagaus – tagein. Neue Beiträge zur Soziologie Alltäglicher Lebensführung. Hampp, München, S 203–217

Voß GG, Pongratz H (1998) Der Arbeitskraftunternehmer. Eine neue Grundform der „Ware Arbeitskraft"? Kölner Zeitschrift für Soziologie und Sozialpsychologie 50(1):131–158

Voß GG, Weihrich M (Hrsg) (2001) Tagaus – tagein. Neue Beiträge zur Soziologie Alltäglicher Lebensführung, Arbeit und Leben im Umbruch. Hampp, München

Weber M (1980) [1922]Wirtschaft und Gesellschaft. Grundrift der verstehenden Soziologie. 5. Aufl. Mohr, Tübingen

Weber M (1985) Über einige Kategorien der verstehenden Soziologie. In: Weber M Gesammelte Aufsätze zur Wissenschaftslehre. 6. Aufl. Mohr, Tübingen, S 427–474

Wetterer A (2003) Rhetorische Modernisierung: Das Verschwinden der Ungleichheit aus dem zeitgenössischen Differenzwissen. In: Knapp GA, Wetterer A (Hg) Achsen der Differenz. Gesellschaftstheorie und feministische Kritik II. Westfälisches Dampfboot, Münster

Weihrich M (Hrsg) (2002) Tag für Tag: Alltag als Problem – Lebensführung als Lösung? Hampp, München

Wendorff R (1993) Tag und Woche, Monat und Jahr. Eine Kulturgeschichte des Kalenders. Westdeutscher Verlag, Opladen

Wilz G, Brähler E (Hrsg) (1997) Tagebücher in Therapie und Forschung. Ein anwendungsorientierter Leitfaden. Hogrefe, Göttingen

Winker G, Carstensen T (2004) Flexible Arbeit – bewegliche Geschlechterarrangements. In: Kahlert H, Kajatin C (Hg) Arbeit und Vernetzung im Informationszeitalter: wie neue Technologien die Geschlechterverhältnisse verändern. Campus, Frankfurt a M, S 167–186

Winker, G./Degele, N. (2009): Intersektionalität. Zur Analyse sozialer Ungleichheiten. Bielefeld: transcript Verlag.

Witzel A (1985) Das problemzentrierte Interview. In: Jüttemann G (Hg) Qualitative Forschung in der Psychologie. Grundfragen, Verfahrensweisen, Anwendungsfelder. Beltz, Weinheim

Witzel A (1996) Auswertung problemzentrierter Interviews: Grundlagen und Erfahrungen. In: Strobl R, Böttger A (Hrsg) Wahre Geschichten? Zu Theorie und Praxis qualitativer Interviews. Nomos, Baden-Baden, S 49–76

Witzel A (2006) Grundzüge des problemzentrierten Interviews. Kommunikationsstrategien 1– 8. Unveröffentlicht

Wörmer, S (2016) Berufliche Mobilität im Alltag. Praktiken und Formen alltäglicher Lebensführung. Lit-Verlag, Berlin

Zartler U, Marhali A, Starkbaum J, Richter R (2009) Familien in Nahaufnahme. Eltern und ihre Kinder im städtischen und ländlichen Raum. Bundesministerium für Wirtschaft, Familie und Jugend, Wien

Zeiher HJ (1996) Konkretes Leben, Raum-Zeit und Gesellschaft. Ein handlungsorientierter Ansatz zur Kindheitsforschung. In: Honig MS, Leu HR, Nissen U (Hrsg) Kinder und Kindheit. Soziokulturelle Muster – sozialisationstheoretische Perspektiven. Juventa, Weinheim, S 157–173

Zeiher H (2017) Zeit und alltägliche Lebensführung. Ein Prozessmodell zur Erforschung der Handlungsgenese. Beltz Juventa, Weinheim, Basel

Zeiher H, Zeiher H (1993) Organisation von Raum und Zeit im Kinderalltag. In: Markefka, M, Nauck B (Hrsg) Handbuch der Kindheitsforschung. Luchterhand, Neuwied, S 389–401

Kommunikative Zeit beobachten. Methodisch-methodologische Implikationen des kommunikativen Konstruktivismus

Ekkehard Coenen

> **Abstract**
>
> This article traces how subject-centred action theories provide a suitable basis for exploring the temporality of action and the subjective experience of time. In comparison, they often lack, among other things, a sense for the significance of materiality within a socio-temporal order. This blind spot can be opened up by communicative constructivism because in its social-theoretical assumptions the subject is decentered and the objections play an essential role. Interactions are not only based on the (linguistic) exchange of subjects (isolated from each other) but also on materiality. Time orders that become socially effective are thus linked not only to a 'communicated' but above all to a 'communicative time'. Consequently, this has an impact on the methodological-methodological level. On the one hand, the focus is on the communicative practice of research and the sequentiality that underlies the constitution of the researching subject and the field. On the other hand, the communicative constructivism shows that researchers can only access the time in the field through objectivations, and thus, the researcher needs to reflect the quality of the data. The focus is now also on methods for collecting data that are not heading to the subjective experience of time, but instead allow the communicative action in situ in its temporality to be observed in different

---

E. Coenen (✉)
Bauhaus-Universität Weimar, Weimar, Deutschland
E-Mail: ekkehard.coenen@uni-weimar.de

ways: audiovisual recordings, ethnographic approaches and participating observations or observing participation and artefact analyses.

Zusammenfassung

Dieser Beitrag zeichnet nach, wie subjektzentrierte Handlungstheorien zwar eine geeignete Grundlage bilden, um die Temporalität von Handlungsvollzügen und die subjektive Erfahrung von Zeit (qualitativ) zu erforschen. Demgegenüber fehlt ihnen jedoch unter anderem oftmals ein Sensus für die Bedeutung der Materialität innerhalb einer soziotemporalen Ordnung. Dieser blinde Fleck kann durch den kommunikativen Konstruktivismus erschlossen werden; und dies gerade weil in dessen sozialtheoretischen Annahmen das Subjekt dezentriert wird und den Objektivationen eine gewichtige Rolle zukommt. Interaktionen beruhen damit nicht nur auf dem (sprachlichen) Austausch von (voneinander isolierten) Subjekten, sondern sind qua Performativität fest mit der Materialität verbunden. Zeitordnungen, die sozial wirksam werden, sind somit nicht nur an eine ‚kommunizierte', sondern vor allem auch an eine ‚kommunikative Zeit' geknüpft. Dies hat Auswirkungen auf methodologisch-methodischer Ebene: Zum einen gerät die kommunikative Praxis des Forschens und die Sequenzialität in den Mittelpunkt, die der Konstitution des forschenden Subjekts und dem Feld zugrunde liegen. Zum anderen verdeutlicht der kommunikative Konstruktivismus, dass Forschende nur mittels Objektivationen auf die Zeit im Feld zugreifen können und somit die Qualität der Daten reflektiert werden muss. Im Vordergrund stehen nun auch Methoden zur Erhebung von Daten, die eben nicht auf das subjektive Zeiterleben zielen, sondern stattdessen das kommunikative Handeln in situ in seiner Zeitlichkeit unterschiedlich beobachtbar werden lassen: audiovisuelle Aufzeichnungen, ethnographische Vorgehensweisen und teilnehmende Beobachtungen bzw. beobachtende Teilnahmen sowie Artefaktanalysen.

Keywords

Communicative constructivism · Communicative time · Qualitative methods · Action theory · Methodology

Schlüsselwörter

Kommunikativer Konstruktivismus · kommunikative Zeit · qualitative Methoden · Handlungstheorie · Methodologie

Einleitung

Zeitsoziologische Feldforschung zeichnet sich dadurch aus, dass sie die Forscher*innen kontinuierlich mit der von Elias (1988, S. 41) so bezeichneten „Wann-Frage" konfrontiert. Um die soziotemporale Ordnung eines Feldes beobachten, analysieren und darstellen zu können, geht es darum, „Ereignisse innerhalb eines kontinuierlichen Flusses von Ereignissen festzulegen, Meilensteine zu fixieren, die relative Anfänge und relative Enden innerhalb des Flusses anzeigen, eine bestimmte Spanne von einer anderen abzuheben oder beide in Bezug auf ihre Länge durch das, was wir ihre ‚Dauer' nennen, zu vergleichen, und ähnliches mehr." (Ebd.) Was als Ereignis, ‚Meilenstein' und Dauer von den Forschenden wahrgenommen wird, ist dabei hochgradig abhängig von den Begriffen und den dahinterstehenden sozialtheoretischen Überzeugungen, die an das Feld herangetragen werden und es dadurch überhaupt erst konstituieren sowie beobachtbar werden lassen.

Jede Beobachtung der soziotemporalen Ordnung basiert auf theoretischen Vorannahmen. Die soziologische Zeitforschung benötigt deshalb handhabbare und klar konturierte Begriffe, um temporale Phänomene sowohl beschreiben als auch – was viel grundlegender ist – überhaupt erst voneinander differenzieren zu können. Zu denken ist hierbei an Termini, wie ‚Zeitinstitution' (vgl. Rinderspacher 1987), ‚performative Zeit' (vgl. Davis 2010), ‚Sequenzialität', ‚innere Dauer' (vgl. Bergson 1920; Schütz 1974), ‚timescapes' (vgl. Adam 2005) oder ‚Temporalstruktur' (vgl. z. B. Bergmann 1981; Luhmann 1981; Rosa 2005). Hinter all diesen Begriffen verbergen sich vielschichtige und historisch gewachsene theoretische Annahmen über Zeit, Sozialität und deren Verhältnis zueinander. Es gehört zu dem alltäglichen Geschäft von Zeitsoziolog*innen, mit einem derartigen ‚theoriegeladenen' Begriffsapparat zu operieren. Zum einen werden die verwendeten Begrifflichkeiten hierbei (leider nicht immer) hinterfragt, stärker herausgearbeitet, moduliert oder eventuell sogar fallengelassen. Zum anderen wird dabei jedoch deutlich, dass auch in der Zeitsoziologie – wie auch in der Soziologie im Allgemeinen – eine ‚unbefleckte Erkenntnis' nicht möglich ist. (Feld-)Forschung ist wortwörtlich nicht ohne Begriffe und Konzepte ‚denkbar'. Kalthoff (2008) stellt diesbezüglich heraus, dass es keine begriffslosen Methoden gibt, durch die die Wirklichkeit uneingeschränkt beobachtet werden kann. Empirische Forschung sei per se theoriegeladen, ebenso wie im Umkehrschluss auch jede Theorie mal mehr, mal weniger implizit auf die Empirie zurückgreifen müsse. Hieraus schlussfolgert Kalthoff „zum einen eine empirische Relativierung von Theorien, zum anderen die Kritik eines positivistischen Methodenbegriffs, denn beides führt zu einer gewissen Gängelung des innovativen Potentials von empirischer Forschung. Das, was methodisch gefordert ist, geht von den Forschungsgegenständen aus, aber auch von den Forschungssubjekten, die ihre Theorien in Anschlag bringen." (Ebd., S. 24). Diese Überlegung lässt sich ohne große Mühe für die qualitativ-forschende Zeitsoziologie übernehmen. Die Methoden, die zur Erforschung von Zeitphänomenen herangezogen werden, sollten einerseits zum Forschungsgegenstand passen. Unter anderem können Forscher*innen sich den Zeiterfahrungen einzelner Subjekte durch Interviews oder Diary-Verfahren annähern, Verlaufsformen und Sequenzen durch teilnehmende Beobachtungen oder Videointeraktionsanalysen beobachten und die öffentlichen Debatten um Arbeits-, Schul- und Freizeitbudgets über Diskursanalysen ausleuchten. Andererseits darf jedoch nicht vergessen werden, dass Forscher*innen aufgrund ihrer wissenschaftlichen Sozialisation auf je andere Theorien zurückgreifen, um Zeitphänomene voneinander differenzieren und entsprechende Daten erheben zu können. System-, Praxis- und Rational-Choice-Theorien stellen beispielsweise divergente Annahmen über die Frage nach der soziotemporalen Ordnung zur Verfügung, die bedacht in die Methodenwahl integriert werden müssen, damit ein kohärentes Forschungsdesign entstehen kann, in dem Theorie und Empirie bestmöglich ineinandergreifen. Während des gesamten Forschungsprozesses ist es demnach angebracht, dass sich die Zeitforscher*innen der ‚sozialtheoretischen Gretchenfrage' stellen: Mit welchen theoretischen Vorannahmen ‚begreife' ich das Soziale? Wie weiter unten erläutert werden soll, ergeben sich aus der Antwort auf diese Frage zeitsoziologische Chancen und Risiken. Einige Phänomene werden beobachtbar und treten vielleicht sogar besonders im Feld hervor, während andere entweder an den Rändern der Aufmerksamkeitsfoki, welche die Forscher*innen im Feld haben, oder sogar in blinden Flecken zu verorten sind. Schließlich ergeben sich durch die zugrunde liegende Sozialtheorie auch methodische bzw. methodologische Überlegungen. Dies lässt sich, wie ich in diesem Beitrag zeigen werde, unter anderem anhand des sozialtheoretischen ‚Umschwungs' verdeutlichen, der sich aus dem Kommunikativen Konstruktivismus ergibt; nämlich die Abwendung vom methodologischen Individualismus und der Zentrierung des handelnden Subjekts zugunsten einer Hinwendung zur Dezentrierung des Subjekts und der Betonung von Figurationen und Interaktionsprozessen.

Im Folgenden zeichne ich nach, 1) wie subjektzentrierte Handlungstheorien, die beispielsweise auf der phänomenologischen Soziologie und dem Sozialkonstruktivismus gründen, zwar eine geeignete Grundlage bilden, um die Temporalität von Handlungsvollzügen und die subjektive Erfahrung von Zeit (qualitativ) zu erforschen. Demgegenüber fehlt ihnen jedoch unter anderem oftmals ein Sensus für die Bedeutung der Materialität innerhalb einer soziotemporalen Ordnung. Daraufhin stelle ich dar, 2) wie dieser blinde Fleck durch den Kommunikativen Konstruktivismus erschlossen werden kann; und dies gerade *weil* in dessen sozialtheoretischen Annahmen das Subjekt dezentriert wird und den Objektivationen eine gewichtige Rolle zukommt. Interaktionen beruhen damit nicht nur auf dem (sprachlichen) Austausch von (voneinander isolierten) Subjekten, sondern sind qua Performativität fest mit der Materialität verbunden. Zeitordnungen, die sozial wirksam werden, sind somit nicht nur an eine ‚kommunizierte', sondern vor allem auch an eine ‚kommunikative Zeit' geknüpft. Dies hat, wie ich abschließend darlege, 3) Auswirkungen auf methodologisch-methodischer Ebene: Zum einen gerät die kommunikative Praxis des Forschens und die Sequenzialität in den Mittelpunkt, die der Konstitution des forschenden Subjekts und dem Feld zugrunde liegt. Zum anderen verdeutlicht der Kommunikative Konstruktivismus, dass Forschende nur mittels Objektivationen auf die Zeit im Feld zugreifen können und somit die Qualität der Daten reflektiert werden muss. Im Vordergrund stehen nun auch Methoden zur Erhebung von Daten, die eben nicht auf das subjektive Zeiterleben zielen, sondern stattdessen das kommunikative Handeln in situ in seiner Zeitlichkeit unterschiedlich beobachtbar werden lassen: audiovisuelle Aufzeichnungen, ethnographische Vorgehensweisen und teilnehmende Beobachtungen sowie Artefaktanalysen.

Subjektzentrierte Handlungstheorien und die Beobachtbarkeit von Zeit

Die Frage, was im Mittelpunkt einer Sozialtheorie steht, hat einen Einfluss darauf, *wie* mit ihr die Zeitdimension betrachtet werden kann. Anders gewendet: Was Forscher*innen auf die anfangs erwähnte ‚Wann-Frage' entgegnen können, hängt enorm von den Begriffen ab, mit denen sie das Feld beobachten. Hieraus ergibt sich das Problem, dass durch den Begriffsapparat und den sozialtheoretischen Zugriff auf Wirklichkeit zwar einzelne Aspekte der soziotemporalen Ordnung erfassbar werden, andere jedoch oftmals fernab des Mittelpunkts, d. h. in der Peripherie, gelegen sind. Umso uneindeutiger scheinen dadurch auch ihre Zusammenhänge zur Zeit. Es ist nur allzu leicht, Verbindungen zwischen temporalen Phänomenen und dem ‚Kern' einer Theorie, d. h. ihren zentralen Begriffen, herzustellen, während das Offenlegen der temporalen Bedeutung untergeordneter Theoriebereiche einiges an konzeptioneller Arbeit erfordert. Dies führt die Forscher*innen auf unwegsames Terrain, das sich nur schwer in Begriffe fassen lässt und dessen Beschreibungen schnell überkomplex zu werden drohen.

Die soziotemporale Ordnung mit bestimmten Aspekten in Verbindung zu bringen, z. B. Materialität und Affektivität, scheint oftmals aufgrund der Theorieanlagen abwegig oder zumindest äußerst umständlich.

In der phänomenologischen Soziologie von Alfred Schütz ist es beispielsweise das Subjekt, das den „Nullpunkt des Koordinatensystems" (Schütz und Luckmann 2017, S. 71) bildet. Es findet sich wiederum in einem spezifischen ‚Hier' und ‚Jetzt' wieder, wodurch jede Wahrnehmung und jedes Erleben zugleich eng an die Zeitdimension geknüpft werden. Dies wird deutlich in einem Passus von Schütz (1974, S. 20; Herv. i. O.), in dem er schreibt, dass „das *Sinnproblem* ein *Zeitproblem*" ist. Sinn sei dabei jedoch von einer astronomischen Zeit losgelöst und stattdessen strikt gebunden an das Bewusstsein „der je eigenen Dauer, in dem sich für den Erlebenden der Sinn seiner Erlebnisse konstituiert" (ebd.). Für Schütz wird es erst durch Sinn möglich, einzelne Erlebnisse in dem Strom der Ereignisse beobachten zu können. Sinn ist „*die Bezeichnung einer bestimmten Blickrichtung auf ein eigenes Erlebnis,* welches wir, im Dauerlauf schlicht dahinlebend, als wohlumgrenztes nur in einem reflexiven Akt aus allen anderen Erlebnissen ‚herausheben' können." (ebd., S. 54; Herv. i. O.) Ohne Sinn können also keine sozialen Prozesse, geschweige denn zeitliche Phänomene beobachtet werden. Die Subjekte würden sich in einem Rauschen wiederfinden, ohne einzelne, klar konturierte und voneinander differenzierte Ereignisse wahrnehmen zu können. Handlungen hätten weder einen Beginn noch einen Schluss, könnten nicht vorausschauend entworfen oder zurückblickend reflektiert werden, würden nicht in kleinere Zwischenschritte untergliedert werden können und wären auch nicht von anderen Handlungen zu unterscheiden. Unser ganzes Handeln beruht für Schütz demnach darauf, dass sinnhafte Zeitunterscheidungen getroffen werden; Vorher-Nachher-Differenzierungen, durch die der Strom der Zeit für das Subjekt strukturiert wird.

Auch wenn Zeit eine Schlüsselkategorie im Denken von Schütz darstellt, so weist sein phänomenologischer Zugriff dennoch blinde Flecken auf. Die Erfahrung von Zeit ist bei ihm zum Beispiel hochgradig immateriell. Sie liegt im Subjekt verankert und scheint losgelöst von materiellen Umständen. Dies liegt im Wesentlichen daran, dass er eine Theorie des Fremdverstehens entwickelt hat, in der Intersubjektivität scheinbar unvermittelt oder zumindest nur durch Sprache erfolgt. Laut Schütz ereignet sich die Welt für das Subjekt in der inneren Dauer, zwischen Vergangenheit und Zukunft, Erfahrung und Erwartung sowie Wissensvorrat und Handlungsentwurf. Sie ist nur von diesen Schnittpunkten aus zu begreifen. Dabei sind die Handelnden in die Verstrickungen aus Weltzeit, Zeitstrukturen der Reichweite und der subjektiven Zeiterfahrung eingebunden. Das Zeiterleben und -handeln werden sowohl durch zurückliegende und erwartete Ereignisse beeinflusst als auch durch Lebens- und Tagespläne, das zwangsläufige Verstreichen der Zeit, Gefühle von Stress und Langeweile oder das Wissen um die (eigene) Vergänglichkeit. Eine ‚gemeinsame Zeit' der Subjekte ist hierbei jedoch strenggenommen nicht vorzufinden. Stattdessen zeichnet sie sich dadurch aus, dass mehrere Subjekte qua Interaktion ihre jeweiligen inneren Dauern auf die gleiche Weise takten, einen ähnlichen Rhythmus aufbauen und somit das Handeln in einer gleichen Geschwindigkeit sinnhaft verarbeiten. Schütz (1972) hat dies zum Beispiel am gemeinsamen Musizieren verdeutlicht, das nur dadurch möglich wird, dass die Musizierenden die gleichen musikalischen Phänomene fokussieren – Takt, Rhythmus, Tempo etc. Er veranschaulicht diesbezüglich den Aufbau einer gemeinsamen Zeit und die Notwendigkeit eines wechselseitigen Sich-Aufeinander-Einstellens. Kollektive Handlungen werden nur dadurch erfolgreich umgesetzt werden, indem die Subjekte das antizipierte Handeln der Anderen vorwegnehmen und in ihre Handlungsentwürfe integrieren. Diese Erkenntnisse haben für Schütz einen allgemeineren Anspruch, da er somit klären möchte, wie die wechselseitige Einstellungsbeziehung auch jenseits des Musizierens strukturiert ist. Hierauf weist er bereits in seinen Ausführungen zur Konstitution einer ‚gemeinsamen lebendigen Gegenwart' hin: „Wir müssen nun in Betracht ziehen, daß das Ereignis in der Außenwelt […] während seines Ablaufs ein gemeinsames Element seiner und meiner lebendigen Gegenwart ist, die somit beide gleichzeitig sind. Meine in Gleichzeitigkeit sich vollziehende Teilnahme am ablaufenden Prozeß des Kommunizierens des Anderen etabliert daher eine neue Zeitdimension. Er und ich, *wir* teilen für die Dauer dieses Vorganges eine gemeinsame lebendige Gegenwart, *unsere* lebendige Gegenwart, die es ihm und mir gestattet zu sagen: ‚*Wir* haben dieses Ereignis zusammen erlebt.'" (Schütz 2003: 195; Herv. i. O.)

Wie bereits erwähnt, bleibt Zeit in den Überlegungen von Schütz jedoch größtenteils von der Materialität losgelöst. Sie wird primär in das Subjekt verlagert, dessen Bewusstseinsstrom sich beispielsweise an die wahrgenommene Musik anpasst. Ein „Wechselseitig-sich-aufeinander-Einstimmen, die Erfahrung des ‚wir', die Teilhabe am Erlebnis des anderen in der inneren Zeit" wird für Schütz „im Durchleben einer gemeinsamen lebendigen Gegenwart konstituiert" (ebd., S. 145). Der Aufbau der Musikinstrumente, die in ihnen eingeschriebenen Gebrauchsweisen und die von ihnen vorgegebenen Körpervollzüge werden von Schütz nicht hinsichtlich der Konstitution einer gemeinsamen Zeit berücksichtigt. Musik ist die klangliche Gestaltung von Zeit und scheint für ihn in diesem Sinne immateriell; so wie auch jegliches andere Zeitphänomen. Da die Sozialwelt bei Schütz vor allem sinnhaft, d. h. im Subjekt, konstituiert ist, scheinen Zeit und Materialität in der phänomenologischen Soziologie kaum analytische Schnittpunkte aufzuweisen. Die materiellen Komponenten der soziotemporalen Ordnung lassen sich vor diesem Hintergrund nur schwer beobachten. Qualitativ-forschende Zeitsoziolog*innen, die sich mit den materiellen Aspekten von soziotemporalen Ordnungen auseinandersetzen möchten, werden mit einer derartigen Sozialtheorie im Hintergrund auf methodologische Probleme stoßen.

Ein ähnlich problematischer Zugang zum Verhältnis zwischen der materiellen und zeitlichen Dimension ergibt sich innerhalb jener sozialkonstruktivistischen Überlegungen, die auf Peter L. Bergers und Thomas Luckmanns (1970) Werk „Die gesellschaftliche Konstruktion von Wirklichkeit" zurückgehen. Dies mag zunächst nicht verwundern, da die Theorie von Berger und Luckmann hochgradig auf der Sozialphänomenologie aufbaut. Zeit ist für die beiden jedoch kein ausschließlich im Subjekt verorteter Phänomenbereich. Sie geht nicht, wie bei Schütz, aus einer egologischen Perspektive hervor. Im Gegensatz zu Schütz heben Berger und Luckmann aber auch die Relevanz der alltagsweltlichen Zeitstruktur hervor. Ihnen zufolge müsse auch der Intersubjektivität eine eigene zeitliche Dimension zugesprochen werden. Dies käme beispielsweise in der Standardzeit zum Ausdruck, die den „Schnittpunkt der kosmischen Zeit mit ihrem gesellschaftlich etablierten Kalender" (ebd.) bilde. Zum einen resultiere sie aus dem unaufhörlichen Voranschreiten der Ereignisse bzw. aus dem kontinuierlichen Fluss des Zukünftigen in die Vergangenheit, zum anderen ist sie aber auch ein Erzeugnis gesellschaftlicher Übereinkünfte. Zeit scheint bei Berger und Luckmann somit etwas sehr Ambivalentes zu sein, das sich sowohl der sozialen Konstruktion entzieht, indem es einen Grundzug der materiellen Welt darstellt, als auch selbst ein soziales Konstrukt ist, das auf einem gesellschaftlichen Wissen um Rhythmen, Dauern und Geschwindigkeiten beruht und erst aus dem Handeln hervorgeht. Zeit liegt einerseits objektiv, quasi unantastbar vor, andererseits wird sie aber auch kontinuierlich durch den Menschen objektiviert. Das Wissen um die Zeit wird dabei in der Trias aus Externalisierung, Objektivierung und Internalisierung hervorgebracht und gefestigt. Zeit resultiert somit aus einem steten Wechselspiel subjektiver und objektiver Wirklichkeit. Die Annahmen des Sozialkonstruktivismus sensibilisieren dafür, dass Zeit nicht ausschließlich aus einer egologischen Perspektive heraus betrachtet werden darf. Sie ist vielmehr ein soziales Konstrukt, das nur in und durch die Handelnden existiert. Berger und Luckmann (1970, S. 29; Herv. i. O.) schreiben jedoch, dass Zeitlichkeit zunächst „eine der Domänen des Bewußtseins" darstellt, wobei sich „jedes Individuum […] des Flusses *seiner* Zeit bewußt" ist. Die Betrachtung von Zeitphänomenen mündet somit letztlich wieder in den subjektiven Bewusstseinsstrom.

Im Sozialkonstruktivismus kommt den Objektivierungen eine zentrale Rolle zu. Hierunter sind „Verkörperung subjektiver Vorgänge in Vorgängen und Gegenständen der Lebenswelt des Alltags" (Schütz und Luckmann 2017, S. 358) zu verstehen. Sie werden in kommunikativen Situationen durch die Handelnden in Form verbaler oder körperlicher Äußerungen erzeugt und dergestalt von anderen Subjekten erfahren. Sie sind, wie Berger und Luckmann (1970, S. 36 f.) es formulieren, „Erzeugnisse [...] menschlicher Tätigkeit, welche sowohl dem Erzeuger als auch anderen Menschen als Elemente ihrer gemeinsamen Welt ‚begreiflich'" und somit „mehr oder weniger dauerhafte Indikatoren subjektiver Empfindungen" sind. Objektivierungen sind dabei zeitliche und äußerst flüchtige Sinnphänomene, da sie nur im Vollzug zu erfassen sind.

Das Problem ist nun, das Berger und Luckmann die Objektivierung subjektiver Sinngehalte primär auf laut- und schriftsprachliche Äußerungen bezogen haben. Mit ihnen lässt sich zwar beispielsweise nachvollziehen, wie über Termine und Fristen gesprochen werden kann oder wie durch Ziffernblättern auf Uhren oder Datumsangaben auf Kalendern Zeit objektiviert wird. Demgegenüber fehlt jedoch eine explizite Auseinandersetzung mit den materiellen Aspekten der sozialen Konstruktion von Zeit. Verschiedene Aspekte der Performativität, d. h. sowohl die Zeitlichkeit der Gebrauchsweisen von Artefakten und Techniken als auch die Temporalität von Körpervollzügen, lassen sich nur schwerlich in den Überlegungen von Berger und Luckmann finden. Stattdessen bleibt der theoretische Fokus auf dem Subjekt, das weiterhin den Dreh- und Angelpunkt der Zeiterfahrung bildet.

Am Beispiel der phänomenologischen Soziologie und des Sozialkonstruktivismus wird deutlich, dass die Verortung einzelner Konzepte innerhalb des Begriffsapparats einer Theorie einen wesentlichen Einfluss auf soziologische Beobachtungen im Allgemeinen und zeitsoziologische Beobachtungen im Besonderen hat. Sozialtheorien, die sich zentral auf das Subjekt stützen, führen dazu, dass auch die soziotemporale Ordnung zutiefst in den Handelnden verankert wird. Zeit scheint aus dieser subjektivistischen Betrachtungsweise heraus jedoch kaum an die Materialität gebunden, sondern ein Produkt semiotischer Prozesse und damit verbundener Bewusstseinsströme zu sein. Das Verhältnis von Materialität und soziotemporaler Ordnung bildet einen blinden Fleck subjektzentrierter Handlungstheorien.

Die kommunikative Konstruktion von Zeit

Einen adäquaten Ausgangspunkt für eine materialitätssensible Analyse von Zeitphänomenen bildet demgegenüber jedoch der Kommunikative Konstruktivismus, der unter anderem auf die Subjektivismuskritik an der phänomenologischen

Soziologie und dem Sozialkonstruktivismus und den in diesen Theorieströmungen fehlenden Einbezug von Materialität in reagiert. Der Kommunikative Konstruktivismus ist als ein vergleichsweise junger Ansatz zur Theoriebildung in der Kommunikations- und Medienwissenschaft sowie in der Soziologie zu verstehen, der erstmalig in den 1990er Jahren erwähnt wurde (vgl. Knoblauch 1995, S. 21–56). Bis heute wurde er in etlichen Debatten und Veröffentlichungen diskutiert, systematisch durchleuchtet und weiter ausgebaut (vgl. bspw. Christmann 2016; Couldry und Hepp 2016; Keller et al. 2013; Knoblauch 2017; Knoblauch und Schnettler 2004; Reichertz 2009; Reichertz und Bettmann 2018). Zu seinen theoriegeschichtlichen Entstehungsherden zählen unter anderem diskurs- und praxistheoretische Ansätze, der Pragmatismus, der Poststrukturalismus, die hermeneutische Wissenssoziologie, die Sozialphänomenologie, die Interaktionsanalyse sowie ethnografische und ethnomethodologische Überlegungen. Ebenfalls übten auch Erfahrungen aus der empirischen Forschung Einfluss auf die (Weiter-)Entwicklung des Kommunikativen Konstruktivismus (vgl. bspw. Keller et al. 2013, S. 9–13; Reichertz und Tuma 2017, S. 7–21).

Im Wesentlichen zielt der Kommunikative Konstruktivismus auf die Frage, wie Sinn handelnd produziert und darauf aufbauend ein gesellschaftlicher Wissensvorrat konstituiert werden kann. Dabei ist der Kommunikative Konstruktivismus als eine *relationale* Sozialtheorie zu begreifen. Sein Zentrum bildet nicht mehr das einzelne Subjekt, sondern eine Triade, in der sich mindestens zwei Subjekte durch Objektivierungen reziprok aufeinander beziehen. Innerhalb dieser Dreieckskonstellation wird subjektiver Sinn externalisiert und für das Gegenüber wahrnehmbar objektiviert. Dies ist das Charakteristikum des Kernkonzepts im Kommunikativen Konstruktivismus, genauer: des *kommunikativen Handelns:* „Es bezieht sich auf Andere, auf das verkörperte Subjekt und schließlich auf die damit verknüpften Objektivierungen, die als Teil der gemeinsamen Umwelt wahrgenommen werden" (Knoblauch 2013, S. 31). Innerhalb des kommunikativen Handelns sind es nicht ausschließlich die Subjekte, durch welche die Welt konstruiert wird. Es ist vielmehr die auf Objektivierungen basierende Kommunikation, durch die, wie Reichertz (2013, S. 51) verdeutlicht, „die Menschen sich selbst, den Anderen und ihre Welt erst erschaffen und immer wieder aufs Neue an Andere weitergeben".

Objektivierungen lassen sich, wie bereits erwähnt, durchaus auch in der Sozialphänomenologie und im Sozialkonstruktivismus finden, jedoch wird ihre materielle Dimension in diesen beiden Theorietraditionen nur sehr vage durchdacht und nicht vertieft. Im Gegenzug unterscheidet der Kommunikative Konstruktivismus aber zusätzlich noch Objektivationen (vgl. Knoblauch 2017, S. 155–170). Diese sind keine flüchtigen, sondern temporal (relativ) stabile

Handlungserzeugnisse. Sie entstehen aus Versachlichungsprozessen, d. h. aus der Entkopplung des Handelns vom Körper des Handelnden und sind dergestalt Ergebnisse sowie Verkörperungen von Handlungen, also „objektivierter Sinn, d. h. zu einem Teil der Umwelt und damit anderen zugänglich gemachter und zugleich materialisierter, d. h. vergegenständlichter und damit auf Dauer gestellter subjektiver Sinn […]" (Pfadenhauer und Grenz 2017, S. 231). Objektivationen sind Resultate von Objektivierungen. Sie bauen auf Körperlichkeit, Performativität und Materialität auf, binden Zeit, formen sie (um) und fungieren dadurch auch wirklichkeitsstabilisierend. Dies bedeutet zugleich, dass Objektivationen auch stets menschliche Erzeugnisse sind. Sie haben weder jenseits der Konstruktionsprozesse Bestand noch werden sie erst in Interaktion sinnhaft aufgeladen. Die Möglichkeit, von Uhren Zeit ablesen zu können, ist zum Beispiel das Ergebnis eines komplexen Deutungszusammenhangs. Genaugenommen, wird durch Uhren nicht die Zeit *angezeigt*. Sie sind stattdessen Artefakte, in denen sich Dinge normbasiert mechanisch bewegen. Sowohl die Uhr als Apparatur als auch das Vorgehen, auf ein Ziffernblatt oder eine Digitalanzeige blicken und eine exakte Uhrzeit ablesen zu können, ist vom Menschen geschaffen (vgl. hierzu auch Elias 1988, S. 96).

Zeit nimmt im Kommunikativen Konstruktivismus eine analytische Schlüsselposition ein, da kommunikatives Handeln stets sequenziell – und somit: in der Zeit – zu denken ist. Als eine Weiterentwicklung der sozialkonstruktivistischen Überlegungen von Berger und Luckmann dezentriert der kommunikative Konstruktivismus das Subjekt und lässt stattdessen den Objektivationen – und somit: den Dingen – eine gewichtigere Rolle zukommen. Interaktionen beruhen damit nicht nur auf dem (sprachlichen) Austausch von (isolierten) Subjekten, sondern sind vielmehr fest mit der Materialität verbunden.

Mit Hilfe von Objektivierungen gelingt es den Subjekten, Koorientierung – d. h. das wechselseitige Bezugnehmen und Abstimmen – als ein zentrales Problem sozialer Ordnungsbildung zu bearbeiten. Schließlich wird hierdurch Sinn externalisiert, dergestalt für die Anderen wahrnehmbar und somit letztlich sozial wirksam wird. Objektivierungen sind „der in einer gemeinsamen Umwelt erfahrbare Aspekt dieses Wirkhandelns" (Knoblauch 2013, S. 29). Durch sie kann es den Subjekten gelingen, Intersubjektivität aufzubauen, sinnhaft in die Welt einzugreifen und sich mit den Anderen zu koorientieren. Koorientierung ist jedoch nur möglich, indem sich die handelnden Subjekte in Bezug auf etwas Drittes – eine Uhr(zeit), einen Sonnenstand, einen Notizzettel, ein Signal etc. – *zeitlich* abstimmen. Ohne eine entsprechende Synchronisation oder (Un-)Gleichzeitigkeit der subjektiven Handlungen, wären soziale Handlungen nicht umsetzbar.

Subjekte koorientieren sich nicht ausschließlich über festgesetzte Termine und Fristen, sondern primär in der Interaktion *mit* den Anderen; und zwar *an den*

Objektivierungen der Anderen: Es wird zum Beispiel über Uhrzeiten gesprochen, und Termine werden in Kalender eingetragen. Die Zeitlichkeit des Sozialen liegt nicht in der astronomischen Zeit begründet, sondern in der „sozialen Zeit" (vgl. Sorokin und Merton 1937). Diese ergibt sich aber nicht aus einer unmittelbaren Intersubjektivität, sondern ist auf ein triadisches Verhältnis zurückzuführen. Soziale Zeit wird stets über etwas Drittes kommuniziert und konstruiert. Um diese theoretische Hinwendung zum kommunikativen Handeln zu betonen, soll im Folgenden stattdessen von der *kommunikativen Zeit* gesprochen werden. Diese ist meines Erachtens strikt von der *kommunizierten Zeit* zu trennen, d. h. von spezifischen Semantiken der Zeitlichkeit, wie Vergangenheit, Gegenwart, Zukunft oder Vergänglichkeit oder Zeitangaben, die auf standardisierten Maßeinheiten beruhen, wie Datums- und Uhrzeitangaben. Statt das Wissen um Zeit zu fokussieren, bezieht sich der Kommunikative Konstruktivismus einerseits auf die Prozesse, die dazu führen, dass dieses Wissen konstituiert wird, und andererseits auf die Zeitverläufe des kommunikativen Handelns. Zeit resultiert nicht nur aus einem spezifischen Wissen, aus sprachlichen Äußerungen, Verstehensleistungen und Deutungen, sondern aus dem kommunikativen Handeln – und somit: aus Interaktionen, Mediengebräuchen, Wirkweisen und Figurationen. Die kommunikative Zeit bezieht sich nicht auf die Synchronisierung innerer Dauern – wie Luckmann (1983) es für die interaktive Zeit festhält –, sondern auf die Zeitlichkeit des wechselseitigen Wirkhandelns. Es geht folglich um die Dauern, Geschwindigkeiten, Synchronisationen und (Un-)Gleichzeitigkeiten des kommunikativen Handelns.

Wie kommunikative Zeit beobachten?

Dies hat selbstverständlich Auswirkungen auf methodologisch-methodischer Ebene: Zunächst gerät die kommunikative Praxis des Forschens in den Mittelpunkt, die der Konstitution des forschenden Subjekts und dem Feld zugrunde liegt; wodurch der gesamte Forschungsprozess in seiner Sequenzialität reflektierbar wird.

Jedem Feld wohnt aufgrund der Dynamik sozialer Ereignisse ein kontinuierlicher Wandel inne. Das Feld kann sich in der Zeit de- und restabilisieren, sich öffnen und schließen sowie be- und entschleunigen (vgl. Dalsgaard und Nielsen 2016b). Aus diesem Grund dürfen sich qualitativ-forschende Zeitsoziolog*innen im Feld nicht an spezifischen Handlungs*orten* orientieren, sondern müssen die gesamte *soziotemporale Ordnung* des Feldes reflektieren. Dies hat zur Folge, dass die Logik der Feldforschung von dem weitverbreiteten methodologischen

Topozentrismus entbunden werden muss. Denn als kommunikativ Handelnde erheben die Forscher*innen die Daten nicht primär *vor Ort,* sondern in *gleichzeitiger Anwesenheit* mit den Feldakteuren (vgl. Dalsgaard und Nielsen 2016a, S. 10, 20 f.). Feldteilnehmer*innen, die den Ort des Geschehens früher verlassen haben oder später hinzugekommen sind, werden eben nicht im Datenmaterial abgebildet. Deshalb kann das Feld niemals holistisch, sondern nur partiell – genauer: in Form von Handlungssequenzen – wahrgenommen werden. Aufgrund seiner zeitlichen Instabilität ist es zudem nicht an fixe Koordinaten, überdauernde Räume oder verortenbare Individuen gebunden. Je nachdem, welche Menschen, Objektivationen, (kommunikative) Handlungen und Wissensbestände in situ vorzufinden sind und mit welchen Mitteln es von den Forscher*innen beobachtet wird, wandelt es seine Gestalt. Es ist das Resultat kommunikativer Handlungen; und zwar sowohl aus emischer als auch aus etischer Perspektive, d. h. aus Sicht der Feldakteure und der Außenstehenden.

Um die kommunikative Zeit im Feld zu untersuchen und eine „Tempografie" (Zerubavel 1979, S. xxi) anfertigen zu können, sollte der forschende Blick nicht mehr auf bestimmten *Sites,* d. h. räumlich abgegrenzten Settings mit feldrelevanten Akteuren oder Ereignissen, liegen. Stattdessen sollten sich die Forscher*innen auf spezifische *Times* konzentrieren, die für ihre Forschungsfrage von Relevanz sind. Statt den Akteuren zu folgen (vgl. Latour 2007) – oder etwas weitergefasst: den Menschen, Dingen, Metaphern, den Konflikten, Storylines und Biografien (vgl. Marcus 1995, S. 105–113) – gilt somit: ›follow the temporalities‹. Um die zeitlichen Aspekte eines Feldes herausarbeiten zu können, muss auf Dauern, Rhythmisierungen, (Un-)Gleichzeitigkeiten und Synchronisationen geachtet werden. Im Fokus sollten dabei nicht nur die Konstitution und Aufrechterhaltung einzelner Zeitphänomene liegen, sondern der gesamte Objektivierungsprozess, der sich im Rahmen kommunikativer Handlungen ereignet, bedarf einer detaillierten Analyse. Was sind die zeitlichen Charakteristika einer Sequenz? Was sind die situativen Bedingungen, die sich auf die Zeit des kommunikativen Handelns auswirken? Wann werden Zeitverläufe materiell und technisch vorgeschrieben? Und welche Rolle kommt spezifischen Körperbewegungen bei der Konstitution von Zeit zu?

Im Zentrum der Erforschung von kommunikativer Zeit steht demnach die anfangs erwähnte ‚Wann-Frage' von Elias. Für die Feldforschung nützt hierbei Luhmanns Überlegung, dass Zeit primär anhand der „Trennung eines ‚Vorher' und eines ‚Nachher', einer Vergangenheit und einer Zukunft" (Luhmann 1997, S. 53) beobachtet werden kann. Diese Differenz kann als ein „sensitizing concept" (Blumer 1954, S. 7) und somit als ein offener und flexibler Beobachtungsrahmen (vgl. Hoonaard 1997; Charmaz 2014, S. 60 f.) dienen, durch den Daten erhoben, neue Konzepte entwickelt und die Theoriebildungsprozesse sukzessiv vorangetrieben werden können. Die Vorher-Nachher-Differenz ermöglicht es, die Zeitdimension zu fokussieren, während die Sach- und Sozialdimension in den Hintergrund rückt. Dadurch stellen sich unterschiedliche zeitsensible Fragen: ‚An welchen Stellen können Vorher-Nachher-Differenzen beobachtet werden?', ‚Wo und weshalb variieren sie in ihrer Dauer?', ‚Gibt es Prozesse, die absichtsvoll be- oder entschleunigt werden?', ‚Lassen sich Muster erkennen, in denen die Trennung von vorher und nachher bestimmte Formen annehmen?' etc.

Durch die Vorannahmen des Kommunikativen Konstruktivismus ergibt sich zudem die *Situation* als eine grundlegende Analyseeinheit, die es ermöglicht, die Prozessualität des Sozialen in den Mittelpunkt der Betrachtung zu rücken und dabei zugleich der Verzeitlichung des Feldes Rechnung zu tragen. Kommunikation, so schreibt Reichertz (2009, S. 98; Herv. i. O.), ist stets „Ausdruck einer spezifischen, einer *bestimmten* Situation, die ein Handlungsproblem hervorgebracht hat, das mittels Kommunikation bearbeitet werden soll". Die methodologische Orientierung am Kommunikativen Konstruktivismus führt somit logischerweise zu einer Abwendung vom methodologischen Individualismus und zu einer Hinwendung zur Situation (vgl. Reichertz 2017, S. 63–68). Im Fokus stehen dadurch nicht mehr die einzelnen Handlungen und die Handlungen Einzelner, sondern, wie Clarke (2016, S. 102) schreibt, „the situation itself becomes the fundamental unit of analysis".

Eine Situation basiert auf der gleichzeitigen Anwesenheit und Wahrnehmung mindestens zweier Individuen. Sie ist eine »environment of mutual monitoring possibilities« (Goffman 1964, S. 135), in der alle Anwesenden, d. h. Feldforscher*innen und Feldakteure gleichermaßen, ihrer wechselseitigen Wahrnehmung ausgeliefert sind. Die Bedeutung der Situation steht nicht von Anfang an fest, sondern sie wird erst durch alle Beteiligten erzeugt, kontinuierlich geprüft und gegebenenfalls geändert (vgl. Ziemann 2011). Die Anwesenden koorientieren sich anhand ihrer Objektivierungen – ihrer verbalen und körperlichen Äußerungen sowie Artefaktgebräuche – und stützen sich auf ein gemeinsam geteiltes Wissen über die jeweilige Situation. Die Situation wird also nicht durch das einzelne Subjekt, sondern vielmehr kontinuierlich durch das kommunikative Handeln erzeugt (vgl. Reichertz 2017, S. 67).

Die Situation zeichnet sich nicht nur durch ein spezifisches Thema oder wechselseitige Bezugnahme aus, sondern unterliegt auch, wie Ziemann (2013, S. 114) zeigt, der Zeitdimension: „Jede Situation ist als zeitlich strukturiert aufzufassen, insofern sie beeinflusst ist von einem Davor, einem (prozessualen) Mitten-In und einem Danach. Das Davor bestimmt unsere Gegenwart, es strukturiert und limitiert die aktuellen Möglichkeiten der Situation. Das Danach bestimmt die Zukunft anderer, neuer Situationen, in denen nicht mehr alles möglich, geschweige denn wünschenswert oder relevant ist. Und das Mitten-in-Situation-Seiend handelt dies alles aus und generiert und legitimiert den bis auf Weiteres verbindlichen und bindenden Sinn."

Aufgrund des ständigen Übergangs zukünftiger zu vergangenen Gegenwarten, wird die Situation dynamisiert. Laut Hempel (2017, S. 231 f.) wird sie „zu einer gleichsam offenen, beweglichen und vorübergehenden Ordnung", die für die Akteure zeitliche Orientierungsmuster anbietet. Zugleich weist jede Situation typische Verlaufsformen auf, also bestimmte Dauern, Geschwindigkeiten und Momente der Synchronisation und (Un-)Gleichzeitigkeit, die einerseits aus der Rahmung resultieren und andererseits aber auch der Situation überhaupt erst eine spezifische Bedeutung zugestehen. Es gibt soziale Übereinkünfte, wie zum Beispiel Trauer- und Hochzeitsfeiern zeitlich gestaltet werden sollten, während sich aber auch von der zeitlichen Gestaltung dieser Rituale auf deren Wirksamkeit schließen lässt.

Des Weiteren verdeutlicht der Kommunikative Konstruktivismus, dass Forschende nur mittels Objektivationen auf die Zeit im Feld zugreifen können und somit nicht nur die die Qualität, sondern auch die Medialität der Daten reflektiert werden muss. Die Überlegungen des Kommunikativen Konstruktivismus führen schließlich auch zu einer notwendigen Reflexion der Methoden, die für die Datenerhebung und -auswertung herangezogen werden. Laut Reichertz geht es im Kommunikativen Konstruktivismus „nicht mehr allein um das Innere eines bewusst und kognitiv gehaltvoll reflektierenden und entscheidenden Egos, sondern Ego wie Alter werden als Akteure und auch als *Produkte eines situativ eingebetteten kommunikativen Mit- und Gegeneinander* innerhalb eines Kommunikations- und Diskursfeldes betrachtet, in dem (zumindest in modernen Gesellschaften) vornehmlich *mit* und *in* Medien kommuniziert wird" (Reichertz 2017, S. 69; Herv. i. O.). Vor diesem Hintergrund erscheinen jene Datensorten, durch die dominant auf subjektive Sinngehalte zugegriffen werden kann, als weniger relevant. So lassen sich durch Interviewaufzeichnungen und -transkripte und Diary-Verfahren zwar bestimmte Aspekte eines Wissens über Zeit sowie Wahrnehmungen und Empfindungen von Zeitlichkeit rekonstruieren, jedoch lassen sich durch diese Daten nur bedingt Interaktionsprozesse nachverfolgen. Beschreibungen von Situationen in Interviews sind lediglich Deutungen und Nacherzählungen dieser Situationen, die zudem in einem ganz anderen Kontext erfolgen. Stattdessen rücken durch den Kommunikativen Konstruktivismus Formen der Datengenerierung in den Vordergrund, die nicht auf die Wahrnehmung und Deutung zeitlicher Phänomene zielen, sondern den Objektivierungs*prozess* und die Sequenzialität von Situationen (detaillierter) beobachtbar werden lassen. Die Untersuchung der kommunikativen Zeit bedarf somit Methoden, mit denen das von Reichertz erwähnte ‚situativ eingebettete kommunikative Mit- und Gegeneinander' aufgezeichnet, konserviert und tiefenscharf durchdrungen werden kann und das kommunikative Handeln *in situ* in seiner Zeitlichkeit beobachtbar wird.

Bettmann (2018, S. 275) verweist darauf, dass unter den Prämissen des Kommunikativen Konstruktivismus „situative Phänomene multiperspektivisch, prozessual und in Korrespondenz mit den situativ-materiellen Verweisungszusammenhängen *in ihrer Dynamik*" erfasst werden müssen. Die Untersuchung kommunikativer Zeit bedarf also eines methodischen Vorgehens, durch die die Sequenzialität einer Situation analytisch handhabbar wird. Hierzu bietet sich erstens die Videographie bzw. Videointeraktionsanalyse an, die die „minutiöse Untersuchung der Sequenzorganisation und die situative Einbettung von interaktiven und kommunikativen Vorgängen" (Tuma, Schnettler und Knoblauch 2013, S. 115) begünstigt. Dadurch lassen sich die (zeitliche) Eigenlogik und die Prozesshaftigkeit der Situation weniger verfremdet erhalten und systematischer sowie detaillierter analysieren. Zweitens bieten sich ethnografische Forschungsdesigns und teilnehmende Beobachtungen bzw. beobachtende Teilnahmen an, durch die die Interaktionen und Prozesse im Feld in der beobachteten Situation für die Forscher*innen wahrnehmbar werden. Die daraus entstehenden Daten – die Feldtagebücher und Beobachtungsprotokolle – halten situierte Handlungsweisen, Umgangsformen und Routinen fest, die Rückschlüsse zulassen, wie sich die Feldakteure in kommunikativen Handlungen koorientierend in Relation zueinander setzten. Zudem kommt in ihnen die „Schweigsamkeit des Sozialen" (Hirschauer 2001) zum Ausdruck, da sie performative Aspekte des kommunikativen Handelns betonen, die beispielsweise in Interviewtranskripten verloren gehen würden. Drittens ermöglicht auch die Artefaktanalyse (vgl. Froschauer und Lueger 2018) einen Zugriff auf soziotemporale Ordnungen, der unabhängig von den Feldakteuren erfolgen kann. Artefakte sind hierbei begrifflich mit Objektivationen gleichzusetzen. Sie sind ‚natürliche' Daten aus dem Feld – und somit nicht durch Interventionen der Forscher*innen generiert worden. Sie ermöglichen einen analytischen Zugriff auf das Wissen im Feld, da sich an ihnen objektivierter Sinn erfassen lässt. Kommunikative Zeit wird hierbei auf zwei Weisen an Artefakten beobachtbar: Zum einen können Objektivationen Zeit repräsentieren, wie beispielsweise Uhren oder Kalender, die eine spezifische Zeitordnung (re-)konstruieren. Zum anderen weisen Artefakte Gebrauchsweise auf, in die eine spezifische Eigenzeit eingeschrieben ist, d. h. eine Dauer, Geschwindigkeit oder Frequenz, die sich im Vollzug auf das kommunikative Handeln auswirkt.

In den zurückliegenden Ausführungen habe ich gezeigt, dass die Sozialtheorie, die Zeitsoziolog*innen aufgreifen, um ihr Feld zu beobachten, einen hochgradigen Einfluss darauf hat, welche Aspekte der soziotemporalen Ordnung – wortwörtlich – ‚begriffen‘ und untersucht werden können. Am Beispiel der Sozialphänomenologie, des Sozialkonstruktivismus und des Kommunikativen Konstruktivismus verdeutlicht sich beispielsweise, dass nicht jede Theorie dazu geeignet ist, die Materialität und Performativität von Handlungen zu fassen und ihre Bedeutung für die Zeitlichkeit des Sozialen auszuleuchten. Während subjektzentrierte Handlungstheorien vornehmlich die kommunizierte Zeit fokussieren, ermöglicht der Kommunikative Konstruktivismus aufgrund der Dezentrierung des Subjekts eine Hinwendung zur kommunikativen Zeit, d. h. den konkreten Handlungsverläufen und Interaktionsprozessen. Die ‚Wann-Frage‘, die sich in zeitsoziologischen Untersuchungen stellt, kann folglich durch verschiedene ‚sozialtheoretische Brillen‘ jeweils anders beantwortet werden. Dies muss unbedingt in der Konzeption des Forschungsdesigns und der Wahl der zugrunde liegenden Theorie berücksichtigt werden.

Literatur

Adam, B. (2005). *Timescapes of Modernity. The Environment and Invisible Hazards.* London und New York: Routledge.
Berger, P. L. und Luckmann, T. (1970). *Die gesellschaftliche Konstruktion der Wirklichkeit.* 2. Aufl. Frankfurt a. M.: S. Fischer.
Bergmann, W. (1981). *Die Zeitstrukturen sozialer Systeme. Eine systemtheoretische Analyse.* Berlin: Duncker & Humblot.
Bergson, H. (1920). *Zeit und Freiheit. Eine Abhandlung über die unmittelbaren Bewußtseinstatsachen.* Jena: Diederichs.
Bettmann, R. (2018). Emergenz und Zukunft des Kommunikativen Konstruktivismus. In J. Reichertz und R. Bettmann (Hrsg.): *Kommunikation – Medien – Konstruktion. Braucht die Mediatisierungsforschung den Kommunikativen Konstruktivismus?* (S. 259–279). Wiesbaden: Springer VS.
Blumer, H. (1954). What is Wrong with Social Theory? In *American Sociological Review* 19 (1), S. 3-10.
Charmaz, K. (2014). *Constructing Grounded Theory.* 2. Auflage. London u.a.: SAGE.
Christmann, G. B. (2016). *Zur kommunikativen Konstruktion von Räumen.* Wiesbaden: Springer VS.
Clarke, A. E. (2016). From Grounded Theory to Situational Analysis. What's new? Why? How? In A. E. Clarke, C. Friese und R. Washburn (Hrsg.): *Situational Analysis in Practice. Mapping Research with Grounded Theory* (S. 89–120). London und New York: Routledge.
Couldry, N. und Hepp, A. (2016). *The Mediated Construction of Reality.* Cambridge: Polity Press.

Dalsgaard, S. und Nielsen, M. (2016a). Introduction: Time and the Field. In Dies. (Hrsg.): *Time and the Field* (S. 8–30). New York: Berghahn.

Dalsgaard, S. und Nielsen, M. (Hrsg.) (2016b). *Time and the Field*. New York: Berghahn.

Davis, T. C. (2010). Performative Time. In C. Canning (Hrsg.): Representing the Past. Essays in Performance Historiography. Iowa City: University of Iowa Press, S. 142–167.

Elias, N. (1988). *Über die Zeit. Arbeiten zur Wissenssoziologie II*. Frankfurt a. M.: Suhrkamp.

Froschauer, U. und Lueger, M. (2018). *Artefaktanalyse. Grundlagen und Verfahren*. Wiesbaden: Springer VS.

Goffman, E. (1964). The Neglected Situation. In *American Anthropologist* 66 (6), S. 133-136.

Hempel, L. (2017). Die Zeit der Situation. Beobachtungen zur Temporalität kommunikativen Handelns am Beispiel Fußballfanverkehr. In J. Reichertz und R. Tuma (Hrsg.): *Der Kommunikative Konstruktivismus bei der Arbeit* (S. 218–255). Weinheim und Basel: Beltz Juventa.

Hirschauer, S. (2001). Ethnografisches Schreiben und die Schweigsamkeit des Sozialen. Zu einer Methodologie der Beschreibung. In *Zeitschrift für Soziologie* 30 (6), S. 429–451.

Hoonaard, W. C. v. d. (1997). *Working with Sensitizing Concepts. Analytical Field Research*. London: SAGE.

Kalthoff, H. (2008). Zur Dialektik von qualitativer Forschung und soziologischer Theoriebildung. In S. Hirschauer, H. Kalthoff und G. Lindemann (Hrsg.): *Theoretische Empirie. Zur Relevanz qualitativer Forschung* (S. 8–34). Frankfurt am Main: Suhrkamp.

Keller, R., Knoblauch, H. und Reichertz, J. (Hrsg.) (2013). *Kommunikativer Konstruktivismus. Theoretische und empirische Arbeiten zu einem neuen wissenssoziologischen Ansatz*. Wiesbaden: Springer VS.

Knoblauch, H. (1995). *Kommunikationskultur. Die kommunikative Konstruktion kultureller Kontexte*. Berlin und New York: Walter de Gruyter.

Knoblauch, H. (2013). Grundbegriffe und Aufgaben des kommunikativen Konstruktivismus. In R. Keller, H. Knoblauch und J. Reichertz (Hrsg.): *Kommunikativer Konstruktivismus. Theoretische und empirische Arbeiten zu einem neuen wissenssoziologischen Ansatz* (S. 25–47). Wiesbaden: Springer VS.

Knoblauch, H. (2017). *Die kommunikative Konstruktion der Wirklichkeit*. Wiesbaden: Springer VS.

Knoblauch, H. und Schnettler, B. (2004). Vom sinnhaften Aufbau zur kommunikativen Konstruktion. In M. Gabriel (Hrsg.): *Paradigmen der akteurszentrierten Soziologie* (S. 121–138). Wiesbaden: VS Verlag für Sozialwissenschaften.

Latour, B. (2007). *Eine neue Soziologie für eine neue Gesellschaft. Einführung in die Akteur-Netzwerk-Theorie*. Frankfurt am Main: Suhrkamp.

Luckmann, T. (1983). Remarks on Personal Identity: Inner, Social and Historical Time. In A. Jacobson-Widding (Hrsg.): *Identity: Personal and Socio-Cultural. A Symposium* (S. 67–91). Uppsala: Almqvist & Wiksell International.

Luhmann, N. (1981). Die Unwahrscheinlichkeit der Kommunikation. In Ders.: *Soziologische Aufklärung. Bd. 3. Soziales System, Gesellschaft, Organisation*. Opladen: Westdeutscher Verlag, S. 25–34.

Luhmann, N. (1997). *Die Gesellschaft der Gesellschaft*. 2 Bände. Frankfurt am Main: Suhrkamp.

Marcus, G. E. (1995). Ethnography in/of the World System: The Emergence of Multi-Sited Ethnography. In *Annual Review of Anthropology* 24, S. 95-117.

Pfadenhauer, M. und Grenz, T. (2017). Von Objekten zu Objektivierung. Zum Ort technischer Materialität im Kommunikativen Konstruktivismus. In *Soziale Welt 68* (2–3), S. 225–242.

Reichertz, J. (2009). *Kommunikationsmacht. Was ist Kommunikation und was vermag sie? Und weshalb vermag sie das?* Wiesbaden: VS Verlag für Sozialwissenschaften.

Reichertz, J. (2013). Grundzüge des Kommunikativen Konstruktivismus. In R. Keller, H. Knoblauch und J. Reichertz (Hrsg.): *Kommunikativer Konstruktivismus. Theoretische und empirische Arbeiten zu einem neuen wissenssoziologischen Ansatz* (S. 49–68). Wiesbaden: Springer VS.

Reichertz, J. (2017). Was ist neu am Kommunikativen Konstruktivismus? Oder: Braucht es neue Formen der Datenerhebung und Auswertung? In J. Reichertz und R. Tuma (Hrsg.): *Der Kommunikative Konstruktivismus bei der Arbeit* (S. 32–76). Weinheim und Basel: Beltz Juventa.

Reichertz, J. und Bettmann, R. (Hrsg.) (2018). *Kommunikation – Medien – Konstruktion. Braucht die Mediatisierungsforschung den Kommunikativen Konstruktivismus?* Wiesbaden: Springer VS.

Reichertz, J. und Tuma, R. (2017). Der Kommunikative Konstruktivismus bei der Arbeit? In J. Reichertz und R. Tuma (Hrsg.): *Der Kommunikative Konstruktivismus bei der Arbeit* (S. 7–29). Weinheim und Basel: Beltz Juventa.

Rinderspacher, J. P. (1987). *Am Ende der Woche. Die soziale und kulturelle Bedeutung des Wochenendes.* Bonn: Neue Gesellschaft.

Rosa, H. (2005). *Beschleunigung. Die Veränderung der Zeitstrukturen in der Moderne.* Frankfurt am Main: Suhrkamp.

Schütz, A. (1972). Gemeinsam musizieren. Eine Studie sozialer Beziehungen. In A. Brodersen (Hrsg.): *Alfred Schütz. Gesammelte Aufsätze II. Studien zur soziologischen Theorie* (S. 129–150). Den Haag: Martinus Nijhoff.

Schütz, A. (1974). *Der sinnhafte Aufbau der sozialen Welt. Eine Einleitung in die verstehende Soziologie.* Frankfurt a. M.: Suhrkamp.

Schütz, A. (2003). Über die mannigfaltigen Wirklichkeiten. In Ders.: *Alfred Schütz Werkausgabe. Bd. V.1. Theorie der Lebenswelt 1: Die pragmatische Schichtung der Lebenswelt* (S. 177–247). Konstanz: UVK.

Schütz, A. und Luckmann, T. (2017). *Strukturen der Lebenswelt.* 2., überarbeitete Aufl. Konstanz: UTB.Zerubavel, E. (1979). *Patterns of Time in Hospital Life.* Chicago und London: University of Chicago Press.

Ziemann, A. (2011). Handlung und Kommunikation – eine situationstheoretische Reformulierung. In N. Schröer und O. Bidlo (Hrsg.): *Die Entdeckung des Neuen. Qualitative Sozialforschung als Hermeneutische Wissenssoziologie* (S. 117–132). Wiesbaden: VS Verlag für Sozialwissenschaften.

Ziemann, A. (2013). Soziologische Strukturlogiken der Situation. In Ders. (Hrsg.): *Offene Ordnung? Philosophie und Soziologie der Situation* (S. 105–129). Wiesbaden: Springer VS.

Rough Relationing Making Time for Analysis in Ethnography

Clément Dréano und Markus Rudolfi

Abstract

In this article, we suggest that ethnographic methods can benefit from playing rather seriously with the temporalities of doing research. We build on a critique of time within the field of Science and Technology Studies (STS) as a linear and singular entity to suggest that, in research practices, temporalities are thriving and are always part of collective and collaborative efforts for ordering knowledge. Following a technique that we call "rough relationing", we foreground in this article that to engage with the different ways temporalities matter during ethnographic fieldwork offers to make time for productive analytical tensions. Such tensions, we argue, may be seen as opportunities to share, talk and write about ongoing concerns one encounters with others in ethnographic work. In the first part of the paper, we show how making time for such tensions has been central for sharing concerns about our previous research: an ethnography of blood donation infrastructures and of an experiment in sustainable living and building that we conducted as part of our M.A. programme. In the second part of the paper, we introduce the technique through a collective game on the temporalities of research that we set up at an ethnography workshop. We linger over some of the pragmatics of the game to

C. Dréano (✉)
University of Amsterdam, Amsterdam, Netherlands
E-Mail: c.m.dreano@uva.nl

M. Rudolfi
Goethe-Universität Frankfurt a. M., Frankfurt a. M., Germany
E-Mail: rudolfi@soz.uni-frankfurt.de

© Springer Fachmedien Wiesbaden GmbH, ein Teil von Springer Nature 2020
E. Schilling und M. O'Neill (Hrsg.), *Frontiers in Time*
Research – Einführung in die interdisziplinäre Zeitforschung,
https://doi.org/10.1007/978-3-658-31252-7_20

foreground playful ways to further tinker with and care for these tensions. We suggest that exploring how temporalities matter in our ethnographic research involves cultivating epistemic virtues such as friendship and playing which are often neglected in social science research.

Zusammenfassung

In diesem Artikel wollen wir den Vorschlag unterbreiten, dass ethnographische Methoden von einer spielerischen Ernsthaftigkeit mit den Temporalitäten der Forschung profitieren kann. Wir bauen auf einem kritischen Verständnis von Zeit im Bereich der Wissenschafts- und Technikforschung (STS) als einer linearen und singulären Einheit auf, um darauf hinzuweisen, dass Temporalitäten bereits während der Forschungspraxis auftauchen und immer schon Teil kollektiver und kollaborativer Bemühungen zur Ordnung von Wissen sind. Anhand einer Technik, welche wir als „rough relationing" bezeichnen, wollen wir zeigen, wie durch die Auseinandersetzung mit Temporalitäten während der ethnografischen Feldforschung Zeit für produktive und analytisch spannende Arbeit gewonnen werden kann. Dabei entstehen auch Spannungen mit anderen, die dazu anregen sich reflektierend über Angelegenheiten in der ethnographischen Arbeit auszutauschen. Im ersten Teil der Arbeit zeigen wir, wie wichtig es war, Zeit für solche Spannungen einzuplanen, um Bedenken über unsere frühere Forschung auszutauschen: Ethnographien über Blutspende-Infrastrukturen und über ein Experiment zum nachhaltigen Leben und Bauen, welche wir im Rahmen unserer Masterarbeit durchgeführt haben. Im zweiten Teil der Arbeit stellen wir die Technik anhand eines Spiels vor, das wir in einem Ethnographie-Workshop durchgeführt haben. Wir reflektieren über die Pragmatik des Spiels, um spielerische und unterhaltsame Wege zu finden, um mit diesen Spannungen umzugehen. Das Erkunden davon, wie Temporalitäten in unserer ethnographischen Forschung bedeutsam werden, beinhaltet das Kultivieren von epistemischen Werten wie Freundschaft und Spielfreude, welche in der sozialwissenschaftlichen Forschung häufig vernachlässigt werden.

Keywords

Time and temporality · Ethnographic methods · Friendship and play · STS · Matters of care

Introduction

Ethnographers are always part of the worlds they research. In particular when it comes to ethnographic methods, it is difficult to keep separate the ethnographers' presence in their fields from the writing-up or drawing of fieldnotes and the re-presentation of ethnographic knowledge in scientific papers, masters' theses or PhD dissertations.

As many scholars, especially in Science and Technology Studies (STS), have argued, methods are not "neutral tools" that clearly separate realities "out there" from a reliable representation of them "in here" within an ethnographic or scientific account (Law 2004; Mol 2002; Verran 2001). For example, STS scholar John Law (2004) urges us to take into account that methods in social sciences no longer "*discover* and depict realities", but rather "participate in the *enactment* of those realities" (ibid., p. 45). In other words, methods, as sets of more or less standardised techniques with their own ideals, materialities, and forms of action, partially perform the realities they aim to study. In that sense, they have politics or, as Law calls it, hinterlands (ibid., p. 27). This paper builds on this understanding of methods in practice to elaborate on a specific aspect of the politics of ethnographic methods.

Throughout the article, we namely attend to a dimension of ethnographic research that is often neglected: time and temporality. We suggest that the practice of ethnography implies both a mode of presence and of knowing that unavoidably render time multiple: there is, to name a few, the time of the field, the time of the desk, of writing, drawing notes or finishing papers, the time of the interlocutors going about their daily businesses (e.g. Fabian 2002). During ethnographic research, whether you like it or not, temporalities thrive, be it during fieldwork or back at the desk. The question we asked ourselves is what to do with this observation? Some might say that this multiplicity should be tamed if we are to bring some coherence in our ethnographies. Indeed, singular time can be a powerful ally in ordering knowledge (Vostal 2016). It can help to trace a thought process, or to reproduce a research design, for example. We suggest however, that to explore multiple temporalities as part of our ethnographic methods also has its virtues.

For example, it can help resist problematic meanings that come with the idea of singular time as linear time. Such as the idea that some societies or groups of people can, in the name of progress, be compared on a same temporal line as being more or less "developed". This concern has been raised in particular within actor-network theory sensitivities, environmental sciences, medical humanities, and feminist and post-colonial (science) studies (M'charek 2014; Serres and Latour 1995; Puig de la Bellacasa 2015; Stengers 2015; Stöckelová 2016; Tsing et al. 2017; Latour and Weibel 2005).

We are thus eager to ask what happens with our ethnographic methods when progress or accumulation is not a wishful temporal metaphor. How, for instance, can we pay attention to different temporalities and ways of relating them across field sites? And how does this bring us to collaborate and know in ethnography? To go about these questions, we offer a modest and hopefully generative technique that we call "rough relationing". "Rough relationing", as we will show in this article, offers to experiment with ways in which temporalities generate tensions in ethnographic work, in two specific ways: Through making us play with time categories and concepts, and through inviting us to slow down and collectively make time for analysis in times of standardised social science methods. We are hopeful that playing with the metaphor of roughness will help us to do this.

The article is structured in two parts and a conclusion. In the first part, we sensitize the reader to "rough relationing" by taking our own examples of an ethnography of blood donation infrastructures and of an experiment in sustainable living and building. We focus on three terms we played with – durability, crisis and synchronicity – and that emerged through roughly relating notes and memories from our seemingly unrelated field sites. In the second part, we introduce the technique through a collective game on the temporalities of research that we set up at an ethnography workshop. Its aim is to show possibilities to collectively experiment with the technique, and to sensitize the reader to its ethnographic pragmatics, playfulness and pleasures.

The two parts foreground a sense that the endeavours that come with practicing "rough relationing" are to be taken seriously. Especially because they involve epistemic virtues, such as friendship and playing, that are often neglected in standardised social science methods, and that need to be granted more space if we want to make time differently for analysis in ethnography (Ballestero and Winthereik, forthcoming). Ethnographic methods, we argue in the conclusion, can benefit from exploring sensitivities for different temporalities. This is our hope that, if cultivated carefully, these sensitivities will help us to get a better sense of how to build and sustain shared concerns and keep caring for them in ethnographic research.

Tensions

Working ethnographically is full of tensions. It requires that quite heterogeneous entities meet in different ways, at different times. This becomes particularly evident as we try to relate our experience during fieldwork to our readings, or to casual or more formal exchanges we have with people from our field sites, colleagues or friends. To be sure, the way we make hold this heterogeneity as we go about our research, and in our analysis is often quite rough. But how to engage with this *roughness* that seems to characterise so well how ethnographers work?

When we look at the meaning of "rough" we first get the following definition: "Rough: (of a person or their behaviour) not gentle; violent or boisterous" (oxford dictionary). In anthropological research, where ethnography remains the main mode of inquiry, to be rough might mean that symbolic or structural violence is done to others for the sake of producing disciplinary knowledge (Fabian 2002). For example, "informants" in the field are made invisible in the research process or in later publications although they helped significantly the ethnographer in obtaining data, and maybe shared personal stories with him or her. Ethnographers can be rough sometimes, even within shared ideals of symmetrical collaboration in ethnography (e.g. Barry et al. 2008; Clerke and Hopwood 2014).

However, if we further scroll down the online oxford dictionary, we find a more promising denotation of the adjective rough. It reads: "Put together as a temporary measure; makeshift" (oxford dictionary). Roughness this time refers to a specific way for things to relate to one another. They do so provisionally, and in an improvised manner. We wondered: how could this other meaning of "rough" be a good metaphor that helps us to inhabit our ethnographic practices? If "relating roughly" is never an innocent practice, it could also invite us to make time for ephemeral, not quite fitting, but nevertheless collective shared moments to be part of our ethnographic research and analysis.

We would like to share with you now how we, the authors of this article, two apprentice ethnographers and long time friends, tried to do this. When we started our M.A. projects in 2015, it soon became clear to us that we could not contribute alone to the formation of research questions and directions within our respective fields – medical sociology and environmental humanities. A crucial part of developing and conducting our ethnographic work consisted in exchange with people in our field sites and at the university, who we like to tell about our research. We, thus, started to share thoughts on our very different research topics. Clément did his research in a blood bank of a big German city on infrastructural practices of blood donation; and Markus did his in a small German ecovillage on experimental sustainable building and living.

Both projects were in different places, the field visits happened at different times during 2017, and most of our literature varied to a great extent. During this period, we kept each other regularly updated about our ongoing concerns. Our exchanges, it seemed, had often rough, uneven edges. They were clumsy, improvised, temporary, and ongoing.

We took a lot of pleasure in these exchanges, in particular because the way we learned to cultivate shared concerns across our different ethnographic projects was through playing with different notions of time. We want to suggest that it is because we played with different notions of time – and because of our friendship over the years – that we could *make* time for analysis in our ethnographies. Instead of taking fixed notions of time such as past, present and future as naturally organising our research, we played with different ones – durability, crisis and synchronicity.

In what follows, we show how the result of such a process might look like in an article. To do that, we play with the form of textual performance, and present the readers with a juxtaposition of ethnographic short stories from our different fieldworks that we call "inter-plays". These are not exactly fieldnotes and neither are they mere abstractions. Rather, they come from the "rough edges" of our ongoing exchanges. The juxtapositions are followed each by a few sentences that more explicitly give a sense to the reader of how we roughly related our empirical stories.

Inter-Plays

Durability

In the ecovillage a group of people has decided to experiment with a different way of living. Part of this experiment consisted in the construction of a building with "waste" materials. When this group started the project they consulted an architect who had previous experiences in building with waste materials and who helped them to plan about the kinds of materials that they could use. In the building industry in Germany at that time "waste" was not a prominent building material. Yet one could hardly find any mainstream advice on the quality, size or shape of the waste materials to be used. Neither were there any useful studies on the performance qualities of waste as a building material. Given this condition, the consultation of an architect proved to be one reasonable option for the group to find out about the possible materiality of their experimental building.

They eventually made use of two waste materials that they thought would be helpful: car tyres and glass bottles. The tyres were used for the construction of building blocks instead of using concrete, a more standard material in building elsewhere. Similarly, the glass bottles were used as bricks for thinner walls in the interior, and were particularly praised for their aesthetics The group and the architect agreed that both car tyres and glass bottles would not decompose within a short period of time and, hence, would serve as quite *persistent* materials. A quality that the group was looking for in their experiment. To be sure, a building that would decompose while living in it would be impractical and wouldn't fit the group's shared ideal of sustainable living.

A concern shared by the doctors and qualified technicians who worked at the blood bank at the time I did my fieldwork is the little quantity and the short life of blood products available in the bank. Blood red cells, especially, that are daily used for treatment of patients with haemoglobinopathies, like sickle cell disease, or Beta-Thalassemia, or during surgeries, can rarely be used beyond a month or five weeks after donation. Furthermore, certain patients may need a very specific kind of blood product. I wondered: how to make sure that there is enough blood in the bank and that every patient in need can benefit from it? With this question in mind, I started to be interested in how technicians and doctors worked towards making the infrastructure of this blood bank durable. I noticed that they relied on different objects and practices to do so. For example, donors' and patients' registries could be used to anticipate the needs in blood of the bank through looking for 'good matches'. Less exceptionally maybe, a doctor would go through the stocks of the blood bank every morning and make sure, with pen and paper, to count what is left and what had been used the previous day in order to get a sense of how to go about the day. Probably, the doctor tells me, they will need to buy blood from another bank after today's counting.

The concern with durability shows the infrastructural complexities of a blood bank. Making a blood donation infrastructure durable may involve gathering health information about donors and patients or looking for particular kind of donor 'populations'; it may also involve selling and buying blood.

To wonder about durability helped me to get a grasp on what it takes to do ethnographic research on resource scarcities and human body parts, two concerns that I explored in my thesis.

The two stories may look quite unrelated. Car tyres, glass bottles and practices of sustainable living have apparently little to do with donors, patients and the infrastructures of a blood bank. As a juxtaposition, they stand next to each other. Roughly so. Fortunately, wondering together about durability gave us also an opportunity to playfully juxtapose these two stories, and to offer them to the reader. Sharing our concerns about durability in relation to our different field sites made us foreground important matters in our research, that, maybe, we would otherwise not have given too much importance. Markus could notice how fragile a sustainable building project would be without durable materials. And Clément could better understand how durability convoked eclectic logics in the blood bank. It let emerge blood not only as a gift that people make to each other, but also as an economic good, and as a potentially data-rich substance about populations, or groups of people.

Crisis

The ecovillage was founded in the year 2010. A group of ambitious people joined together and bought an old castle that was formerly used as a sheltered workshop. The buildings were and some still are quite degraded and most of them needed to be renovated in order to be inhabitable. Within the project of this ecovillage,, the experimental sustainable building required particular attention regarding how to successfully assemble and maintain it. These tasks required constant care. . An instance of this effort is the small carpentry business which was established by the inhabitants of the sustainable building themselves. When I worked there as a "guest helper" the carpenters explained to me that more skilled hands were needed for the renovations and the construction of this building to happen. This is but an instance of the many tasks needed to renovate and maintain that building, and that involved professional know-how.

I heard this story of shortage in needed hands at many occasions during my stay in the field. There were never enough hands to be mobilised, and the fact that people in the ecovillage also needed mine makes me aware of the potential crisis that comes with making this place inhabitable. As an answer to this possible crisis, the carpenters and helpers managed *provisional* ways of habitation. They did so, for example, through continuous monitoring of, and care for renovation work in the ecovillage, and more specifically for the experimental sustainable building. That way, they could prevent that the ecovillage be turned into non habitable ruins. This very mode of working pushed at the same time carpenters and others to create an environment that is sensitized to more than just one kind of crisis for habitation, such as climate change and land degradation.

It is 8 in the morning and I am meeting Emily at the serology laboratory for blood testing. She is a lab practitioner in the blood bank and is responsible for conducting sometimes quite complicated blood tests on donated blood to make sure it matches with the patients. She tells me that the testing is a plastic practice. When blood is needed very urgently, technicians do very quick tests with the machines so that the blood can reach the patient as soon as possible. For other complicated cases for which she and her colleagues have more time, it can take days to make sure that the right blood product will be given to the right patient.

Testing for blood in the blood bank brings about a sense of crisis and care. Emily wants to show this to me. She takes some reagents that they use in the lab for the testing of donors' blood products for matching and disposes a bit of blood with those reagents on a plastic slab. As she moves the slab over the lamp to mix the blood with the reagents, clots appear within seconds. Emily looks at me. "It's beautiful, isn't it ?". She continues: "You know, if we're not careful enough, this will also happen within seconds in the patient's body.". In the blood bank, there is often no pre-established good way to know when a blood product needs more or less testing before getting to the patient. Despite the fact that a lot of activities there are standardized, this part of the job is an uneasy matter. Sometimes, just a basic test is done. Sometimes, machines take over to process more complex testing as quick as possible. Sometimes, in turn, you just cannot speed things up, and a test might take many days to get into the details of blood compatibility between donor and patient. The lesson here is no best answer to how to go about testing the blood of donors. And in the midst of these difficult options, the best you can do is often to keep yourself reminded, as Emily did with me, of how both beautiful and dangerous blood matching can be.

We shared these stories well before we juxtaposed them here. We kept telling these to each other: a curious sense for aesthetics, morals, danger and care in blood testing practices. A surprising, frenetic mode of testing and taste for provisionality in the experimental building. The term "crisis" came quite late in our exchange, as a term that could help us share what we thought did hang together in some way. Crisis was handy to mobilise, because it brought connotations of worry and provisionality that we both encountered in our field sites. It also sensitized us to care, maintenance and repair as activities that people engaged with in situations of crisis. Without the right kind of care and maintenance, sustainability could always get lost in the midst of practices to make it work. And what practitioners talked about as the "gift of life" could suddenly become harmful to its recipient without careful testing.

Synchronicity

Efforts to improve the experimental sustainable building take existing forms of sustainable living that already exist seriously. As a consequence, the group working on it try to implement as much of these alternatives as possible with the lowest costs and emissions as possible. This implies, for example, the use of solar energy for electricity as well as the creation of a greenhouse area in the front of the building. Another instance consists in, using rainwater and wastewater within the sewage system, whenever this is allowed, so that water taps and showers can provide freshwater according to German law. While such efforts constitute a big step forward to a more sustainable future in general, there are also some challenges connected to what the group intends to do..

For instance, solar irradiation, which is needed for gaining enough energy from the sun, depends to some extent on sunny weather. However, in order to harvest rainwater sunny weather might not be the perfect climatic conditions needed. Thus, people inhabiting this building are highly dependent on a *recurring* weather *cycle* and even whole seasons in order to simultaneously harvest enough energy and water. Without a regular cycle they are always lacking or having too much of one or the other.

As the director of the blood bank once asked me about my research, I told him that I want to follow the blood from donors to patients. He seemed surprised and told me that usually social scientists who come to see him are interested in donors' motivations for donating and not in what happens to the blood once it leaves their bodies. I guess his surprise came from the fact that he shares the idea, together with many social scientists, that donation and altruism is graspable in people's mind, in cultural values or in a social contract between people. In my research, I wanted to complicate this question. I had the feeling that altruism and donation may have as much to do with the blood bank's infrastructure. What I learn during my fieldwork, is that not all blood can go to everybody. Despite the willingness to donate, there is no straightforward way between the act of donating and the circulation of blood to a patient's body. Technicians in particular would know that it is the infrastructure that does the synchronization work between donors and patients. And not alone the will of the donor. This becomes invisible when things are going well, and blood seems to peacefully flow from donor to patient. This is where the donor's altruistic story of giving blood to an unknown other become synchronized to what the infrastructure does. As I learnt, this is not an obvious matter. Synchronizing the donor's altruistic self with the working of a blood bank infrastructure is a fragile endeavour that sometimes fail.

The two stories we shared here are centred around synchronization. This term helped us to notice that, in both our field sites, synchronization is an important sensitizer to understand some of the key concerns that people share in our field sites. In Markus' story, synchronization helps to get a sense of how much the group of people working in the experimental sustainable building is reliant on climatic weather cycles. In Clément's story, synchronization helps to grasp a tension that is cultivated in the blood bank, between what the director, and others in social science frame as the donors' altruistic motivations to donate on the one hand, and the demanding, and sometimes conflictual practicalities of making blood flows between distant bodies on the other hand.

* * *

In these inter-plays, we play with three different notions of time – durability, crisis and synchronicity – that help us to build and share concerns in common in our quite different ethnographic fieldworks. To be sure, collectively sharing empirical stories is an important practice in ethnographic work. One that is, however, quite undervalued, because it may seem too rough, too elusive or too temporary. Not strong enough a rendering, or an account, of the reality 'out there'. Or because it contradicts the disciplinary canons of single authorship. As a contrast to this narrative, we want to foreground that the practice of ongoingly sharing and relating ethnographic stories, even if only temporarily, or roughly, is endowed with pleasures and playfulness that are very generative and have the power to breathe life into our ethnographies.

But how to do this well? The inter-plays suggest that one way to do it is through playing differently with the very stabilising, or regulative, and thus powerful ideal of linear time that traditionally divide and organise ethnographic research: from research design, to fieldwork, and back at the desk. There are two ways in which these interplays playfully unsettle this ideal, and we would like to evoke them shortly.

First, they do so through situating ethnographic analysis as a practice of relating empirical stories that does not necessarily take place back at the desk, that is usually considered to be the privileged site of analysis in ethnography. As it appears here, the inter-plays are crafted from the middle of our ethnographic work. They suggest that design work, ethnographic fieldwork and desk work are always intertwined, and never clearly separated in practice. And that ethnographic analysis often brings them together in non-linear ways. Rather than waiting for the time of the desk to come, we suggest that it is a virtue to stay with the many times of ethnographic work, and with their messiness. To say it in other words, when we work and analyse ethnographically, we are caught in multiple times, and the fact that we always stand in the midst of the tensions they bring about is not something we can escape. Instead, we would be better off to make time for these temporal tensions to be patiently articulated in our ethnographic modes of doing analysis.

Second, the inter-plays unsettle the idea of a singular time through nurturing an ethnographic feel for different temporalities. They do so through playing, or tinkering, within the stories we share, with a variety of temporal terms. Through turning them into objects that do not need to be all too stable, we roughly, temporarily share in common and mediate a sense of crisis, durability and synchronicity within our empirical stories. These temporal terms become new sensitizers not only in our ethnographic stories; but also in the way we can engage with time in doing ethnographic research. We thus allow these specific graspings of crisis, durability and synchronicity to become part of our ethnographic repertoire.

This is our argument that making time for analysis in ethnography requires both of these points that the inter-plays foreground. That is, a commitment to non-linearity in relating and analysing ethnographically. And collective efforts to cultivate a multiplicity of temporal terms, or sensitizers, within our ethnographic modes of doing research.

In these inter-plays, playfulness and friendship have gently pushed us to do this through sharing our empirical stories. Friendship, especially, has been important for actually making and taking the time and interest to do so. In that sense, it has always been "at work" in the way we practiced "rough relationing". We leave it here to the readers to start tinkering in similar ways within their academic friendships. As for the second part of this article, it offers possibilities to foreground play as a way to further experiment with "rough relationing".

Intermezzo

In the first part of the article, we set out to show that tensions are always present in ethnographic research and in particular in analysis. We argued that the constitutive heterogeneity in doing ethnography produces quite rough and provisional ways of analysis, and we ask ourselves how to properly deal with this. Taking "roughness" as our terminological starting point, and discussing its' problematic (i.e. violence) and at the same time useful (i.e. temporary measure) meanings, we took a closer look at the insights we get from relationing both of our research projects. What we call "rough relationing" turned out to be an analytic technique in contrast with the standards we know in social sciences.

Considering time and temporality as our analytical focus, we were able to come up with three exemplary terms once we began the rough relationing of our fields: durability, crisis and synchronicity. The terms emerged out of the "interplays", i.e. the mutual and playful juxtapositions of short stories that we shared with each other as part of our friendship and interest in each others work. It made us aware of how standardised social research better fits the temporality of progress while non-standardised techniques such as rough relationing have to make time in order to be practiced. We suggest that rough relationing as a way of doing analysis benefits from the epistemic virtues we set out here: friendship and playfulness.

II. Playing on a Rough Ground. Or: How to Become Ethnographic Through Play

"Rough ground is ground that is not used for any particular purpose, is not even, and is full of wild plants." (Cambridge dictionary)

How to create possibilities to play on a rough ground? This is the question we asked ourselves when we organised the 11th workshop for ethnographers in Bochum, in early 2019. This three-days workshop is self-organised, takes place every year at a different university in Germany, and gathers apprentice ethnographers at different stages of their B.A., M.A. or PhD research all around the country (and beyond). On top of the usual sessions of the workshop dedicated to sharing and discussing ethnographic material and writing, we decided, as the organisers of the 2019 edition, to organise a game that we would play in-between the workshop sessions with the participants.

The aim of the game was to continue to explore what we did in the interplays, that is to sensitize ourselves to different temporalities of and in ethnographic work. We wondered how we could play with other ethnographers around these rough edges that we found ourselves so exciting and pleasurable. We thought that it would be a good idea to specify a location to do so. We set up a rough ground in the common room by putting tables together. This would be our playground where the game that we designed for the participants would take place.

Before we get into the practicalities of the game, however, let us tell you few words on the reason why we thought that playing could help us develop our ethnographic sensitivities. We suggest that play can be a particularly good companion in doing ethnographic analysis. It suspends a sense of getting straightforward to one's aim. As in the "hit and run" strategy of standardised social science methods, for example, that design methods to get straight to the objects they promise themselves to discover. Playing, as an activity, aims thus less at looking forward, than at looking around, and enjoying the detours. This is, we suggest, very much what ethnographers do in practice. We take inspiration here from Huizinga's understanding of play. Huizinga defines play as a multispecies activity that cannot be reduced to concepts such as "instinct" or "mind" (Huizinga 1980 [1949], p. 1), and that foregrounds instead that play is quite of a free activity that stands outside ordinary life, and that absorbs the player intensely and utterly (ibid., p. 13; see also Sicart 2014, 2018).[1]

What we learned with our technique, however, is that playing on a rough ground has some specificities. It is not a detached activity. To be sure, a rough ground is ground that is not used for any particular purpose. This resonates with Huzinga's understanding of play as a free activity. But a rough ground is also ground that is uneven, and full of wild plants. Play, yes, but also: beware! Because playing might not always be possible and desirable. For instance, we would not like to play with nuclear power, toxic remnants, or dangerous animals (e.g. Abildgaard et al. 2017).

To cultivate the metaphor of playing on a rough ground is to be kept reminded of both the importance, and the ambivalence of playing as an activity. In the two "playgroundings" that constitute the core of the second part of this article, we keep reminded of this ambivalence.

---

[1] According to Huizinga, scientific practices tend to assign a function to play. Either in the form of a biological instinct, or as a free play of the modern scientific, lonely mind (Huizinga 1980 [1949], p. 1). In either ways, play becomes an object, but not a ground on which to play and linger for the researchers themselves. We do not need to go with Huizinga here. However, he provides us with the inspiration to further look into how fun, pleasures and passion can become part of experimenting with ethnographic methods.

The different aspects of playing that we present below continue with other means what we started to explore in the inter-plays. That there is not one time, but many times coming together in quite messy ways in doing ethnographic analysis. And that sensitizing oneself to certain temporal terms, or categories, pushes us to weigh up, in open ended ways, how specific temporalities become part of our ethnographic repertoire. At last, playing on a rough ground shows that *taking care of temporalities as objects in ethnographic work* and *taking care of the temporalities of ethnographic work itself* both requires sensitivities that need to be invented, and to carefully make time for different ways of practicing ethnographic analysis.

In what follows, we first present the practicalities of the game we set up at the workshop. It aims at situating the game, and at providing the reader with ways to reproduce it him- or herself within academic, or non-academic spaces. We then recount two moments of playing that we situate with short ethnographic notes that we took during the event, in order to show and reflect on some of the complexities and promises of playing as a way to do "rough relating".

The Game, A Starter Kit

We introduce you now to a possible material set-up to play our game. This is how we did it at the workshop. And if you, the reader, can think of yet another way, we warmly invite you to keep experimenting!

First, a few words on the preparation. We tried to make sure that participants could feel comfortable by providing drinks and snacks, and putting chairs in a circle. That way, we could invite them to make a short introduction round and have the opportunity to present themselves and their research. We also asked them to bring an artefact (an object, a photo, a drawing, etc.) from their research project. The artefacts could have a symbolic value to the person who brought it, and it could also be an object gathered or made during fieldwork. This way, participants would present their research with the help of their artefact, and use them later for the game that we set up.

We decided to play the game after the lunch break on the second day of the workshop. Although we had an idea of how it might look like, it took us some time to figure out how this could work well. We needed some rules first, so we came up with the following three tasks that we wrote on a blackboard in the common room (see Box 1). With the help of these tasks, the participants could already start thinking about the game when they returned from lunch.

> **Box 1. Tasks to practice "rough relationing"**
>
> ---
>
> "Rough relationing". Time categories in ethnographic research
>
> *Propose time categories*
>
> Tell someone about your ethnographic project with the help of the artefact you brought. As you tell, think about possible time categories in your research (e.g. if the artefact you brought is an emergency kit, you may think of emergency as an important time category in your research)
>
> *Talk about the time categories and how they relate to your research*
>
> The person with whom you partnered up picks up one or more time categories that were proposed and tries to link them to his or her own research, with the help of the artefact.
>
> *Temporary agreement*
>
> Choose the time category that seemed to work best during the discussion and write it down on a piece of paper tape. Stick it to the woollen thread and link your two artefacts with the thread and the time category on it.

We then sat down on chairs that we put in a circle and started to read and explain the tasks. The overall idea was clear: Pair up in two, find time categories that you have in common with another person. The artefact you brought will help you with this. Then talk about these categories, or terms, in relation to your own research. It might elicit the memory of good field stories. Finally, write down the term in common you liked most, and use it to connect your artefacts. In order to help the participants to do this final connection work, we provided the necessary tools so that it could materialise on the "rough ground" that we designed (see photo 1). For you, the reader of this text, we also wrote a short instruction on how to create the material space of a "rough ground", so that you can reproduce it easily (see Box 2).

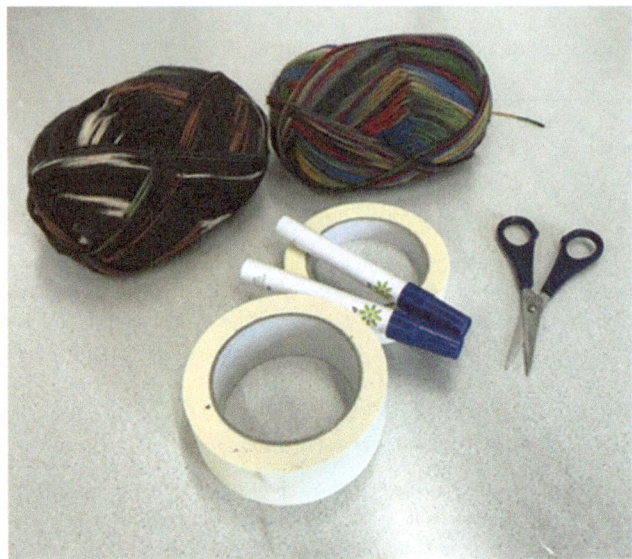

Photo 1 Tape, pen, wool and scissors to do the connection work

> **Box 2. How to create your rough ground?**
> Here is what you need to do it. Find a surface on which you can dispose the artefacts and make the connections. This may be a plane or it can be arranged in 3D space. As a way to take "rough grounds" seriously, we decided during the workshop to put some tables together and to use different heights.

As the organisers of this game, we decided to split up our roles. Clément took the role as observer during the game, and also took some photos. And Markus took the role as participant in the game. The two of us kept exchanging about how the game unfolded during and after it took place. This is why, in what follows, we opt for the use of an authorial "we".

Playgrounding 1. Exploring Time Categories, Telling Each Other Stories

Ethnographic note

We take this photo as the participants of the workshop play for some time already. After few moments of indecisiveness at the beginning of the game, we are both released to see that participants quickly pair up; and quite easily come to talk.

On this photo, some of the players, out of the frame, are still standing, or sitting in the room in pairs, enjoying the talk. It feels really good that, after few moments only of playing the game, the common room suddenly turns into quite a joyful cacophony! The photo shows that, in the middle of this mess, some already started to connect their artefacts, and to write down on a piece of tape the time category that they thought would best fit the stories they just told to each other. Maybe the reason why we took this photo and inserted it here is because we were hopeful. That the participants could get a feel for the game. And that the joyful work of talking and connecting will remind them of the time spent together playing, sharing stories and trying out time words.

Tinkering With Time Categories

We were happy to realise, during the game, that making use of temporal categories, or terms, led the participants articulate and share in a playful way field experiences, stories and concerns that they carried with them. That the mess of it did not feel out of place, but just the right kind of engagement. The players seemed to enjoy and be excited both about the talk and the hands on exercise of connecting their artefacts together on our rough ground. They seemed, in the overall, to enjoy the exercise of sharing these insights from the middle of their project, regardless of how advanced they were, or where they found themselves at that moment in their ethnographic research.

We were especially positively surprised that they could do so easily, without feeling the need of following a clear temporal order. Maybe because the game did not set up a clear place to begin and to end; and because the only limit we set to it was a certain time frame. Nevertheless, within this mess, and collective tinkering, a feeling for "getting it right" could emerge. After all, participants did find a way to tell each other stories, and to connect their artefacts.

The game, so we felt, could thus revive the ethnographic imagination on temporality. It also made us realise that too broad temporal categories, or terms, such as past, present and future were not handy to play with and share stories. The task was thus sometimes very hard, as we noticed that a lot of time-words were not readily available on one's tongue, and had to be actively looked for by the players. In return, too many time categories could be also overwhelming. For example, Carla[2], one of the participants, found herself overwhelmed during the game. She wondered what to do with all these possibilities she could think of.

At last, our impression is that tinkering with time categories during the game opened up possibilities for sharing stories, and for connecting and exploring each others' projects. It proved to be at once joyfully generative, hard and sometimes disconcerting. Time-words did not always come easily on one's tongue. And as Carla expressed it, playing the game sometimes felt like "losing ground".

Asking Questions With Artefacts

Daniel, another participant in the game, found a good way not to fully lose ground during the game. He did so through suggesting ways to ask good questions with the help of the artefacts. He reminded us, for example, that, to find a time category in common, it is not necessary to literally look for them in the artefacts. Instead, it could be done more productively through actively situating the artefact in one's research. He reminded us that context matters. And that the artefact could be used during the talk to specify an exchange, and to ask particular questions about one's research. This could be done, so Daniel, through relating the artefact to specific field situations for example. For the artefact to be generative in the game, it was thus important that it is not used in the first place as an object standing for itself, or as too obvious a representative of one's research. Rather, it worked at its best when it was mobilised to contextualise one's research, to point to specific empirical situations, and to help one's game partner to ask good questions about these.

Abstractions and Sticky Words. The Hardship of Connecting Back Categories to Stories

Finally, we have noticed that some participants during the game also focused their attention towards temporal terms *only*. We realised that this is where the game could become problematic because playing without sharing stories could lead to abstract talk, quite disconnected from one's empirical work.

---

[2]For all names, except of the authors, we use pseudonyms.

We noticed in this regard how important our rough ground proved to be. To a certain extent, it provided the players with a quite specific ecology of attention. The threads and time-words that connected participants' artefacts could remind them not only of the words, and their possible abstract meanings, but also of their talks and the stories they shared during the game, thus adding layers of meaning to them. That these connections could materialise was a reminder that it was important that time categories stick to the empirical research contexts of these playful exchanges. As a way to resist that temporal terms become fetishized entities, standing on their own.

The eclectic impressions and reflections that we recount here taught us that the work of connecting time categories, or terms, to empirical stories within the event of the game is at once messy, joyful and hard work. It is generative, and asks for specifications at the same time. In the following playgrounding, we explore the afterlife of the game. We ask: what does coming back to our rough playground become, after it has been left alone for a while? We suggest that this coming back is still playing. But it is a different kind of play, one that requires to carefully pull threads that are already in place, even if only roughly so.

Playgrounding 2: The Afterlife of a Game: Patiently Pulling the Threads With Others

Ethnographic note

We are sitting in the common room, on the third day of the workshop. We left the messy and joyful cacophony of the game behind us, and the room is now filled with a quiet atmosphere. Imagine that you are now hearing the steady and

relaxing sound of the room ventilation in the background. And how this may contrast to the lively, and loud atmosphere of playing the game the day before. We are alone sitting in the room, chit-chatting, and thinking back of our game. What remains on this photo that we took is our deserted rough ground. Many threads with time-words that connect the artefacts are hanging lose already, and some participants picked up their precious artefact at the end of the day, yesterday, to bring it home. The whole scenery evokes something sad. How to continue getting a grasp on these ephemeral shared stories? What is a good way to do so?

This is day three, and looking back at the game, it seemed to us that it had been a good way to let go, make new connections, and have fun with a lot of different apprentice ethnographers and their research. We remember the time of playing the game quite vividly as a time marked by the light and easy feeling of breaking the linearity of time-thinking. There were so many directions in connecting and exchanging that this game made possible for each of us! But how to get back to them after a while? In order to keep exploring this, we set up a discussion round on the third and last workshop day.

A bunch of the participants from the day before gathered some chairs so that we can sit and think back together. In the meanwhile, the experience of the game had settled a bit in everyone's mind. Our discussion took a very different shape.. It seemed more serious, or concerned perhaps. The lightness had gone. It felt a bit like being back at the desk after fieldwork and its excitement, when one tries to figure out on his or her own what to do with all that lived experience and material collected. Only this time, we sat together *with others*, and we collectively ask ourselves the question: "so what?" What to do now with this rough, and seemingly abandoned ground? In this particularly acrobatic moment, the situation demanded us to be careful about what terms and what stories we want to keep and cherish over time. About the threads we wish to pull, and the one that will stay lose, out of our attention.

Playing this somehow different game elicited some remarks. During our discussion, somebody of the group asked, provocatively: If that game was a method, or a research technique, then "a method for what? How is this of any use for your research?" Someone suggested, tentatively, that the game we played on the day before might be more of a didactics, not to be taken too seriously. It felt strange, thus, that the time of playing yesterday could be radically different from the time of our discussion today.

The authors of this article started to wonder. *When* exactly, had rough relationing happened? Was it during the game yesterday? Or during the discussion we were having in its aftermath? What if, instead, we had been playing all along, during the game, and also now, a while after, trying to pull the right threads, and to remember the stories that made us think? What if, on this last day of our workshop, we were just continuing the same work we had begun the day before, of sensitizing ourselves to different temporalities. And of weighing up and sorting out together what we wished to tell each other and to remember?

Rough relationing, we suggest, is about playing the game, and about playing it again after a while, patiently caring with others for what threads to pull and what stories to remember. Not everybody came on the next day to gather and talk. Even less, maybe, would keep pulling the threads beyond the workshop, and continue explore what they started with the game. As many feminist scholars suggest, continuing to engage with this is, to an extent, a difficult work of love (e.g. Rose 1994). It is also a matter of care, of attending at once, to what we foreground and to what we background. To how we attend and to how we neglect (Puig de la Bellacasa 2011; Tronto 1993)[3]. Our friendship helped us to continue this work over the years, to think about what stories we would like to further tell and share with each other, and to get a sense of which one we left behind.

Rough relationing is thus a matter of how we care, through play and friendship, for the connections we make. A becoming-with (Haraway 2016) through play – a *sym-ludic becoming*[4]. This is, we hope, what the patient work of pulling some threads and not others that we speculated about in the aftermaths of the game can suggest to us.

Conclusion. Making Time for Analysis in Ethnographic Research

In this article, we presented rough relationing as a research technique that offers to play and experiment with the varied temporalities of doing ethnographic work. Building on what STS scholar John Law suggests in his book on mess in social science, we suggested that rough relationing offers an opportunity to think about the messes of reality, and, in doing so, "to teach ourselves to think, to practice, to relate, and to know in new ways." (Law 2004, p. 2). Of course, rough relationing

---

[3]Following Joan Tronto let us recall that care is "a species activity that includes everything we do to maintain, continue, and repair our 'world' so that we can live in it as well as possible" (Tronto 1993, p. 103).

[4]See also M. Wertheim (2018) and the Institute For Figuring for an inspiring example of sym-ludic becoming: https://www.theiff.org/ (accessed: 06.02.2020).

does not engage with all the messes of reality. Rather, it invites us to engage specifically with the question of how time and temporalities 'mess with' our ethnographic practices.

Throughout the article, we argued that time of and in ethnographic work is neither singular nor linear. Rather what ethnographers face in going about their research is a myriad of temporalities that are likely to shape their research practices in different, often surprising ways. Sometimes as the lived temporalities of going about one's ethnographic research, other times as the unruly objects of ethnographic analysis. Instead of looking for ways to clarify from scratch, in the manner of a methods handbook, what is what, and how ethnographers should go about these different times and temporalities that thrive in and 'mess up' their research, rough relationing sets out to offer ways for them to play with these temporal sensitivities.

In this regard, it contrasts with what standardised methods in social science can offer. As a way of tinkering and experimenting, it asks us to make time for new ways of thinking, practicing, relating, and knowing. Standards in social science methods often mean that one can *save* a lot of time during research. In our current academic environments, within which we can observe an increasing interest in saving time (and money), standardised methods look appealing to many. We thus hope that rough relationing can also give hints on the importance of making time in our analysis. Making time for analysis means, at last, that we should not rush or clear up the mess out of our analysis too quickly, but instead slow down, learn to be generous with our methods (M'charek forthcoming), and take a look around, not only ahead (Stengers 2018).

As a way to remind ourselves and the readers of this, we proposed in the article to explore, roughly so, and with care, how time and temporalities matter in doing ethnographic work. We showed in our inter-plays that rough relationing could help, per friendship, to share and cultivate in common long time stories. And that temporal sensitivities in ethnography could be further explored in a collective game that we set up at an ethnography workshop. By reclaiming friendship and playing as epistemic virtues in these specific endeavours, we tried to draw attention to other ways of doing analysis (Ballestero and Winthereik forthcoming). By being good friends, and cultivating a sense of playfulness in our exchanges, we, the authors of this article, learned to praise both the slowness and roughness of our exchanges. We often liked to let them be temporary, inconclusive, and rough. To be taken up and continued for another day. With this article, we hope that you, the reader, will also find some virtue in experimenting with rough relationing.

References

Abildgaard, M.S./A. Birkbak/T. Elgaard Jensen/A. Koed Madsen/A. Kristian Munk (2017): Playgrounding Techno-Anthropology, EASST Review, 36(2).
Ballestero, A./B.R. Winthereik (forthcoming): The Ethnographic Effect. A Companion to Analysis (working title). Durham: Duke University Press.
Barry, A./G. Born/G. Weszkalnys (2008): Logics of interdisciplinarity. Economy and Society, 37:1, 20–49.
Cambridge Dictionary (2020): "rough". URL: https://dictionary.cambridge.org/fr/dictionnaire/anglais/rough?fbclid=IwAR3Es-cbEh4fkePNulVTFP408kWzZ9J9VnobXS5sUZRgIRFDU9R9d49xoM0 (accessed: 06.02.2020).
Clerke, T./Hopwood, N. (2014): Doing Ethnography in Teams: A Case Study of Asymmetries in Collaborative Research. Cham, Heidelberg, New York, Dordrecht, & London: Springer.
Fabian, J. (2002): Time and its Other. How Anthropology Makes its Object. New York: Columbia University Press.
Haraway, D. (2016): Staying with the trouble: Making kin in the Chthulucene. Durham: Duke University Press.
Huizinga, J. (1980 [1949]): Homo Ludens: A Study of the Play-element in Culture. London, Boston, MA & Henley, OX: Routledge & Kegan Paul.
Latour, B./P. Weibel (Eds.) (2005): Making Things Public: Atmospheres of Democracy. Cambridge MA: MIT Press.
Law, J. (2004): After Method: Mess in Social Science Research. London: Routledge.
M'charek, A.A. (2014): Race, Time and Folded Objects: The HeLa Error, In: Theory, Culture and Society, 29–56.
M'charek (forthcoming): What is race? Forensics, Face, and Generous Methods for Studying Race.", in: Special Issue of Social Studies of Science.
Mol, A. (2002): The body multiple. Ontology in medical practice, Durham: Duke University Press.
Oxford Dictionary (2020): "rough". URL: https://www.lexico.com/en/definition/rough?fbclid=IwAR265bJ9YTCQiGE40ebvqsDqmSMQmadngpJDbraYnXipLq1GrzRWo1BssyU (accessed: 06.02.2020).
Puig de la Bellacasa, M. (2011): Matters of care in technoscience: Assembling neglected things. Social Studies of Science, 41(1), 85–106.
Puig de la Bellacasa, M. (2015): Making time for soil: Technoscientific futurity and the pace of care. In: Social Studies of Science, 691–716.
Rose, H. (1994): Love, Power and Knowledge: Towards a Feminist Transformation of the Sciences. Indiana University Press.
Serres, M./Latour B. (1995): Conversations on Science, Culture, and Time: Michel Serres with Bruno Latour. University of Michigan Press.
Sicart, M.A. (2014): Play Matters. Cambridge, MA & London: MIT Press.
Sicart, M.A. (2018): Playing with ethics. In: C. Lury et al. (eds.), Routledge Handbook of Interdisciplinary Research Methods. Oxon & New York: Routledge, pp. 183–186.
Stengers, I. (2015): In Catastrophic Times. Resisting the Coming Barbarism, Open Humanities Press.

Stengers, I. (2018): Another Science is Possible: A Manifesto for Slow Science. Cambridge: Polity Press. (Translated by Stephen Muecke).

Stöckelová, Tereza (2016): Frame Against the Grain: Asymmetries, Interference, and the Politics of EU Comparison. In: Deville J, Guggenheim M and Hrdličková Z (eds.), Practising Comparison. Manchester: Mattering Press.

Tronto, J.C. (1993): Moral Boundaries. A Political Argument for an Ethic of Care. New York/London: Routledge.

Tsing, A./H. Swanson/E. Gan/N. Bubandt (Eds.) (2017): Arts of Living on a Damaged Planet: Ghosts and Monsters of the Anthropocene. Minneapolis: University of Minnesota Press.

Verran, H. (2001): Science and an African Logic. Chicago and London: University of Chicago Press.

Vostal, Filip (2016): Accelerating Academia: The Changing Structures of Academic Time. Palgrave.

Wertheim, M. (2018): Figuring. In: C. Lury et al. (eds.), Routledge Handbook of Interdisciplinary Research Methods. Oxon & New York: Routledge, pp. 57–60.

The Narrative and the Flash Fiction: Ethical and Political Temporalities in the Life Course of an Adolescent Involved with Crime in Brazil

Jacqueline de Oliveira Moreira, Andréa Máris Campos Guerra, Rodrigo Goes e Lima und Ana Elisa de Oliveira Drawin

Abstract

This work is part of the research titled "Adolescences and Laws"(Research funded by Fundação de Amparo à Pesquisa do Estado de Minas Gerais (FAPEMIG – 001–2017, Universal Demand, CHE APQ03220-17).), which aimed to explore subjective-political elements that could favor or hinder an association with crime. Working methodologically with "narrative memoirs" as a research strategy, sixteen interviews were conducted with Brazilian youths aged seventeen to twenty-nine years old, whose narratives were then transformed into artistic works. In this context, we analyze the flash fiction "Bond", aiming to highlight the possibilities that the narrative method, in

---

Research Productivity grantee (PQ2) - National Council for Scientific and Technological Development (CNPq) (Jacqueline de Oliveira Moreira)
Research Productivity grantee (PQ2) - National Council for Scientific and Technological Development (CNPq) (Andréa Máris Campos Guerra)

J. de Oliveira Moreira (✉) · A. M. á. C. Guerra
Belo Horizonte, Brasil

R. G. e. Lima
New York, USA

A. E. de Oliveira Drawin
Porto, Portugal

the interface between art and science, may offer to treat the real. We have thus elected the dimension of time as a privileged aspect that allows for the ratification of the forms of capturing the indeterminable through narrative writing, considering the works of Freud, Lacan and Ricoeur. As a strategy for the research of social phenomena, the narrative memoir shares common aspects with biographical research, but the former allows for the identification of manifestations of unconscious processes, while considering the points of fiction, fixation and fantasy displayed in the narratives. By consenting with the reconstruction of a temporality that is able to encompass the particularities of a subjective experience, it also provides the subject with a new ethical and political position.

Keywords

Narrative · Flash fiction · Temporality · Adolescence · Trajectory

Introduction

This paper is the result of an investigation based on the *Adolescências e Leis* (Adolescences and Laws[3]) research, which sought to explore conditioning[1] subjective-political elements that were favorable and unfavorable to desistance from crime in the lives of Brazilian youths.(*Ana Elisa*) *Ana Elisa*).

In Brazil, the temporal dimension takes an important role when considering the statistics connected to child mortality. The earliness regarding the victims age and the morbid quickness of how the numbers grow and become material in the fate of young people are significant indicators on the seriousness of the situation. According to the Atlas of Violence of 2018 (*Atlas da Violência de 2018* – Cerqueira et al. 2018), "33.590 teenagers and young adults were murdered in

---

[1]The use of the term "conditioning" is justified according to our understanding of the value of the notion of "overdetermination" of psychical factors, as supported by Freud (1900/2011a). Thus, we argue that the subjective-political elements related to one's involvement with crime do not unilaterally *determine* a certain subjective position, but rather, they may (or may not) create *conditions* that allow for a decision to be made by the adolescent. Hence the expression "*conditioning* elements".

2016" there being an increase of 23.3 % in such cases in the period from 2006 to 2016 (Cerqueira et al. 2018, p. 32). Therefore, the observation that follows the data of the Map of Violence since 1998 is still relevant – that "we do not believe that youth produces violence." Rather, the new generations are in fact a result of our societal situation (Waiselfisz 1998, p. 12).[2] In this same social scenario, we observe that the profile of young victims of violence in Brazil repeats itself when analyzing the data of those who are mostly subject to the justice system of the country. The results intensify the scenario of social exclusion: they are mostly low income young black males (Silva and Oliveira 2015). In regards to this population, it is important to remember that since 1990, with the creation of the Statute of the Child and Adolescent (Brazil, 1990) the handling of minors who have infringed the law is done under the Doctrine of Integral Protection (*Doutrina de Proteção Integral*), in which the adolescent answers for his actions through socio-educational measures, decided in accordance to the severity of the offense. These may be: an advertence, the obligation to repair the damage done, community service, conditional discharge (*Liberdade assistida*), semi-liberty and internment in a correctional institution (with a maximum length of three years) (Brazil 1990).

Considering this context and working methodologically with "narrative memoirs" (Guerra et al. 2017) as a psychoanalytic strategy for the research of social phenomena, interviews were conducted with sixteen teenagers and young adults between the ages of seventeen and twenty-nine, through which we sought to learn their life stories. These interviews were transformed into artistic and literary works, then they were analyzed under a Freudian-Lacanian psychoanalytical orientation. From this context, we highlight the flash fiction *Laço,* by Ana Drawin (2017), produced by listening to the narrative of seventeen-year-old G. The teenager was serving a sentence of semi-liberty at the time of the narrative – August 2017. The goal of this paper is to highlight the possibilities presented by the narrative method, in the interface between art and science, to deal with reality, which always seems unattainable. In order to

---

[2]All quotes belonging to works in Portuguese were translated into English.

emphasize such advances in the scientific field, we list the dimension of time as a privileged aspect that allows for the ratification of the ways of capturing what is indeterminate through written narrative. Thus, we make use of Freud's and Lacan's psychoanalytic considerations on time, and Ricoeur's (2012) contribution regarding the correlation between narrative and temporality to draw, from Drawin's (2017) flash fiction, new ways to apply temporal magnitude, in which the *a posteriori* dimension may appear during the act of re-narrating episodes of the story told by the teenager. By allowing the reconstruction of a temporality that can cover particularities of a subjective experience, we grant the interviewee a new ethical and political position, based on the literary discourse. Therefore, writing becomes a methodological resource which forges the meeting with the investigative field and allows for interventions, composing itself as a fundamental instrument, if one intends to touch dimensions of the human experience, which are unattainable through traditional scientific methods of researching life stories.

Before we move ahead with the presentation of the case and its respective literary treatment, it seems important to present the idea behind the method of approximation, used with the teenagers and young adults through an invitation to narrate their story. Such an invitation intends to establish a space of listening and remembrance from which the subjects may slide "through the word writing their own story, in a dimension which includes the Other, its fiction and fixations" (Guerra et al. 2017, p. 1250). Hence, the resource of the narrative memoir – as we have called such methodology of access to the life stories of these subjects – comprehends a psychoanalytic strategy for the research of social phenomena, allowing for the inclusion of the language experience through a narrative outside of rationality or of the linear temporality, which presents the truth of an act through fiction and through points of impossibility of signification. In addition, we intend – through the narrative memoir – to take into account the unconscious experience and the different versions that are combined into the experience of the narrator, presenting its political body and the background design marked by the articulation of power in the discursively constructed scene (Guerra et al. 2017). With this resource we gain access to the story of G., a seventeen-year-old young man (at the time of the narrative, in 2016), who was undergoing a socio-educational measure of semi-liberty. G. says he engaged in trafficking because he wanted to make money. He also got involved in a few robberies. He claims that people usually say that "*if one got involved, he was caught in it*", insinuating that it is usually out of peer pressure, but he affirms that in his case he got involved because he wanted to: "*because I wanted to get out there, I wanted to earn my money, I wanted to make my name*". He then looks for a cousin and asks him how he could start to make money from crime. The cousin – already deceased at the time of the narrative – tries to emphasize that he should study, but the young man is determined, stating that he did not want to ask his mother for money anymore. G. has a twin brother who had also been involved in crime. He says that he was always "too mischievous", he would learn everything through "trouble", and had soon understood that it would be better "to learn from the mistakes of others" and not after making them himself. He is always very attentive to the logics that govern the space and time of crime and is firm regarding his aspirations to criminality. He finds himself liable not for trafficking or robbery, but for shooting an uncle who tried to beat his brother. The young man decided to turn himself to the police after the attempted murder. Let us now know the story of G. from the lens of Drawin (2017).

The Flash Fiction: Listening with Art

Bond (*Laço*) by Ana Drawin

He'd arrive early. It was necessary, with the agility of his soccer feet, to walk downstairs, to pass the alley of soul, to cross Doze street and go down until the end. There were three or two, something that a bit of rage makes we forget about time. They were followed by – despite the almost hoarse sighs – a long, drawn-out moan.

At some point, with the back burning from belt whipping, what he had lived would be reduced by the wheezing of a lung drowning in thick blood. The anticoagulants were, invading the semifinal in the Pavão soccer field – União vs. Floramar –, the delivery of another one:

"Where did you put my aspirin, Pedro?".

"I didn't take it, sir."

"You did, stinky kid. You and your twin are only worth something when I can hear leather cracking on your back!".

Eighteen, with a ten-second pause between them. He'd let it sit to burn more, allowing the pain to stay and feeling the leather pulling some skin. Uninterrupted beating leaves the body soft and numb.

While exposing the hollow of a mouth in gums, as if conducting music, the whipping made a vibrating buzzing sound at the beginning, notes to which the throat resonated, swallowing flesh and mucus in a sound paired with the tempo of violence. After he'd had enough of moving his arm and seeing the buckle of his belt snapping his shoulder, Uncle Abel stretched out – tired of laughter – on the couch of the two-room house and, without intent, found the pink blister pack next to the stacked San Marino cigarette butts that he had piled on the slate floor.

"Can I go to the game now, sir?"

"That whack made you dumber, huh?" Want to get shot in the face now, you shit? The game has started, and you cannot go to the field, you lil' fucking faggot. What time does your brother arrive? Maybe it was that piece of shit who told me to throw the medicine on the floor...

Despite being a drizzle, on a regular basis, when the rain comes to Alameda do Doze, with all the storm drains missing and the dirt track, the street takes the condition of a mire as appropriate. What if through the creek is less dangerous? Car bumpers, nail tips, skull-less animals floating and tyres.

He felt the mud press down so that the air of his chest had escaped before his breathing became the breath for survival. His feet slapped and whipped the mud in dissonance, like a punch after another, to the rhythm of his withered mouth, which drooled for cigarettes, lighting the bottom of one at the end of the next.

"What happened, Pedro?!"

"Is the baby okay, honey?"

"Yes. It's moving alright."

"What's wrong? Why did you come running in the mud? What´s the matter?"

"I shot him."

"What?"

"I don't know how many shots. He tried to beat André, and then I yelled "not my brother" and got the gun."

Temporalities Between Narrating, Telling and Elaborating

In order to highlight the advances made possible by the narrative method in the scientific field, we list the dimension of **time** – as presented by the flash fiction – as a privileged aspect that allows us to ratify the forms of capturing the indeterminable that the narrative resource makes possible, as an investigative method.

In an attempt to demonstrate the importance of written narrative in scientific production, we turn to Paul Ricoeur (2012), who focuses on the subject by seeking to elucidate that the "primordial correlation" (p. 300) between narrative and temporality is not a "dead tautology" (p. 310), as one might think, but rather an important reflection implied in the narrative making process. As a way of elaborating such an argument, the author clarifies that "time is human time insofar as it is articulated in a narrative mood, and stories become meaningful when they become conditions of temporal existence" (p. 300). Taking such a consideration as one of his premises, the author brings us closer to the considerations discussed above from a psychoanalytic outlook, by demonstrating that the exercise of thinking of time in a non-linear and chronological way – as in our human experience when we try to "work out the dialectical relation between past, present and future" (p. 301) – involves a series of structuring paradoxes.

One of them is presented by St. Augustine in his *Confessions,* by saying that "time is not a being because the future is not yet, the past is no more, and the present disappears. And yet we say something positive about time because we say that the future will be, the past has been, and the present is being" (p. 301). To Ricoeur (2012), Augustine's reflection contributes to thinking of "narrative activity as a 'poetic' solution to the speculative paradox," since reciting a poem allows, at the same time, to reveal and to overcome such a paradox, insofar as it "withholds in a single time the intention and the distension." In other words, reciting a poem allows one to experience the anticipation of the whole poem before it is recited, and the progressive narrative journey that makes – as it is recited – the past increase and the future decrease. To St. Augustine, the words of Ricoeur (2012), the recitation of a poem or a psalm would be "like the miniature of ever larger forms of recitation that would involve larger chunks of action, then a lifetime, and finally the whole story of mankind" (p. 302). In this way, Ricoeur (2012) proceeds by demonstrating "how narrative activity – and even more the act of telling a story as well as writing a story – responds and corresponds to these basic paradoxes of time" (p.302).

For this purpose, the author uses the act of "putting-in-intrigue", an act of mediation between event and history, to explain how two temporal dimensions, a chronological (episodic dimension), and a non-chronological (dimension of configuration) are entwined. It is an act-of-intrigue, therefore, which is perceived, not as much by the one who writes or counts, but by the one who "follows" (p. 303) the story, making them understand "how and why the successive episodes *lead* to this conclusion" (p. 304), which is called the "end point". Ricoeur (2012) argues that this end point is not only "the point of view from which history is apprehended as a whole" (p. 304), but also "the act of **re-narrating (re-happening), as opposed to that of narrating, which exhibits this structural function of the final point**" (p. 304, emphasis added).

To re-narrate from this perspective means to point to a "new quality of time" (p. 305), since by knowing the end result, the flow of comprehension changes: "By reading the end in the beginning and the beginning in the end, we have also learned *to* read time itself in *reverse,* as the recapitulation of the initial conditions of a course of action in its terminal consequences" (p. 305). If such positions may not appear new to the reader who is familiar with the Freudian course and recognizes the genius of the Viennese author in his work on the concept of *a posteriori* in the psychoanalytic clinical practice, it is nevertheless significant to witness the breadth of such placement in the narrative field. The idea of "reading time itself in reverse", as Ricoeur (2012) proposes, refers to the fundamental conception of the logical time in psychoanalysis, from which it is established that "truth can only be reached in a hurry" (Vale and Castro 2013, p. 445). A hurry which presents itself as one of the central themes addressed in the narrative that we intend to analyze, as we shall see below.

Time and its Psychoanalytic Foundation

In psychoanalysis, we know that the dimension of time is a fundamental operator in at least two dimensions: in the direction of treatment, since time management – as an "analytic act" (Vale und Castro 2013) – can acquire the status of an intervention; and in conceptual structuring, since there is no possible conception of the unconscious that can dispense considering its atemporal organization, as determined by Freud in 1915. If we find in the unconscious such a singular and important manifestation of the temporal dimension, it is to be hoped that such a conception reverberates widely in the Freudian apparatus for the understanding of psychic processes.

Here we highlight three aspects of the unconscious that are relevant to our discussion: the timelessness of the unconscious and its preconscious and conscious effects; the relation of the unconscious with fantasy and writing; and, finally, the logical dimension of time in its relation with the unconscious and the Other. Freud (1911/2011c, 1915/2011d), in characterizing the unconscious, emphasizes its mobile and drive dimension, explaining its fluid regency by condensation and displacement as its linguistic operators, with a view to obedience to the pleasure principle. It is only by means of the cathexization of the drive by the word, carried out in the passage from primary (unconscious) process to secondary (preconscious/conscious) process, that the rational sense would constitute barriers to pleasure and meaning through language. Unconscious processes, therefore, are exempt from contradiction, pay little attention to reality – which can easily be replaced by fantasy – and are atemporal.

What does this atemporality, central to our discussion, mean? It implies that unconscious processes "are not ordered temporally, are not altered by the passage of time; they have no reference to time at all. Reference to time is bound up, once again, with the work of the system *Cs*" (Freud, 1915/2011d, p. 3010). In this way, while narrating their story, each young person reveals to us the unconscious points that captivate their traumatic experience, making it possible to constitute a field of subjective meaning to the indeterminate that constitutes them. The narrative memoir thus becomes an alternative scientific method that allows for the inclusion of the field of the unconscious indetermination that, rationally, would be invisible to traditional methods. The narrated scene does not lack cohesion, linearity or meaning; on the contrary, it becomes, in the act, the expression of a conflict, of an imponderable event, of a contingency, determinants within each life story – which the narrative method allows us to grasp.

The work of the creative writer in this method implies apprehending and translating the inapprehensible of an experience, historicizing in the universalizing eternity of the story, the singular aspect of a traumatic experience. Hence the importance of the second aspect of the unconscious in the method, concerning fantasy and writing. This confirmation occurs with Freud (1908/2011b) when, in *Creative Writers and Day-Dreaming,* he claims that "the relation of a phantasy to time is in general very important" (p. 1925), since it "hovers (…) between three distinct times" (p. 1925): a desire awakened by a present occasion, the memory of a past experience, and the fantasy itself, based on the expectation of making this desire come true. The reference to this Freudian text is of particular importance as the author not only allows us to bring the writer closer to the figure of the common man by pointing to a more 'mundane' and accessible approach to literary creation, as he also presents a vigorous defense of the power of literary work in the reader's reception, affirming that in achieving the feat of releasing "tensions in our minds", the writer allows us "to enjoy our own day-dreams without any self-reproach or shame" (p. 1929).

The partaking of another reader, between narrator and writer, leads to the dimension of Otherness that Lacan unfolds between the real other, the person itself, and the symbolic Other, a projective screen that organizes each individual's symbolic system to account for the world. According to Lacan (1957/2006b), "the unconscious is the Other's discourse" just as "man's desire is the Other's desire" (Lacan, 1960/2006c, p. 690). Since the human experience is untranslatable in its entirety, we build translation, meaning and creation strategies with the support of language, in order to account for reality from its vanishing points. These are, at the same time, the points of closeness and openness that configure the individual idiosyncrasies through this projective screen that is the Other. The Other is simultaneously screen and hole, since it is missing the final term, the last term, which would give consistency to the being, given that the being is the logical effect of this structural impossibility of a complete translation of itself.

The relation with the Other stands out to the temporality that articulates the unconscious and preconscious-conscious systems. Lacan (1945/2006a) prefers to take it as a logic, distinguishing three times: "the instant of the glance, the time for comprehending and the moment of concluding" (p.167). He retrieves the syllogism in which the director of a prison calls three prisoners and, in exchange for freedom, asks them to solve a problem. Five circles, three white and two black, are presented to them, and on each prisoner's back, a white slice is placed without the chance of knowing their own color. After some hesitation, the three rush to the exit. They explain that after not immediately seeing two black slips on the other inmates, and soon after, seeing the looks of hesitation of the other two, he concludes that he also had the white circle, since his colleagues would not be seeing neither two blacks nor a white and a black. "their crucial value is not that of a binary choice between two inertly juxtaposed combinations – rendered incomplete by the visual exclusion of the third combination – but rather of a verificatory movement instituted by a logical process in which a subject transforms the three possible combinations into three *times of possibility*" (Lacan, 1945/2006a, p. 166).

We are not so interested in the syllogism as in its elements. We have the function of the hurry to conclude, an element of desire (freedom) at stake, the subject in possession of an attribute that he does not know in himself, an interval for signification, and finally the anticipation of knowledge from the Other. What is interesting to our methodology is the ignorance of the subject about himself that precipitates the assumption of a knowledge, which will gain value of significance after some time of working-through. There is, therefore, in our application of the method: a subject alienated to a stigmatized image and, at the same time, a subject who bears attributes that he does not acknowledge. When the other, the writer, (re)tells his story, he recognizes himself in an emptied point that precipitates on him in a kind of non-specular reciprocity, whose logical value moves his desire and resituates him in terms of what he has but does not signify. Hence the value of treatment of the traumatic dimension by the story, through the function of the other, in the (re)composition of the narrative in a logical time whose end – the moment of conclusion – returns as a precipice, and not exactly as a principle. The traumatic abyss of the subject is what reconfigures itself to a new frame of reality.

About the Story and Time

In "Laço", Drawin (2017) proposes a literary treatment for one of the narratives collected during the *Adolescências e Leis* (Adolescences and Laws) research, exploring a valuable part of a traumatic episode narrated by the young interviewee. On the verge of seeing his twin brother being attacked by his violent uncle, the protagonist of the story shoots his uncle, denouncing the end of his tolerance to the history of abuse suffered at the hands of the relative, particularly when directed to his brother. It seems unnecessary to highlight the specular dimension in this shared suffering. By contextualizing the narrative in a given "world of the literary work" (Ricoeur 2012), corresponding in parts to the scenario described by the interviewee, Drawin (2017) assigns a certain rhythm and time to the story, which conceives hermeneutical conditions, openings for analysis and vanishing points of the portrayed subject, which would prove difficult to be contemplated through any plane other than the narrative-literary. It is worth mentioning that the flash fiction is a product of the writer hearing a narration by the adolescent, an important temporal dimension that transcends the mere linking of facts and events of a story, crossing the subjective experience of the character and perhaps only possible in the creative exercise of writing. From the initial sentence "He'd arrive early." to the end of the story, the narrative permeates elements of the young man's past, present and future that shed a light on the story that was heard, on instants of haste, precipitations of the being, incidents of the other and abysses of trauma. In these elements, "the subject anticipates itself on the certainty given by the manner in which the other behaves towards this object" (Vale und Castro 2013, p.443). These same elements announce a possible subjective working-through that could be made possible only *a posteriori*.

The Interplay Between the Young One, The Story and Time

Taking into account how the "re-narration" of the listening of a life story interview allows – in literary form – for the reconstruction of a temporality capable of covering the complexity of a subjective experience, we find that the narrative strategy within the framework of scientific research paves the way for two important results. The first one, as already anticipated by Freud (1908/2011b), consists of the artist's almost enigmatic capacity of revealing certain fantasies, of "overcoming the feeling of repulsion in us which is undoubtedly connected with the barriers that rise between each single ego and the others" (p. 1929). It is not a matter of alleviating or romanticizing the traumatic experience of the account, but rather of allowing one to "enjoy our own day-dreams without self-reproach or shame" (p. 1929). This effect does not banalize or aestheticize the violence described in a narrative such as those of the young people with whom we work. Rather, it allows a reader to approach the described reality, "following the story"

(Ricoeur 2012, p. 303), and empowering a subjective implication that is not hindered by the barriers and defenses of our own phantasies.

Second, we find in Ricoeur (2012) that "the act of narrating a story reflects its development and makes relevant the paradoxes that have led Augustine's perplexity at the proximity of silence" (Ricoeur 2012, 305). In other words, not only does the narrative present itself as a palpable way to approach the inherently contradictory and paradoxical dimensions of human experience, it also allows for something to be spoken, narrated and expressed, opening paths of working-through that are not produced with silence. While they weave this border to the unspeakable, they circumscribe what is impossible to say, giving it a welcome from the outside. In Lacanian terms, conferring it *ex-sistence* in relation to the symbolic.

Thus, the story begins with a short statement on time: "He'd arrive early". An interesting construction to start a story that is based on the narrative of the life of a young one who committed a crime. The choice for "would" reveals an action in the future that is prevented by a tie with a past event. What would he arrive earlier than? Life? Time? Violence? It takes Hermes's agility to arrive before the acts of violence, be it from the uncle towards his brother, or the violent shooting response of G. Which violent act would he be able to outrun? The next sentence announces the ending of the story – the act of shooting his uncle *"There were three or two, something that a bit rage makes we forget about time, followed by – despite the almost hoarse sighs – a long, drawn-out moan."* We may think that the subject would arrive before the tragic outcome, but tragedy is defined by forces of fate. *"Want to get shot in the face now, you shit?"* The phrase updates the tragic destiny, which is lived in reverse.

After that, the writer announces and denounces the daily violence that our non-hero experiences. The rhythm of the belt lacerating a back in a violent scene marks the memory that inscribes a painful time of a sad and neglected childhood. *"Eighteen lashes, with a pause of ten seconds between one and another"*, a marked form that produces marks in body, memory and time.

The past time is mixed with present time in the escape amidst waste. *"Despite being a drizzle, on a regular basis, when the rain comes to Alameda do Doze, with all the storm drains missing and the dirt track, the street takes the condition of a mire as appropriate."* The time of the trauma suspends the barriers of consciousness and adds traits to a single logical temporality. The frame of the flash fiction, which reintroduces the reader in the dimension of time and resituates the young man in relation to his act, humanizes the scene: *"I don't know how many shots. He tried to beat André, and then I yelled" not my brother" and got the gun.*

In making the literary discourse operate on the narrative, the writer uses the artifice of the a *posteriori time to* re-signify and detach the young man from the image of the offender, revealing the complexity of the scene of this adolescent, whose story encompasses the life story of many others in the same Brazilian social scenario. Thus, we can think that such an operation (re)creates the condition for the young ones to re-signify themselves from a displaced point, from an anticipated certainty, from an unknown attribute, all introduced by the other writer. In the constitution of a void of signification, a new condition of subjective possibility arises – one of the values of this method.

Conclusions

Finally, we conclude that narrative is a powerful and fundamental methodological instrument if we are to touch the dimensions of human experience unattainable by traditional scientific methods of researching life stories. When we take time as an index that points to the complexity of human experience in the full extent of its paradoxes, gaps, and incongruities, we find that the narrative experience is a privileged way of considering aspects of subjects' lives which were once inapprehensible. With Ricoeur (2012),

we tell stories because, ultimately, human lives have necessity and deserve to be told. This note gains all its strength when we evoke the need to preserve the history of the defeated, and of the ones who lost. Every story of suffering cries out for revenge and requires narration (p. 309).

Thus, the narrative memoir gains remarkable methodological value, which can be concentrated in seven aspects: 1) the flash fiction preserves the dimension of life, body and time in the interview; 2) it allows for the appropriation of subjective time or time that considers the subjectivity of each young person; 3) it deals simultaneously with subjective-affective time and aesthetic time; 4) it implies trauma as an emptied point of text; 5) it allows for a type of working-through concerning the body and the drive that moves it, historicizing it in logical time repositioned in time itself; 6) it deals with the being and the non-being, from linguistic resources used between narrated and quoted empty spaces; 7) the act of writing withholds its reverse: the significant register on one side, and the living silence of trauma on the other, including the imponderable that science rejects; 8), and finally, it opens itself as a condition of reinterpretation to the researcher, the researched and the research subject.

References

Drawin, A. (2017). *Laço*. Unpublished.
Brasil. (1990). Lei n° 8.069 de 13 de julho de 1990. Dispõe sobre o Estatuto da criança e do adolescente. *Diário Oficial da União*. Brasília: Senado Federal.
Cerqueira, D., Lima, R. S., Bueno, S., Neme, C., Ferreira, H., Coelho, D. et al. (2018). *Atlas da violência 2018*. Rio de Janeiro: IPEA and FBSP.
Freud, S. (2011a). The interpretation of dreams. In I. Smith (ed.), *Freud – Complete works*. Online Edition. (pp. 507–1048). Retrieved from: https://www.valas.fr/IMG/pdf/Freud_Complete_Works.pdf. (Original work published in 1908)
Freud, S. (2011b). Creative writers and day-dreaming. In I. Smith (ed.), *Freud – Complete works*. Online Edition. (pp. 1919–1929). Retrieved from: https://www.valas.fr/IMG/pdf/Freud_Complete_Works.pdf. (Original work published in 1908)
Freud, S. (2011c). Formulations on the two principles of mental functioning. In I. Smith (ed.), *Freud – Complete works*. Online Edition. (pp. 2550–2557). Retrieved from: https://www.valas.fr/IMG/pdf/Freud_Complete_Works.pdf. (Original work published in 1911)
Freud, S. (2011d). The unconscious. In I. Smith (ed.), *Freud – Complete works*. Online Edition. (pp. 2989–3024). Retrieved from: https://www.valas.fr/IMG/pdf/Freud_Complete_Works.pdf. (Original work published in 1915).
Guerra, A. M. C., Oliveira Moreira, J., Oliveira, L. V., & Lima, R. G. (2017). The Narrative Memoir as a Psychoanalytical Strategy for the Research of Social Phenomena. *Psychology*, 8, 1238-1253. https://doi.org/10.4236/psych.2017.88080
Lacan (2006a) Logical Time and the assertion of anticipated Certainty. In J. Lacan (Bruce Fink, Trans) *Écrits* (pp. 161–175). New York and London: W.W Norton & Company. (Original work published in 1945).
Lacan (2006b) Psychoanalysis and its teaching. In J. Lacan (Bruce Fink, Trans) *Écrits* (pp. 364–383). New York and London: W.W Norton & Company. (Original work published in 1957).
Lacan (2006c) The Subversion of the subject and the dialectic of desire in the Freudian unconscious. In J. Lacan (Bruce Fink, Trans) *Écrits*. (pp. 671–702). New York and London: W.W Norton & Company. (Original work published in 1960).
Ricoeur, P. (2012). Entre tempo e narrativa: concordância/discordância. *Kriterion*, 125, 299-310.
Silva, E. R. A. & Oliveira, R. M. (2015). *Nota técnica – O Adolescente em conflito com a Lei e o debate sobre a redução da maioridade penal: esclarecimentos necessários*. Brasília: IPEA. Recovered from https://www.ipea.gov.br/portal/images/stories/PDFs/nota_tecnica/150616_ntdisoc_n20
Vale, S. C. & Castro, J. E. (2013). O tempo e o ato psicanalítico na direção do tratamento. *Tempo Psicanalítico*, 45(1), 439-451.
Waiselfisz, J. J. (1998). *Mapa da violência*: Os jovens do Brasil. Rio de Janeiro: Ed. Garamond, Unesco, Instituto Ayrton Senna.

Temporality in Qualitative Longitudinal Studies on Health Experience: A Review and Analysis

Archana Ramanujam, Christian Bröer, Stefano Giani und Gerben Moerman

Abstract

While the number of longitudinal qualitative studies on experiences of sickness, health and wellbeing has burgeoned, researchers lack the tools to conceptualize of time in our arguments. In this literature review, we examine temporality in different phases of the research process: from the design and analysis through to the discussion and conclusion. We also interrogate the consistency of this temporality across the phases.

Our review draws on four databases and includes an initial sample of 152 studies, of which we reviewed 38 in detail to achieve theoretical saturation. We found four modes of temporality across the studies: interrupted time, phasic time, continuous time and cyclical time. Our results suggest that often temporality remains implicit and is conceptualized inconsistently across the phases of the research process, often lapsing into a more static or cross-sectional approach. We argue in favor of making temporality more explicit in longitudinal studies and in favor of sharpening its conceptualization. Our four

A. Ramanujam (✉) · C. Bröer · S. Giani · G. Moerman
University of Amsterdam, Amsterdam, The Netherlands
E-Mail: archana_ramanujam@brown.edu

C. Bröer
E-Mail: c.broer@uva.nl

S. Giani
E-Mail: s.giani@uva.nl

G. Moerman
E-Mail: g.moerman@uva.nl

modes of temporality can aid researchers to think through this in the design, analysis and reporting of a longitudinal qualitative study. This review is the outcome of the authors' ongoing longitudinal study on health practices in the first four years of a child's life ('Sarphati Ethnography').

Keywords

Longitudinal · qualitative · experience · health · illness · wellbeing · time · temporality · review

Time in Qualitative Longitudinal Health Studies

What defines qualitative longitudinal research? Neale (2019) and others address this question conceptually and in part, practically. In this contribution we take a different approach. While we do spend some time on sensitizing conceptualizations, our contribution is an analysis of studies employing a longitudinal approach. We empirically establish how health researchers reason with time when they report their research in academic articles. Rather than adhering to a typology of methods (longitudinal, cross-sectional) we unearth temporality in use. This attempt stems from our own prior longitudinal research (De Graaff and Bröer 2019), including our most recent project, an ethnographic panel study named 'Sarphati Ethnography'. In this study, we encountered the problem of how to conceptualize and operationalize time during analysis and reporting. We started with a longitudinal design, yet during the analysis, we repeatedly reverted to ignoring time. Therefore, in this review, we also attend to different sequences of temporality within one research article.

Sarphati Ethnography is a project conducted at the University of Amsterdam in collaboration with the municipal health service, involving first-time parents with newborns. This study addresses the development of practices such as eating, drinking, sleeping and physical activity from pregnancy until the child is four years old. Researchers visit over 20 families at home and spend time with them during mundane activities three times a year. On these visits, structured interviews are held and interactions are observed. The study is meant to offer a dynamic, relational and contextualized understanding of children's health. Our longitudinal approach focuses on practices and shows how social and structural factors play out in unfolding lives (Holland 2011).

By observing everyday practices over an extended time, we are able to capture the 'life lived' – the timing and sequence of events based on chronological and biological dimensions of time – and the 'life told', or how health is experienced (Neale und Flowerdew 2003). Our ethnography should bring to the fore ways through which families develop practical solutions for specific challenges and pragmatic concerns during this critical phase. Our research design and the collection of detailed data facilitates a dialogue between our qualitative and quantitative research findings from the Sarphati Cohort (https://www.sarphaticohort.nl/), as the longitudinal data generated in our study will enable the contextualisation of quantitative data on both a retrospective and prospective basis and therefore shed light on underlying mechanisms.

We based the Sarphati Ethnography study design on Neale's (2015) earlier work and tried to attend to both calendar time and experienced time. We also followed recent trends to scale up, standardize and combine qualitative longitudinal and quantitative studies (Neale 2019, p. 12). However, we have to admit that during fieldwork and analysis, we became aware of our own lack of clear thinking about time and changes over time. For example, during our first analysis, we fell back into cross-sectional correlational reasoning, rather than making an argument about developments over time.

Additionally, we seemed to unconsciously oscillate between calendar time and experienced time. This motivated us to look into other studies' conceptualization and use of time in their arguments: in other words, their temporality. Here, temporality is the umbrella concept for all ways in which time is used by fellow scholars. This chapter reports our findings and is meant to help fellow scholars engaging in longitudinal, qualitative research by providing a conceptual scheme and some do's and don'ts.

Time

Social science research can address social phenomena in two ways: as static or as dynamic (Comte 1852). The term dynamic refers to interactions, patterns and changes over time. The term static means that phenomena and (cor)relations are assumed to be stable over time or timeless. A dynamic analysis can range from micro-analysis, for example of conversational turn-taking (Sacks et al. 1978) to the long-term development of social figuration (Elias 1978). Dynamic approaches are generally the preferred way of "researching social change" (McLeod and Thompson 2009). Not all dynamic approaches are based on longitudinal data collection in the strict sense. Tertiary sources and archival material of different sorts can also be combined dynamically, for example in historical research. Oral history or life history – where the longitudinal perspective is established retrospectively, can be considered longitudinal depending on whether one treats the retrospective narrative as a reflection of change or as a present-day account. Other common forms of longitudinal qualitative approaches are extended ethnographies (such as discussed in Breman et al. 1997) and repeat visits of community studies (see for instance Crow 2012 for an overview).

Longitudinal reasoning can be used to establish causal relations. If changes occur over time, the logic used in quantitative longitudinal surveys often presumes a certain causality. Hume (1739/2007) showed us that this is an observation of *a preceding b*, but not per se *a causing b*, let alone that we understand how this mechanism works. Besides, using time for inferences is based on a concept of linear, external or objective time underlying social phenomena. While this chapter is not meant to scrutinize the objectivist approach to time, it is of note that natural scientists also have a hard time establishing a definition of time (Saldaña 2003, p. 5–6; Neale 2019, pp. 24–25). The objectivist approach can be contrasted with time as a topic in its own right (Saldaña 2003, p. 7), an approach that has been developed in sociology, anthropology and philosophy (Hassard 1990; Neale 2019; Wajcman 2008).

Landmark studies of sociology addressed social change both as unfolding in time and affecting social time. Marx' study of capitalism, for example, concerned the phases and revolutions in calendar time and the way society accelerated, as well as how industrial labor disrupted the flow of human experience. This approach, which connects historical change, biographical change and a critical theory of their interrelation has a solid place in sociology (Mills 2000; Rosa 2013). Studies of social time examine long-term changes in time-keeping and time-regimes (Goudsblom 2004), how temporality is part of (colonial) researcher-researched relations (Fabian 2014) and how lived time changes.

Concerning lived time, think, for example, of " biographical disruption" (Bury 1982) due to the onset of chronic disease. Expectations about the future in relation to one's identity are severely altered by chronic diseases. Other examples come from the study of risk and reflexivity: the awareness of risks as such brings the future to the present, and risk prevention is meant to affect the future (e.g. De Graaff and Bröer 2012). In short, the non-objectivist approaches to time encompass lived time, including its micro-construction as much as the large scale socio-cultural construction of temporality. When we attend to social and experienced time, a clock-like steady and linear conceptualization of time makes way for time at different paces, multiple timings and non-linear paths. We may even begin to conceive of time as cyclical or repetitive; economic or revolutionary processes can be cyclical or repetitive as much as the seasons or the passing of a day.

The relevance of attending to time stems from social scientists' interest in change, transformation and modernization at the macro-level and interests in daily life, city life or family life at the micro- or meso-level. Saldaña (2003), who is more interested in the micro- and meso-level, offers a descriptive and data analysis-oriented approach by asking questions about change:

1. What increases/decreases, emerges or vanishes over time?
2. What is cumulative over time?
3. What kinds of surges or epiphanies occur through time?
4. What remains constant or consistent through time?
5. What is idiosyncratic through time?
6. What is missing through time?

These kinds of questions are useful to enhance our descriptions and can be complemented with potential explanations. Explanations for change involve reasoning about effects over time, and there are numerous lines of such reasoning. In epidemiological studies alone based on objective time, Hertzman et al. (1994) have identified 3 ways of conceptualizing time: A) biological time, referring to the development of an organism, B) cumulative time, referring to the exposure of an organism during a certain time and the incremental effects of that exposure and lastly C) historical time, referring to the points in time when interaction between an organism or a group and its environment occur. Note that these basic distinctions by Hertzman et al. (1994) are all applicable to social science conceptualizations of change over time as well: we can understand changes for example (A) in the life-course as rooted in aging or (B) in the duration of a certain period (length of education) or (C) in the way aging is socially constructed (for example, the recent emergence of the fourth age and the fear of becoming frail and dependent (Higgs and Gilleard 2014)).

Neale's work can be used to further refine the types of changes over time; in the flow of time she distinguishes "turning points" and "transitions" (Neale 2019, pp. 39–42). For our purposes, we define turning points as interruptions in the flow of time, as critical events which have asudden impact. Transitions are slower and more gradual connections between phases.

Lastly, we want to highlight two explanatory approaches which are conceptually convincing yet not easily applied, as our study suggests: path-dependency and sequence analysis (Abbott 1995.) Path dependency, for example in the study of revolutions or social protest, addresses the dynamics triggered by contingent events. Early events are relatively important in path dependency, the dynamics are a property of the process itself and are not explained by other factors (Mahoney 2000). Furthermore, the outcomes can be explained. Paths can also be called sequences of events. Sequence analysis (Abbott 1995) points specifically to the importance of time order of events. A simple example is turn-taking in conversations: the order is rather strictly A–B–A–B. Different orders point to markedly different social situations: a therapeutic interaction can have the order A–B–B–B with A denoting the therapist and B the client. This order however does not necessarily explain outcomes, which is an important goal of sequence analysis.

For our purpose of scrutinizing temporality in longitudinal studies, we can now harvest the following sensitizing concepts: dynamic and static approaches, objective/external time or time as socially constructed, and experienced time which can be linear, non-linear and cyclical, and differ in tempo. Change over time can be conceptualized at different scales and due to sudden turning points, gradual transitions, path dependency and sequence effects.

Methods

Our goal in this paper was to review longitudinal health research to reach theoretical saturation in developing our typology of temporality. Therefore, while a full-scale systematic review (Moher et al. 2009) lay outside the scope of our study, we searched in a systematic manner, following the principles of clarity, validity and auditability that underpin a thorough literature review (Booth et al. 2016). We used an abductive approach in developing our typology of modes of temporality, which we will elaborate upon later.

Search Strategy

We ran our search in four databases: *Anthropology Plus* (hosted by Ebsco), *AnthroSource, PubMed* and *Sociological Abstracts* (hosted by ProQuest). These were chosen to cover a range of disciplines and thus address the multidisciplinary nature of the topic. Furthermore, we decided to look at both peer-reviewed and grey literature to minimize publication bias (Kugley and Epstein 2019). No time limits were applied; the whole content of each database was searched. We hoped to find studies that were 1) health-related, 2) longitudinal, 3) qualitative and 4) experience-oriented. These four elements were translated into three search strings for 1) health, 2) qualitative longitudinal studies and 3) experience. The search strings and resulting global search strategy were developed according to the content of each database and its search options and syntax (i.e. subject headings, free-text terms). Maintaining a balance between sensitivity and specificity was the guiding principle (Booth et al. 2016; Petticrew and Roberts 2006). Thus, the search strategy for a medical database such as *PubMed* did not need to include the 'health' search string, while the limited search options and small datasets of *Anthropology Plus* and *AnthroSource* advised the removal of the 'experience' search string.

A total of 566 articles were retrieved. To deal with the overlap of articles included in the various databases, the dataset was imported into RefWorks, a reference management software, where duplicates were removed from the sample. A total of 549 articles remained. Thereafter, the articles were parsed on the basis of title and abstract to retain only those articles that were truly qualitative, longitudinal studies on the experiences of health. A few definitions are relevant here. Health was broadly construed; if 'health' or a wellbeing, illness or disease-related issue was highlighted as the subject of study, then this was enough for it to qualify. However, topics such as breastfeeding, parenting, sexual assault and caregiving in old age that did not have a clearly articulated health-related link, were excluded.

In terms of the descriptor 'qualitative', we chose to include articles with qualitative and mixed methods approaches with a repeated qualitative component. A longitudinal approach was required in order to ensure that researchers began their studies with the aim of thinking in dynamic terms. We defined longitudinal studies as those with two or more time-points where data was collected, with an aim to looking at *change* over time. With regards to experience, studies were necessarily related to the 'experiences' of health or illness of individuals, and those evaluating health education programs or about experiences using health-related interventions (e.g. telehealth) were excluded unless there was a strong emphasis on health experience. The number of articles included at this point totaled 152.

Article Review & Analysis

Articles were randomly selected for review, stratified by database, at first, and later based on abductive reasoning, as described below. A total of 49 articles were reviewed, of which 11 were excluded. Reasons for exclusion were a) that articles

Table 1 Number of articles at various stages of the review process

Database	Number of articles		
	prior to parsing	Post-parsing	Reviewed (excluded)
Anthropology Plus	17	1	0 (1)
AnthroSource	10	9	2 (4)
PubMed	238	68	19 (1)
Sociological Abstracts	284	74	18 (5)
Total	549	152	38 (11)

upon closer reading did not in fact conform to the requirements outlined, b) that only the abstract and not the article were available. In the reviewing process, we first checked if articles fit our requirements. We adjusted our search strategy iteratively according to a close reading of the initial results to arrive at our final sample.

Table 1

We then took an abductive approach to developing our typology (Timmermans and Tavory 2012). Earlier, we had begun a preliminary review with background reading for our own study, and this grew to a larger search for the sensitizing concepts mentioned in the previous section to inform our understanding of temporality. We then drew our sample of longitudinal qualitative studies on health experience, as previously outlined. We tried to use the sensitizing concepts to order our sample comprehensively and introduced new concepts if existing ones did not fit certain articles.

This was an iterative process; we reviewed smaller samples of ten to twenty articles and developed a potential categorization. We then discussed its validity and integrity and compared it to time conceptualizations in the literature again. The first and second author further discussed the difficult cases. Over time we added new cases to further develop the typology. In this process, we also realized that the typology of the articles varied by section (design, analysis, results, discussion and conclusion), and therefore decided to divide up our analysis into these sections. Our categorization was guided by the following questions:

- Design: What was the structuring factor behind the data-gathering moments and schedule? What language was used with regards to time and change in the design?

- Analysis: How did the authors handle the data? Did they organize the data according to particular time units or conceptualizations of time to analyze it?
- Results: What structure and language was used in discussing the results? Were the results discussed according to a particular conceptualization of time; in phases, for example, or using static language?
- Discussion and Conclusion: What language was used in the discussion and conclusion? Was it dynamic? Did it reference a certain type of time conceptualization?

Modes of Temporality

In the introduction to our chapter, we touched upon the literature on temporality and change to tease out conceptual distinctions relevant to the analysis of our corpus. These include dynamic and static approaches, objective and external time, time as socially constructed and experienced time. All dynamic approaches can be linear or nonlinear, and differ in tempo. Furthermore, change over time can be conceptualized at different scales and can be due to sudden turning points, gradual transitions, path dependency and sequences. Aided by these distinctions, we

Table 2 Modes of temporality

Dynamic/Static	Mode of Temporality	Description	Diagram
Dynamic	Interrupted	Time is broken up or interrupted at one or more time-points	—‖—
	Phasic	Time is divided into distinct periods or phases, usually in a particular order.	— — —
	Continuous	Time time proceeds at a constant rate, without any divisions into phases or any interruptions	————
	Cyclical	Time follows a particular repetition or cycle.	◯
Static	Irrelevant	Time is irrelevant.	•
Not mentioned	None/NA	Time is not mentioned/discussed	

have abductively developed a typology of modes of temporality in peer-reviewed articles on qualitative longitudinal health research, presented in Table 2.

As mentioned earlier, we attended to the conceptualization of time in the different parts of a research article: the design, analysis, results and the discussion and/or conclusion. The descriptions of the various conceptualizations of time listed in Table 2 are generalized across the various article sections. The first four conceptualizations are dynamic. They imply a sense of time that develops, whereas the fifth is static, where time is in fact irrelevant. The last category, 'not mentioned', covers articles that did not have the relevant section, be that the analysis, results or discussion and conclusion. Some ethnographic studies do not have a clear analysis section (for example, Béhague 2008), and the three articles purportedly missing a results and discussion as well as conclusion section are written in the style of a methods note (Adler 1999; Foster et al. 2016).

In the following sections, we present single examples of studies that illuminate these modes of temporality. Next we address the distribution of modes of temporality across the different sections of research articles. Lastly we point to sequences of dynamic and static temporality across articles, showing that consistency in the (dynamic) modes across the articles is sorely lacking.

Interrupted Time

The first mode of temporality is interrupted time. This mode refers to significant ruptures or breaks that divide up time. Examples include a move to a long-term care home for dementia patients (Henkusens et al. 2014) or discharge from the hospital (Lohne 2009). The rupture is usually expected to trigger change, reflected in comparisons or dualisms such as 'then-now' or 'before-after'. This change can be either qualitative or quantitative in nature; the experience of eating at the long-term care home might be qualitatively different from eating at home. A quantitative difference might be in the amount of food eaten.

Hargreaves et al. (2010) uses an interrupted time conceptualization throughout the design, results, discussion and conclusion, although this conceptualization is not apparent in the analysis section of the article. The research concerns changes in smoking consumption induced by a ban on smoking in public places. The authors' aim is to examine "the impact of the legislation on individuals, families and communities," (Hargreaves et al. 2010, p. 459) using a mixed methods approach. The introduction of the ban represents a break or interruption in time, and the authors are interested in the change triggered by this. Hence the authors structure their design and data gathering points before and after this change.

This interrupted mode continues in the results, discussion and conclusion, where Hargreaves et al. (2010) discuss the change in smoking consumption between waves of data collection using the terms 'pre-legislation' and 'post-legislation' to signal the interruption and the time-points before and after. Furthermore, statements such as "Some smokers considered that the implementation of the smokefree England legislation had provided an incentive for them to quit," (Hargreaves et al. 2010, p. 463) suggest that the ban, or in other words the rupture, potentially served as a cause for quitting smoking.

That said, this causal aspect is not necessary for an interrupted time conceptualization; rather, it is about the *possibility* of a causal relationship. Hargreaves et al. (2010, p. 464) state, "Structural change instigated by the smokefree England legislation had little effect on the smoking behaviour of people who tended to smoke habitually at home or in outside locations," indicating there was little to no causal effect on quitting for these specific groups. Nevertheless, the authors' entire study formulation and reporting focuses on this pivotal interruptive legislation, and its possible effects.

In their analysis section, they used the framework method to identify main themes. Time was not mentioned and thus irrelevant. Hence, their analysis section was static in nature.

Phasic Time

Phasic time refers to time that is divided into distinct periods or phases, based on unique or different characteristics in each phase. Less attention is paid to interruptions and more is paid to gradual changes, transitions and transformation. This mode of temporality can play out in the perioperative process in replacement surgery (Gustafsson et al. 2007), in decision-making processes about medical interventions (Mitchell 2014), or in the hospital discharge process (Andersen et al. 2017; Carusone et al. 2017). Since the phases can be distinguished based on their unique identity, there are differences between each phase and similarly, there are qualitative changes that trigger the new phase. However, there is always a chronological ordering to these phases.

Gill and Lowes (2008) explore the experiences of donors and recipients in the kidney transplantation process, discussing the giving, receiving and reciprocating aspects herein. They state, "In terms of an exchange model, organ transplantation (particularly live transplantation) is, arguably, psychosocially similar to the dynamics of gift exchange as the process also involves giving, receiving and reciprocating," (Gill and Lowes 2008, p. 1608). Here, they highlight the concepts of giving, receiving and reciprocating as discrete and chronological steps in a process. One cannot receive without another giving, and reciprocating necessitates the prior steps. Furthermore, Gill and Lowes (2008) structure their design and data collection time-points at specific junctures throughout the transplantation process. Interviews were conducted prior to the transplantation, and then three and ten months after the transplantation. While their design may have fit 'phasic' temporality better if they had indicated why these time-points are important, it is clear the time-points are structured at specific junctures throughout a period.

The results, discussion and conclusion sections of this article are also based on a phasic conceptualization of time, as the authors discuss four phases. These are the decision-making process, the transplantation process, the emotional impact of the transplantation and post-transplant relationships. Not only is there a clear chronological order, but each phase is qualitatively distinct and is triggered by qualitative change. In the decision-making process, the transplantation is not definitive yet, and in the transplantation process it is definitive and occurring. The change that occurs between these two phases is that the donor decides to give the kidney, and the recipient decides to receive it. The next phase, the emotional impact of the transplantation and post-transplant relationships both occur once the transplant has already taken place and one person has received it and the other has given it. The transplant occurring is the qualitative change that took place, triggering this phase.

The analysis phase of this article was static, as the authors do not mention temporality in any way, rendering it irrelevant. Although the rest of the article was clearly phasic, Gill and Lowes (2008) also lapse into other modes of temporality. For example, they occasionally talk about 'pre transplant' and 'post transplant'. This positions the transplant as a major change or rupture, fitting better within the interrupted conceptualization.

Continuous Time

Continuous time proceeds at a constant rate, with no breaks or disruptions. For example, Essery et al. (2017) conceptualize of time as continuous in their research on patient experiences of an intervention for intervestibular dizziness. Ellis et al. (2013) also use continuous time in their inquiries into the symptom experience of patients with gastrointestinal cancers in the first year after diagnosis.

In all of these examples, the researchers may be curious about change or stability over the course of time, but they are not as interested in the triggers. Hence, they do not structure the research around such triggers, as was the case with interrupted and phasic temporalities. For example, although Essery et al. (2017) do study change in the form of an intervention, they are interested in patients' experience of it over time, and not necessarily the difference prior to and after the intervention. Changes over the course of time may be qualitative in nature, such as different types of symptoms appearing at various times, or quantitative in nature, such as an increase or decrease in pain. The authors do not focus on any shift or rupture that may cause the change.

Wright et al. (2012) also conceptualize time as continuous in their mixed methods study of ageing HIV patients' despondency in Uganda. Their research design involved visiting patients once a month for a period of a year, a very regular interval. Furthermore, the authors mention that the study was meant to deliver "qualitative insights into changing family situations and relations, older people's tasks and responsibilities, visitors and visits, diet and food availability..." (Wright et al. 2012, p. 323). The word 'changing' indicates a continuous process, and no clear trigger for this change is mentioned. This suggests that this change is a process that occurs over the course of time.

While there was no real temporality mentioned in the analysis section, the results, discussion and conclusion were also written in a continuous temporal mode. In the results, Wright et al. (2012, p. 325) discuss "shifting perceptions and ratings of health", including the case of Linda who reported general weakness and poor appetite at the first interview, and subsequently reported painful muscles without fever, cough and flu etc. The use of the word 'shifting' suggests continuity, and there is a sense that time is progressing at a relatively continuous rate during the 'subsequent 4 months', without specific breaks. There is clearly change, but no real clear trigger for it which structures time.

This continuous temporality is also reflected in the conclusion in the statement, "while worries, sorrow and despondent thoughts were reported in many of the interviews across the year of the study, moods fluctuated with happiness and unhappiness..." (Wright et al. 2012, p. 330). They name the time period 'across the year,' and name the continuous stability of sorrow and despondency, but also suggest changes in mood. However, there is again no clear trigger for this change; it simply happens over the course of time.

Cyclical Time

Cyclical time follows a particular repetition or cycle. There is just one example of cyclical time in our sample, which is no surprise when you consider Munn's (1992) critique of this rather mythical category. Solomon et al. (2015) discuss a series of visits to the doctor's office by autistic children and their mothers where the visits follow a particular flow or cycle. In this temporal mode, there is some degree of structural stability between cycles in terms of the content and order of events. Nevertheless, there may be some change between cycles, such that each repetition does not completely return to its beginning. The trigger for change between cycles occurs in the cycle prior to the change.

Returning to Solomon et al.'s article (2015), not only do the visits follow a flow or cycle, there is not much change in the course of the various visits, further accentuating this cyclical nature. Nevertheless, the authors conceptualize time as continuous in their design section, do not truly present their analytic methods (hence the paper is categorized as 'NA' in for this section), and use time as static or irrelevant in their conclusion. We will return to these inconsistencies later, as they are widespread in our sample.

Irrelevant Time

Finally, irrelevant time means that authors present events as timeless or describe relations as static. Our sample only contains articles which authors have labeled as longitudinal and therefore we expect time to be relevant, yet this is not always the case beyond the design phase. Take Wrubel et al. (2005), who aim to understand pediatric adherence to HIV medication. They begin with a clear goal of wanting to understand adherence as a "dynamic phenomenon" (Wrubel et al. 2005, p. 2424) with "longitudinal factors" (p. 2426). Nevertheless, time is irrelevant in the rest of their article; there is no sense that time is passing as they discuss medication use as static and unchanging, generalized over the period of study.

Clark (2001) states that her study on perinatal social support for Mexicanas in the US states is "longitudinal" (p. 1303). The author conducted 4 interviews throughout the perinatal period with each enrolled woman, and her analysis included cultural domain analysis, content analysis and narrative analysis. Despite this detailed description, she did not mention a temporal component in the analysis.

This continued into the results. Four forms of social support were mentioned; "Helping with Daily Hassles, Showing Love and Understanding, Being There for Me, and My Family Failing Me" (Clark 2001, p. 1303), These themes could potentially be understood as continuous, as the verb is in the present participle and therefore active – 'do-ing' something. However, upon further inspection, time was rendered irrelevant in many of these themes. The following quote describes one of them:

Showing Love and Understanding, the second theme, was more abstract, and involved acts of kindness that may not have alleviated the work of motherhood or hassles of pregnancy, but conveyed concern and affection, sometimes in small but symbolically meaningful ways. Nina's grandmother prayed for her when she was in pre-term labor, for example. Inez's son made her a sandwich before she left for the hospital... Nina's elderly grandmother took special care to explain some of the traditional beliefs that would protect Nina during her pregnancy (Clark 2001, p. 1308).

All of the events mentioned took place at one point in time, and in different mothers' lives. There is no sense of temporality or change, and it is therefore not evident that these events might have come from different interview time-points. Of course, this varied slightly across themes, as 'helping with daily hassles', was described using various events in one mother's experience over the course of the two interviews. This article therefore has some continuous aspects to it, but time was in large part irrelevant. The discussion section solidifies this:

To summarize, the emic results of this research indicate that urban Mexicanas in the perinatal period consider social support to encompass daily instrumental help, emotional support, and the perception that others can be counted on to "be there" for them (Clark 2001, p. 1313).

While Clark (2001) does mention 'the perinatal period', the period appears to occur at one moment in time. There is no explicit mention of change or lack thereof over the course of this period in terms of the forms of social support urban Mexicanas expect, lending an impression that time is distinctly irrelevant.

Inconsistencies in Time

We have now presented the various conceptualizations, and Table 3 shows the frequency with which each conceptualization appears in our sample of articles. If a single conceptualization of time had been applied consistently throughout an article, we would expect the same frequencies across rows. However, there are stark differences which means that the different parts of the article conceptualize and use time differently. We will elaborate on this shortly.

The second-to-last category in Table 3 is 'Other dynamic'. These cases only appeared in the analysis stage. There were many articles where the word

Table 3 Conceptualizations of time in the four sections of the articles

Dynamic/Static	Mode of Temporality	Design	Analysis	Results	Discussion/Conclusion
Dynamic	Interrupted	4	0	4	6
	Phasic	11	1	15	9
	Continuous	23	1	7	4
	Cyclical	0	0	1	0
	Other dynamic/longitudinal	0	5	0	0
Static	Irrelevant	–	27	8	16
Not Mentioned	None/NA	–	4	3	3
Total	Total	38	38	38	38

'longitudinal' was mentioned with regards to the analysis, but there was no further elaboration on how the analysis took temporality into consideration. These articles fall into the category of 'other dynamic', as there is some sense of dynamism but it is vague (e.g. Molassiotis et al. 2010).

In terms of the design, a large number of studies (23) conceptualized time as continuous, whereas in the results section the majority, albeit with a smaller margin (15), conceptualized of time as phasic. In other words, an article does not necessarily maintain the same conceptualization of time throughout, be it continuous, phasic or another mode. This will be addressed in the next section, but it is worth noting that studies may start with a longitudinal design aiming to identify phases through their research. In order to achieve this, a study may start out as continuous, but have a phasic results section. Cyclical and interrupted time conceptualizations were not as frequent.

From Table 3, it is clear that a good proportion of articles do not succeed in consistently applying a dynamic or longitudinal approach. Within the analysis section, the vast majority (27) of articles were categorized as static. These authors avoided any sense of temporality in the analysis section entirely, returning to it thereafter. The static conceptualization of time is less common in the results section, but still relatively prevalent in the discussion and conclusion (16). The fact of the matter remains that all of the articles began with a dynamic design, and do not consistently apply a dynamic approach throughout the article.

Time Through the Course of the Article

As mentioned earlier, the large number of articles that take a static approach to the analysis, results, discussion and conclusion sections points to the fact that dynamic temporality is inadequately maintained in longitudinal qualitative studies on health experience. By mapping the use of either a static or dynamic approach to time through the course of the articles in our sample, as shown in Table 4, we are better able to discern the trends at hand. In the left-hand column, the time pathway through the course of the article is denoted by a series of four characters, each denoting first the design, the analysis, the results and then the discussion and conclusion. The character can either be 'S', denoting static, or 'D', denoting dynamic.

Overwhelmingly, we see that there are few entirely dynamic studies in the sample (4), where a dynamic perspective (irrespective of what temporality subtype) was maintained from design through conclusion. Furthermore, there is a large number of studies (13) that have a static approach to the analysis section, while thereafter reporting dynamic results and discussing it as such in the discussion and conclusion sections. Nine articles have both static analysis and conclusion sections, showing that the longitudinal approach fluctuates throughout the article. These authors did not translate dynamic results into dynamic conclusions. This is reflected in the abstract of Schaffer et al.'s (2008) article, where the study is described as explicitly longitudinal, but the dynamism of the article ebbs and flows through the course of the abstract:

Table 4 Time pathways through the course of the articles in the sample

Time Pathway (design, analysis, results, discussion/conclusion)	Number of Articles
DDDD	4
DSDD	13
DDSD	1
DDDS	2
DSDS	9
DSSD	1
DSSS	5
D(incomplete)/DS(incomplete)	3
note: S = static, D = dynamic	

This article analyses data from a longitudinal, ethnographic study conducted in the United States to examine how 100 mothers of children with genetic disorders used the Internet to interpret, produce, and circulate genetic knowledge pertaining to their child's condition. We describe how they came to value their own experiential knowledge, helped shift the boundaries of what counts as authoritative knowledge, and assumed the role of genetic citizen, fighting for specific rights while shouldering and contesting concomitant duties and obligations. This exploration of e-health use contributes to our understanding of the social practices and power relations that cut across online and off-line worlds to co-produce genetic knowledge and genetic citizenship in multiple contexts.

Towards the middle of this abstract, turns of phrases such as 'they came to value' and 'helped shift' suggest processual and therefore time-related phenomena. The authors are clearly indicating signs of change. However, the concluding summary sentence gives the impression that the study was far more cross-sectional in nature. Instead of being interested in the processes by which mothers 'came to value their own experiential knowledge,' they are seemingly interested in comparing across contexts and not across time. This is evidenced by the phrases 'cut across... worlds' and 'in multiple contexts,' which suggest that the authors are far more interested in comparing across contexts than across time.

Allen et al. (2011)'s abstract, by contrast, starts out with a clear longitudinal intention which dissipates through the course of the abstract, rendered lost by the end:

Our longitudinal (September 2006–September 2008) participatory action research (PAR) focused on a) understanding hemodialysis patients' perspectives on the challenges and solutions to living well with their chronic illness and b) taking action to improve this population's quality of life. The study's participants included seven purposefully sampled patients in two hospital hemodialysis units in Canada. A small sample size was essential to accommodate our commitment to conducting a PAR study with this patient population whose unpredictable health status presented significant challenges to recruitment, follow-up interviews, and participation in data analysis. Data collection and analysis over 2 years included over 100 hours of ethnographic field observation, bi-weekly unrecorded and 12 audio-recorded in-dialysis interviews, five video-recorded life-history interviews, two video-recorded focus groups, and five video-recorded dialysis treatment sessions. Thematic content analysis drew attention to patients' descriptions of adversarial interactions with health professionals. In these interactions, three points of tension were identified: a) between whole person care and "assembly line" treatment,

b) between patient knowledge and medical expertise, and c) between shared decision-making and "digging to find out". The article concludes that these adversarial relationships are indicative of a lack of trust stemming from health professionals' failure to interact with patients as whole persons with unique expertise on their bodies, their experience of illness, and their lives.

This abstract begins with distinctly 'longitudinal' participatory action research, with data collection over the course of two years, including 'bi-weekly... audio-recorded in-dialysis interviews'. Although the research question itself is not clearly worded in a dynamic fashion, we can infer that 'the challenges and solutions to living well with... chronic illness' is a subject well-served by a dynamic approach, as chronic illness is a long-term development. Nevertheless, the analysis in the form of 'thematic content analysis' does not incorporate time, and the 'three points of tension' identified also do not incorporate a longitudinal perspective at all. The concluding sentence about adversarial relationships discusses interaction, but again, this is not over the course of time at all.

Not all articles showed the same fluctuation in temporality in their abstracts as in the body of their text. However, we chose to share those above as they reflect the time conceptualizations throughout their respective articles very well. This critique and the vacillation of temporality evidenced in Table 4 show that there are large strides to be made in consistently applying a dynamic approach to qualitative health experience research.

Discussion

Prompted by our own attempt to set up a longitudinal qualitative panel study, we scrutinized longitudinal studies for the conceptualization and application of temporality. In the literature, we attended to basic differences between static and dynamic temporality and between linear and circular time, as well as addressing tempo. We then analyzed 38 articles (from a collection of 152 in the area of qualitative longitudinal studies of health experience) to assess the specific conceptualization of time in several sections of the the research articles, iteratively consulting the literature and refining our resulting typology. This delivered the basic distinction of static and dynamic temporality, where dynamic modes can be subdivided into interrupted, phasic, continuous and cyclical modes of temporality.

Our analysis shows that many of us struggle to maintain dynamic reasoning throughout a research article. Typically, an article started with a dynamic design and switched to a static approach in one or more other sections. Even if we interpret 'longitudinal' or 'dynamic' broadly, only four articles from our sample of 38 (11%) consistently applied a dynamic approach to time. The switch from a dynamic to a static approach occurs most commonly in the analysis section. This is something we also recognize in our own work. Even with longitudinal data at hand, we switch back to snapshots, isolated themes, correlations and types. In this review, those analysis sections that did include a temporal component often did no more than mention the descriptor 'longitudinal'. We as scholars could certainly pay more attention to our methods sections; the analysis section in particular is often summarized in a line or two. Improvement on this front is a 'quick win' in terms of conceptual consistency.

The conclusions of the articles in the sample were also lacking in terms of dynamism, as just above a third (11 out of 38) had either a static conclusion or both a static conclusion and analysis section. It would appear that outside of the analysis section, the conclusion is the next-most vulnerable part of the article to static temporality, given a dynamic design. Another five articles were in fact static throughout all sections but the design, leaving much room for improvement.

Even though articles discuss the fact that they are conducting a longitudinal study, they sometimes do not specifically address what the time dimension adds to their research. Even if they do, the relevance of dynamic temporality often wavers throughout the course of the article, evading any flow or progress throughout time. Even if data collection time-points are mentioned alongside the quotes ('said at interview 1' etc.), those authors that do not use a dynamic approach do not show any congruent shift, change, interruption or a lack thereof over time.

Beyond the division between dynamic and static conceptualizations, authors often vacillated between the various dynamic approaches to time. This is not always bad, as researchers may not have expectations about what type of time respondents experience until data collection has begun, or they have expectations that differ from their findings. This is particularly the case where continuous time is expected, but breaks or shifts that result in phasic time later in the study may appear in the course of the research. However, with interrupted and phasic time in particular, one would not necessarily expect a shifting mode of temporality from design through conclusion, as the break(s) and change(s) are very much the focus of the study.

Of course, our review is not perfect. Our sample size of articles could have been larger, although we did reach theoretical saturation. Anthropological studies are underrepresented in our review, despite our attempts to include two anthropological databases at data collection. For a future study, the list of search terms should be revisited to address this gap. Additionally, we limited our piece to studies of health experience, in part because we ourselves are undertaking a similar study. This was a conscious choice in order to clearly define and limit the scope of our study, which on the one hand means we cannot necessarily generalize our typology to qualitative longitudinal studies on other themes, but does ensure that our typology and evaluation of the relevant studies is meaningful.

The Future of Time

This chapter contributes usable insights into how time is conceptualized in longitudinal studies, in the form of our typology and the gaps we discovered in the application of time. We mentioned earlier that many authors were not explicit in their use of time. As a consequence, we aim to be more explicit in our own work on Sarphati Ethnography and beyond, and encourage you to do the same throughout your articles and research processes. It increases our analytic leverage when we differentiate between a sudden change such as a health intervention, for example, and a process consisting of multiple phases, such as a treatment course. We should determine what our time conceptualization is (phasic, continuous etc.) in the design phase and keep this in mind throughout the research process and writing the article.

Ultimately, the results of our review leave much to be desired in the field of longitudinal qualitative studies on health experience and in our own research. However, being purposeful, transparent and explicit in the research process and writing will help scholars gain much ground in the quality of these studies. We certainly hope to apply what we have learned to our own Sarphati Ethnography, and the publications that we derive from it.

References

Abbott, A. (1995). Sequence analysis: New methods for old ideas. *Annual Review of Sociology, 21*, 93-113.

Adler, S. (1999). Complementary and alternative medicine use among women with breast cancer. *Medical Anthropology Quarterly, 13*, 214-222. https://www.jstor.org/stable/649645.

Allen, D., Wainwright, M., Hutchinson, T. (2011). 'Non-compliance' as illness management: Hemodialysis patients' descriptions of adversarial patient–clinician interactions. *Social Science & Medicine, 73*, 129-134. https://doi.org/10.1016/j.socscimed.2011.05.018.

Andersen, I.C., Thomsen, T.G., Bruun, P., Bødtger, U., Hounsgaard, L. (2017). The experience of being a participant in one's own care at discharge and at home, following a severe acute exacerbation in chronic obstructive pulmonary disease: A longitudinal study. *International Journal of Qualitative Studies on Health and Well-Being, 12.* https://doi.org/10.1080/17482631.2017.1371994.

Béhague, D.P. (2008). Psychiatry and military conscription in Brazil: The search for opportunity and institutionalized therapy. *Culture, Medicine, and Psychiatry, 32,* 194-218. https://doi.org/10.1007/s11013-008-9090-6.

Booth, A., Sutton, A., Papaioannou, D. (2016). *Systematic approaches to a successful literature review* (2nd ed.). Los Angeles, CA: Sage.

Breman, J., Kloos, P., Saith, A. (Eds.). (1997). *The village in Asia revisited.* Oxford: Oxford University Press.

Bury, M. (1982). Chronic illness as biographical disruption. *Sociology of Health & Illness, 4,* 167-182. https://doi.org/10.1111/1467-9566.ep11339939.

Carusone, S.C., O'Leary, B., McWatt, S., Stewart, A., Craig, S., Brennan, D.J. (2017). The lived experience of the hospital discharge "plan": A longitudinal qualitative study of complex patients. *Journal of Hospital Medicine, 12,* 5-10.https://doi.org/10.1002/jhm.2671.

Clark, L. (2001). La Familia: Methodological issues in the assessment of perinatal social support for Mexicanas living in the United States. *Social Science & Medicine, 53,* 1303-1320. https://doi.org/10.1016/S0277-9536(00)00411-1..

Comte, A. (1852). *Cour de philosophie positive: Vol. 1. Les préliminaires généraux et la philosophie mathématique.* Paris: Borrani et Droz.

Crow, G. (2012). Community re-studies: Lessons and prospects. *The Sociological Review, 60,* 405-420. https://doi.org/10.1111/j.1467-954X.2012.02091.x.

De Graaff, M.B., & Bröer, C. (2012). 'We are the canary in a coal mine': Establishing a disease category and a new health risk. *Health, Risk & Society, 14,* 129-147. https://doi.org/10.1080/13698575.2012.661040.

De Graaff, M.B., & Bröer, C. (2019). Governance and risk in everyday life: Depoliticization and citizens' experiences of cell site deployment in the Netherlands and Southern California. *Journal of Risk Research.* https://doi.org/10.1080/13669877.2018.1501596.

Elias, N. (1978). *The civilizing process : Vol. 1. The history of manners.* New York: Pantheon.

Ellis, J., Brearley, S.G., Craven, O., Molassiotis, A. (2013). Understanding the symptom experience of patients with gastrointestinal cancers in the first year following diagnosis: Findings from a qualitative longitudinal study. *Journal of gastrointestinal cancer, 44,* 60-67. https://doi.org/10.1007/s12029-012-9443-9.

Essery, R., Kirby, S., Geraghty, A.W., Yardley, L. (2017). Older adults' experiences of internet-based vestibular rehabilitation for dizziness: A longitudinal study. *Psychology & Health, 32,* 1327-1347. https://doi.org/10.1080/08870446.2017.1310861.

Fabian, J. (2014). *Time and the other: How anthropology makes its object.* New York: Columbia University Press.

Foster, K., Curtis, K., Mitchell, R., Van, C., Young, A. (2016). The experiences, unmet needs and outcomes of parents of severely injured children: A longitudinal mixed methods study protocol. *BMC pediatrics, 16.* https://doi.org/10.1186/s12887-016-0693-8.

Gill, P., & Lowes, L. (2008). Gift exchange and organ donation: Donor and recipient experiences of live related kidney transplantation. *International Journal of Nursing Studies, 45,* 1607-1617. https://doi.org/10.1016/j.ijnurstu.2008.03.004.

Goudsblom, J. (2004). The worm and the clock: On the genesis of a global time regime. In E. Dunning & S. Mennell (Eds.). *Norbert Elias* (pp. 317-334). London: Sage.

Gustafsson, B.Å., Ponzer, S., Heikkilä, K., Ekman, S. L. (2007). The lived body and the perioperative period in replacement surgery: Older people's experiences. *Journal of Advanced Nursing, 60,* 20-28. https://doi.org/10.1111/j.1365-2648.2007.04372.x.

Hargreaves, K., Amos, A., Highet, G., Martin, C., Platt, S., Ritchie, D., et al. (2010). The social context of change in tobacco consumption following the introduction of 'smokefree' England legislation: A qualitative, longitudinal study. *Social Science & Medicine, 71,* 459-466. https://doi.org/10.1016/j.socscimed.2010.04.025.

Hassard, J. (1990). *The sociology of time.* London: Palgrave Macmillan.

Henkusens, C., Keller, H.H., Dupuis, S., Schindel Martin, L. (2014). Transitions to long-term care: How do families living with dementia experience mealtimes after relocating? *Journal of Applied Gerontology, 33,* 541–563. https://doi.org/10.1177/0733464813515091.

Hertzman, C., Frank, J., Evans, R.G. (1994). Heterogeneities in health status and the determinants of population health. In M. Barrer (Ed.), *Why are some people healthy and others not* (pp. 67-92). New York: Routledge.

Higgs, P., & Gilleard, C. (2014). Frailty, abjection and the 'othering' of the fourth age. *Health Sociology Review, 23,* 10-19. https://doi.org/10.5172/hesr.2014.23.1.10.

Holland, J. (2011). Timescapes: Living a qualitative longitudinal study. *Forum Qualitative Sozialforschung / Forum: Qualitative Social Research, 12*(3).https://doi.org/10.17169/fqs-12.3.1729.

Hume, D. (2007). A treatise of human nature. In D.F. Norton, M.A. Stewart (Eds.), *The Clarendon edition of the works of David Hume: The philosophical works.* Oxford: Clarendon Press. (Original work published 1739).

Kugley, S, & Epstein, R. (2019). Gathering evidence from grey literature and unpublished data. In P. Levay & J. Craven (Eds.), *Systematic searching: Practical ideas for improving results* (pp. 95-123). London: Facet Publishing.

Lohne, V. (2009). Back to life again – Patients' experiences of hope three to four years after a spinal cord injury: A longitudinal study. *Canadian Journal of Neuroscience Nursing, 31*(2), 20-25.

Mahoney, J. (2000). Path dependence in historical sociology. *Theory and Society, 29,* 507-548. https://www.jstor.org/stable/3108585.

McLeod, J., & Thomson, R. (2009). *Researching social change: Qualitative approaches.* Sage Publications.

Mills, C.W. (2000). *The sociological imagination.* Oxford: Oxford University Press.

Mitchell, W.A. (2014). Making choices about medical interventions: The experience of disabled young people with degenerative conditions. *Health Expectations, 17,* 254-266. https://dx.doi.org/https://doi.org/10.1111%2Fj.1369-7625.2011.00752.x.

Moher, D., Liberati, A., Tetzlaff, J., Altman, D.G., Tetzlaff, J., The PRISMA Group (2009). Preferred reporting items for systematic reviews and meta-analyses: The PRISMA statement. *Annals of Internal Medicine, 6*(7), 264-270. https://doi.org/10.7326/0003-4819-151-4-200908180-00135.

Molassiotis, A., Wilson, B., Brunton, L., Chaudhary, H., Gattamaneni, R., McBain, C. (2010). Symptom experience in patients with primary brain tumours: A longitudinal exploratory study. *European Journal of Oncology Nursing, 14,* 410-416. https://doi.org/10.1016/j.ejon.2010.03.001.

Munn, N. D. (1992). The cultural anthropology of time: A critical essay. *Annual Review of Anthropology 21*, 93-123. https://www.jstor.org/stable/2155982.

Neale, B. (2015). Time and the lifecourse: Perspectives from qualitative longitudinal research. In N. Worth & I. Hardill (Eds.), *Researching the lifecourse: Critical reflections from the social sciences* (pp. 25-41). Bristol: Policy Press.

Neale, B. (2019). *What is qualitative longitudinal research?* London: Bloomsbury.

Neale, B., & Flowerdew, J. (2003). Time, texture and childhood: The contours of longitudinal qualitative research. *International Journal of Social Research Methodology, 6*, 189-199. https://doi.org/10.1080/1364557032000091798.

Petticrew, M., & Roberts, H. (2006). *Systematic reviews in the social sciences: A practical guide.* Malden, MA: Blackwell.

Rosa, H. (2013). *Social acceleration: A new theory of modernity.* New York: Columbia University Press.

Sacks, H., Schegloff, E.A., Jefferson, G. (1978). A simplest systematics for the organization of turn taking for conversation. In J. Schenkein (Ed.), *Studies in the organization of conversational interaction* (pp. 7-55). Cambridge, MA: Academic Press.

Saldaña, J. (2003). *Longitudinal qualitative research: Analyzing change through time.* Walnut Creek, CA: AltaMira Press.

Schaffer, R., Kuczynski, K., Skinner, D. (2008). Producing genetic knowledge and citizenship through the Internet: Mothers, pediatric genetics, and cybermedicine. *Sociology of Health & Illness, 30*, 145-159. https://doi.org/10.1111/j.1467-9566.2007.01042.x.

Solomon, O., Angell, A.M., Yin, L., Lawlor, M.C. (2015). "You can turn off the light if you'd like": Pediatric health care visits for children with autism spectrum disorder as an interactional achievement. *Medical Anthropology Quarterly, 29*, 531-555. https://doi.org/10.1111/maq.12237.

Timmermans, S., & Tavory, I. (2012). Theory construction in qualitative research: From grounded theory to abductive analysis. *Sociological Theory, 30*. 167-186. https://www.jstor.org/stable/41725511.

Wajcman, J. (2008). Life in the fast lane? Towards a sociology of technology and time. *The British Journal of Sociology, 59*, 59-77. https://doi.org/10.1111/j.1468-4446.2007.00182.x.

Wright, S., Zalwango, F., Seeley, J., Mugisha, J., & Scholten, F. (2012). Despondency among HIV-positive older men and women in Uganda. *Journal of Cross-Cultural Gerontology, 27*, 319-333. https://doi.org/10.1007/s10823-012-9178-x.

Wrubel, J., Moskowitz, J. T., Richards, T.A., Prakke, H., Acree, M., Folkman, S. (2005). Pediatric adherence: Perspectives of mothers of children with HIV. *Social Science & Medicine, 61*, 2423-2433. https://doi.org/10.1016/j.socscimed.2005.04.034.

The manufacturer's authorised representative in the EU is Springer Nature Customer Service Centre GmbH, Europaplatz 3, 69115 Heidelberg, Germany. If you have any concerns regarding our products, please contact ProductSafety@springernature.com

Printed and bound by CPI Group (UK) Ltd, Croydon, CR0 4YY

25/03/2026

02078196-0006